Political Risk Intelligence for Business Operations in Complex Environments

Macro-level dynamics and modelling are well represented in the mainstream political risk literature. However, not many writings on the subject get their hands dirty in terms of revealing the hard, nuanced and practical work behind knowing what the issues might be for a specific foreign operation in a sensitive or volatile context, and how to plan for them.

Political Risk Intelligence for Business Operations in Complex Environments provides international managers, and by extension their organisations, with a foundational understanding of political risk analysis and planning for on-the-ground operations in challenging times and places. This means having a fluid grasp of what political risk means, and why it matters in the organisation's context, and how relevant intelligence can be gathered and analysed to inform decisions and planning towards an operation's socio-political resilience.

The book explains:

- How and why political risk manifests and the forms it can take
- Company attitudes and operational attributes as a political risk variable
- Understanding the operational implications of socio-political dynamics and trends
- Stakeholder identification and analysis for informed engagement planning
- Scenario analysis to prepare for long-term contingencies and discontinuities
- Holistic, intelligence-driven political risk management planning
- Tactical intelligence exercises to maintain awareness and inform adaptation
- Intelligence management, collection and quality control
- Ethical considerations in political risk management

Rather than being bound by conventional notions of risk, the book emphasises the dynamic relationship between a foreign operation and its host environment and milieu as a source of both challenges and opportunities to manage them. Concepts, frameworks and practises are rounded out with real-world examples and relevant lessons from the author's experience as a political risk consultant.

Political Risk Intelligence for
Business Operations
in Complex Environments

Robert McKellar

Routledge
Taylor & Francis Group

NEW YORK AND LONDON

First edition published 2023
by CRC Press
6000 Broken Sound Parkway NW, Suite 300, Boca Raton, FL 33487-2742

and by Routledge
605 Third Avenue, New York, NY 10158

Routledge is an imprint of the Taylor & Francis Group, an informa business

© 2023 Taylor & Francis Group, LLC

ISBN: 978-1-032-49611-5 (hbk)
ISBN: 978-0-367-71061-3 (pbk)
ISBN: 978-1-003-14912-5 (ebk)

DOI: 10.1201/9781003149125

Typeset in Times
by SPi Technologies India Pvt Ltd (Straive)

Contents

Part II   *The Baseline Intelligence Exercise*

Part III   The Practice of Intelligence

Author

Robert McKellar is an independent political risk consultant. He holds an MA in political science from Canada, completed a master's of international business in France, and studied Arabic in Tunisia for a year. Robert's political risk career began with periodic freelance assignments in the 1990s. He worked as an international strategic marketing consultant and with established risk advisories before creating his independent practice. Robert has conducted advisory, training and assessment cases for business and NGO clients, and has been involved with security sector reform projects in post-conflict environments. He has fieldwork experience in several regions, but particularly North Africa and the Middle East. Robert is the author of *A Short Guide to Political Risk* (2010) and the chapter on political risk in *The Risk Management Handbook* (ed. David Hillson, 2016).

List of Abbreviations

BI	Business intelligence
BOT	Build-operate-transfer
BOOT	Build-own-operate-transfer
CCP	Chinese Communist Party
CIA	Central Intelligence Agency
CSR	Corporate social responsibility
EPC	Engineering, procurement, construction
ERM	Enterprise risk management
EU	European Union
FDI	Foreign direct investment
Govt	Government
HR	Human resources
IP	Intellectual property
IT	Information technology
JV	Joint venture
MENA	Middle East-North Africa
MF	Military faction
Min.	Ministry
MOT	Ministry of Transport
NATO	North Atlantic Treaty Organisation
NGO	Non-government organisation
OECD	Organisation for Economic Cooperation and Development
PPP	Private–public partnership
PR	Public relations
SEIA	Social-environmental impact assessment
TNO	Transnational organisation
US	United States
USSR	Union of Soviet Socialist Republics

Introduction

AN IRAN STORY

When I was a child, my father's employer, a US-based international construction company, along-side its French joint venture partner, won a contract to design and build a highway in Iran, linking Tehran with southern oil ports. In 1976, as a family we were put on notice that Iran was in our near-term future, and in early 1977 we moved to Tehran, where my dad would work from the country office trying to get the project beyond bureaucratic wrangling, a phase it had already been stuck in for a while. By the time we left in early 1979, although a smattering of skeletal base camps had sprouted along the highway route, the design of the route was incomplete, and little dirt had been moved. In a unique new project model, this one started in planning, largely skipped implementation, and went directly to arbitration in the early 1980s as the company sought to recover costs from the now Islamic Republic of Iran, the government of which had bigger things to worry about than a new highway or contractual niceties with an American company.

For us as a family, after the initial shock and awe of moving from small town Ontario to Tehran, it was a memorable experience, marked by late afternoons in shared taxis for grocery shopping and trips to the bazaar, dinners at the local chello kebab hole in the wall, picking up fresh bread each day from the local street ovens, weekend walks in the city's parks and on the foothills north of the city, flying my kite in the empty lot beside our apartment block, and regular get-togethers with friends. The international school we attended was a new kid's nightmare at first, but it soon felt like a second home. The onset of the revolution made it all seem very tenuous, and we eventually had to join the throngs at the airport, in the common ritual of scrambling to find another plane to anywhere after our original flight was cancelled. But even the gloom of the final months did not shade our memories of the good parts of our personal Iran experience.

For the company's project management team, and the international division back in the US, it was a different story, particularly in the sense that after winning the project tender, there were few good parts. The revolution was an obvious reason for operational stagnation, but it could only account for the last few months of the project's malaise. That progress had been sketchy for over two years to that point was more down to ongoing bureaucratic obstacles, misunderstandings with Iranian ministerial counterparts, these counterparts' own indecisive fiddling with the original scope and plan, and an overreliance on "recommended" local partners and advisors who were more interested in their own status with the Shah's inner circle than project performance. Iranian counterparts were hesitant to commit to irrevocable decisions for fear of somehow tripping over the Shah's own latest thinking on the subject of highways and indeed the project itself – a fleeting utterance made over morning tea could trickle back down the system and cause considerable consternation. Iran's government had decided that it needed the highway, and had signed a contract and given guarantees, but formal commitments could not stand up to the apparent whims of the informal system. The intrusion of personal rule and related palace politics had direct effects on necessary design approvals and routinely necessitated time-consuming renegotiations.

By mid-1978, it was apparent that socio-political forces were stirring, but like most other foreign companies, the constructor had no clear picture of the character or severity of growing dissent. The company was getting information from the US embassy, usually lists of incidents such as demonstrations, clashes and the odd bombing or shootout, but this told managers little except that something was happening. Embassy briefs later added indications that dissent was somehow connected to communist or radical socialist groups backed by the USSR. These were alleged to have

DOI: 10.1201/9781003149125-1

networks among industrial workers and universities, and these in turn were organising protests in an effort to undermine the Shah's credibility. Information coming from US-based advisors, including ex-national security officials, was of a similar line. In this view, given that dissent was foreign-instigated, the regime would face little risk of alienating ordinary Iranians with a surgical crackdown, and hence such a crackdown was likely to occur, and, given the vast security resources available, to be effective.

By early autumn 1978, it was clear that much more than leftist agitation was going on, and the evening news was now carrying stories about the Shah's vacillating efforts to appease religious and pro-democracy opposition leaders, even if Khomeini's name was still not quite central to the coalescing picture (as an aside, a couple of weeks before we left, TV news was still on once a day, but the rest of the time TV only showed a very sombre man doing Quranic recital; this was a bit more evocative than our usual morning cartoons and evening *Starsky and Hutch*). The vast demonstrations that now regularly engulfed parts of Tehran were evidence in themselves that dissent had both broad social momentum and direction.

Oddly, given the benefit of hindsight, the company, as with many other foreign firms and indeed foreign governments, still thought that the Shah's regime and stability were recoverable. The period between vague unease, desperate hope and the scramble to leave was a mere two to three months. Getting much more than personnel out proved to be well beyond what was feasible in the time companies had available once managers finally accepted the inevitable. The company that brought us to Iran was not alone in leaving much behind, and in having to walk away from nearly any chance of recovering costs or resuming operations in the future.

The revolution was more than an operational and financial problem. Iran was becoming dangerous. From autumn of 1978 and before the office closed, company managers were still trying to get to and from work, and some inadvertently ended up waiting out the flow of huge demonstrations around their cars after taking a wrong turn. Later, the odd shootout meant a stray bullet or two down a residential street. Foreigners were seldom directly targeted by the protesters, even after the collapse of the Shah's regime, but there was a high risk of being in the wrong place at the wrong time. The last expatriate stragglers to leave in the main wave of evacuations were often chaperoned right to plane by gun-toting youths who were part of the nascent revolutionary defence associations later known as *Komiteh* (Committees). For several months, the company's Iranian personnel faced an urgent dilemma – stick with their job and employer and hope for the best, or quit and even join the revolution to avoid potential repercussions for being "lackeys of foreign agents". On a more basic level, even ensuring that company households had heating and food became a challenge, especially as waves of strikes started to paralyse key industries. In the last chaotic weeks, one company manager had a fatal sudden heart attack, but as with most other companies, no one was directly harmed, expats made it home, and subsequent news from Iranian staff indicated that while life was hard, there had been no direct repercussions for their work with a foreign firm. That people were not harmed was far more a result of luck and on-the-spot adaptation than foresight and contingency plans.

For the company, the full effects of the failed Iran operation included significant, though not catastrophic, financial loss (the Iranian highway was a high-profile project but a small part of total corporate activity and the company eventually did receive limited compensation), short-lived, if serious, anxiety for personnel, and strategic hesitation for some time afterwards with respect to international growth. The latter issue would actually prove to be the most damaging, as the company, once a pioneer in "frontier markets", never quite recovered its sense of adventure and in part replaced international growth with a series of high-stakes gambles to try to retrench in the domestic US market. Had the company been alone in having problems in Iran, its reputation for delivery would have taken a serious dent too, but since most foreign companies were badly affected, no one company stood out as particularly maladroit. Thus, while the nett effect for the operation was total failure, for the company overall it was only serious and mostly recoverable. That no one was directly hurt certainly made the final accounting less dire.

A significant reason for the project's failure, or at least the magnitude of it, was a lack of any serious effort to develop and act on political risk intelligence. Such intelligence would have made a significant difference.

Two questions were critical even before deciding to bid for the job. One was what might change in Iran that would make the project untenable. It would have been hard to predict the revolution, but an assessment of problematic scenarios would have flagged its potential, perhaps alongside other scenarios that did not manifest, such as a military coup and resulting unrest, a serious dispute with the US government that caused the Shah's regime to throw out US contractors, a clash with the USSR (as might have happened had the Shah still been in power when the USSR invaded Afghanistan), or indeed war with Iraq.

The second question was how workable an environment Iran really was. Whom would the company have to rely on and how reliable were they? The experiences of other foreign companies around the same time could have shed light on this. While there was a lot of foreign direct investment flowing into the country, revenues coming back out were another story. Based on the hype of modernisation and bottomless oil money, companies were willing to put up with uncertain payback horizons to get a foothold. There was little clear evidence in the mid-1970s that modernisation plus oil money actually equalled commercial success for foreign firms, and a reasonable hypothesis to draw from this was that Iranian customers, counterparts and regulators, within and because of the wider system of personal rule, often had priorities other than project pace and performance.

With an idea of how the country might evolve and of the actual challenges of working there, the company could have made an informed choice of whether or not to tender in the first place. And if it had decided to, it would have been armed with the necessary insight to design a partnership and financing structure to minimise risks, for example using a consortium of several firms instead of a joint venture between two, and including a state-backed investment guarantee agency in the financing and also for political risk insurance (nascent in those days but still an option). The contract itself could have been negotiated with an eye to minimising exposure at any one point and to putting more onus for project performance onto the government customer. If the Iranian customer had rejected such terms, so be it, since the company's redlines would have been based on intelligence, not gut sense or speculation.

Prior to and in early entry, a detailed understanding of Iranian stakeholder networks and their culture and attitudes would have informed corporate diplomacy and routine bargaining to help overcome bottlenecks and to better align on project priorities. Additionally, bearing in mind the instability scenario, whether a revolution, coup or other violent change, the company could have had pre-planned contingencies aligned with signs of trouble, such that by the time any major instability did manifest, only a skeleton staff was left, and moveable assets had already been taken out. Routine monitoring throughout the operation would have kept the intelligence picture up to date and allowed for ongoing adaptation to the dynamic socio-political context.

Thus, had political risk intelligence been an explicit exercise built into the project's planning, the company very likely would have had a stronger position to start with *if it had gone to Iran*, more effective dealings with Iranian counterparts, and far less exposure once the revolution finally manifested.

The company did considerable prior homework on the commercial, infrastructure and regulatory landscape in Iran. But when it came to socio-political intelligence, while it commissioned some reports about Iran from its US advisors, these were general "about Iran" reports. They were not intelligence; in other words, they did not match insight about relevant socio-political dynamics and actors to specific company interests, exposures and decisions, and they were not integrated with project planning.

The lack of political risk intelligence stemmed in part from a sense of safety within the herd of other foreign investors. The company was going with the flow: Iran was a hot market, and everyone assumed that this was because everyone else was somehow doing well there. Even the US government was touting Iran as a miracle in the Middle East. The company had completed a project in

Iran in the 1950s, when the Shah was still shaken by the Mossadegh interregnum and much more dependent on its alliance with the US, and that job had been quite straightforward. On that basis, the company felt it would be a smooth ride this time around. Finally, although the firm had worked in challenging places before, it had always been a question of dealing with hassles and eccentricities as they arose, and muddling through had seemed to suffice. Some managers had more experience and skill in this regard than others, but their knowhow was not institutionalised as lessons learned.

Knowing the company mindset at the time, an even more banal explanation for a lack of political risk intelligence in the Iran job was that there was no solid concept of political risk in the company. Hassles and delays arose, bad things happened, and projects got derailed, but if it was not through technical and commercial mistakes or misjudgements, then it was just bad luck and the cost of doing business in "crazy places". As for *intelligence*, as a concept and process it was confined to competitive and market analysis where variables were easily quantified. A socio-political environment was too big, abstract and wish-washy to try to analyse. Thus, there was no concept or category to capture and discuss the types of challenges that could arise from socio-political factors, and no process to try to understand them. In this mindset, commissioning a stand-alone country report was sufficient, and even then, it was not standard procedure.

The above point about a lack of concept and process is important, because individual managers, especially those at the front line regularly dealing with Iranian actors, did become very well informed about dynamics that were affecting the company. Had their insights been joined up and assessed at different points in the project, particularly in conjunction with the insights of Iranian staff and trusted local counterparts, there would have been a much clearer picture of the roots of initial and ongoing issues, and of the potential ramifications of encroaching political change. In other words, people were not blind or stupid; there was simply no channel to aggregate and apply what they were learning, and people did not have the conceptual framework to treat burgeoning socio-political changes as a tangible factor in the operation's performance. Socio-political insight remained anecdotal and had little organisational impact.

The company certainly did have bad luck in its timing, but a large part of its disastrous experience in Iran was attributable to an intelligence failure, a lack of explicit recognition of the socio-political variable, and no systematic effort assess and adapt to socio-political indications. It was not alone in being obtuse. Most of "the herd" had very similar problems.

That was the late 1970s. Political risk is a more recognised "thing" these days, and enterprise risk management and sustainability have driven more consideration of uncertainties and potential downsides, and of the interaction of a company with at least its social-environmental context. But in terms of the application of political risk intelligence, not much has changed. With information now more abundant and easily accessible, international managers are more likely to learn about the places they are heading to. But applying an explicit intelligence process that goes beyond general "about this country" information or macro data points is still a rarity. Mainstream business thinking still paints a company's world mainly as itself, markets, investors, competitors and technology, with regulatory change and social-environmental expectations now entering the periphery of this mental picture. For more stable environments where governments work through predictable processes and change is usually incremental, this model of a company's world can suffice. For complex environments, where institutionalisation and national consensus can be nascent or fragile, the model is often too simple and optimistic, and underprepares the organisation for what it could face.

While the overall difficulty of operating in transitional and developing countries has not really changed much over the decades, now as both a result and factor of globalisation, international firms have a much higher proportion of business in emerging markets than before, and this proportion continues to grow. The result is more exposure to potential "Irans" and a range of other challenging situations deriving from socio-political complexity and volatility.

Decades after one of the most instructive lessons in political risk that international companies have had, there is still a need for more explicit and better-integrated political risk intelligence and related planning capabilities. This aim of this book is to provide a practical starting point.

OBJECTIVES

A significant rationale for this book is that while there are many insightful works on political risk, there seems to be a gap around how to actually undertake political risk intelligence and planning, especially for operations on the ground. Macro-level dynamics and modelling are well represented in the mainstream literature. However, not many writings on the subject seem to want to get their hands dirty in terms of revealing the hard, nuanced and practical work behind knowing what the ground-level issues might be for a specific foreign operation, and how to plan for them. Additionally, there has been a tendency to remain somewhat distant from the more complicated, tangled and potentially dangerous problems and conundrums that operations can face in challenging places. The book takes a twofold chance. One is that readers will be interested in and benefit from a relatively nuanced exposition of the relevant thought processes. Another is that readers will appreciate that this does not shirk from discussing some of the more onerous issues that companies can experience. If these bets are borne out, then the perspective herein could usefully augment more macro-level and theoretical points of view.

The objective of this book is to provide international managers, and by extension their organisations, with a foundational understanding of political risk intelligence for on-the-ground operations in complex socio-political environments. This means having a fluid grasp of what political risk means and why it matters in the organisation's context, and how relevant intelligence can be gathered and analysed to inform decisions and planning towards an operation's socio-political resilience. This will be new to some, and for others will hopefully augment a knowledge of relevant practices or at least provide a fresh perspective. The book's aims can actually be further clarified by looking at what it is not trying to achieve.

First, this is not intended as a detailed manual or template. One reason for this is that conceptual understanding is a necessary part of a fluid working knowledge of political risk, and providing this foundation, above and beyond any specific process, is an important task of this book. When we do get into political risk intelligence as an exercise, this will mainly focus on an underlying thought process which is adaptable to a range of operational contexts, not on specific types of challenges that need to be assessed, nor on formulaic assessment methods. There are basic structural similarities between foreign operations in complex environments, but contexts are too variable for a one-size-fits-all focus or approach. For example, compare a small mining company with a handful of operations in remote corners of West Africa, to a global hotel chain serving major emerging market commercial centres. A certain way of thinking is relevant to each, but beyond that their requirements would be quite distinct.

This is also not a survey of current, topical political risks. The focus, rather, is on ways to discern and plan for political risks in a given country operation context. This involves reference to actual dynamics, but only as grist for the mill. Neither is this a survey of current political risk analysis and management practices. One premise of the book, stemming partly from the author's own consulting experience, is that much current practice is not explicit and often fragments the intelligence picture between different functional perspectives. While explicit and holistic intelligence exercises are not always necessary, companies would benefit from having this capability up their sleeve for contexts where it was important, and such a capability is the focus here. Current practices are reflected in the frameworks that we apply, and are discussed, but they do not set our boundaries.

Finally, this is not an academic nor research exercise. It does not aim at theory-building and does not try to position itself within an academic stream of thought. It might end up doing so, but that would be inadvertent, and a by-product of the emphasis on practical thinking to help keep an operation safe, legitimate and sustainable. As for research, arguably if I had to research this topic, then I should not be writing about it, since a book would not bring anything new and would lack the depth of direct experience. The book is primarily based on learning and thoughts accumulated over the course of my work as a political risk consultant. If I could ever remember them all, I could probably attribute much of my own thinking to various instructive writings that I have read over the years, but my own casework and professional interactions have honed and in some ways reshaped any academic learning. As a practitioner, sometimes there is not much time for reflection, or thinking about thinking, but it brews under the surface, and periodically needs to be set forth and examined as a stock-taking exercise. In some ways, this book is such an exercise, and hopefully, having lifted the lid of a pandora's box, I have managed to organise and articulate the results.

That the book is based on experience is an upside, but the obvious downside is that it could be a somewhat narrow perspective. While practical insight from a political risk consultant has its merits, it is a small, and in some ways idiosyncratic, patch of a broader field of practice and thinking. Because this is quite specific to my own experiences and ruminations, as opposed to being a broader review, it will inescapably reflect my own perspectives, including values. As we note later in the part on intelligence practice, perspective is an important criterion when evaluating a source of information. Every source will have its perspective, and we need to account for it in our interpretation. Additionally, any apparent "truths" that a source provides need to be corroborated. Thus, if this is one of the reader's first stops in the political risk journey, many more should follow for a well-rounded grasp the subject.

The above has set some parameters; thus, we can briefly introduce the book itself before we examine the scope. The book begins with an exploration of its constituent themes, to provide a conceptual backdrop for subsequent practical exercises. The heart of the book is a baseline, or strategic political risk intelligence exercise for an operation in a complex environment, aimed at informing operation-wide and cross-functional political risk management planning. While this covers much ground, we also examine other points and circumstances in which political risk intelligence can be useful or indeed critical, and how it can be shaped for different purposes. The practice of intelligence will be explored for a deeper understanding of the capabilities underpinning any political risk intelligence exercise. The book's final thoughts put forward a few key ideas for readers to build upon, not least of which is the relationship between political risk practices and business ethics. A guide to the contents follows the explanation of the book's scope.

SCOPE: WHAT FOCUS AND WHY

Political risk and intelligence are both broad concepts, and we only focus on a narrow part of them. This bears some explanation of what we are focusing on, and why. With a dual purpose, this explanation also provides a quick preview of some of the themes and concepts developed in a more structured way later on. The scope can be defined as the intersection of the following six axes, or perspectives, of the wider panorama, each of which is then briefly explained:

- The concern is foreign companies, in other words those which are foreign to their operating environments.
- We deal with working on the ground in a foreign country, not investing at arm's length.
- We focus on an operation in one country, not the global level.
- Complex emerging markets are the main focus in terms of type of country.
- The emphasis is much more on politics or socio-politics than economics.
- Our concern is intelligence at the local and national level, and the intelligence approach is more qualitative than quantitative.

To start with, we focus on the situation of a company, or part thereof, that is foreign to the country of operation, and which therefore lacks intuitive or innate knowledge of the environment, and also long-standing networks and relationships therein. Political risk can certainly be a challenge in home countries or regions too, but when we are foreigners, we can take far less for granted, and our assumptions about how politics and society work often need significant adjustment.

The focus is on-the-ground operations because these incur more direct exposure than offshore or portfolio investment. Arm's length investors expose money and, in some cases, reputation, but working in a country exposes a greater range of assets, including the most important one, people. As a corollary, it is more work and cost to establish an overseas presence than just moving money around, and hence companies have good reasons to try to persist even when an operation faces challenging times. And when they feel they need to leave, it can be a lot harder than just divesting funds. Political risk is relevant to purely financial investment, and in fact much has been written in that vein, but the political risk of being in a place is usually more acute irrespective of the financial sums involved.

When we say on-the-ground operations, it seems to imply foreign direct investment (FDI). FDI involves taking a stake in a foreign business entity. This can be one we set up ourselves, like a foreign subsidiary, but it can be someone else's entity, or company, too. FDI can therefore range from a major stake and presence in a new country, through to nearly hands-off and only periodic oversight of the investment target. Our emphasis herein is more hands-on FDI. Additionally, on-the-ground operations include a company going to a place to do one specific project or service, with no intention of taking a lasting stake in the country. Depending on country regulations, sometimes this still requires FDI, such as a joint venture with a local partner, but sometimes it really can mean just selling the service and coming in to do it, then leaving. Thus, when we refer to "on-the-ground", it usually means that FDI is involved but not necessarily. We can just stick to the notion of having to actually be there for a while, be it months or years.

As a concomitant to the above, the principal level of analysis herein is an operation in one country. Much commentary on political risk focuses on the geopolitical level, which is about the challenges that international companies and investors face from transnational political dynamics such as trade wars, inter-state and great power rivalries and conflict, and international terrorism. Our preference for the country level, as opposed to the global geopolitical one, stems from the country level being a bigger intelligence challenge. The global picture is a higher level of abstraction, and much insight thereon applies to a wide range of sectors and companies; thus, off-the-shelf, macro-data and open-source information can usefully form a significant part of intelligence inputs. Intelligence for a specific operation in one place requires going well beyond macro-trends, and developing a nuanced understanding of the unique relationship between the organisation and its socio-political environment, including specific actors therein. General or macro-information is useful for some elements of the country operation intelligence exercise, but especially when it comes to socio-political actors, depth becomes critical. We will be looking at the linkages between geopolitical and country operation considerations, but our emphasis is the latter.

It has been noted that the book focuses on complex socio-political environments. In informal parlance, countries which can be characterised as such are sometimes called "complex emerging markets", to distinguish them from emerging markets which have shown steady progress in governance standards and stability. "Complex emerging markets", or "complex environments", generally refers to transitional and developing countries that face a steep climb to becoming well-functioning and stable states, either because they are coming from a very disadvantaged starting point or because they have been through, or are in, a period of very bad governance or traumatic change and have yet to recover. The latter point means that countries can actually move into and out of the complex category. We will get into what makes a country complex or challenging later on. By way of introductory characterisation, suffice to say that such countries or major parts therein tend to be weak in terms of institutionalisation and rule of law, and/or national consensus, in other words shared national values and identity. This general bracket of emerging markets usually presents the most challenges to foreign companies. That said, it is not an ironclad category and its defining characteristics can show up in developed countries during volatile periods; thus, it will be possible to extrapolate from "complex emerging" to other types of environments.

The scope emphasises politics or socio-politics. One might suppose that a book on political risk assumes that politics is an important and unique consideration, but it is useful to make that assumption clear. In particular, an international operation is very sensitive to foreign market economics, so why do we focus on politics? The three-part answer partly explains the rationale for political risk as a specific field of study and management concern.

First, although politics and economics are closely linked, a given political arena, be it global or local, tends to be a tightly interlinked system of actors, values and interests. In economics, as both a field of study and a domain of activity, the predominant player is "homo economicus", an abstraction whose actions only matter in the aggregate. It is very difficult to describe a political system without reference to specific real actors. For example, the global system is driven in part by the interplay between Europe, the US, China and Russia. As another example, politics in Algeria is driven by competing regime factions and the military, unofficial religious institutions, Berber-Arab identity politics, labour activists, pro-democracy activists and disaffected youth. It is hard to get a full picture of either economics or politics without reference to the other, but much explanatory power can derive from a focus on each.

A second reason for a focus on politics is that bad economic bets only hurt one's financial standing. A bad bet on how long to cling to a deteriorating political environment, whom to seek an alliance with for support in dealing with political interference, or how to handle security in the context of a fractured host community, just as a few examples, can severely affect reputation and people too. Losing money is painful for businesses, but it is a routine hazard built into the business paradigm. Politics offers more diverse and dire possibilities outside of normal business experience, and manifested political risk at least indirectly hurts profits anyway.

Finally, politics, which includes a significant dose of faith and fervour as well as tribalism in its broader sense, often trumps economic rationality, and therefore can be a better explanation for economic eccentricity than "homo economicus". Almost any war or insurgency, for example, is bad for the economy, yet influential groups and people routinely start them anyway. Crony capitalism, linking political cliques and in-groups in mutual backscratching arrangements, creates an uneven-playing field and inhibits economic growth and innovation, but again, it is commonplace. When a leader really tries to ram home their own ideology or even personal values in a country, it makes the country look weird and risky and drives away FDI; however, it happens quite a lot. When a populist leadership starts fights with major trading partners to satisfy its hyper-nationalist voter base, it hurts the economy, but this seems to be in fashion lately. These are but a few examples. Economic dynamics, especially in weakly governed states, are seldom mainly driven by classic notions of supply and demand and the rational actor.

Although politics and economics can usefully be analysed as distinct domains, they are closely interlinked, and we will be looking at the linkage. Politics, however, is the source of the more vexing challenges for foreign firms in complex environments, often including economic eccentricity, and hence it is our main concern here.

A final note on scope is on the relevant type of intelligence. There are taxonomies, but for now it is sufficient to note that the focus is on intelligence, as a process and an output, which helps an organisation to sustain operations in a complex socio-political environment. This goes underneath normal business planning factors to shed light on how national and local socio-political values, identities, rivalries, attitudes and relationships could come to bear on a specific operation. Drawing on government analogies, this would be more akin to intelligence supporting a peacekeeping operation in a post-conflict setting, rather than long-range forecasting of a rival country's strategic power using sophisticated data modelling. The focus here is indeed more on the qualitative side; trend and macro-data is used in intelligence analysis, but gathering and "crunching" data is an information processing exercise, whereas intelligence is the formulation of informed judgement.

To hone the above, a rough guiding principle here is that if the electricity goes off and the computer dies, someone should still be able to come up with a useful analysis with a short stack of files containing solid raw intelligence, and a blank notepad and pencil. IT with its data-crunching ability helps, but if its centrality is assumed, it can obscure or distort the barebones logic that underpins the intelligence exercise, and take away the "back of the envelope" option that lets anyone, anywhere, usefully play with insights and ideas without being bound to a server. Technology can also lead practitioners to over-rely on readily available open-source data, to the detriment of more challenging but critical sources, such as people with first-hand insights on the place or situation that we are trying to understand, and indeed our own direct observation, discussions and experiences.

Our focus is where these above six perspectives intersect. It is worth emphasising that other aspects of political risk intelligence are just as important to international companies. The choice of focus is driven by the immediacy of the needs of on-the-ground operations in complex environments, and the intelligence challenge therein. As noted, it also comes from an assessment of the state of political risk literature aimed at business audiences. A company's direct interface with a specific socio-political milieu is not particularly well represented compared to geopolitical and state-level dynamics.

A READER'S GUIDE

The following provides a brief outline of the book's main parts as an overview and navigational aid. Afterwards we provide some suggestions on how to use the book.

Part I introduces the core concepts within the wider subject, and which are actually in the book's title. This covers political risk, complex environments, foreign business operations and their linkages to the socio-political environment, and intelligence. This is a descriptive rather than prescriptive section, but it is a necessary foundation for what follows, and a fluid conceptual understanding is a significant tacit ingredient to any specific political risk intelligence task.

As noted earlier, Part II is the heart of the book. This presents and walks through the baseline, or strategic, political risk intelligence exercise, for example the one that the construction company in Iran would have benefited from after deciding to enter but before finalising plans and commitments. This process yields insights to enable planning for, and around, potential challenges and friction points, and includes a preliminary planning exercise. The stages in the baseline process are illustrated using two distinct hypothetical cases. The distinction helps to see how the baseline process can apply in different contexts. Although hypothetical, the cases are realistic and provide tangible grist for illustration. Without the cases, it would have been hard to unpack and show the thinking and problem-solving that really goes on behind the intelligence frameworks, but a trade-off is that several chapters in Part II are quite long and detailed. The final chapter in this part examines supplementary political risk intelligence exercises, on the premise that an operation will have additional specific requirements both before and during a country operation.

With political risk intelligence applications established, Part III then takes a step back to consider the practice of intelligence, as the capabilities and knowhow that underpin any political risk intelligence exercise. This begins with intelligence management, with emphasis on specific complex tasks and cases. It then proceeds to intelligence sources and collection, and herein we emphasise a valuable but regrettably rare approach, fieldwork and human sources. This part then wraps up with a consideration of intelligence quality pitfalls and remedies. While this part of the book, and indeed political risk intelligence in general, draws on government foreign intelligence practices, it is firmly framed within our private sector, international business context.

The final chapter is labelled "concluding thoughts" and it steps away from immediate practicalities to consider a few broader questions that supplement the core of the book. One is an exploration of the options for establishing a political risk intelligence and management capability within a company, with attention to the need for cross-functional collaboration. Another is the changing global landscape, and how recent major trends are affecting political risk for foreign firms in emerging markets. Finally, this chapter, and the book, concludes with a discussion of ethics in political risk intelligence and management. This extends to a consideration of pressures on good corporate citizenship and how companies could interpret and respond to them.

There are a few suggestions for using the book, and here we also try to help readers to know what to expect. Some chapters are quite intensive, and there are some options if one wants to take a break from a sequential read.

There are some especially tight links and logical routing that would require approaching several chapters in sequence. In Part I, Chapter 2 on complex environments and Chapter 3 on foreign operations are prerequisites for the baseline exercise in Part II. Then, within the baseline exercise Chapters 5 to 10 should be read in sequence, not least because the two illustrative cases are developed through the actual application of the process.

In Part II, Chapter 11 on supplementary exercises could be approached independently. The baseline exercise is complete by then, and the cases are no longer being explicitly used. The whole of Part III on the practice of intelligence could also be a separate read, although if it followed the baseline exercise, then one better could relate practices to specific applications. The last chapter on final thoughts gets away from process and practicalities, and might be a good distraction if one is mid-book and needs a break.

In general, it would be ideal to read the book in sequence, but if readers are like me, they might hop around sometimes. We only counsel that one desists for those chapters which are logically closely linked and which build on each other.

To fulfil the promise of providing nuanced, practical guidance on political risk intelligence and its link to planning, the book is rather long, and so are several chapters. Convention might speak to more, smaller chapters, but when they are complete steps in a thought process, breaking them up would fragment whole ideas and logical links. Length and nuance suggest a patient approach (or making the book one's only distraction on a particularly long flight). The book could have been lighter, but then it would have been less effective. This is a complex and high-stakes domain, and just talking *about* it, as opposed to taking a more experiential walk through it, would have left some critical gaps.

Although there is general adherence to structure and thought process, throughout the book there are discussions of real, practical issues and dilemmas that companies have faced in complex environments. Similarly, political risk management approaches are not just confined to the chapter on planning, but arise through examples along the way. Thus, hopefully readers will have gained relevant substantive knowledge by the end of it, in addition to conceptual and "how to" insight.

Part I

Core Concepts

This part of the book introduces the four principal concepts which come together as the basis of political risk intelligence: political risk, country complexity, country operations and intelligence. These are examined with an eye to providing an introductory understanding of each subject. However, elements of applied political risk intelligence will be introduced herein so that by the time we reach the next section on a baseline intelligence process, there is a reasonable foundation to work from.

DOI: 10.1201/9781003149125-2

1 Political Risk

AS A FIELD AND PRACTICE

The importance of changes in government and society has been well known to international businesses for centuries. One can imagine, for example, traders in the early 1200s watching the Mongol expansion with trepidation. If they survived the various sieges, they eventually had access to a newly secure Silk Road but also the headaches of dealing with a stringent, overarching bureaucracy. Their descendants would face new problems as Mongol power abated, with fractious khanates and warlords exercising tenuous control over different stages of the trade route, and a resurgence in banditry. Each period of the evolution of global links and trading ties had its own unique challenges for businesses. But it was not until the 1960s, with acute academic interest in how international business would adapt to a post-colonial world, that a concept was devised for the challenges that governments and socio-political dynamics could pose. This was political risk.

One of the earliest uses of the term "political risk" seems to be in a 1962 survey of FDI by the International Bank for Reconstruction and Development (IBRD), part of the World Bank group (Fitzpatrick, 1983). By the late 1960s, academics at the interface of international relations and management studies, particularly in the US, were working on defining and honing the concept and its practical implications. Early definitions focused on government interference and FDI policy change, as well as expropriation and nationalisation. The latter were a significant problem for foreign companies in the 1960s and early 1970s as anti-colonial ideologies still guided many newly independent or newly assertive developing country governments, who often saw Western FDI as extortionate and a challenge to sovereign control over national assets. Coups were also prolific in this period as new governments struggled with factional infighting and the civil-military power balance; thus, "instability" soon became an aspect of political risk alongside "government action". However, early theoretical debate occurred on a number of axes, and broader conceptions of political risk pointed to the more systemic relationship between a firm and its environment. The concept of risk itself received considerable attention, in particular whether it was defined by events or actor behaviours, and the difference between estimable risk and qualified uncertainty.

The 1970s saw two events that gave rise to political risk's brief sojourn as a management fad. The first was the oil crisis of 1973, when Arab members of the Organisation of the Petroleum Exporting Countries (OPEC), along with Iran, imposed a partial oil embargo on Western countries. This was undertaken as retribution for perceived support to Israel during the 1973 Arab-Israeli War, and while oil shortages were problematic in themselves, the panic it engendered magnified the effect. The crisis was a very clear demonstration of the relevance of political events and attitudes to business and economic performance, as well as the interdependence that now existed between distant geographies.

The second was the basis of the case in the prelude, the Iranian Revolution, culminating in 1979. Hundreds of foreign companies were taken by surprise, but among these were dozens of multinationals who suffered significant losses, and who had a hair-raising last few weeks in the country. The revolution was a shock, but to add insult to injury, it led to another oil panic as Iran's production nearly halted. The same year the Soviet invasion of Afghanistan significantly raised global tensions, and in 1980, partly as a result of the Iranian Revolution, Iraq invaded Iran, not only severely undermining regional stability, but kicking off eight years of periodic threats to the Gulf's oil exports. By 1979, numerous international firms across banking and industry had already established some political risk analysis capabilities, but the revolution and surrounding events were the start of the brief political risk fad.

Some article headlines from the early 1980s, ironically found in the online library of the CIA, the original home of many early political risk consultants, capture the mood of the time: *The*

DOI: 10.1201/9781003149125-3

Multinationals Get Smarter About Political Risks (Kraar, 1980); *Risk Analysis Big Business for Ex-Aides* (Farnsworth, 1982); *High Times in the Political Risk Business* (Stone, 1982); *Boom Days for Political Risk Consultants* (Stone, 1983). It became almost fashionable among larger international firms to establish in-house political risk or international analysis units, often partly comprised of ex-intelligence and foreign service personnel who retained strong government connections. These units tended to sit within international divisions or in corporate strategy departments, and worked with planning teams to develop processes to screen proposed investments for political risk, plan appropriate diversification strategies, and provide guidance on how to engage with governments in new country markets. This was a far cry from previous approaches to political risk, which had usually involved sending senior managers, often with little international experience, overseas to "have a look around" and, in rarer cases, to commission a generic country report.

The 1980s were a good decade for political risk. It came on the heels of a problematic period that left lingering unease. However, it also saw considerable acceleration in economic and political liberalisation across developing regions. This gave rise to the notion of "emerging markets", developing countries with high growth potential but where political risk expertise was very relevant.

On the economic front, the widespread command economy model of the previous two decades had failed to meet the expectations and needs of growing populations, and the resulting risk of social unrest was one factor in pushing more governments to experiment with liberalisation. A corollary of the failure of state-controlled economies was unsustainable debt, and many governments were compelled to accept liberalising reforms as part of IMF and Western donor bailouts. Not only did this lead to market and financial rules familiar to international companies, but governments began to see FDI as a potential socio-economic development resource that was far easier to work with than the IMF. Thus, ideological wariness of FDI began to give way to investment promotion. A wave of democratisation starting in the 1980s was a corollary of economic developments. Governments that had once been able to use subsidies and state jobs to secure the social contract no longer could, and repression alone to retain authority was both unsustainable and incurred rebukes from Western lenders. Democratic reforms were a practical, if messy, way to maintain legitimacy.

Thus, economically and politically, many developing countries adopted "rules of the game" that foreign companies were familiar with, and emerging markets became a major growth frontier. Political risk as a field and function was there to help navigate this new terrain, which, while more accessible and broadly easier to understand, still presented serious challenges.

The 1990s reversed the fortunes of political risk as a practice. The early 1990s global recession coincided with the business process re-engineering blitz to impel companies to trim non-core functions and staff. At the same time, the collapse of the USSR and Eastern Bloc was underway, giving rise to hyped optimism that the victorious Western economic and political model would soon become universal, making the world a much more stable and agreeable place for international companies. Perhaps few senior executives really believed the hype, but it helped to justify something they were probably going to do anyway, which was to close down political risk and international analysis units in an effort to shave costs.

This might seem short-sighted, but in fact to that point, political risk units and a political risk perspective had often been an awkward fit with business. Writing in 1993, David M. Raddock notes that, coming from government and political science backgrounds, "The new breed of 'political risk analysts' as a whole were slow to make the linkage between political variables and their potential for direct or indirect impact on the corporate bottom line" (Raddock, 1993, p. 3). Much political risk insight seemed rather abstract and not tailored to guide specific projects and initiatives. It was a two-way problem. Senior executives regarded political risk expertise as an exotic appendage, and few tried to understand it for themselves, or to insure its integration with routine planning processes. In intelligence parlance, one would call this a gap between analyst and consumer. The result was that political risk was not seen as a core function, and thus expendable under cost pressure.

The early 1990s did not see the end of history and the advent of an age of universal political and economic values based on the Western model. Capitalism as the mode of production, and the role of private enterprise and exchange within that, is now the predominant economic model, but state-led capitalism and authoritarian or quasi-democratic governance compete with the Western model. In recent years, great power governments have had few qualms about pushing companies to align with the imperatives of geostrategic rivalries. Greased by real-time information exchange, globalisation has significantly accelerated, and with it has come even greater contagion effects from economic and political crises and instability. Globalisation has even facilitated reactions against itself, with traditionalist and hyper-nationalist backlashes in widely separated geographies often singing by the same basic hymnbooks shared through online fora, the dark web and social media. While the Cold War had its share of "basket case" countries, the world now holds an array of failed or fragile states whose problems ultimately affect regional and global stability. Classic political risks such as instability, conflict, terrorism, interference in contracts and corruption have persisted, and new pressures from climate change will intensify some issues and give rise to new ones. Political risk as a challenge did not go away, even while political risk as a field and practice seems to have waned.

Indeed, political risk appears to have hit a dead end. Cecilia Emma Sottilotta, in her 2013 paper on political risk, notes the lack of theoretical progress and consistency in the concept, and suggests that one reason for this is that political risk has remained fragmented between academic fields and the interpretations of distinctly different business sectors (Sottilotta, 2013). A casual perusal of chapters on political risk in modern business textbooks, and recent articles on it in the business press and by management consultancies and law firms, often feels like a trip down memory lane to the 1970s, the last decade when there were significant theoretical breakthroughs. "No other business function has such a variable title", writes Nigel Gould-Davies, about the way that political risk management actually manifests in companies (Gould-Davies, 2019, p. 20). Outside of the insurance industry, it is very rare to find "political risk" in job titles. And despite being a recognised, if perhaps ill-defined, challenge for decades, business surveys persistently indicate that only a small proportion of international firms undertake explicit political risk assessment. At both the theoretical and practical level, political risk seems spectral at best.

This seems to be a dismal state of affairs from the perspective of political risk afficionados, who would appear to be masochistically banging their heads on a wall of their own making. It also suggests that international companies are running blind. But one needs to go behind the "political risk" label to see what is really going on. It is not pretty, but it is not that bad either.

Political risk is indeed an interdisciplinary concern, and it was always prone to getting fragmented between different functions which dealt with political risk in their own terms. Strategic planning, for example, does not ignore geopolitical and country trends in long-range planning; rather, it incorporates these as a normal part of its search for optimal markets and diversification strategies. Legal departments scrutinise regulatory regimes and seek to ensure that contracts are defensible and that disputes would be addressed in places and fora with robust rule of law. Government affairs, external affairs and public relations seek to identify and engage with legitimate socio-political stakeholders, and corporate social responsibility teams directly engage with host communities. Corporate security worries about not only criminal activity but also potential harm from political violence and extremist groups. Business continuity and supply chain managers consider the effects of unrest, strikes and conflict on logistics and critical infrastructure. Senior executives and country managers routinely undertake corporate diplomacy with governments and other socio-political counterparts, and most frontline staff in emerging market operations try to understand members of the socio-political milieu that they come into contact with. Furthermore, many companies still routinely purchase political risk insurance and hedge against currency risks.

Beyond specific management functions, political risk also tacitly manifests in some cross-functional practices. One significant management trend has been the uptake of sustainability, itself a rather ambiguous concept but generally incorporating not just environmental performance, but also fair and legitimate relationships with the societies that a company affects. One aim of sustainability is to reduce friction with the socio-political environment, and in practical terms this is a significant aspect of political risk management. Enterprise risk management, or ERM, has also seen tremendous uptake since the 1990s. While much ERM seems to be trapped in a compliance-centric mode and over-reliant on piecemeal risk registries, its more strategic and problem-solving manifestations help to inspire the questioning of assumptions of success, and this opens the door for hard questions about socio-political conditions that a company would need to contend with in any given growth initiative. Country risk as a practice is alive and well in banks in particular, and its assessment of economic and financial risks often incorporates socio-political variables.

Since the 1990s, then, political risk as an explicit practice area has tailed off, but in practical terms it is still a business consideration and political risk management occurs under a variety of labels and functions. However, there is a badly missed opportunity in not having kept political risk on board as an explicit concept for the socio-political challenges that companies face, and as a way to integrate the diverse functional activities that constitute political risk management.

Outside of a few niche functions such as global threat intelligence, most of the activity that currently relates to political risk management is simply the result of smart people trying to do their jobs well in an international context. They need to look at all factors that could affect their goals, and socio-political dynamics, by whatever label, inevitably come up and become a consideration. But as in the Indian parable of the blind men and the elephant, each function is only getting a piece of the picture. Socio-political challenges derive from socio-political systems, and without a holistic perspective of the relevant system, be it global or country, functional initiatives lack overall cohesion. Not having a sense of the wider whole, delicate balances and trade-offs are not recognised, messaging can be divergent, one part wants to defend and ringfence while another wants to engage, and if a socio-political crisis arises, then everyone scrambles to build a common picture rather than smoothly coordinating around a shared perspective. Experience and creativity, along with more abundant information, have ensured that much de facto, or tacit, political risk management is going on, but while this can work in less volatile circumstances, in complex environments it is far from ideal.

In introducing the concept of political risk, we have come full circle. It is an established concept and has been around for a while, and for a period it was an explicit concern and practice in many international companies. When it fell off the radar, it never quite recovered as "political risk", and while companies now routinely deal with it, they often do so lacking an integrated picture of what they are dealing with. Subsequent chapters focus on how one can get this integrated picture and how to interpret it to see potential challenges and issues that need to be addressed.

DEFINITION AND CHARACTERISATION

Having covered the state of the art, such as it is, it is time to offer a definition of political risk suitable for the context of on-the-ground operations in complex environments.

As noted earlier, various definitions exist and have often been tailored to specific sectors and levels of analysis. To cover these here would lead to getting sidetracked. For interested readers, the 1978 classic *Political Risk: A Review and Reconsideration*, by Stephen J. Kobrin (Kobrin, 1978), and Cecilia Emma Sottilotta's 2013 paper *Political Risk: Concepts, Definitions, Challenges* (Sottilotta, 2013) provide clarity on the main different interpretations.

We first briefly define political risk in our context, and then offer a more nuanced characterisation to help clarify the concept. The basic definition, which uses "organisation" for both the company undertaking an operation and the operational entity itself, is as follows:

> For an organisation in a specific country, political risk is potential harm, disruption and disruptive uncertainty arising from socio-political dynamics and behaviour in the environment, and from socio-political actors' attitudes and responses towards the organisation.

That is deceptively simple, and to operationalise the concept we need some additional reference points.

First, we need to deal with "political", and to clarify that we need a definition of politics. Politics is activity aimed at:

- governing a country, or achieving the position of governing it;
- sustaining, undermining or replacing a particular governing regime;
- influencing a government to the advantage of one's social or economic entity;
- influencing society towards particular subnational, traditional and ideological values; and
- defending one's own social group, be it a subnation, subregion or values-based group, from perceived incursions on its rights and status.

Next, while "political risk" is the short label for the phenomenon of interest, the full label is "socio-political risk", and it is worth briefly seeing why. Social groups and values already arise in our definition of politics. While governments are at the heart of the matter, they impose themselves on, and in turn face expectations and pressure from, society. That interaction is what really drives political dynamics in a country. Additionally, while there is a relatively marked separation of political and social (including business) activity in highly institutionalised countries, in most countries there is an overlap between people's political and social loyalties and activities. Social and traditional bonds cross-cut the public and private domains, blurring the edges between them. As we will see in Part II, when it comes to discerning the challenges that a company can face in a developing or transitional country, the distinction between political and social quickly becomes moot.

The next part is "risk". We actually take pains to minimise use of this term in the assessment process, because it is now so jumbled up with enterprise risk management and the unresolved conceptual confusion therein that it becomes problematic. Political risk as a field was on the scene well before risk became a standard business concern, and hence it had, and retains, a more casual, or common-sense meaning. In general, a risk is a potential challenge or issue, which can arise through interaction with existing dynamics, but also because of potential new events and changes. A risk in our context can also be the manifestation of friction between an organisation and socio-political actors, or harmful behaviour which they might undertake if they see the organisation as a problem, or as a predatory opportunity. Our meaning of risk will become clearer as we proceed in Part II. For now, perhaps just imagine two conceptions of risk, one held by the ERM function in a company, and one held by a foreign intelligence agency. The latter routinely deals with risk, but instead of trying to pigeonhole the concept it just gets on with advising leaders about what could harm national interests and what they could do about it. That it is more our interpretation here.

The above said, we can add one more note about risk in our context of on-the-ground operations, and this is what is exposed to or affected by political risk. It can ultimately affect mission fulfilment or profit, but as eventual, intended outcomes these are not direct on-the-ground exposures. There are different ways of conceptualising what is exposed to political risk, but a holistic perspective emphasises underlying enablers of operational and business performance. Thus, political risk can harm, impede or disrupt:

- personnel – they make the operation happen;
- reputation (and legal standing) – this is the basis of credibility and legitimacy;
- continuity – this enables meeting operational targets; and
- control – this means that we can exercise our legitimate rights, make our own decisions, and retain ownership over our assets.

We explore these four assets, and what can affect them, in more detail in Chapter 3, but at this stage they help to give a flavour of what political risk is about.

The above might seem rather long-winded, but in the author's experience, common modern definitions and characterisations of political risk fail to provide a clear target for assessment and planning, and in particular often fail to actually define what politics means. Even this degree of detail, however, will not always suffice. Politics is a somewhat grey zone in human interaction and sits amidst many other domains of activity, such as business, religion and social activism. At the same time, not everything is politics, and if there is one distinctive feature, it is that governments, or at least predominant authorities in a territory, are close to the centre of it. Elements of this definition and characterisation will come into play later on, but hopefully the above provides a general conceptual foundation for what follows.

THREE ILLUSTRATIVE CASES

Before proceeding to the next chapter on complex environments, some actual cases of political risk are useful to help flesh out the concept. The first one is about a US power company in Georgia, and it illustrates how political risk can arise as a systemic challenge, and entanglement in a deteriorating situation. The next concerns a British retailer in Egypt. This demonstrates how political risk can arise alongside, and partly because of, a company's failure to adapt to its socio-economic, and especially cultural, environment. Finally, the third case about a Norwegian oil and gas company in Algeria clearly shows the overlap between political and security risk. More importantly, though, it demonstrates that while political risk can manifest as a single major surprise, the degree of surprise can vary depending on our own actions. Each case is followed by discussion about what it reveals about the character of political risk, and, as an informal preview of later sections, political risk intelligence. These cases only capture a few manifestations of a diverse phenomenon, but together they at least indicate some important patterns and attributes.

AES in Georgia, 1999–2003: Systemic Challenge and Entanglement

Georgia had been independent from the Soviet Union for seven years by 1998 when AES, a US-based power distribution company, acquired a controlling stake in Telasi, a Georgian state electricity distributor mainly covering Tbilisi. Prior to AES' entry, Georgia's state-building had been disrupted by a coup and two civil conflicts, and the government was eager to show some progress in public service provision. AES' aim was to make the new AES-Telasi profitable, but in responding to a state utility privatisation, it also had a developmental remit in ensuring stable and fairly priced electricity provision for Tbilisi customers.

AES was realistic about some of the challenges, which included widespread corruption in the energy sector and indeed in Telasi itself, and the change for Georgian citizens in now having to pay for electricity, which had been heavily subsidised in the Soviet period. AES took on corruption in its immediate circle of influence and initiated a communications campaign on the merits of paying for power as a way to ensure a safe and stable supply. While AES-Telasi did not operate at a profit at any point in AES' stay in Georgia, it established much of the necessary infrastructure for smooth future operations and was making headway in changing attitudes about paying for electricity. On a purely operational level, after the initial year the project was showing progress.

What AES underestimated was the scale of entrenched opposition to the notion of a profitable, impartial and independent power distributor. It was not just ordinary citizens who found it hard to adjust to paying for power. The Georgian government and Tbilisi authorities themselves were big electricity consumers, and many state agencies now found themselves paying for what they actually used, now that usage was metered. There was considerable overlap between state and local authorities and Georgian business oligarchs who had snapped up cheaply priced state companies after the fall of the USSR and now owned antiquated but power-hungry facilities. When AES-Telasi actually started pressing these major customers for unpaid bills, including through temporary power cuts, this intersection of elites, often organised along clan lines overlapping with mafia groups and ex-KGB, began to organise a backlash. This involved not just circumventing and sabotaging power metres but also coordinating local media and rumour campaigns against AES, and coercing and buying ordinary people's involvement in anti-AES protests.

Another layer to AES' problems was Russia, which sought to keep the newly independent republics dependent on Russia for energy, as a means of continued political leverage. Not only would Russia routinely halt power exports to Georgia, but with the tacit support of the Russian state, Russian mafia and ex-KGB with connections in Georgia assisted with organising the wider campaign against AES. This included using cross-border criminal-political networks to influence power supply from neighbouring countries, making AES look like it was failing to meet its power supply obligations. Watching on the side lines was a Russian power company with informal Kremlin ties, and while the company was not directly involved in the machinations against AES, for the Russian state it would have been a far preferable owner of Telasi than American AES.

Between protests and coordinated pressure, by 2002 AES was losing ground. Pressure escalated to threats, and in August that year the Georgian finance manager of AES-Telasi was assassinated. With increasing security worries, AES sent most of its expatriates home, and it started to look for a way to offload Telasi. The only serious buyer which came forward was the aforementioned Russian power company. AES sold, and by late 2003 had completely withdrawn from Georgia, with a loss of approximately $300 million. Ironically, Georgia's Rose Revolution, which was inspired in part by public frustration with the same issues that had beset AES, occurred shortly after AES left the country, and resulted in reforms that significantly improved governance.

In retrospect, the basic structure of the situation at the time was unfavourable for AES. Drawing on Stacy Renee Closson's research (Closson, 2007), informal social networks within Georgia had become more organised and covert in Soviet times as clans sought to evade Soviet control. These networks, which included an organised crime component, were the de facto power structure upon independence, severely challenging early institutional governance (as occurred in several post-Soviet countries). When combined with a weak and co-opted state and ex-KGB seeking to bolster their own status and gain, AES was up against a shadow alliance that would not allow a lucrative source of leverage like electricity to fall outside its control. Russia's efforts to reassert control over ex-republics, Georgia included, magnified local reactions and added a sub-regional dimension to AES' challenge. One might have thought that more rational elements of the Georgian government could have lent AES some support, since officially AES' role was important, but in AES' own 2004 assessment of the operation, it said of the state's part in the project: "Completely dysfunctional...Impossible to maintain any alignment of interests behind the AES plan...Enormous interference..." (Scholey, 2004). Under pressure and without any national champion, AES was on borrowed time.

AES might have needed a healthy dose of paranoia to foresee the resistance that it encountered, but a sound political risk intelligence question in challenging environments is, "If we did succeed, who would be hurt and how might they respond?" Digging into this question would have raised some red flags and indicated the merits of a more cautious and gradual approach, and perhaps of giving a bigger role to transnational or government donors who could have brought more political and economic clout. The pattern of networked, or systemic, socio-political opposition which this case illustrates is not uncommon, even if AES suffered a particularly severe and irrecoverable instance.

The case illustrates two important attributes of political risk. First, it is not just about things going on in a place. Political risk is often associated with headline trends and newsworthy events. However, while macro-level changes like new FDI regulations, coups, conflict or sanctions can have a big effect, they usually present a relatively clear "take it or leave it" choice. When it comes to stakeholder responses, especially in the context of weak governance and socio-political rivalry, it is often very hard to decipher the phenomena affecting the operation, and companies tend to get entangled, with no clear reason to leave even as their position steadily deteriorates. Thus, political risk is often about relationships, and the socio-political stakeholder variable holds unique intelligence and decision challenges, in addition to being an important factor in an operation's performance.

The second attribute of political risk illustrated by the case is that in political risk, "risk" often needs a more systemic interpretation than in conventional risk management. In typical risk assessment approaches, a risk is seen as an event or change of estimable probability that would have a certain degree of impact on the asset or objective. Risks are identified through scans of potential factors and exposures, then assessed and rated for probability and impact, with the product of the two ratings being the measure of a risk's overall severity. More conventional risk registries include such things as currency and price fluctuations, changes in regulations, a hack of company data, and even internal "failure to" risks such as failure to hire the right talent, or to get the bugs out of a new IT system in time for the business peak. These vary in complexity, but on the whole, they are relatively discrete, and can be captured and assessed as specific occurrences.

In the AES case, a conventional risk assessment could have captured some of the potential issues that AES faced, but AES' ongoing systemic challenge of networked opposition in a context of weak governance, regional power interests and local rivalries would have been hard to capture as a single risk without vastly oversimplifying the problem. Even if there had been a clear and concise way to define the problem as a risk, assessing it as a risk (for probability and impact) would have been a conundrum, because the relevant actors would have had dynamic and adaptive responses, including responding directly to AES's own moves. A conventional assessment would have been too hypothetical and static to capture the possibilities inherent in a dynamic relationship. Trying to break the problem down into an array of sub-risks would have fragmented a holistic picture from which potential patterns of evolution could be identified. Another question is how conventional risk assessment can be applied in cases of entanglement in a deteriorating situation, given the strong element of the principal's own decisions (or indecision).

This is not to say that the conventional concept of risk is irrelevant, but it is more suited to political risks which could be characterised as discrete events, changes or encounters. Alongside such risks, a more systemic assessment would be required to discern potential evolving situations and patterns of interaction between the company and its socio-political environment, and these would look more like situational scenarios than risks. The AES case well illustrates that political risk is not just about "risk" in the conventional sense, and that other perspectives more germane to systems and relationships usually need to augment standard risk assessment.

A brief point to add about this case is that it follows the general pattern of particularly high socio-political sensitivity in projects involving foreign firms and national assets, either critical public services or natural resources that generate public revenue. Foreign provision of, or control over, such assets is often a sensitive issue, even in developed countries long accustomed to a major role for the private sector.

SAINSBURY'S IN EGYPT, 1999–2001: POLITICAL RISK EXACERBATED BY CULTURAL MISSTEPS

Sainsbury's, a major UK grocery retailer, went to Egypt in April 1999 through a few major acquisitions of local grocery chains and distributors which it then transformed into modern supermarkets. Prior to Egypt, Sainsbury's had little international experience and no emerging market experience, yet Egypt's burgeoning consumerism, relative political stability at the time, and sheer market size made it seem like an alluring opportunity.

At the height of its operations in late 2000, Sainsbury's had over 100 stores and 2,000 Egyptian employees, mainly in and around Cairo. During its first few months in the country, Sainsbury's stores met with considerable approval by ordinary Egyptians who welcomed low prices and being able to do most of their shopping in one convenient location, as opposed to spreading it across a variety of small local shops. Staff were also initially enthusiastic about decent pay and stable jobs. Although Sainsbury's had an operating loss of £10 million in 2000, within months of entry it had gained considerable market traction, and seemed headed to longer-term success.

Three factors triangulated to undermine the operation. One was the challenge in dealing with Egypt's bureaucracy, which was slower and more convoluted than Sainsbury's had expected. Getting a licence to open a new store could take months or longer, and in at least one instance Sainsbury's had a licence, opened and stocked a store, and then had to close it and lay off staff after its licence was declared incorrect by Egyptian authorities (Sainsbury's debacle likely to haunt Egypt for years, 2001).

The second factor was Sainsbury's cultural inexperience with respect to Egypt's customers and staff. Drawing on research published by business academics El-Amir and Burt in 2008 (El-Amir & Burt, 2008), which was based in part on first-hand interviews, while customers appreciated low prices and a wide range of choice, many found the shopping experience to be devoid of the human interaction they were accustomed to, while others felt that the mass market approach was blind to Egyptians' own sensitivities to social strata. Staff too were unaccustomed to mechanistic institutional management, and found the lack of informal channels to provide their own advice on cultural adaptation to be frustrating and indicative of foreign arrogance. On the few occasions when Sainsbury's made layoffs, once in response to a labour dispute, local staff were nonplussed at the lack of human touch and consideration in the decisions. When Sainsbury's later encountered direct reactions by hostile socio-political segments, it found itself lacking a support base among customers and staff, who had grown increasingly alienated with what seemed like a maladaptive foreign import even as they continued to appreciate low prices and lucrative jobs.

Finally, Sainsbury's, with enormous purchasing power and mass market appeal by comparison to local family-owned grocery stores, was upending the local market and threatening these smaller businesses, many of which had been part of their local communities for decades. An appeal by a coalition of grocers compelled Sainsbury's to agree not to sell below factory prices (El-Amir & Burt, 2008, p. 25), but this brought small shops only marginal relief. In late 2000, the Second, or Al Aqsa, Intifada in Palestine kicked off, raising Arab and Egyptian sensitivities to perceived Western favouritism towards Israel. Local grocers took advantage of this atmosphere to plant rumours, often via sympathetic local mosques, that Sainsbury's had some kind of affiliation with Israel and was a "Jewish" company, in addition to being an outlet for goods made in the US, Israel's main ally. Even many Sainsbury's customers and staff who doubted these rumours still had sympathy for the campaign against Sainsbury's. As El-Amir and Burt summarise, "Such a significant technical shift [caused by Sainsbury's] in the overall retail culture caused massive market destabilization which was interpreted by both customers and employees as unrighteous…" (El-Amir & Burt, 2008, p. 20).

The rumour campaign led to a round of protests and vandalism at several Sainsbury's stores, and Sainsbury's also suffered from the contemporaneous popular boycott of US consumer goods and outlets (Sainsbury's pulls out of Egypt, 2001). Sainsbury's appealed to the government for some kind of statement that the rumours were untrue, but it took three months for the government to respond, despite keen official interest in sustaining FDI. Eventually, many Egyptians recognised that the charges against Sainsbury's were spurious and the trumped up anger was subsiding, but by early 2001 Sainsbury's decided to exit the country. It sold its stakes in its initial acquisitions back to the principal original owner at a £100 million loss, and in April that year left Egypt.

Many Egyptians, the government included, were sorry to see Sainsbury's go, but were annoyed that the company had cited the difficulty of operating in Egypt as a justification, when it seemed that Sainsbury's had mainly itself to blame for its lack of adaptation and for its decision to leave. Both in Egypt and abroad, Sainsbury's was widely regarded as thin-skinned, and Egyptian observers questioned why it could not have learned from the episode to readjust its position and management style in the country. That this was Sainsbury's first brush with the harder edge of emerging market socio-politics likely explains its seemingly premature decision to withdraw. It was weird, intense and scary, and it had expected more help from its country stakeholders.

As an addendum to the case, in 2014, three years after the fall of Mubarak, the Egyptian businessman from whom Sainsbury's had first acquired its main Egyptian assets, and to whom it resold them on departure, launched an embezzlement case against Sainsbury's CEO, claiming that the company had understated its liabilities, and that the CEO had travelled to Egypt in June 2014 to manipulate evidence. The case went to court in September that year, and the CEO, who was apparently unaware that the case was even underway, was sentenced in absentia to two years in prison. In an appeal, during which it was proven that the CEO had no role in the Egypt initiative and was in London at the time of the alleged trip to Cairo (Garside, 2015), he was acquitted. Thus, on top of a case more about the social aspect of political risk comes a minor lesson about the dangers of weak rule of law, even for individual staff. The Egyptian businessman in question had a track record for spurious commercial disputes and had in fact spent several years in self-imposed exile avoiding his own business problems until regime change in 2011 (Quinn, 2015), yet his questionable case was given credence without any defence, and a foreign national was sentenced as a result. While the CEO easily cleared himself when he travelled to Egypt for the appeal, it was a disconcerting experience which could have had more serious implications.

The Sainsbury's case is relatively uncomplicated compared to AES in Georgia, yet again some of the political risk issues it raises would not have been easy to discern or manage without a serious questioning of initial assumptions. Sainsbury's had two very Western assumptions, one about the universal primacy of "cheap and convenient", the other being "the better business model deserves to win". These only went so far in an Egyptian context before incurring a backlash. Political risk intelligence has a role in questioning assumptions in the socio-political context, to ensure that preconceptions and biases do not blind a company to potential challenges and reactions.

Another insight is that to capture a holistic picture of potential issues, political risk intelligence needs to go beyond the explicitly "political". Bureaucratic delays were a straightforward political risk, but political risk, as this case shows, is not just about the behaviour of explicitly political or official actors. Political risk can derive from purely social, cultural and economic concerns, which only become explicitly political when social actors apply political messaging or align with a political cause to gain wider support for their position (or in other cases when they bring socio-economic concerns to political actors to help seek redress). A negative political label might have little basis in fact, but it can be an effective metaphor for "bad company" generally. The official political actor in this case, the Egyptian government, was only significant for its bureaucratic complexity, and to a lesser extent for its hesitation to go against the mood of the street to try to counter the rumour campaign.

Additionally, again we see in this case that political risk does not just arise from specific changes or occurrences, or "risks". The only explicit political event was the start of the Al Aqsa Intifada. This led to the boycott of US products and outlets, and the product boycott hurt Sainsbury's and could have been a sales challenge for several months. Otherwise, though, it was only a factor insofar as it inspired the notion of linking Sainsbury's to Israel to counter its commercial power, and this was only effective in the context of Sainsbury's having underplayed its cultural integration. No event, or events, were directly responsible for Sainsbury's problems. Except for the bureaucratic challenges, these arose as a confluence of relationships and events, as a system.

Finally, the same question as with AES applies here: "If we were successful, who would be hurt and how might they respond?" It is easy to get carried away with purely commercial success and fail to see unintended consequences and in particular that when someone wins, someone else might lose at least something. In a very institutionalised context where business competition is seen as fair as long as it is legal, this has few ramifications. In a developing country where many people are on the edge of serious scarcity, and where traditional relationships are just as important as institutional ones, blatantly winning can incur a backlash that makes commercial gains unsustainable.

STATOIL IN ALGERIA, 2013: POLITICAL RISK AS SECURITY RISK AND AS A SURPRISE OCCURRENCE

On a brief preliminary note, the subject of this case, the terrorist attack on the In Amenas gas plant in Algeria in 2013, has been widely covered in the news and in at least two publicly available investigations, Statoil's own (Statoil/Equinor, 2016), and a coroner's inquest in the UK (West Sussex Coroner, 2016). The focus here will not be on the details of the event itself, rather on the dynamics around it, and what the case reveals about the character of political risk.

In 2003, Statoil, Norway's principal oil and gas company, had limited international experience and was eager to develop more. That year, it welcomed the opportunity to join a familiar British partner, BP, for joint operations in Algeria, as part of a joint venture (JV) with the Algerian state oil and gas company, Sonatrach. Statoil's stake was officially approved in 2004. The JV developed gas fields in Algeria's southeast, and in 2006 completed the construction of a gas processing plant at In Amenas, approximately 80 kilometres from the Libyan border. By late 2012, the In Amenas facility was processing 11.5 percent of Algeria's natural gas exports, worth around $4 billion a year. At the time of the attack on the plant, on 16 January 2016, the JV had approximately 800 staff, including over 130 expats of whom 22 were Statoil personnel.

When Statoil first entered into the In Amenas project in 2004, Algeria was still recovering from a ten-year civil war that had pitted Islamic extremists against a military-led government. In 1999, after an estimated 150,000 people had been killed, the main Islamist groups were in disarray. The new Algerian president brought in by the military as the civilian face of a post-war Algeria granted an amnesty to remaining insurgents, and the country began to recover from its *décennie noire*.

Not every insurgent wanted amnesty. A hard inner core of Algerian jihadists retreated southward, eventually into the Sahara, where it would take control of smuggling routes and conduct kidnappings to sustain itself as a mobile insurgent force. In 2007, the main Algerian group allied with Al Qaeda to become Al Qaeda in the Islamic Maghreb, or AQIM. In practice, AQIM was a loose federation of different jihadist groups in which the Algerians were first among equals, but it was unified in common resentment against Western influence in North Africa and the Sahel, and against the secular and West-leaning governments of the region, not least Algeria's, which had fought the civil war with brutal tactics and considerable covert Western support.

In 2011, Libya's version of the Arab Spring revolution led to state collapse and violent conflict along tribal and regional lines. This created a stateless vacuum in a large part of the Sahara, and Libyan army weapons fell into the hands of non-state actors. AQIM and other groups benefited by having an ungoverned safe haven and access to new stocks of weaponry. Another effect was that Libyan Tuareg (an indigenous Saharan ethnic group), many of whom had been employed in the old Libyan army, formed armed groups and joined their brethren in Mali in their fight for autonomy. In 2012, Tuareg rebels seized control over much of Mali's north. Within the wider Tuareg rebellion in Mali, the Islamist element aligned to AQIM began to predominate, giving AQIM and its sub-groups yet another haven in the region from which to initiate attacks, including several launched into southern Algeria.

AQIM wanted to shore up its position in the Sahel and Mali in particular, but France and the US were quietly seeking to increase intelligence and counter-terrorist capabilities among Sahel governments. AQIM believed that it needed a strong statement of its own capability in order to deter regional collaboration with Western security efforts, and it also wanted to take advantage of the opportune circumstances afforded by the power vacuum on Algeria's southeast to strike a humiliating blow against Algeria. It is not certain if AQIM's command or a specific sub-group came up with the idea to attack the In Amenas gas facility (Guidère, 2014), but a specific sub-group led by an experienced commander took on the task and undertook intensive planning that included developing detailed target intelligence (Barak, 2016).

On the eve of the attack, at the In Amenas gas plant expat managers were facing a disconcerting spike in a long-running labour dispute among locally contracted drivers. On 15 January 2013, one group of drivers angrily pressed their demands in a meeting with expat managers. Evidence for the UK inquiry states that this meeting was "heavy and explosive" (West Sussex Coroner, 2016, p. 113). In Amenas' managers probably felt that their week could not get much worse.

The attackers struck the gas facility the next morning. In Amenas had three layers of security, with Algerian military patrols keeping an eye on the surrounding area, a locally based gendarme unit for perimeter surveillance and response, and unarmed civilian guards and barriers for the facility itself. The attack force got through the first two layers without being noticed, upon which the third layer was irrelevant. The four-day crisis had begun.

In total, 39 expats, of whom 5 were Statoil personnel, and 1 Algerian were killed. This was tragic but it could have been worse. The attackers had planned on maximal destruction if the Algerian government did not negotiate (demands included a prisoner release and safe passage to Mali) (Barak, 2016, p. 13), but in the end they procrastinated, hoping that hostages' phone calls to media outlets and their companies would increase pressure on the Algerian government, and at least draw out the siege for prolonged publicity. By the time it was clear that no negotiation would occur, the attackers were too busy dealing with the army's response to find all the hostages, many of whom had managed to escape and hide, often with the help of Algerian staff who were left unguarded.

The locally based gendarme got into sporadic shootouts with terrorist lookouts on the first day of the siege, but the army only responded in force on the 17th. When it did, there was no pretence of negotiations, and no surgical raid. The majority of hostage fatalities occurred when troops and helicopters engaged from a distance. In the most lethal incident, 26 hostages died when Algerian forces attacked a convoy of trucks in which the terrorists were transporting hostages from one site to a defensive perimeter at another section of the facility (Statoil/Equinor, 2016, p. 29).

On the 18th, when the attackers saw that they were out of time, they blew up the central processing plant in order to leave lasting damage before they were killed. Sporadic fighting continued, and the army declared operations over on the 19th, the fourth day of the crisis. Only three attackers were taken alive. The Algerian investigation later led to the capture of an accomplice who had once been employed at In Amenas, and this helped to explain how the attackers knew the plant layout (Statoil/Equinor, 2016, p. 59). It remains unclear whether there was a connection between the labour dispute and inside help for the attackers, or if such additional help would have made much difference.

In addition to the human tragedy, the attack led to a costly pause and slow recovery of In Amenas' production. It took a year before Statoil and BP personnel came back to In Amenas. The plant resumed gas processing only weeks after the attack, but it took over three years to reach pre-attack production levels, and a planned expansion of the plant was shelved (Attack on In Amenas Gas Facility – Special Report, 2018). The financial effect, in terms of lost revenue and repair costs, was billions of dollars, of which Statoil's share would have been in hundreds of millions. AQIM thus achieved not just terror and lingering unease but also a significant economic strike on Algeria and Western companies.

There were also repercussions at home. Statoil decided to clear the air by releasing its own detailed investigative report in late 2013. Several home countries of expats killed in the attack conducted inquests, but because of BP's significant role in the project, the UK's Coroner's Inquest, concluded in early 2015, was particularly detailed. Both the Statoil report and the UK inquest did not directly blame the JV partners for negligence, but they did find several failings and misjudgements in risk assessment and security that contributed to a lack of preparation for an attack contingency. This led to criticism by bereaved families who felt that the JV partners had not taken duty of care seriously enough. In 2015, several families launched a lawsuit against BP. BP settled in 2019 before the case went to court, but the publicity around the case was damaging. By comparison, Statoil's transparency in releasing its report, which was a serious and self-critical assessment, and its overall transparency in dealing with affected families, reduced its reputational damage even if it did not escape some harsh criticism.

Political risk is often equated with newsworthy surprises like coups, expropriations or indeed terrorist attacks, and the In Amenas attack was an example of how political risk can manifest as a one-off harmful surprise. At the same time, the case also reveals that in political risk, surprise can be a matter of degree over which we have some control. This becomes clear in briefly examining why the attack was such a surprise for the JV.

The JV was not blind to the possibility of an attack on the In Amenas plant, and incoming intelligence from external monitoring services also noted the possibility (Statoil/Equinor, 2016, p. 57). But the scenario was not developed and tested, nor was it directly accounted for in planning.

One reason was organisational. In Statoil alone, there were at least three functions dealing with risk assessment for the In Amenas operation, and the overlap in their responsibilities "can potentially hinder security from being addressed holistically" (Statoil/Equinor, 2016, p. 51). The problem was multiplied across the JV, in which the three main partners each had its own processes but little formal coordination in terms of sharing and weighing up intelligence. If the possibility were taken seriously in some corners, the channel to explicit organisational consideration was not clearly defined.

Another reason was related to over-reliance on a basic risk map, a depiction of the outcome of a conventional risk assessment using probability and impact as the axes of risk prioritisation. In the In Amenas case, because an attack had no precedent and was an ambiguous prospect, it was not separately defined, and instead aggregated within terrorism risk in general. Thus, it was obscured, and its importance was dragged down by less severe but better understood terrorism risks such as kidnapping and pipeline sabotage (Statoil/Equinor, 2016, pp. 47, 58; West Sussex Coroner, 2016, p. 103). Once it was somehow accounted for on the risk map, even if it was not clearly depicted, further exploration and testing was not deemed necessary. The risk map was the final word in planning priorities (linking to the organisational question, different units in the JV even had somewhat different risk maps).

As a side note, ironically, while one role of risk assessment is to provide warning against surprise, in emphasising probability, or likelihood, as one axis of assessment this role can be undermined. Simply put, by definition, any surprise was "unlikely" before it happened. Sometimes something is unlikely because it is an estimable type of risk and reliable information points to it not happening. However, sometimes we are actually uncertain, and this gets translated into "unlikely" by the available logic of the risk framework. Especially for high-impact but low-likelihood risks, further testing is critical, and this would need a framework better suited to handling uncertainty, and to structured exploration of the outside possibilities. The JV might have misused the risk map by lumping too many things into the same box, but relying only on that approach was a risk in itself. This is especially relevant to political risk and its security aspect, because together, the vagaries of social and group psychology, complex causal interactions, and deliberate deception by hostile actors often lead to ambiguous possibilities.

Finally, assumptions about the Algerian army were badly flawed. As we saw in the previous cases, the stakeholder aspect of political risk can be critical, yet in a conventional risk-centric perspective focused on potential events and occurrences, it can be overlooked. Statoil and BP had premised their security plan on army responsiveness, yet "There was, however, only a limited exchange of information with the army. The joint venture was not therefore in a position to test its own planning assumptions." (Statoil/Equinor, 2016, p. 70).

The Algerian military had taken an *éradicateur* approach to Islamist terrorism during the recent civil war, and to put it mildly, it had prioritised the elimination of terrorists over minimising collateral damage. That they would prioritise the JV's people over an expedient end to the siege and the elimination of terrorists would have seemed highly questionable, had anyone decided to really look into their position. The military's capabilities were also not questioned in detail. While Algeria's military presence in the sub-region was significant, it was stretched by the dual imperative of securing far-flung borders and chasing down remnant terrorist groups. In its strategic picture, the gas processing plant competed with pressing priorities. The army was an essential stakeholder for the JV, but rather than being treated as such, it was more or less regarded as a fixed condition, or feature, of the operating environment, not as an actor with its own values and limitations.

In summary, three adaptations could have reduced the degree of surprise. One was better coordination and a simplified intelligence and security structure. Another was additional, more creative and assumption-busting analysis to augment the usual risk assessment, including an interpretive hunt for new and unusual patterns in the ongoing intelligence feed. The third was reframing the army as a stakeholder rather than a cog in security plans. Simulation exercises around the outside possibilities, incorporating role-playing "bad guys" and ideally real Algerian army and gendarme officers, could have made some apparently remote contingencies seem much more plausible and worth at least some adaptation of security arrangements.

Note that in the above, actually having a clear warning of the attack would not have been essential for better preparation against surprise. There have been instances when an intelligence service, for example, has known about an impending incident, which then enabled either forestalling it or quickly managing it. Usually, though, intelligence monitoring feeds in fragments of a picture, and creative interpretation leads to possible pictures, or scenarios, which cause us to adjust our preparations. In the In Amenas case, as Statoil summarised, the high degree of surprise came not from a lack of raw intelligence, but rather from "failure of imagination" (Statoil/Equinor, 2016, p. 70). This case was about a relatively discrete occurrence, but what it illustrates about the surprise aspect of political risk also applies to bigger potential events or changes, such as the Algerian civil war and the Arab Spring, which together shaped the context of the case.

To conclude with a broader point, the case clearly illustrates the overlap between security and political risk. Threats can be political actors, and their targets can be selected because of their ideological symbolism and/or because they represent an extortion opportunity for the political group. Additionally, personnel and assets can be harmed by political violence in their vicinity. These are classic security risks, but it is briefly worth noting another important part of the political risk and security overlap.

This is the potential effect of security arrangements on the reputation and moral standing of a company. One reason why the JV in the In Amenas case did not want its own armed private security for the facility itself was that it could potentially lead to a dangerous escalation of otherwise manageable disputes such as the driver strike, as well as accidental shootings. There have been numerous cases of company security, whether provided by the state or private contractors, exacerbating tensions with host communities and labour activists through ostentatious and heavy-handed behaviour, and in the worst cases through excessive use of force or using company security as a cover for violence against local political opponents. Companies can face a backlash from an array of stakeholders when abuses occur in their name. The In Amenas case seems to highlight the problem of a lack of security, but from a political risk perspective, security capability can be a double-edged sword that requires careful balancing.

REFERENCES

Attack on In Amenas Gas Facility – Special Report. (2018). *Gulf Oil & Gas (dot) Com*. Universal Solutions S.A.E. Retrieved April 29, 2020, from https://www.gulfoilandgas.com/webpro1/projects/3dreport.asp?id=100122

Barak, M. (2016). *The In Amenas Gas Facility Attack – An Analysis of the Modus Operandi*. Herzliya: International Institute for Counter-Terrorism. Retrieved April 29, 2020, from https://www.ict.org.il/UserFiles/ICT-The-In-Amenas-Gas-Facility-Attack-Barack.pdf

Closson, S. R. (2007). *State Weakness in Perspective: Trans-territorial Energy Networks in Georgia, 1993–2003*. Doctoral dissertation, London School of Economics, International Relations. Retrieved from http://etheses.lse.ac.uk/1941/1/U226529.pdf

El-Amir, A., & Burt, S. (2008). Sainsbury's in Egypt: The strange case of Dr Jekyll and Mr Hyde? *International Journal of Retail and Distribution Management, 36*(4), 300–322. doi:10.1108/09590550810862697

Farnsworth, C. H. (1982, October 28). Risk Analysis Big Business for Ex-Aides. *New York Times*. Retrieved from https://www.cia.gov/library/readingroom/docs/CIA-RDP99-00418R000100190001-1.pdf

Fitzpatrick, M. (1983). The Definition and Assessment of Political Risk in International Business: A Review of the Literature. *The Academy of Management Review, 8*(2), 249–256. doi:10.2307/257752

Garside, J. (2015, June 11). Sainsbury's CEO acquitted of embezzlement charges in Egypt. *Guardian*. Retrieved April 22, 2020, from https://www.theguardian.com/world/2015/jun/11/sainsburys-ceo-acquitted-embezzlement-egypt

Gould-Davies, N. (2019). *Tectonic Politics: Global Political Risk in An Age of Transformation*. Washington DC: Brookings Institution Press.

Guidère, M. (2014). The Timbuktu Letters: New Insights about AQIM. *Res Militaris*. Retrieved April 29, 2020, from https://hal.archives-ouvertes.fr/hal-01081769/document

Kobrin, S. J. (1978). *Political Risk: A Review and Reconsideration*. Working Paper #998-78, Massachusetts Institute of Technology, Sloan School of Management, Cambridge, MA. Retrieved June 16, 2022, from https://core.ac.uk/download/pdf/4413271.pdf

Kraar, L. (1980, March 24). The Multinationals Get Smarter About Political Risks. *Fortune*. Retrieved June 16, 2022, from https://www.cia.gov/readingroom/document/cia-rdp91-00901r000500150058-7

Quinn, I. (2015, April 29). Mike Coupe, Sainsbury's CEO, flies to Giza after Egyptian conviction. The Grocer. Retrieved April 22, 2020, from https://www.thegrocer.co.uk/supermarkets/mike-coupe-sainsburys-ceo-flies-to-giza-after-egyptian-conviction/517732.article

Raddock, David M. (1993). *Navigating New Markets Abroad*. Maryland: Rowman & Littlefield Publishers, Inc.

Sainsbury's debacle likely to haunt Egypt for years. (2001, April 18). *Mena Report*. Al Bawaba. Retrieved April 22, 2020, from https://www.albawaba.com/business/sainsbury%E2%80%99s-debacle-likely-haunt-egypt-years

Sainsbury's pulls out of Egypt. (2001, April 9). BBC. Retrieved April 22, 2020, from http://news.bbc.co.uk/1/hi/business/1268099.stm

Scholey, M. (2004). *What Happened to AES in Georgia and Where Do We Go from Here?* World Bank Energy Week 2004. Retrieved April 22, 2020, from http://siteresources.worldbank.org EW04_Georgia (link no longer active at 16 June 2022).

Sottilotta, C. E. (2013). *Political Risk: Concepts, Definitions, Challenges*. School of Government. Rome: LUISS. Retrieved June 16, 2022, from https://sog.luiss.it/sites/sog.luiss.it/files/SOG%20Working%20Papers%20Sottilotta%20ISSN_0.pdf

Statoil/Equinor. (2016). *The In Amenas Attack: Report of the Investigation into the Terrorist Attack on In Amenas*. Stavanger: Statoil/Equinor. Retrieved June 23, 2022, from https://www.equinor.com/content/dam/statoil/documents/In%20Amenas%20report.pdf

Stone, P. H. (1982, December 25). High Times in the Political Risk Business. *The Nation*. Retrieved June 16, 2022, from https://www.cia.gov/readingroom/document/cia-rdp90-00806r000100500006-9

Stone, P. H. (1983, August 7). Boom Days for Political Risk Consultants. *New York Times*. Retrieved June 16, 2022, from https://www.cia.gov/readingroom/document/cia-rdp91-00901r000500150019-0

West Sussex Coroner. (2016). *In Amenas Factual Findings Conclusions*. London: Transcript. Retrieved April 27, 2020, from https://www.westsussex.gov.uk/media/8874/inamenas_factualfindingsconclusion.pdf

2 Complex Environments

This chapter is aimed at providing an understanding of what complexity means in the context of a socio-political environment, and hence the country dynamics that one considers in identifying and assessing political risk. This will not be a rote breakdown of risk types, rather a consideration of broad factors and patterns that can make a country or part thereof challenging for a foreign business operation.

It is important to note that this chapter only looks at one side of the political risk equation – what is going on in the socio-political terrain that we might enter, irrespective of our prospective presence or identity. Country and local dynamics can affect anyone exposed to them, and we can learn a lot from understanding how a place works in general. But different organisations can have very different experiences depending on whom they are and how they relate to the socio-political terrain and actors within it. Thus, this chapter provides a general terrain map, while the next chapter adds nuance by looking at how an operation's own unique attributes and relationships can affect its particular experience.

The chapter unfolds as follows. As a precursor we look at the concept of "complexity", and how this term applies to the kinds of places and issues under consideration. We consider state fragility as an observable proxy of socio-political complexity, and use the analogy of the individual citizen for a tangible, human-scale introduction to the effects of complexity. The rest of the chapter is then about the factors and attributes that create complexity, and in turn political risk, for a company, without getting into who the company is and what it is doing. At this level, being foreign and having a local footprint is sufficient. This begins with an overview of the system of socio-political complexity, and then examines the elements of the core system within that, and how weaknesses in these lead to behaviours and dynamics that can affect foreign companies. By the end of this chapter, we will have established what to look for to identify general sources of political risk in a given terrain, and this will be an aspect of the baseline political risk intelligence exercise in Part II.

Note that when we begin the baseline exercise, there will not be a discussion of indicators of political risk. This chapter constitutes that discussion, not by listing and describing indicators, but by elucidating systemic weaknesses that can give rise to problematic phenomena and behaviours.

A SENSE OF COMPLEX

While not part of a standard political risk lexicon, the term "complex" is apt for the types of environments under consideration, because it implies that even in the absence of newsworthy or obvious challenges, one can still have a lot to worry about and a range of imperatives to balance if the operation is to be sustained in good health. To only say "politically risky" fails to capture the actual experience of a company in a complex environment. One can enter a place suffering a terrorist bombing campaign, or which could soon be subject to international sanctions, in other words a politically risky place, and not notice the risk because the bombs are sporadic and on the other side of the city, and sanctions never quite manifest. Day-to-day operations could be relatively smooth and require little explicit consideration of the socio-political domain.

Big and obvious risks such as terrorism or sanctions certainly happen and affect companies, but unless or until they manifest, they are often only distractions, while the problems that bite tend to derive from a dynamic mix of more subtle issues, like incurring a bad relationship with one's host community because one did not understand local social tensions, while at the same time facing persistent corruption pressure that wears down staff and ultimately risks legal liability and extortion, perhaps all in the context of anxiety about staff security. When managers become overwhelmed, mistakes happen, and these reduce credibility and incur backlashes. Issues can then coalesce and feed each other. The result can be entanglement in a deteriorating situation. This in itself is manifested political risk and makes the operation more vulnerable to further risks, but complexity made this situation possible. In relation to political risk, one could say that the more complex the environment, the more acute political risk tends to be, not just because of things that could happen there, but because issues are harder to foresee, and because of higher and sometimes overwhelming demands on management attention and judgement.

There is no standard index of socio-political complexity for countries, so to get a sense of what range of places are relevant to a focus on complex emerging markets a proxy is useful. There are commercial political risk indices, but these tend to focus on narrowly defined political risks of interest to a certain clientele. There are also "ease of doing business" indices, but they tend to look at the steps and timelines involved in business bureaucratic procedures, not at how unpredictable or open to socio-political interference such procedures might be. That leaves indices of state fragility, which for purposes here is a reasonable, if imperfect, proxy for socio-political complexity.

Assuming that a government were genuinely concerned about its country's viability as a well-functioning socio-political entity, it would hope to maintain human security, people's trust in each other and in the government, legitimate state authority, and national sovereignty, including territorial integrity. Fragility means that these bases of being a viable and functioning country are prone to disruption or dysfunction, often for the very same reasons, such as weak governance, social fragmentation, conflict and instability (which we get into later) that make a place complex for a foreign company. Thus, as a proxy for complexity it is workable at least on broad scales.

A fragility scale with some indicative countries at different general brackets is illustrated in Figure 2.1, drawn from one such index, the Fund for Peace *Fragile States Index 2020* (there are other fragility indices, and the World Bank's *World Governance Indicators* are similar, although phrased in terms of government behaviour and capacity).

One can find 178 countries on the *Index*, using aggregate scores from 12 sub-indicators. It would be evident to most readers that there would be a world of difference between the complications facing an operation in Switzerland, and one in Somalia. In Switzerland, one only has to obey the transparent and seldom-changing law in order to avoid socio-political issues or interference. In Somalia, one would need to balance inter-clan rivalries, pay bribes to officials and militia, hire and manage armed security, and somehow convince home country regulators, investors and

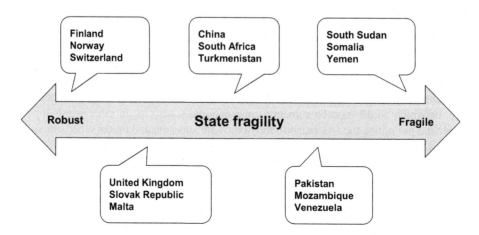

FIGURE 2.1   Illustrative state fragility scale.

critical non-governmental organisations (NGOs) that the company was meeting ethical expectations. In other words, Somalia is much more complex. Distinctions in this respect are quite clear
at widely separated points, for example between Malta and Venezuela, but they become finer
within brackets, and places are fragile, and complex, in different ways. By and large, it is safe to
say that we are interested in at least the countries on the more fragile half of the scale, but this
needs qualification.

For one thing, as we will see in the next chapter, the attributes of a specific company and operation are significant variables in how complex the relationship with the socio-political environment
might be. For example, two companies want to enter Country A, a fragile emerging market. One
company is going to fulfil a contract to operate the prison system, the other is opening an organic
yogurt plant. The prison outsourcing operation would likely be far more open to complication than
the yogurt plant.

Another qualification is that countries can become more or less robust depending on their own
internal dynamics and how they adapt to global and regional change. For example, according to
the *Index*, both Turkey and Jordan became considerably less robust between 2012 and 2020, while
Uzbekistan and Kyrgyzstan significantly improved. Aside from the extremes on either side of the
fragility scale, countries tend to move around and "fragile" describes a time period as much as a
place.

On the above note, as an important aside it is worth emphasising that even long-established
democracies and the upper half of the Organisation for Economic Co-operation and Development
(OECD) can become more fragile or show attributes of fragile countries. For example, the US and
the UK ranked 159th and 158th, respectively, in 2012. In 2020, they shared the 149th position, a significant regression. Several Western European countries showed a similar, if less-marked, pattern.
At the time of writing in 2020, the US, as one example, has been experiencing massive anti-racism
protests met by heavy-handed police responses, armed militia wandering the fringes of protests,
right-wing protests against state governments over covid restrictions, intense left-right antipathy
and a weakening of governing institutions because of continued presidential aspirations to personal
rule. If an alien entrepreneur were to drop in from another planet and look for fragile countries to
avoid, without knowing that the US has been a long-standing and usually stable democracy, the
alien could be forgiven for thinking it was fragile. In a few years it might be a different story. Thus,
one should bear in mind that while both "fragile" and "complex" usually apply to developing and
transitional countries, this is not always the case, and again fragility is not just about where but also
when.

While fragility is not a perfect proxy for complexity, it is workable. Imagine, for example, two
sets of monkey bars (or climbing frames) in a children's playground. One is made of wood and is
very sturdy. It is intricate and would take time to understand and negotiate, but it is solid and we
can look at it from afar and plan for it, knowing that by the time we start climbing it will not have
changed. The other is made of rope and is equally intricate, but it is in a state of disrepair and has
been frayed and tangled by a recent storm. It is harder to make sense of it in advance, and when one
starts climbing, one is more likely to slip and to get tangled. Thus, the more fragile monkey bars are
also more complex from our perspective as a climber. In a sense, fragility exists independently of
our interests or actions, but translates to complexity once we engage with a fragile system. In general, fragility as a tracked and indexed phenomenon helps to depict the broad bracket of countries,
and periods in countries' evolution, most germane to a concern about socio-political complexity
and risk.

THE INDIVIDUAL CITIZEN ANALOGY

Before moving on to what makes a country complex and politically risky, it helps to first consider
the question at a more manageable human scale, that of an ordinary person living in a complex
socio-political environment. By and large, the factors that complicate their life are often the same

as those which affect a foreign business operation. As we proceed, one can try the mental thought experiment of substituting the individual for one's own company.

First, for useful contrast, we start with the converse. Imagine a hypothetical law-abiding middle-class citizen A living in northern Europe. She can choose her friends on the basis of personal preference. She likes to wear outrageous T-shirts now and then, and no one seems to lift an eyebrow. She will probably never see the inside of a police car unless she does something really out of character. When she deals with the bureaucracy, the process can be slow but it is exactly as expected and nearly automatic. When she applies for a job, no one asks about her ideology or religion and she does not have to name relatives in high places. She is more likely to be struck by lightning than killed by human action. She generally distrusts politicians but has seen them come and go without any significant effect on her day-to-day life or indeed on the country's wider governing institutions, and if she really disliked a particular leadership or policy, she would feel entirely safe in joining a protest movement or an opposition party that actually expressed a sharp critique. For citizen A, her life seems to happen in one domain, and politics in another, and the domains only seem to intersect via a staid civil service that she rarely has to deal with. If life were complicated for A, it would not be because of politics.

A's relationship to politics and its influence on her can be summarised in Figure 2.2 below on this page.

By contrast, in Algiers in 2001, the author interviewed an Algerian manager working with the client foreign company as part of a case to see how the company was adapting to political changes as the civil conflict went into a new, cooler, phase. It was a freewheeling discussion, and it provides a useful example of life for an ordinary citizen in a complex socio-political environment (this individual, B, was not entirely ordinary in terms of economic status, since he had a good professional education and a fairly lucrative job, but his case will suffice).

B had had a wide circle of friends before the 1990s. During the 1990s and still in 2001, he only had a few. Early in the war years, B had broken off contact with friends who had regime connections, partly because he loathed the regime for its corruption and repressive tendencies and partly because it was dangerous to be associated with friends of the government, which the armed groups regarded as a viable target. He walked on eggshells with the few acquaintances he still had, because anyone could be a police informer and casual conversation was risky. For B as for many Algerians, politics had enforced a degree of social fragmentation, and he became socially isolated.

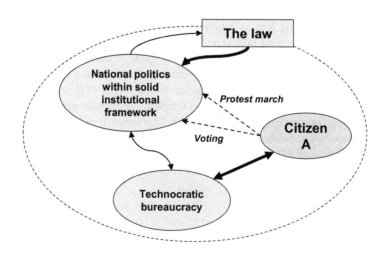

FIGURE 2.2   Low complexity for citizen A.

B was relieved to have a job with a foreign company. It was risky, because the armed groups had threatened Western companies and their workers, but it was worth it if only to escape the intense office politics that had arisen during the conflict. B had been a university teacher for part of the 1990s, and during the conflict universities had fallen under tight state control in an effort to identify insurgency sympathisers among students and staff. There had been an unhealthy rivalry among staff to appear more pro-regime, especially during organisational reshufflings and promotion competitions. B had often felt like his position was hanging by a thread, and managing the office politics had been a far more intensive job than the one he actually got paid for.

Security and fear of violence had weighed heavily on B throughout the 1990s, and by 2001 he was still quietly traumatised. The armed groups had apparently found worthy targets even among his banal neighbours, and he had seen bodies in his neighbourhood on the way to work. His daughter refused to wear a head scarf, and he eventually got her to go and stay with relatives in France. His son was "fighting age" and like many Algerian youth subject to random police detention. B paid for him to continue his studies in Egypt. B and his wife both dreaded the daily commute, not just because of potential terrorist attacks, but because at the frequent police roadblocks they both felt a cold knot in their stomachs, knowing that even as middle-aged professionals they were not immune to arbitrary suspicion or rumour.

The bureaucracy in Algeria had always been a convoluted blend of French, state-socialist and traditional (Ottoman) styles and processes, and creating redundant positions had long been a way for the state to try to control unemployment among educated youth. Even then, whom one knew was just as important as qualifications in getting a civil service job; hence, civil servants' work skills were often sketchy. B had to routinely interact with the bureaucracy for a variety of permits and registration renewals, and each time the process seemed different, his papers were lost or somehow "incomplete" despite what the last person had told him, and sometimes he was offered the chance to ensure that papers were not lost the next time by paying a small assurance fee (grand corruption was less of an issue at the time because of politically motivated "transparency" campaigns but at lower levels it persisted). B, along with many Algerians, spent a lot of time poring over applications and standing in line behind counters, and it added to his daily frustrations and anxiety.

B did not like the armed groups, and when the government gained the upper hand and reduced terrorist violence in Algiers, he was relieved. But that did not ameliorate his attitude towards the regime. It was hard to assign responsibility for corruption and repression, because despite President Bouteflika's appointment in 1999 and his apparent self-confidence, the regime was still a shifting web of competing "clans" and factions with muscle derived from links to different security agencies, connected by family and crony ties to business oligarchs who helped finance their respective factions, all ultimately paid for by siphoned oil proceeds. Despite its nebulous character, though, what the people at the top, *le Pouvoir*, thought or felt on a given day still had direct implications for ordinary people. B resented this whimsical power, and was also concerned about Algeria, which seemed to lack any consistent guiding hand or institutional bedrock beyond these shifting cliques.

B's life was complicated indeed, and this was wholly because of politics. B's case might be a somewhat extreme example, partly being based on life during a brutal civil conflict. Nonetheless, as an individual analogy his case is useful because it illustrates the multi-faceted character of socio-political complexity and its potential to have myriad niggling effects that add up to a very high-pressure situation.

Figure 2.3 is a quick summary sketch of what made individual B's life complicated.

If one replaced a person with a company, there would be more factors at play, and the overall picture would be more complicated. But a complexity picture for each of the three cases in the last chapter, for example, would share broad similarities with B's situation, especially the Georgia case. Now we turn to the matter at hand, the socio-political dynamics that can make life complicated for a foreign business operation.

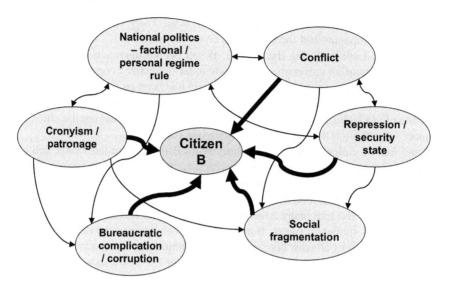

FIGURE 2.3   High complexity for citizen B.

A SYSTEM OF SOCIO-POLITICAL COMPLEXITY

There is a variety of taxonomies of political risks, and creating another taxonomy is not the aim here. Rather the focus is on what makes an environment complex and hence politically risky. In this section, we provide an overview of the wider system of socio-political complexity, or the process by which a place becomes fragile and complex. In subsequent sections in this chapter, we will then examine each main part of the complexity system, including external and long-term influences, the core socio-political system, and the symptoms of socio-political ill-health along with their implications for foreign companies. Note that this will not go into detail on socio-political actors or specific issues for companies, since they will be considered in the next chapter, which focuses on how an operation relates to its environment.

Two brief points are in order before starting. One is that academics, NGOs and political risk thinker-practitioners continue to generate considerable detailed research about the factors responsible for state fragility and complexity. What follows in this chapter does not draw from a particular theory; rather, it is a distillation of relevant knowledge aimed at practical brevity. It might not seem brief, but by comparison to the scope of the phenomenon it is just a sketch, and to try much more would need a corollary book just on socio-political dynamics.

The other point is that in spite of the aforementioned research, there is no grand or unified theory of complexity or of what ultimately makes a place politically risky. This is because of nuanced cultural and historical variations, and because of the importance of very specific but uncertain conditions, such as the psychology of a given leader at a sensitive time in a country's evolution. Thus, as we posit a system of complexity and factors within it, one must bear in mind that it is fuzzy and indicative. As with any model aimed at simplifying a complex reality to make it manageable for analysis, it is still necessary to adjust one's lens, to not get too attached to labels and categories, and to look at specific nuances and potential twists of fate, when assessing a particular case.

Figure 2.4 depicts a simple map of the system of socio-political complexity. Between countries, the parts would vary in intensity and nuance, but it broadly applies to most countries experiencing a degree of fragility. The map provides a reference point and guides the subsequent discussion.

On the left are influences. These are long-term or external conditions, trends and changes which affect the evolution of the *core* socio-political system and can cause shocks that perturb it. In the centre are the three elements of the core socio-political system. Governance is how the country is

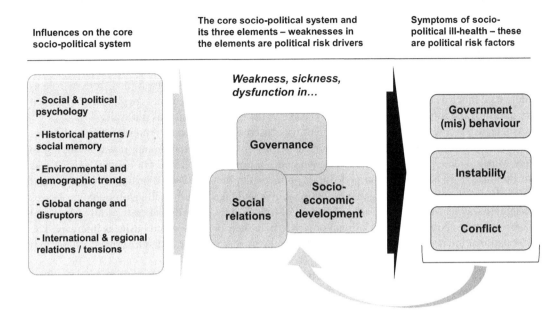

FIGURE 2.4　Socio-political complexity system map.

led and administered. Social relations are the mutual attitudes and interaction between different groups defined by sub-culture or other axes of affiliation, and the relationship between people's group identities and their identity as citizens of the country. Socio-economic development is about people's economic security and social mobility. If all three are reasonably robust, a country can endure pressures and challenges without significant disruption, and will be capable of bouncing back from the odd crisis and resuming its more normal evolution. In practical terms, this means that citizens and companies can get on with life without much concern about how politics could affect them. When these elements get sick or weak, their converse, weak governance, social divisions and socio-economic regression or stagnation are ultimately responsible for political risk, and hence we can call these political risk drivers.

Because these three core system elements closely interact with and affect each other, when one or more is problematic or weakens, it can infect the others, and acute manifestations, or symptoms, of socio-political ill-health can arise, as depicted on the right. Government misbehaviour is intentional and unintentional activity that harms or hinders law-abiding people and non-state organisations, including companies. Instability means pressure for regime change outside of electoral or other institutional processes, and carries the potential for lingering political uncertainty, unrest, disruptive change and violence. Conflict is rivalry and violent confrontation between groups, and between the government and groups opposed to it. Note that symptoms can affect each other. If an aspect of government misbehaviour, for example, is widespread corruption, this can undermine a government's legitimacy and intensify pressure for regime change. In analytical terminology, we can call symptoms political risk factors, since they constitute the conditions and dynamics that could directly affect a foreign operation depending on its profile and behaviour.

If not resolved, symptoms in turn further damage the elements of the core system, just as a severe fever can harm a sick patient. If a feedback loop forms between damaging symptoms and weak elements and this is not broken, the ultimate result is state failure. Failure means that although a country might persist as an internationally recognised sovereign territory, inside it becomes so devoid of structure and cohesion that it is barely recognisable as a state. As we saw earlier, there is a spectrum of fragility, and many countries, meaning both governments and societies, manage to break or weaken this loop, although it can be an ongoing and perilous struggle.

As a brief illustration of the complexity system process, we can look at a country that went through it, from seemingly very healthy to deathly ill, and then to a precarious, partial recovery. In the 1960s and early 1970s, Lebanon seemed to be doing very well, and its capital, Beirut, was even known as the "Paris of the Middle East". The country was a financial hub servicing oil-rich regimes in the region, and linking European and Middle Eastern business. Lebanon profited from its role as middleman, much as Dubai or Singapore does today. From an outside business perspective, it looked very alluring, and foreign firms did indeed partake in the boom. But all was not well.

As a legacy of French rule, the government was based on confessional representation and domi-nated by Christians. Leaders did not bother changing this system even though it was annoying to many Muslims and kept religious distinctions under a political spotlight. On another axis, it was also dominated by both Christian and Sunni political families who were business oligarchs and clan leaders at the same time. A game of factional give and take undermined institutional processes and inhibited coherent responses to problems. Politicians and senior bureaucrats of all stripes had no compunction about using their official power to help their own clans and business interests. The wider national interest mattered only insofar as it converged with their own. Governance, then, was weak.

Social relations were partly based on sectarian identity. Christian, Sunni, Shia, Druze and other sects differentiated people, and within sects families and clans were important. There was sub-regional affiliation too, for example Christians mainly lived on the affluent central coast around Beirut, while most Shia lived in the much poorer south. Even Beirut was divided on sectarian lines. The notion of a Lebanese national identity was abstract by comparison, and the government played no unifying role.

Socio-economic development was not an explicit government priority. Public services and basic education worked, but much de facto development happened through the country's unplanned eco-nomic boom. As such it was uneven. Politically connected clans and families could send their kids abroad for a good education, and they came back to take up lucrative positions in the expanding trade and finance sectors. Beirut was a construction zone, with new luxury high-rises casting long shadows over urban slums populated in part by poor Shia who had come to Beirut for menial work. Social mobility was like riding a rocket for those with connections. For the poor it was a remote dream.

Muslims were becoming more aware that demographic shifts were eroding the justification for Christian political dominance. Christians were conscious of this, and some factions decided that they had to prepare for the contingency that Muslims could try to restructure the political order by force. This led to the nuclei of what would later become militia forces. In 1971, when Jordan expelled the Palestinian Liberation Organisation (PLO) and they moved to Lebanon, the contingency seemed fulfilled. Not only was there a surge in the Muslim population, but the PLO were wandering around with guns, and the government, unable to manage far lesser problems, did little about it. Christian leaders, with the support of Christian politicians and army officers, scaled up their militias.

When clashes between Christian forces and the PLO and its Lebanese Sunni allies finally broke out in 1975, all sides, and indeed many neighbourhoods and clans, organised armed groups. Early on, the Shia, poor and disorganised, unliked by both Christians and the powerful PLO, were for the most part victims of the ensuing violence, but in 1979 the revolution in Iran brought a radical Shia regime to power. Lebanon's Shia got a helping hand, and Hezbollah in particular became a power-ful new force. Syria and Israel invaded and fought directly and through proxy groups, intensifying destruction. Lebanon had become a failed state by 1976, and it took 13 more years before a com-bination of international pressure and exhaustion drove the antagonists to the negotiating table. By 1991, the militias had stashed their guns to take up positions in the new power-sharing government, and with regular serious hiccups the country began rebuilding.

Going back to the complexity system map as an interpretive lens, each of the three elements of the core socio-political system had serious weaknesses. The government was dominated by elite factions who ruled in their own interests. Social relations were weakened by sectarian divisions.

Development was ad hoc and unequal. These problems bled into each other. Social divisions were worsened by Christian dominance of the government, and by economic inequality along sectarian lines.

Long-term and external influences had a major part. Census figures before the war were outdated, and it was becoming clear that demographic shifts were afoot, reducing the overall acceptability of Christian political dominance, and putting Christians on the defensive. The 1967 Arab-Israeli War led to the PLO fleeing to Jordan, and when Jordan forced them out, they moved to Lebanon, severely upsetting what was left of the sectarian power balance. Syrian-Israeli tensions were a factor in each side's invasion of Lebanon. Iran's revolution led to the rise of well-armed Shia factions.

There was a feedback loop. Had it endured as an actual institution, the government might have been able to pull together international support to help end the war and act as a credible mediator. Instead, the government's fragile cohesion was further eroded by conflict. The army became a militia in itself, and the government fragmented on factional lines. The initial clashes also intensified social divisions, causing all sides to organise for war. The economy, based on Lebanon's role as a stable, open hub in a turbulent region, fell apart and became a war economy instead, and many warlords actually found it to be quite lucrative and had a vested interest in not going back to legal, transparent business. The system, then, was too weak to endure the symptom of conflict.

Fast forward to recent years, and a major factor in Lebanon's routine political crises is the influence of historical patterns and social memory. Lebanon has new pressures now, but some patterns that got the country into civil war are repeating. The government and political elites, again locked in power by a rigid sectarian power-sharing formula, are behaving in much the same way as their pre-war predecessors, and this is not surprising given that many of the same families are still at the top. And at least one major armed group, Hezbollah, keeps everyone else on edge and thinking about self-defence. The knowledge of what sectarian conflict can do injects some restraint into power ambitions, but it has also instilled a tremendous wariness of being on the back foot when someone else makes a power play. The past is alive and well, for better or worse.

As for what Lebanon's fragility meant for a foreign company, even before the war, market entry and setting up a business operation were not a simple matter of applications, registration and compliance. One needed the right connections, and having those connections probably meant that someone else did not like you, so connections had to be chosen carefully. Any agreement with powerful interests might have had some form of legal documentation, but for the most part it was spoken, maintained through reciprocity and mutual favours, and adjusted based on this give and take. That made a presence tenuous, and many foreign companies accumulated skeletons in the closet in terms of their business practices. By 1975, Lebanon was just too dangerous to be in, and it only got worse. There were hopeful foreign firms that hung on until the last minute, but in the end the best they could do was to pass the controls to Lebanese managers and hope for the best. Some legitimate commerce did keep going through the war years and some firms managed to maintain at least a foothold, but after the war Lebanon's role as a regional hub never recovered, and many initial business ambitions were ill-suited to the conditions that emerged in the 1990s. Lebanon's fragility and failure directly translated into political risk for companies who had taken a stake in the country, and indeed the ghosts of war are an indirect political risk factor for more recent entrants.

Lebanon was a handy example because it started out as such a seemingly normal place, indeed one of the few in a region known for strife. It is also handy because it forms a complete story, from normal to tenuous to severely complex, and back again to the land of the living but badly scarred. It is a uniquely Lebanese story, though. As we proceed through the factors of complexity and political risk, we will be looking at other variations in their interplay, although these can only be a handful of reference points in a varied phenomenon.

We now turn to the complexity system's parts. First, we briefly examine influences, not by defining each one but by general illustration, since they can be very diverse. Then we proceed to the three elements of the core socio-political system, namely governance, social relations and socio-economic development. This will consider what constitutes good health in each, and how they can weaken and affect each other. Next is symptoms of ill-health, or in analytical terms "political risk factors". We will focus on government misbehaviour, instability and conflict for reasonable parsimony, although within each we will note some key sub-types. Implications for foreign companies will be drawn out where appropriate, though again we hold off from delving into specific issues until the next chapter when we get a better idea of what is at stake for a foreign operation.

INFLUENCES

Any given core socio-political system, comprised of the three aforementioned elements, generates change within itself, and in the absence of significant forces beyond it, it would still continue to evolve and experience ups and downs. One could look just at the immediate system and still get some idea of the socio-political challenges that the country, and by extension a foreign company, could experience in the short term. But for a more holistic picture, one needs to look beyond the immediate system at external and long-term influences. These help to explain how the current core system came into being, the enduring effects of past experiences, perturbations that might arise from outside the system, and how the system could evolve in the future. The map above suggests several types of influences, but in practice these considerably vary by case, and hence a couple of top-level illustrations serve better than explaining each point.

China, for one, can be characterised as a one-party authoritarian state with increasingly centralised, personalised control under Xi since 2012. The Chinese Communist Party (CCP) sees itself as guardian of the nation with a mission to lead it to strength and prosperity, but based on China's tumultuous past, the party has a deeply rooted fear of unrest. Thus, while it relies on its stewardship of economic prosperity for legitimacy, it also exercises stringent socio-political control. This control is partly rationalised with reference to the Chinese nation and its struggle against foreign rivals and detractors, and this message in turn relies on an activist foreign policy that actually sustains a degree of international tension. This control equation of prosperity, coercion and nationalism lies at the heart of the system. Some relevant influences that one might examine in assessing the sustainability of this equation over time include the following:

- foreign trading partners' increasing wariness of China's foreign policy and security ambitions, and the effect of this on the international trade component of China's economic growth (less important but still relevant are foreign reactions to human rights issues arising from the coercive element of the CCP's control strategy, especially as it applies to ethnic minorities);
- US-China tensions in East Asia, including the risk of conflict and its potentially severe effects on the economy and on the regime's credibility as the national guardian;
- China's relations with Russia, which are based on mutual wariness of the West but which are vulnerable to the over-reach of either side's regional ambitions;
- pandemics, such as coronavirus, and their long-term effects not just on the economy but also on social perceptions of the government's approach to dealing with crises;
- aridity, made worse by climate change, in northern China, as a direct economic inhibitor, and an indirect one as it increases the potential for resource conflict with neighbours, with implications for economic relations and the risk of actual war;
- ageing demographics as a result of the old one child policy, leading to higher social care costs, lower productivity and higher labour costs, thereby affecting economic growth and potentially challenging China's shift out of middle-income status; and
- increasing tension between social acceptance of the CCP's controlling paternalism based on its historical legitimacy, and an evolving private sector culture of self-organisation, creativity and innovation.

China might manage and even find opportunity in these factors. However, together they challenge the current system, and especially because of a lack of legitimate channels for dissent and leadership change, if the carrot element of the control equation were to weaken, coercion alone would need to be totalitarian in scope and could risk a serious backlash. Thus, achieving enduring prosperity (the carrot) is a very urgent priority, and the regime is quite willing to risk international friction if it sees other countries as constraining its growth potential and access to resources. Going beyond the immediate system, then, helps to see how it could evolve and some of the issues that could arise for Chinese society, and in turn for foreign companies with a long-term interest in China.

A dramatically different example is Chad, in the Sahel region of Africa. (As a post-script, after originally writing this, long-standing president Deby was killed in a rebellion launched from Libya in April 2021, and a military emergency council took control. The situation could be quite different by the time of publication, but in some ways this makes the example, though now outdated, even more germane to our subject). The country is led by strong-man Idriss Deby, who came to power through a rebellion in 1990. The regime rules an ethnically divided country through a combination of patronage and repression. Despite having become Africa's ninth largest oil producer, the country remains desperately poor because of severe regional droughts, and while oil proceeds benefit regime patronage networks and the armed forces, they have little effect on development. Chad faces routine ethnic clashes, especially between Arab and non-Arab groups, and has seen several ethnic insurgencies, often involving ex-army officers. Despite development challenges, Chad has become noteworthy for having one of the most capable militaries in Africa, and in recent years has collaborated with French and US regional counter-terrorism initiatives, as well as regional peacekeeping missions. Western strategic interest has led to support for the Deby regime and to economic assistance. The country is seldom stable, however; and lacking a solid socio-political core, it is very vulnerable to influences from beyond the immediate system. These include the following:

- the persistence of, and social reliance on, historical ethnic affiliations, which, along with weak governance in the immediate system, challenge the development of a cohesive Chadian nation;
- conflict in bordering countries, because of their potential for spillover into Chad's own ethnic conflicts, and in the case of Boko Haram in Nigeria because of direct violence against Chadian communities in the border region;
- relations with, and stability in, Sudan and Libya, which have provided safe haven for Chadian rebel groups in the past and even now, and from which future rebellions could be launched;
- French and US perceptions of Chad's strategic significance in the war against jihadist terrorism and Boko Haram, and their attitude to the Deby regime as an ally versus their concern about the regime's human rights record;
- less importantly, Gulf Arab, Egyptian and Turkish interest in Chad as a potential ally in achieving their ambitions for influence in Libya;
- the price of oil, and Chad's relations with Cameroon which is host to much of the Chad-Cameroon pipeline and to the port from which Chadian oil is shipped;
- the price of cotton, Chad's second most important export after oil; and
- desertification and climate change, which have already severely reduced Chad's arable and grazing land, harmed agricultural exports, and increased ethnic clashes over resources.

Unlike China, which is a huge and relatively stable country with important internal dynamics that drive much of its socio-political evolution, when considering Chad's evolution and prospects, influences are actually of paramount importance. Just looking at Chad's immediate socio-political system would offer limited insight. This is typical of fragile countries, which, because of weak governance and low national cohesion, tend to be very vulnerable to external dynamics, and to pre-state, historical sub-national loyalties.

To some degree, influences are inseparable from any discussion of a given socio-political system, and many observers and analysts automatically think about the wider picture when they examine a country. But influences become a more explicit focus when a situation is difficult to explain with reference to the current picture. For example, the Iranian Revolution, the Algerian civil war of the 1990s, and Libya's implosion in 2011–2012 each seemed to have few preconditions in the observable timeframe. A series of "whys" leads back in time to historical patterns and social memory, events and periods with significant reverberations, and old socio-political fault lines. For example, while Libya's implosion seemed anomalous given what we knew about the country over the prior two decades, comparing Qaddafi's highly engineered state with socio-political groupings and relationships in the decades preceding his rule would have revealed a sharp contrast, and the potential fragility of the superstructure he sought to impose on society.

Likewise, when we want to see what might happen in the next one or two years, looking at a current socio-political system might suffice. But the further out we project, the more we need to consider influences from outside the system to understand how it might evolve. Jordan's future, for example, depends in part on long-term shifts in the historical legitimacy of the monarchy, the prospects for Palestinian statehood, the outcome of the Syrian conflict, and the ambitions and rivalries of regional and international powers in the Middle East. As we see in the next part of the book, scenario analysis, which projects beyond the observable horizon, places considerable emphasis on influences and how they interact with dynamics in the current system.

CORE SYSTEM ELEMENTS: POLITICAL RISK DRIVERS

We now shift our perspective back to the here and now, to the current socio-political system and its three constituent elements. A few introductory notes are in order. When we say current system, "current" does not just mean the government of the day or this week's news. What a system looks like today is just the latest twist in the fabric of broader forces and interests that have been shaping it for some time. Thus, while we are returning to the here and now, the now in particular is somewhat fuzzy, and there is always an implied historical perspective in examining the politics of a country, even if we do not go back very far in time to look for the deeper "whys". This is not just relevant to more enduring socio-political systems, but it also holds for very fragile or failed states such as Yemen or the Central African Republic, when the apparent chaos at any one time is meaningless to the observer without looking back to see how it started, or what system was in place before and why it fractured.

The three elements of the system – governance, social relations and socio-economic development – seem to encompass much that goes in a country. Our interest, however, is in the aspects of these which ultimately lead to political risk, and that will vary by country. Religion in India, for example, is not entirely an individual matter, and religious identity can mark a person as "the other". Religious friction can complicate a foreign company's local interactions, and sectarian clashes are distinctly hazardous if one is caught in the vicinity. Conversely, this is not the case in Brazil. Likewise, in many countries private sector business and entrepreneurialism cross-cut social boundaries and have no particular political meaning. In other countries, the private sector is dominated by regime cronies who benefit from political connections, and business leaders are self-consciously political players. Generally, the less institutionalised, or rules-based, a country's politics, the more it spills over beyond government into other domains of life. In short, while the three elements touch on a lot of human activity, only some aspects of each are relevant to political risk, and those aspects can considerably vary by country.

Finally, in positing a socio-political system, it is useful to have a sense of what overall health or ill-health means, and according to what reference point. To begin with the reference point, this is the cumulative effects of the system on an individual citizen or private organisation, including a foreign company. A healthy system has nett positive effects, in terms of a person's or organisation's safety, baseline economic security, opportunity to pursue legitimate interests, and sense of relevance as a citizen or participant in social interaction. In turn, people's behaviour contributes to system health, through their economic productivity, civic and political participation, and mutual support. When the system works for people, they do not need to resist or undermine it to survive or have a meaningful existence. They do not have to defend themselves or fight the government or each other, and they have better things to do than plot power grabs, criminal enterprises or revolutions. An unhealthy system, by contrast, leads to insecurity and constrains legitimate opportunity, and at the private individual and organisational level, this motivates anti-system behaviour, whether consciously or through survival instinct.

The three elements can be regarded as interactive subsystems of the wider socio-political organism, much as a human body has subsystems such as digestion, circulation and neurotransmission. When one weakens, it affects the others as well as the whole organism and each of its cells, the citizen or company.

Positing the system's effects on a private citizen's or organisation's wellbeing as the main benchmark of system health could be contentious. One could, for example, say that the power and grandeur of the nation is the benchmark, or human or social advancement towards some ideal type (like "New Soviet Man"). The notion of a private entity's wellbeing leaves plenty of room for ideological and cultural interpretation, but as much as some regimes, politicians and ideologues would prefer us to believe otherwise, ordinary people are the bedrock of any positive human evolution. Ultimately, they not only fund states and drive economies, but far outnumber politicians, bureaucrats and soldiers. An engineered system, like the USSR's or Libya's under Qaddafi, can only go so far on abstract goals and concepts before it is pulled back to reality by misalignments with the citizenry (the contradiction is one reason why highly ideological or puritanical regimes are so repressive). Thus, positing the effects on private entities' wellbeing as a measure of system health is not just a philosophical position. The importance of this has been confirmed in cases of post-conflict reconstruction and counter-insurgency, which have poor and unsustainable results if the day-to-day experience of ordinary people is not a planning priority.

The above does not suggest that a strong state, nationalism and shared values or ideologies, in other words grand-scale structures and ideas, are bad for ordinary people or ultimately backfire on the country's system. The international system divides people into countries, and they are stuck with each other inside borders. A degree of broad-based nationalism mitigates social group conflict and also leverages the wider national group as a basis of mutual support and collective endeavour. Additionally, the international system, while not quite anarchic, is not particularly rules based. Hence, there is some predatory threat from other states, and national cohesion and organising for self-defence and international influence help safeguard citizens' wellbeing. In a healthy system, all of this can happen at the same time that the "person on the street" feels reasonably unoppressed and has no strong reason to attribute his or her day-to-day problems to the state or society.

In the above, it is worth emphasising that private organisations or private entities include foreign companies. A foreign firm is different from a local citizen or even a local business, in that it is in a place for a limited time and purpose. But it too benefits from a healthy system and in turn gives back to it. It also faces constraints and danger when a system weakens, hence our equating weaknesses in the three elements to political risk drivers.

From these broader characterisations, we move to the first, and in many ways central, element of the socio-political system, governance.

GOVERNANCE

Before getting started, it is useful to clarify two terms that will recur in this chapter, government and regime. We use common-sense notions instead of dictionary definitions. Government refers to the wider set of governing institutions, including the executive, legislature, courts and civil service, and in democracies it can also mean the elected government of the day. Regime applies to less institutionalised systems. It suggests a degree of factional or personal rule, and refers to the ruling party, clique or individuals at the top of a government, along with their unofficial support networks outside of government. The more personalised a country's governance, the more normal it sounds to use the phrase, "the [person's name] regime". The distinction is a matter of degree, and the context should help to clarify it as we proceed.

Governance is the exercise of public authority in a country. This means making and enforcing laws and regulations, taxing in exchange for public services and infrastructure, negotiating with other countries' governments, defending the country from external threats, and ensuring fairness and non-discrimination in the state's relationship with society. When these are done well with an eye to the long-term national interest, societies benefit from peace and stability, and people and businesses can focus on personal and economic objectives without much distraction. Foreign companies likewise benefit from calm and rational governance. Good governance does not always mean an easy ride for a company. Sometimes rational governance leads to higher taxation and tighter regulations. But if these are known in advance, remain stable over a reasonable period of time, and change by transparent rules and processes, then companies can plan for them and they are, like the wooden monkey bars in our previous analogy, workable.

Good governance is a matter of degree, and standards somewhat vary by level of overall development. In general, though, there are several characteristics of a government that add nett value to society without becoming a threat or hindrance to ordinary people.

One is institutionalisation and the rule of law. Institutions are principles, rules and structures that stand above any individual leader or office holder, and which constrain people in government to act within their professional mandates. The rule of law means that everyone, leaders included, needs to obey the law and that laws change by formal, legal processes, not on a leader's whim. Together these help to smooth over human eccentricity and prevent the abuse of government power. They also prevent serious mistrust of a government because even when it might seem incompetent, at least people know it cannot start acting like a self-interested mafia using the coercive powers of the state for its own ends. Importantly, institutions that endure beyond a given leadership mean that while leaders can get frail or die, the government itself remains and still functions, and there are clear processes by which vacant leadership positions are filled.

The second is accountability and adjustment mechanisms, in other words ways to get governments to listen to and act on citizens' concerns and ways to change a government's leaders. These help to ensure that governance is self-correcting and that there are pressure valves to accommodate social frustration. Leaders stay more or less committed to the national interest because they know that they are accountable and could lose their positions even while the government, as a set of institutions, endures. As alluded to earlier, formal leadership transition mechanisms also prevent messy power plays and succession struggles. Genuine democracy is a tried and tested approach to accountability and adjustment. However, even in non-democracies there can be workable, if less robust, mechanisms, for example regular discussions between central government officials and local leaders who represent different sub-regions or social interests, broad-based plenary sessions to select new leaders and traditional consultative assemblies linked to formal government structures.

Finally, governments need to have the capacity to fulfil their roles. This means professional and technical skills and professionalism, the latter a factor of institutionalisation. But it also means money to pay for personnel, fund civil service infrastructure like offices and information systems, and provide public services and national security. Money comes from taxes, which depend on a productive citizenry and private sector, although there are other, less sustainable, sources including debt, the sale of government-controlled natural resources and state company revenues.

A government does not have to be a high performer in each of the above to be acceptable to most citizens. It does, though, need to have a critical mass of legitimacy, or citizens' agreement that the people holding office have the right to exercise public authority. Legitimacy can derive from respect for and trust in long-standing institutions even if people do not like specific office-holders, from a government's economic and public service performance, and, much more tenuously, from the popularity of specific leaders. A government or leadership can endure with only moderate legitimacy if people generally perceive it as doing at least slightly more good than harm; but if it further erodes, the relationship between government and society can become confrontational.

On the whole, established democracies of the upper OECD have reasonable strength in the above pillars of good governance, and despite their own pressures, they continue to be the most stable and straightforward places for ordinary citizens and foreign companies. Developing and transitional countries face varying degrees of weak governance by comparison. What follows is both causes and forms of weak governance, since weak governance tends to be self-reinforcing. This is a very nuanced phenomenon, and the discussion here is necessarily top level.

A serious challenge to good governance is personal or strongman rule. This is the concentration of government power in one or a few hands. It makes a political system vulnerable to the eccentricities, personal interests and, in many cases, grandiosity of specific individuals. The psychology of a given leader or clique is a factor in this phenomenon, which is often associated with a sense of personal entitlement and of historic destiny or mission. It can arise in both authoritarian and democratic systems, and after periods of conflict or national trauma. We examine each instance in turn.

First, while authoritarian systems can be institutionalised, within such systems, such as single-party states, monarchies and hybrid systems like Iran's are pathways to personal rule. There is already an intense concentration of power at the executive level; hence, by comparison to functioning democracies it is a short step to a total factional or personal power grab. This provides an incentive, but also anxiety that another faction will get there first. A lack of accountability and public transparency means that machinations to enact personal dominance bear little risk of public disclosure and opprobrium. Additionally, weak institutional checks and balances mean that other levels of government will struggle to deter or counter a factional takeover bid.

For those reasons, even in long-standing authoritarian systems that have shown reasonable institutional resilience, power grabs occur. For decades after Mao, for example, the CCP in China contained its own checks and balances and adjustment mechanisms, and leaders had to ensure a critical mass of party support. Yet since assuming power in 2012, Xi was still able to become the first president for life (should he so choose) and hold or control all key party leadership positions. To stay on top, he has enacted party purges on a scale unseen since the fall of the Gang of Four. Likewise, in Saudi Arabia, the monarchy has long ruled through internal consensus and consultation with traditional elites, but in 2017 Mohammed bin Salman emerged as a strongman and conducted unprecedented crackdowns within the royal family and its elite networks, and took personal control over the security apparatus to help safeguard his singular dominance.

Personal rule, or degrees of it, has proven feasible in democracies too, when their institutions are too weak to counter forceful politicians who, with a national vision that justifies all means, weaken accountability and adjustment mechanisms to stay in power once they get elected. The usual route is through nationalist or traditionalist populism, whereby a candidate actually runs on the promise of ignoring institutional niceties in order to work for the "real people" against the elites and outside, or inauthentic, groups. Riding a wave of emotional support among a majority, they face little initial risk in dismantling checks and balances and judicial oversight. By the time of the next election, the opposition is constrained by new election laws, the regime has control over the media so can pump out its own spin, and it has developed plans to at least try to fiddle with the vote. A stronger majority means that constitutional changes to further entrench the strongman are possible. At the time of writing, there are various countries in every region with strongmen who at least started out as democratically elected, with Duterte in the Philippines or Modi in India being somewhat typical. It is worth noting that established democracies have seen an increase in populist politics, and had Trump in the US been able to achieve his ambitions, the US might have been another example. Institutional resilience prevailed, but it was a near miss and plainly reminds us that what stands between well-functioning democracy and de facto dictatorship is institutions, not some ephemeral national wisdom or sense of fair play.

Finally, countries that are in or just pulling out of conflict or traumatic change can suffer from a total fracturing of institutions and be ripe for the rise of a strongman. For example, Kagame in

Rwanda and Afwerki in Eritrea both became strongmen rulers directly following their military leadership roles in civil wars, and both are strict authoritarians. In Russia, Putin came to power on the heels of the chaos of Yeltsin's post-Soviet presidency, and leveraged a near vacuum of institutional cohesion to firmly implant himself and his clique in power. Being a national saviour buys post-chaos strongmen considerable time to build a system around themselves to perpetuate and extend their control, before social memory of the dark days before their rule starts to fade, along with their historical legitimacy.

Another challenge to governance is that weak institutions open the way for political interference by organisations that, according to the institutional framework at least, should not be involved in governing, with the result of parallel or shadow government. The military is the usual culprit. Political development often sees the military and related security forces backing away from politics, but when the army has ruled in the past, it usually entrenches at least some influence in government to ensure that future civilian leaders do not intrude on its interests. These interests can be power for its own sake, a concern about national security, and control over major state companies and whole economic sectors. In some cases, the civilian element is the real shadow, and just a veneer for de facto military rule. The military is either a parallel force or indirectly running the government in Egypt, Sudan, Algeria, Pakistan, Iran (with the Revolutionary Guard as opposed to the official military), Thailand (in alliance with the monarchy), Myanmar and, to a lesser extent, in Indonesia, to name a few. Parallel government can involve other actors too. In Turkey, for example, after coming to power in 2002, the AK Party government neutralised a politically powerful military with the help of the Gulen movement, a close-knit and influential religious association. The movement became so embedded in government that it controlled several key ministries for over a decade until it was eventually removed in a purge that had considerable collateral damage.

Governance can also be affected by traditional sub-national interests. In less institutionalised systems where traditional loyalties compete with state authority, a regime often needs to cater to traditional power bases, such as clans, tribes and sects in order to maintain its position and influence. In Africa, this manifests as Big Man politics, wherein a leader gains traditional and sub-national support through a web of patronage networks. In Central Asia, governments need to continually balance the interests of powerful clans. In much of the Middle East, the support of important tribes and families, and in some cases religious authorities, remains a factor in a regime's overall legitimacy. These are just a few examples of a widespread phenomenon. It can lead to distortions and apparent irrationalities in official policy as a regime tries to balance contradictory interests, and it can amplify sub-national friction as groups vie for the ear of the regime.

Governments and regimes can be sub-nationally divided within themselves. Sometimes sub-national or factional representatives proactively agree to create a power-sharing structure in the government or a ruling party, but more usually this arises from brokered peace deals following a period of civil conflict. In a context of continued group rivalry, this can result in awkward inter-factional bargaining and contestation as each side tries to defend its own group's interests. The result, as in Lebanon for example, can be chronic dysfunction, and as seen recently in Ethiopia, infighting can even escalate to armed conflict.

A sheer lack of resources also hinders good governance. Tunisia provides an example. Prior to 2011, the country had strongman rule under Ben Ali, but the state was relatively functional. Since the revolution in 2011, despite being a functional democracy, the country could not recover from the economic paralysis that occurred during and following the revolution, and terrorist attacks on tourists did not help. Without sufficient tax revenue, the government failed to meet social expectations. There were successive leadership changes and cabinet reshufflings as politicians floundered to get socio-economic progress back on track, and democratic politics itself has lost some credibility as a result. Unlike Tunisia, some countries start from severe scarcity. The Sahel countries, of which Niger is the poorest, are examples of the challenge of even getting off the ground as functional governments. In Chad's case, and more recently Mali's, this is partly attributable to the effects of conflict, which usually corrodes an economy and severely distracts leaders from development challenges, but it is also very much attributable to the sheer paucity of resources, including technical expertise, in relation to the development challenge.

Of the three socio-political system elements, governance is the most important both to foreign companies and to the lives of ordinary people. Put simply, governments make the rules and hold the guns, or usually most of the guns. More broadly, though, governance is at the heart of the matter when it comes to state fragility and complexity. Weak governance can, either directly or inadvertently, lead to official discrimination against sub-national groups, thereby raising the stakes in inter-group rivalries and reducing national cohesion. It can also lead to skewed, inconsistent and poorly implemented economic and development policy, increasing frustrations and a perception of injustice. As we will see, social divisions and socio-economic weaknesses both in turn affect governance. However, governance is the critical variable. If a government is functional, fair and respected, it has the means and credibility to address weaknesses in the wider system. If not, then it is not just incapable of guiding society to address systemic challenges, but itself can be a major cause of friction and socio-economic malaise.

Social Relations

Governance involves state-society relations and the government's effects on people and businesses. Within societies themselves, however, group relations can have a significant effect on ordinary people's security and day to day concerns. Ideally people, and companies, would not have to worry much about the effect of group identities. Smooth social relations tend to persist when national cohesion and pluralism are balanced. In other words, people share a general sense of citizenship and broad national values, but within this they exercise specific subcultural values, traditions or other group distinctions, and do not feel threatened or affronted by people different from themselves. When social relations are smooth, then acute rivalries either do not arise or are ironed out with reference to shared values. People might still have to worry about the effects of weak governance, such as corruption or arbitrary law enforcement, but they do not need to acutely worry about each other, or about the government clamping down on them specifically because of their sub-national or cultural affiliations. This balance between national cohesion and pluralism might sound like an ideal, but degrees of it have helped to maintain social peace in numerous countries with high social diversity.

The converse of smooth social relations, social divisions, is unfortunately just as common. Social divisions are problematic in that they instil a motive to boost one's group at the expense of wider society or the nation-state, thus undermining national cohesion. Social divisions are also the cracks which can widen into unrest or violence when groups feel particularly vulnerable or alienated from each other and the government, and hence mutual social group antipathy is in effect latent conflict. Here we examine three common axes of social divisions.

As a preliminary note, while our focus is developing and transitional countries, what is discussed herein also applies to developed countries of the upper OECD. Even the Nordic countries have seen their reputed social tolerance perturbed by immigration, and a result has been an increase in support for far-right parties. Right-wing nationalism in many established democracies posits a true nation in relation to outsiders as defined by aspects of a person's origins, subculture and values. Thus, although what follows is oriented to complex emerging markets, social divisions challenge countries at all levels of development.

The first axis of social division is sub-nationality, referring to traditional group identities that were historically the principal bases of social affiliation and organisation, and which persist despite the imposition or creation of the modern nation-state. Sub-nationality can be based on ethnicity, tribe and clan, and religion. Different groups often coexist with each other and the nation-state, but rivalries arise for several reasons and on several axes.

Scarcity, particularly of basic resources such as water and arable land, can cause localised friction as different groups vie for access and control. For example, much ethnic friction in the Sahel and east Africa is driven by land competition between herdsmen and farming communities, a division that often overlays tensions between Muslims and non-Muslims. This has increased with climate change, which has accelerated desertification. A government's maldistribution of the burdens and benefits of extractive or industrial farming operations can also increase ethnic friction if some groups seem to be favoured or disadvantaged, and this often occurs in a context of local poverty. For example, among Nigeria's Delta populations, frustration about oil pollution in the absence of economic benefits has driven sub-national rebellion, and similar concerns about gas operations are a factor in Mozambique's insurgency in Cabo Delgado. There is not a strong ethnic axis in Mozambique's insurgency, but local frustrations sharpened a north-eastern regional identity which was partly articulated as shared, and among insurgents puritanical, religious adherence.

When the government is dominated by a particular group and favours it, it increases tensions with others, as do government efforts to impose its cultural identity on other groups in the name of national unity. Myanmar has faced this problem since independence, and ethnic rebellions are nearly continuous. Another example is Turkey, where the Kurdish insurgency in the south-east rekindles when government commitment to sub-national rights falters. Similarly, the Tuareg in Mali and Niger periodically rebelled against southern ethnic repression even well before the rise of Al Qaeda in the Islamic Maghreb (AQIM) and other regional jihadist groups.

Demographic shifts and migration are significant triggers of sub-national rivalries, as we saw earlier in the Lebanon example. When population shifts seem to threaten the cultural integrity and way of life in the traditional homeland of a sub-nation, tension between immigrants and incumbents increases. Burkinabe immigration and economic competition was a factor in Ivory Coast's descent into conflict starting in 2002, for example. Urban migration in particular can create tightly packed agglomerations of people from different sub-national groups, who are suddenly in competition with each other for scarce jobs and resources. Ethnic and sectarian clashes and riots periodically flare up in many large cities in the developing world. Delhi, Karachi, Cairo (with a Coptic minority), Lagos and Johannesburg are just a few examples of urban centres where the phenomenon recurs.

Tribe and clan can be a sub-factor in broader sub-national rivalries (tribes are larger groups and clans are more like large extended families, but clan sometimes just refers to tightly knit groups based on mutual interest; for example, in Algeria regime factions are often called clans). Somalia's initial descent into state failure in the 1990s was partly a result of clan warfare following the fall of the Barre regime. In 2011, Libya originally fractured on tribal lines and the conflict only later coalesced onto an east-west axis. Tribalism plays a significant role in Iraq's continued violence, and is a factor in the shifting alliances in Yemen's civil war. Clan rivalry manifests as criminal violence in the Caucasus, where covert resistance to Soviet cultural homogenisation transmuted into clan-based mafia groups after the fall of the USSR.

Age-old social fault lines are a link to a country's deeper past, often beyond the formation of the current nation-state, and in many places they have endured even as technology changes societies in many other ways. Since World War II, sub-national divisions have been a factor in nearly all civil conflicts and much low-level violence, and while there has been a gradual evolution away from old roots, this axis of social division will continue to affect socio-political systems in every region, especially where governments are too weak or too one-sided to mediate.

Another social division is the split between traditionalist and cosmopolitan, or inward and outward facing, attitudes in society. Some areas and social classes, partly by historical accident, for example by being situated on a trade route or near a coast, have been at the forefront of cross-border commerce. As countries become more integrated into the global economy, people in these segments tend to prosper and become more exposed to global ideas and values, while those in the traditional heartland begin to feel as if the social structure they are used to is under threat and become frustrated by the emerging development gap. A split thus emerges. The acceleration of globalisation in recent decades has widened this split in many countries, leading to a degree of polarisation on the traditionalist-cosmopolitan axis. It can both become acute in itself and intensify sub-national divisions.

In democracies, nationalist conservative politicians acting as defenders of traditional values have exploited the split to gain a loyal traditionalist base, in the process raising consciousness about differences in social values, and in some cases, as noted earlier, also differences between the "real" nation and outside groups. This phenomenon has eroded social cohesion in some of the largest emerging markets, including Turkey, India, Sri Lanka and Brazil. In authoritarian countries, including Iran, Russia and China, leaders have catered to traditionalist concerns to justify their lack of regard for "foreign" human rights and democratic values, and likewise played on xenophobia to hype traditionalist support.

The traditionalist-cosmopolitan divide by itself can remain a quirk of socio-political evolution and mild tension between sub-cultures, but when exploited for political purposes, it can define actual sides in a "war" of values and create tangible animosity. In the examples here and many more, including Eastern and Western European countries and the US, even when ethnicity or sect is not part of the narrative, people can loath the notion that they share citizenship with someone at the opposite pole. Additionally, when the government or leadership is an antagonist in this contest, segments opposed to its values can regard it as one-sided and illegitimate. This division can thus manifest not just as social unrest, but also political protest and the government's suppressive riposte.

The last axis of social division that we examine here is inequality, which is directly linked to socio-economic development. Inequality in wealth and social mobility can overlay sub-national divisions to make them worse, and it can contribute to friction between globally integrated and homebound segments of society. However, it can be an axis of social division in itself, particularly in cities where it can be starkly visible. Urban migration from poor rural areas can create an underclass living in close proximity to socio-economic elites and, hence, acutely aware of the gap. Most urban poor have more immediate concerns than organising revolutions or insurgencies, but they can constitute a pool of willing participants in dissent once it manifests. Additionally, youth among urban poor, unable to find meaningful social roles, can be drawn to activities that allow them to express their frustration while at the same time earning some form of livelihood. Organised crime and terrorism can offer status, relevance and income, despite the severe moral and physical hazards they entail.

In Algeria, for example, the numerous *hittistes* (those who spend their days leaning against walls, referring to unemployed young men) living in proximity to the *chi chis* (slang for rich kids whose parents benefit from regime connections) gave momentum and energy to the 1988 protests that led to the failed 1991 democratic experiment. They were subsequently the recruitment pool for the jihadist insurgents. *Hittistes* and *chi chis* have their local variants throughout the developing world. Inequality in itself is only an unhealthy characteristic of an economy, but when it becomes self-conscious and connected to a wider story of right and wrong, it severely strains the significance of shared citizenship, and, at least for those on the bottom, the legitimacy of the people in power.

Before concluding social divisions, we should note gender exclusion, not as an axis of rivalry, but as an influence on social divisions. Gender exclusion can affect other types of tensions by making men, concerned about status in their own more aggressive social roles, the main arbiters between groups. Gender inclusion, by contrast, means that women, who tend to be more concerned with family economic security, are engaged in inter-group life, with a consequent reduction of male status competition that exacerbates tensions. Women's active participation in peace-building initiatives has long been recognised as an important factor in the sustainability of results. This issue can be culturally sensitive, but gender exclusion often has tangible effects on social divisions and their propensity to devolve into conflict.

Social divisions can have a serious effect on the other two elements of the core system. While weak governance can intensify or even create divisions, governments can also get sucked into social rivalries, thereby exacerbating fractionalisation within governments themselves. Additionally, acute divisions can be severely distracting for governments who are already managing a variety of development challenges. As we will see next, the socio-economic element affects social divisions when development is unequal, but divisions in turn impede economic collaboration and exchange.

Furthermore, when group rivalry extends to resource competition, it leads to economic inefficiencies and the mismanagement of resources, thereby impeding wider national development.

For foreign companies, even short of violence, social divisions can create problems. Like governments in fragmented states, companies too can import social divisions into their own organisations through local hiring, and, if unmanaged, these can be severely disruptive. Likewise, when taking on local partners or suppliers, if a company seems to favour one group over another, perhaps through nepotism pressure brought to bear by government officials, the company can be seen as taking sides. In dealing with host communities, corporate social responsibility (CSR) programmes need to carefully consider social structures and inter-group rivalries lest the company end up supporting an unfair status quo or inadvertently empowering some groups over others. Even where an operation is situated can be contentious if it affects rival groups differently. In divided societies, cultural slights are magnified and consultation with the right people, including traditional leaders, can be both difficult and necessary if the operation is to gain local acceptance. Finally, taking on state contracts or dealing with state-connected partners in countries where the regime forms one side of a sub-national rivalry can trigger local and international criticism that the company is tacitly supporting sub-national oppression.

Socio-Economic Development

As a preliminary point, the focus here is on development as an element of the socio-political system and as a driver of political risk for companies operating on the ground, not on economics as a factor in the returns on financial investments. Country risk is a field which focuses mainly on economic challenges to financial returns, and it would be a useful corollary for readers interested in both on-the-ground and portfolio investment in complex emerging markets (a useful introduction is *Guide to Country Risk*, by Mina Toksöz [The Economist, 2014]).

"Socio-economic development" puts social and economic together, because of the tight linkage between society's general sense of wellbeing and a country's economic performance. Whatever else a country's development trajectory does, to work for ordinary people it needs to improve two aspects of their lives. One is economic security, or being able to pay for the essentials of household life, including food and housing as a minimum. The other is social mobility, in other words the opportunity to legitimately improve one's economic circumstances if one is motivated to try. Social mobility is a matter of degree, and in less developed countries the opportunity might be slim, but any realistic hope of even slightly bettering the household is a significant factor in contentment. Affordable health and education, the main social aspects of socio-economic development, are closely linked to economic wellbeing. If one needs to spend the household savings or go into deep debt to pay for a health crisis, for example, then economic security is tenuous. Likewise, if education is financially out of reach, then social mobility is a scant prospect for all but the rich, who are already at the top anyway.

Development has a crucial role in the socio-political system. If people's basic needs are met and they feel like they have a fair opportunity to better their economic status, there is less basis for group-based competition and rivalry over scarce resources. This means less chance of conflict. Second, development creates a productive citizen tax base. This provides stable funding for public services, and this improves trust in the government. Trust in turn reduces the chance of violent dissent and unrest. The more a government depends on productive citizens for its revenues, the more incentive it has to ensure that ordinary people and the private sector have what they need to be productive. This makes a government more responsive and further improves its legitimacy. When a government needs to worry less about social tensions and conflict, and social frustration with its own performance, it can better focus on the job of governing without serious distractions. Thus, socio-economic development is tightly bound up with wider systemic health.

Turning to sicknesses in the socio-economic development element, and hence its role as a political risk driver, we examine some broad inhibitors. Conflict, instability, global downturns, pandemics and other trauma harm development, but this is self-apparent. The focus here will be on governments' roles in weakening development, since among all of a country's organisations and entities, governments have by far the most influence on it. Much development occurs as the national aggregate of small-scale socio-economic interaction and innovation, and is not guided or planned, but governments are the elephant in the room, for better or worse.

General economic mismanagement, particularly inconsistency and ill-coordinated policy flip-flops, is one cause of stalled or intermittent development. Argentina, for example, has been in and out of debt and currency crises since the 1980s, partly because of contradictions between liberalisation and previous but lingering state-led development patterns, and partly because of crises-driven, reactive policy lurches. Egypt is another case of inconsistency. After a state socialist model under Nasser, in the 1970s Sadat implemented the *Infitah* (openness) economic liberalisation policy. Without commensurate changes to the vast state sector, the policy failed and led to severe hardship and unrest. Since then the country has continued to struggle with the contradiction between entrenched state-connected economic interests, not least the military, and genuine liberalisation. Turkey had similar challenges and faced a serious financial crisis in 2001. IMF-guided reform led to a more robust economy but some years into the AK Party's administration, an emphasis on credit-funded growth and an aversion to interest rates undid the gains. The currency has faced years of downward pressure and the country has been on the edge of a currency crisis since 2018.

The above are only three examples of ill-planned policy shifts and the phenomenon is widespread. There are two main patterns. One is that a country with a legacy of heavy state involvement in the economy finds itself struggling with debt and related challenges, and under immediate pressure decides on quick liberalisation, but without commensurate institutional reforms and support for domestic industries to prepare for global competition. Panic is a bad mode for high-stakes planning, and rounds of reactive firefighting can recur for years or, as in Argentina's case, decades. The other pattern is that a government knows what it should do for sustainable reform, but quick, high growth, often along with subsidies, are politically expedient, and credit-funded growth is incentivised at the expense of resilience. While reforms for long-term sustainable resilience can be unpopular in the short term, the alternative of ongoing economic fragility ultimately has far worse human consequences, and as economic security declines, so too does the legitimacy of a government or regime. If, in a context of economic insecurity, a government suddenly tries to redress financial weaknesses, for example by cutting subsidies or raising the retirement age, it can face acute and dangerous social frustration. An ultimate economic reckoning can be disastrous for ordinary people, and in turn for governments seen as responsible for the ensuing hardship.

Related to the above is government prestige projects that divert attention and funding from meaningful development. Debt-heavy mega-projects, such as Egypt's New Administrative Capital outside of Cairo, result in symbols of national prestige, but the money would usually be better spent on improving existing basic infrastructure and public services. Similarly, luxury townships and office blocks near capital cities, such as outside Luanda, Angola, often have little demand and are unaffordable for ordinary people. Airports, hydro-electric dams and other infrastructure are often over-scaled and aimed more at prestige than addressing social needs. Pet projects of a regime can be rushed through with inadequate social-environmental planning, leading to population displacements and long-term environmental degradation. A related prestige-based eccentricity in cities is razing shantytowns, banning street vendors and moving people from decaying but centrally located apartment blocks to newer but distant housing. This makes a city look neater, but severely damages its informal economy on which many people rely, and means long and costly commutes for relocated people.

Another impediment to development is regime favouritism among economic actors. Cronies, patronage networks and state companies run by close regime contacts or insiders can all benefit from easy credit, lax regulatory oversight and protection from private business competition. Regime-connected business oligarchies might seem like one of the few initial options to create national economic entities with sustainable scale. In Japan and South Korea, for example, government-connected *keiretsu* and *chaebol* led those countries' initial global competitiveness. But as those cases demonstrated, after a certain point state-linked conglomerates stifle more focused, efficient and innovative independent players. Favouritism often creates an exclusive enclave that leaves businesses and entrepreneurs on the outside struggling to stay afloat. State companies are usually not supposed to have special advantages beyond their specific remits, but because of personal regime connections and nepotism they often do. They include military-owned companies, which are major players where the military still has a political role, such as in Egypt, Thailand, Indonesia, Myanmar and Pakistan. Military-owned conglomerates are often deeply engaged in purely civilian sectors, and one basis of their dominance is access to cheap conscript labour. For ordinary people trying to better themselves through entrepreneurship, being on the outside of the regime's extended circle can put a low and absolute ceiling on their ambitions. This affects them and also hinders their ability to employ others.

Over-reliance on commodity exports is a common problem for developing countries with natural resource wealth. Dependence on agricultural exports has proven to be unreliable and governments in countries with a large agricultural base often seek diversification for more stable growth. But oil, gas and minerals are another story, and can seem so lucrative that not only does a country not have to diversify, but the government can rely on exports and royalties for its revenues and largely ignore the challenge of fostering a productive tax base. This is an aspect of the resource curse or Dutch disease. An ordinary citizen of Angola, Equatorial Guinea or Chad, to name a few, will be well aware that their country has grown far wealthier in the last decade or two because of oil, but if asked how it affected their lives, they might reply that if they noticed it at all, it was because the police were more numerous and better armed if no less abusive, and the regime's friends had bigger houses and cars. Money in the absence of institutions and political commitment does not lead to development, and can exacerbate inequality, including between rival sub-nations.

Socio-economic development is a complex issue, and the above is not the whole story by any means. We will, however, add one more challenge. This is governments' pressure on civil society organisations (CSOs), including NGOs. Since about 2005, partly in response to the Colour Revolutions, regimes and governments with any concern about their legitimacy have been clamping down on CSOs for fear that they go beyond social issues and start to act as enablers of organised dissent. Crackdowns intensified after the Arab Spring. Dozens of countries have implemented severe limitations on CSO formation, funding and activities. One effect has been a decrease in local mutual support networks and the ability of communities to self-organise in response to environmental change, economic hardship and natural disasters. By weakening CSOs without providing commensurate support structures, governments have reduced socio-economic resilience and increased vulnerability.

All of the above constraints on development contribute to inequality. That inequality can be addressed by redistribution, including through progressive taxation, is somewhat ideologically contentious. What is less contentious is that economic stability and a focus on enabling grassroots economic activity with supportive credit access, infrastructure, legal frameworks and non-discrimination are enablers of at least the opportunity for ordinary people to better themselves. Crucially, as noted earlier, affordable health and education are also essential. When these enablers are absent, inequality increases. The earlier discussions of traditionalist-cosmopolitan friction and inequality as an axis of social division indicate the possible effects if inequality becomes acute and highly visible, and if inequality occurs between sub-nations, it also increases sub-national rivalry.

Another result of a lack of socio-economic progress is that much of a whole society can sense that for want of better governance, they are well behind peer countries in terms of prosperity and opportunity. This is known as relative deprivation, in other words the feeling that one's society is living below a standard which it is capable of or should be achieving. This feeling can unite large segments of a population in frustration towards a government, and is often a significant factor in large-scale social unrest and protest.

We have already discussed connections between socio-economic development and the other two elements, governance and social relations. It is worth emphasising, though, that institutionalisation and the rule of law are critical factors in development. Governments need to be able to plan without individual and clique self-interest impeding clear assessment and effective resource allocation, and a lack of institutionalisation makes this difficult. The rule of law is ultimately what creates a level-playing field, and makes ordinary people and businesses feel sufficiently secure and confident that they can get on with economic life without fear of arbitrary law enforcement, extra-legal political interference, corruption pressure and other hassles in their business activities. Institutions and the rule of law are in fact tremendous economic assets for a country, but because both can challenge the control and advantages of an entrenched leadership, they are often deliberately weakened.

In addition to its destabilising effects on the wider system, socio-economic development, or lack thereof, has direct implications for foreign companies. Overall, socio-economic progress means that there are more diverse market opportunities and domestic economic activity to plug into. More specifically, it means that a company has access to a pool of qualified or at least willing local suppliers and workers, and does not need to rely on dubious regime cronies for local inputs. A vibrant local business scene enables a range of legitimate learning relationships and sources of friendly advice. Finally, a foreign business operation often has a very high profile. When people have economic security, this profile might still attract attention and local interest in jobs and social investment, but it will not attract desperate hope that a company cannot fulfil. When development is stalled or regressing, the converse of these applies.

Each of the three elements of the socio-political system is nuanced in itself and varies by level of overall development, culture and national history, but hopefully this section has provided a reasonable baseline for extrapolation to specific cases. As noted throughout this section, the elements are tightly linked, and if one is weak, it affects the others. Together weaknesses in the three elements are the bases of fragility in a country, and hence of complexity from a foreign company perspective. The main linkages are summarised in Figure 2.5.

Within the governance section we noted that governance was the most important of the three elements. A government can help to heal fractures and can guide fair and rational development,

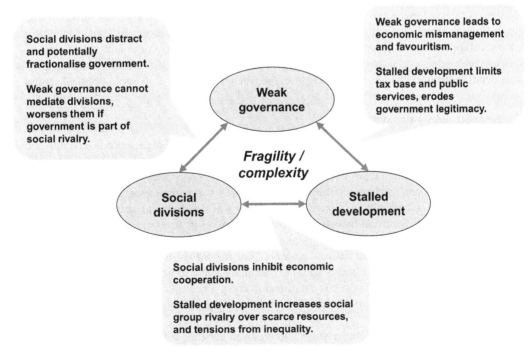

FIGURE 2.5 Links between core system elements.

or it can do the opposite to devastating effect. From a foreign company's perspective, a government is both the gatekeeper to its society and market, and the business rule-maker and enforcer. A government might not always be FDI-friendly, but if it upholds and adheres to the rule of law and changes policies in predictable ways, at least a company is on stable ground. If a government is eccentric, personalised or illegitimate, it makes life considerably harder for a foreign entrant. But although governance is central to the system, it is in many ways a reflection of what goes on around it. Absolute scarcity or economic shocks reduce its resources and make it hard for it to gain credibility through effective service provision. Social fragmentation makes it hard to satisfy all sides, and managing cracks in national cohesion can be severely distracting as a government walks a fine line between building national consensus and enforcing it through repression. Governance might be central, but it is bound to the other two elements in a tightly linked system, and any illness in one quickly spreads if it is not managed. Illness leads to acute symptoms, which are directly responsible for political risk that derives from just being in a particular socio-political terrain. Symptoms are thus political risk factors, which we examine next.

SYMPTOMS: POLITICAL RISK FACTORS

Within the wider complexity system, influences affect what goes on in a country but they do not directly affect a foreign company. What goes on within three elements of the core socio-political system, on the other hand, have broad implications for a foreign entrant. But it is the symptoms of ill-health within the core system that have the most acute effects, and hence which are reasonably regarded as political risk factors. These are not political risks in themselves, since whether or not something is a potential challenge depends on a foreign operation's profile and exposures. But these first-order dynamics are what could directly impinge on an operation.

There are different ways of conceptually organising these factors, and some political risk taxonomies are very detailed. The focus here, however, is on broader patterns and dynamics that give rise to political risk, and hence, as noted, we will confine this to three main factors. To reiterate, these are government misbehaviour, instability and conflict. By this point, the discussion of system elements has already covered much ground in terms of how these can arise, and as we get further towards specific causes of political risk, nuanced variations between countries increase. Thus, what follows is top level, providing an interpretive framework that applies to a range of complex environments. This will include general implications for foreign companies, but specific challenges are covered in more detail in the next chapter, which examines the foreign operation in its socio-political setting.

GOVERNMENT (MIS-) BEHAVIOUR

With considerable control over a foreign company's access and overall experience in a country, how a government behaves is a significant factor of political risk. Government misbehaviour might be a short way of naming this factor, but the "mis" is not always appropriate. As noted, governments can have sound reasons to change policy or regulations in ways that cause problems for foreign firms. Sometimes, for example, a country reaches a stage of development at which it is attracting considerable FDI and its current incentive structure underplays its hand in terms of the taxes, local content or other advantages it could gain. Dealing with governments making legitimate and rational changes is much like dealing with business partners – one needs to be flexible and respect the other's interests. Much of what follows in this section is about misbehaviour in the sense of weakly managed or driven by factional as opposed to national interest, since this is less predictable and more problematic. We examine five sub-factors herein: erratic policy, convoluted bureaucracy, corruption, cronyism and repression.

Erratic policy-making and policy changes derive from personal rule and a lack of clear institutional decision processes, from the continued firefighting that follows ill-thought reactions to economic crises, and from government efforts to sustain short-term public support at the expense of long-term resilience. A foreign company decides to go to a new country on the premise that relevant policies and regulations are workable. These range from government attitudes to economic liberalisation and the relative importance of FDI in development plans, through to local ownership rules, intellectual property protection and taxation. If these change, so can the business premise. Additionally, a company might enter on the understanding that business is somehow sacrosanct and left out of a government's foreign policy and domestic political calculations, only to find that the government begins to expect foreign firms to toe the line, for example by not voicing concerns about weak labour standards among state company suppliers, or by echoing the government narrative on certain foreign policy issues. If significant shifts in policy and attitudes occur after an operation is underway, a company often faces a scramble to comply with new rules, unanticipated costs and even a weakening of its overall legal status and protections.

Convoluted bureaucracy derives from weak institutionalisation, including direct political interference in the civil service, from under-capacity arising from a lack of resources and training, and quite often from overstaffing as a way to reduce graduate unemployment. It can also arise from the awkward coexistence of different bureaucratic models. For example, in ex-colonial countries the old colonial model, say French, can linger beside a Soviet-inspired model adopted after independence, and these can impede the full adoption of the most recent reforms. Just like ordinary citizens, foreign companies rely on the civil service for access to public services and need a range of other approvals, including business licences, work permits, import permits and environmental approvals. A slow and convoluted bureaucracy can hinder operating schedules that depend on timely approvals for specific activities or stages. Political interference in the bureaucracy can be especially problematic, since delays, via application denials and regulatory inspections, can be ways in which a regime pressures a company for better terms or compliance with political imperatives, or to back off from direct competition with regime cronies. Sometimes delays are a way to send a message that a bribe or other inducement could be needed to clear an application, and there is some overlap between bureaucratic convolution and the next subfactor, corruption.

The type of corruption of interest in this context is mainly a foreign company's bribery of politicians and civil servants. Grand corruption involves large sums for significant favours, such as exemption from certain regulations or even obtaining a public contract. Petty corruption involves facilitation payments or other small inducements to speed up routine approvals or for access to public infrastructure. Foreign companies are one half of the corruption equation, but corruption is more pervasive where institutional oversight and the rule of law are weak, and where bureaucratic processes are sufficiently convoluted that there is a steady market for "special services". In many cases, corruption is itself nearly institutionalised, being so common and well understood that it works like an actual market. When the rules of the game are easy to learn and one gets what one pays for, it can seem very alluring.

But there are dangers. One is legal liability in one's home country, and possibly in third countries where one does business. The US Foreign Corrupt Practices Act has a particularly long reach. Less obviously but more seriously, paying bribes can get a company and its staff caught up in politicised anti-corruption campaigns in the host country. Such campaigns are often an aspect of political purges, and being anywhere near them can lead to severe complications. Particularly with grand corruption, being known as willing to pay bribes can mark a company as susceptible to pressure, and having paid a bribe a company is also vulnerable to blackmail. Petty corruption is more ambiguous, but being exposed as a serial briber can have a serious effect on a company's reputation.

Cronyism, discussed earlier under favouritism, is another type of government misbehaviour that affects foreign firms and their host country independent business counterparts. In the absence of robust institutional checks and balances and rule of law, senior political figures can give advantages, such as public contracts, regulatory laxity and anti-competitor protections to companies willing to provide favours in turn. These favours lead to returns including nepotistic hiring, kickbacks, bribes and political campaign funding. There is often some personal or sub-national connection between senior officials and heads of favoured companies, and indeed state companies can be cronies connected through shared official contacts. However, even foreign firms can buy their way into a regime's circle of friends if business ethics are a low priority, and if a company is willing to make political games as central to its endeavours as actual business operations.

Cronyism is problematic for the clear reason that if one tries to compete with a crony, the playing field is not level to start with and a regime can cause considerable hassle if their business friends face stiff competition. Additionally, cronies can control so much of the economy that it is hard for a foreign company to have local partners or suppliers without dealing with a crony; and because they are inherently corrupt, there is potential liability in the relationship. Cronyism is often pervasive in countries with deep social divisions and where regimes heavily rely on repression to safeguard their tenure. Thus, when a foreign company develops close links to a regime-connected firm, it can appear, both domestically and to overseas observers, as though the foreigner is taking sides in social rivalries and tacitly colluding with a repressive regime. A company can try to manage a relationship to avoid perceived collusion, but if a company premised its entry on links to a well-connected local partner, it only has so much bargaining power to influence the relationship.

Repression is the last form of government misbehaviour that we will address here. There can be a fine line between law enforcement and protecting the state from illegitimate threats, and repression. Governments in socially divided countries can face the ongoing threat of sub-national rebellions, and these could utilise terrorism to cause harm beyond the rebels' home areas. A high-security footing looks unpleasant and makes people wary, but in many cases the alternatives could be worse (and successful rebellions seldom lead to better governance). Security gives way to repression, though, when a regime relies on fear more than legitimacy to stay in power. State terrorism has the same logic as the non-state kind, that is, hurt a few to scare the rest into quiescence or reluctant support, and like non-state terrorism a degree of arbitrariness can amplify the resulting anxiety.

Repression has clear implications for ordinary citizens, but foreign companies also suffer from it. The author is familiar with several cases in which a foreign firm's local staff were "disappeared" in security sweeps, creating severe moral conundrums for expat managers. Expat staff might not be targeted in sweeps, but they too can suffer detention or other hassles if they are not careful about their political views or inadvertently associate with "subversives". Repression also goes hand in hand with the use of threats to help resolve business disputes, and foreign companies can face serious pressure if they fall out with a regime crony. Repression can manifest as "hostage diplomacy", or the arrest of expat staff from countries with whom the host country government has a dispute. Finally, if a foreign company is required to rely on state security forces or regime-connected security companies for their own security, it can be difficult to ensure that they do not commit human right abuses while contracted or assigned to the company.

INSTABILITY

Analysts, journalists and even intelligence agencies have used "unstable" as a catch-all for "problematic", and it can mean anything from messy governing coalitions to civil war. The term, though, means something specific for our purposes. First, the thing that is unstable is a government, whether a whole system or a specific regime (note that while instability and fragility sound similar, the latter applies to an entire country including its social structure and national cohesion). Second, the kind of change that instability can ultimately lead to is quite sudden, and is outside of routine and institutionalised adjustment mechanisms. In other words it is change by force or compulsion, not evolution or formal process. Third, and importantly, instability does not mean such change itself, but the potentiality for such change, or being in a precarious state. Sudden change can be very disruptive to citizens and companies, but the preceding build-up can also be problematic. It often includes spikes of tension in long-standing political rivalries, and creates anxious uncertainty that can linger for years or decades before an unstable situation is resolved one way or another.

There are two principal forms of the phenomenon. One is bottom-up instability, in which an increasing number of people in a society feels growing distrust and frustration towards a government and eventually mobilises to try to force change. The end logic of this type, if reached, is revolution. A second type is intra-regime instability (we will usually just call it regime instability), wherein factional infighting within the regime leads to a power contest and sometimes a sharp, violent contest. There is overlap between these two forms, especially whereby factional infighting or coups weaken a government's legitimacy among a populace. We address each type in turn, along with their political risk implications.

Bottom-up instability starts as frustration with a government among a sizeable part of the population. Frustration usually has a significant socio-economic component, but it also comes from building resentment to government misbehaviour, particularly corruption and self-preserving repression. As a government or regime begins to lose legitimacy, people become more sensitive to its underperformance, and protests can break out for myriad reasons, for example subsidy cuts, tax increases, ethical scandals or the mismanagement of a disaster or crisis. Early in the process of bottom-up instability, protests usually aim at specific grievances, but if a government mishandles the situation, for example by excessive use of force or by denying that problems exist, then protests can escalate to calls for regime change. Dissident groups might already exist and begin to coordinate a protest movement, although in recent years social media has enabled spontaneous initial coordination and dissident groups sometimes play catch up with unplanned protest movements.

In response to widespread protests, governments usually mix negotiation with constrictions on Internet and mobile networks, arrests and crowd control, trying to find the balance between carrot and stick to defuse the situation. Dissidents can increase pressure by organising strikes and setting up physical defences. A standoff, with periodic spikes in protests and government suppression, can last for weeks or months.

The outcome varies. If a regime has control over capable security forces and sees protests as an existential threat, it could eventually crush a movement rather than risk it getting out of hand. More usually, there is an ambiguous outcome that combines partial accommodation to protester demands and some changes in government composition with a heightened security presence on the street. Core issues might not be resolved, but both sides agree to back off for a while. This can lead to future rounds of protest, which can become a regular feature of the national political scene until something else changes.

Protest movements can also lead to significant change. Full revolutions that change an entire system of government are rare, with the last clear example being Iran in 1979 (the fall of communist Eastern Bloc regimes was more an implosion than a revolution). In most cases, although the leadership and some of the architecture of government changes, at least part of the old government remains intact. Partial revolutions can result in better governance in the long run, but because they lead to some dysfunction and disrupt the economy, the issues that initially led to protests can linger. In countries where the military has political influence, revolutionary governments can also be vulnerable to military manipulation, and even a coup, as occurred in Egypt in 2013 for example. Thus, despite a major change, a country does not necessarily become more stable, at least in the short run.

Bottom-up instability can also lead to armed conflict, if a regime is intransigent and maintains control over the security forces, and if protest groups can make a transition to armed insurgency. The latest example of this at the time of writing in 2021 seems to be in Myanmar, where urban dissidents have been getting guerrilla training from long-standing rural insurgent groups (this case coincides with regime-level instability, since protests followed a coup). Syria is a severe case of how bottom-up instability can open a pandora's box of social fissures, existential anxieties and pent-up fear and rage. Although early protests were peaceful, they were all it took to trigger a spiral into multi-sided civil war.

There are several implications of bottom-up instability for foreign companies. On the upside, a successful revolution can lead to a more transparent and well governed operating environment, as in Georgia in 2003. Even a protest movement met with partial government accommodation, such as in Morocco's Arab Spring, can lead to more accountable and transparent governance.

There are several downsides though. An obvious one is the unrest that ensues during periods of manifestation. Protests are not always violent, but they are disruptive and lead to transport hub closures, roadblocks and other logistical problems. They can also involve strikes that impede public service provision. When there is violence, including police action, staff risk getting hurt and company facilities could be damaged. Regime change, while sometimes a good thing in the long run, can lead to bureaucratic confusion and worse-than-usual delays, the replacement of officials whom a company is used to dealing with, and in some cases changes to business regulations. Finally, instability can create long-term uncertainty, whether in the lead up to protests, or in ambiguous outcomes that hold the potential for further unrest. Foreign companies can often endure through periods of political unrest and resume operations once calm returns, but the severity of the phenomenon varies, and even if a return to business as usual is feasible, such periods can be costly and even dangerous.

Intra-regime instability derives from factional power contests, which can be on various axes including sub-national, family, ideological and civilian-military. Nearly any government, or indeed large organisation, has factional contests within it. The difference in complex emerging markets is weak institutionalisation. When institutions, which include the principles that underpin them, are weak, there is more opportunity to operate outside of, or bend, the rules to try to achieve one's interests. Conversely, there is also a risk that one's factional opponents will try the same thing. Institutions not only constrain, but they also protect, and when they are weak or manipulable, people feel vulnerable, and this intensifies their threat perception of other groups. In many cases, for a long-time intra-regime contests can be contained by a combination of albeit limited institutional oversight, informal bargaining and personal relationships. But when either an opportunity for greater power arises or a group's position comes under increasing pressure, factional power plays can occur, whether short-lived like a coup or a power grab or drawn out as competing sides intensify manoeuvres for tactical advantage. Both variants disrupt the normal process of governance and further undermine institutions, and even slow-burning contests can flare into violence with the potential for lingering unrest.

Coups, power grabs and purges are the visible manifestations of intra-regime instability. While coups involving regime change are the most well known, power grabs within a regime can be just as disruptive, involving violent crackdowns and at least a temporary spike in overall repression. Purges are a tool of new leaders trying to clean out old networks to install their own, and of established regimes trying to thwart would-be plotters in the government and civil service. While purges can be targeted and selective, they can also affect hundreds or thousands of people across government agencies and institutions. Purges often have a secondary aim of frightening possible opponents into quiescence, which is why they tend to recur, often dressed up as anti-corruption or similar "clean government" campaigns. The fear motive is also why they can be both arbitrary and brutal, destroying careers and even leading to victims spending years in prison, or getting executed.

There are several implications of intra-regime instability for a foreign firm. The violence that can spill over from regime power contests, particularly during coups and attempted coups, is dangerous, though usually short-lived. A successful coup can also lead to temporary international sanctions that affect operations. Just as serious is the spike in repression that occurs when power contests heat up, and if local staff have the "wrong" personal connections, they can become targets, as can personnel among local partners and suppliers. Legitimate government contacts and friends can become politically sensitive to the point of near paralysis, and they can be inexplicably replaced. As noted earlier, being too close to people who become victims of a factional rivalry can drag a company into it, as the company itself is scrutinised for potential affiliation with opposing factions. Intra-regime power games play out in the shadows for the most part, but they can have tangible effects on a company's networks and its own operations.

CONFLICT

Conflict is violent confrontation between groups. All forms of conflict can make life, including for foreign companies, difficult and hazardous. For our purposes, we broadly define three types: routine low-level violence, armed conflict and state failure.

Even in the absence of a specific armed conflict, low-level, routine violence can make a country insecure. As noted earlier, when a protest movement stalls but the driving issues are alive and well, protests can recur, and hard-core elements often bolstered by unemployed youth can turn protests into violent riots which are met with a heavy police response. Ethnic and other sub-national clashes, often occurring in cities with diverse sub-national migrant populations, are usually short-lived but intense. Mob clashes can happen quickly, giving bystanders little time to leave the scene. In resource-scare rural areas, for example in the Sahel in Africa, ethnic rivalries can involve informal armed militias and cycles of raids and retaliation. Criminal violence is not usually regarded as conflict, but it can be endemic and affect ordinary people. Organised crime and gang violence in Mexico and Central America, for example, has led to some of the highest homicide rates in the world. Where law enforcement is weak or corrupt, there can actually be police collusion with crime groups. Terrorist groups, often aspiring insurgents who get stuck at the terrorism stage, collude with or become crime groups for funding, and can cause periodic mayhem through attacks on civilian targets. Lurking amidst these actors and issues are the state's security agencies, which often apply their own form of terrorism to try to keep a lid on other forces. Thus, even when there is "peace", a country can still experience considerable insecurity on a routine basis.

Armed conflict encompasses insurgencies and civil wars. Insurgencies usually arise from sub-national friction and begin as a low-level guerrilla war in the sub-nation's home territory. Sub-national repression or discrimination is a common driver, but in resource-rich areas, there can be a strong motive to try to directly control the resource trade, not just to fund the quest for autonomy but as an end in itself. When insurgencies remain small and localised, as most in fact do, they can endure for years or decades with little effect on broader national security. They move beyond the local nuisance stage when they represent a sizeable sub-nation in a large contiguous territory that has its own resources for funding, when there is a regional arms trade, and when the state is too badly organised to contain it early on. This is the path to civil war, which pits two roughly equal sides against each other, and moves beyond guerrilla attacks and counter-insurgency to include a conventional war aspect. Clearly defined civil wars, such as the past ones in Sri Lanka or Angola, are actually a rarity in civil conflict. Usually, victory is elusive for either side, the rebel side fractures and it becomes hard to track all the forces involved, civilians as opposed to armed forces are the main targets and victims, and all sides suffer from economic disruption. Some conflicts, like Algeria's civil war of the 1990s, see far more covert violence and terror tactics than actual battles.

State failure is the most serious form, and also result, of civil conflict. If a government is weakened by bottom-up instability or becomes ineffectual through its own internal divisions, it can leave a power vacuum that sub-national factions or raw opportunists violently compete to fill. In other cases, insurgency or sub-national clashes increase anxiety among uninvolved factions, and because the government is too weak to provide security, all sides take up arms to protect themselves. A spiral of mutual insecurity and a free-for-all for control over any valuable resources ensue, leading to a multi-sided conflict in which the government is just one faction among others. When there are diverse axes of conflict, and myriad conflict actors including remnant government forces, factional warlords and gangs, no single group has the scale required to achieve victory and re-establish order. The country has thus gone from fragile to failed state with a war/criminal economy, and at this stage only outside intervention can end the violence. There are numerous examples, but stark archetypes include Lebanon's civil war, Liberia and Sierra Leone in the 1990s and early 2000s, the eastern Democratic Republic of Congo (DRC) from 1997, and the ongoing conflicts in Libya, Yemen, Syria, Somalia and the Central African Republic. Despite the Taliban's victory, Afghanistan teeters on the edge, a situation most Afghans are regrettably familiar with.

Low-level violence affects ordinary citizens, and it can be disruptive and dangerous for foreign companies too. Violent protests and sub-national clashes can occur in major urban hubs where a firm has country offices. Staff can be exposed, property can be damaged and local logistics can temporarily close as police clamp down on incidents. Criminal violence can affect personnel, and both organised crime and terrorist groups can see foreign firms as lucrative kidnapping targets. Terrorism can cause direct harm, and by definition it is hard on the nerves and can affect staff's willingness to work in a given country. Local workers are just as exposed to covert state repression as any other citizen and can be the victims of arbitrary detention or disappearance.

An insurgency can be localised and remote from an operation, but if it affects the area of operation, it can lead to severe security strictures that impede movement, and if a foreign company is seen to be somehow colluding with the state, even just by working on a state contract, the company can be a target. Insurgents also extort foreign companies for funding. Civil war presents physical hazards to foreign companies, and also moral hazards around potential collusion with conflict actors and human rights abuses. Additionally, even if civil wars do not affect a company's operating area, they can affect logistics and infrastructure, such as ports, transport links and pipelines that become important rebel targets. State failure makes security nearly impossible to attain. The country can become a no-go zone, and companies already there can be forced to leave behind half-completed projects. Sometimes companies try to hang on, as did Firestone Tire and Rubber Company during Liberia's civil war and Talisman Energy in Sudan's, but in so doing they can be forced into acute moral dilemmas and face considerable danger.

In general, of the three political risk factors, conflict takes the highest price for mistakes. On the surface it might seem mainly like a security and business continuity challenge, but the intense rivalries that drive it make it the ultimate political hotplate. A company could well have to contend with amplified sensitivities and mutual hostility between the stakeholders it needs to relate to, while at the same time securing itself without triggering heightened threat perceptions of people around it or inadvertently making conflict in its vicinity worse.

That concludes our tour of complex terrain. To summarise the thought process, after exploring the concept of complexity, we examined the system by which it arises and perpetuates. Long-term and external influences affect the core socio-political system either over time or through perturbing shocks. The core system itself, comprised of governance, social relations and socio-economic development, can experience illness in any one of these elements, which can infect all three. Core system ill-health in turn gives rise to symptoms, which are most directly responsible for political risk. If symptoms are unmitigated, they feed back into the core system, and state failure could be an eventual result, making a country impossible to operate in.

Even without accounting for who and what a foreign operation is, it is clear that complexity in the socio-political terrain presents challenges to any organisation. There is a risk in just being there. However, if we stopped here, our understanding of what gives rise to political risk would be quite elementary. For a fuller picture, we need to go beyond the terrain itself to understand what is at stake there, namely a foreign operation and assets thereof, and how it is exposed to and interacts with its socio-political milieu. That is the focus of the next chapter.

3 Country Operations

The last chapter provided an aerial map of socio-political terrain, looking at the broad dynamics and patterns that make an operating environment complex, and therefore politically risky for foreign companies. It also outlined in general terms how complex dynamics affect foreign company operations. This chapter adds nuance to the emerging political risk picture by examining how an operation's own attributes, including company behaviour and relationships, shape the socio-political challenges that an operation can face. Anyone operating in a place is subject to the effects of terrain dynamics, but whom someone is, what they are doing and how they behave are significant factors in their own unique experience. Additionally, this chapter considers in more detail an operation's exposures to political risk, and how these can be affected.

The chapter proceeds as follows. First, we characterise country operations and how different operational attributes relate to political risk. We then introduce the notion of stakeholders, in other words socio-political actors with specific attitudes towards an operation, or whom an operation relies on. Next, we examine the attributes that make an operation significant to socio-political actors, in other words an operation's socio-political profile. Following this, the assets that a company exposes to a complex environment are examined. Finally, we briefly consider how company attitudes and behaviours can affect vulnerability to political risk. That is an important theme, but it is explored at various points throughout the book, and hence our discussion of it here is only introductory. As with all chapters in Part I, this one is the basis for nuanced intelligence processes that we apply later, and most elements herein will be expanded on through actual application.

There is a clear challenge in this chapter in trying to establish a baseline picture of a country operation without being too generic or over-relying on a narrow set of sectors for examples. What follows probably will not achieve the ideal balance, but a more modest aim is that at least readers will be able to apply the conceptual framework herein to develop a sense of their own types of operations in relation to political risk.

CHARACTERISING COUNTRY OPERATIONS

A consideration of political risk remains abstract until there is an object exposed to it; hence, we need a characterisation of that object, a foreign company's operation in a complex emerging market. First, we briefly examine the origins of an operation in terms of motives and decision process, in other words why and how an emerging market country operation arises in the first place. This proceeds to a consideration of how political risk can vary according to an operation's phases, the sector of the operating company, and the mode of entry (or type of presence). Finally, for a holistic view of an operation in its context, we picture an operation as a system of interaction with the socio-political environment and actors therein.

ORIGINS

A country operation is usually a manifestation of a company's international ambitions, which in turn derive from strategic imperatives. On the growth side, a company might seek new markets, or new sources of inputs either for its own production or to sell to users in other sectors. On the efficiency side, if a company already has international markets, then getting closer to them can reduce sales and servicing costs, and the increased proximity also builds customer loyalty. Labour or materials might be cheaper somewhere else, and it might make sense to offshore certain processes. There

DOI: 10.1201/9781003149125-5

might be alluring overseas targets for integration across the industry value chain or for acquiring new skills and technologies. Longer-term considerations include denying opportunities to competitors, geographic diversification to manage the corporate risk-reward balance, and creating backups and redundancies in key supply chains and processes in case of business continuity issues in current geographic hubs.

For companies based in mature markets, emerging markets are often attractive with respect to several of the above imperatives. Established markets tend to have relatively higher market saturation and weaker demographics, as well as more intense competition. Many emerging markets, through demographic and economic growth, have growing educated middle classes which are both potential markets and skilled labour pools. Skilled and unskilled labour is usually cheaper than in mature market regions. There is relatively higher demand for infrastructure expansion and modernisation because of a low initial starting point in relation to growing populations and domestic business activity, and competition for foreign investment. Natural resources can be relatively untapped by comparison to international companies' home regions which companies have already been trawling for decades. Finally, the very fact that emerging markets are challenging gives early movers a significant advantage over subsequent competitors. Especially for firms in mature industries, emerging markets can represent a badly needed growth horizon, and an early mover advantage is valuable.

Internationalisation imperatives plus the allure of emerging markets impel the search for specific emerging market country opportunities. Strategy, marketing and business development work on opportunity identification, and a given country opportunity is then assessed for feasibility and against risk-reward criteria (these often include some permutation of political risk). If a prospect passes these tests, it is handed from prospecting to operations. In the case of tender opportunities, for example for an infrastructure project or oil concession, the company starts the bid phase, which involves not just the bid itself but also establishes the bases of contractual negotiations, and gets prospective delivery and financing partners on board. Once the bid is won, the prospect moves to initial planning. If there is no bid involved, say if a company wants to open a country subsidiary or partner with a local company for sales reach, the prospect moves directly to entry planning. When the first team that will stay for a while arrives on the ground, the country operation is born. In larger firms, it might only be one small node in itself, but it is the ultimate outcome of corporate strategic ambitions which in turn rest on the success of a number of such operations globally. For smaller firms, such as small mining firms built around one or a few projects, one operation could be make or break.

PHASE

Some foreign operations are project-based, and hence have an exit planned from the start. Others are intended as a "permanent" presence in a new market or supply chain node, but even so they eventually face an exit stage at some point if only as a result of evolving corporate strategy. Thus, while operations vary considerably in form and intent, they all go through several phases from pre-entry to exit, and different phases tend to have different political risk implications.

Pre-entry planning, when there are few people and assets on the ground and most work is done from head office, entails little exposure, but this is the stage when intelligence and plans that will guide operations are formed. Mistakes and misjudgements in this phase can have serious consequences later on, leaving country management blindsided by gaps in corporate's assessment. More seriously, there is often still considerable hype and optimism about having won a project or launched a new initiative, and this can lead to a disinclination to look hard at potential challenges and friction points, or to take warnings seriously.

Launch and initial set-up are when a company gains its first real experience with the local bureaucracy and any forms of corruption pressure that might be prevalent. The firm will be seeking a raft of initial permits, and its first tangles with the bureaucracy could be a shock. It is also when a company still lacks cultural knowhow and has no innate sense of the values and social structures that sit alongside and affect commercial and organisational thinking. Opportunists and predators in the local terrain know that the company is still new and ill at ease, and can exploit this for their own ends. Plans laid at HQ might seem too academic against the reality on the ground, and there is a need for more practical insights. Hopefully, after initial entry the company will have trustworthy host country staff or other contacts on board, and they can help the operation to navigate towards a socio-political fit, but this phase still presents a steep learning curve and high vulnerability.

The operating phase is ideally when things seem routine. Challenges can still arise, but a company would have learned how to diagnose and manage the more mundane issues, and its information networks will be better developed and more capable of providing warnings about potential socio-political changes or shifts in attitudes that could affect the operation. There are potential issues in this phase, though, partly arising from the company's adaptation. Depending on the degree of localisation, the country team could be too flexible in adapting to local ways of doing things, and see corporate policy as unrealistic or inapplicable. This can lead to corrupt interactions and to relationships with politically connected but ethically dubious partners or influencers. Complacency can also make political risk and related monitoring seem unnecessary or burdensome, especially when managers feel "plugged into" the local scene and get their information from local networks, some of which might not have the company's best interests at heart. Thus, when things feel too smooth, vulnerabilities can arise.

It is also worth noting that the corporate team can be the ones who are complacent once an operation appears to be in a routine phase. The experience of Talisman Energy, a Canadian oil company, in Sudan in 1998–2003 is a useful illustration. Not long after entry, country management was expressing serious concerns about the operation, which was in a war zone. The main issue was that army units guarding Talisman's operation were also engaged in military action, which included raids on local villages and other abuses, sometimes using the company's helicopter pads for army gunships. It was clear to country managers that the situation was unsustainable, yet HQ failed to budge on the issue because the operation was on target and senior management saw non-commercial matters as abstract and immaterial. The country-HQ disconnect can therefore work both ways. If HQ sees an up-and-running country operation making targets, it can become complacent and not take country-level concerns seriously. "Out of sight, out of mind" can apply as long the commercial aspect is working. This is a formula for delayed reactions to building problems, and for considerable stress and even hazard for staff on the ground.

The late operating phase preceding exit can be sensitive. In government contracts, or when working with state company partners, the foreign firm can appear ripe for some arm-twisting to hand over more assets or technology than contractually agreed, or to accept late contract changes. This is because much of the work has been done, rare foreign expertise has already been used, and local staff have learned how to run the operation; thus, the company's bargaining power is diminished. Another issue is how the operation handles its local labour and local corporate social responsibility (CSR) programmes when workers and the host community are aware of the firm's impending departure. Ideally, workers would be equipped with new skills for future opportunities, and CSR and social investment programmes would have been designed with an eye to a careful handover, but even so, the company can face concern that its departure will leave others high and dry. This can lead to friction. For example, in 2016 both Coca Cola and Sony faced strikes at plants in China when they announced the impending sale of the affected plants to Chinese companies, who, staff feared, would not provide the same benefits and working conditions (Strikes in China over foreign employers selling out to local companies, 2016).

Exit can be smooth when there is no unfinished business, but if there is, then it can be a vulnerable time. If there are lingering disputes with partners or suppliers, these can flare up as the other parties see this moment as their final chance for redress. Disputes with governments, for example over unpaid taxes, or, in the case of government projects, over contractual terms of a final handover, have led to trumped-up charges against the company and staff to complicate departure. Repatriating cash and physical assets can also be difficult in the context of a dispute. In unstable or hazardous contexts when a company might have to temporarily scale back operations or even withdraw, it is ideal if only essential personnel are left on the ground, but a small team in a complicated situation can feel particularly isolated and actually be more vulnerable because of fewer human resources, and eyes and ears, to manage any potential crises.

Different operational phases thus have different political risk profiles. Upfront assessment can provide general guidance, but if intelligence and planning are not updated by phase, an operation could end up flying blind not long after it commences. Even if the socio-political environment does not change much, the original assessment would be obsolete in relation to operational exposures and vulnerabilities.

Sector

Different business sectors face different types and degrees of political risk in country projects because of the character of their product or service, and the attributes of the operations they undertake. There are numerous distinctions between sectors, and we only outline a few key ones that are most relevant to political risk exposure, along with a few illustrative sectors.

One axis of distinction is how embedded typical operations are. An operation that needs to embed expatriate staff and heavy equipment for years represents a high commitment. It can be harder, or more costly, to withdraw in the event of harmful change or unrest, and the company's physical assets can become bargaining chips in the event of disputes with the government. Oil and gas, mining, infrastructure and manufacturing all require well-embedded operations that need to be sustained over several years or more. Retail operations are somewhat less embedded, and business-to-business sales and service (with products imported) and professional services are relatively light-footed by comparison. For example, a professional service firm has little to leave behind, and could fly people home without having to first mothball complex physical facilities.

Another distinction is how regulated a sector is. Regulations vary by country, but sector variations in overall regulatory intensity tend to be similar across countries. Oil and gas, telecoms, media platforms such as Google or Twitter, and chemicals, for example, are tightly regulated and therefore highly reliant on regulatory clarity and consistency, as well as bureaucratic performance in regulatory implementation and oversight. Financial services and TV media can also be heavily regulated depending on the extent of their presence. Less regulated sectors, such as facilities management, private education, and fashion retailing, can still find regulatory change and inconsistency to be a hassle, but since fewer regulations apply to their operations, the overall effects are less onerous or potentially disruptive.

Sectors also differ in how closely they are linked to or reliant on governments. When a government is a customer or requires state company participation, or when a project is initiated by a government, an operation might gain the benefit of political support, but is also more exposed to regime whims and political pressures. Oil and gas, mining and public infrastructure operations have strong government ties, and thus more directly feel the effects of weak or eccentric governance. These sectors also attain some control over sources of national wealth or public services, and governments can be very sensitive to the public perception of an operation. In extractive operations, the resource a company came for sits under government-owned or controlled land, and rights to the site, namely the concession, can become a bargaining chip in a dispute with a government. Manufacturing operations can sometimes be regarded as key to a national development strategy, and hence be overseen by the relevant ministry. Hotels, retail and professional services, by contrast, are more firmly in the private domain, and while they need to deal with the bureaucracy, generally they seldom need to deal with politicians, at least if there is not unofficial political interference.

How labour-intensive a sector is also matters. Governments often apply more stringent local content regulations to labour-intensive operations to ensure that people benefit from jobs and job training. A local labour force also entails more scrutiny of local health and safety and labour code compliance. In many countries, it also means dealing with unions which use can use strike activity and their own media relations as bargaining chips in disputes. For once, the oil and gas sector is not among the more affected sectors – it tends to be much more capital than labour-intensive. Mining is quite labour-intensive and manufacturing can be, and the construction phase of infrastructure projects also has high labour requirements. On a side note, while local content and union participation often apply to foreign labour-intensive projects, in recent years Chinese companies working in developing countries, particularly in Africa, have been allowed to shirk the rules, largely because of Chinese state loans that go hand in hand with the ingress of (often state) Chinese firms. Most international companies are not following or bearing the flag, and competing with those who are can be frustrating. We bring up this point again in the book's concluding chapter.

Finally, the importance of consumer branding is relevant. Branded clothing, phone, food manufacturers and retailers, for example, are at risk of weak intellectual property and brand protections, making them susceptible to product piracy. Because of the importance of corporate identity in customer retention, branded consumer sectors are also especially hard hit by scandals involving ethical lapses such as labour abuses. A company is often held to account not just for breaches in its own facilities, but across its wider supply chain. That could extend to various emerging markets where relevant regulations are weakly defined and enforced, or relaxed for regime cronies among supplier networks.

There are more axes of variation, in particular how disruptive a sector's operations tend to be for host communities (e.g. industrial agriculture), and how ethically controversial a sector is (e.g. "sinful" industries or those which seem to profit from basic human needs, like pharmaceuticals). Of the above, oil and gas and mining recur, and it is no surprise that much political risk literature either is for the extractives or heavily draws on them for case studies. A company's sector is indeed a factor in a typical operation's political risk exposure. But it is also the case that more inherently politically risky sectors are usually better at managing political risk because they have more experience with it. Thus, an experienced oil company might not find a relatively fragile country to be especially problematic, whereas the same country could lie well outside the comfort zone of a branded appliance manufacturer.

Mode of Entry

The mode of entry on which an operation is premised also shapes political risk exposure. Again there is a range of variations, and we only outline some key reference points.

Projects are one entry mode. A company wins a tender and then establishes a temporary project office and the required facilities to execute the work, with no intention to set up a long-term presence. Especially on government contracts, projects face contract change, cancellation and payment risks, for example if a new political leadership changes the policies that led to the requirement. Especially in complex projects, such as infrastructure construction or e-government systems integration, there can be considerable scope for charges of underperformance or incompletion, and if a case goes to arbitration, it can take years to resolve and leave both parties with some lingering resentment. One irony that construction firms in particular have faced is that missed deadlines, a common charge levelled by government customers, often occur because of government interference and politicised design changes.

A design and build (or EPC – engineering, procurement and construction) project is often just the initial phase of a longer government-contracted operation in which the government grants a concession or is the customer and/or partner. Public-private partnerships (PPP) using the build-own-operate-transfer (BOT or BOOT) model, independent power and other utilities provision, and large-scale extractive projects are examples. These often start with a construction or field development project, but then move into an operating phase that can be intended to last over two decades. Because revenues only accrue after operation commences, financing is required for early phases, and in developing countries project financiers often include donors and transnational lenders such as the World Bank or a regional development bank, whose presence helps to deter and arbitrate contract disputes in early phases. However, even 5, let alone 20, years of government-contracted operations in a volatile political context is a long time. Government leaders and their spending priorities can change several times, and once the operating phase is smoothly under way, a government can be tempted to change contract terms or to increase its own control or stake to the detriment of its foreign partners. The sheer temporal exposure is thus one challenging characteristic. The other is that projects involving public service provision or national assets are inherently political and subject to shifting political attitudes. These two traits combine to make a degree of political pressure or interference at some point in the operation nearly inevitable.

For a long-term presence beyond a specific project or contract, there are several entry options. A manufacturer, for example, who finally decides to produce in a country, as opposed to just exporting to it, can license or franchise production to a local manufacturer, or sub-contract production to local companies. Both are quick but entail a potential loss of control over quality, intellectual property and ethical and environmental standards. In places, such as Bangladesh or Indonesia, where weak governance leads to gaps in regulatory enforcement and also to governments ignoring bad habits among crony companies, weak labour standards in particular have vexed branded consumer goods manufacturers.

Acquisition of a local firm offers more control. Many developing country governments make joint ventures (JVs) easier because of the skills and technology transfers that occur between the foreign and local partners, and in some cases a nationalistic attitude leads to limits on foreign stakes in a local business entity. But where acquisitions are feasible, they can be a relatively quick way to gain a strong foothold. Challenges include the fact that due diligence can be very difficult in emerging markets because regulations governing company records are often weak or poorly enforced. An acquisition target might be well embedded in regime-linked crony networks and accustomed to corruption, and the foreign firm faces not only the usual cultural hurdles but also the challenge of unlinking the company from illicit influence (this was, for example, one of AES' first tasks with Telasi in the Georgia case in Chapter 1). If the target is close to political interests, there could be political interference in the deal and subsequent pressure to prevent changes that could affect the company's position in crony networks. Additionally, while the acquisition target might meet local labour and environmental standards, or be able to elude them because of political ties, after the acquisition the company is more likely to be assessed against norms and standards in the buyer's home region, and failure to meet these can incur reputational damage in core markets.

JVs, as noted, are often preferred by developing country governments because of the developmental benefits for the local partner, and hence official approvals can be easier. Even though a JV is a legal entity, the partners remain distinct, thus unlike with an acquisition, the foreign firm does not bear direct liability for the partner's overall ethical standards outside of the specific JV activity. A close partnership with a local firm in an unfamiliar political environment has risks though. One challenge is that the host country partner applies local political connections as leverage in disputes. For example, in 2008 when there was a growing divergence between BP and its Russian partners in the TNK-BP joint venture, the Russian side was able to call on regime friends to initiate investigations into BP as a pressure tactic, and the JV was ultimately adjusted to grant the Russian side more control. Manufacturing JVs can face the risk of intellectual property and brand piracy when the local element gains access to the foreign firm's knowhow and labels. In 2007, for example, French company Danone saw its China JV directly competing with itself when the Chinese partner started independently selling products under the same brand, taking advantage of weak intellectual property laws and jingoistic perceptions of foreign-local disputes to dodge legal liability.

Subsidiaries are another option. Wholly owned subsidiaries offer more control than other entry modes, but implanting a part of the company is often a complex and time-consuming endeavour, especially since no local partner who knows the environment is formally on board to assist. Being wholly owned is also no guarantee that a subsidiary will adhere to corporate standards. Walmart, for example, faced corruption charges in the US in 2019 after several of its emerging market subsidiaries were found to be using local agents to pay bribes to speed up local approvals. This is a familiar story in various sectors. Localisation, or letting a foreign subsidiary adapt to local conditions for a closer fit with market preferences and culture, can accelerate a foreign firm's local footprint, but it also runs the risk of the subsidiary playing by local rules, and in weakly governed environments this can risk corruption and other ethical and legal pitfalls.

Partly owned subsidiaries can be even more problematic. The foreign stakeholder bears the brand name and therefore is publicly held accountable for the subsidiary's actions, when in fact the foreign firm might not have much control. The Bhopal disaster in India in 1984, for example, is often directly attributed to Union Carbide, but Union Carbide India, 49.1 percent Indian owned (including a sizeable government stake), controlled the Bhopal plant. Similarly, Shell is often directly held to account for environmental damage and company security abuses in the Niger Delta, but it is the Shell Petroleum Development Company of Nigeria, 55 percent owned by the Nigerian state oil company, that runs onshore Delta operations. In weakly regulated jurisdictions, partial ownership can be insufficient to ensure adherence to ethical and environmental standards and hence expose a firm to breaches and consequent fallout. When companies try to deny full responsibility for breaches on the premise that they do not have full control, critics and even the company's own shareholders can see some hypocrisy in a firm putting its brand on a venture yet trying to hide behind a lack of full ownership.

There are more variations and nuance in mode of entry, and the above is only indicative and does not necessarily suggest which type bears more nett political risk exposure. This is because there is a trade-off between control, which can be applied to reduce ethical and legal breaches, and exposure in terms of people and assets on the ground. However, as with phases and sectors, a consideration of how mode of entry affects exposure helps to set broad initial hypotheses on the types of issues an operation might face.

It should be noted that in the heyday of political risk theorising in the 1970s, entry mode was often discussed in relation to the risk of government expropriation or nationalisation, and these discussions are still reflected in more recent musings. A wholly owned subsidiary, for example, had higher expropriation risk because it had more company assets exposed and few local stakeholders who would be hurt by expropriation. Correspondingly, a JV involving a local partner had less risk. These days, expropriation and nationalisation are far less common than more subtle forms of manipulation and interference, which can be motivated by a range of interests including crony greed, and affect any kind of foreign stake or presence. While there is still some relationship between entry mode and the risk of expropriation or nationalisation, it is far weaker than it was in the 1970s when many governments still had one foot in statist economic models. Having local stakeholders on board who would be hurt by government interference can help when there is such a risk, but even a wholly owned subsidiary can develop such ties, for example through local supply contracts, and CSR programmes and social investment. Furthermore, the partner in a JV or other partnership model can act as an inside agent for a regime faction seeking to skew a venture towards its own specific interests, and from this perspective a wholly owned subsidiary is actually easier to shield from manipulation.

AN OPERATION AS A RELATIONSHIP SYSTEM

We now step away from specific operational and company attributes to consider an operation as a relationship system, or ecosystem. Any foreign operation that involves a direct presence can be conceptualised as an entity sitting within and interacting with a wider socio-political milieu, and a high-level system perspective is a useful way to grasp some of the key linkages and dependencies that exist between the two. As we will see in Part II, at a more detailed level of analysis these nodes of interaction can represent exposures and potential friction points, and hence they help to inform hypotheses about issues that might arise. For now, this simply helps to see an operation in broader socio-political and relationship terms, as opposed to just commercial and technical. The ecosystem in Figure 3.1 is necessarily top level and generic, but for purposes here we can imagine a manufacturing operation that relies on both local labour and partners.

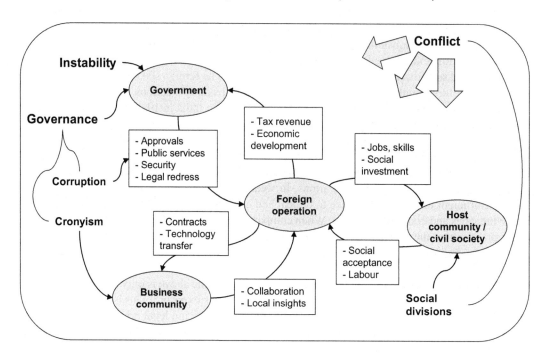

FIGURE 3.1   Country operation ecosystem.

There are a variety of ways to map an operation in its socio-political context. For example, one can focus only on socio-political stakeholders to see how the operation fits into, affects and is affected by networks, or one can map critical operational dependencies to relevant socio-political dynamics and actors. In this basic hybrid depiction, interactions and exchanges appear to be smooth and to provide what the company needs for pace and endurance. Factors of complexity, however, such as social divisions or corruption, can affect the entities that the company interacts with and disrupt the equilibrium of exchanges.

What is not showing in the diagram is the factor of company behaviours and its attitude to the host society. If the company were insensitive or obtuse to its local effects and cultural acceptability, this would also affect the exchanges going on, ultimately reducing the benefits returned to the company. We will discuss company attitudes and behaviours in relation to political risk at various points in the book. For now, we can just bear in mind that the relationship system is two-way: an operation is affected by dynamics and actors around it, but it in turn affects the system, and therefore is a factor in how the system responds to the company. We address this point again at the end of the chapter.

The illustration depicts what seems to be ordinary, or non-political, commercial relationships with the local business community, but local businesses can be political players to varying degrees. Even in upper OECD countries such as in Western Europe, companies have a socio-political aspect, both receiving laws and social reactions, and in turn influencing through lobbying, bargaining and corporate communications. In many emerging markets, as the last chapter noted, large local companies and business leaders are often closely linked to, or overlap with, politicians or other political actors, and can seek to benefit their own factions or social groups. Customers too could be relevant to a socio-political perspective. For example, farmers buying agricultural equipment or genetically modified seeds might be represented by influential farmers' unions. The depicted ecosystem also does not include local competitors, but as we saw in the Sainsbury's case, they can organise to apply political pressure if they feel squeezed, and if they are regime cronies, they could exercise regime connections to their advantage. Thus, it is not safe to assume that the business domain is apolitical, and parts of it often are relevant to a socio-political perspective of an operation.

There is not much about a country operation that does not eventually touch on socio-political actors and dynamics. For example, expat staff depend on work or residence permits to be at the operation, and this ultimately rests with policies set by the ministry of interior (or another depending on specific institutional models), itself under the oversight of the political leadership. Logistics might include port transit and, therefore, depend on customs for relevant permits and port clearance, as well as labour relations and union activism among port workers. On an even more basic level, a company's operation has to be situated somewhere, and in many cases this is in proximity to a host community affected by any inconveniences but also hopeful about getting jobs or other benefits from the company's presence. A negative host community reaction can lead to NGO and media criticism and regulator intervention. In short, even when a socio-political system is calm or changes incrementally, the relationship between a company and the socio-political environment is itself dynamic and needs to be managed. This is all the more so if weak governance, instability and conflict rattle the whole system and stress actors within it, the company and its immediate socio-political contacts included.

To summarise our characterisation of operations, an emerging market country operation is a manifestation of strategic imperatives, and part of a wider international portfolio which can constitute a significant part of a company's profit-making activity. Operations go through several phases, and each phase has a somewhat different political risk profile. Political risk implications also vary with business sector and mode of entry. Finally, a socio-political ecosystem perspective reveals the systemic exchanges between an operation and socio-political entities, and these in turn represent potential political risk exposures. When we proceed to Part II, this characterisation will help to sketch the object of the intelligence exercise, in other words the thing of value (the operation) that is subject to harm or disruption from political risk.

SOCIO-POLITICAL STAKEHOLDERS

The operational ecosystem just discussed indicates that socio-political actors and relationships constitute a tangible element of an operation. Thus, when considering political risk, it is insufficient to only look at country-level factors and dynamics, which we covered in Chapter 2. A traveller is certainly affected by the terrain they cover, but their encounters with people along the way often have more immediate and nuanced implications. Indeed, most cases of manifested political risk have mainly been the result of socio-political actors' direct responses to an operation. Relatively few issues are only attributable to a worsening of the terrain, for example conflict or the rise of a government with a hostile attitude to foreign investors in general. That being said, terrain dynamics do not just affect foreign companies, but also socio-political actors with whom companies interact, and hence even though actors' responses are often most directly relevant to political risk, the attitudes and pressures underpinning those responses are in turn shaped by broader factors in the environment. Indeed, many actors that a company deals with are directly involved in broader country dynamics. Thus, there is a link between terrain factors and specific socio-political responses to a company.

The term "stakeholder" is commonly used for a relevant actor or contact, and hence we apply it here with some adaptation of meaning. In most guides on stakeholder management, stakeholders are defined as an individual, group or organisation whose interests would be affected by one's activities (hence, they have a stake) and who could have some influence over the operation. "Stakeholder" is a bit of a misnomer in our context, however, because not every relevant socio-political actor will have a stake in an operation. We might have a stake in *them*. For example, a company will need to rely on the police as an aspect of its security, but the police might not care what the company is up to as long as it is acting within the law. Additionally, having one's own influence is not a prerequisite for being a socio-political stakeholder. For example, if a foreign company gets a permit to build an access road through a farmer's field, the farmer certainly has a stake, but might have no influence. However, the company's behaviour towards the farmer could be reported to someone who does, such as an NGO or a traditional authority, and they could exercise influence on the farmer's behalf. Thus, we adapt our definition of stakeholder accordingly:

> Socio-political actors with an interest in the operation, and or / whom the operation relies on, with direct or indirect influence over the operation.

One could premise the whole definition or its parts with "potential" since stakeholder interest can be contingent on specific company actions, and influence can be latent until organised or mustered as a response.

The distinction between socio-political actors in general and stakeholders can be confusing because country dynamics that can affect an operation all derive from human behaviour. It is important to note that socio-political stakeholders are those actors with whom we have some relationship or whose actions derive from their perception of us. For example, the author recalls a case of a foreign mining company in the Philippines which was threatened by an insurgent group because of the operation's negative effects on the local community, and this actually led to indirect engagement to try to learn how genuine the group's concerns were. The insurgents were a stakeholder. On the other hand, a terrorist group that plants a bomb in the city where we have a country office might not even know about us, and the bomb is a manifestation of conflict dynamics in the environment, not a specific response to us even if we were affected. When we have no relationship with or meaning to someone, then their behaviour can be regarded as a manifestation of a terrain factor. We might assess them to better understand what is going on in a place, but not to see how we could shape and manage a relationship with them, as we would with a stakeholder.

The above makes another useful distinction from conventional notions of stakeholder. The language of stakeholder analysis and engagement is usually influenced by a company's sustainability aspirations and tends to focus on positive relationships. But stakeholders can be bad actors too, or those with predatory or innately hostile attitudes towards the operation. When an actor is both potentially violent and intractably hostile, such as regional Al Qaeda in the Statoil case, or Russian mafia racketeers targeting foreign firms back in the 1990s, then in practical terms they can be regarded as threats and addressed by the security function. However, if they notice us and we have meaning to them, then they are still stakeholders, and security approaches, such as protection or deterrence, are actually a form of stakeholder engagement. Threat assessment is a specialist drill-down exercise, but it is informed by stakeholder analysis, which in a political risk context also considers threats.

Operations vary considerably in terms of who matters, in other words what types of socio-political actors become stakeholders. It is possible, though, to provide some typical examples. Table 3.1 captures some recurring types and how they can be relevant, but it is only a top-level and indicative snapshot.

Many of the examples in the table would not apply to a given operation, and no doubt many types would be missing in the context of another. The choices a company makes in how it sets up its operation are a factor in which actors become relevant. For example, a company might outsource much of its production activities to local firms, in which case they handle interaction with local labour. CSR programmes widely vary and entail diverse interactions. For example, an educational programme might rely on the participation of local schools or technical colleges, and this in turn makes the Ministry of Education a stakeholder, while others focus on grassroots development that requires the support of local NGOs and traditional authorities. As we will see in the next section, an operation's socio-political profile, or identity, is also a factor in stirring the interest of different actors, and no two operations have exactly the same profile. Thus, unlike terrain factors, stakeholders can only really be identified once operational attributes are known at least at a general level.

TABLE 3.1
Common Stakeholder Types

Category	Type	Our Interest in Them	Their Interest in Us
Government/official	Regulators and tax authorities	Official permits, legal status, timely responses	Compliance, possibly corruption
	Ministry responsible for our sector (e.g. Industry)	Tacit approval and support, non-interference	Alignment with development goals, possibly corruption
	Ministries whose remits we affect (e.g. Agriculture)	Tacit approval, non-interference	Respect for their goals, possibly corruption
	Local authorities	Local permits, support in host community interaction	Local effects, development, possibly corruption
	Police/security/emergency response	Responsiveness, joint planning for special hazards, security human rights compliance	Security interest in potential political effects of operation, possibly corruption
	Regime/political leadership	Tacit approval, non-interference	Developmental impact, effect on crony networks, possibly corruption
Civil society	Host community	Social acceptance, potential labour pool	Potential effects on livelihoods and group rivalries, development benefits
	Traditional authorities (e.g. village elders)	Social acceptance, guidance in community engagement	Potential effects on their constituents and status
	NGOs (local, national, international)	Social acceptance, partnership for CSR programmes	Potential effects on environment, human rights and livelihoods
	Labour unions	Labour pool, support in labour negotiations, minimal disruption	Members' jobs and benefits
	Media	Fair coverage, reporting of operation's positive effects	News interest, professional curiosity, possibly regime favour if reporting on disputes with government
Business community	Partners/suppliers	Required inputs and collaboration, local content fulfilment, local insights	Revenue, skills and technology transfers, possibly our intellectual property
	Business associations	Joint lobbying, local insights, acceptance	Member opportunities as suppliers and partners, international ties
	Politically connected competitors	Effects on operation through hostile lobbying	Effect on their market share and prices, effect on competitive landscape

(*Continued*)

TABLE 3.1 (CONTINUED)

Category	Type	Our Interest in Them	Their Interest in Us
Other/threat actors	Insurgent and terrorist groups	Security of personnel and assets	Potential symbolic target; local insurgents could seek to influence operation's impact on their constituent social group
	Organised crime groups	Security of personnel and assets	Potential target for kidnapping or other extortion; theft of assets
	Political security agencies	Security of domestic personnel if detention risk, and human rights adherence in any security support provided to the operation	Potential political implications of the operation or spillover of foreign political values; security of the operation if it is of importance to the regime

A particular interaction with effects for the operation could involve only one stakeholder. For example, between 2016 and 2020 a Spanish hotel group trying to build a new hotel in Cancun, Mexico, repeatedly butted heads with the local authorities over environmental impacts and the additional burden on waste treatment facilities (Riu Hotels challenges order to halt construction of project in Cancún, 2020). It was a costly dispute, but it was quite simple in that it only involved two main parties, the company and the local council. In another example from 2019, suffering from falling oil prices, the Nigerian government under President Buhari sought an extra $62 billion from foreign oil companies which had allegedly failed to allocate the appropriate share of revenues to the state over the preceding decade or so (Nigeria Demands $62B from Oil Majors, 2020). Again, this was a potentially costly dispute, but it was easy to see who was involved and why.

In other cases when stakeholder responses manifest as an issue, a network of stakeholder interests is involved. Both the AES Georgia and Sainsbury's Egypt cases illustrated networked stakeholder responses. Another example is that of a Canadian mining company in the Democratic Republic of Congo (DRC) in 2009–2010 which had its licence revoked only to see the concession sold at a fraction of its value to a Central Asian mining group, after what one can surmise was a conspiracy ultimately enabled by, and benefitting, corrupt elite networks in the regime's inner circle (RAID UK, 2019). Even in more basic and localised cases, networks can be involved. For example, in the early 2000s a foreign mining company in Indonesia found that local elites assisting with its CSR programmes were actually linked to government-funded civic associations whose role was partly to keep an eye on community activism, and they used this semi-official status to harass and threaten local activists concerned about the mine's environmental impact. This severely compromised the company's local trust and incurred reputational damage (Welker, 2009).

Even if an issue only involves one group or organisation, stakeholders are linked to others, and to understand one actor's attitude and influence, one often needs to see where it fits in a network. Linkages, whether cooperative or competitive, can affect an actor's position towards an operation, and actors can draw on each other for support in shaping a response if they feel a need. That explains our inclusion of indirect influence in our definition of stakeholders. We will examine stakeholder networks as part of stakeholder analysis in Part II.

Before moving on, it is worth highlighting that although the wider context here is political risk, positive stakeholder relationships are an essential element of an operation's success, and a committed and adaptive company can do a lot to avoid friction and create positive bonds. For example, even within a government that is on the whole quite corrupt or run by personal power interests, there are almost invariably champions of good governance who see legitimate, "clean" FDI as a pillar of national development. Stakeholder analysis is not just about looking for potential problems but also about with whom and how to form mutually beneficial legitimate relationships. A book on political risk might read like a corporate horror story to some extent, but companies manage to successfully work in very challenging places, and a significant reason for this is robust stakeholder relationships. We will see in the chapter on political risk management planning that such relationships are an integral part of approaches to addressing challenges.

SOCIO-POLITICAL PROFILE

An operation's socio-political profile means its visible or perceived attributes and effects in the socio-political context. The profile is what socio-political actors notice, and some actors become stakeholders based on their interpretation of the profile in relation to their own values and interests. We make extensive use of the socio-political profile in the chapter on stakeholder analysis, since it provides a basis for extrapolating potential stakeholder attitudes and responses towards the operation.

An individual-level analogy might help to explain the concept of profile. The author once went to Tyre (or Sour) in Lebanon, which at the time was quite off-the-beaten track. This is a useful example because my presence was an oddity and definitely noticeable. From initial responses to me, I can surmise that, first, people thought I worked for the UN, which had a role in supporting Palestinian refugees in the permanent "camps" in the area. When they learned I was travelling on my own, they thought I was somewhat weird because I came there at all, since there was not much to do and the town was still in tatters from conflict. Some suspected that I was a writer looking for the right place to inspire me. Some saw my relative wealthiness and ignorance as a potential opportunity. Others were eager to connect with a representative of the world beyond the town. My profile changed quite quickly once I got my feet on the ground, but on arrival and in the initial few days my stakeholders included several individuals and groups in the immediate vicinity who took an interest in me based on aspects of that profile, or the profiles which they created to explain my presence. The aspects I could control had to be managed to avoid inadvertent suspicion or friction.

A foreign operation also has a socio-political profile, or perceived characteristics and implications from the standpoint of socio-political actors. Alongside whom the operation relies upon and needs to work with, the profile is a significant factor in defining who stakeholders are or will be once they notice the operation and have time to shape feelings about it. What matters about a foreign operation varies to some degree according to the cultural, political and developmental context, but the following four main elements capture some relevant considerations:

Physical attributes

- The areas and locations that the operation affects, and respective time periods
- Physical hassles and disruptions, including noise, traffic and dust
- Environmental effects, most noticeably on air and water quality in the affected area but also on the wider ecosystem (changes to the appearance of local landscapes, whether natural or historical, are also important)

Socio-economic implications

- Potential effects on host communities, for example constrained land or resource access, land acquisition, community relocations and effects of company security zones and procedures
- Employment, training and local business contracts
- CSR and social investment

- The operation's role in/contribution to national economic development
- The operation's contribution to government earnings and foreign exchange
- Effects on local business competitors

Company public identity and reputation

- The company's nationality, and its home/HQ country's reputation in the host country
- The company sector's reputation for integrity and social and environmental performance (sector reputation can transfer onto the company)
- The company's own track record with respect to the above
- The reputation of significant partners (foreign and local)
- The company's experience in emerging markets and the region (less experienced can mean more interesting from an opportunistic or predatory perspective)

Political aspect

- If on a government contract, a transparent, open, tender versus a back-door deal
- Any political affiliations, domestic and foreign, used or consulted to help gain entry or win a contract
- Potential gains or benefits for regime-affiliated actors or other socio-political elites
- The company's relationship with its home/HQ country government and its stake or interest in the operation
- Any transnational or national donors/development banks associated with the operation

A couple of real examples of socio-political profiles help to flesh out the concept. The first is the ProSavana project in Mozambique. This was initiated in 2009 by the Mozambican government in agreement with the Japanese and Brazilian international development agencies, and foresaw the conversion of 14.5 million hectares of land in Mozambique's agricultural heartland from subsistence to industrial export-oriented farming. The intended crop was principally soybeans. The Mozambican government thought that the plan would provide better-paid jobs for subsistence farmers and that the export proceeds would fund the import of more diverse foods than people could produce themselves. Additionally, the foreign exchange earnings were a clear benefit. Japan's and Brazil's aid agencies also had an eye on the socio-economic benefits, but their respective governments foresaw their own countries' corporations getting first rights as project operators. As of the time of writing, the project has been considerably scaled back from its original concept and has seen only limited implementation, mainly because of a coordinated anti-ProSavana Mozambican and international campaign that has reacted to the project's profile and has put considerable public pressure on the foreign development agencies involved. The profile elements included the following:

- Prior industrial farming initiatives in the Amazon and Africa had seen multinational agricultural firms engage in land grabs, evictions and the compulsion of local farmers to switch crops or work on company farms (ProSavana would have had private foreign companies lead on implementation even though it was positioned as a development initiative).
- The focus on export crops triggered concern about village and local economies, in which surplus production drove local markets that not only enabled economic exchange, but also social exchange and cooperation that increased the capacity for self-help and resilience.
- Farmers and their supporters worried about their own food security, since thus far they were growing their own food and there was no guarantee that soybean exports would somehow translate into both money to buy food and access to varied food sources (Suzui, 2017).

- Past industrial farms and agricultural companies had a bad track record for environmental sustainability, and there were concerns about soil depletion, chemical pesticides and deforestation.
- Some large Brazilian multinationals which were likely candidates to come to Mozambique had poor reputations for integrity, sustainability, and respect for host communities, and indeed the Brazilian government itself had a mixed track record for conservation in the Amazon.
- Communities in the path of the project started to hear about it only after the government started testing reactions by sending teams to knock on doors trying to get farmers to sign up to the plan, raising suspicions because of the project's lack of transparency (Parenti & Liberti, 2018).
- The Mozambican government was a principal stakeholder and ultimately would have been responsible for ensuring that the project had real socio-economic benefits for affected communities, and public trust in the government was low, since it had a reputation for corruption, cronyism and inefficiency.

Just with respect to the involved development agencies, had they taken more time to reflect on the project's profile early on, this might have helped to shape a more palatable variant of it, for example one that included smallholder farmers and host communities as partners instead of passive recipients. It took the activist campaign to act like a mirror and actually spell out what the project's profile was. As it currently stands, ProSavana has been considerably modified to reflect campaigners' concerns; thus, in effect the socio-political profile has been modified to reduce friction. Once the project enters the implementation phase, no doubt there will be further modifications based on local stakeholders' direct experience with the project.

Another example comes from a consulting case that the author was involved with in 2013. The client was an American oil and gas company that was launching conventional gas production in southern Morocco, but this operation was small-scale and was only an entry point for what the company hoped would be much more extensive shale gas production in the medium-term future. In shaping the initial profile, we had to do two, one for conventional operations and the other for shale. Even prior to detailed research, it was clear that the socio-political profile for each phase would be very different, especially in the context of water scarcity and desertification in the area of operation (shale gas extraction uses high-pressure water to fracture rock to release gas, and shale operations are supposed to be capable of recycling the water, but the industry's track record is mixed).

As research progressed, hypotheses based on the initial profile sketches were borne out. Conventional operations hardly raised an eyebrow, and most stakeholders saw them as usefully contributing to economic development. The regime and certain elements of several ministries (ironically the ministry responsible for energy also handled the environment, leading to a sort of split personality) welcomed the long-term economic potential of shale gas, but the Ministry of Agriculture, local authorities in the south and environmentalist groups representing host communities saw very high risk in shale operations in a water-starved sub-region where agriculture was the basis of local economies. The company therefore had fair warning that it would be an uphill struggle to get widespread acceptance for the intended shale phase of its operation, despite its expertise in water recycling.

Other aspects of the company's profile were relevant, if far less so than the implications of shale gas. The company was American, and while at the ministerial level this was not an issue, many ordinary Moroccans regarded the US occupation of Iraq and support for Israel to be symptomatic of a bias in American attitudes, and this image rubbed off on US firms to a degree. The company also had concurrent and planned operations in Algeria, with whom Morocco had a tense relationship, and while this was not particularly problematic, some stakeholders found plying both sides of an axis of tension to be disloyal and opportunistic. At a more basic level, a lucrative foreign operation in a relatively poor area of the country attracted considerable attention among job seekers, when in fact operations were not labour intensive. The company experienced what it called "job mobs" outside its local offices from time to time when rumours of hiring circulated, and these had to be delicately handled. On the positive side, the firm had a track record for managing the environmental effects of its operations and was not in the news for the wrong reasons, and government stakeholders looking for an uncontentious and reliable partner in energy development would have had no particular concerns based on the firm's past performance.

For readers familiar with the exercise, social and environmental impact assessments (SEIAs) might seem to be the process which develops a socio-political profile, or at least its social aspect. As we note again in Part II, SEIAs can be useful inputs when developing a profile and also in stakeholder identification, but they are not the same process and their outputs are very different. SEIAs are compliance-centric, and hence their audience is twofold: company engineers who use the outputs to ensure compliance with relevant health, safety and environmental regulations, and regulators who need to see a completed SIEA before granting relevant approvals. They are certainly not intended to provide a basis for estimating stakeholder interest and reactions, and there is nothing about them that requires developing a political profile nor a consideration of a firm's track record and reputation. Indeed, given that host country regulators, who report to political bosses, will be reading an SEIA report, putting in political and reputational insights about the company could be problematic. Finally, at least in the author's experience, we would not take several weeks or months, and create a report of hundreds of pages, to develop a socio-political profile. An initial sketch can derive from informed brainstorming, and subsequent refinement is embedded within the stakeholder analysis process.

The most important point to draw from this section is that whatever we think about ourselves, when it comes to political risk, it is how we appear to others that matters. Foreign operations in emerging markets are noticeable, and their socio-political profile is a significant factor in who takes an interest, what their attitudes are and how they might respond.

ASSETS EXPOSED TO POLITICAL RISK

Risk only exists in relation to something that we seek to achieve or preserve. This section examines the assets that a foreign business operation exposes to political risk and how assets can be affected. This will apply both "asset" and "exposure" in somewhat expansive terms. An asset in this context refers to anything, whether an aim, a thing, an enabler or a characteristic, that is valuable to us. An exposure means an asset that is in a place or situation where it could be harmed or diminished, and exposure means an asset's condition of being in a volatile or precarious place or situation. This precursor is necessary because other well-known business interpretations of these terms focus on tangible goods like money and equipment, whereas our concern stretches to our very ability to do anything, let alone what constitutes our material possessions at any one point.

Many political risk definitions only focus on socio-political effects on profit. Profit is a company's raison d'être, and most foreign operations have a profit target, so it is an exposure. However, when considering political risk in on-the-ground operations, as opposed to portfolio investment, profit is a longer-term intended outcome of the operation and is not itself directly exposed to dynamics and stakeholder responses. Furthermore, one can make a profit and still lose in the long run because of political risk, for example through reputational damage or harm to staff, both of which could hinder the ability or willingness to undertake future international ventures (the case of Talisman in Sudan cited earlier is an example – its Sudan operation was profitable but the reputational damage and subsequent risk aversion spelled the beginning of Talisman's decline).

A more tangible focus is on the assets that enable the operation to function and to endure long enough to reach profit targets, and which are important to the firm's ability to conduct future international operations. There are different ways of breaking these down, but we will apply the framework in Figure 3.2, bearing in mind that other variations are valid. Note that this traces exposed assets back to both profit and corporate international capability.

The four principal assets, people, reputation, control and continuity, all enable the operation to proceed on track and to endure until profit targets are met. But people and reputation are also factors

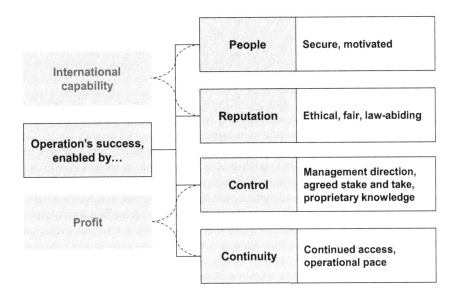

FIGURE 3.2   Assets exposed to political risk.

of a company's long-term capability to succeed in international initiatives. People will move onto other projects and bring their experience with them, and they need to remain motivated to undertake future overseas operations. Reputation gained in a country operation similarly is transferable and brings higher credibility to other international initiatives. An operation's profit, on the other hand, is enabled by management control, which includes retaining rights over one's agreed share of the earnings, and by continuity, which translates to operational efficiency. We will only focus on the country operation as we proceed, but it is noteworthy that two operational assets are also wider corporate enablers, and have only an indirect link to profit.

There can be close linkages between the four main assets. Going back to the Sainsbury's Egypt case, for example, the company's reputation was hurt by its lack of cultural adaptation and its effect on local grocers, and subsequent protests not only hurt continuity but also posed some risk to staff in the affected stores. Oil companies in the Niger Delta in Nigeria face heightened security risks because of their poor reputation among Delta communities who are constituents of the main insurgent groups in the area. Conversely, if company staff are anxious about security, they might want to leave, and this affects continuity, and manifested harm can give a company a reputation for being unable, or too cheap, to look after its staff. An erosion of control, for example through a dispute with a state company or regime-connected partner, can affect continuity if the company becomes susceptible to less efficient management direction and can affect reputation if the partnership starts to assume more of the identity of a less upstanding partner. We will be addressing each main asset in turn, but it is worth bearing in mind that they are often linked, and together constitute the foundation of an operation's success.

As a final introductory note, while almost any on-the-ground operation will rely on the above four main assets, the sub-elements of each one will considerably vary between types of operations. This is especially the case for continuity, the sub-elements of which can be as specific as access to certain roads and ports, and the timely granting of very different types of permits. As we consider each main asset, we can sketch a general picture, but in practice there is a wide range of nuanced variations.

PEOPLE

People include expatriate and local staff. The proportion often shifts over time towards a higher local contingent, as local hiring proceeds, local content quotas are attained, and local staff gain the necessary know-how to keep the operation on track. From a duty of care perspective, expat staff represent a higher liability or obligation, because they transferred from home and lack their own contacts and networks in the host environment. However, the wellbeing and morale of all staff is important to the operation, and discrepancies in treatment risk leading to friction within the operation's organisation (pay discrepancies, sometimes a source of friction, are nearly inevitable since local staff are usually paid according to host country benchmarks).

People enact the operation, and if they are demoralised, anxious or hurt, the operation falters. Indeed, without them, the operation would exist only in name, not as productive activities. Thus, for purely operational reasons they are the principal asset, and in moral terms they are by far the most important one. Their wellbeing is closely linked to the reputation of the company as a responsible and committed employer, and this in turn underpins talent retention, and makes people more willing to undertake assignments abroad. Political risk can harm human assets in several ways.

People can face physical harm. When there is unrest, rioting, armed violence or a terrorist attack in the vicinity, harm to personnel can occur inadvertently or as collateral damage. A less-dire example comes from an old client project: in 2013, in Tunis the assassination of political activist Belaïd led to violent protests, and the client's staff were caught dodging blockades and police tear gas on the way to the office. Another challenge mainly affects local staff: in periods of high political tension or security crackdowns, local staff can be caught up in security sweeps, or loosely match a regime's broad definition of "suspicious person" and be detained. For example, in 2018 when a German energy company decided to exit Turkey, one of the reasons was the arrest of ten local employees on terrorism charges, a fate shared by thousands of Turks following the 2016 coup attempt (Filippakis, 2018). Similarly, foreign companies in Hong Kong saw local staff detained in the context of widespread protests and security crackdowns in 2019–2020.

Perhaps more seriously, foreign company personnel can be directly targeted by political groups. In cases of terrorist attacks, such as Al Qaeda's bombing of HSBC's Istanbul office in 2003 or the In Amenas gas plant attack in 2013, the perpetrators might have no particular feelings towards the company, rather the firm symbolises hostile or invasive foreign values, and FDI in general can be seen as helping to economically prop up an enemy government. When local insurgent groups target foreign company staff, attacks are usually more directly motivated by grievances against the company. For example, in Niger, expat managers of foreign mining operations have been abducted by Tuareg rebels because of the perceived collusion between the foreign firms and an ethnically discriminatory regime. In the Niger Delta in Nigeria, insurgent groups have abducted foreign oil company personnel not just for ransom, but as retribution for perceived harm to host community livelihoods and reliance on abusive state security forces to safeguard oil operations.

Organised crime can likewise target foreign companies, again because of what the company represents, in this case wealth. Kidnapping is a common form of attack. Targets are opportunistically chosen as good balance between accessibility and the likelihood of a high ransom. A colleague in kidnap consulting once recounted to the author a case in East Africa. A foreign telecoms firm was targeted merely because the crime group had an associate (a relative of a one of the gang's leaders) working in the company's operation, and this made it easy to obtain intelligence on specific targets and security arrangements. Cases of maritime piracy and the seizure of crews for ransom, as was common off the coast of Somalia and remains a risk in the Gulf of Guinea, are likewise motivated by the wealth that foreign companies represent.

Staff can also become pawns in disputes either between the company and host regime or between a firm's home and host governments. An infamous case involved Sergei Magnitsky of Hermitage Capital, whose arrest and death in Russia in 2009 was the impetus for the US Magnitsky Act targeting specific officials involved in human rights abuses. In the aftermath of the detention of Huawei's finance director in Canada in 2018, two Canadians, one a businessman, were arrested in China in what most observers regarded as tit-for-tat retribution, and dual Chinese-foreign citizens are especially vulnerable to detention during international political disputes. Regime cronies are also not above using threats and violence to thwart foreign competition or control. Recall the AES Georgia case, in which the Georgian AES-Telasi finance director was murdered in 2002.

In addition to physical harm, personnel can face legal entanglements. In developing and transitional countries, laws can be obscure and arbitrarily enforced, and individual expats can face legal hassles and even detention for inadvertent infringements. In other cases, corrupt officials can claim that a law was broken in order to extort a "fine". When legal systems are weak or manipulable, disputes with well-connected local partners can end up with charges levelled against specific expat managers. Recall, for example, the Sainsbury's Egypt case in which the CEO, unbeknownst to him, was found guilty of fraud in a case trumped up by the old local business partner. While legal hassles short of detention are not physically dangerous, they are stressful, and if someone is arrested, prison conditions can make even a brief stint in jail traumatic.

Finally, especially for expats, working in weakly governed and volatile environments can entail considerable stress and anxiety. Dealing with corruption pressure, balancing social divisions within the workforce, worrying about security issues and struggling with an opaque bureaucracy all add up to a stress load far higher that what managers are used to back home. Moral dilemmas can also arise, in particular in trying to balance social and political relationships, and in the trade-off between company security and its potential effects on the host community. If HQ does not appreciate the socio-political complications, it can press for business performance that seems impossible in the local context without cutting some corners, and this can add to country managers' stress.

As with other exposed assets, people can be harmed by forces and actors that do not involve political dynamics or stakeholder behaviour. For example, one of the most notorious hazards for expat staff in developing countries is dangerous traffic and roads. What makes political risk to personnel different from health and safety hazards is that it is, in one form or another, about actor behaviour, not accidents or physical conditions. Managing risk to personnel needs to integrate both the political-criminal and health and safety aspects, but when the political-criminal aspect is particularly acute, as in many complex emerging markets, it needs considerable share of mind and specific approaches. This was one of the findings of the Statoil In Amenas report, for example, which found that an overemphasis on health and safety had obscured risks arising from actor behaviour and politically motivated threats.

REPUTATION

Reputation is the basis of an operation's and company's credibility, which in turn underpins legitimate relationships. Reputation usually includes legal standing, although not always, for example if a social media platform caves into host regime pressure to allow the monitoring of its customers' accounts, it is legally compliant, but the firm can get a reputation among core audiences for selling out its values. For purposes here, we will simply focus on reputation as the underlying character that legitimate stakeholders perceive and respond to. Compliance is only a part of this when it is in relation to laws designed to enforce genuine corporate integrity and sustainability performance.

Reputation is an intangible asset and bears some clarification. One can consider, at a basic level, the contrast between greedy, arrogant, uncaring, deceitful and opportunistic/"short-termist" on the one hand, and conscientious, fair, honest and far-sighted on the other. There have been companies, and company leaders, who have not really cared how they were perceived as long as they were known to make above-average profits. From a purely capitalist economic perspective, that is more or less the strict definition of a "good" company. But from the late 1980s onwards, companies with a singular and short-term profit orientation tended to paint themselves into corners, becoming unacceptable or too risky to all but likeminded partners and host governments, and hence on a slippery slope to isolation and potentially the hazy edges of corporate criminality. Even before sustainability gained traction on the corporate agenda, international companies were finding that being known as clean and conscientious helped with stakeholder trust, moral bargaining power and reducing the perceived risk of dealing with a company. Reputation thus made it easier to work with legitimate stakeholders, and broadened a company's horizons by opening doors. Attention to reputation also helps to avoid legal liability, since many laws around company behaviour align with principles of corporate integrity and social and environmental performance. Thus, while intangible, reputation is a critical asset which has important strategic implications in the long term.

We discussed socio-political footprint earlier, and while this can evolve and actually be managed, part of it is baggage that the operation brings along from corporate reputation, which at least initially can be hard for a specific operation to control. Unlike the other assets, though, reputation at the country level is largely affected by one's own decisions, attitudes and behaviours while there. This makes risk to it more manageable in some ways, since it is partly a matter of self-control. But self-control itself can be difficult in weakly governed and confusing environments. Foreign operations have incurred bad reputations despite initial good intentions, and in turn this has had consequences for corporate reputation.

One of the most common reputational issues that international companies face is ethical breaches in the global supply chain. This is a global challenge but it is an aggregate of specific country operations and supply contracts. While this is seldom directly caused by socio-political factors, weak governance, including weak or under-enforced regulations and cronyism, contributes to the problem. Electronics manufacturers, for example, have faced ethical criticism and home country regulator scrutiny because of the leakage of conflict minerals, particularly from eastern DRC, into supply chains. The eastern DRC is notoriously complex socio-political terrain, and certifying supplies as conflict-free (in other words, revenues do not fund conflict actors) has been fraught with difficulty. Clothing and food manufacturers, such as Nike and Nestle, have faced criticism about poor labour standards and child labour along their supply chains. Among their challenges is that developing country suppliers are often able to elude their own governments' labour regulations because of crony connections or bribery, or, as in Chinese cotton production, the government is actually involved in labour abuses and limits access to information on relevant labour practices. Managing ethical, and also environmental, performance among emerging market supplier networks is complex and costly, but not doing so, especially for branded consumer goods companies, carries the higher cost of eroded brand image and market share.

Reputation also suffers because of an operation's perceived manipulation of dubious regime ties for its own business interests. This is closely linked to corporate lobbying, which is often a necessary form of diplomacy to ensure that political stakeholders understand company perspectives, but taken too far it can verge on acting as a regime crony for unfair advantages. For example, in South Africa during Zuma's presidency, several Western companies, including IT and consulting firms, became well ensconced in the Gupta family's crony network and gained lucrative contracts as a result. However, they eventually faced considerable international scrutiny. One, ironically a public relations company (Bell Pottinger), became so toxic that its shareholders, clients and staff deserted it. The firm collapsed in late 2017. Another example is an international tobacco company in Uzbekistan in the 1990s. The firm's entry strategy was largely premised on becoming, in effect, a regime crony to thwart competition (Gilmore, McKee, & Collin, 2007). Regime ties were subsequently used to influence health regulations that could affect the domestic cigarette market, as Gilmore, McKee and Collin note: "The chief sanitary doctor was powerless next to BAT, particularly given its close alliance with President Karimov" (Gilmore, McKee, & Collin, 2006). Especially given the Uzbek regime's bleak human rights record at the time, it was a risky strategy. Generally speaking, when a company gets a reputation for hazy ethical red lines, in future operations in weakly governed environments host regimes can expect more of the same, and by comparison to its more conscientious peers, a company can face higher pressure to align with dubious regime interests as a pre-condition of doing business.

Corruption is another reputational issue. It can incur liability, but also considerable reputational damage. Canadian construction company SNC Lavalin, for example, came under investigation by Canadian authorities in 2015 for bribery in Libya between 2001 and 2011. The case became messier in 2018 when it seemed that senior politicians in Canada were actually trying to assist the firm to avoid maximum charges so that it could still receive Canadian government contracts. In a 2019 plea deal, SNC Lavalin pled guilty to fraud, and its share price sharply declined, but the political fallout from the case continues to stir controversy. This came just over a decade after the company was involved in a major corruption scandal in India. That too had political implications, specifically for the Kerala state government. In both cases, the resulting political scandals amplified public awareness. In some cases, corruption allegations and charges hardly make the news, but when they do, a company faces reactions from a range of stakeholders and wariness among prospective partners and investors. Additionally, for unprincipled regimes where the firm might one day do business, the company can look like an easy mark for corruption pressure, since, again, its moral red lines seem to be flexible.

Another significant reputational issue concerns the link between country operations and human rights abuses. Host communities and labour and environmental activists have been harmed by the security forces safeguarding foreign operations. Talisman in Sudan was previously mentioned, but BP in Colombia until 2010, and Shell in Nigeria for decades and currently, are also examples in which at least some allegations of security abuses seemed to be well founded. In these and many other cases, the companies in question did not order or want human rights abuses to occur, but reliance on armed or state security force protection in a conflict zone in a weakly governed country comes with clear risks. All three of the above and a considerable number of other firms, mainly in the extractives and natural resource sectors, have faced reputational damage and court cases over abuse allegations. There is a variety of related ways that company operations can harm host communities, including, for example, forced displacements, local pollution and deforestation, local price inflation as wealthy companies spend locally, and the exacerbation of social rivalries through uneven hiring and CSR activities. Company taxes and a government's take in extractive operations can also help to sustain an abusive regime which, with hard currency flowing in, has even less incentive to be acceptable to its own citizens.

There is a body of well-publicised guidelines and standards on business and human rights, as well as on community stakeholder engagement, and much of this is actually incorporated into many companies' own policies. However, when operating in weakly governed countries, the lack of host government concern or oversight, not to mention governments' own nonchalance towards human rights, can make it easy to overlook host community impacts. The result can be host community rejection of the operation and escalating friction. This easily becomes a tangible operational problem, and since friction usually requires more security, it can lead back to the risk of perceived collusion with human rights abuses. Once local NGOs and media become involved, it is a short step to negative international attention. Companies can brazen their way through particular cases, but a reputation for host community harm becomes a ball and chain in the long run and erodes staff and other core stakeholder loyalty.

Political risk can affect reputation in a number of ways, and we confine ourselves to only one more here. This is smear or disinformation campaigns organised by political or politically connected interests. Drawing on the AES Georgia case, politico-mafia pressure included the use of local media and other information channels to portray AES as an extortionate foreign profiteer, and we also saw how disinformation was used against Sainsbury's in Egypt. Another well-known example is Bechtel's involvement in the water privatisation and network upgrade project in Cochabamba, Bolivia, in 1999–2000. The project introduced water price increases and usage monitoring, and also cut subsidies for heavy consumers. Poor household users were affected, but the aggregate cost differences were greatest for politically connected large landowners and local industrialists. Similar to the AES case, these interests used their media clout to portray the operation as a profiteering foreign conspiracy. This amplified and partly steered grassroots opposition in a context where "American imperialism" still had some resonance, and where a degree of social unrest had already created a volatile public mood. In April 2000, Bechtel withdrew amidst violent protests against the project. In more authoritarian contexts, regime cronies can use state media as one attack vector, and regime-linked oligarchs often deliberately acquire media outlets to use as reputational attack dogs. Thus, while reputation is often a factor of the company's own behaviour in a complex socio-political context, it can be directly targeted by stakeholders affected by an operation.

Reputation might be intangible but it is a cornerstone of trusting relationships, social acceptance and moral bargaining power, which together expand a company's freedom to manoeuvre and reduce the likelihood of damaging friction and liability. It is noteworthy that while reputation can be directly affected by socio-political factors and responses, the above makes it clear that it is largely a factor of company decisions and behaviour, albeit in often confusing and difficult environments. We have mainly discussed reputation in ethical terms in this section, but because it is linked to mistakes and poor judgement, it is also about a company's perceived competence. When a company gains a track record for issues in complex environments, it appears to be shooting from the hip, not taking risks and sensitivities seriously, and incapable of learning from its mistakes.

CONTROL

Control refers to the foreign company's retention of contractually agreed management direction, stake, compensation and physical and intellectual property (IP) in a country operation. Aspects of control are directly linked to profit. An operation can be on track and hitting production targets, for example, but if the foreign firm's stake, share of revenue, or after-tax margin erodes, then operational progress fails to translate to commensurate financial gain. Control is also indirectly linked to personnel security and reputation, because when a company cedes management direction, it holds less sway over security policy, and integrity and sustainability safeguards. Control can be affected by socio-political dynamics and behaviour in various ways, a few of which we outline here to provide reference points.

If a company commits to an operation on certain premises about relevant government business and economic policy and these then change, its anticipated earnings can be affected. Upward changes in general corporate tax rates are not common, since most emerging market governments seek FDI and even compete for it, but tax rates, subsidies and royalties can change for specific sectors and types of operations. A common pattern is that a country is relatively liberal when it has a limited track record for FDI in a given sector, and hence still appears risky. Once the country gains a record for successful foreign operations, or in the case of extractives, early foreign operations have made significant discoveries, then the government's bargaining power increases, and it adjusts relevant policies to grant itself a bigger slice of the earnings. A related policy change that countries undertake once they have more a confident position is more rigorous local content stipulations, meaning that foreign operations need to utilise a higher proportion of local staff and supplies. Such adjustments can be sound economic policy, and indeed even the IMF is sometimes critical of FDI incentive schemes that underplay a government's opportunity to boost public revenues.

Less predictable are changes that limit foreign ownership or control. These can be a government's instinctive response to economic crises, or motivated by economic nationalism. Changes can require a scramble for local partners in order to remain compliant. For example, in the wake of the 2008 financial crisis, Indonesia necessitated partial local ownership in several "strategic" sectors, leaving foreign firms little time to find and forge deals with the most appropriate local partners. Similarly, when Algeria implemented the 49/51 rule in 2009 (which stipulated that any business entity needed to be at least 51 percent Algerian-owned), foreign oil companies ended up competing for the attention of Sonatrach, the state hydrocarbons company and the only viable local partner, whose bandwidth at the time was already severely constrained by a politically motivated anti-corruption investigation aimed at influencing factional control over oil revenues. A reduced stake also affects overall take, since another partner is now on board, and while the partner shares the costs, they also share earnings.

Government contract cancellation and expropriation are two well-known control challenges, and are often linked because a cancelled contract could result in fixed assets being left behind and transferred to the state, then perhaps onto the next contracted operator. Contract cancellation, which pertains to government-contracted projects, can be motivated by a straightforward concern that a company is underperforming or underinvesting in a concession. It can, however, also arise from a regime preferring another company, sometimes because it is more willing to pay bribes or offer inducements, as we saw with the Canadian firm's licence revocation in the DRC. While less of a motivation in recent years, economic nationalism and ideology have still been drivers, as clearly exemplified in Venezuela and Bolivia under their recent leftist populist regimes (in Bolivia up to the end of 2019), which nationalised a range of operations in the extractives and infrastructure sectors. Both risks have been a significant focus of political risk management literature for decades and both are insurable, but they still occur, and when they do, they effectively terminate control. Recourse to a dispute settlement process is then an option, but the process can be protracted and distracting, and can increase friction with a government that might still be relevant to a firm's future aspirations.

Currency controls can arise when a government faces a foreign reserves shortage, which in turn is linked to a foreign payment crisis. In Egypt, for example, the economic downturn following the 2011 revolution led to caps on foreign exchange withdrawals and transfers for businesses, among which were foreign manufacturers who relied on imported parts and materials that had to be paid for in foreign currency. Import-reliant operations had to periodically scale back production, and profit repatriation was intermittent, until caps were lifted in 2017 as part of a wider economic reform process which included a currency floatation. Argentina is notorious for periodic currency crises and controls, and there has been considerable speculation that Turkey, facing a protracted currency crisis, might also initiate controls.

Tax and related disputes about the state-company earnings split can come as a surprise and threaten anticipated profit. Particularly when facing an economic downturn, governments can develop a strong incentive to go back over tax records with a keen eye to any potential loophole that a company might have used, and audits can lead to charges of underpayment. South African mobile operator MTN, for example, faced several audits and tax evasion allegations in Nigeria between 2015 and 2019, as the government sought to plug holes in its budget from the decline in oil prices (as noted earlier, foreign oil firms faced similar allegations). For the oil and gas firms, the domestic supply obligation in production agreements, which gives the government a right to divert a certain proportion of production from export to domestic consumption, can also become contentious during economic downturns. Again, looking at Egypt, in 2014 British Gas was one of several foreign operators facing breach of contract with overseas buyers because so much gas was being diverted to the domestic market. The government, facing a currency crisis and socio-economic frustration, felt that its problems were more acute.

Discrimination against foreign firms can also occur. Economic nationalism can be a motive, but more commonly in recent years a government facing economic pressure can see international companies as wealthier, and thus more capable of absorbing the damage from state incursions on their earnings. In the aftermath of the 2008 financial crisis, for example, the government in Ukraine delayed VAT refunds to several foreign firms for months (refunds were automatic for producers who exported), leading to serious cash flow problems. One, ArcelorMittal, seemed to be particularly singled out, suffering approximately $300 million in VAT refund arrears by mid-2010 and pressure to pay corporate income tax upfront, while domestic companies faced no such hassles (Wellhausen, 2012).

A foreign firm's control over its intellectual property can be challenged by government pressure to share expertise with local partners, and when there are weak IP protections, local partners can try to steal IP knowing that sanctions would be light if they were caught. China presents a unique IP challenge. While the legal protection of IP is improving, it is still relatively weak. More concerning is that in many sectors, joint ventures, often with state companies, are the most feasible or indeed the only permitted mode of entry, and to obtain official approval, deals often need to explicitly include technology transfers. Thus, losing control over one's IP is in effect the price of market access.

Politically connected local partners can also challenge control, using their connections to try to compel the foreign side to cede management direction. The AES Georgia case included elements of this phenomenon as oligarchic and factional interests vied for influence over electricity distribution and sought to reduce their own power bills. BP also faced political pressure in its TNK-BP joint venture, as previously noted. Another example comes from Norwegian Telenor's experience in Ukraine and Russia in 2004 to 2010. The case is too complex for a full explanation here, but in short, Telenor's Russian partner, a regime-connected banking group, sought to use the partnership as a cloak to make dubious acquisitions in Ukraine and Russia. The deals were motivated by the bank's oligarchic rivalries and Kremlin ties rather than any legitimate commercial logic. When Telenor exercised its stake to try to resist the deals, it was hit with a series of spurious court cases and even hostile public relations campaigns. The disputes with the bank were resolved by 2010 through two separate international arbitration proceedings, but the episode cast a long shadow over Telenor's regional ambitions. Similar to the AES Georgia case, Telenor was dealing with a hydra of political and oligarchic interests for whom contractual obligations were somewhere between a useful veneer and an inconvenience. The case is instructive, and a fuller summary is available on Telenor's website (Telenor Group n.d.).

The last control challenge that we examine here is rather obscure but potentially serious. An old case that the author worked on, involving an international consulting company in a post-Soviet country in 2004, provides an illustration. The company was on a government contract to implement new management practices at a state utility company. The brief was somewhat contentious because it included measures to reduce nepotism and increase transparency, and this challenged some well-ensconced "clan" interests. Additionally, violent crime, in particular kidnapping, was a hazard. The country team asked its ministerial counterparts to suggest a security provider, which the company then hired for personnel and facility security. To make a long story short, it turned out that the security firm was owned and staffed by not-exactly-ex secret police with their own factional interests. By the time the foreign company sought an independent review of the situation, the security team had been busily increasing its influence over not just security procedures, but also over management decisions, starting with casual and friendly advice that became more specific and assertive the more the security firm understood its client's operation. Some of this advice made sense, but some did not.

To generalise from this case, local agents, advisors and even law firms can gain considerable access to company and operational details, and potentially insinuate themselves to try to steer decisions towards their own specific interests. In the initial weeks and months after entry, expat managers can feel vulnerable and heavily rely on local support and knowledge, but it can come at a price beyond just the fee.

Several control-related issues are more economic than political and are par for the course anywhere. When a government adjusts economic policy to maximise its own interests, and by extension the public services it can provide, this is often normal and rational even if it is inconvenient. Such changes can be sudden if they are driven by unanticipated economic shocks, since governments scramble along with everyone else to respond to crises. When infringements on control, whether stake, take or management direction, are motivated by specific socio-political perceptions of the company, they can be economically irrational and potentially more serious, leading to complications beyond just lost earnings. Thus, control is exposed to both state reactions to economic conditions, and to more specific stakeholder interests deriving from ideological values, opportunism and in some cases predatory interest.

CONTINUITY

Continuity refers to the operation's ability to stick to schedules and maintain pace. Its opposite would be delays, intermittency and a longer-term stall or halt. Like control, continuity is also directly linked to profit. The operation might be under control, but if it is stalled with costly assets sitting unutilised, then control alone does not lead to projected earnings. Of the four types of assets, continuity varies the most between different sectors and specific operations. As noted earlier, even one specific logistics route can be critical for one project, while for another smooth labour relations could be far more important. Thus, what follows is necessarily top level, though hopefully it suffices as an indication of the wider set of potential continuity challenges arising from socio-political dynamics and relationships.

As noted in the section on bureaucracy in Chapter 2, approval delays can lead to operational gaps. A company can prepare to execute a project phase or a specific element on the premise that relevant approvals will be forthcoming and end up in "hurry up and wait" mode. The World Bank's *Doing Business* index and similar sources can help to discern how long a given procedure *might* take in a specific country, but these provide averages, and where bureaucracies suffer from politicisation and under-capacity, there can be wide variations.

A project the author worked on for a European oil company in Algeria in 2010 provides an example. The company, with a sizeable Algiers office, had fully prepared to move on a substantial project in the south but faced repeated rejections of their environmental, and also workforce migration (from expat to local), applications. Some firms in the same sector had similar problems, but others felt that Algeria's procedures were quite straightforward. In fact, while there was bureaucratic underperformance, different foreign companies were treated differently depending on how they, and the importance of their respective projects, were perceived by the regime. In this case, it turned out that an old arbitration case against the Algerian government was still an annoyance to the regime and it had "deprioritised" the company's approvals. While delays from under-capacity might be broadly estimable, the intrusion of political influence on bureaucratic decisions is more of a wildcard. Additionally, delays can be a form of corruption pressure, and if one is not aware of the possibility, then instead of seeking legitimate support to deal with the problem, one can end up trying the process repeatedly or simply waiting.

We should note that customs delays are a special sub-set of approval challenges. Operations that rely on routine imports of the same production inputs can learn and adapt to customs procedures over time. Those that require a series of one-off imports of specific equipment or materials, for example for a construction or field development project, could be facing a range of different customs regulations that complicate the clearance process. This is in addition to general bureaucratic approval challenges, as well as port capacity and infrastructure limitations.

Labour strikes can affect infrastructure and public services that a country operation relies on. The Iran case in the book's prelude might be old but it is not outdated in terms of how general strikes can affect companies and even their personnel. In that event, the whole country was paralysed for weeks and there was a scramble to find alternative access to even basic amenities. Strikes can also affect specific logistics hubs. For example, in 2010 South African Transnet, which held government contracts for a range of port and rail operations, faced a weeks-long strike that severely constrained both domestic and international logistics. Several foreign mining companies were forced to delay ore exports, while manufacturers faced supply shortages.

Strikes also affect specific foreign operations. Vietnam, for example, saw a significant increase in "wildcat" (spontaneous and non-union-sanctioned) strikes from 1995, as Vietnam adopted free market reforms which increased workers' reliance on private sector salaries. There were nearly 1,000 strikes in 2011 alone, with nearly 80 percent of them affecting operations with an FDI component (Chi & van den Broek, 2013). The number has decreased since then, partly because of labour reforms in line with Vietnam's international trade agreements, but strikes remain a feature of the manufacturing sector in particular. Strikes have clear continuity implications, but they can also lead to violent unrest. The strike at the Marikana platinum mine in South Africa in 2012 is a notorious example, with 34 striking workers killed in police intervention. The operator, a British-South African firm, faced allegations of serious errors that contributed to the clashes, and the loss of trust with its South African workforce was a factor in another strike in 2014. This was an extreme example of how strikes can go from a business continuity problem to a reputational one, but even less dire instances of violence, including police responses, can erode worker trust and increase labour activism.

Government-contracted projects, such as the construction and/or operation of public infrastructure, or e-government information systems integration projects, routinely experience delays because of government design changes and contractual wrangling after the project has commenced. Construction projects, as one sub-set, are notorious for delays because of contractors underestimating the complexity of the work, and this is related to the common approach of awarding bids to the firm or group with the lowest cost estimate (other approaches put more emphasis on evidence of proficiency). But when the government is the customer, projects can also directly experience eccentricities inherent in the culture and style of national governance.

The Iran case in the prelude noted the influence of palace politics on the constructor's ministerial counterparts, resulting in hesitation and vacillation in design decisions. A similar recent case involved a Spanish consortium working on the Haramain high-speed rail project in Saudi Arabia. As a Spanish executive put it in 2015, speaking about their Saudi government customer, "the contract is the starting point in negotiations, not the end point. We have been negotiating with them for three years [since the contract was signed] and this has caused a lot of headaches" (Gomez & Mendez, 2015). Delays were finally resolved in re-negotiations that led to more time without penalties in exchange for lower fees. The informal relationship networks that often constitute the wider regime in developing countries can present opportunities for back-channel communication and building legitimate political support, but they also mean that the project needs to contend with ongoing behind-the-scene consensus-building that can affect what seemed to be firm agreements.

Local protests against an operation are another continuity challenge. We already noted how host community protests driven by a company's poor social performance are linked to reputation. Local protests also affect continuity because they often involve roadblocks or human barriers around company facilities or logistics routes. Foreign mining companies in Peru, for example, have been the target of numerous local protests in recent years, including in 2019 when protesters in Chumbivilcas province severely disrupted ore shipments by blocking a highway (Aquino, 2019). Simply calling local protests a law and order issue and letting the police handle them can lead to violence and further damage host community trust, and more experienced companies accept that delays to listen and respond to issues are often better than trying to blindly stick to schedule. In one case the author worked on, for an oil company conducting exploration in Kenya in 2014, the company's field teams had had some difficult encounters, and it became clear that not proactively consulting with tribal elders in survey areas would lead to mistrust and local activism. Consultation was built into the project process, and although initially it caused some variability in the schedule, over time the company got better at local interaction and likely saved itself greater delays in the long run.

We limit this to one more continuity problem, the effects of violent unrest and conflict. We have noted at several points how anti-government protests and police responses, as well as security measures in response to insurgency and terrorism, can lead to temporary lockdowns and impede logistics. Not only do normal business interactions slow or come to a halt, but company personnel sometimes have to stay at home until unrest subsides. NGOs, which routinely work in conflict-prone environments, call this "hibernation", and it is a standard phase in NGOs' graduated response to insecurity.

The worst case for continuity is when a country or area of operation becomes too dangerous to remain in and a company needs to leave. This does not necessarily mean that it has to terminate an operation (some operations can be mothballed), but the company might not be certain when it could return and if old contractual arrangements and regulations would still apply. For example, prior to 2011, Libya had thousands of expatriates in the country working on various infrastructure, oil and gas, and government planning projects. When the revolution occurred in 2011, companies scrambled to get people out, and several foreign governments launched their own evacuation efforts. Projects were mothballed or simply abandoned, and since then many companies have tried to pick up the pieces with whichever government is now in charge in their old operating area. Companies can try to sustain operations during a conflict, as Firestone did in Liberia during the 1990s civil war, having negotiated its continued presence with rebel leaders. But even when this is feasible, operations are routinely slowed or halted because of security concerns and the effects on required infrastructure.

By way of concluding this section, we can summarise what probably became apparent in the above examination of how political risk affects different assets. This is that one particular dynamic or twist in a socio-political relationship, in other words a manifested challenge or issue, can affect several assets. This is depicted in Figure 3.3, using only two contingencies for illustration.

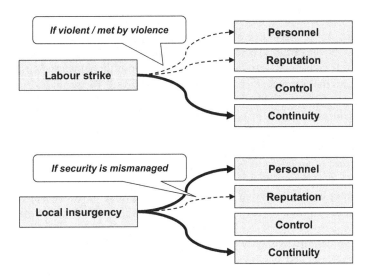

FIGURE 3.3 One challenge, multiple effects.

In the case of a strike, the main implication is halted production, which affects the continuity asset. But if a strike is violent, or if a violent fringe of strikers targets managers, then they could affect company personnel too. If they are met by violence and strikers are injured or killed, then the company's reputation would likely be damaged. In the case of an escalation of a local insurgency, for example a heightened tempo of attacks or a shift of conflict activity towards the operating area, the main implications are for personnel, who could get hurt, and continuity, which could suffer from security lockdowns or periodic "hibernations". However, reputation could also be affected if the company's security contingent becomes paranoid and harasses local people, or in the case of state-provided security, if protection details actually take part in aggressive counter-insurgency efforts.

Most political risks, as specific socio-political changes, events or dynamics, or as a turn for the worse in a socio-political relationship, do indeed affect multiple assets, and there is no standard set of risks associated with each asset. Asking what could affect a particular asset or sub-elements thereof is a useful hypothesis generation exercise, but in any given context one would likely find the same risks (potential causes of harm or disruption) arising several times. The author has seen assessments that interpret every effect on an asset as a separate risk, and the results are too unwieldly and piecemeal to help much with planning. We address such questions in more detail in Part II. For now, it is simply worth underlining what likely became evident in this section: a given risk or issue could and often does have a range of different effects on an operation.

COMPANY ATTITUDES AS A POLITICAL RISK FACTOR

This chapter took several angles on country operations, and hence prior to considering the effects of company attitudes and behaviours, a brief summary up to this point is in order.

We began with a characterisation of country operations and the principal axes of variation with respect to political risk. That section also posited an operation as an element in an ecosystem of socio-political interaction, partly as a means to generate hypotheses on political risk exposures, as we do later on, but more generally to illustrate how an operation's socio-political fit matters to its performance and endurance.

The chapter then examined socio-political stakeholders, the actors that an operation would affect and who would likely respond, and upon whom the operation would need to rely. Stakeholder attitudes and reactions were seen to be a significant source of political risk, but just like the foreign company, stakeholders are affected by wider socio-political dynamics, and hence their responses are partly shaped by the terrain factors examined in Chapter 2. We briefly made the important point that stakeholders are not just a source of risk but can be supportive allies and partners too. Linked to stakeholders was the operation's socio-political profile, or the attributes that socio-political actors notice and react to. If considered early on in planning, the profile helps to identify relevant stakeholders and also helps the company to manage how it is perceived. The profile becomes an important reference point later on in stakeholder analysis within the baseline exercise.

Finally, we considered the four principal assets that foreign operations expose to political risk, namely people, reputation, control and continuity, with illustrations of some of the ways in which socio-political dynamics and relationships can affect them. Two of these assets, control and continuity, are directly linked to an operation's commercial performance, while personnel and reputation matter just as much to a firm's long-term international capability. In considering political risk's effects, we saw that a manifested issue can affect more than one asset. This speaks in part to the linkages between assets, which together enable an operation, but also to the multifaceted character of political risk.

One would not necessarily explicitly consider each facet of an operation discussed in this chapter in an intelligence exercise, and as with terrain factors in Chapter 2, what matters depends in part on the unique operational context. However, knowing the different ways in which an operation could be analytically parsed provides a range of reference points to generate hypotheses on relevant potential challenges. Both this and Chapter 2 were not yet about an intelligence process, but we will be applying these themes and concepts when we enter into processes in Part II.

We now turn to the principal focus of this final section. Having explored operations in relation to political risk, we already have some indirect indications of how companies contribute to their own negative experiences. Here we flesh these out somewhat and characterise three attitudes that can both create political risk, and make a company more vulnerable to it. This is only introductory, since these will come up again in different contexts.

One is a business-centric mindset. A company that sees its environment purely in terms of markets and competitors could be unprepared for the forces and interests that intrude on and distort this idealised commercial domain. A business-centric mindset also leads to overconfidence about the primacy of commercial logic. "Win-win" does not mean the same thing to everyone, and political rationality can be very different. Assuming that everyone will think about mutual profits first and foremost can be a formula for at least disappointment, and sometimes for a rude awakening to the fact that power imperatives, rivalries and "our" rights often carry far more weight. To put it starkly, in business, it is not profitable to kill or get killed, but in politics it can be. If we cannot think beyond commercial logic, we could fail to understand important interests and values that shape both the business environment and responses to the operation.

Over-optimism is another potentially problematic attitude. As noted in the section on phases, businesses, unlike militaries, intelligence agencies or humanitarian NGOs, often thrive on optimism, and motivate people through creating a sense of momentum towards goals. In this atmosphere, a consideration of the potential downsides and of intricate non-business factors can seem out of place or like a ball and chain. Again, this attitude is not problematic in some places, but in complex emerging markets, it often leads to operations getting blindsided when complications do arise. In its more extreme manifestation as hyper-positivity, this attitude can even inhibit people from asking about the potential downsides in the first place. When raw ambition and energy are touted as all that matters, no one will want to stick their neck out to say that they beg to differ.

Finally, company tribalism can be a significant challenge. Ethno-centrism can be an element of this, but the attitude more commonly arises when there is a strong sense of loyalty among staff and management, and a commensurate sense that what is good for the company is good generally. Very few corruption cases have arisen because individual managers were seeking personal gain. Instead, most cases have been attributable to people trying to boost their company's performance, even if they risked liability in doing so. Similarly, taking shortcuts in sustainability compliance and responsible security is seldom motivated by malice; rather, if these help the company to do better, then such shortcuts contribute to the greater good of the tribe. Tribalism, in particular its element of faith that the company is uniquely smart, right and legitimate, can also lead to disdain for those who seem to oppose the company's interests. Thus, governments are "inept" when they harden regulations, and host communities are "parochial" when they express concern about an operation's effects. The nett effect of tribalism is that a company positions itself in opposition to its socio-political milieu. It is one tribe competing for turf and influence with others.

Companies afflicted by acute manifestations of the above attitudes can create political risk by inspiring hostility and wariness towards the operation, either through perceived arrogance or by riding roughshod over socio-political sensitivities. They also make themselves more vulnerable by inadvertent or wilful blindness to the potential downsides and the opportunities to manage them. All three of these attitudes can converge, and indeed they can become mutually reinforcing. Sustainability and corporate ethics have much more share of mind than they did a couple of decades ago, and not many companies based in established democracies acutely manifest these attitudes. But they exist in nearly all companies to varying degrees. They are actually necessary for a company to function effectively. But corporate cultures can take on a life of their own, and cultural aberrations still account for much manifested political risk that could have been avoided with greater self-awareness.

For the most part, political risk is an environmental concern, in that it arises from what is going on around the company, not from within it. But we should avoid the notion that political risk is only something that happens "out there". The organisation is a significant part of the political risk equation, beyond simply containing the assets that political risk can affect. Thus, self-knowledge is one critical underpinning of resilience. The other is knowledge about the world around us, in other words intelligence, the subject of the next chapter.

REFERENCES

Aquino, M. (2019, October 16). Peru government Taps Armed Forces to Unblock Copper Protests. *Reuters*. Retrieved December 30, 2020, from https://www.reuters.com/article/us-peru-copper-protest/peru-government-taps-armed-forces-to-unblock-copper-protests-idUSKBN1WV1TR

Chi, D., & van den Broek, D. (2013). Wildcat Strikes: A Catalyst for Union Reform in Vietnam? *Journal of Industrial Relations, 55*(5), 783–799. doi:10.1177/0022185613491685

Filippakis, L. (2018, May 22). Foreign companies 'flee' Turkey due to political and financial instability. Independent Balkan News Agency IBNA. Retrieved December 20, 2020, from https://balkaneu.com/foreign-companies-flee-turkey-due-to-political-and-financial-instability/

Gilmore, A. B., McKee, M., & Collin, J. (2006). British American Tobacco's erosion of health legislation in Uzbekistan. *BMJ, 332*(7537), 355–358. doi:10.1136/bmj.332.7537.355

Gilmore, A. B., McKee, M., & Collin, J. (2007). The Invisible Hand: How British American Tobacco Precluded Competition in Uzbekistan. *Tobacco Control, 16*(4), 239–247. doi:10.1136/tc.2006.017129

Gomez, L., & Mendez, R. (2015, February 6). *Saudis Kick up Storm Over Spanish Group's High-speed Desert Rail Project*. El Pais. Retrieved December 22, 2020, from https://english.elpais.com/elpais/2015/02/04/inenglish/1423052376_326956.html

Nigeria Demands $62B from Oil Majors. (2020). *Rig Zone*. Retrieved December 14, 2020, from https://www.rigzone.com/news/wire/nigeria_demands_62b_from_oil_majors-10-oct-2019-160030-article/

Parenti, E., & Liberti, S. (2018, February 12). Mozambique's Farmers Battle to Keep Land in Nakarari. *Al Jazeera*. Retrieved December 14, 2020, from https://www.aljazeera.com/features/2018/2/12/mozambiques-farmers-battle-to-keep-land-in-nakarari

RAID UK. (2019, September 16). DR Congo: The Forgotten Victims of Dan Gertler's Corruption. Retrieved December 14, 2020, from https://www.raid-uk.org/blog/dr-congo-forgotten-victims-dan-gertler%E2%80%99s-corruption

Riu Hotels challenges order to halt construction of project in Cancún. (2020, November 5). Mexico News Daily. Retrieved December 13, 2020, from https://mexiconewsdaily.com/news/riu-hotels-challenges-order-to-halt-construction/

Strikes in China over foreign employers selling out to local companies. (2016, November 25). The Guardian. Retrieved December 10, 2020, from https://www.theguardian.com/world/2016/nov/25/strikes-in-china-over-foreign-employers-selling-out-to-local-companies

Suzui, G. (2017). *Development for Whom?: From the Case of the ProSAVANA Project in Mozambique*. Berkeley: Berkeley University Development Program. Retrieved December 17, 2020, from https://mdp.berkeley.edu/development-for-whom-from-the-case-of-the-prosavana-project-in-mozambique/

Telenor Group. (n.d.). Retrieved June 20, 2022, from https://www.telenor.com/media/vimpelcom-ltd/historical-background/

Welker, M. A. (2009, February). "CORPORATE SECURITY BEGINS IN THE COMMUNITY": Mining, the Corporate Social Responsibility Industry, and Environmental Advocacy in Indonesia. *Cultural Anthropology*, *24*(1), 142–179. doi:10.1111/j.1548-1360.2009.00029

Wellhausen, R. L. (2012). *When Governments Break Contracts: Foreign Firms in Emerging Economies*. PhD thesis, Massachusetts Institute of Technology, Political Science.

4 Introduction to Intelligence

Thus far, we have introduced three of the four key themes that together make up political risk intelligence for operations in complex environments. A brief recap is in order. First, we explored political risk as a field and concern oriented around the issues that companies can face as a result of socio-political trends and behaviour. Political risk is relevant in nearly any business operation, since laws and social perceptions affect companies anywhere, but a political risk perspective is particularly relevant in complex socio-political terrain where less about the environment can be taken for granted. We then delved into complex terrain, introducing socio-political complexity and mapping the factors and patterns that give rise to complexity and thus to political risk. Finally, we looked at foreign business operations, how they related to the socio-political milieu and how they were exposed to, and in some cases created, political risk through their interactions.

This final chapter within the part on core concepts introduces intelligence, the fourth strand of the book's title and focus. Readers will be happy to know that this is not as extensive as the last two chapters, since intelligence is a way of learning and type of knowledge rather than the substantive issues or domains of human activity that are the subjects of an intelligence method. The best way to illustrate intelligence is to actually examine an intelligence exercise, and we do that in Part II. Nonetheless, intelligence is sufficiently nuanced and distinct as a concept that a prior introduction is warranted before we get into the details of a specific intelligence process. Additionally, having a contextual understanding of intelligence will help readers to go beyond what it just in this book, since an intelligence perspective is applicable to a range of situations in which an organisation is facing difficult choices, uncertainty, challenges and competing or hostile interests. Note that this introductory chapter steers clear of the operational and organisational aspects of intelligence, since we cover these in detail in Part III.

The chapter proceeds as follows. First, we characterise intelligence, by examining the development of intelligence as a practice, and providing a definition appropriate for our purposes with some brief illustrations. Next, we examine some other intelligence-like practices in the business world, to see where intelligence, as we use the term, fits with these and to forestall potential confusion arising from apparent overlaps. The last section examines the main roles of intelligence in an organisation, and the thorny question of how much intelligence is enough, or indeed too much.

CHARACTERISING INTELLIGENCE

There has been considerable popular attention paid to the historical roots of intelligence, including its position in ancient military and political manuals such as Sun Tzu's *The Thirteen Chapters*. While certain progressive thinkers in ancient states did recommend that military and foreign policy decisions be based on structured insight, these were brief sparks in a world still committed to religious observance. Even for much of the history of the Roman conquests, generals planning campaigns were at least as concerned about the results of divination as they were with information on the enemy. Intelligence as a practice was ad hoc and mainly took the form of reconnaissance. This began to change in Renaissance Europe, when diplomacy became an institutionalised practice. This enabled official espionage and made code-breaking a valuable court asset. It was not until the late 1800s that more or less stand-alone intelligence agencies were established, and thus that there were organisations dedicated to honing and standardising intelligence practices. World War I and the Russian Revolution paved the way for the modern intelligence agency. Three main variants now

DOI: 10.1201/9781003149125-6

often reside under different ministries in the same state: internal security, foreign political and military. A separate signals or communications intelligence agency might support the other three or be embedded in one of them.

There are a variety of axes of specialisation within and between the main types, and larger intelligence agencies are similar to multinational companies in having a matrix structure. Functional divisions align with the intelligence process; hence, for example, there are the collectors who get required information and the analysts who turn it into intelligence reports. There are divisions according to the type of information source; thus, we have a range of "-*ints*", including sigint (signals), humint (human), osint (open source) and imint (imagery). Region and subject, for example South Asia and bio-chemical weapons proliferation, are two more axes. In Western models broadly based on the intelligence structures of the UK and US, there is a final layer of analysis sitting above all of these specialisations, known as all-source analysis, which cross-checks and integrates all relevant reporting from across the whole intelligence community (the collection of distinct intelligence agencies) to provide both regular policy guidance and insights on specific emerging issues. Policy-makers see a range of intelligence reports, including even raw material such as transcripts of an agent's notes or a phone intercept, but reports and briefings from all-source analysis are specifically produced for senior leaders to inform them about national threats and challenges.

Another distinction that has been made is between strategic and tactical. Strategic intelligence informs long-term planning towards achieving a particular position some years hence. Tactical intelligence is about the challenges along the way, including specific localised, near-term problems. It has shorter time horizons and less emphasis on dealing with uncertainty, and more need for hard facts about the here and now. The distinction can be useful but in practice it gets blurry. An immediate, localised challenge can have strategic ramifications, and involve a number of moving pieces that require a holistic, or strategic, approach. It is also a matter of perspective. For example, for national security planners in the capital city, the problems encountered by an infantry battalion in a far-flung country might hardly register, but for the battalion commander, they could seem quite complex and require nuanced forward thinking. This is broadly parallel to the perspectives of corporate HQ and the on-the-ground management team running a particular overseas operation. There is a practical distinction in level of abstraction and time horizons with their associated degrees of uncertainty, but one person's tactical problem is often another person's strategic one, and changing circumstances can give seemingly tactical challenges strategic significance.

Like governments and armies, companies and their predecessors have long been using intelligence in ad hoc and opportunistic ways, and from Venetian traders to British colonial companies, even espionage was a valid tool of learning about competitors. But as a formal practice, intelligence began to enter the business domain following World War II. During the war, industrial manufacturers, especially in the US, had applied military operations research in an effort to optimise war production. Operations research widened into management science after the war, but even its more holistic view of the firm did not escape an industrial engineering mindset. By the late 1960s, though, it was becoming clear that the business arena was more complicated than just monolithic firms striving for scale and efficiency. The increasingly rapid cycle of technology and innovation was enabling companies to get a jump on each other not just in efficiency but in adapting to market preferences. Furthermore, although with the current focus on China's rise it is easy forget, Japan was becoming a serious disruptor, supporting and coordinating its industrial companies for a new approach to global competition. Management thinkers began to posit strategy in terms that would have been somewhat familiar to military campaign planners. Companies were increasingly seen not as complex machines, but as players in a competitive, dynamic game. To win the game, one needed a strategy, and that had to be premised on robust insights about the other players, and the terrain they contended for – markets. Competitor and market intelligence became recognised practices closely linked to strategic planning.

While strategy itself has seen numerous fads over subsequent years, the importance of intelligence about the world beyond the firm's boundaries has only increased with globalisation, and currently intelligence activities are undertaken for an array of purposes across a typical multinational, including political risk analysis and aspects thereof where these explicitly occur. "Intelligence" can mean different things in a company, but those activities that focus on actionable learning about the business environment and actors within it are quite similar in spirit, and even broadly in method, to the classical notion of intelligence developed in the context of national security and diplomacy.

Not all information-gathering and processing, nor research and analysis, in companies or indeed governments is intelligence activity, at least as we use "intelligence" here. Organisations generate, process and use vast amounts of information just in the act of remaining coordinated and cohesive, not to mention in technical or process innovation. Intelligence is distinguished from other information activities and uses by at least the following three features.

Intelligence directly informs planning and decisions that initiate actions. Intelligence as a process gathers and uses information, in other words transferrable or communicable facts or knowledge, but intelligence products are structured, purposeful insight and foresight about the situation being acted upon. Intelligence goes through production stages from raw to finished, but it ultimately ends up as coherent reports and briefings in the hands of those tasked to navigate and safeguard the organisation (the company or country operation, for example). Old, or used, intelligence can revert to being information, for example stored in a library as historical background material, when it is no longer actionable. A key feature of intelligence, then, is actionability.

Intelligence is about the world beyond the boundaries of the organisation. Organisations need information about themselves to function. Resources and assets need to be counted and their flows measured to ensure efficient operation. But developing and maintaining a view of the organisation is not an intelligence activity; rather, it is accounting for and keeping track of what is under our noses. In complex organisations, this can be a challenge, but it does not involve reaching out into the world to see and assess what we did not know about before. Internal insights and self-knowledge are necessary for effective planning, but the job of intelligence is to provide the other half of the planning equation, insight about the external environment. As we see later, "intelligence" is often used for internal management information, but the term starts to become meaningless when it is simply equated with the information managers use for their day-to-day jobs.

Finally, intelligence shapes new insight. For example, a manager arrives at a new country operation and is responsible for handling the importation of equipment. She reads the necessary procedures and reviews the relevant documentation, and asks a local counterpart for help in understanding some nuances. The manager did not undertake an intelligence exercise. She simply learned existing information. If, after using what seemed to be the correct procedures, she found that imports were delayed, she would try to find out why in order to solve the problem. That would be an intelligence exercise. Thus, intelligence is not simply learning what is given; rather, it involves a degree of investigation and discovery.

By way of further characterisation, intelligence can be both intensive and routine. Intensive processes are often aligned to planning cycles or strategic reviews, and they can also occur based on indications of significant change or in response to manifesting urgent situations. Intensive processes produce specific insights to guide significant decisions. Routine intelligence, on the other hand, comes after an intensive process has identified relevant factors and actors, and monitors these to keep the organisation abreast of minor developments which, if ignored because they are minor, could eventually add up to render the organisation's perception of its environment out of date. Intensive processes tend to yield stand-alone reports, briefing sessions and workshops, while routine monitoring manifests as dashboards, newsletters or other brief updates. There is a systemic relationship between intensive and routine. Intensive processes reveal what needs to be routinely monitored, but monitoring can detect significant changes that require an intensive review of a situation. We look more closely at these modes and their role in the wider intelligence cycle in Chapters 11 and 12.

As a final point on the character of the phenomenon, unlike intuition, opinion or impressions, intelligence is processed and checked for quality on the assumption that misperception and misinterpretation are common problems (news can be quality checked too, but unlike intelligence, news is for such a general audience that it can seldom inform the actions of any one organisation). For example, if a management team goes to a country to get a better idea of the place, as was not uncommon in the 1960s and 1970s as a way to "assess political risk", they could come back with impressions which, if not challenged or corroborated, become the main basis of the company's perception. It is possible that the people they met were spinning their own agenda, that the local chaperone, perhaps a prospective partner, chose only the best sights, that the newspapers available at the hotel were state-owned, and that the management team had a five-star experience in a divided and unstable country. Even relying on one or a few experts on a place or situation can be problematic, since experts are not exempt from bias and often cling to particular paradigms that can define their niche within the information market.

An intelligence process contains corroboration, critical reviews and self-challenging to ensure that the final product is not just impressionistic or based on a narrow set of perspectives, and that uncertainties or speculation are properly qualified. This goes hand in hand with the feature of shaping insight from obscurity – when a situation is unclear, the scant information that is readily available can lead people to infer too much and jump conclusions, or people fall back on popular theories or prior experiences. We examine some of the cognitive pitfalls in Chapter 14, but for now an important distinction between intelligence and other types of insight is its self-conscious and self-critical aspect.

The character of intelligence emerges from the above, but a definition is still useful to pin down the concept. This takes into account our particular focus and draws on the classical notion of intelligence; hence, this is not generic enough to fit all conceptions of the term.

Intelligence, then, can be defined as insight and foresight enabling the organisation to act with clarity about the external factors and actors relevant to the organisation's aims and institutional health.

There are a few things to note in the definition. One is that intelligence is about current situations, but also how these might evolve; hence, it involves facts about the here and now as well as informed hypotheses about what lies beyond the observable horizon. The second point is that while it is tempting to say that intelligence *ensures* that the organisation acts on relevant knowledge, we can only say that it *enables*. Whether or not intelligence is taken on board is partly a matter of how useful and user-friendly it seems to be, but there is nothing inherent to intelligence that can ensure that leaders use it. That is up to organisational culture and governance. Finally, the definition includes both aims and institutional health. Intelligence helps to achieve objectives, but also to defend or safeguard the institution, in other words the organisation's parts and principles, from threats and hazards. Intelligence often does both at the same time by helping to find feasible and advantageous objectives, and then helping to pursue them with awareness of the challenges that the journey entails.

Other definitions of intelligence characterise it as the organisation that produces intelligence, as in, "Intelligence says that if we take that route we'll run into a tank division", or the activity that produces intelligence, for example, "Carry out some intelligence (conduct an intelligence exercise) to see which route is safer". Our definition looks at intelligence as a product or output, as in "We need some intelligence on this or we might be in trouble". All three perspectives are facets of the same concept, and we will be using all three as appropriate.

A few hypothetical examples help to illustrate intelligence. A personal computer manufacturing company's biggest two competitors merge, creating significant efficiencies and market power and posing a potential threat to the firm's market share. However, it is unclear if the merged competitor will remain in the computer business, since the merger was preceded by statements about the synergies between the two sides' IT services and outsourcing capabilities. They might even spin off the computer business to focus on higher growth services. Using game simulation and workshops with industry experts and observers, the company develops a few key competitive scenarios as well as indicators of their potential emergence. The company devises several strategic options and adjusts preparation on the basis of ongoing monitoring. Intelligence thus fed into strategy formulation to enable the firm to respond to its mega-competitors' moves, rather than reacting on impulse or remaining in wait-and-see mode.

As another example, a coalition of international humanitarian NGOs working in a post-conflict environment carried out a security review, and this discerned a significant risk of an increase in armed violence in several sub-regions, with consequent hazard to staff in those areas. The coalition establishes a monitoring network, using intelligence feeds and incident reports from NGO bases and also from friendly peacekeeping detachments, to monitor early warning indicators of armed violence. NGOs then use this for travel planning and local withdrawal contingencies to reduce the chances of staff being hurt by armed clashes.

Finally, a European oil company's project team in a foreign country is concerned about an upcoming national election. The challenger has a track record of economic nationalism and a preference for Chinese investment, while the incumbent sees FDI as a development accelerator and feels that Europe is a better long-term economic partner. Country management tasks several staff to undertake an exercise first to try to discern each candidate's electoral chances, and then to explore how the challenger might act towards foreign oil firms and the company in particular, if he won. Managers use the latter to develop contingency plans, including a new and reinforced bargaining position in case the company's stake in the country comes up for discussion. After early indications that the incumbent would probably win, some on the management team wanted to stop the exercise, but others prevailed with their argument that it was better to carry on than to be caught by surprise if the challenger managed to achieve an upset.

There is a subtle but noteworthy distinction in each example between intelligence and decision-making. It can be hard to distinguish the two processes, but intelligence serves an agenda set by the organisation's leadership and key stakeholders, and that agenda in turn derives from the organisation's mission and values. If NGOs, for example, saw no reason to risk staying in a dangerous country, intelligence on the security situation would not be necessary. Intelligence can be very bound up with decisions and direction-setting, but it is distinct. We consider this in more detail later when we examine the difference between intelligence and strategy.

As with politics, the boundaries of the concept of intelligence are not always cut and dried, and as a mode of information gathering and processing it sits in a crowded space. With constant evolution in business uses of structured information, the concept and value of intelligence can get lost in the haze. The next section examines three closely related business functions and processes, to help distinguish intelligence from these but also to elucidate its relationship to them.

RELATED BUSINESS PRACTICES

Various activities and management functions in an international company generate and use intelligence. Public relations, for example, monitors media trends to understand how to focus company communications; government relations researches political stakeholders to plan engagement and lobbying approaches; legal and compliance track changes in relevant laws and regulations. Much of this is intelligence in the sense described above. There are other processes or functions, however, that seem close to intelligence but which actually have different purposes. These have sometimes subsumed the concept of intelligence in companies, and in so doing led to confusion about what intelligence means and how it can contribute to plans and decisions. These related practices are business intelligence (BI for short), risk management or enterprise risk management (ERM), and strategy, or more precisely strategy formulation. The following examines each with an eye to the distinction from, and relationship to, intelligence as we conceptualised it in the last section.

BUSINESS INTELLIGENCE

BI and business analytics together refer to the capture, processing, correlation and presentation of data from around a company to help managers to make informed decisions. BI implies more of a sense-making aspect, with user interfaces that enable managers to manipulate data to devise specific insights, while analytics is more of a catch-all label for the wider data management capability and has several sub-fields, such as predictive analytics. For our purposes, BI and analytics are different aspects of the same function, and we will just call them BI for convenience.

Companies have always created, stored and used information, but prior to modern information networks and business computing, managers seldom used more than a fraction of what existed in a company when doing analyses that informed plans and decisions. It was just too cumbersome. Even after companies were electronically networked in the 1970s and 1980s, information systems were too underpowered to provide firm-wide data access and analysis, and management users were still reliant on IT experts to manipulate or query data and generate user-friendly reports. In the ensuing years, BI eventually led to firm-wide data access, and to user-friendly tools and interfaces that allowed non-IT experts to generate their own reports and track relevant data in real-time using instant queries and online dashboards. In recent years, BI has been merging with data mining to make use of Big Data, or the vast amount of data points and information generated by tracked online activity within a company and its connected ecosystem (or the "extended enterprise").

BI has had a significant effect on companies' ability to optimise performance. It is used by nearly all management functions on both the efficiency and sales growth sides. Logistics, for example, can track the progress of individual electronically tagged shipments from the factory to the buyer, to analyse bottlenecks along the route. Sales and marketing can correlate data on customers, pricing, product options, sales volumes, sales office activities and advertising to discern how to maximise sales in any given season and area. Staff profiles and performance can be correlated to better inform future hiring decisions. Data slices can be razor thin for nuanced insight on priority segments and activities, or macroscopic for a wider view of company performance. BI systems are now embedded in nearly all larger firms, and many managers could not imagine doing their jobs without BI.

The very label, "business intelligence", gives the sense that BI contains or constitutes the intelligence capability in a company. This is partly reinforced by BI's ubiquitous usage, which makes managers far more familiar with it than with external intelligence exercises. BI and especially Big Data are also relatively new and still somewhat faddish, and tend to absorb considerable management attention. Thus, BI has partly overshadowed other conceptions and uses of "intelligence" in a company. There are, however, significant differences between BI and classical intelligence.

First, BI is a capability, not a product or output. It is a very capable filing system with an additional layer of user interface that allows one to slice and correlate information. As a tool, BI can be applied to a range of analytical problems, but it is not the analytical process itself nor its resulting insight. Second, BI enables the use of quantifiable information. Anything that a BI system derives for a user is ultimately based on an aggregation of tracked units, transactions or specific physical characteristics, and hence it is not well suited for the analysis of complex human dynamics and ambiguous problems. Finally, BI is about information inside the organisation or generated in its interaction with others, not the world beyond the company's own circle of influence.

Despite the label, then, BI is not intelligence in our sense of the word. Planners and leaders can obtain useful insights on the inner workings of the firm from BI, but they would still need intelligence on relevant actors and dynamics beyond the organisation to plan initiatives that went beyond just internal efficiency and relationships with current and known customers and suppliers.

The above conclusion is not meant to suggest that data analysis and real-time online monitoring are not relevant to classical intelligence. BI is mainly inward-looking because companies logically first networked themselves and then started to expand slowly outwards to those whom they interacted with, such as customers and suppliers. A BI-like system using relevant external data is a possibility, and would be valuable in a range of intelligence tasks. It is harder to attain than internal BI because most companies cannot run around plugging everyone else into their own data stream.

While the above applies to most companies, Google, Facebook and other big online service providers actually are plugged into the external world, and social and news media monitoring tools allow others to leverage their data flows for insights on relevant social networks, trends and attitudes. For most companies, social and news media analytics would not attain Big Data scale, but it does present the opportunity for real-time analysis of some important dynamics beyond the firm. Indeed, social media analysis has become a tool in the repertoire of political risk analysts, who use it for a range of purposes, such as sensing the mood of "the street" in cases of instability. There is also a universe of static, if routinely updated, online data available for intelligence analysis, but while some commercial intelligence providers package certain indicators into user-friendly platforms, thus far only social and news media provides the basis of a real-time BI-like external data flow.

It is likely that more external data will turn into real-time flows, but this will present its own challenges if companies are not judicious about what is relevant and manageable. The company and its ecosystem have a natural, if hazy, limit, but when one looks beyond, there is a strong potential for data overload. Communications intelligence agencies, for example, are adept at scooping up information, but analytics to make sense of it still lags behind collection capabilities, and the excess of data can lead to relevant correlations getting lost in the wider morass.

ENTERPRISE RISK MANAGEMENT

ERM has emerged as the principal label for systematic risk management in companies, and is now such a common buzzword that it is easy to forget how recently it became a corporate concern. Prior to the 1950s, risk was only formally talked about in the context of insurance, and the first academic books on risk only appeared in the 1960s. In the 1970s, as financial markets became more complex, banks and other financial players began to apply systematic risk management. In most other sectors, outside of a few specialist functions, companies for the most part tacitly managed risk through caution, quality control, decision analysis, common sense and strategic thinking, and risk was accorded no special place in the management pantheon.

This changed in the early 2000s when several corporate scandals and bankruptcies in the US rocked investor confidence and led to risk management and internal control regulations. While initiated in the US, European and other governments soon followed with similar standards. The principal aim of the new wave of regulations was to prevent economic disruption because of corporate and banking failures arising from financial over-extensions, and the covering up of these through bad or fraudulent accounting. However, both corporate boards and influential management consultancies saw an opportunity to extend the spirit of the new provisions to loss minimisation in general. The Committee of Sponsoring Organizations of the Treadway Commission (or COSO, a US-based joint finance sector initiative to combat corporate fraud) published its guidance on ERM in 2004, and this provided the ERM label and framework for the kind of systematic risk management that proponents claimed would ultimately make companies more profitable and less prone to embarrassing failures. ERM saw rapid uptake among larger firms in particular. By the 2008 financial crisis, ERM meant more than just financial prudence and accurate book-keeping, and it emerged from the crisis more or less unscathed.

ERM had entered into the corporate psyche, for better or worse. On the side of better, before ERM there was no explicit channel or process beyond the finance and safety functions to discuss risk. Hyper-positive corporate cultures and groupthink often made people counselling prudence appear as curmudgeons and naysayers. ERM provided the channel, occasion and sometimes obligation to discuss uncertainties and downsides. The notion of risk appetite, when appropriately contextualised for different types of decisions, helped leaders and planners not just to scope financial bets but to establish red lines and limits with respect to the feasibility of new initiatives and the kinds of problems that the company could live with. Strategy as a field and practice had long accounted for risk, but a more explicit concept of risk provided a connective framework for relevant notions like trade-offs, uncertainty, strategic gambles and "real options". Risk management at the operational level, when really focused on hazards and not just problems or incompetence, drove a search beyond the obvious for factors that could affect operations, and made challenging assumptions a normal part of operational plans and reviews. A mature, un-hyped interpretation of ERM and its service to strategy and operations helped many companies to become more self-aware and better at making nuanced decisions.

On the worse side, when companies caved into the hype about ERM as the fix to nearly all corporate problems ("in identifying and managing risks we'll make better choices, avoid liability, and be more efficient"), their interpretation of ERM could be so broad and ill-defined that it began to be everything. On the strategic level, risk went beyond just potential downsides to include upside risk, in other words potential opportunities, the very thing that companies exist to find and exploit in the first place. Thus, strategic marketing and business development teams were somehow doing risk management when they identified and pursued new prospects. At the operational level, there was a sense that the more risks identified, the better it was for performance and avoiding compliance breaches. Managers felt pressure to report risks and started seeing them everywhere. As a result, alongside actual hazards were mundane problems and numerous "failure to" risks that were little more than checklists of basic competencies or steps in a process. This led to enormous, discordant risk registries and matrices that were hard to track and nearly impossible to interpret for planning purposes. Faced with the challenge of making sense of risk when it seemed to be everything, senior managers often just got on with their jobs and let ERM run in the background, separate from real decision-making but still weighing on time and conscience.

The better and worse manifestations of ERM are sometimes regarded as a matter of risk maturity, in other words how sophisticated and integrated risk management is in the organisation. The "worse" illustration above, however, often arises when companies are well beyond risk immaturity. Rather, it is the maturity mid-point where many companies get stuck, often because senior management initially construes ERM as a new way of working rather than supporting what companies already do. The ERM revolution never quite yields the promised results but no one wants to be a heretic by calling for a basic reconsideration.

There is a natural link between risk management and intelligence, and they fluidly relate in companies with a mature and pragmatic conception of ERM. Actionable risk identification and assessment, at least with respect to the external environment, is an intelligence exercise in which the organisation strives to see beyond the known to understand how change could affect it, and the hazards and threats it could face. Risk intelligence is not constrained by rigid ERM systems and can be scoped and shaped for the best fit with a given decision context. Strategic risk assessment involves horizon scanning and scenario analysis, for example, while risk assessment for specific initiatives focuses not just on downside occurrences but also on how the relevant environment might evolve and the relationship between the company and other actors. Intelligence exercises in support of risk management are thus flexibly tailored for specific purposes, and designed with decisions and action in mind, as opposed to just contributing to a risk registry where many recorded risks can lie dormant until the next round of risk reporting.

Intelligence as valuable, action-oriented insight gets distorted where ERM remains caught between being a self-consciously explicit function and also the wider way a company should be working. This occurs because risk frameworks, such as COSO's Integrated Framework or ISO 31000, are prescribed as the only way to structure a risk intelligence exercise. Intelligence agencies, which routinely deal with risk and uncertainty, have myriad approaches to different challenges and, like strategy consultants, often premise an approach on the specific decisions that they must inform. A standard risk framework, by contrast, has a rigid, limited logic which does not lend itself well to more ambiguous, complex or in-depth problems. If results need to be captured on a standard risk registry and matrix, there is not much room for an examination of alternative futures, dynamic interactions or nuanced insight on specific actors. Simply put, when intelligence is crammed into a rigid risk box, much relevant insight can be lost or obscured.

As a tangible illustration, in one political risk case for an upcoming operation in a developing country, the author and project team designed the approach in the proposal stage, taking into account what we knew about the operation and the country in question. When we presented it, the client in turn handed us a risk framework and said, "Your approach looks great from a purely logical standpoint and it covers all the bases, but whatever you do it needs to fit into this – the team at HQ wants to be able to log the results in the risk registry". The client was actually head of international ventures, not a risk manager, and he regretted having to forego an approach that fit better with his own concerns. Thus, what made sense was secondary to adherence to ERM protocol. As an aside, "risk" in political risk sometimes sets expectations about its relationship to ERM, even though the political risk label was developed decades before risk became a standard business term.

Intelligence as a process and output can apply to a range of challenges involving ambiguity or uncertainty about the outside world. It can be, and indeed often is, risk assessment, and when ERM is interpreted as adding value to strategy and operations, intelligence can have a fluid and practical relationship with it without being subsumed. Along with other functions and processes, though, intelligence can become distorted by overly ardent and mechanistic interpretations of ERM. Intelligence is a natural friend to risk assessment, but when it is forced under a risk rubric, its potential for actionable insight can be severely diminished, especially when the problems it addresses do not readily lend themselves to dissection into what can be rated and mapped.

STRATEGY FORMULATION

A strategy is a plan that sets an organisation's major objectives and how to achieve them. Objectives are designed to contribute to the realisation of the organisation's mission (what it is trying to do for whom) and as stepping stones towards its vision (what the future would be like if the organisation succeeded in enacting its values, and the organisation's status in that future). A strategy is not just a statement of broad goals or values-based aspirations. It is also distinct from policy, which is more about the principles and rules that guide behaviour in a given context. Strategy is action-oriented, and a good strategy not only defines what the organisation should do, but how to make itself capable of the journey and how to navigate the obstacles ahead.

Intelligence has a critical role in strategy formulation and strategic reviews. Situation analysis, in one form or another, is the starting point of strategy development. While the SWOT (strengths, weaknesses, opportunities, threats) framework is sometimes derided as "so what analysis", its four boxes at least capture the fundamentals of a company's situation. Strengths and weaknesses are about the capabilities of the company, while opportunities and threats are about its external environment. A strategy aligns the company's capabilities with what it needs to do to develop and exploit opportunities and manage threats (threat in this context is what we would call a risk factor, whereas a threat more precisely refers to a hostile actor). Intelligence is how the company gains actionable insight on the external environment. The familiar PEST (political, economic, social, technological, sometimes with legal and environmental) framework refers to common types of relevant factors, and analysis of these would combine with market and competitive analysis for the outward-facing element of the situation assessment.

One might expect that with sufficient high-quality information and rigorous analysis, the intelligence exercise would actually result in the strategy. After all, intelligence indicates where the opportunities are, the obstacles and risks that need to be managed, and how relevant factors could evolve. With map in hand, the organisation need only prepare itself and then start the journey. This might be facile, but in practice there is actually some confusion about the distinction between strategy and intelligence. It is significant, if sometimes subtle.

We examine the intelligence cycle later in the book, but as a brief precursor the first step in the cycle is setting intelligence targets, or giving the intelligence capability a direction. Intelligence, now speaking of an agency or unit, does not set its own direction, or not all of it anyway. The organisation's leaders do. Their direction is partly based on their reading of intelligence reporting, for example on opportunities and challenges. However, they combine this with the organisation's mission and vision, which leaders and key stakeholders set, to decide what the company should try to do, and hence what it needs to learn about. Intelligence, unlike leadership, is not responsible for aligning objectives with mission and vision.

Second, intelligence cannot decide what risks are worth taking. It can provide insight on potential challenges, but assessment does not extend to deciding whether or not to go ahead anyway. Using a political risk example, a company is considering a major contract in a country, and intelligence indicates that any operation would face persistent corruption pressure, periodic violent protests in the vicinity and possibly violent regime change with consequent unrest and even international sanctions. The intelligence manager, or at least the person assigned to the task, tells the leadership that the project is not worth the potential difficulties. The leadership replies, "We'll have to try anyway because our traditional markets are stagnant and we need to get used to operating in frontiers, plus if we don't try to get this major opportunity then a competitor will. We'll just have to take your advice on board to manage the risks as best we can." The parameters of the take-it-or-leave-it decision and the risk-reward equation are not set by intelligence. Indeed, a strategy can be deliberately risk-taking, and this is decided through not just rational analysis but also corporate cultural attitudes to risk and the expectations of company stakeholders. Such considerations are not in the intelligence job description, even if intelligence can have some effect on them.

Finally, intelligence is about the external environment and not about the company's own capabilities, which are fully one half of the considerations relevant to strategy formulation. This seems obvious, but sometimes it is not to strategic marketers and other outward-facing specialists, who can regard the company as a piece in a board game and plot strategy based on its position relative to other players. Strategy consultancies have sometimes been criticised for basing recommendations on this perspective, leaving client managers to decipher their results in the context of the company's actual strengths and limitations. Intelligence exercises should consider the firm's capabilities, but only to ensure that insights are relevant. Then strategy formulation brings internal and external insights together.

To help sharpen the distinction, one can consider what intelligence would look like without an organisation needing it. Collectors and analysts would probably study personal interests and perhaps publish the odd paper. In other words, intelligence would be academic. The user organisation thus gives intelligence its meaning. If intelligence is partly defined by being actionable, there needs to be someone doing the action, and they do not just wait for intelligence to tell them what to do. They already have a sense of direction because of their values and ambitions. These are at the heart of any strategy. Intelligence just helps to make strategy realistic.

Intelligence, then, is not strategy-formulation. Strategy integrates the organisation's values, self-knowledge and worldly knowledge, while intelligence only provides worldly knowledge.

Note that the above does not address a basic "should" about intelligence, which is that it should be reasonably independent from leadership and office-political dynamics so that insights are not skewed by factional contests, ideological or other subjective values, or career agendas. This is a point about intelligence quality control, not its distinction from related functions, and we address such issues in Chapter 14. The independence of intelligence, though, is relevant to its relationship with strategy. Just as intelligence is not strategy formulation, those conducting strategy formulation need to keep their ideas and ambitions in check until the relevant intelligence is in. In other words, strategic visioning is not intelligence.

ROLES AND LIMITS OF INTELLIGENCE

Having characterised intelligence and clarified its sometimes confusing relationship to mainstream business processes, we conclude the chapter with some conceptual refinement, through a brief examination of intelligence's general roles, and also its limits. Roles are presented as advantageous insights that intelligence provides for its customer organisation, and note that the seven roles that follow are only a few indicative possibilities. The subsequent section on limits examines at what points or in what contexts more intelligence could become "too much of a good thing".

ROLES

Opportunity

The organisation has a mission and knows its capabilities and limitations. It needs to find opportunities to fulfil its mission, and these need to be feasible given what the organisation can do. In some cases, intelligence applies mission and feasibility as parameters to search for relevant opportunities. In others, the organisation envisions opportunities. Intelligence then tests critical assumptions about the success of envisioned opportunities to see which are feasible, or how an opportunity would have to be reshaped to have an acceptable chance of success. In a business context, identified opportunities are also assessed for their effect on the global portfolio of investments and operations to see how they would affect the corporate risk-reward balance and diversification.

Intelligence-led, as opposed to vision-led, opportunity identification is exemplified in how extractive and infrastructure companies get new overseas business. While they sometimes proactively approach foreign governments with ideas and proposals, they usually "keep an ear to the ground" to learn about requirements for foreign participants in resource or infrastructure development, and then test the feasibility of prospective operations before tendering or bidding.

China's Belt and Road Initiative, announced in 2013, is a good example of the outcome of an opportunity identification process that started with visioning, since there was no one asking for such an initiative or offering China an opportunity to partake. China was seeking ways to increase global influence, economic growth and access to commodities, and planners envisioned a way to meet all three mission parameters. Intelligence indicated that the Initiative would have favourable reception among a significant number of prospective trading partner countries, and hence that overall the idea was feasible.

Critical Factors

The organisation or part thereof has defined an objective. This could be positive, such as fulfilling a new growth opportunity, or it could be defensive, such as holding a position in the face of pressure or opposition. To achieve the objective, the organisation needs to know what enablers, obstacles, friends and adversaries could significantly affect its progress. Intelligence identifies these critical factors (which we use to include relevant actors as well), and maps them against the impending journey to guide the organisation towards advantages and away from harm and impediments. Intelligence then monitors these factors to keep the organisation's awareness of them up to date.

Note that this holistic function of intelligence can apply to different tiers of objectives. For example, a company's vision is an objective in itself. Strategy formulation assesses critical factors to discern how to advance towards the vision, and this results in strategic objectives, which in turn are planned with an eye to their own critical factors. It is safe to say that at any level, whenever there is a conscious objective, there are critical factors involved in achieving it, although this is more apparent in dynamic or volatile contexts and when the stakes are higher.

A peace-keeping mission provides a basic example. The objective is to maintain a truce and reduce violence. Intelligence examines factors that could affect the capabilities of the peace-keeping forces, such as climate, terrain and logistics routes. It also discerns potential spoilers, such as groups who benefit from a conflict economy, and supporters, such as community leaders trying to end violence in their areas. These and other factors are accounted for in operational planning to increase the chance of mission fulfilment. Political risk intelligence exercises for foreign operations that make it past the approval stage are actually similar in shape, although a peace-keeping operation's core activity is itself a type of risk management, whereas political risk management supports a different core activity.

Foresight

The organisation recognises that its technological and market environment is so dynamic that if it does not start planning new capabilities now, it will be a latecomer in the future. It needs to have a sense of how the environment might evolve in order to seed a portfolio of innovation options. On another level, the organisation is trying to decide if a particular investment is worth the financial and opportunity cost, and needs an idea of how relevant external success factors might play out in the future. Finally, an operation or investment could be approved but its success depends on proactive adaptation to change. Again, a peek into the future helps with planning.

In each instance, intelligence carries out foresight exercises to provide at least a sense of how relevant factors could evolve. Sometimes straight-line forecasting is appropriate, but dealing with longer time horizons or more dynamic or volatile contexts, intelligence applies horizon scanning, alternative futures, scenario analysis and other tools that can account for uncertainty. These derive not specific predictions, rather hazy possible futures that at least reveal the magnitude and direction of potential change. Intelligence also develops observable indicators of each general possibility to enable users to foresee which directions seem to be manifesting, and periodically revisits the analysis to retest and modify hypotheses as uncertainties clarify with time.

As an example, oil and gas companies heavily rely on scenarios about the future of supply and demand. Just speaking of oil, as reserves become scarcer companies need to be ready with new technologies for more challenging extraction, and as renewables supplant fossil fuels, companies need to be prepared for a well-timed shift to new energy offerings. Both trends are uncertain, and innovation takes time. In specific oil and gas operations, which can last for a decade or more, companies need to understand how a given country environment could evolve before investing and need to be able to align with impending changes in the environment once they have committed to a project.

Actors and Interests

The organisation faces a range of sometimes contradictory social, investor and regulator expectations, and needs to understand the different interests it is dealing with in order to avoid friction that could result in disputes or liability. In other cases, it needs partners, staff and suppliers for a specific project, but prior analysis has indicated considerable overlap between the local business scene and political and criminal interests. The organisation needs to understand the interests and connections of prospects before it can decide whom to engage with. Intelligence provides stakeholder analysis, on the one hand, to better understand the positions and influence of interested actors and thus enable coordinated engagement and communications planning. On the other hand, when nuanced insight is required, intelligence conducts due diligence investigations to unearth any potential red flags around political and criminal ties so the organisation can avoid potentially damaging associations and select genuine and legitimate partners.

While companies routinely undertake due diligence and, though to a lesser extent, stakeholder analysis, humanitarian NGOs in post-conflict environments provide a good example of the use of actor-specific intelligence. Because of lingering tensions between ex-conflict actors, NGOs need to be careful to have a balanced impact, and this means knowing local groups and their sensitivities in detail. They also often need local partners, and in divided and weakly governed environments local NGOs can be formed to serve particular factional interests, including by diverting aid. Taking on the wrong local partner can be disastrous, and international NGOs often carry out vetting to ensure that local partners are legitimate and share universal humanitarian values.

Warning

The organisation understands that certain negative, indeed catastrophic, contingencies are inherent in their context or operating environment. Such a contingency might not manifest as an actual event or action, but if it did, then the organisation would need to be prepared to withstand its effects. The flip side is that a massive potential opportunity might arise, and the organisation would not be able to exploit it without prior preparation. Maintaining a prepared stance is too costly over a long period of time; thus, the organisation needs to know in advance if and when the contingency might arise. Intelligence establishes a warning system which monitors observable indicators of the contingency's shift from latent to manifesting. The organisation can adjust its stance in line with indications, thereby balancing the cost of preparedness with the likelihood of occurrence.

The nuclear stand-off between the USSR and the US provides clear examples of warning systems. Both sides had an array of indicators of a nuclear attack and constantly gathered intelligence on them. As more indicators shifted from green towards red, nuclear launch preparations went through more layers of safeguards towards a hair-trigger stance. Evacuation planning is another clear warning system example. An NGO or company working in a conflict or disaster-prone environment will not keep three large aircraft and a fleet of trucks on permanent standby. Instead, it increases preparation in line with indications of a severe event or escalation of conflict, thereby not wasting resources but ultimately being ready for evacuation if need be. In another vein altogether, seasoned short-sellers do not keep a pile of money on hand; rather, they keep an eye out for stock bubbles, and when they see one starting to form, they borrow to be ready to exploit it.

Risk

In any given initiative and even in routine operations, things can go wrong, and the organisation can incur harm. Much of what could go wrong is par for course given human and technological limitations, but there are also actual hazards, or potential harmful occurrences that are not inherent in the organisation's normal activities and which cannot be managed just by routine quality control. The organisation needs to understand what these are in order to minimise loss and setbacks. With only finite resources, including human attention spans, risks also need to be prioritised so that risk management focuses on the more serious ones. While the organisation will examine risk within its own boundaries, intelligence provides an assessment of risks that arise in the external environment. Intelligence identifies relevant risk factors, such as natural disasters, crime, economic downturns or regulatory change, then examines the potential intersection of these with the organisation's exposures to derive risks. Risks are then assessed for severity, and priorities take centre stage in risk management planning, while less important risks are monitored and managed by minor adjustments to routine processes.

A useful example of risk assessment comes from civil engineering. A company is tasked to design an office complex, and in so doing it needs to consider risks to structural integrity. Risk factors include the quality of materials and of the actual construction, but even before deciding what the structure should look like and be made of, the company needs to know environmental risk factors. These include weather and earthquake patterns, terrorism and other armed violence, the potential for gas explosions or industrial accidents in the vicinity, and the structure of the ground including earth stability and the potential for sink holes. The company learns about each factor and relates the findings to the initial building concept to derive and assess risks. The final building plan includes blast damage protection, earthquake-proofing and an encompassing traffic barrier. Thus, risk intelligence led to tangible design changes that made the overall level of risk to the structure acceptable.

Threat

A critical factor analysis indicates that the organisation faces hostile or adversarial actors, in other words threats, defined as actors with potential or actual capability and intent to cause harm (note again the difference from the use of "threat" in SWOT and similar casual usages). In a purely business context, threats might be competitors in one's core segments. In a military setting it would be opposing forces and their allies. For a company or NGO in a complex environment, it might be terrorist, crime and insurgent groups that target foreign organisations. Most organisations face the risk of opportunistic cyber-attack, but some are also targeted by specific threats. The organisation needs to understand the threats in the relevant domain or environment in order to plan effective avoidance, protection and deterrence. It also needs to understand what threats might do, in other words the risks arising from threat behaviour, to be able to prepare against specific actions. Intelligence conducts a threat assessment, identifying potential hostile actors and prioritising them according to capability and intent. Intelligence also derives risks from threat activity so that the organisation can plan not only threat management but also threat incident mitigation and recovery. Finally, a monitoring system tracks threat activity to provide warning of an attack.

Most companies do some kind of threat assessment, particularly for cyber-threats. A clean-cut example of the use of threat intelligence, though, would come from an international hotel chain in a city with some track record for terrorist attacks on foreign targets, for example Karachi or Jakarta. The regional or country security director would scan for relevant groups and learn their behaviour, including targeting patterns and modus operandi. This would feed into a capability-intent framework to prioritise threats, and their potential actions become threat-related risks. Security plans derived from intelligence aim at plugging vulnerabilities and mitigating risks. Plans could include tailored perimeter and access controls, structural strengthening, incident response capabilities, and evacuation and medical response planning. Threat incident planning would include business continuity and crisis communications. Monitoring would indicate how to adjust security and crisis management measures in line with changing threat profiles.

It is worth noting that all of the seven roles of intelligence outlined above can have a political risk aspect, and the socio-political environment is a potential target of each role. Thus, we need to take the "risk" in political risk in a somewhat general sense. Political risk intelligence can take different forms depending on the concern and context, and is not just bound to the risk assessment role.

There is a dual opportunity and risk persona to intelligence. It can help to identify opportunities while at the same time looking for holes in ideas and busting assumptions that do not stack up. It can help to make initiatives more feasible, but still brings attention to the downsides. It can help to identify allies and partners, but it also warns about possible ill-intentions. If intelligence were a person, he or she would be invested in the success of the organisation, but also somewhat detached from enthusiastic idea-generation, at least mildly sceptical about any proposed initiative, and highly attuned to the fact there is a wider world out there that is not always sympathetic. Without intelligence, life might be fun for a while, but inevitably enthusiasm alone would lead the organisation into a quagmire. Intelligence thus sounds indispensable, and this would seem to indicate that more is better. But can there be too much intelligence, or can it have too big a role? The next section considers this question.

Limits

To help set the scene, years ago, as a strategic analyst intern in HP's business desktop computing division, the author heard the first-hand story of the development of the e-PC, a very small desktop computer (just the box) that saved space, could be carried in a briefcase, and made office moves or reconfigurations a logistical breeze. This became a big seller, and HP remained the market leader in small desktops for some time. The e-PC was not the outcome of market research or competitive analysis. A handful of engineers were playing on their own time, and made the prototype before senior management even knew about it. It did not take much investment to get to that point, but it still took some, particularly in human resources as the side project became something of an obsession for the people involved. According to established process, regular innovation workshops gave people a chance to put forward ideas, and the ideas earning higher initial scores went through a validation stage, which was in effect an intelligence exercise aimed at testing assumptions and feasibility. Had the e-PC followed that route, some months down the road it *might* have had development approval, and by then the e-PC team would have become somewhat bloated and bureaucratic by comparison to its original renegade geek squad.

In their 1998 work, *Strategy Safari*, Mintzberg, Ahlstrand and Lampel devote Chapter 7 to what they call the "learning school", one of several perspectives on strategy formulation covered in the book (Mintzberg, Ahlstrand, & Lampel, 1998). The chapter reviews management research which indicates that strategy and its implementation are actually the collective result of many people trying to do their own jobs more effectively without necessarily thinking about the big picture. The result is not chaos, rather aggregate learning by doing which in time leads to organisational evolution in line with what seems to work best. Detailed, assessment-driven planning and execution, then, is not the only way that successful companies innovate and grow. Given the link between strategy formulation and intelligence, these indications are germane to a consideration of the limits of intelligence. First, we explore some issues with intelligence overload, looking at both intensive upfront intelligence processes and intelligence monitoring. Then we consider the question of appropriate balance.

Heavily front-loading intelligence on a place or situation before deciding to try something, or exactly how to try something, can be problematic. It takes a while, and from the start of an intelligence process to its conclusion, the relevant situation might have changed. If the situation has not changed by the end of the intelligence exercise, it probably will soon enough after the initiative is underway, and over-reliance on upfront insight can lead people astray later on. Second, no amount of estimation can catch how an experience will actually play out, because companies are change agents themselves, and learning and adaptation are not accounted for in front-loaded insight. Deliberation that tries to account for every detail and contingency can simply be oppressive, eroding shared urgency and momentum. Excessive insight and commensurate fine-tuned planning can force front-line managers to "paint by numbers" at the expense of exercising experience-based problem-solving. Finally, intelligence is only useful when it is clear and oriented to action. It stops being intelligence when it becomes information overload or a library of complex models, and this easily happens when one fixates on gaining ample prior knowledge.

Similarly, imposing nuanced and extensive intelligence monitoring systems on an initiative or operation can be constraining if people are expected to routinely read them and act on changing indicators. If people are not really expected to, then such systems are just costly window-dressing. Detailed monitoring systems, as a cross-check on experience-based learning and adaptation, can in effect become the management of management, with the intelligence team acting as de facto shadow government. As with upfront intelligence, there is the problem of information overload and the reversion of intelligence to data and stored information when it becomes too much for the relevant people to take in and make sense of in the context of their day-to-day jobs. The problem becomes similar to rogue ERM – either one takes it all seriously and spends the whole day "acting on intelligence" or one gets on with the job while extensive information dashboards just take up space on a server.

The above might overstate the case, but it is not that far off from real misalignments in many international companies. Planning processes can require insight on myriad factors and indicators when in fact only some are relevant to a given initiative. Experienced managers often sense what the critical questions will be, so in addition to the box-ticking intelligence, which they might barely use, they commission targeted drill-down reports from external experts. Intelligence specialists, meanwhile, can be fixated on their own trade and subjects, churning out voluminous and nuanced insights or dashboards without really knowing how they will be used or what their impact could, or should, be. The worst, yet not uncommon, combination is processes that enforce intelligence usage, and intelligence outputs that do not align with meaningful concerns or actionable questions.

As an illustrative anecdote, the author was once responsible for reviewing an analyst team's report on a country, for a powerplant client. By the time I had hacked my way through two-thirds of it, I had to wonder why the client did not just buy two or three academic books on the place for a minor fraction of the cost. I finally asked the person who sold the project if this was really what the client had asked for, and apparently it did indeed "tick all the boxes". Some process in the client company required this *information*, but I could not see how any specific person or team could use it to make a decision or how it could substantively change what was already planned. In another case, involving stakeholder identification and analysis, the brief stipulated a standard framework that did not discriminate whatsoever between what, or who, was more or less relevant. The suggestion of a screening stage to focus on the most pertinent actors was met with a shrug. The final results were like a who's who for the country, and likewise it was hard to see how more than a few elements could have been useful for planning (going beyond the brief we did include a section on actionable findings, but this only referred back to a small part of the overall results). There are often opportunities to take shortcuts in an exercise for more focused, relevant results, but because of cookie-cutter processes and anxiety about compliance with these, it can be all or nothing. Intelligence thus gets lost in a sea of information, the sheer volume of which can be off-putting to would-be users.

There are some tried and tested ways of reducing the intelligence burden, or in other words making it more intensive only where it is most required. Going back to the learning school of strategy, some companies have a new venture process designed to seed ideas that could one day develop into major innovations or strategic initiatives, but which are initially approached as learning experiments. This can even apply to new country entry projects, when a small subsidiary has low- or no-profit targets and plenty of time to learn the environment through direct interaction before scaling up. In both cases, low-risk learning by doing precludes the need for detailed prior insight. Another approach is to pre-screen an initiative for the degree of intelligence it requires. Lower-risk, lower-stakes initiatives are assigned less intensive intelligence exercises and only periodic monitoring, while more significant undertakings get a full intelligence package. This is actually used for political risk intelligence among some extractive and infrastructure firms, who set intelligence requirements based on an initial top-level assessment of risk in the target country. Finally, efficient investment or project screening processes apply only top-level intelligence in early feasibility testing, saving more intensive exercises for initiatives that become more serious prospects. As noted earlier, even in specific intelligence exercises, a screening stage could be used to focus intelligence on more important factors. These are only some ways to limit intelligence overload in general while still getting the goods where they matter most.

As the roles outlined earlier would indicate, intelligence is valuable to an organisation, and even a matter of survival in some contexts. If a company does not pay much attention to it, initiatives are vulnerable to foreseeable mistakes and disruptions, as well as to group-think and hype. The converse, heavily embedding intelligence into management processes, is safer, but as this section suggests, it is not ideal either. When intelligence becomes a box-ticking exercise or takes on a life of its own in absence of genuine needs, it loses its actionable character and becomes just information. For a process or output to be intelligence, by definition it needs to be linked to decisions and actions. As long as that link is consciously maintained, the amount of intelligence flowing in an organisation and for specific initiatives will be proportionate to actual needs. Thus, rather than managing intelligence overload, another way of stating the challenge is how to maintain a clear distinction between intelligence as actionable insight and guidance, and information which might or might not be required or used.

This is a fitting handover to Part II on the baseline political risk intelligence process, which early on will discuss the challenge of scoping an intelligence exercise for actionable insight and minimal clutter. We will return to the subject of intelligence in Part III, when the focus will be on more practical questions about intelligence management and quality control.

REFERENCES

Mintzberg, H., Ahlstrand, B., & Lampel, J. (1998). *Strategy Safari*. London: FT Prentice Hall.

Part II

The Baseline Intelligence Exercise

Part I introduced the core concepts within the theme of political risk intelligence for operations in complex environments. This part of the book brings these together in an intelligence process that addresses the question, "What are the socio-political challenges that we could face and what could we do about them?" This is the most holistic political risk question for a country operation, and the process that answers it is likewise holistic, examining both the terrain and stakeholders, how the political environment could evolve, the issues that the company could face and how it could avoid or manage them. We call this process the baseline intelligence exercise.

It is baseline in that it provides a strong foundation for political risk management planning, but it would still need follow-up nuanced insight on specific variables and challenges that it identifies. One can see it as providing the strategic hilltop perspective. After that, specialists might have to go down for a close-up look at features that the hilltop observer sketched. In practice, the outputs of a baseline exercise are usually reviewed by a range of management functions, such as security, legal or community relations, who look more closely at the issues that affect their particular piece of the political risk management puzzle, while the full set of findings continue to provide a joined-up perspective that enables coordinated planning. The country or project manager is the one who keeps the big picture front of mind so that they can ensure that different political risk management initiatives align and have strategic coherence. Thus, the results of the baseline exercise are like a large-scale map. It helps to plot the journey and navigate, but smaller-scale maps will need to augment it along the way.

As the coming chapter discusses, the baseline exercise is a thought process rather than a template, and there are different design choices depending on the stage and character of the foreign operation. By way of comprehensive illustration, in this part of the book we will be applying one particular framework comprised of several stages, but while it does directly apply to certain contexts, it should also be regarded as a set of reference points that can guide the development of tailored approaches.

Note that within Part II, Chapters 6 through 10 are stages in the baseline exercise, while Chapters 5 and 11 are supporting and supplementary material. Part II proceeds as follows.

DOI: 10.1201/9781003149125-7

Chapter 5 provides an overview of the baseline intelligence exercise, including when and why it happens, considerations in its design, and how the overall process works.

Chapter 6, the first stage in the baseline exercise, develops the context and focus of subsequent stages. It is mainly about how to go from a blank initial slate to relevant variables and intelligence targets.

In Chapter 7, terrain analysis derives specific challenges for an operation from broad factors in the environment.

Chapter 8 examines stakeholder analysis, which reveals key socio-political stakeholders, challenges and opportunities in stakeholder relationships, and what drives the principal stakeholder attitudes to the operation. This is the most nuanced chapter, because understanding specific actors is an intensive undertaking that goes well beyond just learning about broad dynamics and interests.

Chapter 9 moves directly into top-level political risk management planning, on the assumption that more detailed implementation planning will need to follow. Planning could actually follow the next stage, scenario analysis, but we bring it directly subsequent to terrain and stakeholder analysis to maintain continuity of focus, and add in long-range planning once scenario analysis is complete.

Chapter 10, as noted, presents scenario analysis, which looks beyond the foreseeable future to see how the wider operating environment could change, and how an operation can plan its adaptation.

The baseline exercise concludes with Chapter 10, but there will be a need for other types and levels of intelligence before and during a foreign operation. Thus, Chapter 11 examines several supplementary intelligence exercises.

We noted in the book's Introduction that two hypothetical cases will be used for illustration in this part of the book. Their application begins in Chapter 6 and continues through to Chapter 10. They are not introduced beforehand, rather they are developed through their usage within the wider process.

5 Baseline Intelligence Exercise Overview

This chapter introduces the baseline intelligence exercise and provides an overview of the process by which it is undertaken. First, we address what the exercise is for, and when it is useful. Then we examine some of the considerations that underpin the design of the exercise. These include a fundamental problem in intelligence targeting, and the strengths and weakness of three common approaches to strategic political risk intelligence. Finally, we outline the specific approach that we will apply. This outline forms a roadmap for Chapters 6 through 10, each of which is a stage of the baseline exercise.

WHAT, WHEN AND WHY

The baseline exercise is a research and analytical process that results in insights that managers can apply to make an operation safer and more resilient, and to safeguard its legitimacy and integrity. The relatively comprehensive variant that we will use results in knowledge about the socio-political terrain, stakeholders, longer-term change scenarios and relevant implications for the operation within and across each of those elements. This is not the only variant that makes sense, depending on the phase and attributes of the operation, but any baseline exercise would provide a holistic foundation for political risk management in the given operational context. This makes it distinct from tactical or functional intelligence. For example, a renewable energy company might know that there is contention within a government over how much to subsidise the development of renewables. The company needs to know how this debate might play out and the implications either way. That would be a tactical exercise that only affects one aspect of the operation. Similarly, the corporate social responsibility (CSR) manager might hire an anthropologist to map out clan and tribal relations in the operating area to better know how to balance local social investment. That insight might be useful for other functions, but it is primarily CSR-specific intelligence. By contrast, the baseline exercise looks at the whole operation within its socio-political environment.

The main reason for a baseline exercise is that however much tactical and functional intelligence activity is going on, it is unlikely to add up to a total intelligence picture of the operation. If a country manager put all tactical and functional reports on the desk and drew out and aggregated key findings, he or she would still not have a full basis for a political risk management strategy and the coordination of relevant activities. As noted in the Iran example in the prelude, the US constructor had no shortage of insight, and various people and functions were becoming specialists on Iran in their own right. But the silos of expertise never joined up, and even if they had, it would have taken an explicit effort, and probably some additional research, to connect the dots for coherent planning. The baseline exercise provides this foundation, and forms the bigger, integrated picture which encompasses, at a top level at least, the tactical and functional issues being addressed in various corners. It is only as extensive or detailed as it needs to be, but it is always holistic.

There are several points in an operation's inception and execution at which a baseline exercise can be valuable if not critical.

One is when an operation is still under consideration. We discussed intelligence overload, and a full baseline project can be overkill to assess feasibility. There are options for more concise, quicker political risk feasibility assessments, which we consider in Chapter 11. But if the decision has particularly high stakes, a more detailed and comprehensive assessment might be required. For example, a branded IT manufacturer might be trying to diversify Asian operations to become less dependent on its presence in Taiwan and China, and after selecting a few options for regional hubs, it will need to make a very big decision. It would benefit from visualising an operation in each prospective location and conducting a top-level, hypothetical but realistic baseline exercise for each. The simulated country presence that seems to go most smoothly would be the best bet. The exercise would also inform the company of the issues it needs to consider in scoping and planning its new regional hub, early on before critical decisions have already been made.

Another pre-entry scenario is tendering for significant public sector contracts. Imagine, for example, a company looking at a tender for a powerplant in a south Asian country. A quick feasibility assessment might help them to decide whether or not to bid in the first place. If they proceed to bid, though, the tender itself needs to take political risk into account, since it will set contract stipulations which would provide at least some political risk safeguards. If, instead of going straight to tendering, the government customer is initially asking for expressions of interest and preliminary discussions, the company can factor political risk into financing and partnership considerations that would create the eventual tendering entity. When a company recognises it as such, the tender phase, or its expression of interest prelude, is actually a crucial moment in political risk management, and a baseline exercise can inform early decisions that will have implications across the life of the operation.

As an aside, in both of the above instances, if early on the company has a solid understanding of the challenges it could face, it can negotiate an eventual political risk insurance policy tailored to its own concerns and required safeguards, and not just based on the insurer's assessment. For example, a construction company took an African government to arbitration over a payment dispute. The government failed to provide an arbitrator to the process and its intentions were unclear. Normally, the insurer, in this instance the US Overseas Private Investment Corporation (OPIC, the predecessor of the US Development Finance Corporation), would have acted on a non-payment claim only if the company won arbitration, and there was still a chance of that happening. But a negotiated policy clause defined the government's non-participation as an "unresolved dispute", a trigger to a claim. OPIC was thus obliged to act on the claim even before the case had been heard. Knowing that the government in question might stonewall in any dispute process or try to drag one out, the company had sought to cover its bases, even if the cost of insurance was slightly higher as a result.

Pre-entry and during an operation's initial launch, when important decisions remain to be taken and the company needs to quickly come to grips with its new environment, are perhaps the archetypal occasions for a baseline assessment. Ideally, decisions to that point, as discussed above, would have been based on relevant political risk intelligence. But starting an operation, and the first presence on the ground, is when a nuanced fit with the socio-political environment needs to be shaped. This can involve, for example, decisions around specific locations, CSR, local hiring and suppliers, security, government and business relations, public communications, business continuity and integrity assurance. Political risk intelligence that preceded entry will be relevant, but it will need to be updated and expanded for the latest concept of operations, and for the reality of day-to-day operations with people on the ground.

During an operation, significant shifts in the socio-political environment, or in the profile and exposures of the operation, can mean that the company's political risk picture needs to be reformulated. In the last chapter we discussed the relationship between monitoring and intensive intelligence projects. Monitoring can be sufficient to remain up to date between baseline exercises, which themselves run on approximately a 12- to 18-month cycle (we discuss time frames later on). However, if monitoring detects major changes, then a fresh baseline exercise can be required to ensure alignment with an emerging new context. Previously mentioned, for example, was a project the author worked on for a company in Algeria, which was trying to adapt to very different circumstances following the 1990s civil war. Similarly, if an operation enters a new phase, for example if it moves from a representative office to sales and service, or from design to construction, its attributes can change so much that prior assessments seem more suited to an entirely different operation. Again, a new baseline exercise can help to maintain alignment between the operation and its environment.

A final occasion might be if the company is facing problems and cannot identify the source of them. In Chapter 11, we examine problem diagnosis, which can help if the problem is relatively discrete. If we refer back to the AES Georgia case, though, the problems were numerous, serious and opaque. The author worked on a similar, if far less dire, case when the client company seemed to be standing still with respect to permits, disliked by state media, distrusted by its state company partner, and facing friction with its local workforce. When nothing seems to be going well, a baseline exercise can re-build the political risk intelligence picture from scratch, ideally with no preconceptions or mental clutter, and in so doing it stands a good chance of explaining the roots of the issues, which are often connected. In Chapter 1, we mentioned entanglement in a deteriorating situation as a broad manifestation of political risk. A baseline exercise can help to untangle the picture, and thereby inform a plan to untangle the operation, or indeed the decision of whether or not to leave.

Not each of the above situations needs a baseline exercise. It depends on the context, specifically the stakes involved, the relative complexity of the environment in question, how much early decisions could affect the operation later on and the company's uncertainties around mission-critical questions. The one phase when the baseline exercise would almost always apply, at least in our context of complex environments, is entry and launch, when an operation moves into its temporary home.

One point that might be apparent from the above is that political risk intelligence can, and often should, accompany the steps of the country operation planning process, from conception through to launch and execution. Deciding where to go or whether or not to tender takes some political risk insight. Then as the company moves closer to an entry decision and an actual presence, intelligence becomes progressively more nuanced. At any given point, there could be a body of prior intelligence that an exercise can draw on. But a caveat is in order. One attribute of the baseline intelligence exercise which makes it particularly credible and useful is that it is "baseline", in that it starts from a blank slate, without preconceptions and without just welding together previous assessments from within the last year or so. From initial interest in a country to an actual presence, both the socio-political environment and the operational concept can significantly change. Tacking more nuance onto, or just updating, old assessments can quickly result in a disaggregated hodgepodge, like a book with an interesting title, but that turns out to be mainly addendums that actually contradict parts of the core text. Prior intelligence can certainly be used, but like any other source it needs to be assessed for currency and relevance, and at any point in time the exercise needs to be premised on the latest operational concept and socio-political situation.

DESIGN CONSIDERATIONS

Prior to introducing the approach that we will apply, this section examines a few basic options in designing a baseline, or strategic, political risk intelligence exercise. These could be useful in themselves in specific circumstances, but the broader aim is to introduce some of the considerations which shape the approach that we will be using. First, though, to set the scene we examine a basic challenge that affects nearly any design choice in strategic intelligence assessment. This has been known as breadth versus focus, or the problem of "unknown unknowns".

A BASIC PROBLEM

It is uncontentious to suggest that an ideal assessment framework would point as quickly and concisely as possible to pertinent factors, actors and issues. Casting a wide net and then sifting through the catch for relevant insights can take too long and end up burying important findings in tangent but irrelevant information, known as "noise". However, if we cast too narrow a net, we will catch something, but it probably will not be the only relevant material. The problem is akin to the one of "unknown unknowns" made famous by US Defence Secretary Donald Rumsfeld in 2002. If, perhaps on the basis of over-confidence, we focus too narrowly too early, we risk missing relevant variables that we did not even know existed. But addressing that problem by looking at *everything* is not feasible either.

An example helps to illustrate the challenge. In this case, the problem that affected the company working in Libya was the worst one they had prior to the 2011 revolution and conflict. Yet it was a very nuanced and obscure issue that would have been hard to catch without first knowing how or why the factors around it could be relevant. Note that the case has been simplified and somewhat adjusted to preserve the privacy of the company involved.

In Libya in 2006, an international consumer food manufacturer had a local plant and distribution operation run by a third-country franchisee. He relied on his relationship to one of Qaddafi's sons for help in negotiating the country's byzantine bureaucracy. Another son had a personal rivalry with the first one, and the plant became a pawn in their dispute. The rival son ordered security forces under his control to blockade and close the plant and it remained inactive for several months. He also made death threats against the franchisee, forcing him to flee back to his country. Eventually, mediation by one of Qaddafi's daughters healed the rift and operations resumed, but the pause was costly, and the episode was dangerous.

It is not known what kind of assessment the company did, but a typical Libya political risk analysis at the time might have focused on factors such as FDI policy changes, corruption, human rights issues, bureaucratic delays, labour relations, jihadist terrorism, a coup and regime behaviour that might have triggered new sanctions. Just for the sake of illustration and without getting into the nuts and bolts, one can assume that the company's analysis examined these factors. It is unlikely that this focus, however relevant it was, would have provided much useful insight to help avoid or plan for the issue that arose. The problem was too nuanced and too far outside the "usual suspects".

Next, imagine that an analyst felt that the country, being so new to non-oil and non-infrastructure FDI, was ripe for a wide variety of challenges, and he or she cast a very wide net that included family rivalries among myriad other factors. This could have caught the rivalry factor, but it could well have been buried amongst many others and not seen as especially important. In other words, the analysis yielded too much noise for any one sound to stand out. Note that in the Statoil Algeria case in Chapter 1, a similar problem arose: the relevant variables were caught, but crammed alongside too much else to be particularly noteworthy.

Finally, perhaps a maverick analyst decided that all of the usual factors were too run-of-the-mill, and that the analysis should just drill down on dynamics within the eccentric Qaddafi regime. After all, it had a hand in almost anything that went on in Libya. This might well have caught family rivalries and led to an investigation of their implications, but potentially at the expense of other factors that could well have caused problems too, such as a labour strike or a terrorist attack near the plant. The challenge of scoping in this example is illustrated in Figure 5.1.

There are ways to catch relevant but obscure variables, and of course in this case one could have done a stakeholder analysis too, or looked at political risk from different angles. But the trade-off between coverage and focus is always a challenge, arising largely from time, attention and resource limitations, not just on the intelligence team's side, but also among intelligence consumers or users.

We now turn to examine three basic reference points in assessment design, and how they compare in terms of this trade-off and other considerations. With growing awareness of the value of sustainability insights in foreign operations, social stakeholder analysis is often a concomitant of political risk assessment, but it is usually undertaken separately, and for the sake of illustration we will just focus on explicit political risk approaches. These are not standard frameworks with specific labels, but they do catch common ways that baseline, or strategic, political risk assessments are done. In practice, there would be more steps in each of these, but what follows suffices to outline their basic logic and the main distinctions between them.

BOTTOM-UP APPROACH

The bottom-up approach generates comprehensive information about the socio-political environment and afterwards extracts relevant insights for the operation. Initially, the operation's attributes, exposures and profile would only be sketched at a top level for a broad research direction. Then the intelligence team would list the variables that they think could be relevant, or they might have a

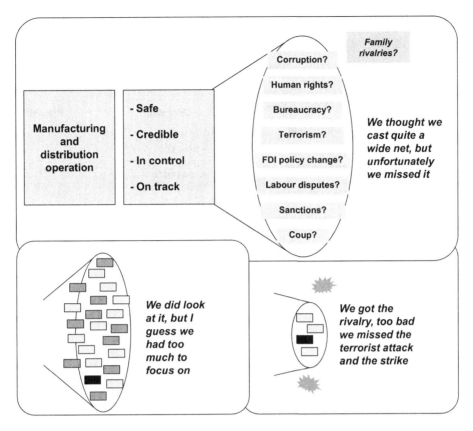

FIGURE 5.1   How wide a net to cast?

standard list of factors which is adaptable to different contexts. The team then develops a detailed characterisation of each factor. This approach might or might not have an explicit division between terrain factors and stakeholders, and in practice it usually phrases stakeholders as factors (e.g., labour unions would be covered under labour activism). Once the socio-political environment has been broadly illuminated, the team goes back to the operation in somewhat more detail, looking at how it fits into the picture. Implications and specific potential issues, or risks, are articulated and assessed, and priorities are defined. The general bottom-up approach is depicted in Figure 5.2, and note that factors therein, while typical, are purely hypothetical for illustration.

Starting from a sizeable swathe of information about a country, the bottom-up approach can yield results that only indirectly address a company's actual relationship to its environment. But if consciously applied specifically because it does yield a broad perspective, it can have its uses. For one thing, it can be an exploratory method. Going back to the problem of unknown unknowns, in the absence of a prior understanding about a place or situation, targeting diverse aspects of it for detailed characterisation can help to develop this understanding, and might well catch variables that no one initially imagined would be relevant. In other words, this approach casts a wide net. In particularly opaque or complicated cases, perhaps a bottom-up project could actually be an initial stage that then feeds into a more targeted one. Second, this approach can provide users with a tailored education about the country they will be working in. If the written outputs are compelling and digestible, then users will gain a broad and fluid understanding of the country, and they might well draw on this at various times during their assignment if only for useful context to situations or discussions they find themselves in. A more focused problem-solving process on its own might not provide that broad fluency.

The above said, as the main or only approach to informing political risk management, the bottom-up method is not ideal. Because it takes only scant direction from operational attributes and

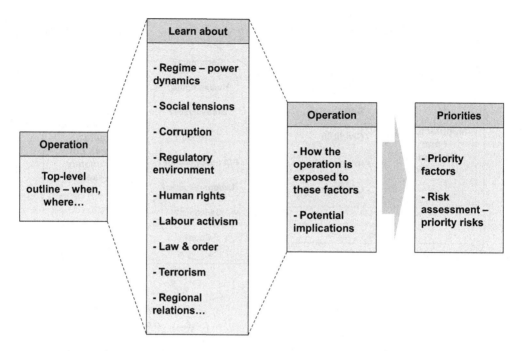

FIGURE 5.2 Bottom-up approach.

exposures before it dives into the subject matter, it lacks a clearly defined object of the exercise. Without an object, what is relevant is unclear, and the intelligence team scoops up reams of information to ensure that they catch something that matters. There is such a morass of information at the end that the priorities extracted from it necessarily come more from mental osmosis than explicit consideration, and hence tend to be fuzzy. At the same time, if the approach is oriented around risk assessment, it can generate a very large, disaggregated list of separate risks. In summary, the net is usually too wide, cast without sufficient consideration of what could matter to the operation, and the noise generated can obscure relevant findings.

In spite of its shortcomings, the bottom-up approach seems to be a very common way of conducting a baseline exercise. There are several reasons for this. In Chapter 1, we discussed the analyst-consumer gap, or how political risk experts and business managers sometimes do not share a common perspective or language. User questions can thus be phrased too broadly and analysts might not know enough about the operational side to ask narrowing and scoping questions. Another reason is that analysts can be experts in a place or phenomenon, but they might not have had much exposure to problem-solving approaches, and breaking a study down into "about the country" subject headings feels more familiar. Finally, this approach can be quick to get started and seem comfortably straightforward. There is not much up-front questioning to shape the exercise. Once it gets going, it runs until the defined topics have been covered, and only then do the analysts need to go back and check in with the users, if indeed they do not just hand over a report. The philosophy seems to be, "Before we complicate things, let's do some research and see what we have." As noted, there are occasions when a bottom-up approach is suitable at least as one step in a wider process, but on its own it is more of an information exercise than an intelligence one.

Risk Checklist Approach

The risk checklist approach posits a list of generic political risks and then undertakes research about the environment to see how each of these could manifest for the operation. The process then articulates more specific risks and assesses them for probability and impact, thereby defining priorities

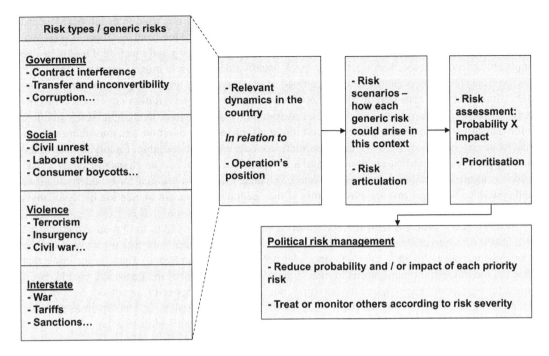

FIGURE 5.3 Risk checklist approach.

for political risk management. Conceptually this is nearly the opposite to the bottom-up approach. Rather than first developing a broad picture of the environment and then seeing what the issues might be, this approach starts with assumptions about relevant general risks and then looks at the environment to see how they might arise. Figure 5.3 depicts the checklist approach, and again this is top-level and the specific entries are hypothetical.

This approach often applies taxonomies of political risks that are based partly on a reading of the "usual suspects" that have often affected foreign operations, and partly on the specific risks insured by government and private insurers. If a company is considering using political risk insurance, it makes sense to apply the insurer's definitions for at least a part of the assessment. If some generic risks turn out not to be relevant, this is simply reflected in their rating. For example, if civil war is on the checklist and it is nearly irrelevant to the context, then any civil war risk scenario would be rated as improbable, although it would probably still get a relatively high impact score (that might seem odd for a risk that is largely irrelevant to a place, but that is the logic of this approach). Since the approach aligns quite closely with standard risk management, if political risk management recommendations are included, they tend to derive from generic risk management options such as avoidance or exposure limitation, risk transfer and sharing, and impact mitigation.

The risk checklist approach is quite widespread partly because it seems efficient, coming pre-armed with hypotheses about what could affect the organisation, and it also meshes well with ERM practices. Its effectiveness as an intelligence process depends very much on how flexible it is. If there is exploration around each risk, and a search for background factors and actors, then it can yield insights about the wider socio-political system and stakeholders relevant to the company. In other words, the analysis can connect the dots (risks) for a broader explanatory picture.

In practice, because part of the allure of this approach is that it seems like a shortcut to political risk insight, it is often applied in a rather mechanistic way. Shortcuts can be risky when trying to learn about a high-stakes and complex situation, and as the only approach to a baseline exercise, a rigid checklist approach has several shortcomings.

First, there is excessive a priori reasoning in positing a risk before even seeing what is going on in place and without context. It is unlikely that any pre-ordained list of risks would actually catch all of the nuanced factors that would be relevant in a given context. If one tried to develop a standard checklist that covered a range of types of environments, say for anything from advanced transitional economies through to weak post-conflict states, it would be very long and much in it would not be applicable to a given case. Second, the approach usually does not yield much insight on stakeholders, because stakeholders cannot be characterised as risks and hence are not explicit intelligence targets. Third, since the approach divides the analysis by each type of risk, it does not connect the dots between them to discern broader dynamics, for example ethnic tensions, that could be relevant to a wide range of potential issues. The end result might refer to aspects of ethnic tensions under various risk headings, but this is hardly a coherent picture of an important variable. Finally, as discussed in Chapter 1, assuming that every challenge a company could face can be characterised as a risk, which is a relatively discrete, estimable event or change, can fail to account for broader situations and systemic challenges that arise from a mix of factors and interests, not to mention the company's own behaviour and relationships.

In short, if the problem with the bottom-up approach is that it yields too broad a picture, the risk checklist approach has the opposite problem. The intelligence picture that it provides will be like someone cut holes in a piece of paper and held it up to a landscape. They might think that they cut the holes in the right places to make the most relevant parts of the landscape visible, but it might have been hit and miss, and the resulting image will be abstract and fragmented. Imagine, for example, that looking through the paper one sees rock through several holes. One assumes there are several rocks lying around. Take the paper away and it might turn out that there is an uneven, rocky ridge running across the landscape, a feature with broad implications for any journey.

OPERATION-CENTRIC APPROACH

This is not a common method, but the author has worked with variants of it in workshops when the company had already been in a country for a while and wanted to clarify their political risk situation and hone their political risk management approach. Between the intelligence and company teams there was already considerable country knowledge, and the operation was up and running so what was at stake was easily sketched. Even in a workshop context this still was a baseline exercise framework, and one could envision applying it to guide a more detailed research process. The approach is illustrated in Figure 5.4. There are different ways of breaking down operational assets. This loosely

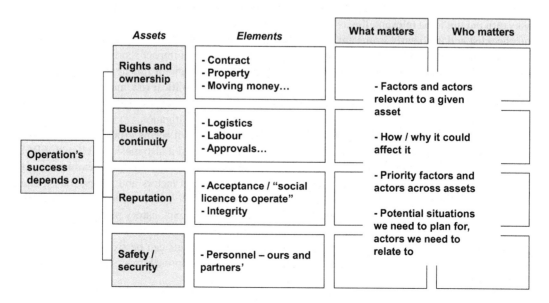

FIGURE 5.4 Operation-centric approach.

applies the framework we used in Chapter 3. Specific elements are again only illustrative and in practice can be broken down further into sub-elements.

The first premises in this approach are what the operation relies on to be successful. This is broken down into several main assets, and then each of these is broken down further to elucidate particular dependencies, or elements, which an asset relies on to remain intact and healthy overall. These are akin to critical success factors. Then for each element, but with an eye to the assets, a scan is conducted for relevant terrain factors and stakeholders. The exercise then explores how terrain dynamics and stakeholder attitudes and responses could affect a given element and in turn each main asset, and defines plausible situations that could result in harm or disruption. These become the basis of both risk management and stakeholder engagement planning. However, because the exercise develops a cross-asset perspective on factors and actors, planning includes a holistic strategic perspective and the outline of a core political risk management strategy.

The operation-centric approach has the benefit of being directly about what matters to the operation. It starts with what the operation relies on to succeed, then looks at the environment to see how these elements could be affected. Unlike the risk checklist approach, there is no prior assumption about the risks that the operation might face, and assessment is not constrained to what is in an initial checklist. The operation-centric approach could apply a conventional risk assessment to help define priority challenges, but it does not oblige the intelligence team to shape every challenge as a risk. Because the process was designed around what keeps the operation safe and effective, the outputs will not include much noise that could obscure important findings.

This is a looser process than the risk checklist, and there is more room to explore potentially relevant directions discerned along the way. Still, it shares the problem that factors and actors are at least initially parsed out according to imposed categories, in this case operational assets. For a part of the process, then, there will not be a picture of how relevant variables relate within the socio-political system, and again the view of important broader dynamics would be fragmented. In cross-asset analysis, a more holistic picture emerges, but if at least a top-level systemic picture were developed earlier, it would provide very useful context that would support interpretation throughout the whole assessment. In the aforementioned workshop settings, much was already known about the environment, but if this were not the case, the problem of initial lack of context would be more acute. Thus, while this approach is much more focused than the bottom-up one, it could actually benefit from having some bottom-up thinking at an early stage.

Another potential problem is combining terrain and stakeholder analysis. These are quite distinct. Terrain dynamics occur independently of the company's presence, and when the company drops into the terrain, it gets affected by these dynamics just like anyone else there. Stakeholders, on the other hand, are only such in relation to the operation, and their attitudes and responses are partly shaped by it. Stakeholder assessment is more nuanced and needs more prior understanding of the environment. Thus, it is useful to stage an assessment from terrain to stakeholders. This not only provides insight on the socio-political situation that drives much stakeholder behaviour, but the terrain stage can be partly tailored to identify relevant actors, since it will already be discerning some socio-political players within national and local dynamics.

As noted earlier, each of three basic ways of framing the baseline exercise discussed above is only intended as reference points, and in practice there are variations and more steps in each. For example, most baseline exercises also include scenario analysis, usually after the core assessment. For purposes here, however, they suffice to illustrate some of the considerations that go into the design of an effective baseline exercise. It cannot try to cover everything and needs some initial focus, or it can yield fuzzy results and excessive noise. It cannot assume too much too early, or it risks missing some important variables. It should provide some wider contextual understanding early on so that the intelligence team has a sense of the bigger picture as it proceeds to discern specific potential challenges. Finally, trying to do too much at the same time can be confusing, and it makes sense to stage an analysis from general to nuanced, and in our context this means moving from terrain to stakeholder analysis. These indications inform the design of the process that we will apply in Chapters 6 to 10. The next section provides an introduction to this process.

ELEMENTS AND PROCESS

It is useful to begin with what the process is aiming for, thinking backwards from the results and then looking at how they are obtained. For example, putting oneself in the shoes of someone managing a construction, extraction, manufacturing or services operation in a challenging country in Africa, Central Asia or the Middle East, I might want to know the following.

First, I would be interested in the general character of the country. I might have experience in other places, and I would like to know how this country was distinct in terms of overall difficulty and stability. How it got to where it is now would be useful historical context. I would like a sense of the most pressing issues that the country was facing, and the direction it seemed to be heading in. The overall character of the leadership and power structure would add useful nuance. While this general characterisation might not directly tell me what I need to do, it would give me useful interpretive background.

I would then want to know what was going on there that could directly affect the operation. The company is moving into new terrain, and I know that it will be exposed to certain conditions, trends and dynamics once it hits the ground. What these factors are, and the challenges that could derive from them, would help to shape our presence to avoid or minimise problems, and to align routine risk management and contingency planning with the more pressing potential issues.

The company will rely on certain groups and people, affect others, and represent a problem or a target for some. Who matters for the operation, their attitudes towards it, and how they could influence it are critical to how we build and manage relationships and protect ourselves. We might be able to build useful ties to some actors who could help us to fit in and learn the place. Others might become hostile if we did not know their concerns, and it would be ideal to forestall friction before it developed. We should also know if we are facing innately hostile or predatory actors, since they could do considerable damage if we did not counter their influence.

Knowing the issues and stakeholders is one thing, but I would need an idea of what to do about it. I do not want a piecemeal approach to political risk that fragments knowledge and creates silos of activity. I need a strategic, holistic approach that addresses the most complex sets of issues, while ensuring that all challenges are accounted for. I know that relationships are a big part of how we will stay resilient. Thus, plans should include stakeholder engagement, not as a separate activity, but integrated with how we manage issues and our socio-political fit.

Finally, although my immediate interest is the current stage of the operation, it would be useful to know how the whole socio-political environment could evolve over the next few years. It would give me some forewarning about potential turns for the worse, and help the operation to prepare in advance for directions that the country might take. We should also be able to quickly adapt if the overall situation seemed to be deteriorating. Conversely, if the country seemed to be changing for the better, then we could take this into account in future business planning.

The approach applied here considers all five sets of questions: context, terrain, stakeholders, medium-term planning, and scenarios and longer-term planning. The result is holistic insight from broader dynamics to nuanced interests and attitudes, and guidance for avoiding and managing potential problems. This can be regarded as the "full menu". In the author's advisory experience, in any given case not all elements need equal emphasis, and indeed no two intelligence cases have quite the same design. Thus, as we proceed, one can interpret the full baseline exercise as a holistic framework in itself, but also as a refence point for tailored project design, and as a menu of potential sub-projects that could each yield value in their own right, depending on the intelligence user's specific needs and uncertainties. That said, and to be clear, as we proceed we will be treating the elements as linked parts of a single broader process, which is depicted in Figure 5.5.

Subsequent chapters have their own introductions to each stage, but an overview helps to grasp the wider process and how the steps link together. The first stage, context and focus, is mainly about setting the direction of the assessment. This outlines the operation, including its backstory and relevant attributes, to define the thing at stake and which we seek to enable and preserve. From that

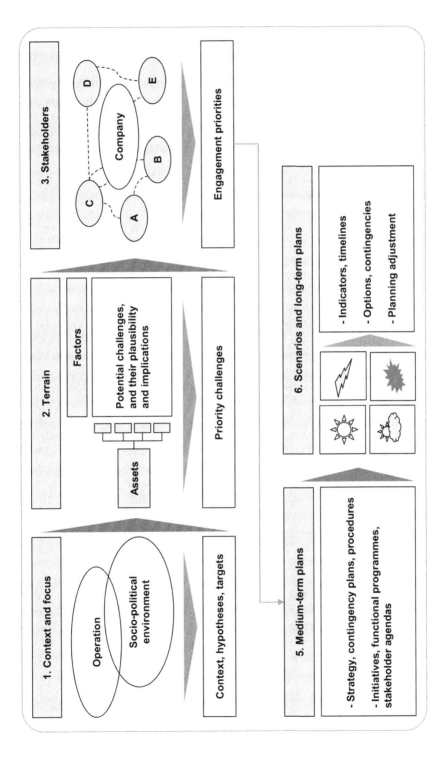

FIGURE 5.5 Baseline intelligence exercise process.

we can extrapolate very preliminary hypotheses on the kinds of variables could affect the operation. Next, we broadly characterise the socio-political system to develop contextual awareness, but then using our initial hypotheses as a guide, we scan the system for actual variables that could be significant. This results in a list of potentially relevant factors and at least general types of actors, which are our preliminary targets for the following stages. The link to the next stage, terrain analysis, is a reasonably strong sense of the terrain factors that could matter to the operation.

The context and focus stage forces us to face our initial uncertainty head on, and to put shape to ambiguity. That is uncomfortable and messy. Thus, there can be a temptation to skip or minimise it to quickly get into research on the basic subject matter, as the author has seen on too many occasions. That temptation needs to be controlled, because without investing in this explicit intelligence targeting stage, the rest of the exercise will meander, and the results will seldom constitute actionable insight.

Terrain analysis begins with factor investigation to understand the drivers and sources of a given dynamic, and how it might lead to new events or changes. We then examine the operation's intersection with each factor to discern potential challenges, both from current factor dynamics and from potential new events. Challenges are assessed for their plausibility and implications, and then, after considering other relevant variables, are prioritised to provide clear planning targets.

As noted earlier, terrain analysis precedes a focus on stakeholders because by comparison it is quite macroscopic. As such, it provides a sense of the socio-political dynamics that act on potential stakeholders, and in which they are participants. Thus, when we examine stakeholders, our knowledge of the terrain helps to explain some of the roots of their attitudes and behaviour.

We arrive at stakeholder analysis. Without terrain analysis we would not know how broader trends and pressures in the environment could affect us. But as noted earlier, terrain factors are like the weather or a landscape, in being relatively broad, observable and affecting most people exposed to them in roughly the same way. Stakeholders, by contrast, although partly shaped by terrain pressures, arise via their perception of the operation, and hence they are a far more dynamic and nuanced variable.

Stakeholder analysis starts with a detailed actor identification step, leveraging but going beyond our initial hypotheses and what we learned from terrain analysis. We then define and analyse the principal domains of stakeholder interaction, so that we have a sense of their socio-political milieus and their roles within these. Stakeholder investigation then discerns actors' potential attitudes towards the operation, and the forms and degree of influence they could bring to bear. We map stakeholder networks to understand relationships and rivalries that could affect their responses to the operation. Finally, we summarise key findings from this stage. These include a map of stakeholder attitude and influence positions as a basis for initial engagement planning, the main potential stakeholder issues that we might need to plan for, and the principal drivers of positive and negative attitudes towards the operation.

For the political risk management planning stage, there are two options in the baseline exercise. One is to do scenario analysis first, and then conduct both medium- and long-range planning as a single exercise. The other is to make the most of our working memory of terrain and stakeholder analysis by moving directly to medium-term planning, and then augment planning later on after conducting scenario analysis. Here, we take the second option, since there will be a lot of accumulated insight after terrain and stakeholder analysis, and waiting for yet another analytical stage before planning risks losing the thread. Medium- and long-range planning are in any case somewhat distinct and need not be handled in a single stage.

With the above noted, the next stage is political risk management planning. Planning begins by integrating issues according to general management approaches, to create a smaller and more coherent set of planning targets. Among these will be core issues that lie at the heart of a political risk management strategy. An initiative is formulated to address each target issue, and oversight ensures that the trade-offs and overlaps between initiatives are managed. Coordination is based on cross-functional collaboration, and the formulation of clear stakeholder agendas that integrate engagement priorities across different initiatives. While the resulting plan would still need refinement for implementation, it provides the basis for strategic coherence and senior management guidance and oversight.

In our chosen arrangement, scenario analysis is the final stage. Because scenarios are about the broader country context, scenario analysis mainly draws on terrain insights, along with a deeper consideration of influences on the current system. However, stakeholder insights can add nuance to the resulting storylines. One could argue that scenario analysis is not essential as long as we regularly redo the baseline assessment and conduct monitoring in between. However, there is still much that an operation can do in the here and now to "future-proof" itself. Knowing what the relevant preparations should be requires having a sense of how the future might unfold. Another point is that although scenarios are usually characterised as long-term systemic changes or future states, in more volatile countries instability can quickly manifest. Thus, scenarios can inform not just future-proofing, but preparation for major change in general. Plans to address scenarios augment the medium-term plans from the previous stage.

The above has outlined the stages of the baseline exercise, but we also need to address the important question of its timeframe and currency. In our context of complex emerging markets, socio-political volatility means that the resulting intelligence might only be current and reliable for approximately 12 to 18 months, even with monitoring and incremental updates. That suggests that the baseline exercise runs on a 12- to 18-month cycle; in other words it is redone every 12 to 18 months. There are exceptions to this, which we noted. To reiterate, one is that the environment changes and we need to reset our baseline perspective sooner than anticipated. The other is that the operation enters a new phase and its profile and exposures significantly change. Within the baseline exercise, scenario analysis might seem to need redoing less frequently, since it projects out to three to five years, but the assumptions on which scenarios are built also lose currency. Thus, a fresh scenario analysis is included in each baseline exercise.

In general, a significant error is assuming that once we have done the baseline exercise, we are covered for the duration of the operation and that incremental updates will suffice to keep it current. This results in an outdated intelligence picture that no amount of tweaking can rectify. It is better to have no hard intelligence at all than to plan on the basis of stale intelligence, because at least then people will not have a false sense of confidence and will likely be more observant and cautious.

There is variation in how long it takes to conduct a baseline exercise. If an operation is up and running, and the environment and operational attributes have not significantly changed, then the exercise could be relatively light. This might involve bringing together different perspectives in the organisation and among partners and external specialists to refresh the socio-political picture and revise planning. That could actually work as a series of workshops interspersed with reflection and research to clarify key uncertainties, and might only require a month or so of periodic team effort. At the other end, if the company is new to a place or is facing a very different situation, then it could require a small full-time team for three months of intensive research and analysis. If an exercise would need to be intensive, its duration should be factored into the cycle discussed above to ensure that the operation was not left without solid, current intelligence for the weeks or even months that it took to get refreshed insights.

The next five chapters in this part of the book are each a stage in the baseline exercise. Each will illuminate the overall logic of the respective stage and walk through the main steps and assessment frameworks. We need tangible grist for illustration along the way, and there were several options when considering how to approach examples. In the end, the best choice seemed to be two imaginary but realistic cases involving distinct types of operations in countries at different levels of development. Using the same cases throughout gives a better sense of how the assessment frameworks build on each other. That the cases are imaginary provides the opportunity to develop them to explore different types of issues. By using two very different modes of operation and levels of country development, we can provide a wider range of reference points from which readers can extrapolate to their own companies' contexts.

The cases will be developed through application, but we can briefly introduce them here. One represents a project mode of operation and takes place in a developing country. This envisions a European company about to launch a highway construction project which has mainly been funded by official European donors. The project is in a West African state with its capital city on the coast of the Gulf of Guinea, and its northern edge bordering the problematic Sahel subregion. The case country is a loose hybrid of Benin, Nigeria and Burkina Faso, in terms of socio-political dynamics, but these are only general reference points. The case will draw upon some of the issues relevant to a capital and labour-intensive project, government contracting and dealing with social divisions and conflict risk.

The other case sees a European IT consultancy seeking a long-term presence within a transitional country in the Middle East or North Africa (from now on we use MENA for short), loosely drawing on socio-political dynamics from both Egypt and Algeria. This case will allow for discussion around the challenges of ensconcing oneself as a new participant in a somewhat problematic business milieu, and it will highlight complications arising from the overlap between business and political players and interests. It should be stressed that while both the case companies and countries are imaginary, they are realistic and draw on actual company experiences, and real attributes of their respective regions. That said, neither case will be form a comprehensive story; rather, they will only provide a pool of general attributes and issues for illustration. The principal focus will be on the intelligence thought process.

A final preparatory note is that as we proceed into the baseline intelligence exercise, there will be occasional reference to the intelligence team, when it is useful to mention who is undertaking the exercise. We discuss who an intelligence team can be in Part III and in the book's final chapter. The point to bear in mind now is that while it can mean a team of intelligence specialists separate from operational management functions, in practice frontline managers are often part of an intelligence team. Even when they are not, as intelligence users they are still part of the overall intelligence exercise, and, more importantly, frontline managers implement political risk management based on intelligence. Thus, one should not regard what comes as being aimed just at intelligence practitioners. It is relevant to anyone who will be creating or using political risk intelligence for a specific country operation.

6 Context and Focus

The aim of the context and focus stage is to go from a blank wall to knowing enough to focus the rest of the baseline exercise on what could matter to the operation. It is almost inevitable that by the time a company needs a baseline assessment, the relevant management team will have developed some knowledge about the country and potential challenges therein, but tacit knowledge, ideas and notions do not add up to a clear picture of the right focus and questions until we sort them out and see what they mean. By the end of this stage, we will have an initial picture of the operation in its socio-political setting, and an idea of at least the general types of factors and actors that could be relevant to safely sustaining the operation. These constitute our intelligence targets. Hypotheses will change and be refined in later stages, but this stage provides a solid starting point.

This stage is often necessarily messy. Even when it seems possible to take a straight line to relevant variables, availing ourselves of the opportunity to make a mess is useful. We might find that there were unknown unknowns, that some of our assumptions were not as strong as we thought, or that our sense of the place was fuzzy or outdated. It is possible to truncate this stage, and there is no point in meandering if we are rightly confident that we know what needs scrutiny, but to rush or omit it risks gaps and uncertainties later on. The approach that follows assumes that we are not particularly confident and welcome the chance to test and prod from different angles. Note that because this stage has a strong brainstorming aspect, what follows is not a rigid prescription, and there are different approaches that could fulfil the same objective of intelligence targeting and clarifying the scope of the baseline exercise. Thus, as well as outlining a thought process, the approach herein also provides general guidelines that could help to shape a customised method.

The chapter proceeds as follows. First, we examine the operation to define the object of the baseline exercise and to derive initial hypotheses on relevant socio-political variables. The next step develops a picture of the socio-political environment both as broad contextual insight and as the subject of a scan for actual variables relevant to the operation. Finally, we take stock of the results of the first two steps, and test ideas and assumptions derived to that point. The outputs of this stage are informed hypotheses about relevant terrain factors and stakeholders, key questions and contextual awareness of the socio-political environment. Reasonably robust hypotheses about terrain factors are the link to the terrain analysis stage which follows.

As noted in the last chapter, illustrations will mainly draw on the two hypothetical cases. To reiterate, one is a highway construction project in a developing West African country and the other is an IT consultancy entering a transitional MENA country.

ABOUT THE OPERATION

This step answers the question, "political risk to what?" Without at least a concept of a prospective operation there is nothing at risk, and the baseline exercise would be academic research as opposed to intelligence formulation. Depending on the stage of the business initiative, there might not be a very solid notion of an operation, for example if a company is conducting the exercise to help decide whether or not to proceed with a country initiative, or what country to go to. In such cases, the profile we sketch here would be very top level, but still realistic and indicative. As we proceed, we will assume that an operation has been decided and is in the pre-entry or early launch phases; in other words, it exists in nascent form or soon will, since this provides more grist for illustration.

Before proceeding, one can bear in mind that Chapter 3's *Characterising Country Operations* section, which looked at how different business sectors, operational phases and modes of entry can have their own unique exposures and challenges, is relevant background here.

DOI: 10.1201/9781003149125-9

Various questions, brainstorming tools and perspectives can be used to develop a useful sense of the operation. Here we will start with the journalistic questions of who, what, why, when, where and how to develop a rounded profile. We then look at the operation's backstory, or how it came into being and any potential concerns which might arise from its origins. Next, the operation's main assets and dependencies (conditions that assets depend on) are broken down to generate hypotheses about what could affect them. Finally, we consider how the company generally handles political risk in similar contexts, so that we have at least a high-level concept of political risk management when interpreting potential challenges later in the baseline exercise. It is also possible at this stage to create a preliminary socio-political profile, as introduced in Chapter 3, but we save that for the stakeholder analysis stage where it directly feeds into stakeholder identification.

A final note before proceeding concerns the required degree of detail about the operation. This will vary. One might be able to catch all of the relevant operational attributes in a one-day workshop or it might take a week or so of reviewing relevant sections of operational plans. One can bear in mind that at this point we are trying to focus a strategic-level assessment, and this does not need a detailed operational blueprint. As noted in the introduction to Part II, the baseline exercise is not the final word, and after it provides strategic insights, specific management functions will likely be following up on tactical issues relevant to their parts of the operation.

THE SIX BASIC QUESTIONS

Who, what, why, when, where and how together provide a basic framework to sketch out the operation. It is not sophisticated, but it compels us to consider the operation from several different angles. From each question, attributes relevant to political risk and to scoping the baseline exercise will arise.

"Who" is a preliminary question, and even precedes the scoping of the baseline exercise. It is about the entity or organisation that forms the object of the exercise, and by extension which will undertake it and use the resulting intelligence. The more focused and concise the object of the exercise, the more parsimonious it is from an analytical perspective, but the choice will need to consider shared exposures, concerns, interests and trust between the members of any wider operational entity. As the Statoil Algeria case in Chapter 1 indicated, vulnerabilities can arise when assessments are divided between operational actors. However, one can imagine a situation in which an assessment is watered down or sanitised for fear of upsetting partners, some of whom might be relevant intelligence targets themselves. In some cases, there might need to be a distinction between joint assessment and planning, and what the company undertakes specifically for itself.

The "what" puts boundaries on the operation. The more focused the "what", the more targeted the assessment, but foreign operations can be complex and multi-stranded, or related to other company activities in the country and even neighbouring ones. Thus, exactly what the baseline exercise is covering might not be self-evident. Explicit definition helps to ensure that eventual results are about specific activities and exposures, and not just about a general country or regional presence.

"Why" has two aspects. One is the commercial stake. Ultimately this includes profit, but other considerations, such as getting a foothold in a high-growth market or becoming a respected regional player, are just as relevant. The other aspect is the "why" from the host country perspective. The construction company is fulfilling a need for better logistical connectivity, for example, while the IT consultancy is helping organisations in the country to become more agile and efficient. The host country "whys" are a potential factor in how the company is received and its perceived value to socio-political actors, and hence form part of the overall strategic stake.

"When" also has two sides. One is the overall operation from start to finish. While a baseline intelligence exercise, even with scenario analysis, might not cover much of it, the full timeline is still important since political risk management in the here and now should consider not just near-term issues, but how it could help with an operation's future position. For the highway project, there might be five years of actual work on the ground, starting in a few months. The IT consultancy aspires to actually become a part of the business milieu in the host country, and it might expect to be there for at least 20 years. The total time frame puts the operation in a temporal context.

The other aspect of "when" is which specific operational phase the exercise covers. Our focus here is entry, set up or launch, which for both case operations would probably fit the 1-year to 18-month currency of a baseline exercise. In other contexts, the exercise might apply to ongoing operations, an expansion phase or even exit. Whatever it is, specifying the relevant phase and its expected duration helps to focus the baseline exercise both in time and in relation to specific activities that occur in the given phase. If the relevant phase and the time horizon of the baseline exercise misalign by just a few months, we can probably afford to adjust the baseline's time horizon, although as the results of the exercise start to lose currency, monitoring and updates should become more intensive.

"Where" is the host county, but operations vary in terms of their geographic spread and exposure. The highway project, for example, might be spread across different local jurisdictions, cover the homelands of different ethnic groups and, at some points, come into proximity to a regional insurgency. The IT consultancy, by contrast, will be mainly confined to the capital city during its entry phase, and a rebellion in a remote province might not touch life in the capital. Some national-level socio-political dynamics affect an operation wherever it is in a country, but specific areas of operation can present their own unique local challenges.

"How" is about the company's main activities in the relevant operational phase. The highway constructor will be getting necessary permits, importing equipment, setting up base camps, residencies and offices, getting local labour and subcontractors on board, and beginning actual earthworks. If there are necessary relocations of people living in the path of the planned work, these will probably start in this phase as well. The "how" for the constructor not only helps to tell us how the operation could be exposed in terms of people, equipment and facilities but also provides an early indication of attributes that might shape socio-political actors' attitudes. Relocations, if necessary, are certainly one red flag in that respect, but so too would be disruptions and hassle created by major works, particularly in the towns on either end of the planned route. For the IT consultancy, they will be seeking permits, establishing offices, getting local staff on board, and developing initial partnerships and business development discussions with private and public sector prospects. Their plan is to initially work with well-connected host country partners for access into the business scene, while trying to make their own brand stand out for the day when they can operate independently. This already points to a potential conflict of interest and perhaps awkward relationships with partners who might be politically connected, and hence even at this basic level of enquiry we start to get hypotheses about potential issues.

Following the six basic questions, one can summarise operational attributes relevant to scoping, and any political risk hypotheses garnered to this point. For example, drawing on the highway context, a summary might include the following.

- Considering potential sensitivities and distinctions between project partners, our company needs its own assessment and is the principal object of this exercise. We will collaborate with our donor agency partners (the main project lenders) on joint assessments, but reserve this exercise for our own use.
- The operation is the highway construction project linking towns A and B as well as urban access roads in both towns.
- The project's anticipated profit would be a decent contribution to the bottom line, but success would also mean a strong reference case which would help to shore up our position in the high-growth African market, particularly with respect to aggressive competition from Chinese firms. The project is also high stakes for the host country, since it is fundamental to the economic integration of the underdeveloped northern region, and also to increasing the allure to foreign mining companies who have thus far been deterred from prospecting in the north because of logistical constraints.

- We have been notified that our firm has provisionally been selected subject to final contractual negotiations; thus, the project start date would be approximately — and its completion date —. The first phase, set up and launch, will cover the initial 12 to 15 months, which is the general time frame of the baseline exercise.
- The project will establish a country office in the capital to manage government relations and imports, project offices and residencies in towns A and B, and three basecamps along the highway route, which runs between the Central and Northern administrative departments. The geographic scope of the exercise includes rural and township operating areas within the two administrative divisions, in addition to the national level.
- The project aims for simultaneous completion of the highway and urban access roads on either end; thus, construction will occur along the length of the route. Urban works will require route clearance and relocations of communities near the planned route on town outskirts (refer to the donor committee's social-environmental impact assessment). Despite prior donor agency and government consultations with affected communities and planned assistance with relocations, it is reasonable to anticipate that urban disruption and relocations would still engender considerable concern, and implications need to be assessed in the exercise. Additionally, a significant factor in schedule adherence is equipment imports via the capital's port, and factors that could affect logistics are an important consideration. Finally, local content stipulations plus our own labour requirements mean that hiring, and labour and supplier relations, will be another key intersection with the host environment, and will need to be considered for potential challenges.

A summary for the IT consultancy case would focus less on physical and geographic attributes and more on relationships and business positioning. The six questions do not yield the whole operational picture, but already there is at least a tangible operation at stake, a temporal and geographic scope for the exercise, and a few early indications of variables that could be relevant.

OPERATION BACKSTORY

Our illustrative focus is the early stages of an operation, and hence the backstory would include activities, relationships and commitments that led up to the decision to proceed. If the operation were already underway, then a backstory would still be instructive, but it would focus more on the operation's recent history, including problems it had experienced, as opposed to its origins.

We have noted how political risk intelligence follows, or should follow, an initiative from concept through to execution. Ideally intelligence, and due diligence on prospective partners or other relationships, would have steered the company away from potentially risky liaisons and commitments on the path towards a final decision and entry planning. This does not always happen, or at least not as well as it could. In the rush to win business or get access to a country, there can be a tendency to downplay the risks and difficulties, to engage with actors who can help to overcome initial hurdles without sufficient caution, and to be very liberal in espousing the mutual benefits of the planned initiative. Additionally, a company can knowingly take risky decisions that could have implications later on. Thus, even before starting, an operation might have accumulated some political risk baggage. If this is not elucidated and examined in the baseline exercise, the resulting intelligence could have some serious blind spots.

By casting a critical and honest eye on the backstory, potential baggage can be discerned. There are various potential issues, and we only look at a few types for illustration. First, especially on government contracts or concessions, a company might cut a backroom deal, either in absence of a bidding process or to try to gain an advantage in the process. It is nearly an axiom in political risk that the more transparent the method of business acquisition with a government, the less risky the operation, first because a government faces more hurdles if it wants to renege or try to force the company to accept new terms, and second because it forestalls allegations of corruption or other impropriety. If there were a backroom deal, the implications would bear exploration.

Second, and relevant to both public and purely private sector operations, a company might overstate an operation's job creation, partnership and developmental merits to try to increase support and make entry smoother. In many emerging markets and especially in poorer developing countries, there are already high expectations of foreign companies, and hyping the benefits can set a company up for apparent under-delivery. Not just governments, but local unions, host communities, NGOs and the business community can be resentful if what seemed like promises go unfulfilled.

Another issue is that a company might have scrambled in the early stages of an initiative to find well-connected local partners to increase the chances of a smooth entry and early wins, without knowing enough about them. In many emerging markets, the biggest and seemingly most capable prospective partners are also part of a regime's crony networks and beholden in some ways to the regime or specific cliques in it. If entry is premised on a particular partnership of unknown political significance, then this is a factor that the baseline exercise would need to cover.

Corruption is another possibility. Paying bribes just to get into a country certainly sets a company up for complications later on. It is unlikely that this would be discerned just by considering the operation's backstory, since presumably the people seeking political risk intelligence are the same ones who decided to use bribery. However, it is still worth asking the question at this stage, since sometimes it is simply not considered, and bribe-paying can happen in corners of a company without senior managers being aware of it. Needless to say, if corruption is discerned, it is best to clear the air and deal with liabilities before putting people and assets in the country. Dealing with corruption in the firm is actually a broader integrity and governance concern, and if someone used bribery to bring the operation to this point without it being discerned, it would indicate a deeper corporate problem.

Potentially awkward or constraining relationships, irrevocable decisions made without sufficient awareness, and difficult expectations revealed in the backstory can be summarised at this point and flagged for inclusion in the relevant analytical stage, which would usually be stakeholder analysis, since political risk baggage mainly derives from prior interactions with specific actors.

Drawing on the example of the IT company entering the Middle East or North Africa, a summary of its relevant backstory might focus on discussions that it has had with prospective local partners. It has not yet formed a partnership, but in its initial haste to open doors with a local company with strong credentials, it has made promising sounds to one firm in particular. The local company is very interested in brand association with a respected international player, and possible skills and technology transfer through close collaboration. But at this point it is clear that the IT consultancy has not yet considered the socio-political implications of a partnership, despite having raised expectations. There would likely be more than just one red flag, but this is the kind of issue that the backstory can help to uncover.

The above might indicate that the backstory step is a rather awkward self-criticism exercise. For best effect, though, it is important that it is positioned as a chance to identify potential vulnerabilities so that the operation can proceed from any given point with the best possible preparation. Knowing the relevant backstory in advance is the only way to ensure that the implications of early misjudgements or indeed deliberate risk-taking are accounted for in the assessment.

ASSETS AND DEPENDENCIES

The concept of assets was introduced in Chapter 3. To reiterate, they are what the company needs to sustain in order to succeed in the operation and to maintain or boost its overall international standing and capability. When implanted into their new environment, assets also become exposures. This step in the process clarifies the operation's assets, and then looks at what these depend on within the socio-political environment. Then by asking what and who could affect these dependencies, we generate additional hypotheses on relevant factors and actors.

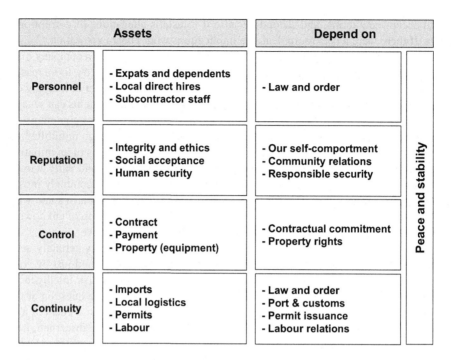

FIGURE 6.1   Assets and dependencies.

Using the highway project example and applying the asset types from Chapter 3, a top-level sketch of the operation's assets and socio-political dependencies is depicted in Figure 6.1.

Bearing in mind Chapter 3's general discussion of assets, only a few points bear clarification here. Personnel mainly means the security of people. Law and order is a general way of stating an absence of unrest or threats in the relevant vicinity, and effective, legitimate policing. Subcontractors would be responsible for their own staff from a duty of care perspective, but all workers are relevant to the operation. Reputation, largely being about the company's behaviour, is harder to delineate but one can still posit some variables that the desired reputation depends on. Within control, contractual commitment refers to the government's commitment to both the highway project and its own contractual obligations. Under continuity, law and order is again relevant because unrest or violence can affect logistics and required infrastructure. Finally, peace and stability in areas of operation are germane to all assets. A widespread insurgency or a coup, for example, could put pressure on the entire operation.

Having used exposed assets to identify dependencies, now we use dependencies as the starting point and ask what, and who, could affect them, thereby discerning pertinent types of factors and actors. This is illustrated in Figure 6.2 at a general level. Note that if some dependencies occurred more than once in the previous exercise, they can be aggregated in this step.

Even though this is hypothetical, a few explanatory points are in order. First, not every factor has a corresponding actor. Actors in this context are actually potential stakeholders; in other words, they would have some relationship to the operation. Thus, unrest, for example, while carried out by people, does not have a corresponding actor because it would happen regardless of the company's presence. Second, at this stage the results will be imprecise and just act as pointers for research later on. For example, crime and terrorist groups are obvious actors to list in the context of personnel security, but once we start looking at groups in or around these general categories, we might later see that local ethnic militias or insurgent groups are the relevant specific types. Note too that a factor can point to broader behaviours or dynamics in the environment, and then actors indicate

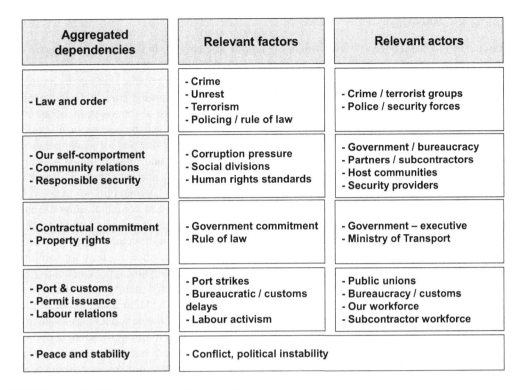

FIGURE 6.2 Variables that could affect dependencies.

specific entities that could channel that behaviour directly to the operation. Thus, for example, we have the factor of government commitment and rule of law, but general attitudes and behaviours would be tailored for, and applied to, the operation through specific government agents. Finally, the broad potential dynamics of conflict and instability probably will not involve stakeholders, but that is unclear at this point, and we leave the question to later stages.

The result of this two-step thought process is initial hypotheses on intelligence targets. To recap, we articulated and listed the operation's main assets. Next, we asked what these relied on in the environment, to derive dependencies. Then we asked what and who could affect the dependencies. The answer to that question is our preliminary targets, although since no in-depth research has been undertaken yet, the results are only types and categories, and even these could change as we learn more. Stakeholder analysis in particular includes an explicit stakeholder identification step which will likely obviate some of the results we derive now.

To keep up with our other storyline, the IT consultancy in an Arab, or Arab-Berber, country, we can briefly see what the exercise might have derived for them. Some general outcomes, for example those concerning personnel security, would be similar. However, the company would be less concerned about a specific contract, property, logistics and labour activism. Rather, if the company aspires to a wholly owned subsidiary, rules around foreign ownership would be relevant, and given the plan to initially rely on well-established partners, so too would cronyism. Actors would include the business community and prospective partners, in addition to government agencies overseeing FDI regulations. Depending on hopes of getting government work, government contractual adherence and relevant aspects of the rule of law could be relevant factors. The exercise might also have listed human rights, as did the constructor's, but in this vein because the IT company was aware that authoritarian governments sometimes rely on and even pressure foreign IT specialists to assist with repressive surveillance capabilities, a potential red flag for a European firm.

POLITICAL RISK MANAGEMENT

As discussed in Chapter 1, very few foreign operations in emerging markets happen without any political risk management, whether explicit or tacit and ad hoc. Political risk management for the operation in question will be based on intelligence from the baseline exercise, but having an initial top-level sense of how the company usually handles political risk in similar contexts helps to interpret potential issues and challenges later in the assessment. There are distinctive approaches even within the same sector. For example, some companies prefer to safeguard the operation and limit its contact with the socio-political environment in order to minimise exposure and focus on operational efficiency. This ring-fencing approach can include insurance, security and anti-corruption measures, for example, but would exclude high-profile or interactive local engagement. Others use the same tools but make social acceptance, transparency and local engagement a strong pillar of their overall approach, in order to increase situational awareness, and build trust and communication channels that can help to foresee and forestall potential issues or friction. There are a range of philosophies between these and they derive as much from corporate culture as from the actual challenges faced.

There is no point in taking this too far or trying to get too detailed, since it is only for soft interpretive background. In the author's experience, relevant insight on company approaches can derive from just a few good discussions. Without some concept of political risk management, though, the assessment would be conducted as though the company did not have the faintest idea about political risk. There is a tendency in conventional risk analysis to assess raw or inherent risk first, and then go back and see how company plans affect the level of risk. This works in some contexts, but in political risk it can feel absurd to assume that the intelligence user is flying blind, especially since they asked for and will soon receive targeted intelligence. It could even be that the company has experience in the target region or even the country in question, and this would clearly be relevant to how prepared it is for potential challenges there.

ABOUT THE SOCIO-POLITICAL ENVIRONMENT

This step has a dual role. One is to develop a contextual overview of the country, so that the intelligence team has a broad perspective of the environment as it proceeds through subsequent stages. As part of the final reporting from the baseline exercise, the overview would also provide intelligence users with useful background insight. The other role is to refine and flesh out initial hypotheses and thereby derive clearer targets for the forthcoming analytical stages.

This step proceeds as follows. First, a snapshot of relevant published indicators helps for an initial characterisation of the socio-political environment. This is followed by the country's backstory, or how it came to be at the current point in its evolution as a socio-political entity and business environment. Next, we apply the socio-political system framework from Chapter 2 to develop a more nuanced country characterisation and to establish the basis for testing and refining hypotheses formed in the "about the operation" step. Finally, we look at other companies' experience in the country for any transferrable insights. At the conclusion of this step, we will have a reasonably fluid, if still top-level, understanding of the socio-political environment, and a better sense of actual variables that could matter.

INDICATORS SNAPSHOT

Published indicators do not provide much insight on their own, but when used comparatively they give a sense of how challenging the country could be compared to known benchmarks, and they can broadly indicate problematic variables or attributes. Benchmarks could include the company's home country, and any emerging market countries in which the company has significant experience. Without benchmarks, indicators lack a frame of reference and are hard to interpret.

There is a variety of indicators and data relevant to socio-political evolution and stability. Economic and demographic datasets, for example, can be useful when trying to estimate instability and low-level conflict, since economic stagnation and youth demographics are often important factors. For now, though, the aim is only to provide a very preliminary snapshot, and hence just a handful of descriptive indicators suffices. Some political or country risk research providers compile their own indices, but those published by transnational organisations, NGOs and donor agencies are freely accessible and often sufficient. It is important to bear in mind that nearly any index or dataset has limitations in terms of the quality or granularity of the information it was built upon, and the judgements behind the modelling that produced specific scores and ranks. This is not a serious concern for this step as long as more reputable sources are used, but in fine-tuned modelling, cross-checks, corroboration and the analyst's own judgement to reconcile discrepancies are usually par for the course.

There are a number of possible indices relevant to this step, including, for example, the World Bank's *World Governance Indicators*, the Fund for Peace *Fragile States Index*, Transparency International's *Corruption Perceptions Index* and, for a sense of the country's socio-economic situation, the UNDP's *Human Development Index* (HDI). Since 2010, the HDI has also had inequality-adjusted human development scores, which are useful given the role that inequality can play in social divisions and instability.

We can provide an illustration of how indicators can be used, drawing only on the *World Governance Indicators*, which in practice would be one of a few indices packaged for a rounded perspective. This applies to the IT consultancy case. While the country, X, is imaginary, for the example we use the figures for Egypt. The company's Western European home country, which we leave unspecified, is represented by France. We can imagine that the company has considerable experience in India and Saudi Arabia, and hence they form the emerging market benchmark countries. Figure 6.3 shows the comparison.

The indicators are reasonably self-explanatory and definitions can be found online. Note that for country X there are figures for different intervals for an indication of recent trends. The first thing that stands out is X's low voice and accountability, which broadly equate to civil rights. In recent years, Saudi Arabia has been nearly an archetype of authoritarianism, and X is quite close. If X really were Egypt, 2009 would be before the Arab Spring and the subsequent events leading to Sisi's presidency; comparing 2009 with the following years shows not only areas of recovery but also continued decline, notably in regulatory quality. Just based on this snapshot, it would be reasonable to conclude that country X is a more complex environment than the two emerging markets that the company knows well, and much more challenging than the company's home country.

World Bank, World Governance Indicators	Country X at intervals, percentile rank			Benchmarks 2019, percentile rank		
	2009	2014	2019	Home country	India	Saudi Arabia
Voice and accountability	14	15	8	88	58	6
Stability / non-violence	26	8	13	59	21	30
Govt effectiveness	47	20	37	89	60	64
Regulatory quality	47	26	19	91	49	52
Rule of law	52	29	38	89	52	59
Control of corruption	36	31	28	89	48	63

FIGURE 6.3   Comparative governance indicators.

Fleshing this out with the other indices mentioned above, one would find a similar gap between X and the benchmark countries. One exception, again if the country were Egypt, is that human development scores improved from even the year before the Arab Spring revolution, partly as a result of economic reforms from 2016 aimed at tackling Egypt's currency crisis, which coincided with and helped the recovery of FDI.

Indicators do not tell much of a story without some historical background, but for the purposes of this step both the intelligence team and eventual users would have a sense of the overall degree of challenge posed by the socio-political environment, and even of some of the more worrying variables that bear examination, like corruption or regulatory ambiguity.

COUNTRY BACKSTORY

Just as the operation can have political risk baggage from its past, so too can a country, and a historical overview is instructive background. A picture of only current or recent dynamics is static and two-dimensional and lacks meaningful context. A backstory provides historical context, and also helps to understand what events or periods still resonate as influences on the current system. This can take the form of a timeline of key events and change points, but it should also characterise distinct periods in the country's socio-political evolution. Alongside, the state or character of the business climate in different periods, from an FDI perspective, brings an additional layer of business-specific nuance. One does not have to write a history essay for this step, and detailed research is not necessary for a characterisation. But especially in more volatile contexts, it can take some patience to discern the key evolutionary threads, and one should be asking "why" when significant twists or changes arise in the story.

Figure 6.4 is a very top-level illustration of a backstory summary, drawing on the example of the West African country that the highway constructor will be working in.

Period	Character, key episodes	Business environment	Formative episodes
Pre-modern state, 1700s to 1960	Pre-colonial socio-political order, slave trade, French rule	Colonial monopoly	Key shapers and enduring influences, e.g. northern rebellion, long period of personal rule, success of democratic protests in effecting reform
Chaotic state-building, 1960 – 1972	Northern rebellion, coups and counter-coups, junta rule	"At your own risk" – limited FDI, high risk of expropriation and regime interference	
People's Revolutionary Party, 1972 – 1990	K's coup, Marxist, Soviet ties, eccentric, repressive rule		
Fledgling democracy, 1990 –2006	Loss of Soviet support, democratic protests, multiparty system and first real elections	FDI laws, bilateral investment treaties	
Poor but stable 2006 – 2018	Workable democracy, slow but even development	Convoluted but workable business framework, FDI take-off from small base	
Regression, 2018 – 2021	Northern unrest, regional jihadist influence, presidential erosion of democratic safeguards, pandemic, increasing dissent		

FIGURE 6.4 Country backstory.

The imaginary country for the constructor case partly draws on Benin, which thus far has actually avoided the sharp ethnic and north-south tensions common in much of the region, although the broad changes in governance are reflective of real periods, as is the current friction around the erosion of genuine democracy. As an interesting aside, an illustration of what could happen in the People's Republic years of the "at your own risk" period was the case of a US constructor. During a dispute with the Beninois government over contract changes, the army confiscated the constructor's equipment, which was effectively held for ransom, after which the government claimed that the company breached its contract because of the ensuing delays. That was the end of the project. The business environment has considerably improved along with more pragmatic governance.

In this example, the initial period of democratic transition is a potential harbinger of popular responses should the current regime press on with its apparent ambitions to entrench itself. To enhance the case, we added a past northern rebellion, which would have seen a Muslim population trying to resist the cultural encroachment of a southern (mainly Christian) majority. Past conflicts do indeed leave scars and old wounds can reopen, a current example being Igbo separatism in Nigeria, drawing on memories of the 1960s Biafra War to articulate a sense of subnational grievance. In the context of our imaginary country, actual jihadist activity in the region could act as a catalyst to rekindle social memories of past conflict.

For the IT company example, if the country were Egypt, following the transitions from Nasser to Sadat and Mubarak, and the awkward and incomplete shift to a liberal market economy, particularly topical insight would have included the 2011 revolution, Morsi interregnum, military coup and Sisi's rise. His presidency has brought some economic pragmatism, but it still represents the abrupt slamming of a lid on the aspirations unleashed in 2011, and thus far the principal answer to lingering pro-democracy activism has been more stick than carrot. Even a top-level reading of recent history highlights potentially serious unresolved socio-political pressures. If the country were Algeria, another source for the imaginary case country, there would be even more twists and turns significant for the current situation, not least the 1990s civil war and power clan contests in its aftermath, an Arab Spring reaction that laid the groundwork for the current democratic protest movement, and the regime's floundering response to change pressure. On the business climate side, like Egypt but more so, Algeria has struggled to shed its statist past, and the current business environment retains considerable baggage from a period when the state directly controlled most economic activity.

There might not be clear hypotheses on sources of political risk from the backstory, but without it, there is no basis for understanding the depth or significance of relevant dynamics in the current system. Just as with trying to know a person, one could learn their current interests through casual conversation, but the whole person, including deeply embedded traits and views, only reveals itself when their past experiences are understood. Additionally, once we have a historical baseline, the "why" behind current dynamics tends to come more fluidly.

CURRENT SYSTEM OVERVIEW AND SCAN

This step develops a picture and conducts a scan of the current socio-political system as outlined in Chapter 2, which posited the system as follows:

- governance, social relations and socio-economic development, as the three core system elements, weaknesses in which are political risk drivers; and
- government (mis)behaviour, instability and conflict, as three symptoms of socio-political ill-health and which constitute political risk factors.

There were also external and long-term influences. Historical influences were partly derived in the country backstory and they will tacitly factor into thinking now, but, as noted in Chapter 2, influences are more directly relevant to scenario analysis and they will be explicitly examined in that stage. For now, bearing in mind preparation for the terrain analysis stage, a view of the current system suffices.

The dual remit of the "about the country" step, to provide a contextual overview and to further focus the assessment, shapes the approach here. On the one hand, we are interested in explaining the character of the socio-political environment, to answer what is sure to be a basic question among intelligence users: "What is this place like and how does it work?" This also helps the intelligence team by developing a wider perspective on the situation before getting absorbed with specific variables. On the other hand, we still need direction for subsequent analytical stages, the immediately forthcoming one of terrain analysis in particular; thus, the intelligence team's analytic question is, "What specific system dynamics could affect the operation?"

First, we develop an understanding of the current system with an eye to general characterisation. This should be quite broad, elucidating important trends and behaviours affecting the system's overall health and stability. Next, we apply our insights and hypotheses from the "about the operation" step and revisit the system with the aim of discerning actual variables relevant to the operation. Imagine having a futuristic scanning gun programmed with assets, dependencies and hypotheses. We move the beam across the system, and when it pings, we stop, adjust the beam for higher resolution and then record the picture for subsequent study. The two sub-steps, characterisation and scanning for variables, are depicted in Figure 6.5.

To develop the overview, initially it can help to posit specific questions for each system component. In answering these, the blanks are filled in and a basic picture emerges, at which point one has more confidence and can start to sketch around the answers, connecting the dots and developing a more detailed image. For the core element of governance, for example, starting questions might include the following:

- Who (really) runs the country?
- What is their authority or power based on?
- What are the constraints on rational governance in the national interest (even established democracies have such constraints, so this is not a loaded question)?

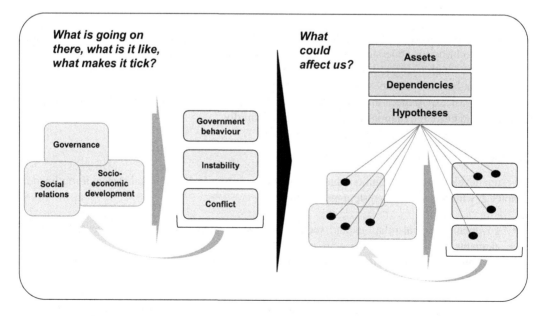

FIGURE 6.5   System overview and scan.

Jumping to the symptom of government misbehaviour for another example, initial questions could be the following:

- Is there favouritism or discrimination in how the law is applied, and, if so, who benefits?
- How pervasive is corruption and how does it manifest?
- Does the government interfere in legitimate business activity, and, if so, why and how?
- What is the government's attitude to human rights, and how does this manifest?

Questions will vary by country, and one might know a place well enough to focus questions on specific gaps. When we are not confident, initial questions should be quite broad. Overall, the main output of the characterisation is a holistic sense of how the socio-political system works, the main challenges to system health and integrity, and how it is distinct from places that the intelligence team and users might be familiar with. We will also have a sense of how the parts of the system interact and of dynamics, such as social polarisation or ethnic tensions, that cross-cut different elements. This will be especially useful later on in scenario analysis, although systemic interactions will be revisited in that stage after we have insights from terrain and stakeholder analysis.

The next step, as noted, is to take this picture, or map, and conduct the scan for what could affect the operation. This would also develop ideas on relevant actors, although we reserve explicit stakeholder identification for the stakeholder analysis stage. The starting point is the hypotheses on relevant variables developed in the last section. For example, the highway constructor posited crime, unrest, weak policing and terrorism as potential variables relevant to the dependency of law and order and the asset of personnel. When we look at how these or similar factors actually manifest in the environment, we might find ethnic clashes, sub-regional jihadist insurgency, banditry and corrupt policing to be the real-life variants. Similarly, social divisions were a hypothesised factor relevant to reputation. The scan reveals that these manifest as north-south ethnic and sectarian rivalries that are particularly acute in the areas of operation, which span the central to northern zones of the country.

Not knowing much about the country before, our earlier hypotheses, however broad, might have been incomplete. Thus, we go beyond our initial hypotheses and scan for what else could affect dependencies and the assets they support. This could reveal new variables. For example, in the highway case country, the port is on the Gulf of Guinea, and we learn that around 40 percent of global sea piracy incidents occur in the gulf. Our initial hypotheses on logistical challenges derived from the dependencies of the port and customs, but looking more broadly at what could affect the logistics asset, sea piracy becomes a relevant factor.

In addition to the system as it is now, this step should also ask what relevant planned events are on the horizon. These are not scenarios or potential new events, but scheduled or at least intended occasions like elections, the introduction of new laws relevant to FDI and the operation's business sector, peace talks, or regional diplomatic summits. Events that could have implications for the operation within the time horizon of the baseline exercise should be included as additional variables to investigate later.

There is probably a temptation to clean up the messy longlist of variables that we have at this point. There is one more step though, which takes a very direct look at the potential problems that foreign companies can have in the country.

CASES AND REAL EXPERIENCES

Looking at what other foreign companies, and even private domestic businesses, have experienced in the country is instructive, and hence we should examine available case studies. There are some caveats. First, newsworthy, and therefore easily accessible, cases are not necessarily indicative of common challenges. If something makes the news, there are usually very high financial stakes involved, or a significant but rare occurrence of serious mishap, misunderstanding or manifested hazard. An obvious exception would be if there is a string of similar publicised cases, like those involving racketeering in Russia in the 1990s, expropriation in Venezuela under Chavez, or current Chinese government pressure on companies that voice concerns about forced Uighur labour in their supply chains. Second, as noted in Chapter 3, different sectors and types of operations have different exposures, and when learning from a case, it might be necessary to filter out unique challenges from more transferrable lessons.

As an example, if the IT consultancy were going to Egypt, and reviewed the Sainsbury's case in Chapter 1, bureaucratic delays and uncertainty would seem relevant, especially as exemplified in the instance of opening a new store only to be told that the approvals were somehow invalid and the store had to close. On the other hand, Sainsbury's problems with local vendors, public distrust and the consumer boycott are not readily transferrable lessons. Sainsbury's had a public-facing operation with a highly visible local socio-economic impact, while the IT consultancy would have a lower profile and mainly be dealing with Egyptian managers out of public view. We can learn from any political risk case but should not infer too much from niche or specific circumstances.

Another approach is to ascertain common challenges among foreign companies in general. There are myriad easily accessible "doing business" guides for specific countries, but they tend to be quite generic, and to focus on official procedures which in practice might not be applied as they appear on paper. Instead, it is more instructive to look for the practical issues and routine distractions that companies have experienced. Much of this will not come up in the news or other media, and it might be necessary to talk to commercial attachés in the country, members of bilateral business associations, experienced country managers or other sources for useful insights. It is worth it, though, for the nuance it can provide. For example, if Algeria, as opposed to Egypt, were the target market for the imaginary IT consultancy, this enquiry might discern that common experiences of foreign companies include the following:

- bureaucratic opacity and delays, and the awkward balance between the need for a personal touch and, in the context of past politicised anti-corruption campaigns, bureaucrats' concerns about looking like they are doing favours;
- regulatory ambiguity, ironically arising from the government's renewed effort to bolster the private sector and FDI through more streamlined regulations – because the regime is very distracted by its own political problems, these efforts tend to get stalled and it can be hard to know whether the old or new rules apply to any given situation;
- being approached by *sous marins* (submarines), business agents with regime or military connections offering support, liaison and advisory services that sound very useful but which can represent potential liabilities, including the risk of inadvertently getting onside with one or another regime clique;
- disgruntled Algerian workers, perhaps frustrated by lack of promotion or training, calling on relatives in the bureaucracy or even the police for help – while this usually does not lead to serious problems, it can entail some hassle and be disconcerting;
- problems with in-company labour "syndicates" which every private company over a certain size needs to establish – companies often find that their bargaining approach is abrupt and that they go to the labour inspectorate with grievances before trying to resolve them with company managers;
- and a somewhat nationalistic press, even including more independent papers, which is quick to convey foreign companies as the wrongdoer in any dispute with a local partner or the government.

These kinds of issues are day-to-day distractions and challenges faced by foreign firms in a range of sectors. Some of these are very nuanced and would need to be somewhat generalised or repackaged into analysable variables. A final thought on cases and company experiences is that it is useful to relate insights back to the system overview and scan, to see which system dynamics they derive from, or if they represent previously unnoticed and more nuanced patterns that could augment the system picture.

STOCK-TAKE AND FINAL CHECKS

At this point we have a sense of what matters to the operation. Terrain factors will be more apparent, since stakeholder insight still requires an explicit identification process, but there will ideas about relevant actors too. In this step, first we pull indications together to take stock of what we have. Then we conduct some final tests to try to catch anything important that we might have missed.

STOCK-TAKE

Bringing ideas together in one place gives us the first full list of potential variables. The first attempt might be messy and there will be evident overlaps, or the same things stated in different ways. We can aggregate where possible, and group variables under broader conceptual labels where they seem to be aspects of the same dynamic or type of actor. The list will still be rough, and we can save the task of organising variables under analytical rubrics or domains for the terrain and stakeholder analysis stages. For now, assuming that we have done a basic clean-up, the results could be as depicted in Figure 6.6, for both the constructor and the IT consultancy.

For the IT consultancy, there are a few question marks in the list, indicating weaker hypotheses or unknowns that still bear testing in the following stages. In addition to the above, as noted earlier there could be specific planned events or change points that need to be considered, and these would be an addendum to the set of variables.

One can likely see how both factors and actors could be grouped or sequenced for analysis, either according to the assets and dependencies that they could affect or by their position in the socio-political system. Additionally, some factors and actors overlap. For example, would we assess political commitment to the project as a factor, or as an attribute of the government stakeholder?

Constructor, West Africa		IT consultancy, MENA	
Factors	**Actors**	**Factors**	**Actors**
- Banditry / crime			
- Policing	- Host communities / ethnic groups		- Business community – prospective customers
- Ethnic clashes		- Terrorism	
- Host community divisions	- Local authorities		- Prospective partners
	- Insurgents	- FDI laws / regulations (*also capital controls?*)	
- Human rights			- Politically connected competitors – *relevant?*
- Bureaucratic & customs delays	- Government customer	- Bureaucratic delays	
		- Rule of law – interference in business	- Relevant government agencies
- Labour activism	- Relevant regulatory agencies and customs		
		- Intellectual property protection	- Capitol city local authorities
- Cronyism (local subcontractors)	- Prospective local subcontractors		
		- Cronyism	- Potentially government as customer
- Corruption	- Local labour / unions	- Corruption	
- Political commitment to project	- NGOs	- Human rights	
			- Labour – professional / graduate
	- Donor agencies (project sponsors)	- Potentially government behaviour as customer	
- Rule of law – contractual commitment			- Security providers - *required?*
	- Police / security providers	- Instability – dissent, regime factional	
- Instability – dissent, regime factional			- Media – national business press
	- Media – national / international press		
- Conflict / insurgency (north)			
- Sea piracy			

FIGURE 6.6 Initial targets.

Again, though, organising variables can come later. For now, this stage has done its job of identifying intelligence targets.

There could be a temptation to rank or score the variables by relevance, in order to further focus the subsequent analysis. We have not done detailed research, though, so comparing relevance could be premature. However, some earlier hypotheses might seem increasingly irrelevant or superfluous after going through the steps to this point. If we are confident that some early ideas do not matter, then they can be removed. By this point, the list should contain qualified hypotheses, and not be a grab bag.

The distinction between variables relevant to the two operations arises from their very different profiles and types of operating environment. The constructor will be operating in a wide area, including rural zones. It is more physically exposed, and the environment is relatively insecure. It will also have considerable visibility within, and effects on, host communities, and thus both they and NGOs are relevant actors. On the other hand, the constructor is going to the country for one project which has largely been negotiated, so it will not have to worry about changes in FDI laws and regulations, or government interference outside of the contractual relationship. The IT consultancy, by contrast, will be in one urban hub that is reasonably secure, and will have low visibility and few direct effects on host communities. However, in seeking a long-term presence, it will need to worry about FDI regulations and government interference in business, as well as its relationships within the business community. The important point here is that, although the two cases share some variables, we have managed to find targets that are specific to each operation, rather than relying on a generic shopping list of factors or risks.

It is worth reiterating that the variables we have now are still subject to change as detailed exploration gets underway. This is only a starting point, not rigid parameters.

FINAL CHECKS

The thought process that brought us to this point started with the operation, then developed a picture of the socio-political system and finally directly looked for relevant variables in the environment. That was a relatively linear process and we have an opportunity to probe around its edges and test new angles to see if we missed anything important.

First, intelligence users, the managers planning the operation, might have specific concerns and anxieties. These can derive from past negative experiences, or from hints that they picked up through business contacts and discussions. It might be too early to know if and how these concerns matter, but operational experience is worth listening to, and a user-friendly intelligence process can flex to look at specific questions. We might also have discerned concerns from the operation's profile and backstory. For example, the constructor was especially worried about the reaction to relocations, and the IT consultancy was anxious about expectations it might have set when talking to prospective partners. These too should be flagged for explicit investigation, rather than assuming that we will automatically cover them when exploring the identified variables.

More broadly, it is also useful to test assumptions shaped to this point, using creative thinking tools that go beyond the linear logic that led to the list of variables. For example, one could test two competing stories. One is about the operation running smoothly over the assessment period. The other has the opposite plot, that it would not go well. The discrepancies in reasoning, use of available facts and degrees of confidence between the two stories can point to weak assumptions and new uncertainties. One could also apply devil's advocacy or "red teaming", having part of the intelligence team or even outside associates examine the focus of the assessment and pose hard questions about its coverage and relevance.

There are several other possibilities for final testing, and we posit two additional tests for illustration. The first takes a wide-angle snapshot of the operation, using the ecosystem model introduced in Chapter 3. We project into a time when the operation is established and running smoothly. This brings key dependencies and linkages into relief. Figure 6.7 is a top-level example for the highway project in West Africa.

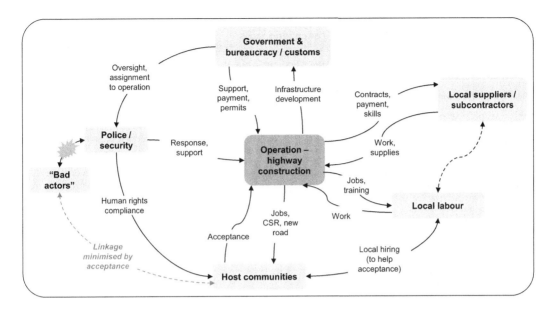

FIGURE 6.7   Operation ecosystem test.

The links, or flows, between the operation and groups around it are in effect the socio-political circulatory system of the operation. When critical flows get blocked or distorted, the ones moving back into the operation decrease or turn from positive to harmful. For example, local hiring helps to increase host community acceptance. If, for whatever reason, the company could not hire locally, then acceptance could decrease or turn to animosity. Similarly, the police, who would be responsible for aspects of the operation's security, are respectful of human rights, and this also helps to sustain the flow of host community acceptance. If police human rights compliance weakened or indeed became its opposite, again acceptance of the operation would be affected. By sketching critical flows, a natural question is what could affect them, and this could yield additional hypotheses.

Next, from the ecosystem test in addition to previous insights on assets and dependencies, we can list critical assumptions about success, and then ask how political risk could affect them. Political risk question marks are drawn from the earlier list of target variables, but we can go beyond that to posit new possibilities. Again using the construction project example, Figure 6.8 on the next page illustrates this test.

We see here that each assumption could be challenged by certain factors and interests. They represent intelligence targets, which we will investigate to see if, how and to what extent they matter. While this test might not yield many new variables, it is a straightforward perspective on targets and questions directly relevant to the operation's experience.

There are other options for testing new angles, but the above suffices to indicate the possibilities. Testing might not add more to the list of targets, but it does add a fresh point of view and sharpens some important questions that the assessment will need to examine.

By the end of the context and focus stage, we will not have answers about what the operation needs to address, but we will know what to examine to get the answers. Stakeholder analysis will rely on terrain intelligence and its own identification process for specific targets. However, we are reasonably well equipped to proceed with terrain analysis. That stage will refine and hone targets defined in this one, and then proceed to discern potential challenges that could derive from them. In addition to target variables, we have a contextual understanding of the operation and socio-political system, and this will support interpretation throughout all subsequent stages.

Key success assumptions	Political risk question marks
People safe and secure	Insurgency, banditry, ethnic clashes, weak policing
No major ethical breach	Corruption pressure, reliance on weakly governed protective security, linked to local subcontractors (how much control?)
Host communities accept us in return for jobs, CSR, respect	Local divisions make it hard to balance interests; reliance on government for relocations; human rights and security issues; would unions prioritise own members and make it hard to hire locally? (Could we avoid using unions?)
Local labour relations are smooth	Activist unions (see above), reliance on subcontractors for their managing their own labour relations
Local subcontractor relations are smooth	Possible crony links to regime and corrupt relationships, weaker labour relations and social responsibility standards
Government abides by contract, committed to project	Weakness in rule of law, past cases of contract breach, election or regime change lead to new government priorities / attitudes
Permits, customs and port logistics are timely / functional	Bureaucratic and customs delays, port strikes, sea piracy
Country will remain accessible / viable	Bottom-up instability / anti-authoritarian dissent; regime instability – coup potential (unrest, sanctions); insurgency as potential civil war

FIGURE 6.8   Assumptions test.

There are other possible approaches to initial intelligence targeting. Any robust process that takes a hard look at both sides of the political risk equation, the operation and the environment, and where they intersect, would provide actionable results. The most critical point to draw from this chapter is that upfront targeting makes the difference between focused hunting and simply filling in the blanks in a template. We saw that by making the unique operation the clear object of the exercise, we derived different questions and variables for each of the two cases. A thorough targeting step is sometimes seen as a hurdle, holding back the intelligence team from delving into the subject matter. Without it, though, it is doubtful if subsequent research would focus on what really mattered, or yield much more than a slightly customised country report.

7 Terrain Analysis

As a preliminary clarification, in this chapter "factor" is broadly used to mean relevant trends, conditions and dynamics in the socio-political environment (the terrain) where the operation takes place. It is just a handy label to distinguish between things going on in an environment from actors who could respond to the operation.

From the context and focus stage, we have a reasonably clear picture of the operation, the environment and how the two generally intersect. One output from that exercise was qualified hypotheses on relevant terrain factors. Thus, we have our targets for the terrain analysis stage, the subject of this chapter.

To recapitulate, "terrain" means the environment that exists and evolves irrespective of our presence. A traveller can encounter new weather patterns and diseases, craggy mountains or barren deserts, inadvertently walk into an ongoing fight between local rivals or seem like a target to opportunistic criminals who are on the prowl for any lucrative mark. The traveller's presence did not create the conditions or give rise to the behaviour, but they could affect him or her all the same, and to plan a safe journey these factors need to be understood. Likewise, a company going to a new country drops into different conditions and dynamics and needs to learn how these could affect the operation in order to plan for its resilience and safety. There will also be specific actors, or stakeholders, who respond directly to the company, and later on terrain and stakeholder insights are combined for nuanced planning insights. The focus now, though, is terrain, and insights from this stage are in themselves a significant part of the overall political risk picture.

The aim of this stage is to learn how relevant factors in the environment could affect the operation. A factor, like corruption or ethnic tensions, is a microcosm of interactions, dynamics and behaviours. By themselves, they are only attributes of the environment, and while they can help to explain how a country evolves, it is only through their interaction with the operation that they generate specific challenges. We will examine how to derive potential challenges from the factors identified in the context and focus stage, and how to assess and prioritise them to provide political risk management planning direction.

The rest of this chapter follows the terrain analysis process, as summarised in Figure 7.1 on the following page.

The first step is factor analysis, which aims at understanding what gave rise to a given factor and how it works. We see in the next step, challenge formulation, that potential challenges to the operation come from its intersection with factors. Thus, we need a clear characterisation of a factor to be able to see how it could touch and affect the operation, both through ongoing factor dynamics and through potential new events or changes that a factor could generate.

Challenge formulation identifies potential factor-operation intersections and discerns how a factor would manifest in a given intersection to produce certain implications, or effects. In this step, we will examine the logic of challenge formulation, and then proceed with six examples to illustrate the thought process and some of the analytical problems therein. Following these, we will examine the steps required to clean up overlaps and account for particularly close linkages between challenges, so that we hand over a manageable set to the next step, assessment and prioritisation.

Challenge formulation would have indirect indications of how relatively important or serious different potential challenges are, but it does not explicitly make that assessment. Thus, in the next step we turn from deriving challenges to comparing them, towards a prioritisation that will later help to inform political risk management planning. This involves assessing and rating a challenge's plausibility and implications, correlating these with a basic prioritisation matrix, and then refining the results to derive a tiering in order of severity.

DOI: 10.1201/9781003149125-10

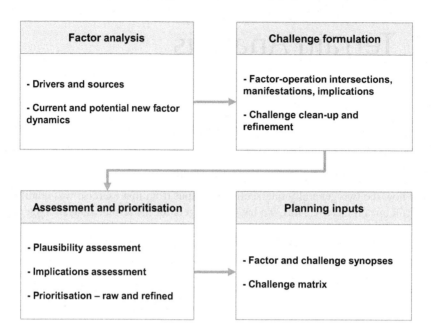

FIGURE 7.1   Terrain analysis process.

Finally, the results of the analysis are packaged in a handover to planning. We examine planning in detail in Chapter 9 when we have both terrain and stakeholder insights, but we can still examine some outputs that help to kickstart planning considerations based on terrain analysis alone.

A preliminary note on the organisation of work in terrain analysis would help readers to conceptualise how the wider approach works. Factors would be grouped according to their linkages in the wider socio-political system or based on an efficient sequence of learning. Each intelligence team member would deal with a group of related factors. A team member would first analyse a factor and then look at how it could intersect with the operation. These touchpoints are where potential challenges could arise, and there might be several for each factor. The team member would then develop each challenge, deriving a story of its manifestation and implications. Following this, the full list of challenges would be streamlined to account for overlaps, and then the team would work together on assessment and prioritisation.

FACTOR ANALYSIS

Before we can discern specific challenges from a factor, we need to understand how a factor works. A preliminary step is to put clear parameters on the factor so that we can focus on the aspects that matter. For example, from the context and focus stage we might sense that policing is important. But we are not worried about everything to do with policing. Our interest derives from certain concerns. One is police capacity in responding to security incidents affecting personnel. Another is police corruption, which could affect company interactions with the police and incur disconcerting hassles. Finally, police human rights behaviour could affect both personnel and also the operation's host community and labour relations if police were to intervene in serious disputes. These aspects of police capacity and professionalism are the broad intelligence target, and in defining this we restate and clarify the relevance of the factor, or why it is included in the assessment. The "why" is actually our hypotheses about the challenges that could arise from the factor, and like any hypothesis they might be proven wrong but they provide a research direction.

With a clear target, we turn to painting a relevant picture of the factor. To understand its depth and prevalence, we discern what gave rise to the factor and sustains it, or why it exists in the first place.

Next, all political risk factors are ultimately driven by human actors and the interplay of different interests. Knowing the players involved, a factor goes from being an abstraction to a human phenomenon with motivational drivers based on needs, values or aspirations, which affect the factor's force or intensity. How a factor actually functions, or its mechanisms, reveals the kinds of behaviours and actions that could intersect with and affect operational assets. Where it happens is also germane, since its geographic proximity to the operation increases the chances of us being affected by it. Finally, knowing the factor's origins, players and dynamics, we can reasonably address the question, "What new occurrences could it give rise to?" Current dynamics could be problematic, but we also need an idea of potential spikes of intensity or significant new events, since these could cause problems in the future.

While all of the above tacitly relies on an understanding of the wider socio-political system, there are two important points at which the system directly comes into play. One is in discerning sources of the factor. These will often relate to systemic dysfunctions, and if we see these as forces, their strength and depth help to explain the endurance and intensity of a factor's dynamics and manifestations. Loosely drawing on the West African case country, we can see how reference to the system helps to explain a factor's sources, using two very different factors, cronyism and banditry, as examples. This is illustrated in Figure 7.2.

Note that the two factors share one common source, social relations or, in this case, ethnic divisions, although with respect to cronyism the relevant divisions would be among southern groups close to the regime, while banditry is affected by the wider north-south ethnic and sectarian divide.

The other point when we need to explicitly examine the system is in trying to discern what problematic new events, or spikes of intensity, could arise from a factor. Again drawing on the

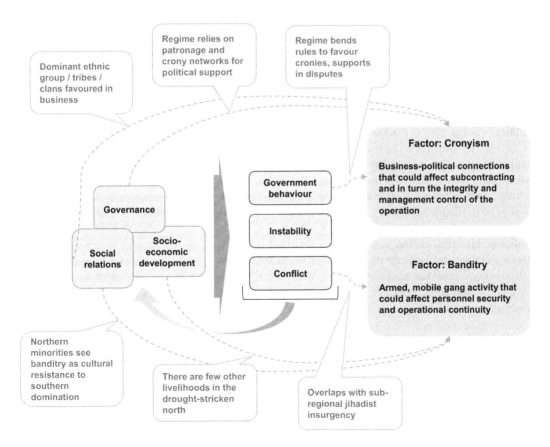

FIGURE 7.2 System reference for factor sources.

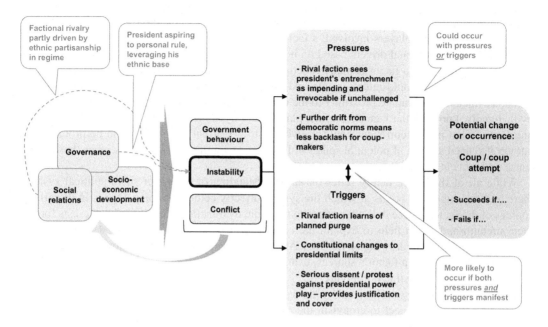

FIGURE 7.3   System reference to derive potential events from factors.

West African case, we can use the factor of regime-level instability related to a factional rivalry as an example. It could have current dynamics which indirectly impinge on the operation, perhaps by increasing bureaucratic dysfunction as rival factions vie for control over the civil service. But if the rivalry became acute, it could also give rise to a coup attempt, which would be a significant event with distinct implications for the operation. In discerning a potential event, we sense a new possibility from factor sources and dynamics and posit a change hypothesis. Then we apply a combination of scenario-like story development and research on relevant pressures and triggers to see why and how the event might occur. This thought process leans on our understanding of the wider socio-political system. This is depicted in Figure 7.3, using the example of a possible coup.

In this example, a coup or coup attempt might look plausible at first glance, but this step does not explicitly assess the plausibility of the event. We will do that later when prioritising challenges, by which point we will have a better understanding of the bigger picture. For now, after developing and testing a mini scenario of an event's manifestation, if it does not seem too farfetched, we develop a picture of its distinct dynamics and manifestations should it occur, and retain it as a potential challenge deriving from the factor.

Factor investigation has two broad results. One is how a factor works now. Its current mechanisms and their intensity are what could harm the operation where it intersects with the factor. The other result is potential new, significant events that a factor might give rise to, and how they could play out. Using this foundational insight, the next step of challenge formulation continues factor analysis as it hunts for specific ways in which a factor could affect the operation.

CHALLENGE FORMULATION

Challenge formulation both refers back to factor analysis and actually continues it by looking at the factor in direct relation to the operation. A potential challenge forms from the intersection of the operation with a factor. How the factor manifests will vary between intersections, and each manifestation will have certain implications for the operation. The intersection-manifestations-implications chain forms a challenge. One factor could yield several distinct challenges, both from current factor dynamics and from potential discontinuities that it gives rise to.

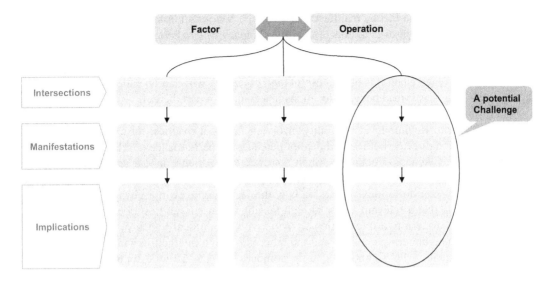

FIGURE 7.4   Challenge components.

Figure 7.4 illustrates the basic analytical components of a potential challenge deriving from a factor.

We examine the three components of the challenge chain in turn, starting with intersections. There are three general types of intersections, as shown in Figure 7.5.

Interactive intersections come from the operation's direct dealings with entities in the socio-political system, as broadly illustrated by the ecosystem depiction in the last chapter. These include permit applications, regulatory compliance and inspections, local hiring and partnering, host community interaction, and reliance on police and public services, to name a few. These links are potentially a factor's ingress points. The factor of corruption, for example, could manifest in permit applications, and police and public service interaction. A touchpoint with ethnic tensions, as another example, might be local hiring (importing tensions) and host community CSR initiatives.

Geographic intersections are where an operation is physically close to problematic factor dynamics, both in space and time. Operational facilities and activities are situated in certain places, which

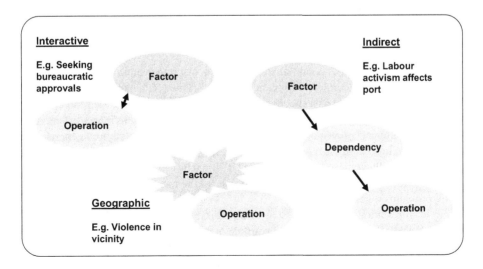

FIGURE 7.5   Factor-operation intersections.

could overlap with where factors manifest. For example, bottom-up instability that involves urban protests and police responses could occur near the company office. Police corruption, manifesting as traffic stop shakedowns, could occur along certain roads used by staff to get between areas of operation. Just as an ecosystem map can help to find interactive intersections, a geographic map with factor "hot spots" marked on it is often a useful tool, especially when an operation has a significant physical presence or is spread between locations in a country or part thereof.

Finally, intersections can be indirect, not touching the operation but touching what it depends on in the environment. Regime-level instability involving factional rivalries, for example, might not touch the operation directly, but it could disrupt bureaucratic performance or relations with a state company partner. Likewise, a company might not directly experience labour activism, but strikes could affect infrastructure on which the operation depends.

Next, we have manifestations. These are how the factor behaves in a given intersection. For example, imagine that a relevant factor is high tensions between the host country and a neighbouring one. We discern two intersections. One is with operational logistics, which partly rely on a port in the neighbouring country, and the other is through interaction with the host country government customer, who is annoyed that the company also has activities in its rival neighbour. A manifestation in the logistics intersection could be transport closures between the two countries in periods of especially acute tensions. For government interaction, it could be pressure on the company to confine its regional operations to the host country. Thus, one factor can manifest in different ways depending on how the operation intersects with it. Note that there is a significant distinction between factor manifestation from current dynamics and from discontinuities or new events, but we will address that separately, since it impinges on the wider challenge formulation process.

Finally, we have implications, in other words what the factor's manifestation means for the operation, should both an intersection and manifestation occur (that "should" is one crux of plausibility assessment later on). This derives from some form and degree of negative effect on operational assets, which again are people, reputation, control and continuity.

We need to take an aside to consider an important question, which is why we use "implications" for potential negative effects instead of "impact", which is nearly ubiquitous in conventional risk management. The short answer is that "implications" is a common sense and somewhat flexible concept that better lends itself to the complex and rather hazy domain of political risk. But this bears further explanation.

An impact is a singular effect, which can usually be quantified in time or dollar terms. Thus, the risk which creates an impact needs to be a discrete event, with one tidy story leading from occurrence to measurable effect. This works well in some contexts, such as finance, health and safety or engineering, where bad bets, accidents or technical failures are one-off events. It can work in political risk too for some types of issues, like an increase in tax rates or new investment regulations. But many political risks are more like potential situations than discrete events. They can often unfold in different ways, depending on certain contingencies or "ifs". One could explore each "if" branch and characterise each potential effect as a specific challenge, but this fragments one problem, and this in turn would fragment the approach to managing the problem. "Implications", as a softer, more interpretive notion than "impact", does not try to measure an effect; rather, it assigns a general magnitude of harm or difficulty. In so doing it can account for several "if" branches as long as the overall degree of harm would be broadly similar. When plausible "if" branches would have very distinct outcomes, then different challenges would need to be derived, but for the most part, "implications" allow us to keep holistic problems together.

Returning to implications as a component of a potential challenge, we noted in Chapter 3 that one challenge can affect several assets. For example, a strike would affect business continuity, but it could also affect the company's moral standing depending on the grievances involved, and if it caused serious delays, then it could affect contractual standing. Implications account for the effects on all assets touched by the challenge. We will also later see that where we draw the line in the sequence of a challenge's knock-on effects also matters for deriving implications. There is a tricky balance between trying to catch the full effects of a challenge, and projecting so far out in a cause-effect chain that the implications become entirely speculative, subject to myriad contingencies, or "ifs", which are hard to foresee.

The three challenge components are the bases of challenge formulation, but we also need to consider the distinction between challenges arising from current, ongoing factor dynamics and challenges deriving from new changes or events. The two types are dealt with quite differently.

Bureaucratic corruption is a good example of a factor which is an ongoing dynamic. It is happening in the background. One intersection in which we might encounter it is seeking permits. We would enter into a situation where we might experience the factor's manifestation, which in that case would be bribery pressure. We might not experience the corruption factor every time we seek a permit, and when we are not seeking a permit, we drift away from the factor for a while.

By contrast, a coup, an extortion attempt, or the introduction of a new law, would derive from ongoing factor dynamics, and might even be recurrent, but they are specific new events. If an event happens, we are automatically affected (we are only looking at events that could matter). Thus, intersection and occurrence are one and the same, and manifestation occurs in every instance. Compare this with bribery pressure. Just because bribery pressure is happening, it does not mean we experience it. We need to put ourselves in a situation where it can happen, and even then it might not manifest depending on how prevalent the problem is.

The distinction comes into play when we formulate challenges. For those arising from ongoing dynamics, the intersection is a specific interaction or touchpoint. From those arising from new events, the intersection is the event's occurrence. The distinction also matters when we assess challenges' plausibility later on. For challenges from ongoing dynamics, how common the intersection is and how common factor manifestation is per intersection are probability variables. By contrast, for new events we would look more at what would cause them to happen.

As we proceed, the thought process will become more concrete, but this hopefully helps to see the sub-text of what we are doing in challenge formulation. The basic framework outlined above is not always tidy, and there are other ways of deriving potential issues. If it does not seem to work for a specific problem, one can use an ad hoc narrative approach, as long as the logic is sound. We now turn to some specific examples for illustration. The cases being hypothetical, the substantive issues are only illustrative, and the examples are quite top level. The main emphasis is on the analytical problems and dilemmas that can arise. The first three examples mainly concern ongoing factor dynamics, and the next three focus more on potential new events.

CHALLENGE FORMULATION EXAMPLES

We begin with a relatively straightforward factor that we have already touched on, corruption. The derivation of implications and sketching of potential challenges is depicted in Figure 7.6 on the next page, and this could broadly apply to either of the hypothetical cases.

In this illustration, there are three ways that the operation could encounter corruption. In seeking permits, corruption manifests as pressure for a bribe in exchange for the timely processing or granting of a permit. This manifestation, or specific actions, has implications, which are either some liability and an accumulation of costs if bribes are paid, or delays if they are not. As noted earlier, there can be conditions, or "ifs" in implications, and we would not gloss these over even if they did not affect the overall magnitude of the problem.

There is a noteworthy difference between bureaucratic bribery pressure and the next intersection, approaches by agents. Bureaucratic corruption might not manifest every time the company seeks approvals or permits. Perhaps it is not an especially pervasive problem, and only some bureaucrats press for bribes some of the time. An approach by an agent, by contrast, might not be very common, but when it happens, it is specifically to press for an illicit relationship, and the manifestation

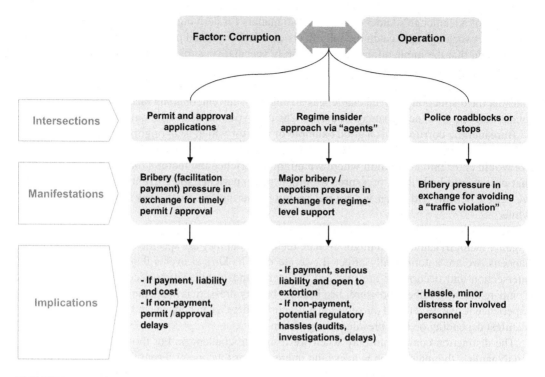

FIGURE 7.6   Deriving challenges from the corruption factor.

of corruption occurs in 100 percent of intersections. We know that agents are a fact of life in the environment; in other words, they are a current dynamic, but each approach is a new event even if it might be recurrent.

The final intersection of police stops and roadblocks is similar to bureaucratic corruption in that the manifestation might not happen every time. The noteworthy point from this intersection is that, if we were using the West African highway example, policing has already been selected as a factor in itself, and bribery pressure from the police would come up there too. Factors can cross-cut, and we might see the same challenge arise more than once. During challenge formulation, redundancies are not problematic, and identifying factor linkages can be useful. But at some point we need to deal with clear duplications. That could happen now, if analysts notice the redundancy and then decide which factor to cover it under, or it could happen later in the clean-up step once we have a full view of all derived challenges.

The above example of the corruption factor was relatively straightforward. We now examine a more nuanced factor, ethnic divisions in the host community, one that we identified for the highway project in West Africa. The derivation of challenges from this factor is shown in Figure 7.7.

Again, there are three intersections. Local hiring is one. We might know from factor investigation that the northern towns along the highway route have mixed populations from northern and southern ethnic groups, between which there is considerable friction. The company hopes to hire locally in order to increase local acceptance and would in effect be importing ethnic tensions into the workforce (only hiring from one ethnic group might negate this problem but ethnic discrimination would lead to even bigger problems). Additionally, it would have to use some union labour from the south, and these southern workers will also not mix well with local northern ones.

The basic manifestation of ethnic tensions in this intersection is friction or mutual hostility between groups of workers. To derive implications, some informed storytelling or visioning is required. For example, if work teams were mixed, tensions could make them dysfunctional because

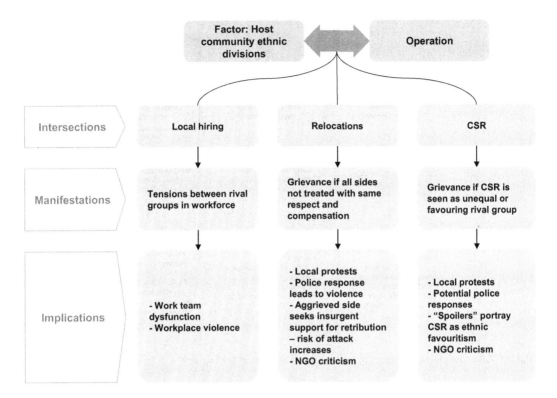

FIGURE 7.7   Deriving challenges from the ethnic divisions factor.

people stick to their own cliques when a task requires a team effort. Tensions could flare up under certain circumstances, for example because of jealousy over promotions or pay rises, or if a local supervisor denigrates workers from the opposing group. This could lead to violence. Thus, we used plausible "ifs" to generate implications.

The next intersection is relocations. Recall from the context and focus stage that people living near or on the planned construction site in the towns on either end of the highway route will need to be moved, and relocations were one of the company's key concerns. The manifestation of ethnic divisions in this intersection is ethnic group grievance *if* there is a perception of unfair treatment relative to other groups. Thus, a condition, or "if", is attached to the factor manifestation, not just to specific implications as with the above example. Implications in turn are derived from this "if" being fulfilled. We mentioned conditionalities earlier, but this bears some examination.

Imagine that I want to understand what could start an argument during a family reunion, so I can help to keep things smooth. There could be myriad possibilities, and at first I do not have a clue. So knowing what I do about the family, I mentally test a number of contingencies, like Uncle Jim getting drunk and talking politics. I run through a few more possibilities. The Jim contingency seems most plausible. When we find a reasonably plausible "if", and it would steer factor manifestation in a distinct direction, then we can develop the challenge on that basis. In the relocation example, the "if" of a perception of unfair treatment seems to be the right course to take, given what we know about the government attitude to northern communities, and the friction between ethnic groups where relocations will occur. Again, all "ifs" in the development of challenge are taken into account when later assessing plausibility, so at this point we do not have to worry about getting it exactly right.

The third factor example discerns challenges from intersections with current factor dynamics, and from a potential new event which could arise from the factor. This is regime-level instability, drawing on the West African highway case. The challenge formulation process is depicted in Figure 7.8.

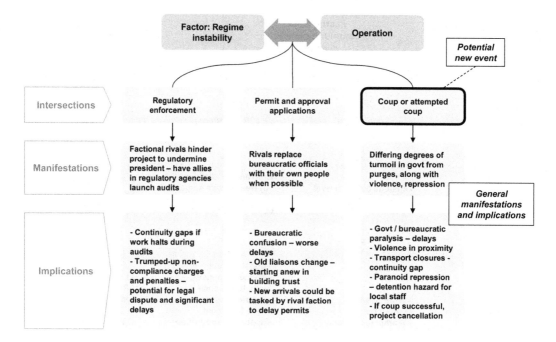

FIGURE 7.8   Deriving challenges from the regime-level instability factor.

We can imagine that factor investigation revealed a rivalry between two factions in the regime. One is the president's clique, which, while having an ethnic patronage base and increasingly authoritarian aspirations, considers itself the progressive and "modern" side. The other has different ethnic affiliations (although both are southern, not Muslim northern) and is nostalgic for the old people's republic days. If it had its way, the government would have a much more statist approach, and China's CCP regime represents a broad aspirational model. The presidential clique is more interested in ties with Europe and the West, and this was one reason why it sought Western donors and a European constructor for the highway. This is an annoyance to the rival group. It would have preferred a Chinese contractor, not just for the other perks that come with Chinese investment, but because it would have been a step towards integration in China's Belt and Road Initiative, and hence towards a relationship with what it sees as an admirable political system.

There are three intersections between the operation and this rivalry. One is regulatory enforcement. As is often the case when there are regime-level rivalries, one axis of factional competition is influence over the civil service, and the rival faction might use whatever influence it has in regulatory agencies to try to create problems for the project as a way of getting back at the president for seeking a European constructor.

As with corruption, another intersection is dealing with the bureaucracy (regulatory agencies are a part of this but a unique subset because of their investigative and enforcement powers). There could be factional influence over bureaucratic behaviour, but equally important the rivalry could simply have a corrosive effect on bureaucratic motivation and performance. This could worsen delays. One might recall that in the constructor case we had weak bureaucratic performance as a separate factor, and hence this intersection with regime-level instability is another factor overlap. In the later cleanup step, we might decide to integrate this particular intersection with the issue of bureaucratic delays since it is a nuanced aspect of the that problem.

The last intersection is a potential new event, a coup attempt (which could be successful or not), derived from factor analysis wherein the event looked reasonably plausible. The intersection is actually the occurrence of the coup attempt, which would affect the entire operating environment and certainly touch on the operation. As this example illustrates, the operation can intersect with current and ongoing factor dynamics, but those same dynamics could also give rise to new events that have their own distinct implications.

A more important point here is that a coup attempt is a clear archetype of the "if" branch problem. There are two very different possibilities inherent in the event: the coup attempt succeeds or does not. Earlier in factor investigation when looking at the coup possibility, we did not illustrate an analysis of how a coup attempt might turn out. If we had, we would have derived some variables and conditions, such as factional links to different security agencies and how good each side's intelligence and preparations were. If that sub-analysis had had very definitive results, perhaps we could now discount one of the branches and just focus on the implications of the more likely one. For illustration, we can assume that we do not feel especially confident about which branch would unfold, and that is often the case when an event would involve covert action and deception.

There are two main ways of dealing with multiple branches from the same initial occurrence. First, one could say that whether or not it were successful, any coup attempt represents considerable overall disruption, and hence we can assess it as one phenomenon and just note the potential range of variation. That might be workable in some cases, when an event would incur a similar degree of mess and worry either way. This was the approach taken in the diagram above. There is a broad characterisation of manifestations and implications, with reference to "different degrees of turmoil" and an "if coup successful" contingent implication.

That last "if" though is too big to let lie. There is a substantive ideological and policy difference between the two sides, and this difference is germane to how the construction project would be dealt with depending on who came out on top. With the presidential faction, it would be continuity after some short-lived turmoil, but if the rivals gained power, they would likely cancel the contract and invite a Chinese state company in to finish the job. The new regime would not have to worry about repercussions from the involved donor agencies, because Chinese involvement would effectively replace the Western donor relationship. Thus, upon reflection, we should probably take the other approach, which is to deal with the two branches as separate potential challenges. This approach, recognising distinct outcomes, is depicted in Figure 7.9.

When we later get to prioritising challenges, a successful coup is a relatively high priority partly because of its more serious implications. An unsuccessful coup attempt is still problematic, but it would not be irrecoverable.

The coup attempt intersection was a useful initial foray into potential new events, but there is still more to be explored when it comes to things that could happen, as opposed to bumping into current factor dynamics. We now look at three more examples that emphasise new events. The first one is terrorism, which we discussed earlier in a different context. This draws on the IT consultancy case, and for illustration assumes that the country is Egypt. Its challenge formulation process is illustrated in Figure 7.10.

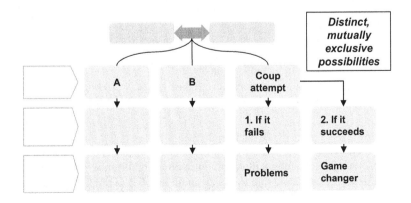

FIGURE 7.9   Distinctive event branches – coup attempt example.

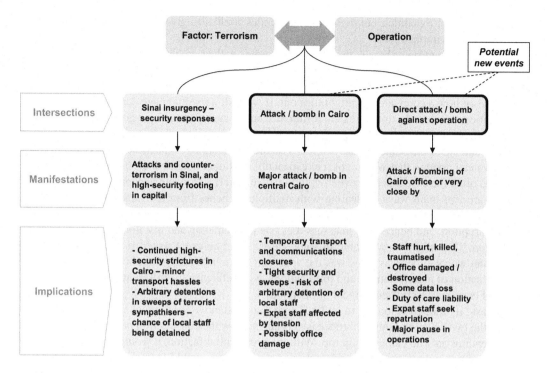

FIGURE 7.10   Deriving challenges from the terrorism factor.

There are again three possible intersections. One is with the security strictures that derive from current factor dynamic of the Sinai insurgency, carried out by jihadist groups but in the context of, and related to, Bedouin subnational grievances. The Sinai might be remote from Cairo, but the rebellion heightens security measures in the capital where the company will be working (this is a geographic intersection). As a direct challenge to a regime which already sees itself as a bulwark against Islamist revolution, the insurgency inspires some regime paranoia. The high-security footing is partly aimed at preventing an attack in the capital, something that has occurred in the past and which the jihadists likely would try again if they saw it as at least somewhat feasible.

Next, the possible attack in the capital is another geographic intersection with the operation and is a potential new event. If it happened, the company might suffer some damage, and also the effects of even more stringent and repressive security measures. The implications in the above diagram do not catch the full range of possible effects; rather they catch generalised midpoint effects, based on two counter-balancing considerations:

- Cairo and even just its downtown are large areas and the company would have to be quite unlucky to be directly hurt by a bomb or an attack;
- but in the built-up urban environment, any major attack would still have serious logistical effects, and the concomitant effects, including anxiety among staff, would still be significant.

These considerations are reasonable, but when there is a wide range of possible effects depending on uncertain variables, then just catching a plausible midpoint might not be enough. Intelligence users might latch onto that as the only outcome to worry about and fail to prepare enough for the outside but very serious possibilities, for example that an attack happens close to the office, or that company personnel are working near the location where a bomb explodes. Thus, while the implications

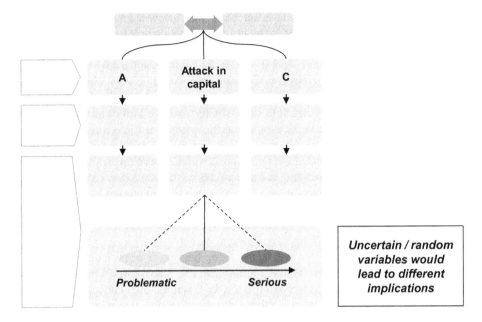

FIGURE 7.11   A range of implications.

summary can be based on a general midpoint, it could still be necessary to at least sketch different outcomes based on how key uncertainties could swing. Figure 7.11 depicts this level of analysis as an extension of the baseline one.

The baseline implications reflect the midpoint, while a few other levels of implications are also developed. In practice, a company would put most preparation into the plausible midpoint, but based on this extended analysis it would develop contingency plans for the more serious outcomes. Monitoring after the intelligence exercise would target the variables that affect implications severity, for example terrorist targeting patterns, and perhaps readjust the plausible midpoint over time. The merely problematic implications are only useful as a reference point. We would not underprepare just because we might get lucky and experience very mild effects.

This example makes apparent that probabilities can be tightly bound up with the judgements about implications. One could assess the basic probability of a terrorist attack in the capital, but then in looking at what it could mean, the questions of "precisely what, to what degree, where, when…" all come into play, and there are probabilities in each. However, while it is useful to sketch some outside possibilities, we would not create specious arrangements of variables just to generate more things to worry about. Once committed or on the ground, hazards are assessed within the broad limits of what is at least conceivable, not speculative "what ifs".

The final intersection, again a new event, is a direct attack on the company as the intended target, and again plausibility comes into play in how we approach implications. We have not yet explicitly conducted plausibility assessment, but from factor analysis we could have a sense of how plausible an event could be. In our example of the IT consultancy, assuming that it would be operating in Cairo, the notion of a direct attack is very tenuous. Targeting patterns make an attack on a low-profile IT consultancy seem very remote. Terrorists would almost certainly not waste the planning and resources involved in penetrating the capital's defences on such an obscure target, instead far preferring one with higher public impact or an effect on tourism revenues.

For the above reason, it might seem like a stretch to even posit a direct attack on the company. We do so, however, because while it is implausible, it is conceivable in a context where terrorist attacks happen now and then, and where terrorists generally perceive the intrusion of Western cultural values to be problematic. But constructing the direct attack scenario and implications in detail is not particularly useful. The implausibility of the event means that one would need to speculate on nearly every relevant variable, and a detailed plotline would be too hypothetical to provide useful guidance. The hazard needs to be on the radar, with at least a sketch of its potential significance, but unlike with the potential attack in the capital, general implications suffice, at least for now.

In practice, implausible, if still conceivable, events that would be very serious would warrant a top-level contingency plan, but for the most part they would be left to intelligence monitoring. Monitoring would track changes in the event's plausibility, and if it looked increasingly plausible, then more detailed analysis would be warranted and this would feed into more nuanced preparations. Recalling the Statoil Algeria case, a direct attack was posited, but not defined clearly enough to make it onto the mental radar of security planners. We will not fixate on the direct attack possibility, but we want to avoid Statoil's mistake, and at least ensure that the issue is visible and tracked.

After considering coups and terrorism, we turn to a very different kind of factor, the government's commitment to a project for which it is the customer, drawing on the West African highway case. This presents some unique analytical problems. The thought process to get to the challenges from this factor is shown in Figure 7.12.

We can assume that in the context and focus stage, there were some indications that despite seeking the highway project the government's commitment to it could waver. Perhaps it had made difficult budgetary trade-offs and was worried that the debt incurred might not actually pay for itself over time. It was also discovered that while the rival regime faction agreed with the merits of the highway, it disagreed on who should build it. Project commitment thus became a target factor.

While it seems like an obvious thing to include in the assessment, this is actually a difficult factor to deal with in terrain analysis. It is very close to being a stakeholder attribute that would only exist in relation to the project, which has not yet even begun. In stakeholder analysis, we will examine interests and motives in detail, and will be able to extrapolate government responses to the project's projected profile. In terrain analysis, the commitment factor seems to be quite hypothetical, since it is not part of the current terrain. Additionally, at least for the foreseeable future the government is committed to the project, since it is moving ahead with contract finalisation. Thus, while we suspect that commitment might waiver over time, we have little to base that on right now.

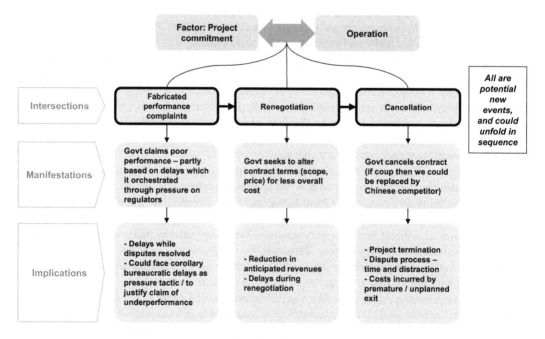

FIGURE 7.12 Deriving challenges from the factor of project commitment.

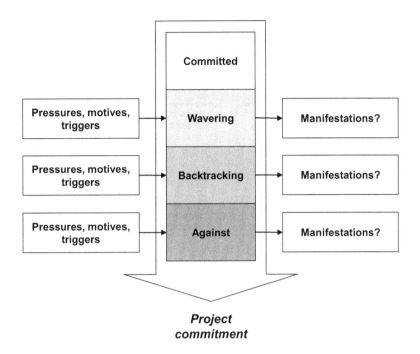

FIGURE 7.13   Sub-process developing potential levels of factor intensity.

Despite the above problems, we can imagine that the intelligence team still decided that it was useful to examine the question as a terrain factor. For one thing, this would help to develop a picture of the dynamics and pressures around the issue, as useful context when later assessing the government customer as a stakeholder. For another, some of the dynamics around project commitment could be entirely exogenous to the specific relationship between the company and the government.

Before deriving implications, since this factor does not yet concretely exist, one needs to deal with the central question of what future potential levels of project commitment could be. We can derive a range of commitment levels, behind each of which is a mini-scenario explaining how the level could occur. Then for each level of commitment, a manifestation can be formulated. This sub-process is illustrated in Figure 7.13.

We can now build implications from the manifestations of potential degrees of future commitment, and this brings us back to the original factor diagram, which in practice would have followed the forward-looking sub-process. Getting a head start on analytical clean-up, it might seem appropriate to integrate the complaints and renegotiation challenges into one, and just call it political pressure on the project. Cancellation, on the other hand, is quite distinct and would be kept as a separate challenge. Specific challenges aside, the wider scenario based on this factor, moving from complaints through to cancellation, should be retained. It might not unfold in sequence, but it represents a plausible route to intensifying pressure and ultimately cancellation. In planning, this sequence could be the basis of discussion about how to forestall the scenario in the first place or prevent it from reaching its full conclusion.

The final point in this example is that again there is a factor overlap. The challenge of cancellation occurs here under the project commitment factor, in which a coup is a variable, and also as an implication of a coup under the regime-level instability factor. This is a clear redundancy. It would be reasonable to remove coup-related cancellation from the weak commitment story and keep it all with the coup story. Then here we retain only the prospect of cancellation as undertaken by the current (or any future elected) leadership. Later when assessing the plausibility of cancellation by the current leadership, it would be based on economic and budgetary anxieties, whereas the plausibility

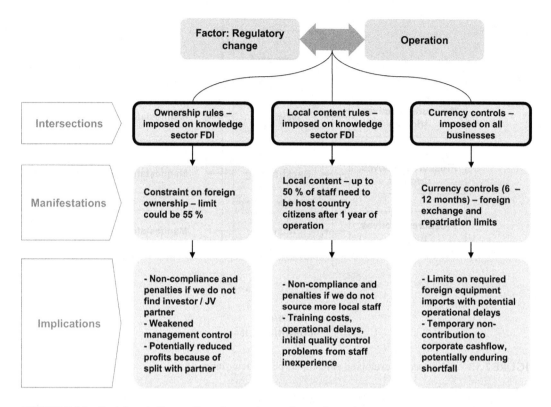

FIGURE 7.14 Deriving challenges from the regulatory change factor.

of coup-related cancellation would be linked to the plausibility of a successful coup. We could deal with this overlap now, or later in the clean-up step that follows challenge formulation.

The last example is the factor of regulatory change, one derived for the IT consultancy in a MENA country. The formulation of challenges from this factor is illustrated in Figure 7.14.

We can imagine that the factor investigation step found that the government's development plan includes fostering the domestic knowledge sector, including consulting and IT services. This is seen as valuable not just for the jobs and revenues it would create, but for the development of domestic expertise that could be applied to support other sectors of the economy, such as manufacturing, without firms having to source overseas providers. This interest ties in well with the IT consultancy's aspirations to make a mark in the national market, but it could also lead to regulatory changes which have implications for the company.

One could be a sector-specific change in foreign ownership rules that leads to a need for a JV partner, on the premise that this would increase knowledge transfer to domestic firms. Related to this could be more stringent local content rules, specifically around staffing, aimed at developing the sector's human resource base. There would be implications for the company from each potential change: on the one hand, reduced control and somewhat reduced near-term profit and, on the other, continuity problems as the company takes on and integrates more local staff than initially planned.

Another possible regulatory change is the introduction of temporary currency controls to stave off a foreign exchange shortfall. If the case country were Egypt, perhaps another round of controls might be required before economic reforms have taken effect. If it were Algeria, even though the price of oil has increased, the country is still suffering from years of low prices and its foreign reserves are depleted. For an IT consultancy, the implications of currency controls would not be especially serious compared to more import-dependent sectors, such as manufacturing, but it could still present at least some problems.

This factor and its resulting potential challenges are relatively straightforward by comparison to some others, but there are still points worth noting. The actual contents of the potential changes are unknown, since none of them has even been planned yet. In the above depiction, we can assume that the intelligence team used available indications to construct a reasonable direction and degree of change and applied these for midpoint estimates. One could develop each potential regulatory change in more detail, deriving a spread as we did with the case of the terrorist attack. However, given that the changes might not happen at all or for a long while, it is probably safe to use midpoint indications for now. Then after entering the country, regulatory changes can be assigned to monitoring, which could pick up on changes in specific government plans and the plausibility of their rollout.

Note that from that last point, and as indicated elsewhere in the examples, it is clear that baseline assessment often heavily relies on the fact that monitoring will occur afterwards. It effectively continues the assessment as potential challenges become nearer in time, and hence more concrete and observable. Given that monitoring will occur, there is no need speculate now on myriad possible contingencies.

That completes the tour of factor examples, which were a useful basis for illustrating some of the analytical dilemmas that can arise. Some of these are not easily resolved and require the analyst to use considerable judgement, or to apply some additional creative problem-solving.

Together, the six examples indicated several analytical problems and lessons. A brief summary is instructive:

- Factor overlaps happen when we formulate or draw on the same cause-effect implications story under multiple factors and intersections. Overlaps can usefully indicate systemic linkages but can also lead to duplications and skew later prioritisation, and hence need to be managed. The coup and project cancellation were examples. Cancellation was a coup implication, but that same story arose under the factor of project commitment, from which we decided to remove it.

- When a factor or specific intersection is highly nuanced, one might need to make considerable use of visioning and storylines to see how the resulting challenges might play out. This can involve the same kind of judgement and plot development that is associated with scenario analysis. Workplace friction and violence was an example where plausible contingencies had to be posited and developed to see what could happen.

- In a given intersection, we might want to test contingencies to see what factor manifestations could arise. An "if" branch is worth developing when it is reasonably plausible, but we would not posit speculative or frivolous contingencies just to add to the list of potential challenges.

- When specific contingencies, or "if" branches, would lead to broadly the same degree of difficulty, they can be incorporated into the broader implications of one challenge. But when "if" branches are dichotomous or would have very distinct implications, then the branches should be developed as separate challenges.

- When implications could considerably vary in their seriousness, depending on uncertain or random variables, then it is worth developing a range of potential implications to reflect this uncertainty. We might not label each set of implications as a separate issue, but they still need to be noted. For example, for the terrorist attack in the capital, we developed a reasonable midpoint, but we noted the more dire possibilities to ensure that intelligence users did not overlook them.

- When the above is the case, but the given intersection or event is somewhat speculative or seems quite implausible, then fine-tuned implications could be too hypothetical to be useful, and indicative midpoint implications suffice unless or until monitoring later clarifies what could happen. The terrorist attack on the company illustrated this point.

- When an entire factor is not based on current dynamics but would exist in the future as a direct result of the operation occurring, one can posit different degrees of future factor intensity to see what challenges could arise.

- When a factor is in effect a stakeholder attribute, it might be more straightforward to address it in stakeholder analysis where it can be assessed in the context of motives and interests in relation to the operation. It might be useful to try it as a terrain factor, though, because this could provide context for subsequent stakeholder analysis.
- When a potential challenge is ambiguous, rather than trying to develop it in detail, we can provide a reasonable sketch and then assign it to monitoring, which will shape a more robust intelligence picture as the relevant variables clarify over time.

CLEAN-UP AND REFINEMENT

If this were a real intelligence exercise, at this point we would have our initial list of challenges. We do not show interim results for the cases, but if one is curious, Figure 7.26 towards the end of the chapter depicts the final set of challenges for each case operation.

Factor analysis and challenge formulation did not yield a brain dump, but there is some stream-lining to do. As we saw in the previous section, a challenge under one factor can include or refer to a challenge developed from a different factor, whether as a contributing cause or as an implication. Factors often do cross-cut and their interactions are instructive, but cross-cuts can lead us to derive the same challenge in different places. We need to weed out duplications because later on they can be double-counted and skew prioritisation, and they could also create clutter that impedes clear-sighted political risk management planning.

This tidying process can be messy, like sifting through a big pile of old playing cards trying to make at least one full deck, but after some initial sorting it starts to come together. Using only a few outputs relevant to the West African construction case, Figure 7.15 depicts this sorting and tidying process.

By the end of this process, we might have aggregated or adjusted some challenges, but the main effect is to keep specific cause-effect and implications stories from bubbling up in several places.

Just to keep up with the IT consultancy case, one clean-up would be to aggregate local staff detentions from where they occur as an implication and turn it into a single challenge. This would

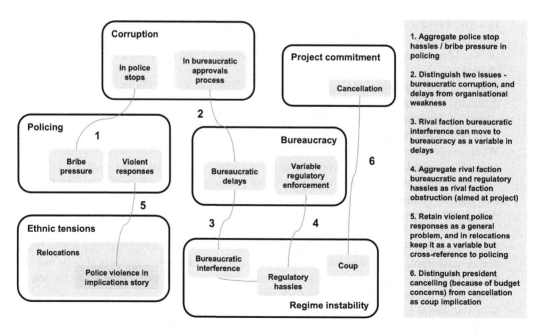

FIGURE 7.15 Cleaning up overlaps.

refer back to its originating factors, including weak human rights, weak rule of law, terrorism and revolutionary unrest, but because the problem has a basic story affecting one particular asset (staff get arbitrarily detained in broad security sweeps or crackdowns), it makes sense to distil it into one issue. It can remain as an implication of other challenges without redundancy. Causal linkage is not the same thing as duplication, and in fact in final prioritisation causal links are a consideration in relative challenge severity.

After cleaning up, some challenges will be quite discrete. A terrorist attack is an example. Although terrorism has its own causal links in the socio-political system, it is not closely dependent on how other challenges manifest or evolve. Other issues, though, could feed into each other, and could be so closely related that they form a system of challenges. We should look for such systems, because if intelligence users ultimately end up trying to manage parts of a system in isolation, they will probably fail to manage any of them very well. Using the West African highway example, we can imagine that we scanned for systemic linkages and found the challenge system shown in Figure 7.16.

Host community distrust and association with human rights abuses, which themselves are causally linked, are in effect the system outputs. Two significant causes of both are relocations going badly and police violence, the latter as a response to unrest during relocations, and to any local dispute with the operation. Outside of but related to the system are other challenges that could affect it. This systemic view helps us to see what has to be managed together, and looking ahead to planning, challenge systems do indeed form holistic planning targets. For now, and in the next step of assessment and prioritisation, it can make sense to treat a tightly interactive challenge system as one aggregate problem, since the implications are closely related, and because if one part of it manifests, it can drag the others into manifestation.

Along with systems of challenges, this step should also clarify other key challenge relationships that would help both when tracking an issue's manifestation later in intelligence monitoring, and when deriving political risk management approaches. These might not form systems, but they could at least form causally linked pairs. For example, in the IT consultancy case, one challenge is crony partner manipulation for control over a partnership, and this could lead to cronies using their political connections to worsen the separate challenge of bureaucratic delays, as in, "We can help with delays, but only if we have more control." As another example, a change in foreign ownership rules

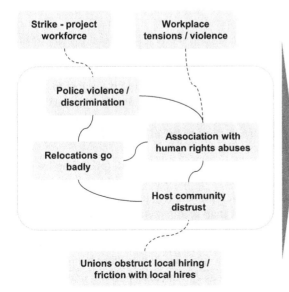

FIGURE 7.16 System of challenges.

could worsen crony partner manipulation, because new JV rules might force a closer relationship than the consultancy had initially envisioned.

At the end of the clean-up step, we would have a list of well-defined potential challenges. We can now begin deriving their relative severities, so that political risk management can allocate time and effort appropriately.

FINAL ASSESSMENT AND PRIORITISATION

We conduct assessment now, after having the full set of challenges, because we can better see how they are linked, and can bring a comparative perspective to bear.

Assessment is towards prioritisation, which indicates how to allocate political risk management attention. For example, if a team had 20 people, and faced 10 challenges, it would not make sense to just allocate two people to each challenge. Some issues are simple and somewhat implausible, and some are complex and would almost surely manifest. Team allocation would favour the more important issues, while still ensuring that all of them were covered. One could also think in terms of person-hours, the seniority or experience of the people assigned to different challenges, or budget for specialist expertise. Prioritisation should not set rigid parameters on attention allocation, and we will see in the chapter on planning that we often group issues not by their priority level, but according to what is more efficiently managed together. However, planning needs a reasonable sense of priorities, or we risk serious resource misallocation.

It is probably apparent by now that country-level political risk involves complex human phenomena that do not lend themselves well to quantified assessment. Theoretically, with enough information it is possible, but for practical purposes, prioritisation is a qualitative exercise that relies as much on informed judgement as on measurable indicators. Accordingly, the approach that we will apply here is mainly qualitative.

We proceed as follows. The first step is assessing plausibility and implications. These are the two most fundamental components of a challenge. For example, if something were implausible and would have minor implications if it manifested, then it is not worrisome. If it were plausible and would be disastrous, then it is worrisome. We approach each component in turn. We then see how plausibility and implications can be correlated for an initial prioritisation. With this in hand, we explore some complementary approaches to refining the prioritisation, taking it to a point where we feel that there is a reasonable balance between modelled outputs and our own informed sense of an appropriate tiering.

PLAUSIBILITY ASSESSMENT

Before we consider assessment, a conceptual prelude is why we use plausibility instead of probability, which is much more common in conventional risk assessment. We already discussed why implications are preferred to risk impact. It is a broader notion that flexes for a degree of uncertainty in the effects of a situation or event. For similar reasons, for our purposes plausibility is more suitable than the standard risk assessment variable of probability.

Put simply, probability is an estimate of the chance of an event occurring in a given time frame, and in percentage terms it is between zero and one. The concept itself is not problematic, but in a political risk context it can be, for two reasons. One is that probability, and its more casual twin, likelihood, can involve a strong element of frequency, and analysts often attach too much weight to this facet of probability. Indeed, the lowest probability bracket on risk matrices in political risk is often labelled "rare". If this were only a convenient label for "very improbable", it would not really matter. But often by default, significant potential events that have never or seldom happened in a country are stuck in this bracket, even if there might be forces and interests pushing towards their occurrence. Probability itself is quite straightforward, but its association with frequency can be hard to get past, and this can lead to potentially serious errors.

The second problem is that probability looks at an event as a block occurrence, as in "the probability of X within two years is low". But in political risk, X is seldom a discrete, either/or event. Rather, it is often a potential malleable situation with an array of moving parts, some of them random or subject to human whim or eccentricity. Situations can play out by degrees over time, and their plotlines can drift. Unless clearly qualified, the notion of probability is often too mechanistic for the fuzzy world of political risk. An analogy might be trying to use Newtonian mechanics to describe subatomic interactions or black holes. It assumes too clean-cut a world to apply to a stranger domain.

Plausibility seems better suited. Every potential challenge has an element of a story, or a plot, behind it. We build a plot to make it happen in our imaginations so that we can see how it might arise and what it would mean. Plausibility includes a measure of our confidence in the plot, based on the reasoning and the weight of evidence behind it. Probability is an aspect of a plausibility judgement, but alongside the assessment of a storyline.

Turning to assessment, first, we examine plausibility considerations for different types, or categories of issues, and see how these can help to derive initial broad-brush estimates. Then we apply a fine-tuning process that tests and solidifies these to assign plausibility ratings.

Figure 7.17 on the next page depicts three broad categories of challenges along with examples, some of which span categories. Under each type of issue are two sets of applicable considerations, one for probability and one for storyline reasoning.

Rather than proceeding by types of challenges, we will examine probability and reasoning considerations in turn. Probability relates to the chance of having a given challenge in the first place. For challenges from intersections with ongoing factor dynamics, probability arises from the frequency of intersections and the timespan over which they occur, and the frequency or commonness of factor manifestation in intersections. For example, if we will need to routinely apply for permits, and if bureaucratic corruption is pervasive, then even within a few months we can expect to encounter bureaucratic corruption pressure at least once. If the phenomenon is less pervasive, perhaps we might not experience it in a short period, but if we are in the country long enough, with the same tempo of permit applications, our chances increase.

With the second type of challenge, a new event, frequency might have a role. For example, if terrorist attacks in the city happen now and then, then we might be there for the next one. For the most part, though, the probability of events comes from the strength of the indicators of what would cause them. An event does not come out of the blue. There will be motives and pressures, and a trend of intensification in these, before an event happens. At any given time, an event's probability is effectively the balance of driving and restraining forces. When restraining forces prevail, the event remains latent. As restraints give way to drivers, probability increases. Triggers are the wildcard in event probability. Some triggers are more like manifested preconditions, such as a regime changing the constitution to be in power longer, and thereby inducing mass protests. Others, like a symbolic suicide or a tax on WhatsApp messaging, are hard to predict. It is possible, though, to understand at what point triggers become relevant to an event's occurrence. The higher the pressure, or the closer something is to an edge, the less of a prick or a nudge is needed to unleash pent up potential. In other words, the potential event or change has a hair trigger.

Probability assessment for the third category of challenges, complex situations, relies less on exogenous indicators and track record, and more on actor behavioural patterns. This is partly because complex situational challenges often have a strong aspect of actor intentions and game-like interaction. Past and typical behaviours are one indicator of challenge probability. For example, in the IT consultancy case, do regime-linked partners typically use their political connections to vie for more control? We would know some of this from factor analysis, but we revisit the question now with a critical eye. As well, triggers to act in ways that would give rise to the challenge are relevant. If project renegotiation pressure could arise because of a bad cash crop harvest and government concerns about debt, then the probability of a bad harvest comes into play. For complex challenges, probability is much more fuzzy, but one can still test a challenge against these variables for an initial sense of its chance of happening. For this kind of challenge, though, the second type of plausibility variable, reasoning, is usually a major element.

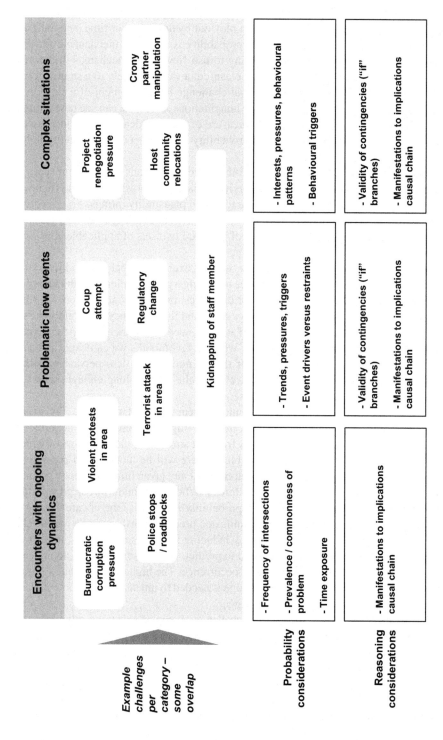

FIGURE 7.17 Plausibility variables for three types of challenges.

We already mentioned how potential challenges are in effect a story of how the operation would encounter and be affected by a factor. Stories involves plots, which can be more or less robust. In our case, plots are derived as far as possible from facts and insights, but there is still reasoning involved, and along with probability this needs to be assessed for a full picture of how plausible a challenge is.

For all three types of challenges, a significant part of the story is the causal chain from manifestations (harmful actions or events) to the posited implications. We might have a sense from probability assessment of how likely we are to have the problem at all, but part of the challenge is how it affects the operation, and we originally derived this by imagining how the challenge would play out inside and on the operation. In the earlier example of ethnic friction in the workforce, for instance, there were different posited contingencies that would trigger or intensify dysfunction and perhaps violence, such as discriminatory supervision or jealousy over pay or promotions. Now we can ask how realistic these contingencies are.

When we do so, we should not be assuming that managers have already received and absorbed political risk intelligence. Rather, we assume the current operational concept and the company's normal political risk management measures (which we characterised in the context and focus stage). Managers will start thinking about options as soon as they hear about problems, but unless or until the concept of operations and specific plans change, the original concept is our reference point.

The above process might identify some highly implausible implications that require a rethink, but on the whole it should not cause us to reformulate the core implications of a challenge even if they do seem implausible. If they are at least conceivable and are something that intelligence users would need to be aware of, then they stand, and their overall seriousness is still used when deriving a final challenge prioritisation.

The other main aspect of reasoning, contingent "if" branches, applies to the manifestation of events and complex situations (it applies less to challenges from ongoing dynamics, because they are already happening and do not depend on something else happening first, although there often "ifs" in their implications stories).

Drawing on the IT consultancy case, the event-type challenge of regulatory change was posited as an outcome of a government plan to develop the domestic knowledge sector. To develop the challenge, we had to explore what would happen "if the government decided that regulatory enforcement of skills transfer was the better policy". We were uncertain that the government would decide this, because it might worry about scaring away foreign companies. Now, this marginal confidence around the central contingency is accounted for in the assessment of plausibility.

It is worth noting that some challenges can overlap all three categories, and consequently be subject to several types of plausibility assessment. In Figure 7.17, the kidnapping of a staff member was used as an example. It is spread all the way from "encounters with ongoing dynamics" to "complex situations". The issue might have been flagged in the first place because of a relatively high incidence, or frequency, of kidnapping in the area of operation. In other words, kidnapping is an ongoing dynamic. A kidnapping is a specific event, which could depend on bandit or insurgent targeting patterns and perhaps specific intentions towards foreign companies. Then if the victim survived that long, the kidnap resolution phase is a complex situation, very much game-like with moves and countermoves. Plausibility assessment for a whole kidnap case, if that was how we defined the challenge, would use approaches relevant to each of the three types of challenge.

Related to the above is that for some complex situational challenges, we will need to clearly define the parameters of the challenge, specifically where we stop in a chain of events and what we include in the challenge story. In a kidnapping, for example, are we assessing an attempt, a seizure, a killing, a botched negotiation, or all of these? We would have defined this in the manifestation to implications chain when shaping the challenge, but if a challenge is still fuzzy, we need to set boundaries, or what exactly we are assessing for plausibility will be unclear.

While the above thought processes present some difficulties, they would give us at least initial indications of plausibility. At this point, a comparative review might reveal outliers, or challenges whose plausibility seems too high or low in relation to comparable reference points. This can call for some rethinking and adjustment.

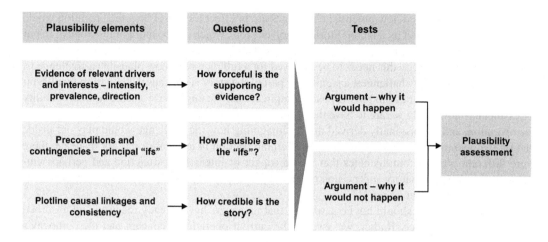

FIGURE 7.18 Plausibility assessment check and finalisation.

The next step in plausibility assessment is testing and refinement. This is a relatively quick thought exercise done for each challenge. It integrates our thinking to this point towards honing our initial plausibility assessment. This is illustrated in Figure 7.18.

This is very general, and other frameworks could work just as well, but bear in mind that we have already considered plausibility variables in detail, so this final exercise should be quite top level. The aim is to test our confidence in the plausibility assessments we have formulated thus far, not redo them. What is noteworthy, and often underutilised, is the final test of competing arguments, one in favour of the challenge happening, and the other for why it would not happen. We can then see how the arguments stack up against each other. Refinement would favour the stronger argument.

Now, for the sake of subsequent prioritisation modelling, we need to assign plausibility scores or ratings. There is a variety of probability rating scales in use. One five-point scale used in the US intelligence community for many years is somewhat typical, and it also has the advantage of not using frequency-related probability terms. Since this kind of one to five scale is probably most familiar to readers, we present it here as an option, but alongside it we also posit a commensurate plausibility scale. These are depicted in Figure 7.19.

In both, there are not just single scores for a label, but ranges. Although in both government intelligence and political risk, one would not usually derive fine-tuned statistical estimates, sometimes

Common probability labels	Percentage indicators	Plausibility labels	Plausibility scores
Remote	7, +/- 5	Speculative	1 – 2
Unlikely	30, +/- 10	Conceivable	2 – 4
Even chance	50, +/- 10	Plausible	4 – 6
Probable	75, +/- 12	Credible	6 – 8
Almost certain	93, +/- 6	Convincing	8 – 10

FIGURE 7.19 Probability and plausibility rating schemes.

there will be enough confidence for more granular comparisons, and the "give or take" margins in each scheme allow for finer distinctions.

The plausibility terms do not have associated percentages; rather, they have simple scores from 1 to 10. We can imagine that 0 would be something like "inconceivable/entirely speculative" and 11 "self-evident/obvious". Having numerical scores allows for basic data manipulation and graphing. The same can be done with probability ratings, and in conventional risk assessment a basic one to five scale (low to high) is usually used for that purpose.

There are two nuanced considerations. One is how to account for frequencies that we might have used in assessing plausibility. The above scale is only about having the challenge at all, but we might have found that the challenge is likely to arise multiple times or even regularly. Frequency matters because the effects of a recurrent problem can be cumulative. We will include frequency as an adjustment variable in final prioritisation, but it should still be clearly noted when a challenge is likely to be recurrent so that intelligence users can derive appropriate plans to reduce frequency or cumulative effects.

The other consideration is how to handle uncertainty. Looking at the probability labels above, in those terms an uncertain event is 50–50. However, that suggests considerable confidence. Like flipping a coin, we at least know that the situation is not remote and indeed that we should not be surprised if it manifested. The plausibility approach is better at capturing at least the sense of uncertainty. But with both scales, when there is high uncertainty arising from complexity, the number of pre-conditions, and potentially also secrecy and opacity, involved in a potential challenge, like frequency it should be noted alongside a given score. A note attached to a rated challenge would read something like the following: "The score reflects a reasonable midpoint, but confidence is only moderate and depending on random or inestimable variables plausibility could be, or become, higher. The challenge bears monitoring to adjust plausibility as indications clarify." As we will see later, uncertainty will also be among the variables that adjust raw prioritisation.

IMPLICATIONS ASSESSMENT

We already derived implications, since they are inherent in potential challenges. Thus, we do not need as extensive a process to assess them as we did for plausibility. A tricky thing about rating implications is that one set of effects can mean different things for different organisations. Organisational culture, brand identity, risk attitudes, experience in challenging environments, corporate stakeholder expectations and the personal attitudes of staff assigned to an operation all impinge on how a manifested challenge would be perceived. Thus, benchmarks of seriousness should be defined within the organisation, not taken from a standard guide.

That said, there are some basic considerations in assessing and rating implications. These include the following:

- Personnel, both expat and local, are the principal asset because if they feel anxious or demoralised, an operation could unravel. Additionally, companies have an especially high duty of care for expat staff assigned to volatile environments. Thus, harm to personnel carries considerable weight when assessing implications.
- Adding to the above personnel effects, implications ratings should account for the stress and anxiety in managing a situation. If I face bureaucratic delays, I might lose 30 minutes' sleep per night. If a colleague is kidnapped, I am not going to sleep at all for a while. The effect on personnel is not just about who is directly affected. If angst in managing a challenge is not accounted for in implications, then it needs to be an adjustment variable. It is better to include it in implications assessment, as an additional personnel effect, since it is very closely related to direct personnel implications.
- Reputational effects are interpreted quite differently, with some companies having thicker skins in terms of bad press or simply not being well liked, but when reputation begins to

affect essential relationships, or incurs liability, weakened bargaining power or dangerous hostility, it starts to affect the wider set of operational assets.

- Recalling from Chapter 3, control and continuity are the main commercial performance assets, and when these erode beyond a certain point, the commercial logic of the operation does too (it is possible to put a dollar figure on some issues). Eroded control, however, is a broader problem, because it can mean less control over the preservation of people and reputation, as well as other sub-assets such as brand and intellectual property.
- We also noted that a given challenge can affect multiple assets, and the aggregate effect across assets needs to be accounted for in assigning an implications score.
- In deriving implications, for some there was a story of unfolding effects over time. The full chain of implications within the challenge should be accounted for (as discussed earlier with respect to plausibility, any time limit or limit on cause-effect branching of a challenge needs to be reasonably explicit, for the assessment of both plausibility and implications).

While a company should develop its own implications seriousness benchmarks, Figure 7.20 is an example of what this might look like at least in structure. The benchmarks themselves are purely illustrative. This also depicts a rating system, using a scale of 1 to 10 as with plausibility. If one were to use a five-point probability scale, then implications scores should also be 1 to 5, with the opportunity to use fractions for finer distinctions if need be. Theoretically, the highest bracket that any one asset-related implication reaches would define a challenge's implications rating. For example, if an operating permit were withdrawn and the operation faced an indeterminate halt, then the implications score would be in the "dire/tragic" range, even though no other assets were seriously affected. That is the theory, but in practice any rating scheme is only a guide, and the meaning that we attach to given set of implications matters more than a strict reading of the benchmarks. For example, for some companies, a halt might be bad, but it is taken as stride as a normal business problem, and would not come close to a staff member getting kidnapped. If we look at a challenge in isolation, it can be hard to decide how to score it, but by comparing as we proceed, we get a sense of the relative seriousness of challenges, and this helps to zero in on a given rating. Again, benchmarks are just there to help, and are less relevant than the significance that we attach to something.

Note that there is room for finer distinctions between ratings. For example, in "dire/tragic" for the personnel asset, there would be a significant difference between one person being killed, and two, or ten. We could fine-tune, perhaps creating benchmarks for each integer, but at some point, for

Implications label	Implications scores	Indicative reference points			
		People	**Reputation**	**Control**	**Continuity**
Inconvenient	1 – 2	- Minor hassle	- Unfair press coverage	- Minor concessions	- Minor delays
Distracting	2 – 4	- Low-grade stress	- Minor dispute / incident	- Increased oversight	- Temporary holdup
Disruptive	4 – 6	- Worried / anxious / minor injury	- Suspicion / wariness	- New rules or partners	- Major delays
Disturbing	6 – 8	- Threatened / hospitalised	- Erosion of moral standing / trust	- Unwanted equal partner	- Long-term halt / major slowdown
Dire / tragic	8 – 10	- Maimed / killed / kidnapped / jailed	- Major ethical scandal / moral liability	- Junior partner / forced handover	- Indeterminate halt

FIGURE 7.20   Implications seriousness rating scheme.

practical purposes it is splitting hairs. Again, common sense and our own internal reference points are the ultimate adjudicator.

Prioritisation

At this point, we have plausibility and implications scores out of 10 for each challenge, and now it is time to relate the two components for a baseline prioritisation. We will adapt a tool that is probably familiar to many readers, the probability-impact matrix, which we have discussed at several points.

The matrix has been around for decades, but with the exploding interest in enterprise risk management, it has gone from being a handy summary picture for presentations, to a widespread tool for final risk prioritisation. The more risk assessment being done by ever more functions in a company, the greater the demand for a simple approach that non-specialists can use, and the matrix method is certainly simpler than statistical models. Many casual users seldom question its logic, while some experienced specialists think that the matrix is nearly useless. For domains like political risk, that deal with informed judgements about complex human dynamics, the matrix is still one of the few tools that can wed qualitative estimates of the two risk components, probability and impact, or in our case plausibility and implications. It can be problematic, but that comes more from how it is used, and how much is expected of it, than its barebones logic.

It is worth looking how the matrix approach is commonly used to see, and thereby avoid, some of its weaknesses. Figure 7.21 summarises the conventional application. As we have been, we will talk about the matrix in risk terms for illustration, since risk is its original context.

The typical matrix has five positions, from low to high, for each of probability and impact. We know a risk's probability and impact scores, and these are coordinates by which we can map it on the matrix to see its position in relation to other risks. More precisely, though, a risk's position forms the outer corner of a quadrilateral; the bigger its area, the more severe the risk. On a typical 5 × 5 matrix, a maximally severe risk has an area of 25. We can divide other risks' areas by this number for a percentage of the maximum. A risk of 2 × 2, for example, would be 16 percent of 25, a relatively

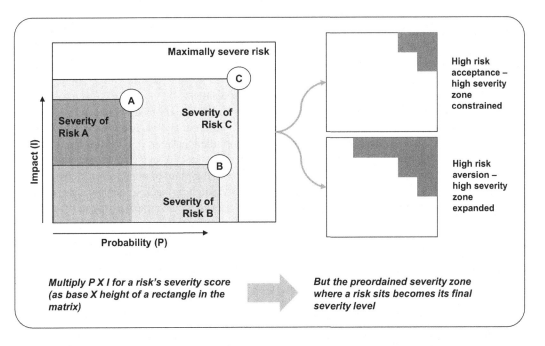

FIGURE 7.21 Conventional matrix application.

low-priority risk, while one of 4 × 3 would be 48 percent, a significantly higher priority. Thus, a risk's severity is derived from its probability (P) score multiplied by its impact (I) score.

This seems fine at first glance, and multiplying does yield a reliable raw tiering of risks. But the spreads between risks get skewed by multiplication. For example, imagine that I think a risk is quite likely and serious, so I rate it 4 for probability and 4 for impact, for a severity (P × I) score of 16. But that is only 64 percent of the possible maximum of 25, and proportionally this is rather tame by comparison to the axis scores (4 is 80 percent of 5). If I think a risk is somewhat less likely and less serious than the 4 × 4 one, I would give it a 3 × 3, one stop less on each axis. But the product of 9 is only 36 percent of the total maximum of 25, despite each score being 60 percent of its respective axis (and the 3 × 3 risk comes out at barely over half as severe as the 4 × 4 one despite being only one stop away on each axis). This skewing effect means that the outcomes often do not align with an analyst's sense of how important a risk actually is.

In fact, while probability and impact are the two main criteria of risk severity, there is no mathematical relationship between them. A review of completed matrices from across myriad organisations and initiatives might show a similar pattern, with most higher-impact risks less probable and most lower-impact ones more likely, but this is the anthropic principle at work: absurdly dangerous proposals seldom even make it to the risk assessment stage. To get a basic tiering of risks, one could just as well add probability and impact scores as though they were distinct assessment criteria. While that has quirks, it is no quirkier than multiplying.

Looking at the right-hand side of Figure 7.21, we can see how the multiplication problem is commonly addressed. Users pre-define severity zones in the matrix, often using colour-coding. For example, red, or very high severity, might cover P × I scores of 15 to 25, orange for moderate-high might cover 8 to 12, and so on. There are usually four or five coloured severity zones, from very high (red) to very low (green). Organisations spend a lot of thought on trying to get these zones right, specifically on aligning zone coverage with their attitude to risk. A risk-averse organisation might have six or seven red squares on the matrix, while a gambler might have only three red squares in the upper-right corner. Colour-coding makes sense in that it is based on a coordinate's proximity to the maximally severe intersection, the outer corner of the whole matrix. But most colour schemes are somewhat arbitrary and ambiguous when it comes to real-world application. Additionally, different contexts or types of decisions would have different significance from a risk perspective, yet once a company creates a colour scheme, it tends to get used for every initiative and level of decision, from routine IT upgrades to a merger. Finally, colour-coding is usually used alongside multiplication. Colour-coding is a de facto admission that multiplication does not really work, yet the two are there side by side, with each box, and risk therein, having its P × I score in addition to a colour. This is confusing for users, most of whom are not risk analysis specialists.

That companies try so hard to finesse colour schemes and the relationship between P × I scores and positions suggests that they are trying to do too much with the matrix. A matrix is a basic tool, and no matter how much we tweak it, it will not yield more than a sketch of issues' relative importance. It is a useful starting point, though, if we just stick to its skeletal logic. That logic is not about P × I products or pre-ordained zones, it is simply proximity to the point of maximum severity, where the maximum *P* line intersects with the maximum *I* line. Switching back to our own language, if we map challenges using their plausibility and implications scores, the simplest way to derive their relative severities is to get out a ruler and see how far they are from the upper right corner. The closer ones are more severe, and the more distant ones less. Figure 7.22 shows a matrix designed for this basic interpretation.

The matrix could be more refined, and it is just to illustrate the logic. One might notice that colour-coding a matrix actually uses the same logic. Red is always closer to the top right corner, orange somewhat more distant, all the way down to green (negligible severity) near the bottom-left corner. In our case, we will dispense with colours and just take the band as our severity level. Plausibility and implications are the critical components in challenge assessment and prioritisation, so the resulting map has meaning in itself, even before we add more layers of interpretation.

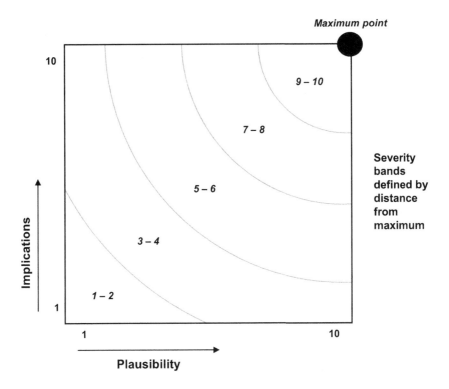

FIGURE 7.22   Matrix with severity bands.

Even though we shed some conceptual baggage, we are still left with two matrix-related problems. One is that the matrix will show a challenge with low plausibility and high implications as being no more important than one with high plausibility and minor implications. For example, a coup might be implausible, but it would be very problematic if it happened. It would end up in the 3–4 (low severity) band. Bureaucratic delays, by contrast, are nearly inevitable but they would only be inconvenient. They too end up in the 3–4 band, or perhaps even a higher one. If we just go by matrix position, we could end up assigning less importance to issues that could actually get us killed while spending more time managing minor hassles. If we consider the aforementioned frequency bias in probability assessment, and the tendency to equate uncertainty with a low probability, this is especially dangerous. Thus, whatever the scores say, the challenges that sit in the upper-left corner need to be flagged. They might be remote, but they are still conceivable.

The other problem is one we discussed. There is overlap between the two axes. A challenge might have three implications, each with its own "if" branch, and if we did a detailed analysis, we might see that their plausibility scores are different. A probability distribution or other mathematical method could capture these distinctions. We cannot really ignore this problem, but it is hardly a showstopper in our context. There is seldom enough hard data for such a fine-tuned analysis, we already caught reasonable midpoints and separated very distinct outcomes into different challenges, and it would be impractical to try to manage every permutation as a separate issue. This problem needs to be recognised, but frankly, as long as challenge formulation was reasonably nuanced, we can live with it.

Imagine that we did our mapping. A useful way to depict the final results is to take each challenge's score and divide it by the most severe challenge's score, for a relative depiction in percentage terms. This clearly shows the spreads between challenges, which is a useful complement to the visual map. We could call the prioritisation complete and move on, but what usually happens is that there is some lingering unease with the results, both in positions and in spreads. The process was mechanistic, and we can usually think of other things we should have thought about. Thus, we can try a few more exercises to see what other arrangements come up, if only to assuage that unease. We will walk through three, and bear in mind that these do not form a package or a process, nor are they part of some standard toolkit. They are only illustrations of possible interpretive testing, and readers could probably think of other tools that would make sense in their own contexts.

One possibility is to adjust the matrix band scores by adding in some other challenge attributes. For example, we mentioned how frequency (or recurrence) and uncertainty should be noted alongside assessed plausibility. They could be part of an adjustment model. How suddenly a challenge would manifest also matters, because less warning time means that we need to be more alert and prepared. Finally, we mentioned linkages between issues. We accounted for some and actually created systems when causal links were very strong, but we can still include a challenge's contribution to causing other ones. Taking these four variables into account, an adjustment model might look as shown in Figure 7.23. The challenges therein are only illustrative and this is not drawn from one of the cases.

In this example, we tried to give the matrix band its due as the heart of prioritisation by ensuring that possible scores for the other variables did not add up to more than 10, the maximum severity band. Uncertainty and suddenness were deemed more important than the other two variables, so they were assessed out of three, as opposed to two. The final scores were converted to a score out of 10, so that we can see how they vary from the raw matrix scores, and we have been using 1 to 10 scores so this just retains interpretive consistency. The adjustments are relatively minor, but if we were to revisit the relative ranking, challenge positions would shift, some moving up in the scale and some down. Bureaucratic delays, for example, become less important because their manifestation is like a drip feed (low suddenness), and they are a well-known phenomenon so we were confident in our estimation of them (low uncertainty). A coup, by contrast, goes up, because: given the secrecy surrounding coup planning, we are not especially confident that we got the assessment right (high uncertainty); a coup would manifest very suddenly; and it would affect the plausibility of several other issues (strong linkages), for example pro-democracy protests or international sanctions.

	Bureaucratic delays	Violent street crime	Change in tax levels	Coup	Local staff detained
Matrix band: n / 10	5	5	4.5	3.5	5
Uncertainty: n / 3	0.5	0.5	0.5	2	1.5
Suddenness: n / 3	0.5	3	1	3	3
Linkages: n / 2	1.5	0.5	0.5	2	1
Recurrence: n / 2	2	2	0.5	0.5	1
Sum	9.5	11	7	11	11.5
(Sum / 20) X 10	4.3	5.5	3.5	5.5	5.8

FIGURE 7.23 Matrix band prioritisation adjustment.

Agreement on scale of 1 to 10	Bureaucratic delays	Violent street crime	Change in tax levels	Coup	Local staff detained
We have little experience in managing this kind of challenge	2	4	2	9	7
It would need novel, intensive management approaches	3	3	3	5	6
We would need to be ready to manage it very soon after arrival	8	9	3	3	4
How we manage it would make a big difference	3	8	4	5	7
Sum	16	24	12	22	24
(Sum / 40) X 10	4	6	3	5.5	6
Matrix band for comparison	5	5	4.5	3.5	5

FIGURE 7.24   Prioritisation from a management perspective.

The results of the above or some variant thereof might stand as a final outcome. But we can try an entirely new angle for a fresh reference point. We can even dispense with an explicit consideration of plausibility and implications in order to get our heads into a new space. A possibility is to take a political risk management perspective and ask how hard or intensive management efforts would have to be for each challenge. Figure 7.24 is an illustration of this kind of exercise, using the same example challenges.

The precise questions could vary, but whichever are used could be presented to the operation's management team in a workshop or interview format. The basic question is to what extent they agree with the four statements with respect to each challenge. This could be also phrased as, "how applicable is this statement to…". When comparing to the matrix band positions, there are some changes in prioritisation. Bureaucratic delays are run-of-the-mill for the company, and hence not particularly problematic. Street crime could affect people as soon as they hit the ground, and managing the challenge, for example through basic security procedures, would make a lot of difference. The team has little experience in dealing with the risk or event of a coup. It would need to be intensively planned for to avoid the worst effects, although there is some time to do this since the challenge is still somewhat latent. The nett effect is that the coup's score goes up. It would be possible to combine the scores from this exercise with the matrix band scores, as we did with the adjustment model. However, as it is, it provides a fresh point of view, and might be better left as food for thought for when we make our final, refined assessment.

Finally, for purposes here anyway, we can ditch scores and try an approach based purely on informed common sense and team discussion. This could be called bracketing, whereby we keep taking finer prioritisation slices of the full set of challenges until we end up with a reasonably nuanced breakdown. This approach is illustrated in Figure 7.25.

In a team workshop setting, we would work our way down the pyramid, from two severity brackets to five, making decisions about where to allocate challenges at each tier. At the final layer, we can assign one of the two possible scores to a challenge or use paired comparisons ("which one is

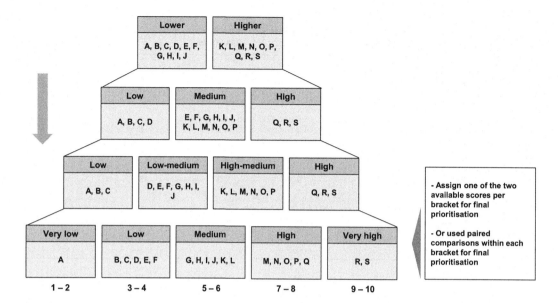

FIGURE 7.25   Prioritisation from bracketing.

more important, this one or that one?") for a final, refined prioritisation, and again derive a relative spread. Final pinpoint scoring might be splitting hairs but it could be interesting. It is likely that the team doing this would know the plausibility and implications scores and the given matrix severity band for each challenge, but it would be ideal if they did not refer to them again until afterwards. It can be surprising how closely the outputs of this kind of exercise correspond to assessed matrix positions. What is more interesting, though, are the discrepancies. Because this was done wholly through reasoned debate, there would be a rationale attached to each challenge's final position, and if that position is different from the matrix band, then the matrix band score might need to be adjusted.

One could add more exercises, or other ones. The important point is that we do not just take the matrix as the final word. We can dress it up in a number of ways, and it still cannot do more than provide a raw initial prioritisation. There will be different results from each follow-up exercise, and they need to be reconciled for a final tiering. One could imagine a mathematical approach, perhaps averaging scores out of 10 from across the different frameworks, but in any such process quirks are bound to arise. We need to bite the bullet at some point and just go with what feels sensible, taking scores and outputs into account but not being bound by them.

As a part of this final sense-making, a devil's advocacy element would help. Indeed, reviews from outside of a group which has been working together on the same problem is a fundamental quality control measure in intelligence, and it could apply to any intelligence exercise.

Except for devils' advocacy, the author actually applied each prioritisation exercise, including the initial plausibility-implications mapping, to both cases, but depicting various results is too detailed for purposes here. We will see the matrix for each case in the next section, where it has been converted into a planning, as opposed to assessment, format. Based on the baseline prioritisation and adjustments, the final results for each case are presented in Figure 7.26.

We can note two points in the prioritisation. First, recall that in the clean-up step we discerned one challenge system for the highway case, and this was indeed assessed as one integrated issue, labelled as host community friction. It became the constructor's most severe potential challenge. Second, a couple of similar issues across the two cases are in different severity brackets. A given type of challenge in one operational context can have different significance in another. For example, bureaucratic corruption is less of a problem for the constructor because it is working on a government contract and can probably expect some support with the issue from its customer, the

	Very high	High	Medium	Low	Very low
West African highway project	- Host community friction (system of four challenges) - Strike – workforce - Workplace friction - Bandit / insurgent kidnap	- Unions obstruct local hiring - Successful coup - Violent street crime - Local elections ethnic clashes	- Violent democratic unrest - Insurgent attack on operation - Political pressure on project - Rival faction bureaucratic obstruction	- Local contractor corruption - Coup attempt (failed) - Port strike - Customs delays - Corruption pressure - Project cancellation - Bureaucratic delays	- Police roadblock hassles - Donor-president friction over non-democratic tendencies - Sea piracy – lost shipment
MENA IT consultancy	- Crony partner manipulation - Crony competitor retribution - Local staff detention	- Change in FDI ownership rules	- Govt pressure for surveillance projects - Revolutionary unrest - Bureaucratic corruption - Bureaucratic delays - Terrorist attack in capital - Socio-economic protests	- Organised criminal extortion attempt - Change in local content rules	- State nepotism pressure - Terrorist attack on company - Local neighbourhood friction - New currency controls

FIGURE 7.26 Challenge prioritisation for the two cases.

Ministry of Transport. Conversely, an attack on the operation is a more severe issue for the constructor than it is for the IT consultancy. While the overall plausibility of an attack was assessed as low, uncertainty was a significant adjustment variable because of the jihadist insurgency in the Sahel to the north of the country, which routinely has unexpected twists and turns. In the IT consultancy's MENA country context, what we learned about terrorist targeting and behaviour made an attack seem remote, and at least for the time being there is little uncertainty about its implausibility.

The full tiering of challenges would start at the top of the "very high" box and proceed down each until we reached the last challenge in the "very low" box. In practice, using relative scores with the most severe challenge as 1.00 or 100 percent, we would group challenges by proximity. Having five boxes suggests that each one covers a 20 percent spread, but if we had one challenge at 0.39 and one at 0.41, it would make little sense to stick them in different pre-ordained categories. Thus, we would let natural groupings define the brackets, and we could end up with more than just five.

We noted in assessment that frequency and uncertainty deserve special mention, and this remains the case even if we included both as adjustment variables. More importantly, as noted, we cannot let the challenges in the upper-left corner of the matrix fall from view. These are the ones that are implausible but whose manifestation would be very damaging. An appropriate label for this category, or section of the matrix, would be "potential nasty surprises".

A final point before moving on from this section is that by prioritising challenges we can also prioritise factors. Factors were, in a sense, a vehicle to get us to challenges. But they are also broad targets for follow-up monitoring. For example, if ethnic tensions or regime infighting were drivers of important potential challenges, one would keep an eye on them to see how they evolve, and how changes therein could affect the operation. For each factor, one could add up severity scores for the challenges deriving from it and convert the sum to a score out of 1.00, or 100 percent, by dividing each factor's score by the biggest sum. This would again clearly depict a severity spread, or put another way, the spread between factors' overall contribution to the operation's political risk.

One problem that is likely to come up in factor prioritisation is that some challenges derived from more than one factor, or in the clean-up step were integrated from the storylines of challenges under different factors. This could complicate factor prioritisation, but since this step does not directly feed into planning, some reasoned fudging is not problematic. It is mainly for a sense of which broad dynamics are more worth keeping an eye on.

FINAL RESULTS AND PLANNING INPUTS

Chapter 9 addresses planning in detail, using the results of terrain and stakeholder analysis. Thus, here we only provide a flavour of the results from terrain analysis and how they can be applied to generate at least initial planning considerations.

As noted, terrain analysis can be a stand-alone exercise, or there might be a need for interim results during the wider baseline exercise. Combining the outputs of the prior context and focus stage with terrain analysis, we would have a robust picture of the operational context, key dynamics in the socio-political system, and the challenges that could arise from those dynamics. Even in the absence of further stages, this would provide some confidence in planning for how to make the operation more resilient. There would be different kinds of documented reports and briefings in the handover to planning. We will not cover the gamut here. Instead, just for illustration we will briefly examine three outputs, which are aimed at the briefing and workshop level of reporting rather than extracted from a main report. These are a factor synopsis, a challenge synopsis and the challenge matrix.

Figure 7.27 is an example of a factor synopsis, using the factor of ethnic tensions from the West African highway case.

Main sources and links	Assets affected
- National-level (principally north-south) ethnic and sectarian divisions, worsened by government discrimination - Particularly acute in central-northern sub-region, where southern and northern groups cohabitate, and where migration imports ethnic and sectarian sub-nationalism from both ends of the country - Linked to ethnic clashes, jihadist insurgency, human rights, policing and labour activism	- Principally reputation – moral standing - Secondarily continuity and personnel

Intersections	Principal challenges
- Local hiring – importing ethnic tensions into the workforce (linked to labour activism – union obstruction of local hiring) - CSR initiatives – CSR could be perceived as unfair and advantaging one group over another - Relocations – sensitivity to perceived favouritism or discrimination	- Workforce friction – between workers from rival groups - Host community distrust – rival groups perceive unfairness or discrimination in treatment or operational impacts - Perceived collusion with human rights abuses – police intervene in host community protests or are heavy-handed in responding to local hostility to company - Host community relocations go badly – mistrust and mutual hostility severely disrupt process, incur protests and clashes

Overall importance and why	CRITICAL: High sensitivities and mutual distrust could be affected by and linked to the operation, which could suffer serious reputational damage and continuity and security problems if tensions escalate in the areas of operation – this is particularly the case during relocations in the initial phase

FIGURE 7.27   Factor synopsis, ethnic tensions.

We do not provide much detail on the sources and drivers of the factor. The "Context" section of a synopsis report would have positioned ethnic tensions within the socio-political system, and readers would have the main report for more background. The synopsis sets up the discussion of challenges deriving from the factor, by outlining the main operational intersections and the challenges that these could give rise to. Finally, we have a brief assessment of the factor's overall importance. In this case, ethnic tensions are at the heart of the challenge system (labelled "host community friction" as discussed earlier) which is the constructor's most severe potential issue, and hence the factor was appropriately assessed as critically important.

A challenge synopsis is illustrated in Figure 7.28 on the next page, using the challenge of crony partner manipulation from the IT consultancy case.

Note that the summary does not review the thought process and the precise judgements which led to prioritisation. That would be too detailed for a quick reference piece, and the main report would contain key rationales. There are two noteworthy points in this example. First, there are two sets of implications, just as there would be for corruption pressure (pay bribes or do not) or a labour strike (acquiesce to demands or do not). Here, the implications also vary according to the company's response. However, the overall difficulty or harm is approximately the same either way, and our implications rating would have covered both the baseline and contingent scenarios. The baseline is called that because it is the scenario that would unfold in the current concept of operations, which sees the company forming a partnership and trying to sustain it. However, it is very likely that the company would resist illegitimate crony pressure, and hence that contingency had to be examined too. Recall our earlier discussion of how to treat plausible "if" branches. Even if they do not affect the magnitude of the issue, they should be noted for planning purposes.

The second point in this example is the note that "we have not yet committed…". This strongly implies that an obvious way to handle the challenge is just to use an entirely different approach to country entry. For example, if the company abandoned the idea of working with a major local partner

Mechanism / story line	Main sources and linkages
- We partner with a local company that is a regime crony, perhaps via military links or family ties to regime insiders - They legitimately use brand association with us to increase their own credibility, but then push for increased control, using the brand but without adherence to partnership protocols or the contract - They also seek to obtain our intellectual property (IP) for their own use - We challenge these efforts, and they activate regime ties to try to pressure us to go along, or to put us in a situation of total dependence on them for market access	- Arises from the fact that the most well-entrenched and capable prospective partners are regime cronies – they are hard to avoid if we want rapid market access - Linked to corruption (via partner corrupt practices), bureaucratic hassles (as crony pressure tactic), IP risk (via pressure to obtain IP beyond contractual agreement), pressure to partake in repressive surveillance contracts, and possibly security threats if a partner activates intelligence or criminal contacts to increase pressure

Baseline implications – if we do not challenge pressure	Contingent implications – if we challenge pressure
- Loss of control over management direction and potentially some IP - Increased corruption / moral liability via partner practices and collusion in repressive technology projects - Isolation from / mistrust of independent business community	- Trumped-up regulatory and bureaucratic hassles - Potentially squeezed out the country because of operational paralysis from the above issues - Potentially threats to personnel

Overall severity and why	CRITICAL: Our plan was to enter via well established local partners, who seem important to our rate of expansion, but it is very plausible that such relationships could backfire and either incur significant loss of control and integrity issues, or lead to marginalisation NOTE: We have not yet committed to this entry strategy – it is not irrevocable

FIGURE 7.28 Challenge synopsis, crony partner manipulation.

and took a more gradual approach to entry, it would make the issue highly implausible, thereby reducing its severity. As we will see in the next chapter, the IT consultancy decides to do exactly that on the basis of terrain findings. But even if a solution to a challenge seems obvious and necessary, a challenge is still assessed according to the current concept of operations, not possible alternatives. Until the IT consultancy firmly decides to change its approach, the current concept is the one that involves working with a major national partner, and in that context the challenge is very severe.

Both synopses would not be particularly robust as planning inputs without the main report to back them up, but for the purposes of a quick guide during discussions they contain the key reference points. The next output we examine is the plausibility-implications matrix, or challenge matrix for short, reformatted as a basic planning tool.

When we derived the final challenge prioritisation, plausibility and implications ratings were the main variables, but not the only ones. We took several angles on challenges' severities, and the final result was an integrated judgement. Thus, it is important to bear in mind that the challenge matrix, which is simply the original plausibility-implications matrix in a different format, is not meant to depict priorities. Rather, it is intended to inspire thinking around two very broad means of making a challenge less severe, reducing its plausibility, and/or reducing its implications.

Recall that the original matrix was a box with the upper-right corner as the intersection of maximum plausibility and implications scores. The closer a challenge was to that corner, the more severe it was. Here, we turn the box into a cross, with the two axes intersecting at their midpoints, creating four quadrants. This seems like a minor tweak, but it effectively creates a map of challenges and helps with visual interpretation. We could add in two other pieces of information. First, it is possible to show challenges' final rankings, either by colour-coding them or just giving them rank labels. Second, we could draw links between challenges to show causal relationships. However, adding in more information can lead to visual clutter. For purposes here, we omit these and just depict the challenges mapped according to their plausibility and implications positions. The challenge matrix for the West African highway case is shown in Figure 7.29, followed by the matrix for the MENA IT case in Figure 7.30.

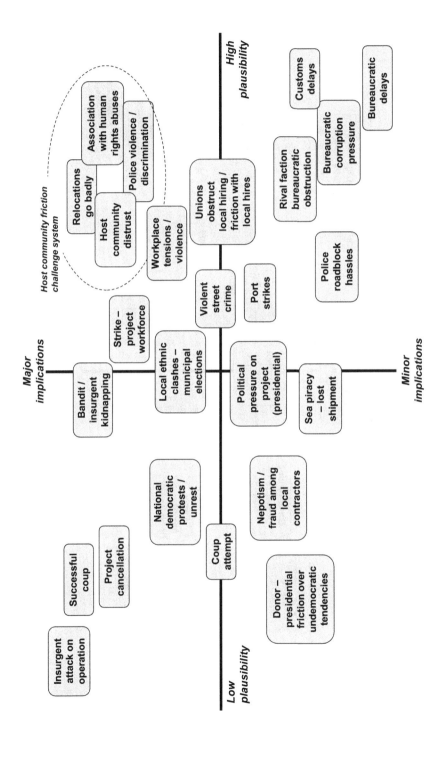

FIGURE 7.29   Challenge matrix, West African highway case.

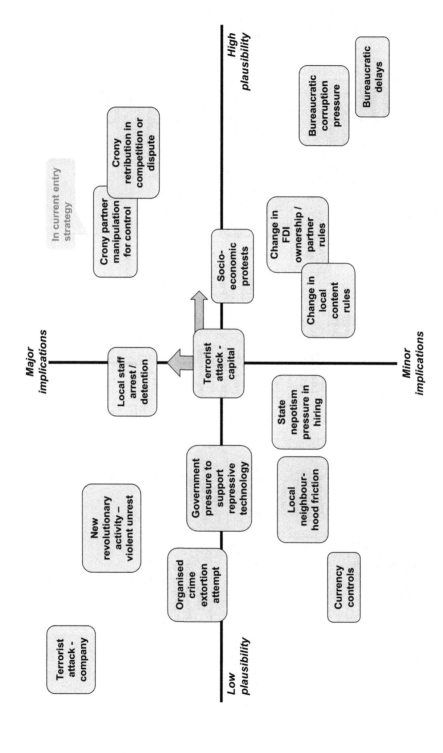

FIGURE 7.30   Challenge matrix, MENA IT consultancy case.

In Figure 7.29, the four closely linked challenges in the challenge system of host community friction (assessed as one issue) are grouped by a dotted perimeter. Note that the challenge of "insurgent attack on the operation" is on the low plausibility end, but we noted earlier how the uncertainty around it made it more severe than its baseline plausibility would suggest. As this demonstrates, we need to be careful to keep in mind that the matrix does not show final severity assessments, and it would be a good idea to keep the final prioritisation in hand, or posted on a wall, while using the challenge matrix.

In the matrix for the IT consultancy case in Figure 7.30, because the terrorist attack in the capital has such variable parameters, the variability was depicted even though the uncertainty around it would have been accounted for in the adjusted prioritisation. Another point is the note, "in current entry strategy", added to the crony partner manipulation challenge. This is just to remind people that the challenge's position is based on the current operational concept, not possible alternatives that might have sprung to mind immediately upon learning about the problem.

A way to apply the matrix for initial planning is to focus on overall de-prioritisation, initially emphasising priority challenges but also easily manageable ones. Plans would aim to move challenges further down and left, until the whole map looked less troublesome, or indeed looked quite tolerable. This would involve developing top-level options to manage challenges and screening them to select those with the greatest cost-effectiveness. Then, with reference to links between challenges, approaches can be refined and integrated into a smaller set of more holistic initiatives. At this stage we can even test sequencing, to see what should be addressed first for the greatest effect on other issues. At a workshop level this would not yield robust plans, but it would provide an outline which could then be the basis for deeper ruminations. As we see in Chapter 9, we will ultimately apply a holistic approach that addresses closely related challenges together, and within a wider political risk strategy. That will take stakeholder insights on board as well, and hence will be different to what we have discussed here.

If terrain analysis were undertaken as a stand-alone exercise, the next step would be detailed planning. However, in the context of the wider baseline exercise, drawing solid management conclusions at this point is premature. Lacking a perspective on relationships and attitudes towards the operation, insights are still somewhat two-dimensional. Stakeholder analysis adds another critical dimension, and the next chapter examines how.

8 Stakeholder Analysis

Terrain analysis has provided a detailed picture of the socio-political environment and the challenges that could manifest from dynamics within it. Terrain challenges are specific to the operation but arise from many of the same factors that would affect other companies in the country. To some extent, they are the risks of just being there. But as we have noted, there is another source of complications, and of opportunities to manage them, socio-political stakeholders, entities with which the operation will have some kind of relationship, for better or worse. Actors whom we rely on and affect, who have expectations of us and who see us as a problem or a predatory opportunity are a significant variable in a company's foreign experience. This is particularly the case in complex emerging markets, where institutional boundaries between business and other domains of social interaction can be very porous. Terrain analysis can be a stand-alone exercise, but in more sensitive environments it often lacks the nuance needed for confident navigation. Stakeholder analysis, the subject of this chapter, can be an essential facet of the political risk intelligence picture.

While stakeholder analysis can be an independent exercise, as we proceed in this chapter we will be conducting it as part of a wider baseline intelligence process, and continuing with the two cases, namely the highway constructor in West Africa and the IT consultancy in a MENA country.

The objectives of stakeholder analysis are the same whether it is a stand-alone exercise or a stage in a broader one. These are to discern who matters to the operation and why, key potential friction points, the challenges that stakeholders could present, and indications of how to engage or otherwise deal with stakeholders for a smooth country experience. The last point bears expansion. We try not just to foresee problems but also to discern potential opportunities for positive engagement towards managing specific challenges and reducing overall political risk, if only by stakeholders accepting the company's presence, or sharing local insights to help better understand the country. This is an important distinction from terrain analysis, which was mainly about challenges inherent in the environment.

Figure 8.1 on the next page is a depiction of the stakeholder analysis process that we will apply here.

The first step, identification, is easier if we have done terrain analysis, but the process starts from scratch. A preliminary socio-political profile for the operation forms an interpretive backdrop. Then we look for broad types of actors that could be relevant, using a series of identification frameworks to generate hypotheses. Types are then researched to find actual actors who might matter. When we discuss this step, a prelude is what exactly the unit of analysis is, since every actor is actually part of a larger one, and delineating relevant actors can be challenging.

We now have stakeholders to investigate, but first we need to know how they interact in their immediate domains, which are arenas of especially close socio-political interaction, such as a national government or a business community. An actor's role and relationships in its primary domain help to explain its baseline values, interests and behaviour. Domains also help to estimate potential aggregate responses to an operation, and socio-political niches that a company might fit into. We will consider how to define domains, and how to map them to discern relevant relationships and dynamics.

Next, stakeholder investigation and assessment go hand in hand, because we investigate towards discerning an actor's attitude towards the operation and its potential influence, which are the main assessment criteria. Along with targeted assessment, though, investigation yields a characterisation of a stakeholder, so that we also have a more holistic understanding of them. This step also discerns actors' cross-domain linkages, which we bring to bear in the next step, linkage mapping.

DOI: 10.1201/9781003149125-11

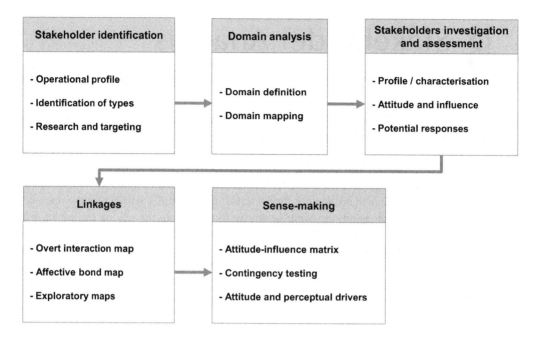

FIGURE 8.1   Stakeholder analysis process.

Linkage mapping follows the investigation of all stakeholders. We already have domain maps that we developed prior to stakeholder investigation, but after investigation we really know how actors relate to each other both within and across domains. Mapping these linkages reveals potential groupings and networks that could respond in similar ways and leverage each other's influence, and also lines of friction and rivalry that the company would need to be aware of in forging relationships. Links are important intelligence in themselves, but they also adjust our initial assessment of a stakeholder's attitude and influence because now we have a clearer understanding of the effects of alliances and rivalries.

Finally, we move onto sense-making, or extracting top-level findings. The assessment of attitude and influence yields a stakeholder matrix, which, like the plausibility-implications matrix from the previous chapter, provides the basis of early considerations on engagement options and strategies. Another valuable planning handover is the key reasons for both positive and negative perceptions of the operation. Finally, potential stakeholder issues are summarised. In planning, they will be integrated with terrain challenges to yield a holistic view of the issues that the operation could face.

As we did in the last chapter, having a sense of how stakeholder analysis works in practice would help to picture it as we proceed. Note that while we will deal with domains in one section for a cohesive explanation, in an actual analysis after defining domains we would allocate them between members of the intelligence team. Whoever is responsible for a given domain would do the domain mapping, and then armed with that contextual awareness would investigate the stakeholders within the domain. Thus, rather than doing all domain mapping as a precursor to stakeholder investigation, there would be several concurrent domain-stakeholder workstreams, as illustrated in Figure 8.2.

On a more practical note, we have mentioned that stakeholder analysis is the most nuanced stage in the baseline exercise, and the most demanding in terms of intelligence collection. For actionable insights, fieldwork and human sources are required. We do not address the practicalities here, but Chapter 13's discussion of human intelligence particularly applies to stakeholder analysis.

We now proceed with the first step in the process, identification and targeting.

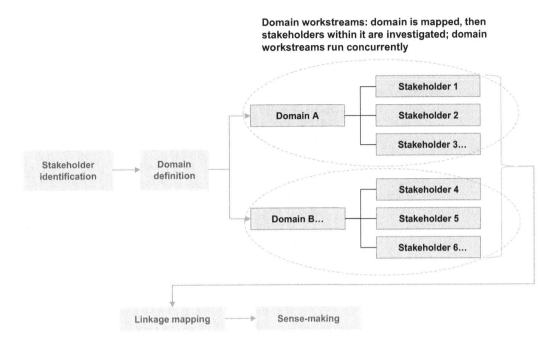

Domain workstreams: domain is mapped, then stakeholders within it are investigated; domain workstreams run concurrently

FIGURE 8.2   Domain-stakeholder workstreams.

IDENTIFICATION AND TARGETING

Chapter 6, on context and focus, set some parameters on who might matter to the operation, but it was quite top level and aimed more at guiding the immediately following step, terrain analysis. Terrain analysis in turn would have disclosed some relevant actors, but not as a primary aim, and not every terrain factor or challenge would have a commensurate stakeholder attached to it. For example, instability of either type is driven by actors, but their behaviour in dissent or factional rivalry would not usually be motivated by their perception of a specific foreign company. Thus, even after considerable country research, we need an explicit stakeholder identification step, or intelligence targets will be too generic to guide investigation.

This step proceeds as follows. First, we address the conceptual problem of what constitutes an actor and a stakeholder, so that we know what kinds of units could be relevant. Then we develop a preliminary socio-political profile for the operation as an aid in identification. Identification frameworks follow and take several perspectives on the socio-political milieu to derive relevant types of actors. Research then discerns who fits the identified types to discern actual actors.

CLARIFYING THE UNITS OF ANALYSIS

We discussed what constitutes a stakeholder in Chapter 3. To recapitulate, the basic criteria that an actor has to meet for being a stakeholder include:

- we will need or depend on them, and/or they could potentially support us;
- we could affect their interests by carrying out the operation as planned; and/or
- they could otherwise have an interest in the operation because of values, symbols or opportunities, including predatory, that we represent to them.

Note that the above criteria would exclude socio-political actors whose actions could affect us, but who are not acting towards or on the company. A stakeholder, again, has or could have some kind of relationship to us, either directly or via perception.

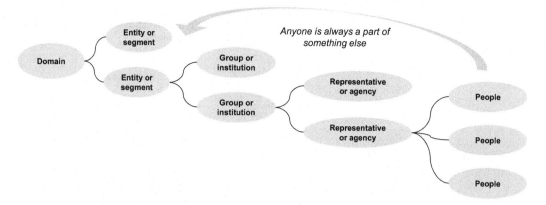

FIGURE 8.3   Actor breakdown.

Knowing what makes an actor a stakeholder is one thing. More challenging is what constitutes an actor. This is because no matter what or whom we select, they are always part of something bigger than themselves, and hence there are actors within actors. This makes it hard to put boundaries on any given "who". Consider Figure 8.3, which illustrates levels of actor breakdown.

A domain or broad entity, like a government or a host community, could be seen as an actor, but it is too abstract and internally differentiated to behave cohesively. We can look for specific groups or institutions, like a certain neighbourhood or a ministry, and they come closer to being cohesive, engageable actors, but they still might be quite abstract and differentiated. If we started on the other end, with smaller, discrete agencies or even specific people, they would behave more as one unit and there would be specific individuals to talk to. However, they would likely be parts of a larger unit and answerable to it. In focusing on the smaller unit, we could inadvertently pass inappropriate or confusing messages further up the actor chain or interpret personal or narrow perspectives as representative of a wider whole.

We need to consider bigger entities and groups, since their broad perception of the operation could be a factor in the company's experience, but we also need specific ingress points, representatives and conduits, and these would be much more discrete units. Balancing these imperatives requires flexibility in what we call an actor, and at least an initial understanding of how the relevant social-political milieus actually work. There are several common possibilities that we can use as reference points, again bearing in mind that any actor unit is part of a larger one:

- An institution or organisation, like a ministry, company, NGO, religious establishment, local council, business association or independent press outlet – these are cohesive through a hierarchy and have shared organisational interests, although when it comes to engagement we would still need to identify the most relevant ingress points or channels.
- A relatively autonomous or special purpose sub-unit of a larger organisation, such as an investment promotion agency within a ministry of industry, or a particular mosque or church in the area of operation – these might be bound to a larger organisation but have a somewhat unique internal perspective and some leeway to forge their own responses to a foreign operation.
- A segment of a wider population, for example environmental NGOs within the wider NGO community, or the independent business press within the media – when a swathe of similar organisations could take an interest in the operation, they can be treated as a segment, similar to how marketers apply segmentation to understand large tranches of customers. There will be some organisations that could act as direct conduits to a segment, but on the whole, interaction with a segment is by broad mutual messaging, not direct interaction.

- Proxies and conduits within a social entity, for example a tribal council, neighbourhood association or local tradesmen union in the host community in the area of operation – these are cohesive units and we could get their perspective on shared interests. However, we would need to ensure that the set of actors identified as channels to the wider milieu together represented all relevant groups in the community, or we could end up with a biased or incomplete view of how the company was locally perceived, and in engagement we could appear to be favouring certain interests over others.
- An established and cohesive network, such as the *makhzen* in Morocco which consists of business-political elites linked to the king through traditional ties, the power "clans" in Algeria based on sub-regional and ideological affiliations, and kinship networks in Africa, the Middle East and Central Asia – elite networks and "clans" might be informal, but more established ones can be as unified and influential as any ministry. Again, there can be specific conduits, whether families or people, into a network, but the network itself would be a relevant actor unit.
- Specific individual people, such as informal presidential or ministerial advisors, and influential traditional leaders – in more institutionalised countries, we deal with whoever fills a role and do not think too much about the specific person, but in complex environments individuals can be at the nexus of different social and political networks, and have influence well beyond their overt roles. When they are employed as political advisors, they can become de factor gatekeepers to official power holders and have a significant effect on policy and even on a government's attitude to a particular foreign operation.

The above can help to define relevant actors, but if actor breakdown cannot be resolved in the identification step, given our limited knowledge at this point, it is perfectly permissible to pass the buck to stakeholder investigation. There we will develop enough insight for confident choices on the relevant actor units.

Actor delineation is particularly relevant when we begin research on actual actors that fit the relevant types discerned in initial identification, but it is useful to be aware of the possibilities early on so that we can at least visualise them as we develop hypotheses.

PRELIMINARY OPERATIONAL PROFILE

We introduced the concept of a socio-political profile in Chapter 3. When we get to stakeholder investigation, one key question is the stakeholder's potential attitude to the operation. The operation's profile is a reference point for that assessment, enabling us to extrapolate what the operation, or relevant facets of it, could mean to different actors. However, a preliminary profile is also useful in identification, because it helps to generate ideas on who might take an interest based on operational attributes. Thus, before using identification frameworks, we can develop a top-level profile as an interpretive aid, drawing on terrain analysis insights for a general idea of what attributes could trigger socio-political interest.

To briefly refresh from Chapter 3, the main profile elements are as follows:

- the operation's physical properties and effects;
- the operation's socio-economic implications for society and government;
- the company's public identity and reputation, including nationality and socio-political symbolism; and
- the operation's political aspect, through ties to foreign and host country government actors.

A profile for the West African highway operation provides an illustration. First, it will cover a sizeable area and affect both the towns it is connecting and rural areas between them. As with most construction projects, it will cause noise, dust and traffic disruption, and because of security issues its protective cordon will be another physical impact. As an aside, if there is a social-environmental impact assessment (SEIA), it could be very useful for ideas about relevant physical attributes and socio-economic implications, although again beware of the difference between an SEIA and stake-holder intelligence.

The operation's positive socio-economic implications include jobs and local company contracts, as well as the benefits of having a modern highway strengthening trade and transport links to a remote part of the country. With respect to host communities, the company plans on local hiring and CSR initiatives to garner acceptance and offset hassles caused by the project. There could be intense competition for jobs and local CSR, and there is considerable scope for disappointment and a sense of injustice if expectations and the distribution of benefits are not handled carefully. On the socio-economic downside, the relocations of host community members close to the construction sites could be harmful if not carefully handled, and in the north the security cordon could disrupt the livelihoods of nomadic herder communities.

The company has no particular reputational burden, and it is accustomed to donor agencies' integrity, developmental and environmental expectations. We can assume the company is French, and this can be a double-edged sword in ex-French colonies. On the one hand, there is some cultural affinity via *la francophonie*, and the common language of business helps. But there is still some lingering resentment of colonialism, and indeed the country's post-independence mutation into a somewhat anti-Western, Soviet-allied people's republic was partly driven by this sentiment. Being from the ex-colonial power carries some old, but still meaningful, baggage. If the company does make mistakes, its nationality might amplify public reactions.

Finally, the political aspect includes the company's affiliation with the donor agencies funding the project. While one such agency might be African, we can assume that another is European (European Union level), and a third is the French aid agency. Donor affiliations thus put the project more or less in the "Western/European camp" and give it some association with French foreign policy. The customer is the current government, led by the president and his faction. We know from terrain analysis that the country is a democracy but a tenuous one lately given the president's bent for centralising power. We also know that the government has a reputation for favouritism towards the south, and that this has contributed to resentment among northern Muslim populations. We do not know this now, but among northern communities this aspect of the profile might generate some suspicion about the rationale behind the highway. It is possible that they will see it as a government attempt to extend tighter control over the north (e.g. a highway makes it easier to deploy security forces). When combined with French anti-jihadist military action in the neighbouring Sahel, there could even be a fringe notion that the highway project is part of a government-French joint conspiracy to maintain southern dominance. Linking back to the company's French origins, this perspective could be problematic.

There would be more nuance in the above, but it suffices to illustrate a reference point to help generate ideas on who might take an interest. It would be useful to briefly consider how the profile for the IT consultancy planning to enter an Arab/Arab-Berber country would differ, since it represents a very different type of operation.

For one thing, the IT consultancy's operation would have a limited physical footprint. To spare its staff daily traffic hassles, it wants to situate its office in a quiet suburb. This might mean some minor disruption for residential neighbours, who might also be concerned that if a terrorist group wanted to bomb the company, neighbouring households could be collateral damage. We know from terrain analysis that an attack on the company is a remote possibility, but we should be aware of the concern among neighbours. The operation's socio-economic implications are more significant. It represents knowledge and skills transfer, some good jobs even if it will not be a major employer, and potentially stronger business performance among its local customers, assuming the consultancy's projects are effective. On the downside, the operation could represent competition for domestic firms trying to grow their own IT service businesses and might appear to some players to be a potential partner of convenience for the acquisition of IP and a veneer of association with global best practice. The company is from Europe but does not have any colonial baggage in the country, and in general it has a respected brand and track record. Thus far, it has no strong political affiliations, although if it had proceeded with a partnership prior to an intelligence exercise it could well have ended up being linked to a regime crony and a political-business faction prior to entry.

Note that both companies share the attribute of being foreign to their environments, and hence could represent ignorance or gullibility that makes them an opportunistic target for manipulation, scams or predation. Both of our imaginary companies have some emerging market and regional experience, but they could still be seen as naive, and relatively wealthy, newcomers.

We will not explicitly apply the profile in the next steps, but it forms interpretive background for all identification frameworks. Different aspects of the profile will be expanded and highlighted later in stakeholder investigation, when we home in on certain facets to help discern potential attitudes to the operation.

IDENTIFICATION FRAMEWORKS

This step applies identification frameworks, which are brainstorming tools designed to make us think about who matters from several different perspectives. We present five frameworks here. In practice, frameworks can be tailor-made for the context, and perhaps only two or three would be used. The five frameworks herein can be seen as reference points. Note that this sub-step is primarily aimed at deriving types of actors, not specific, actual ones. In practice, there would be some research, but this is mainly a brainstorming exercise. Once we have general targets, research will be applied to derive actual actors within categories and types.

We will proceed from more fluid, top-level frameworks to more nuanced and detailed ones. The five frameworks include the following:

- mind mapping;
- an identification matrix;
- proximity mapping;
- stage mapping; and
- derivation from terrain challenges.

Mind Mapping

Mind mapping is a general term for making mental associations. It starts with a central question, situation or entity, and then expands from there to related elements or ideas, which then branch off into other correlations, until we finally run out of ideas on what comes next. The results show what we currently know about the variables relevant to the problem at hand. This might not be much, but it is a starting point and indicates avenues for more research. Figure 8.4 on the following page is an illustration, using the IT consultancy case.

Even in the absence of solid information, if one knows what foreign operations in the region usually involve, it is possible to derive relevant types of actors. The exercise can even inspire new ideas. For example, the consultancy could have been prodded by the "local staff/labour" trunk to think about how the company would find local staff, and universities came up as a possibility. Some results, like business customers, do not necessarily point to socio-political actors, but we know that there is considerable business-politics overlap in the country, and hence we do not discard that result even if it might seem more relevant to business development.

Identification Matrix

Matrices are widely used in business for idea generation, with the classic Ansoff Matrix being one well-known example. The matrix depicted in Figure 8.5 is somewhat more comprehensive than a

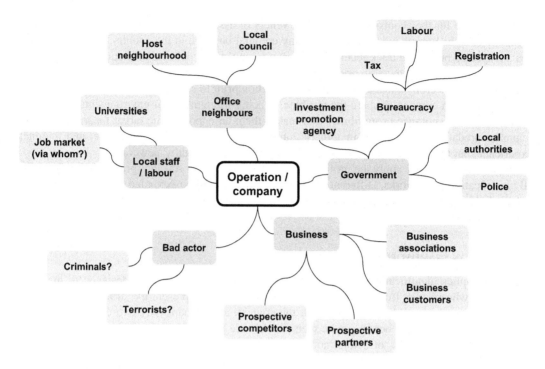

FIGURE 8.4 Mind mapping.

basic two by two. It has both the national and local levels, and in each of those there are three actor categories, one being "other" to catch outliers. Then the three categories on the other axis directly utilise stakeholder criteria as possible identifiers. The national-local breakdown would not apply to some operations, like our hypothetical IT consultancy's. However, it is useful for operations with a degree of geographic spread in a country, such as the West African highway case, which is applied in Figure 8.5 for illustration, as shown on page 187.

Entries are derived in part from extrapolation from the prior terrain analysis and show some knowledge about the context. For example, there is national labour, referring to the main skilled labour pool. The company knows this is principally comprised of southerners because most of the formal economy is in the south and the unions are southern-led. Local labour, by contrast, refers more to would-be workers in the less-developed north where the operation will occur. Some of the entries are closer to being discrete actors than others. The government customer, for example, would be known, and one could even put a name to it at this point (e.g. the Highways Department of the Ministry of Transport). Others are still just general types.

Note that there is some repetition of actor types, and this could occur in several frameworks. One can put an actor type wherever it fits for now, because we will aggregate redundancies when we clean up the identification framework results to develop research targets.

Proximity Mapping

Another way to derive relevant types is to use the operation itself as the anchor point, and then ask what kinds of actors stand at different degrees of proximity, in terms of both interaction and geographic distance. This forces us to think about who we will be in contact with, and to think far beyond our immediate circle. Figure 8.6 is an example, again drawing on the West African highway case.

When compelled to stretch beyond the immediate, the company derived some actor types that they had not thought about before. For example, even though it is a developing country with a limited formal sector, there could be business associations that might be able to provide useful local contacts and advice. Going beyond that, politically connected competitors might matter. It is unknown now,

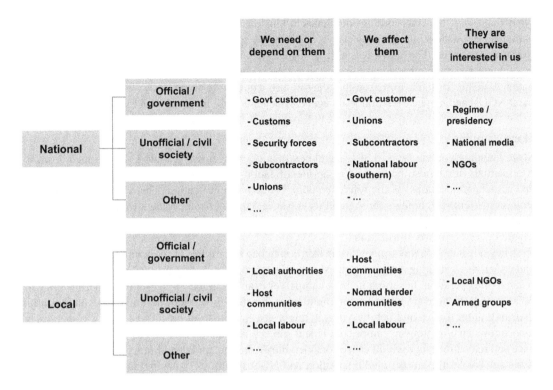

FIGURE 8.5 Identification matrix.

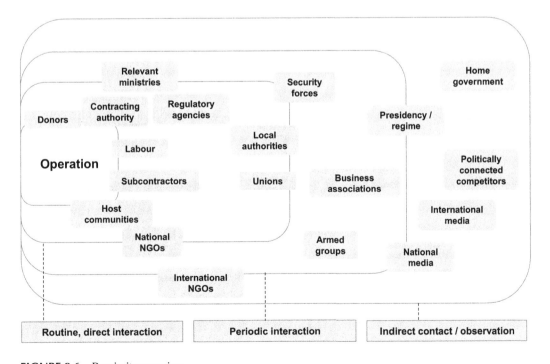

FIGURE 8.6 Proximity mapping.

but perhaps there are other foreign companies lurking on the sideline hoping that the highway project is transferred to them, and perhaps even ready to apply some persuasion to this effect. International media also come up. The highway is a sizeable investment for the country, and how it proceeds could be of interest to international news organisations. Host communities would likely have some links to national NGOs. It stands to reason that they in turn would have some ties to international development NGOs, and maybe even donor aid agencies beyond those involved with the project.

Stage Mapping

Stage mapping is often used in SEIAs and community engagement planning, but stripped down to its essentials, it can also be applied as an identification framework. It uses an operation's stages, and associated locations, as the reference point for actor identification. The operation would have some consistent stakeholders throughout its presence, but other stakeholders would be more or less relevant to a specific phase. Stage mapping lends itself well to highway constructor's operation, and Figure 8.7 is a top-level illustration.

A key advantage to this framework is that it matches actor types to a schematic of the operation and its activities, making it easier to envision not just who actors might be, but how they might really relate to the operation. In setting up base camps, for example, a security cordon and perimeters will be necessary. If there are nomadic communities in the area, they might find that these encroach on their migration routes, and nearby villages might also face disruptions. Thus, even the seemingly innocuous step of putting up camps could incur stakeholder interest. We already knew that the clearance and relocation stage would cause considerable disruption, and in addition to host communities, this stage might also attract media attention and NGO scrutiny. By having an explicit look at the exit stage, we are also reminded that CSR programmes would come to an end, at least in the current plan. Depending on how exit is handled, host communities and local NGOs could be adversely affected and could respond, risking any reputational gains the company might have made by strong CSR performance.

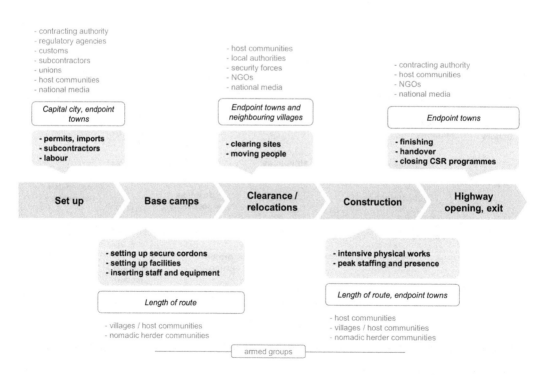

FIGURE 8.7   Stage mapping.

Stage mapping usually extends beyond the timeline of the baseline intelligence exercise. For example, the highway project might last five years, while the exercise's time horizon is only a third or so of that. What the baseline's time horizon really means is that given the volatility in the country, another blank slate exercise should happen after a certain point or it risks becoming outdated. It does not mean that we should not look at the future, since political risk management, including its stakeholder aspect, also includes forward planning, laying foundations now for what could be necessary later.

Derivation from Terrain Challenges

The last framework that we examine derives potentially relevant types of actors from terrain challenges. The starting point is to simply ask who would be involved in any given challenge. Not all of the results would be relevant, but we obtain more possibilities to investigate. We will apply the IT consultancy case for illustration, taking only a few challenges from the total set identified in the last chapter. This is depicted in Figure 8.8.

One thing to note is that because terrain analysis was not about "upside risk" or opportunities, the basic question of who is involved in a challenge is likely to yield only potentially neutral and hostile actors, and we do not even bother listing those who would in no way be a stakeholder. However, in this example and in practice, one can also ask what kind of actor might be able to help with a given challenge. The investment promotion agency, business community and business associations come up in this vein. Some actors could come up for different reasons. For example, under the challenge of new revolutionary activity, security forces are relevant because the company might need to interact with them more in planning its own security. But security forces are also related to the issue of staff arrests or detentions, which would be more likely in the event of dissent because of increasing regime paranoia. Terrorists have a question mark. We know from terrain analysis that terrorist groups probably would not take action against an obscure foreign company, but this could change, and terrorist groups might warrant consideration as a potential stakeholder.

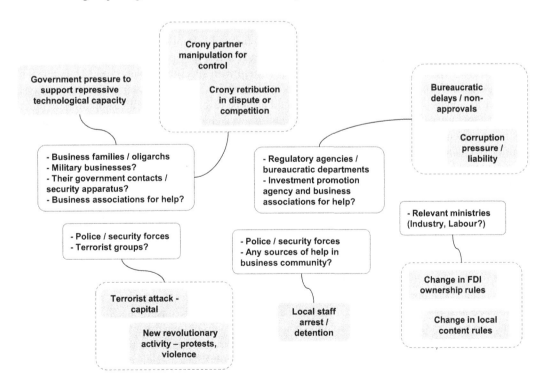

FIGURE 8.8 Deriving actor types from terrain challenges.

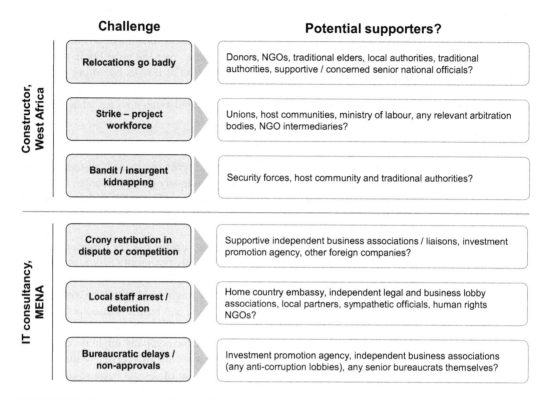

FIGURE 8.9   Types of actors who could help with terrain challenges.

As a subset of this approach, we can directly ask who might be able to help with different challenges. This is illustrated in Figure 8.9, using three different challenges for each case.

This approach would not identify types of actors who could simply assist with the operation, as did the mind mapping framework when it derived universities as a potential conduit for sourcing staff. Rather, it yields ideas on potential sources of help with specific problems, and by extension with political risk management. Some types of actors who could be problematic in some ways, like security forces or bureaucratic officials, could even be revealed as possible supporters in other contexts. This formulation is actually our first hint of a stakeholder engagement and even political risk management strategy. A strategy seeks to align stakeholder relationships with the management of priority challenges, while at the same time reducing friction. Types of actors identified in this approach could well become central in the political risk management planning stage later on.

At this point, we can clean up redundancies and create a list of relevant actor types. The next step in identification then discerns who fits the types, to yield actual actors who could be relevant to the operation.

IDENTIFICATION RESEARCH: DISCERNING REAL ACTORS

Aside from specific actors we already knew about, the identification frameworks have mainly provided types and categories of actors. We now use these as parameters to search for real ones.

We need to apply two basic judgements in the research process to ensure that we derive relevant targets, and not a hodgepodge of amorphous socio-political blobs or long lists of small groups or individual people. One is about actor delineation. We want cohesive targets, but at the same time we want representatives of relevant larger entities. This can be a difficult balance, but if we get it wrong now, it is not problematic, since stakeholder investigation will clear up any remaining delineation questions.

The other judgement is whether or not an actor meets the stakeholder criteria. These were reiterated earlier. There is one important exception. If an actor is not a stakeholder but a potential influence on stakeholders, then it would be worth examining at least as a part of a stakeholder domain.

The outputs of this step would be a categorised list of actors. For each, there would be a clear indication of the wider group, organisation or entity that it most directly stemmed from. Along with that should be a brief explanation of why the actor was deemed relevant, either as a stakeholder or as a potential third-party influencer. Illustrating specific actors for the two cases is too detailed for purposes here, but some for each case will emerge as we proceed, and the domain maps that follow provide a sense of actors relevant to each case.

DOMAINS

Once we have identified relevant actors, we will parse them into domains. We noted that in practice different intelligence team members would develop the picture of their assigned domain and examine the stakeholders within it, in one integrated workstream. For conceptual clarity, we cover the discussion of domains in this section, and leave stakeholder investigation for the one that follows.

This section proceeds as follows: First, we discuss what domains are, and their utility in stakeholder analysis. Then we move onto domain definition. The main part of this section is then walking through five very different types of domains, using examples from the two cases, to provide concrete illustrations of what domain mapping can reveal.

THE CONCEPT AND UTILITY OF DOMAINS

We have touched on domains, but they bear clarification. A domain is a distinct arena or milieu of human interaction along a particular nexus, whether geographic, social, political, professional or institutional. Within a domain, actors cooperate and compete, and often know about each other, even if they do not actually know each other personally. Domains are the mini worlds that stakeholders inhabit, and success and advantage in their domain are often significant drivers of socio-political actor behaviour. People and groups can be in more than one domain, but their primary one usually consumes most of their attention.

Domains are invaluable context when trying to understand specific actors. The immediate socio-political pressures, relationships, rivalries, territoriality and fiefdoms in a domain are significant shapers of actor interests, values and behaviour. Thus, analysing actors within domains is much more instructive than looking at each actor in isolation.

Domains do not just provide context, though, but can matter in themselves. A company will not always be interacting with specific actors one by one, and in a given situation there could be a web of domain interactions around a particular issue. Imagine, for example, that a driver speeding along a rural road accidentally hits a goat. The driver pulls over. The farmer comes to remonstrate. Discussions enter the negotiation phase, with compensation on the table. A neighbour joins in, adding their arguments to the calculation. Things get tense, so another neighbour calls the police. They come and try to calm things down. Meanwhile, a village elder hears the fuss and comes to arbitrate. From one farmer we get a handful of people and a multi-way discussion. The community domain, via several representatives of it, is now what the driver is talking to. Thus, domains can be a type of loosely aggregated actor in their own right, and knowing how they work can help to understand how they, as entities, might form responses to the operation and to particular issues.

DOMAIN DEFINITION

In initial stakeholder identification we derived relevant categories and types of actors. One approach to defining domains is just to use these generic classifications. However, this would risk inaccuracy, since in a given country the actual arenas of interaction will not always fit into generic boxes. Thus, we need to try to shape domains as they actually manifest on the ground.

At this point, we have some ideas and insights to work with. In the context and focus stage, the socio-political system overview would have indicated at least some socio-political groupings and arenas. As well, we had an initial crack at an ecosystem map for the operation. Terrain analysis would have provided an important layer of insight, since players involved in terrain factors were part of the investigation. The types and categories derived from actor identification, despite being somewhat generic, are another baseline. With the addition of identification research, we can define domains with reasonable confidence. Our initial domain definition could be somewhat patchy, but it can be refined and revised as learning accrues.

One approach to definition is to start with general actor categories, and if it is relevant, then also different geographic levels, like national or local. Actors will fit into the resulting boxes, and this gives us at least a starting point. We can draw on the West African highway case for an example and note that for the sake of brevity this mainly uses actor types rather than specific actors. This is illustrated in Figure 8.10.

This basic breakdown yields 12 preliminary domains, and in the absence of further consideration these would be better than having no domains at all. But there is likely room for more accurate, or realistic, definition, based on how actors really relate on the ground. We can ask what is wrong with this picture and keep adjusting it until we feel that the result is reasonably reflective of real hubs of routine interaction.

In the above, based on what we know about the country thus far, one thing that strikes us is that at the local level geographic proximity will be very significant to how actors relate. It is a developing country with a sharp distinction between a more urbanised and interconnected southern coast, and more remote smaller towns and rural communities in the centre and north. In more remote areas, socio-political interaction is highly localised. It thus makes little sense to parse all local host

| Geographic levels | Category | | | |
	Government	Civil society	Business	Armed group / criminal

National	- Regime
	- Ministries A, B
	- Security forces
	- Courts
	- Regulators C, D
	- Ruling party
	- Opposition party
		- Unions
		- NGOs
		- Media
		  - State
		  - Independent
			- State
			- Regime-connected / business-political "clans"
			- Independent
			- Small
			- Business associations
				- National elements of regional groups (see regional level)

Local / host community	- District authorities - Local councils A, B - Local party representatives / youth organisations	- Civic associations / local NGOs - Traditional authorities - Religious institutions - Neighbourhoods / villages	- Small / micro - Informal	- Local bandit groups
Regional / international	- Company's home government / embassy - Donor / transnational agencies - Competitors' home governments / embassies	- International NGOs - International media	- Competitors - Other major FDI participants	- Regional jihadist network A - Smuggling group B

FIGURE 8.10 Preliminary domain matrix.

community members into four separate functional domains (the ones that run across the top of the matrix). Whatever an actor's function, its most intense interactions will be with others in the same location. There are at least three specific relevant communities in this case, the two towns on either end of the highway and a rural (nomadic and village) one, and they are quite distinct. Thus, we can make these sub-domains of the wider host community domain and allocate actors according to where they reside. Some local actors, like town authorities, party youth groups or the local police, might be parts of national institutions, and this will be accounted for in stakeholder investigation, but since most of their interaction is at the community level, their locale is their primary sub-domain.

Other changes to the baseline matrix seem useful too. International NGOs with a significant presence in the country could be transferred to the national civil society box, since they work closely with national NGO partners and have very similar roles. NGOs can then form a sub-domain, or segment, within national civil society, along with national unions and the media. It seems parsimonious to integrate national jihadist and smuggling groups with the regional networks they are connected to. It also makes sense to add foreign companies to the national business box, since there is close interaction with national counterparts, and some foreign firms with a long presence could be well integrated into the national business landscape.

With those changes made, the other boxes still work as domains. We have one outlier, international media. There is no harm in having outliers, but we can also put them where they most closely relate, and in this case it is with media in national civil society.

The result of this thought process is the domains and sub-domains shown in Figure 8.11 on the following page.

This example is relatively complex because of the relevance of company interactions with different locations. An operation's geographic spread increases the number of distinct areas that it would affect and interact with. Our example is a highway project, but rail projects would be similar in this respect, as would operations that span production and transit. Some pipeline projects even cross several countries. The host community and local aspect would be simpler for a project in one general location, and simpler still for an operation with a minor impact on local communities, such as in the IT consultancy case.

The IT consultancy in MENA is a useful contrast, since its operation has a very light physical footprint, and is based in one city. If we undertook a somewhat similar thought process, domains for this operation might be as depicted in Figure 8.12 on page 195.

This example clearly has less emphasis on host communities and only minor reference to different locations. The host neighbourhood is in the city where most projects will happen. There is a distinction between different city and municipal authorities, but they would be closely integrated in the wider city governance structure. More noteworthy is that there is some implied overlap between domains. The military sits in the national government domain, but its business arm is in the business domain, and some business players are indicated as being close to the regime. While we parse actors according to their primary domain of interaction, in less institutionalised countries, domain membership is seldom mutually exclusive. Stakeholder investigation will examine all of an actor's links and interactions, within and outside of its primary domain.

Now that we can see selected stakeholders from both cases, an interesting distinction is that for the IT consultancy, more indicated stakeholders seem relevant to enabling business operations and relationships, as opposed to avoiding friction or anticipating negative responses. This is often the case when a company is trying to actually become a long-term business player. By contrast, a project operation, like the highway, needs to know more about how to get that one job done as smoothly as possible, with assets, including reputation, intact.

Based on the author's consulting experience, and accounted for in the emerging case stories, is another reason why the indicated actors in the IT consultancy example are as much about fitting in as avoiding or managing issues. While it is convenient for the purposes of political risk analysis to focus on a consistent concept of operations, in practice certain interim findings can cause company managers to revise their strategy. Based on the results of terrain analysis, the IT consultancy's managers have sketched a new concept: a close fit with independent actors might offset the

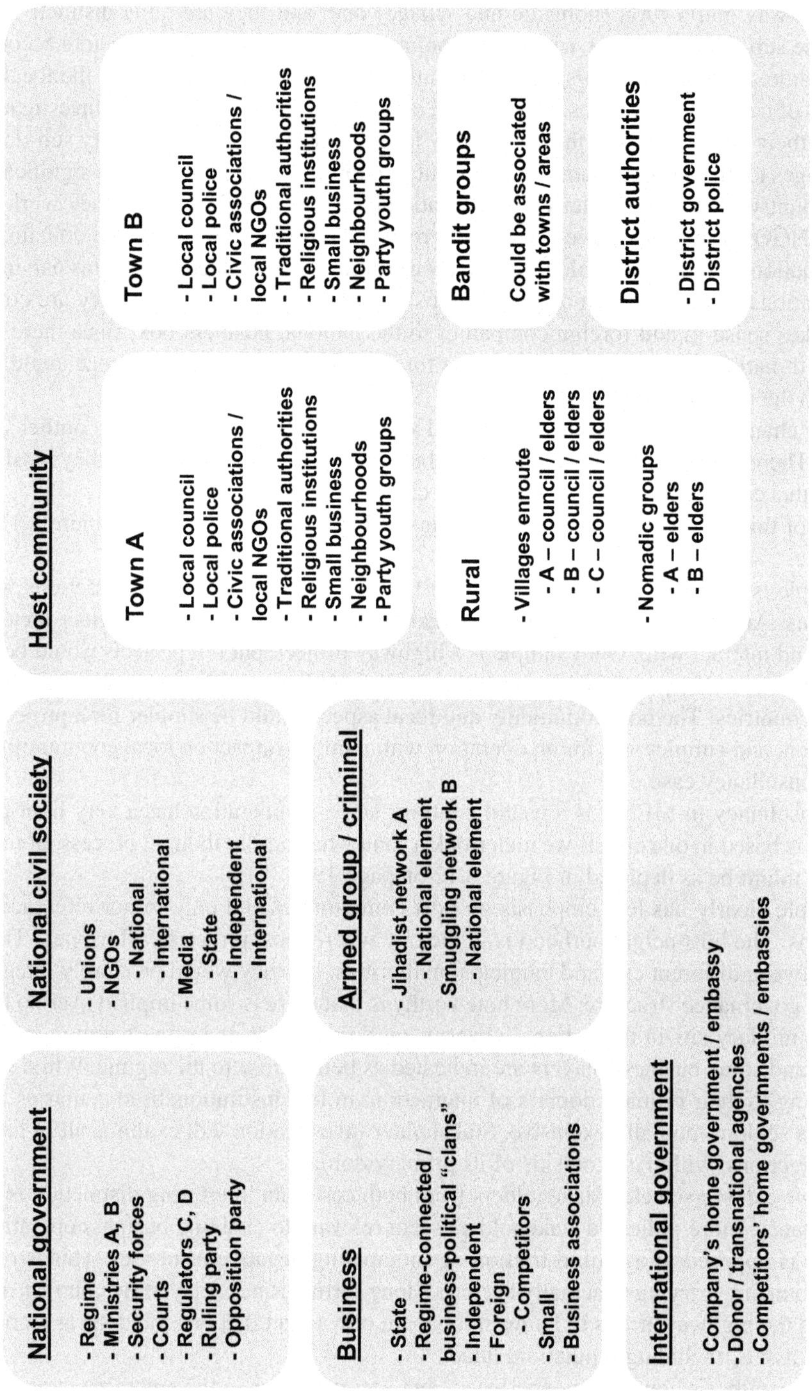

National government

- Regime
- Ministries A, B
- Security forces
- Courts
- Regulators C, D
- Ruling party
- Opposition party

National civil society

- Unions
- NGOs
  - National
  - International
- Media
  - State
  - Independent
  - International

Host community

Town A

- Local council
- Local police
- Civic associations / local NGOs
- Traditional authorities
- Religious institutions
- Small business
- Neighbourhoods
- Party youth groups

Town B

- Local council
- Local police
- Civic associations / local NGOs
- Traditional authorities
- Religious institutions
- Small business
- Neighbourhoods
- Party youth groups

Rural

- Villages enroute
  - A – council / elders
  - B – council / elders
  - C – council / elders
- Nomadic groups
  - A – elders
  - B – elders

Bandit groups

Could be associated with towns / areas

District authorities

- District government
- District police

Business

- State
- Regime-connected / business-political "clans"
- Independent
- Foreign
  - Competitors
- Small
- Business associations

Armed group / criminal

- Jihadist network A
  - National element
- Smuggling network B
  - National element

International government

- Company's home government / embassy
- Donor / transnational agencies
- Competitors' home governments / embassies

FIGURE 8.11   Domains, West African highway case.

National government

- Regime
  - Political clans A, B
  - Military
- Ministries A, B
  - Investment promotion agency
- Security forces
- Courts
- Regulators C, D, E
- City authorities

Business

- Military / military-connected conglomerates A, B, C
- Regime-linked business families C, D, E
  - Holding companies C, D, E and
    relevant operating companies in each
- Mid-sized independent IT and management
  consultancies
  - E, F, G, H as representative
- Business associations
  - National state-linked
  - Independent
  - Small-medium
  - International-national

Civil society

- Job seekers (grads, professional)
- Universities
  - A, B, C as representative
- Employment channels
  - University-linked youth
    career NGOs A, B
- Media
  - State media
  - Independent business press
  - International business press

Host community

- Office neighbourhood
  - Neighbourhood association A
- Residence neighbourhood
  - Neighbourhood association B
- Municipal council (office area)

Armed group / criminal   Organised crime networks A, B; terrorist groups C, D

FIGURE 8.12   Domains, MENA IT consultancy case.

disadvantages of not having a well-connected (crony) partner, and regulatory changes aside, a higher degree of localisation could be a good way to make the right kinds of friends. Thus, stakeholder analysis is now more aligned to the need to find a sustainable niche, a strategy which is effectively political risk management, in that it avoids the most severe terrain challenge within the original operational concept.

DOMAIN MAPPING

We have our defined domains and sub-domains. At this point, we map them to reveal broad schematics in terms of key players and interactions. There will likely be a need to revisit and adjust domain pictures when we later learn more about specific stakeholders within them, but the initial results will be sufficient to contextualise stakeholder investigation and to characterise domains themselves as macro-entities.

Bear in mind as we proceed that we would not analyse non-stakeholder influencers in detail, but if they are important to what goes on in a domain, then they should be included in domain mapping. For example, an important political-business family might not know or care about an operation, but they might have considerable sway in the business world. If we did not include them as an influence, we would miss an important variable.

The following begins with a somewhat detailed discussion of Town A from the highway case, as an example of a sub-domain that is a tangible and dynamic ecosystem, as opposed to a broader and less-integrated set of actors. That will illustrate how a domain picture can reveal potential integrated responses and issues, in addition to providing context to better understand actors. Then, more briefly, we will examine four other domains which, together with Town A, demonstrate some of the main problems and approaches in domain characterisation and mapping. This will include some real-world, if top-level, domain characteristics along the way, to help visualise what can really go on in complex emerging markets. We will also be expanding on the case stories here, to provide grist for subsequent steps both in stakeholder analysis, and in later stages of the baseline exercise.

Town A: The Case of a Dynamic Local Ecosystem

Town A, with a population of 45,000, is a sub-domain of host communities from the West African highway case, in which the planned highway will connect two towns, thereby linking the north-central and northern areas of the country. Town A is the southernmost town, and thus, unlike the mainly Muslim Town B in the north, it has a diverse mix of southern and northern groups and cultures. Town A is already connected to the capital by highway. The new highway will extend the existing one, skirting around the town, but linking to its main street with a new access road through what is called the north gate, once a gate in the historic walled city's fortification. Around the gate is a mainly Muslim neighbourhood. It is also a local business hub, consisting of tradesmen, a truck station that tends to transporters heading north on the old road and a small market. This community is the main one facing relocations to make way for the access road. The domain map for Town A is shown in Figure 8.13.

Relocations are the most relevant aspect of the operational profile. They will affect about 600 people and tens of micro-businesses and are to take place about eight months after the operation's launch. A separate regional company has been granted the contract for new housing and business amenities, and units are supposed to be complete when relocations start. Another profile element is simply the disruption caused by construction, especially for the north gate area. Truckers, a key local sector, will be particularly affected, although there are plans for a temporary access road skirting construction, and the highway will leave the old northern road intact. The highway's

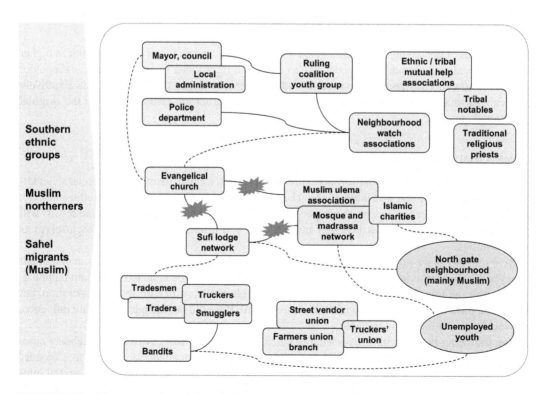

FIGURE 8.13   Host community sub-domain, Town A.

symbolic aspect, including its connection to the southern-dominated government, could be problematic to some of the Muslim population, but at the same time unemployed youth will be very hopeful, if not desperate, for jobs, and small tradesmen will expect business opportunities. Given the profile, the central questions about this sub-domain would be what dynamics and mobilisations could arise if the project is ill-received, and what could trigger a bad reception. We would get into these questions directly when examining specific actors, but they form a backdrop to sub-domain characterisation.

For centuries, Town A, situated on an old trade route, sat at the nexus of several tribal territories and was a cultural melting pot. Islam coexisted with local religions and with early Christian converts, and while people were culturally distinct, they shared a sense of community and commercial interests. The slave trade and French colonialism strained the social fabric but did not fracture it. This legacy of tolerance survives among groups and families with long roots in the area, and manifests in easy relations between the local Sufi lodge, southern tribal notables, traditional religious priests and non-Muslim ethnic mutual aid organisations founded by early southern migrants. Constituents of these actors tend to be small and micro business owners with little interest in identity politics. This position is becoming harder to sustain because the town has grown considerably in recent years, and northern and southern migration has brought ethnic and sectarian sub-nationalism with it.

Sectarian friction partly manifests in the bad relationship between the evangelical Christian church and Muslim religious institutions. The friction is not just theological. The church is the local branch of a large national network, and has a close relationship to the regime via patronage ties, making it a symbol of southern sub-nationalism. But another religious division is intra-Muslim, between the local Sufi network and the conservative Sunni ulema. Sufism has a long history in the region and incorporates pre-Islamic traditions. The ulema, by contrast, are partly funded by conservative Gulf Arab religious foundations, and leading ulema have been to the Gulf for scholarly training, or what Sufis and others regard as Wahhabist indoctrination. With Gulf funding for social programmes and more strident dogma, the mosque has a special appeal to unemployed Muslim youth, while the Sufis still appeal to older, more established segments.

The local and mayoral authorities are southern dominated, although with minor northern representation. They have a close relationship with the southerner community, which tends to be the more affluent ethnic segment. Official authority is exercised institutionally and through the police, but it is extended by the relationship with southern neighbourhood associations, whose main role is neighbourhood watch, which in practice means keeping an eye on Muslim activism and deterring Muslim encroachment on southerner neighbourhoods. The local branch of the national ruling coalition youth group also has an informal enforcement role and has worked with neighbourhood watch associations to harass Muslims who get too active in local politics. It has been involved in electoral violence in the past, instigating attacks against local northern politicians and their followers. The evangelical church likewise has a close relationship with the authorities and is highly sub-nationalistic.

Small businesses are both southern- and northern-owned and -operated and tend to be located near or in their respective sub-national communities, with a rough north-south division in the town. There are some local branches of national companies in the agricultural and manufacturing sectors, and these mainly employ southerners. The northern population, by contrast, is especially dependent on local and regional trade, including smuggling. Muslim micro-businesses, such as mechanic shops and metal working, tend to service the trading sector, at the centre of which is trucking.

Around the town, banditry is a problem for outsiders and for southern commercial trucking, but the local bandit groups have extended family connections to the northern trucking and smuggling businesses and leave them in peace. Unemployed Muslim youth are attracted to banditry as a way to make ends meet and to give a slap in the face to the authorities, and for some of them banditry is a stepping stone to eventually joining regional jihadist groups. The bandits themselves claim some insurgent credentials, but by and large they are more opportunistic than political. They do engage in kidnapping high-profile targets, including foreign aid workers, but this is actually a commercial activity for them, since they make money by selling victims onto jihadist groups.

Countering the bandits, and dealing with other crime, is the local police department. It is not a very effective force. For one thing, it has a bad reputation among Muslims, partly through its connection to, and leniency towards, the neighbourhood watch groups which sometimes engage in violent vigilantism. Another factor is the merger of the police and gendarmerie two years prior. Before that, the police patrolled the town and the gendarmerie, a military unit, patrolled the surrounding rural areas. The merger was partly a result of the national regime's factional rivalry. The rival (non-presidential) faction is well represented in the army, and the president thought he could reduce their influence if he shifted the gendarmerie to the police under the ministry of interior. One result was a diminution of the old gendarmes' capability. Not fully trusted, the old units were slimmed down, subordinated to the civil police, and their military vehicles and weapons replaced with civil police equipment. In Town A, this suits the police chief. He has more people under his command even if some are disgruntled by the transfer, and his fiefdom built up over years was given a boost. But the capability for off-road patrols outside the town is weaker, and bandits, smugglers and regional insurgents have had an easier time.

The above is the basic schematic of key actors and dynamics. Among the actors would be several stakeholders, and the map and characterisation provide an understanding of their immediate socio-political context and pressures. On the one hand, groups with shared roots in the location find themselves at odds with increasing sub-nationalism, a result of migration from both ends of the country. Local cultural bonds that cross the ethnic and sectarian divide are becoming an anachronism. Northern Muslim and southern Christian have become the predominant socio-political identities, and much local actor behaviour is driven by sub-national friction. Traditional commerce carries on and remains the town's lifeblood, but there is now an increasing separation of northern and southern commercial activity. Anyone the company deals with or affects in the town will have some stake in the north-south rivalry, even if they would prefer not to, and this would be a factor in stakeholder attitudes and responses to the operation.

Going beyond actor context, and adding in some other variables that might have been discerned, one could also get a sense of domain-level dynamics that might ensue once the operation's presence is felt. For one thing, we know how important the transport sector is, and any significant disruption to it could bring an integrated reaction from local business owners and the unions that represent them. With small business connections to the Sufi lodge and smuggler links with bandits, this could extend from moral opprobrium to threats. If relocations go badly, the mosque could get involved, widening the response. On the other hand, while proffered support to displaced people might assuage northerners' concerns, southern segments could feel that they are getting a bad deal when they see the north gate community moved into better accommodations and compensated for disruptions to livelihoods.

Relevant here is a common source of disputes in developing countries, namely customary, in other words not legally registered, property titles. Even if an affected household or business in Town A did not have a land or property title, the operation would still need to treat them fairly. But weak claims leave open a channel of attack for southern groups seeking to portray compensation as one-sided and even illegal. The government itself, politically reliant on its image as the defender of southern interests, might provide at least tacit moral support for this position. A legal challenge would likely fail because fair compensation was a clearly specified donor funding condition. But the rhetoric around it would raise the issue's profile and sharpen attitudes. Between the church, neighbourhood watch associations and the party youth group, the reaction to perceived favouritism to Muslims could entail a degree of violence. The authorities and police, not exactly neutral arbiters, might not be able or willing to prevent clashes, and could well be biased in their response.

Finally, recall that violence in the upcoming local elections was a terrain challenge. These will occur about ten months after the operation starts. Town A has seen electoral violence in the past, with clashes between Muslim youth and sub-nationalistic southern organisations. Coming shortly after the relocations, electoral tensions could coincide with southern ire at perceived company favouritism and become a pretext for targeting the new properties around the north gate.

These are only initial indications, but they illustrate that for more tangible ecosystems, the utility of domain mapping and characterisation goes beyond providing context to actually estimating patterns of responses to the operation. Additionally, we might identify opportunities to group some actors according to shared roles and values, and this streamlines subsequent actor investigation. In this case, for example, we could group unofficial southern sub-nationalist organisations and treat them as elements of the same broader interest group, since they are closely linked, and would likely respond to the operation as one entity.

Government Domains When Institutions Are Weak

In both hypothetical case countries, and indeed in many, if not most, countries that fit the complex emerging market bracket, governments exist both as sets of official institutions and as informal networks and fiefdoms. Governments are almost always a significant domain for a foreign company, containing ministries and agencies that directly and indirectly impinge on an operation. It would be nice to be able to just use official organisational charts to see how these actors fit together and interact, but while that is part of the picture, the non-institutional side, and its relationship to the formal structure, need to be accounted for as well. The notion of dual structures is depicted in Figure 8.14 at a purely conceptual level. One can imagine that among the operation's stakeholders are several departments and agencies in the bottom two tiers in the formal organisational chart.

The above roughly corresponds to the government in the West African case country, wherein there is a factional rivalry, with the president's clique on one side, and an *ancien régime* holdout embedded in the military on the other. The relevant aspects of the operation's profile are its contribution to national economic integration, and its identity as French and European. The latter is a boon to the president, but bad news for the rival faction which seeks inclusion in China's Belt and Road Initiative and a closer relationship with China, a model of effective state-centric development that harks back to the country's own pseudo-Marxist days.

One of the reference points for the case country is Benin, which is far less volatile, having only shades of the case country's issues. Nonetheless, to understand the pressures on any given stakeholder department or agency in Benin, one would need to look beyond the official structure.

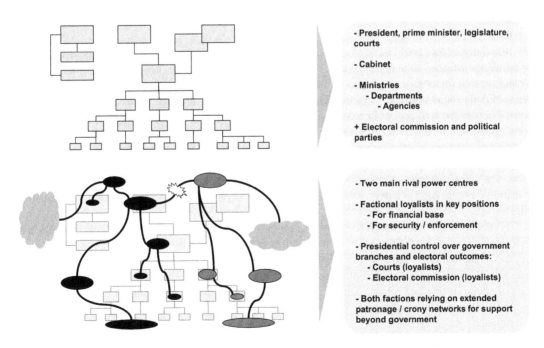

FIGURE 8.14 Government domain with formal and informal power structures.

Following a new democratic constitution in 1990, institutionalisation increased. However, since the current president's electoral victory in 2016, he has managed to assert personal control over the courts and electoral commission, the two bodies that were most capable of ensuring adherence to the constitution. This has allowed the president to personalise governance, using networks of loyalists on the inside and patronage ties externally to thwart checks and balances and sustain broad, if transactional, political support. Any given organ in the government, from a ministry to an agency, is guided as much by presidential power imperatives and personal vision as by its official mandate. For a company, this means that in dealing with government stakeholders it is actually indirectly dealing with the regime itself. There are several West African countries that have at least the same degree of systemic stress as the case country, but Benin is a useful example because it shows that even when things seem reasonably normal or straightforward from the outside, the institutional framework can still be insufficient to explain domain dynamics.

As noted, two reference points for the IT consultancy case are Egypt and Algeria. Egypt is less complicated than Algeria, but the government domains of both countries layer institutional hierarchy and other power networks. In both countries, the military is at the centre of power in spite of having no formal governing remit; there are close relationships between the regime and political-business "clans"; and factional competition can include vying for control of parts of the bureaucracy, state companies and security agencies. Both countries have a far better-resourced government than most sub-Saharan African states, but institutions are not commensurately stronger, and again, relying just on the formal design would shed little light on how things really work.

We should note that particularly when examining official institutions, we might need to include non-stakeholder actors in order to understand a domain and the influences on stakeholders within it. We might not ever deal with a certain agency or clique, but if our stakeholders are somehow answerable to them, or under pressure from them, then these third parties are relevant to the domain picture. For example, an operation might have nothing to do with the intelligence service, but if it is the de facto enforcement arm of a regime faction and makes other agencies nervous, then it needs to be accounted for. On a more basic level, few foreign companies have anything to do with a president and the upper reaches of a regime, but especially where there is a degree of personal rule, they can be very significant influences on government stakeholders.

Civil Society Domain Segments

We noted that actors could be segments of a wider population of similar types of units. Businesses are long accustomed to using market segmentation, and a priority market segment is like a stakeholder, in that the company tries to build at least an indirect relationship to it. Segments can also be useful in socio-political stakeholder analysis, when the company needs to relate to broad sets of actors but will probably have direct interaction with only a few. Segmentation is particularly applicable to the national civil society domain, which can consist of myriad organisations of varying degrees of relevance. We would know at least the key actors in each segment, and there will be a few organisations that the company might deal with as segment representatives. However, segments themselves can give a reasonable top-level picture of domain constituents and dynamics. Figure 8.15 is a hypothetical example using segments grouped within sub-domains for illustration.

The above is general enough to apply to a range of countries, although where governments are more repressive, some NGO segments might be very weak, and press independence is a matter of degree. There are often links between sub-domains, and some players can be hubs. In Tunisia, for example, the Tunisia General Labour Union (UGTT) is not only an actual union, but a strong advocate of social justice and related causes, and maintains close ties to like-minded NGOs and media outlets. Following the revolution in 2011, it was a staunch opponent of Islamic fundamentalism and coordinated secular civil society responses against it.

All sub-domains could be relevant to some degree, but which segments matter depends on the operation's profile. For example, environmentalist, labour rights/social justice and sub-national

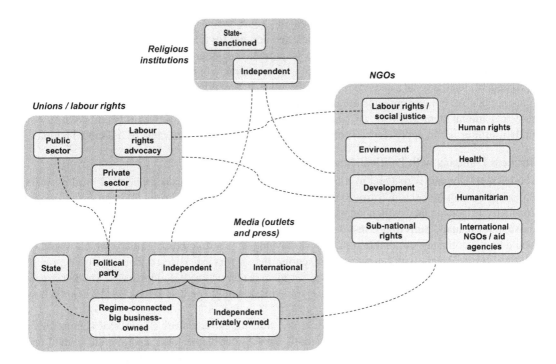

FIGURE 8.15 Civil society domain as segments.

(indigenous) rights NGOs often figure prominently in the scrutiny of extractive operations in rural areas, and their critiques can be taken up by sympathetic independent press. Many countries only have a few main unions, but others have myriad sector-specific unions that would seek to maximise their members' bargaining power in jobs with a foreign company. In countries without much media freedom, the state or state-allied media could be the only relevant one, and in operations based on state contracts, press coverage can be a way to pressure or advocate for the foreign company depending on the health of its relationship with the government.

An important aside about media is that press ownership is critical to understanding what kind of coverage to expect, or how much it might vary from the government line. State papers and those owned by regime cronies support the regime on any given issue. In the context of more authoritarian rule, if a press owner has other business interests that could expose them to regulatory and tax hassles, then they too tend to toe the line. In other cases, business oligarchs buy or launch papers to gain some influence over public opinion, and reporting can be weaponised when the owner has a commercial dispute or faces stiff competition. In most countries, partly because of restrictions on media freedom, there are relatively few press outlets that only focus on independent professional journalism, but they are often regarded as quite credible, and their coverage of a foreign company can carry weight with interested audiences.

In the West African case country, a prominent civil society player would be the relevant national union, which was identified as part of the terrain challenges of union obstruction of local hiring, and strikes. As in Tunisia, in many post-colonial countries labour unions played a significant role in the independence movement, and afterwards had such strong nationalist credentials that it was difficult for even strongmen regimes to repress or ignore them. We can assume for the sake of the case that the relevant union has such a legacy. Other pertinent segments could be national and international rights and environmental NGOs with an eye on the effects of the operation, and state, regime-linked and international media. We saw that religious institutions mattered at the local level, and we could extrapolate from this that national-level organisations could be relevant too, perhaps by supporting their local branches in any issues around relocations.

There are also civil society sub-domains in the IT consultancy case. For example, universities are potential collaborators when seeking local staff, and perhaps for related CSR initiatives. Educational NGOs could also be relevant partners. A socio-political segmentation could apply to universities in particular, and might segment by ownership (state, regime-connected businessperson, religious, independent, international), and academic independence. Sometimes a socio-political segmentation is not applicable. For example, job seekers were another civil society sub-domain in the consultancy case, and among them would be various socio-political distinctions. However, it would not be especially useful or fair to apply a socio-political segmentation to a broad swathe of individual people.

Business Domains with Political-Business Networks

The business domain is relevant to most operations, since foreign firms often need local partners and suppliers, not to mention trustworthy liaisons. But it is far more relevant to companies, like our imaginary IT consultancy, which are trying to actually ensconce in a country for the long term. The consultancy actually aims to become part of the domain. A relevant aspect of the operational profile would be the company's global best practice knowledge and strong brand, both of which would be alluring to big players with an eye to augmenting the IT services slice of their portfolios, and to focused companies already in the IT services or management consulting industries. Another aspect is that the company is new to the country, and some players might perceive its lack of local knowhow to be a useful vulnerability.

The business domain in many developing and transitional countries is a mix of state/military companies, regime-connected oligarchs, tycoons with insider connections, and an independent private sector that ranges from smaller medium-sized companies to micro and informal businesses. In countries where a statist legacy remains strong in spite of plans to privatise, such as Algeria, there can be a sizeable tranche of salaried jobs in state and semi-privatised companies. Elsewhere, including in Egypt, another reference country for the IT consultancy case, a significant majority of jobs are in small and micro firms and the informal sector (Egypt too had high state company employment in the past, but it has been dwindling since the 1980s, and the civil service now accounts for most formal salaried jobs). In both countries and in many emerging markets, most private businesses are family-owned, but when privatisation of state companies occurs, a common pattern is that retired and well-connected regime or military figures acquire, or are granted, control and privatised companies remain in the regime's extended network.

Figure 8.16 is a top-level depiction of a business domain, showing at least a preliminary understanding of links between different elements. In practice, the domain map would contain more named stakeholders, but this suffices to illustrate broad dynamics.

This is hypothetical but broadly reflective of both Algeria and Egypt, and indeed it captures some widespread phenomena. The nexus is where the political and financial power is, and it includes regime cronies and oligarchs with direct links to, and actual overlaps with, powerful regime cliques. In Algeria, active and retired senior military officers have important business interests, and military-owned conglomerates are major players in Egypt. In both countries, the ministry of industry or its equivalent has some effect on industrial policy, but since it has little control over financial flows, it is outside the nexus. In Algeria, there really is a business leader's association which is recognised by the government as the principal private sector representative. It acts not only as a liaison between the regime and big business but also as a place where business leaders negotiate to ensure that competition does eat too much into mutual gains. There is a tycoon class in both countries, which has regime links, but unlike cronies no direct regime representation or overlap. Private companies that lack any regime connections seldom get beyond the small end of medium size and tend to have their own representative bodies outside of the big boys' clubs. Ironically, these truly private sector firms are what many governments have their eyes on as they ponder reforms to boost jobs and overall growth and competitiveness, but a lucrative status quo hinders the political will to level the playing field.

The map helps to contextualise actors, not only in terms of where they fit but also with respect to concerns and interests. Insiders would be very alert to any changes in the fortune of their regime-level

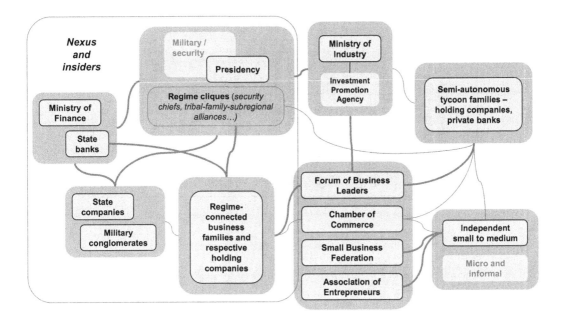

FIGURE 8.16 Business domain with political overlaps.

champions, and would be part of, and affected by, any clique rivalry or regime change. In Algeria, for example, several cronies of the old Bouteflika regime are now facing corruption charges, and in Egypt companies associated with the old Morsi government have suffered serious crackdowns. Tycoons maintain a tenuous balance between independence and regime connections. Independent smaller businesses are on the receiving end of a loaded game but are not exposed to the vagaries of courtier politics, and if liberalisation accelerated, they at least know how to innovate and how to survive genuine competition. The different business associations cater to their constituents and reflect their anxieties and ambitions.

More broadly, the map helps to characterise the player dynamics that the IT consultancy would encounter upon entry, and it provides an early indication of a key strategic consideration. This is the trade-off between access to the nexus, and freedom from power games and the baggage of being seen as an "insider".

Armed Group/Criminal Domain

Armed and criminal groups can be difficult to delineate because of their shifting memberships under different umbrellas, the overlap between political and criminal networks, and their cross-border regional or international dynamics. This delineation problem makes domain maps particularly important, since they provide a clear schematic before tackling the analysis of any one actor. We will look to the West African highway case for an armed group/criminal domain at a regional level, with emphasis on its elements in the area of operation. This draws on real dynamics, but it is for illustration only, since the regional situation is so fluid that any rendition is quickly out of date, and anything specifically about the case country is fictive.

An international terrorist and organised criminal nexus is often portrayed using network maps, showing intertwined hierarchies, transactional flows and key hubs. However, insurgencies are usually tied to a specific territory, and an actual geographic map overlaid with relevant groups is a useful perspective. For purposes here, we use a basic hybrid for a very top-level depiction of the domain in and around the case country, as shown in Figure 8.17.

Al Qaeda (AQ) and Islamic State (IS) are the two main jihadist umbrella groups in the Sahel and West Africa and are good examples of how nebulous regional insurgencies can be. With both

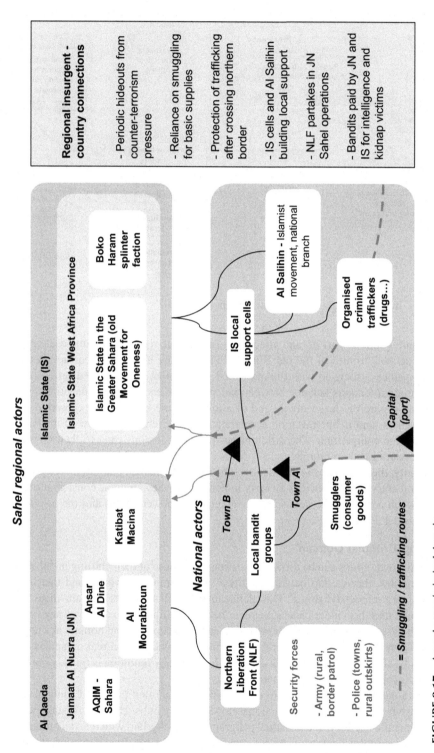

FIGURE 8.17　Armed group/criminal domain.

AQ and IS, the main regional groups were constructed to wrap around and demark regional affiliates, as opposed to being cohesive command structures. AQ's affiliates coordinate but are still quite
independent and have close ties to specific areas and ethnic groups. The main element in regional
IS is a splinter from Nigeria-based Boko Haram. It was joined by a breakaway faction from the old
Movement for Oneness (or Unity) and Jihad in West Africa (MUJAO using the common French
acronym). The other part of MUJAO merged with Al Mourabitoun, which allied with AQ. While
the AQ and IS networks sometimes coordinate, despite their common jihadist ambition they also
routinely clash. Since jihadist insurgency first entered West Africa after Algeria's *décennie noire*,
the splintering and reshuffling of groups and alliances have made specific group labels somewhat
ephemeral. The human players, however, are real, and some, especially on the AQ side, have been in
the game for over two decades. Note that the domain map does not show government-armed ethnic
militias, which in the affected countries are also important conflict actors, although their influence
is mainly confined within national borders.

Several West African countries share with the case country the tenuous condition of not being
part of the Sahel conflict but being touched by it and increasingly at risk of being drawn into it.
Sufism, a significant strand of Islam in West Africa, has been a buffer against extremism, but it is
under pressure from imported Wahhabism and other Salafist (one could just say puritanical) ideologies. These strands, while not inherently militant, challenge local cultural bonds that used to
attenuate sectarian differences. Northern poverty, discrimination by southern-dominated governments, and increasing resource competition with southern farming communities increase the allure
of jihadism as an ideology of self-defence and rebellion. Added to this is government under-capacity
that hinders effective responses. Just as importantly, government corruption can lead to enforcement
agencies turning a blind eye to smuggling and trafficking, which, through tariffs and protection fees,
are sources of jihadist funding. These illicit trade routes head north into the conflict zone, and in turn
become a conduit for conflict actors trying to stir up insurgency further south. These factors make
conflict spillover a serious prospect for a number of countries, including the case country.

In the case country, smugglers and traffickers use bandits and their own armed units for protection further north, and their routes pass close to the areas of operation. Their main concern is the
transit of goods and drugs, but they are not averse to kidnapping if an opportunity presents itself.
Bandits operate throughout the north including the areas of operation. They specialise in armed rob-
bery, and also have links to regional insurgents who pay well for high-profile kidnap victims. The IS
presence is mainly concerned with providing safe havens for IS operatives hiding from French-led
counter-terrorism operations across the northern borders. However, they also work with the local
branch of the Al Salihin movement to proselytise in northern communities (Al Salihin is fictional,
but loosely based on the regional branch of the Yan Izala movement, which has sought to weaken
Sufism to enable the spread of Salafism). In the northwest is the NLF, linked to a northern ethnic
group and Sahelian migrant communities. Thus far, it acts more as a local recruiter for JN, sending
fighters northwards to partake in the Sahel conflict, but its long-term aim is to launch an insurgency
at home with JN's participation, and it has conducted the odd raid on border patrols and police units
to build its credentials.

For the more ideological of these actors, the relevant aspects of the highway operation's profile
include the company's Western and French origins, and the fact that the highway would make the
north more accessible to government security forces. Jihadist groups' operational capabilities in the
country are nascent, but they would likely harm the company if it were easy to do. Smugglers and
traffickers are less problematic as long as company staff do not bump into their convoys. Bandits
present a more immediate hazard because they have a well-developed grassroots infrastructure that
rests on northern clan and tribal ties, and the "wealthy foreigner" aspect of the operation's profile
makes its staff alluring targets for kidnapping. However, the intentions and capabilities of all local
actors depend to a large extent on the fortunes and plans of the AQ and IS groups to the north. The
Sahel conflict influences much armed group and criminal activity in the country, and to varying
degrees local actors are extensions of the two main Sahelian insurgencies. Thus, even though they

are over the border and mainly operate some distance to the north, the Sahel combatants are a key element of the host country picture.

Other domains can also stretch beyond borders, but in volatile regions and where governments lack the capacity or, through corruption, the will to enforce territorial integrity, conflict and crime in particular tend to be a regional, as opposed to national, phenomena. A depiction of the armed group/criminal domain in the case country would have been strangely devoid of context and explanatory power had it only focused on the country itself.

A final note about this example is that it, along with a subsequent investigation of specific armed group/criminal stakeholders, is not unlike threat assessment. Threat assessment is a drill-down exercise focused on innately hostile and predatory actors, and it informs security planning. In practice, when dealing with threat actors, stakeholder analysis yields somewhat contextual insights, and then threat assessment follows up with greater nuance. We will examine threat assessment in Chapter 11, where we will see that it is actually a detailed continuation of stakeholder analysis.

The above five examples together illustrate that domain mapping and analysis is a relatively fluid exercise, rather than a formulaic process. Approaches need to adapt to a domain's distinctive characteristics. Likewise, the insights that can derive from the exercise vary, ranging from actor context to schematics of complex arenas, and even initial scenarios of domain-level responses to an operation. When we start investigating specific stakeholders, we are well armed with context, and have a range of hypotheses on relevant interests and influences to guide investigation.

Before proceeding with stakeholder investigation, an important point can be drawn from the above examples. This is that several stakeholders were active in more than one domain. There was an overlap between actors in the government domain and the political-business one. Media outlets owned by oligarchs or tycoons were in both the political-business and the civil society domains. Bandits were part of Town A and part of the armed group/criminal arena. In practice, while actors might have a primary domain in terms of interactions and influence, they can have a role in other ones too. If domains are supposed to reflect reality rather than just be discrete categories, then some overlaps are inevitable. In practical terms, this can make it hard to pinpoint where an actor should be situated for the purpose of analysis. The simplest approach is usually to cover an actor in what we see as their primary domain, where they have the highest interaction or share the most similarities with other actors. We can draw on an actor's relationships and behaviour in other domains to inform that investigation, but its primary milieu provides the most direct context.

STAKEHOLDER INVESTIGATION

The most basic objective of stakeholder investigation is to understand how a given actor might affect the operation, through their perception of it and how they could behave towards it. That only scratches the surface though.

Imagine that I got a new job as a senior manager in a different, and somewhat awkward, company. In stakeholder analysis terms, the company could be regarded as a domain, and the business unit I work in is my immediate sub-domain. There is an urgent to-do list and high expectations from the big boss. I am going to have to convince people that my objectives are good for them, dodge extraneous office politics and thwart would-be spoilers, make the right friends for help and influence, and avoid looking like an office Machiavelli or my support could dwindle. If I cannot do this, then I will probably fail. To be able to do this, I need to know what makes people and cliques tick, their concerns and ambitions, how they are linked or in contention, and how they might see me and what I am trying to do.

To generalise from the above example, stakeholder investigation is aimed at having enough knowledge about actors such that we can avoid or manage friction, anticipate harmful intent, appeal to interests and values, and build trust where appropriate. We only need to know these in relation to the operation; thus, compared to all there is to know about an actor, this is actually modest in scope. But it is still more than just developing a mechanistic indication of attitude and influence, the main prioritisation axes in stakeholder assessment and sometimes the sole focus of analysis. Attitude and influence will come out of investigation, but by themselves and if not backed up with relevant characterisation, they do not provide much tangible guidance beyond raw prioritisation.

By now we would have an emerging mental picture of stakeholders, but now we directly explore their potential relationships to the operation and what these could mean. First, we make some guiding points on the analytical approach. Then we walk through the thought process of stakeholder investigation. Finally, an illustrative example of an investigation summary, using an important stakeholder from the West African highway case, concludes the stakeholder investigation step.

ANALYTICAL APPROACH

For all stakeholders, the overarching analytical target is their likely attitude towards the operation, and their potential influence on it. Attitudes derive from the intersection of their interests and values with the effects and symbolism of the operation, in other words its socio-political profile. As noted earlier, influence can be direct or indirect. Direct influence is the power an actor has on its own to affect the operation and the moves it could make independently. Indirect influence is the power that it could mobilise from alliances and connections, and also by manipulating others into supporting its cause. Indirect influence can be passive too, as when an actor faces hardship and another one helps out of sympathy or conviction. Attitude and influence together tell us how much difficulty or help we might get from an actor, and the kinds of actions they could take. The above comes with the caveat that we should not assess attitude and influence in a mechanistic way that limits what we can learn about who someone is. We will proceed towards an assessment of attitude and influence via a flexible route that also leads to a characterisation.

It is worth noting why attitude, sometimes equated with interest, and influence, sometimes called power, are the criteria we use. If someone feels indifferent to an issue, then no matter how influential or powerful they are, they would probably not bother to do anything about it. If they feel strongly about something, then they would find a way to exert their influence to steer outcomes towards their own interests. Influence on its own can be latent, for example someone might have friends in high places and considerable sway in a community, but unless stirred by attitude these assets can remain dormant. An assessment of influence will disclose what an actor's available levers are, and attitude indicates if and how these could be applied. Attitude and influence are thus intertwined, and together are the most fundamental lenses for assessing a stakeholder's meaning to an operation. There are other possible stakeholder assessment criteria, but these two together get to the crux of who matters and why.

On a more practical note, because stakeholder analysis is nuanced and resource intensive compared to other stages in the baseline exercise, we would not give all stakeholders the same degree of scrutiny. There would have been accruing confidence about who matters more, and by now we will have a sense of where to apply resources for the best effect. For stakeholders who are less critical, or somewhat peripheral, to the operation, we could just expand somewhat on their domain role for some additional nuance. Recall from the Town A example in particular that we actually learned quite a lot about specific actors just by doing domain mapping and characterisation. Another approach is to form a set of closely related or similar actors and treat them comparatively. By contrast, for stakeholders that we sense are relatively important, we would seek more insight about their internal workings, including influential personalities and internal factional lines, and a deeper understanding of their organisational culture and values. Some would even warrant being treated like a sub-domain, so that we understood the different players and dynamics within the stakeholder unit.

Having addressed some preliminaries, we can outline the general thought process that we apply in investigation. This is depicted in Figure 8.18.

There are two levels to the exercise. One is the core assessment, wherein we seek to discern an actor's likely position towards the operation, and how they might act on it. The second is supporting insight, which we might not use in actor prioritisation but which provides a tangible sense of who

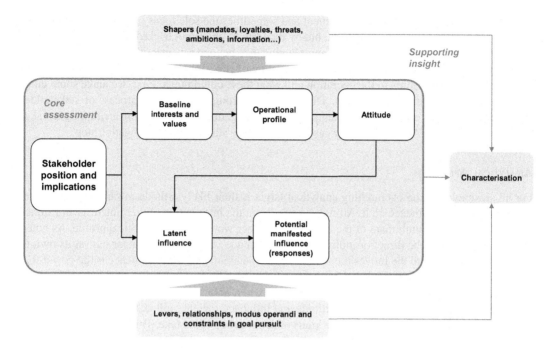

FIGURE 8.18   Stakeholder investigation thought process.

the actor is as an intelligent, motivated entity. These levels are linked. Supporting insight feeds into the core assessment, providing the requisite nuance to make judgements about values and interests, perceptions, and influence and how influence might be wielded. The core assessment and supporting insight both lead to a targeted characterisation, which is the essential "who is this actor" accompaniment to the basic assessment of why, how and to what degree they matter.

In exploring the thought process, first we will head in the direction of attitude. Once we reach it, we will make a preliminary judgement on the intensity and direction of an actor's attitude towards the operation. Then we come back to the start and take the path towards influence, again forming a preliminary judgement once we get to the terminus. Then we consider potential manifested influence and conclude by briefly examining the elements of a supporting characterisation.

THE PATH TOWARDS ATTITUDE

A stakeholder's baseline values and interests constitute the motives behind its routine socio-political behaviour irrespective of the operation's presence or effects. This baseline needs to be established before we can gauge a potential attitude, since attitude derives from the actor's perception of the operation's implications for what matters to them.

From domain analysis, we would have learned something about an actor's day-to-day roles, interactions and pressures, or put another way, other games in which the actor is a player. We expand on domain insights and take a direct look at what motivates the actor. Actors have ambitions, they try to stave off threats and rivals, and they have day-to-day concerns about their autonomy and relevance, and even survival. These all shape an actor's sense of self-interest and related objectives. Values are another layer of motivation. Beyond power or survival imperatives, actors can have ideologies, loyalties and cultural legacies which guide a striving for self-realisation or the furthering of a cause. Loyalties point to the effect of relationships on values, and indeed relationships can be important to perceived self-interest too. For example, a business family with instrumental ties to the presidential "clan" might not agree in principle with the regime's policy or ethics, but because the relationship helps business, the family would have an interest in regime stability and in being seen as supportive. Once we understand baseline interests and values, we have a solid reference point for the analysis of what the operation could mean to the actor.

That last point about our meaning to the actor is instructive. We, the operation and company, want to know how they could react to and affect us, and/or what benefits could derive from a relationship. Actors aware of or affected by the operation want to know the same thing about us. Seen this way, stakeholder analysis is a two-way street. We are actually trying to see into their stakeholder analysis. And their analysis of us is premised on the operation's socio-political profile, oft discussed and indirectly informative in preceding sections but now explicitly applied.

We have defined the elements of a socio-political profile, which range from physical effects to symbolism. A general and comprehensive profile was sketched as a prelude to stakeholder identification. When it comes to specific actors, not all elements of the general profile will be meaningful. Once we understand an actor's baseline interests and values, we can see what profile elements are relevant, and extract and expand on them to test their significance. For example, among the key values and interests of a host community, represented by civic associations and NGOs, could be preservation of the local landscape, which people sense is threatened by unplanned development. They might not care much about the foreign company's commercial and financial track record, but what it is doing on a physical level would matter. Therefore, we focus on the operation's physical effects when discerning community perceptions. Conversely, a particular business family might be in an intense rivalry with other ones and is desperate to secure advantages. It might not care about an operation's physical effects but would be acutely interested in the company's brand and financial strength, which would be a boon if the family secured a partnership, or a serious problem if a rival did. The relevant profile element is therefore the company's business position.

In many cases, multiple profile elements will be relevant to an actor's interests and values. In the West African highway case, for example, the operation's physical effects would at least temporarily affect basic interests, such as local livelihoods and movement. But the company's nationality and its relationship to the government customer could be interpreted through values too, such as lingering anti-colonial sentiment and, among northerners, concerns about an erosion of cultural autonomy once a major link with the south is established. Interest-based and value-based perceptions would interact. The operation will be at least somewhat disruptive. That would be annoying for people, but, with help to offset hassles, recoverable. However, the company's French-ness and its role in a government contract could amplify attitudes, from merely annoyed to suspicious and hostile.

Ideally, we would flesh out the relevant profile elements as the given audience would perceive them. In other words, we have a crack at interpreting their view of us, taking into account not just their value lenses but also the information they have access to. Information about the operation can be inaccurate or rumoured. More significantly, it can also be spun by another stakeholder seeking to sway others' opinions. The ability to get others to learn and believe one's preferred interpretation of an issue is a source of some stakeholders' influence. When an operation is the target of this capability, it can significantly skew stakeholder perceptions. Imagine that stakeholders hear that the operation is giant conspiracy to recolonise the country. This operational profile would have very different implications for values and interests than the actual concept of operations, hopefully anyway. Recall that in several real cases cited in earlier chapters, including AES in Georgia, Sainsbury's in Egypt, and Bechtel in Bolivia, manipulated information was a factor in widespread anti-company reactions. Discerning what stakeholders are hearing or could hear about an operation is easier for current, ongoing operations, since one can plug into the relevant grapevines. For planned operations, stakeholder investigation would discern who has the means and motive to manipulate information, and this would need to be accounted for in extrapolating other actors' perceptions.

In the author's experience, stakeholders' direct experience of a foreign operation is usually the most important shaper of perceptions, in the sense that it leads to the most intense feelings either way. An out-of-the-blue barrage of negative media on an operation is often seen for what it is, an attempt to manipulate opinion. It starts to stick, however, when tangible problems for people arise and seem to at least partly validate hostile interpretations, as occurred in each example above. Thus, while it can be important on its own, the problem is usually linked to wider issues. In all cases, though, the information factor warrants consideration. As an aside, information coming from a company can also be skewed, either from excess positivity or a deliberate attempt to downplay potential negative operational effects. This can delay the formation of negative attitudes, but it worsens them in the end through raising false expectations and incurring a reputation for dishonesty.

Discerning stakeholder perception is largely an extrapolative exercise. We learn what matters to them, look at how we and our actions could affect that, and account for the factors that influence their perception. Then we extrapolate the resulting attitude. But fieldwork is an opportunity to directly ask stakeholder representatives how they feel, or would feel, about the operation and why. That can be a delicate discussion, but it can augment and cross-check extrapolation, which on its own can have considerable margin for error, being based on an indirect reading of people's thoughts and feelings. We examine fieldwork as an intelligence collection stream in Chapter 13.

Using supporting insight, we have discerned the stakeholder's baseline interests and values, accounted for factors influencing their perception of the operation, and discerned what the relevant operational profile elements mean to them. This brings us to the derivation of attitude, within the core assessment logic. This is different from what we have done to get to this point, which was exploratory and investigative, yielding a nuanced but hazy picture. However useful that impressionist portrait could be, we need a clearly defined reference point for later comparisons and for an eventual strategic perspective. Thus, we assess a degree and direction of attitude and clarify the key reasons for the assessment. This judgement is only a preliminary baseline and is subject to adjustment after the investigation of all stakeholders and network mapping. As with terrain analysis, all stakeholder assessment could be saved for the end, but because it draws on considerable nuance about an actor, it is useful to form preliminary judgements while the details are still fresh.

When we arrive at the final sense-making step, we will see that the stakeholder matrix uses attitude and influence as axes. There is only one direction for influence, low to high, since an actor cannot have influence less than nil. For attitude, though, the axis has two directions, negative and positive, or unfavourable and favourable. The intensity of attitude is reflected by the position in either direction. The attitude component of the matrix, with scores and supporting descriptors and labels, is shown in Figure 8.19.

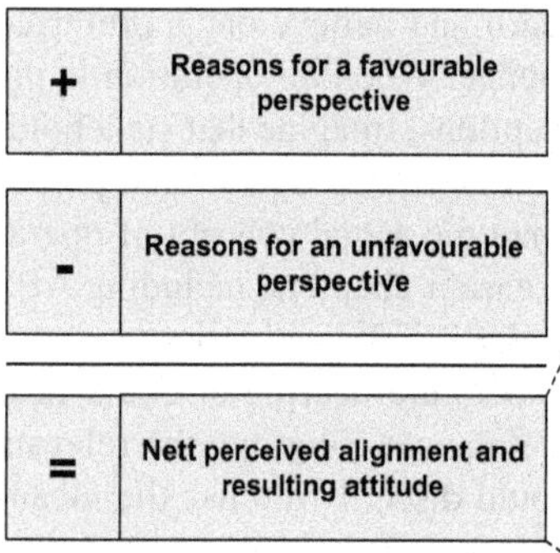

+	Reasons for a favourable perspective
-	Reasons for an unfavourable perspective
=	Nett perceived alignment and resulting attitude

Rating	Perceived alignment of operation with interests and values	Resulting attitude to the operation
+ 5	Highly beneficial	Supportive
+ 3	Beneficial with few / minor downsides	Benign
+ 1	Operation does more good than harm	Mildly optimistic
0	No discernible effect either way	Neutral
- 1	More hassle than benefit / reasons for concern	Annoyed / wary
- 3	Problematic / predatory opportunity	Opposed
- 5	Threatening / predatory target	Hostile

FIGURE 8.19   Attitude assessment ratings.

Included in this is a basic logic for making the assessment when, as often happens, an actor has different attitudes towards an operation. For example, in the Town A sub-domain illustration it was noted that while the Muslim population in general would be wary of the implications of the highway project, tradesmen and unemployed youth would welcome any work opportunities, which the company does plan on offering. We saw a similar combination of attitudes in the Sainsbury's case in Chapter 1. Workers and customers liked the company for its jobs and convenient one-stop shopping, but they did not like its displacement of local shops nor its cultural gaucheness. Thus, it can be useful to list the main reasons why an actor would like to see the operation progress and succeed, and alongside that why they would like it to simply go away, change in ways that would impede safety and success, or fail. These can be compared for a reasoned nett attitude assessment, and the results of this thought process can be summarised as the supporting rationale.

The descriptors and labels in the scale will not always properly characterise an attitude and should just be regarded as brackets or reference points. A key point to note, though, is that for the bottom brackets, -3 to -5, there is a distinction between a negative perception of the operation's significance, and a predatory interest in the operation, but they have the same practical meaning. Someone might see an operation as problematic because it complicates their lives or threatens their values. This leads to a negative attitude. Someone else might welcome the operation but for the wrong reasons. For example, a racketeering mafia group might be pleased to see a wealthy company land on their doorstep, but they would only benefit if the operation's safety and success were diminished, making them opposed or hostile. Note that predatory interest can mix with other attitudes, such as when a civil servant who is on the whole favourable towards an operation sees a chance to press for a bribe.

At this point and indeed throughout the baseline exercise, one should not fall into the trap of seeing a modelled assessment as the final word and the only thing that matters. It is just the tip of the iceberg, and, as noted earlier, on its own it is not especially useful when it comes to actually doing something about an issue or actor. However, assessment tools do yield reference points, and when dealing with myriad units and complex dynamics, we need some clear signposts or else we can end up floundering in a sea of impressions and details. Assessment results are like marks on a map and help us to navigate the big picture.

We can almost move onto stakeholder influence, but one important question about attitude remains. This is the potential effect of contingent "ifs", which are especially germane to stakeholder attitude because while an actor's influence can change, attitudes can be very capricious. The current operational concept is our principal reference point, but even within that, things do not always go to plan. There might be delays in particularly disruptive phases, or accidents, or perhaps the operation needs to scale back and shed local staff because of a drop in the price of its product. We cannot estimate all potential contingencies, but just as with terrain analysis we can posit and test a few plausible ones that would be particularly relevant to the given actor. The ones that would have a significant effect should be noted alongside the baseline judgement. Later, when considering potential stakeholder responses, estimated from both attitude and influence, plausible contingent responses can be included alongside the likely reactions to the baseline operational profile. In the sense-making step, we can also test the whole stakeholder matrix against plausible potential changes in the operation.

THE PATH TOWARDS INFLUENCE

This brings us to influence, the ability an actor has to affect the operation. As with attitude, we need to establish a baseline before considering how influence could be applied. The initial focus, then, is on latent influence, the assets and capabilities that an actor is sitting on, or has available, until stirred to action. They might never use all of this, but it sets the range of possibilities in terms of potential responses and provides an overall measure of how weighty they could be as a factor in the company's experience. Recall that influence is both direct, what an actor possesses on their own and by virtue of their role and position, and indirect, or lent to it by another actor. We examine both types in turn.

There are actually myriad sources of direct influence, which can range from the personality traits and relationship skills of specific people inside stakeholder groups or organisations, to just knowing how a legal system works and how to manipulate it. Thus, there is no standard checklist of sources of influence by which to gauge what a stakeholder possesses. However, there are some common forms of influence that can at least serve as general guidelines on what to look for. These include official and unofficial authority, the control of information, the control of valuable assets and a coercive capacity including violent means.

Note that wealth can buy influence in some contexts, especially where corruption is prevalent, but we leave wealth aside since it is, paradoxically, both too obvious and deceptively obvious. Any reader who works with a large and comparatively wealthy company would know that money alone seldom guarantees an easy ride for the organisation.

The first main form of influence, official authority, is held by and within state institutions, and is exerted through the making, enactment and enforcement of policy, laws and regulations. A given organisation or agency can wield this power, but so can individuals and cliques within it. State institutions are hierarchical; the higher one's rank, the more discretionary power, or decision authority, one has. Ironically, institutional rank also matters when institutionalisation, in particular adherence to rules and principles, is low. In that case, not only does a ranking official or politician have discretionary powers, but they can also manipulate the levers of state to pursue personal aims or forward unofficial values. Official authority is not just a tool of state organs and officials, but could be used by non-official actors, like clans or tight business-political networks, who have representatives or agents in the state apparatus.

Unofficial authority is another form of influence. It gives an actor the ability to influence group perceptions and even mobilise collective action through appeal to its credibility and status, as opposed to compulsion or simply paid inducement. Unofficial authority can be held by various types of actors, but common ones include sub-national and religious traditional hierarchies, political parties both electable and fringe, NGOs, unions, trade and business associations, and press outlets with a strong ideological or sub-national bent. Unofficial authority varies with the size of the actor's following or membership, and the strength of its affective bonds therewith. For example, a socially progressive newspaper might have a wide readership and some influence on people's perceptions, but for most readers the paper is not really a guide to socio-political behaviour. A traditional clan leadership, by contrast, might only have a few hundred constituents, but they might be fiercely loyal and see their leaders as far more worthy of obedience than any state institution.

Moving from authority to capabilities, another source of influence is control over information. This is often associated with the media, and some independent media players are solely in the business of journalism. But when news outlets are owned or controlled by other interests, whether business or political, news can be spun to influence or manipulate an audience. Troll farms and social media manipulation can be part of an information apparatus, and along with Internet controls are prevalent in the toolkit of state repression and foreign subversion, which can be directed at companies too. Traditional authorities, including religious leaders, can use traditional fora, such as sermons and consultative assemblies, as their own information apparatus, which is often extended by social media usage. Any organisation, including companies, can create and disseminate information, but there is a difference between feeding this into media channels, where journalists can be an important intermediary, and direct transmission to the intended audience, whereby messages and "truths" are unmediated and undiluted.

The ability to directly harm others is another source of influence. Governments have this, and when institutionalisation and the rule of law are weak, the bureaucracy and security services can be used against anyone who is inconvenient to the regime or to cliques within it. Insurgents and terrorists also have a capacity for targeted violence and coercive extortion, and more sophisticated criminal groups combine this with proficiency in fraud, cyberattacks and data theft. Actors that are not primarily armed groups, such as kinship-based clans, religious groups and political parties, can also have an armed or "street" wing which they use to protect members and intimidate rivals. Actors can borrow other actors' capacity for violence, as when a political-business family gets help from the police or intelligence service to investigate or intimidate competitors. Even short of actual harm, the possibility of it can influence other actors' cost-benefit calculations in seeking their objectives, and hence too their behaviour.

A final source of influence that we will mention here is simply control of something that others need. A union, for example, might control the availability of labour in a given sector. Bureaucracies, and by extension governments and regimes, control access to permits and public services. A state oil company might be the only potential partner for foreign firms. Control over an asset or an enabler confers bargaining power and leverage.

An actor can possess various combinations of the above forms of direct influence, and different forms to different degrees. However, direct influence is not the whole story of an actor's latent influence. We now turn to indirect influence, a factor of extended relationships. Most forms of direct influence involve and utilise relationships, but these are inherent in an actor's primary role. A union or religious hierarchy, for example, only really exists through its relationship to members and adherents. Extended relationships, on the other hand, can allow an actor to call on or mobilise support from beyond their routine circle of interaction and even well beyond their home domain.

An explanatory example of indirect influence derives from one of the previously cited Algeria projects that the author worked on. The foreign company needed a trucking firm to assist with an operation in the south. Normally it would have put a contract out to tender. However, the local Wali (head of the Wilaya, which is like a *région* or a province), who had considerable clout over local approvals, got a call from a powerful retired general in Algiers who insisted that a particular trucking company get the contract. The Wali felt compelled to pressure the company to forego a tender process and assign the contract accordingly, and the company did, in order to smooth its relationship with the Wali. It turned out that a local trucking firm was owned by a member of a specific regional clan from the north. When he heard about the contract, via mutual liaisons he contacted the ex-general, a fellow clan member, for help. Neither the ex-general nor the trucking boss had lived in the clan district for decades, they did not personally know each other and had no routine interaction, and they were hundreds of miles apart. But with that clan link, the boss's influence on the company, via the Wali, went from low to high.

Extended relationships can be via intermediary organisations. For example, a national NGO can have a link to transnational donors via their international NGO partner, who might be directly funded by donors. That link could be put to use if, for example, the national NGO had a serious issue with a foreign donor-funded project. Relationships can also be based on backchannels that organisations cultivate for the event that they could come in handy. A common example is companies becoming political party donors and developing party relationships in order to have a friendly ear once or if the party gains power. As the Algerian example illustrates, relationships between specific people can also give their respective organisations a mutual backchannel. In short, indirect influence derives from memberships and affiliations which cross-cut the routine relationships inherent in actors' roles and positions. The more intense these cross-cutting relationships are, the more likely it is that they can be used for meaningful support. Especially when it comes to individuals, affiliations can be deceptively mundane. For example, just having gone to the same school or served in the same military unit can be a strong enough basis to ask for help from well beyond one's immediate walk of life.

As noted earlier, indirect influence can also be passive, whereby one side does not call for support or even realise that it has any friends, but someone helps anyway because doing so fulfils their own interests or values. In a political risk context, the most common passive actor is host communities affected by an operation. They might have no capability to respond on their own and little media or lobbying knowhow, but other actors could take an interest in their plight and respond for them. NGOs, sympathetic media, religious organisations and local insurgent groups are among those who keep an eye out for affected communities and act on their behalf. A company might assume that no one is affected by its operation because it did not hear any concerted complaints, only to find out the hard way, via committed activists, critics and even sub-national rebel groups, that it was having a negative effect on people.

We have considered direct and indirect influence, and from this we have a broad indication of latent influence. But we need one more step in the thought process to narrow it down. "Latent" suggests that something is sitting unused and can be brought to bear whenever needed. We have looked at sources and forms of an actor's influence, but we have not yet asked how much of that is actually available.

Actors spend influence on a variety of things, ranging from regulatory laxity for their business to their followers' help in proselytising their values. They usually have to offer something in exchange, such as favours, support or effective leadership, to keep the help coming. If they ask too much, their socio-political capital is depleted. Many aims that an actor pursues are not immediately urgent, and they could shelve some in order to reallocate influence should something pressing arise. But there is one expenditure which most socio-political actors, and indeed people generally, are loath to cut back on. This is successful contention in a rivalry and countering perceived threats. Some rivalries are not existential or very serious, and an actor could swallow their pride and negotiate a resolution if they saw a bigger problem coming. Others, though, seem irreconcilable and too dangerous to ignore even for a short time. An actor will not stop spending influence on such rivalries unless an even more pressing threat comes along. They will also be hesitant to start new battles, which in influence terms could break the bank. Rivalries are thus an influence subtractor.

Another important consideration is an actor's capability to marshal their influence. Rivalries with other actors subtract from influence, but so too do rivalries within the stakeholder organisation or unit. For example, if a regime is divided between two factions and each controls part of the government apparatus, it would be hard for the regime to apply the levers of state in a coordinated way. Slow recovery from traumatic change, or getting bogged down in a failed reform process, also inhibits the capability to apply influence. One can consider, for example, a seemingly powerful state company that has recently experienced the effects of a political purge and is now in the midst of a messy corporate restructuring. It will be discombobulated and weak in ways that are not apparent from the outside, but which add up to make it incapable of coordinating its resources. A lack of internal cohesion, then, is another influence subtractor.

We now have the three pieces we need to assess latent influence, namely the direct and indirect forms that an actor possesses, and influence subtractors. The basic logic is to add the first two and subtract the third. Again, this is preliminary and we can adjust later after we have the big picture and more points of comparison. The influence axis of the stakeholder matrix is shown in Figure 8.20.

As with attitude assessment, behind the basic assessment logic would be considerable nuanced thinking drawing on the supporting insight element of stakeholder investigation, and the bare

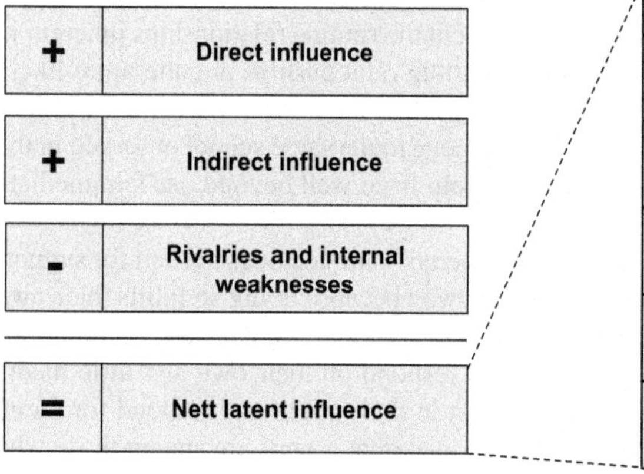

+	Direct influence
+	Indirect influence
-	Rivalries and internal weaknesses
=	Nett latent influence

Rating	Influence descriptor
5	Major influence / consequential
4	High influence / weighty
3	Moderate influence / noticeable
2	Low influence / minor
1	Marginal influence / negligible

FIGURE 8.20   Influence assessment ratings.

assessment is only the tip of the iceberg in terms of relevant intelligence. A brief rationale for an assessed position should again be constructed, not only as a test of our own confidence but also to assist in sense-making later in the final interpretation step.

Before moving onto the integration of attitude and influence, we can briefly note that with influence too contingencies can affect an actor's position. In the West African highway case, for example, there was a possibility of a coup. As it stands, the rival, military-based, faction in the regime is somewhat on the sidelines, powerful but not willing to challenge the elected president, and thus it has limited control over the levers of state. If a coup happened, it would gain total control. Rivalries and contests, including coups and purges, elections, conflicts and revolutions can all alter the balance of power among stakeholders, even seemingly innocuous ones if they have strong links to the winning side. We noted previously that influence is less volatile than attitude, which can sometimes change on a dime. Within any given power structure, that is usually the case. But power structures themselves can change. We would have accounted for such change in terrain analysis, which examined instability and conflict. Thus, we do not need to develop change contingencies again here, but now we are much better equipped to understand their implications for particular actors, and we can take note of plausible potential changes in status and influence.

POTENTIAL STAKEHOLDER RESPONSES

Returning to the process of stakeholder investigation, attitude dictates the latent influence that an actor's draws on in response to the operation, and the shape and direction of the response. We now understand both attitude and influence, and hence at this point we can consider potential responses. As opposed to terrain analysis, we will not usually be able to pinpoint specific potential actions or events. We will have some kind of relationship with stakeholders, and their responses will often depend on the status of the relationship at any given point. Thus, potential responses have more "if" contingencies than typical terrain challenges and can be gradual and malleable. Later in planning, we will combine terrain challenges and stakeholder responses into integrated issues for more coherent political risk management, and therein most stakeholder responses shape issues rather than constituting specific issues themselves. All of that said, we can still posit general and indicative responses as a means of gauging the magnitude of an actor's potential effect.

In addition to attitude and influence, when shaping potential responses we need to consider two other variables. One is an actor's inhibitions about using their influence. Not everyone likes to pick an argument or take a stand, even if they have resources to, and some actors are more patient and cautious than others. The other, related, variable is modus operandi, or how they typically behave in a given situation. For example, some play the long game, while others are impulsive. Some prefer messaging and indirect influence, while others prefer direct confrontation. We would have a sense of both variables from the supporting characterisation, and this is helpful now.

A final point is that we are mainly looking for potentially negative or hostile responses. Neutral and positive responses are the baseline, or norm, for any legitimate organisation. We are looking for potential aberrations in the baseline. That will help us to plan to prevent them from arising, to smooth them out again if they do occur and to prepare for ones that cannot be reset. Especially with favourable actors, there is not much to be gained by estimating specific responses, since we will have an opportunity to directly listen to them, and in turn to shape their responses towards us.

Three brief examples help to illustrate response characterisation. Based on attitude and modus operandi, a particular NGO might monitor an operation, conducting observations and interviews within affected communities, and publish a "*Company X* Watch" page on their website to keep other interested observers informed. They might not do more if the current concept of operations plays out. It is just a way of letting the company know that it needs to be careful.

Mid-ranking officials in a key regulatory agency might see us as a predatory opportunity and have few inhibitions about pressing for an illicit relationship involving bribes and nepotistic favours in exchange for help with approvals. If we decline, they have several levers to pressure us, including stalling approvals, starting trumped-up audits and spreading rumours that we are disrespectful of the culture. They might apply any combination of measures, but they would be somewhat constrained by their fear of drawing too much attention to themselves in a context where mid-ranking officials are themselves routinely under the spotlight for failing to implement government policy.

A political-business family might be inclined to call friends in high places to make life difficult for a foreign entrant, but the government regards the foreign firm's presence as important to building the country's allure to FDI. The family does not want to cross the government, and hence would be inhibited from using its full clout, instead perhaps using its business connections to try to deprive the foreign firm of local allies.

Again, we would not have the prescience to know exactly what an actor would do. But we can develop realistic benchmark scenarios reflecting the magnitude and direction of responses, and these are valuable later when we define integrated issues as political risk management targets.

Supporting Characterisation

We reached assessment, but to get there we heavily relied on supporting insight. It was guided by the assessment requirement, but it was also somewhat exploratory, and partly aimed at developing a profile of the stakeholder so that we know who they are, in nuanced and practical terms. Thus, we have what we need to develop a targeted characterisation. This will be top-level for less relevant actors. For those which we feel are important, it could be quite detailed. The exact types of insight in a characterisation vary, but in general the following are indicative:

- background and history – the events and experiences that led to their current form and situation;
- domain roles – their position in their immediate socio-political ecosystem, what they do, whom they interact with;
- structure and internal dynamics – important sub-units and people, the hierarchy if relevant, internal dynamics including alliances and rivalries, organisational culture;
- interests and values – principal ambitions, concerns and motivators, and key cultural, traditional and ideological values;
- routine behaviour/goal-seeking behaviour – what they are doing on a routine basis, how they act on interests and values and pursue objectives;
- principal alliances and loyalties, and how they act on these; and
- principal rivals – actors whom they perceive as hostile to/problematic for them, and how they deal with rivalries and threats.

Missing from this is how they feel about the operation and how they might behave towards it, since those are integral to the assessment and would be captured in supporting rationales. Instead, the characterisation looks at the actor as a subject in their own right. Consider the colloquialism, "Who is he when he's at home?" We can see someone everyday and never really know who they are, because we see them in certain situations that require particular behaviours and a social or professional veneer. If we really want to understand them, we need to see them in their habitual setting. Likewise, when we deal with a given stakeholder, the very context of our interaction with them modifies their behaviour. If we do not try to know them outside of this, then we only see one narrow aspect of them. Thus, the characterisation that we extract from supporting insight gives the actor substance and dimensionality.

There is one thing in the characterisation which will directly feed into later assessment and planning, as opposed to being soft interpretive insight. These are the summaries of positive and negative relationships. These were accounted for as variables in attitude and influence assessment, but they are the principal input into linkage mapping, and both are relevant to stakeholder engagement planning. Knowing rivalries either helps to avoid becoming involved with one or enables a company to plan for the hostility they might incur if taking sides, say through a partnership, is a risk they are willing to take. Knowing alliances, we can estimate networked responses to the operation and understand the full set of actors we might be indirectly engaging with on a particular issue. Note that if a company does end up on a side in a rivalry, then it does not make much difference if the rivalry subtracts from a stakeholder's influence stock, since the company will be among the targets that the influence is spent on.

STAKEHOLDER INVESTIGATION OUTPUT EXAMPLE

The above was mainly about the barebones of the stakeholder investigation and assessment thought process, rather than using the case examples to illustrate the logic along the way. That was a necessary change of gear because the thought process is quite intricate. However, an example would help to put some meat on the bones, and we will use the rival regime faction from the West African highway case for illustration. Several actors from both cases would be particularly interesting, but the rival faction is useful because there is a significant contingency in its assessed position, namely a possible coup. For realism, the example is illustrated as an analyst's own notes prepared towards the end of the investigation step, for an intelligence team coordination meeting. There would be more detail on the actor than what appears below, and while it contains all relevant insights, it does not strictly follow the thought process that would have led to them:

Regime Rival Faction (Military Faction – MF)

Who / What

- MF core is defence chief of staff, military leadership and senior officers. Army is principal branch. Strong ties to elites in southwestern ethnic base. Represented in national ruling coalition through major southwestern parties, and in official opposition through minor ones. MF senior leaders are southwestern ethnicity, but military overall contains sizeable minority of southeastern ethnic group members.
- Legacy dating back to colonial era, when French gave preference to southwestern tribes in colonial forces. After independence successive coups until 1972 coup, when General K took power. He "civilianised" himself but remained de facto head of military in addition to being president. Initiated hybrid form of state socialism and forged ties with Eastern Bloc and USSR. After Soviet collapse, shift to liberal model deemed necessary, and democracy was seen as prerequisite for Western economic support. Genuine democracy and westward drift followed, but military leadership retained autonomy and "guiding hand" role, used this partly to try to sustain balanced foreign relations (MF retains lingering suspicion of ex-colonial powers).
- MF has cabinet representation through minister of defence (appointed with MF approval). Chief of staff leads national security committee of which president is part. Much routine MF activity is military administration and security operations, intelligence on Sahel and jihadist actors.
- Military command has cohesive organisational culture. Military was never purged, and leadership changes since 1990 have been incremental. Promotions are based in part on conformity with enduring organisational self-image, which is more ideological and nationalist than ethnic. It remains a distinct socio-cultural entity with roots in the past.

Values and Interests

- Southwestern ethnic affiliation, but southern nationalist, concerned about Muslim immigration and national security issues from Sahel conflict.
- State socialist affinity – accepts that People's Republic days are long gone, but sees embrace of Western model as sell-out to neo-colonialism. Western ties would be tolerable

with a balanced development track, but president is firmly in Western camp, partly because it helps to guarantee a strong "international community" backlash against any coup attempt (deterrence). MF feels that this policy makes country open to Western exploitation – no counterweight means no bargaining power.

- Prefers Chinese cooperation – China represents successful statist model, would be lucrative partner, and, if MF ever regained power, would be uncritical of necessary political "reengineering" and entrenchment of paternalistic rule.
- Raw status and financial interests – takes a cut from cotton exports, allegations that control over rural borders is used to elicit bribes from regional smuggling groups, and takes kickbacks from defence contracts (spending has increased with Sahel insurgency). Eyes set on eventual mining exploration licenses as potential source of lucre.
- Threatened by president's powerplay. MF sees genuine democracy as a nuisance but it kept president on a short leash. Now he is eroding democracy and entrenching his own southeastern clique. MF has lost ground, e.g. transfer of gendarmerie from ministry of defence to interior, creation of civilian intelligence service to rival military intelligence, presidential loyalists in many institutions including key ones of judiciary, electoral commission.
- Preferred modus operandi was avoiding confrontation with democratic leaders while playing national security card and using entrenched state network for behind-the-scenes influence. Now being squeezed out of non-military institutions. Principal concern is how to sustain / regain influence, outlast president to facilitate preferred development and foreign policy vision, ideally under more malleable figurehead president.

Rivalries and Relationships

- Principal rivalry is with presidential faction. Thus far, rivalry has not led to serious tensions between respective ethnic bases, since both factions play the southern nationalist card, the president for broader political base, MF to justify bigger defence budgets with respect to the "northern problem" and Sahel conflict.
- Ethnic and tribal ties with important business leaders including owners of main southwestern newspapers and construction firms, loyalists in state companies (cotton, cement...), ministries of industry, labour and agriculture. Has ethnic network across other ministries, but president is squeezing it through aggressive appointment of his own loyalists.
- Close ties to southwestern ethnic faction in national industrial union, which itself is prone to intra-southern ethnic friction.
- Allies include national ruling coalition southwestern bloc, and southwestern main opposition parties, but these are weakening - president's southeastern bloc gained ground through electoral manipulation (see loyalists in electoral commission and judiciary).
- Russia – pre-1990 diplomatic defence ties maintained, MF ensures that some token defence contracts go Russia's way.
- China – cultivating defence ties as precursor to closer commercial and political engagement, mainly buys Chinese armaments even though president cuts side deals with French contractors. MF has insinuated to Chinese diplomatic and defence contacts that if it were in control, it would ensure China's first rights on northern mining development.

Attitude to the Operation

- Highly favourable towards highway itself – would enable quicker troop movements to north, facilitate mining exploration, and MF agrees with original premise of increasing south-north economic integration.
- Sees missed opportunity for major Chinese investment. Country does not have many big infrastructure projects and the highway would have been a significant step towards inclusion

in China's investment sphere. Annoyed that president tailored tender to favour European firms (partly through local content stipulations, which China would have balked at).

- Would strongly prefer contract given to Chinese contractor. Credible allegations that MF maintains discussions on this possibility with Chinese commercial attaché and defence backchannels.
- Company's involvement is very disappointing and annoying in being symptomatic of MF's loss of status, but is not an existential threat.
- Preliminary assessment of nett attitude to the operation: OPPOSED-HOSTILE (-4).

Influence

- Overall, influence in socio-political system is waning as president uses solid electoral position to implant loyalists, erode electoral challenges, and create counter-balance security apparatus in ministry of interior.
- President still somewhat cautious, however, in reducing military power base. Quiet convention since 1990 was that military would retain autonomy in defence affairs, and MF has loyalty of southeastern ethnic base. To openly challenge MF would risk: mutiny; intra-southern ethnic tensions; weakening of military capability with respect to northern threats. Additionally, military has southern nationalist credentials stemming from defeat of northern insurgency in late 1960s, a memory rekindled by current northern jihadist threat which has all southerners concerned and vigilant.
- Military also controls military intelligence, original national intelligence service. Despite president forming civilian agency under ministry of interior, military intelligence remains strong, and credible indications that it has collected "dirt" on presidential loyalists as deterrence against direct challenge to its remaining power.
- Instead of direct challenge, president is nibbling at the edges, trying to hem MF into a purely national territorial defence role. This has been successful. MF's power has considerably eroded, particularly through losing influential networks in ministries of finance, foreign affairs, interior. Pre-2018 when president began powerplay, MF was partner in power. Now struggling to hold position.
- Although overall role in socio-political system diminishing, MF remains second most influential national actor. This in itself does not directly translate to influence on company, since MF has no formal remit to deal with company. However, via remaining tribal and ethnic ties it has significant networked influence which could be applied to hinder operation (see available levers below, accounted for in this judgement).
- Preliminary assessment of nett influence: MODERATE-HIGH (3.5).

Contingent Change in Influence: Coup

- Prior to 2018 MF was content to be in the shadows, accepted some erosion of power as long as it retained defence policy, influence in national strategy, and core interests.
- President's ambitions and manoeuvring now a serious threat. MF cannot fight back electorally because its ethnic base is minority and president has eroded electoral oversight. Current trajectory is towards president gaining total control over military budgets, and from there appointments. MF would be subject to de facto piecemeal purge.
- MF has means to execute a coup, even with stronger counter-balance in the ministry of interior. President's erosion of genuine democracy would provide some pretext.
- But conscious of risks. Planning/timing needs to be meticulous. MF would need to ensure that it could quickly return to at least façade democracy after a coup in order to avoid serious economic damage from sanctions and backlash from southeastern ethnic groups. But this would need to be done in such a way that MF retained control. Risks of a rushed coup

are high in terms of messy aftermath, and a failed attempt would incur a purge and mean the eradication of MF as a political entity.

- MF would risk a rushed coup attempt if the presidential threat became existential (see coup d'état in terrain analysis for potential redlines and triggers).
- If a coup were successful, MF would have near total political control even if it faced serious challenges. Influence would become MAJOR (5).

Potential Responses to the Operation Under Current Power Structure

- MF's available levers to affect operation include:
  - Influence in labour ministry – instigating / manipulating labour inspections, official support for strikes / labour agitation
  - Influence in union – supporting / requesting labour agitation
  - Influence with southwestern tribal representatives in southern migrant communities in north – supporting / requesting social agitation
  - Influence with media outlets – requesting negative media coverage
  - Influence with southwestern-led private construction firms and state cement company – deny access or manipulate partnerships
  - Control over military intelligence – covert investigation to disclose potential embarrassments (link to media influence)
- Serious lever is MF's ultimate control over security presence outside area of operations. Would be capable of contriving to permit jihadist attack on operation, since once past the military any jihadist force has fair chance to avoid detection by police patrols, therefore would meet only minor resistance from immediate protection details. However, judged that MF would be strongly inhibited from using this tactic. Disclosure of involvement would be politically crippling, and successful jihadist attack in centre of country would damage MF's credibility.
- MF responses would therefore likely consist of coordinated use of five above levers, with the aim of:
  - Causing delays that could add up to contract abrogation
  - Causing reputational damage to company
  - Making it embarrassing for president to continue working with company, thereby opening door for cancellation and handover to Chinese competitor (for whom MF would try to pave the way)
- Presidential faction would try to limit MF influence on operation, but without additional countermeasures MF likely would cause at least moderate delays and reputational damage.
- If successful coup, MF could remove company by decree, but would likely fabricate pretext involving illicit collusion with previous regime.

Preliminary Indications for Engagement

- One common interest with company is successful completion of highway – company should play on its track record for successful execution and quality in indirect messaging.
- Another common interest in avoiding jihadist attack on operation – security planning could be forum for soft engagement and building interpersonal respect, and some of this could filter upwards to influence MF attitude.
- Possible that sub-contracting / supplier ties to MF-linked companies would mitigate MF attitude, but could also expose operation to interference.
- Otherwise, company's presence and MF's preferences are antithetical, and planning should mainly focus on blunting MF response.

The rival faction, "MF", is a relatively cohesive actor, with a generally coherent set of interests and values, disjointed only by indications of some illicit activities, and potential friction between its southwestern and nationalist identity. The main assessment complication is the faction's direct link to the coup contingency, which would represent a major power shift. Note how the interim summary extended to at least top-level ideas about engagement. These would be revisited in the political risk management planning stage, but emerging options can be sketched as they form.

Other types of actors might be more straightforward because they are not linked to major contingencies, but some will be hazier in terms of cohesion, interests and values. This especially applies to actor segments, as illustrated in the civil society domain earlier. There will usually be a few organisations in a segment that warrant individual focus, but for the overall segment the language of analysis will need to reflect generalisations: for example, the human rights NGO subsegment "on the whole would be highly critical of" or the state-connected media segment "generally supports the regime in any dispute". When a generalisation is too much of a stretch, the key exceptions should be noted, or if certain segment members seem to go against the herd, then they could warrant extraction for separate analysis.

At this point, we would have investigated each stakeholder. The intelligence team would have used summaries like the "MF" example above to compare notes and address any inconsistencies or contradictions that might have arisen (e.g., between how the actor appears when under a singular microscope in their own domain and their roles and relationships in other domains). With intelligence on actors in hand, we now turn to relationship and linkage mapping.

RELATIONSHIP AND LINKAGE MAPPING

As part of investigation, we elucidated each actor's main relationships. As it stands, those only exist in actor profiles and assessment summaries. We now need to extract and assemble them to connect the dots, in order to obtain a big picture schematic of different sets of links and rivalries. Knowing these, we can then visualise networked responses to the operation, frictions that would need to be accounted for in engagement planning, and potential backchannels and conduits to indirectly communicate with otherwise inaccessible actors.

We begin with the concept of a master map, a comprehensive stakeholder linkage tableau. Next, we examine exploratory mapping to address specific questions about responses and engagement opportunities. That includes a discussion of the challenges in making sense of cross-cutting rivalries, and the use of a top-level summary map as a big-picture, digestible schematic.

Master Linkage Maps

A master map applies information about relationships and rivalries from investigation to visually depict the links between all stakeholders, as well as key third-party influencers. Master maps are not always necessary in stakeholder analysis, but they provide a bird's-eye view that facilitates pattern recognition. They are also a repository, in a sense, from which one can extract particular networks, using zoom-ins on particular nodes and clusters. As an aside, making and manipulating such a map is challenging without software designed for that purpose, but with sufficient time and a blank wall or large blackboard, it is certainly feasible.

There are two main, and complementary, approaches to master mapping. One uses domains and functional roles as the main grouping principle, and emphasises ties based on interaction. The other uses affective bonds, such as loyalty, cultural affinity and shared membership in social or subnational entities, as the mapping axis. The following examines both approaches, mainly with an eye to top-level patterns that they can yield. Note that the term "clan" will frequently appear, and its meaning is broadly a tightly related unofficial in-group that could be based on extended kinship ties, shared sub-national identity or simply shared interests, including illicit ones.

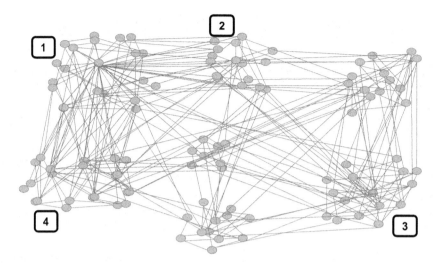

FIGURE 8.21 Domain-based master map.

Figure 8.21 depicts a domain-based map. It is not drawn from a real case and should only be regarded as a representative illustration.

Clustering, or proximity of actors to each other, is based on domain membership, which reflects overt roles, like official governance, business and national and local civil society activism. Links are mainly based on routine interactions and tangible cross-influences, but they can derive from affective relationships, as when a government agency lends a hand to a business because of kinship ties between individual members of each actor unit.

Even without knowing details in the above depiction, patterns emerge. For example, there is a central player in domain 1 with dense ties to 2. This player could be the presidential clique in a relatively personalised regime, and it would be typical that it would directly oversee much of the civil service and security apparatus (2) and appoint loyalists as agency heads. Another thing that stands out is the web of links between 1 and 4. If 1 is the central government and extended regime circle and 4 is business, this would indicate political-business clans spanning government and business. 3 could be the relevant host community. Its ties to 1 and 2 (government) would partly be based on the exercise of state authority and policy. However, ties to 1 in particular, which normally would have little to do with a local community, would likely indicate some kind of unofficial affiliation, perhaps based on sub-national traditional relationships between local leaders and members of the regime inner circle.

The strength of the domain-based map is that we do not lose sight of actors' day to day roles and overt interactions while we lay out and examine linkages. It helps to show how the wider stakeholder milieu operates, and while affective bonds are not explicitly revealed, they can be inferred in interactions between groups that have no clear functional relationship.

The second type of map, based on loyalty and affective bonds, addresses a question that can arise in domain-based maps: What accounts for the dense links between different domains that seem to have no clear functional reason to be so closely intertwined? Consider the prior example of the southern Algerian trucking company and the retired general in Algiers. They were in very distinct domains and had little or no functional interaction, yet their link had significance. If we make affective bonds the principal axis in mapping, then the trucking boss and the general would not be sitting in opposite corners connected by a long thread. Instead, they would be sitting side by side in the same clan or other loyalty-based cluster. If we take the actors in the domain-based map and apply the affective axis, we might get a very different picture, perhaps like the one in Figure 8.22.

The main clusters, as represented by 1 and 2, could be based on sub-national loyalties or patronage ties. At the centre of each would be a clique or senior hierarchy with considerable unofficial

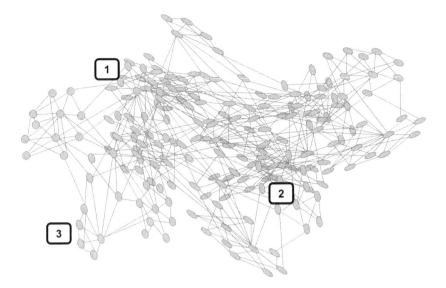

FIGURE 8.22   Master map based on affective bonds.

influence over the cluster. Some clusters, such as 3, are relatively isolated, and these could indicate geographically remote communities mainly consisting of sub-national minorities. Especially for the main clusters, or clans, it is likely that, given their strong group identity, there is a degree of rivalry or at least "us and them" sentiment between them. Sometimes a regime manages such rivalries and keeps its own would-be rivals from accumulating too much power by dividing key positions between clans. If one were to highlight key state institutions in the affective map, especially the security apparatus, financial institutions, state banks and large state companies, one might see a kind of clan division of power. If we had a very granular breakdown extending to the level of individual people, we might even see clan rivalries played out as factional splits within specific organisations. The map could provide some interesting answers if one were to look for potential patterns in stakeholder responses. If an actor were well connected within an affective cluster, then regardless of its formal status, it might be quite capable of mustering others to support it, just based on loyalty.

In a relatively pluralistic society, with an extensive array of cross-cutting affiliations and loyalties, a map based on affective bonds might not make sense. It would just be a haze of more or less equidistant dots, and we would have to revert to the domain-based map to discern meaningful networks. But in many developing and transitional countries where sub-national and unofficial loyalties remain strong, this alternative perspective can be very instructive. The domain-centric one keeps actors in their role boxes, so that we can still see what their main activity and role-based interactions are, while the affective map better reveals underlying patterns of affinity, and some potentially surprising sources of actors' indirect influence. It should be noted that a map based on affective bonds can be much more challenging to make and use, because it requires deeper insight on specific actors and even individual cliques within them, and it can lead to actor units being split to depict internal clan factional rivalries. Thus, an affective map might be limited to exploratory sketches, but even this can yield useful complementary insights.

One way that master maps have been used is to add up the links feeding into and out of actors, and then simply say that those with a higher number of direct links are more influential or important. This can even extend to complex linkage modelling. These "hard" approaches can yield some insights, but they generally run up against nuanced exceptions to the mechanically derived findings.

A more tangible application of a master map is to extract from it tight webs and clusters, and lines of contention, to define a few key networks and rivalries relevant to the operation's likely interactions and potential issues. However, a master map can be too abstract and complex on its own to see patterns around more focused questions. Thus, while it is an instructive baseline, smaller maps can be developed to explore particular dynamics and to develop a more holistic perspective on specific milieus. The following considers a few possibilities by way of example.

EXPLORATORY LINKAGE MAPPING

One exploratory question could be about the networks that would be involved in a particular potential issue. For the West African highway case, we found that a significant potential challenge was host community relocations not going well, because of a perception of unfair treatment among local groups. We might want to get a schematic of the actors who would ultimately be involved in a response, and how they are linked. This is illustrated in top-level format in Figure 8.23. In practice, it would be more detailed and would be done for each affected location.

As discussed in the Town A domain example, members of the host community could react to the project on their own. But they are linked to a wider potential response network. Southerners in the host community are linked to sub-nationalist networks that would ultimately extend to both the military faction and the presidential faction and regime inner circle. Local northerners might ultimately get support from national Muslim ulema, who in turn have supportive ties in Arab Gulf countries (those ties could translate to financial and public relations support). Insurgent groups could also respond to perceived injustices against affected northerners. Another set of links is with civil society and international ethical observers. Responses would flow from national NGOs and media outlets to the international community, and along that chain ethical criticism would be disseminated to wider audiences. The map does not show the strength of linkages, but it still provides a sense of how the challenge of "relocations go badly" could actually manifest through three main response chains, namely southerner, northerner and third-party ethical observer.

Maps can be used not just to shed light on negative contingencies but also to better understand potentially friendly networks that the company might try to fit into. Turning to the case of the IT consultancy in a MENA country, it now has a notion that forging ties with independent actors, or those relatively unconnected to the regime's extended circle, could be a way to gain a foothold without the risks of being tied to regime cronies. We might ask what the independent actor network actually consists of, to get a sense of how and where the company might integrate with it. The network is illustrated in Figure 8.24.

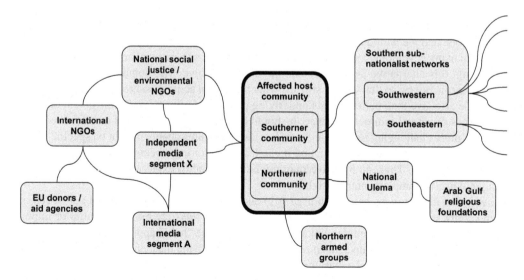

FIGURE 8.23   Host community response network.

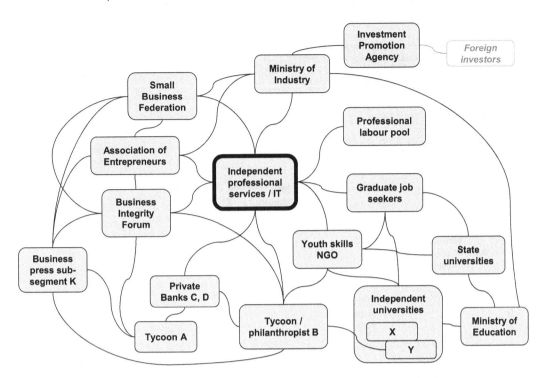

FIGURE 8.24   Independent business network.

For this, the intelligence team purposely put potential local partners at the centre, since that is more or less where the company would be if it pursued a non-crony entry strategy. There are potential opportunities to plug into the network, for example by supporting educational and job skills development, and through membership in relevant business associations. While cronies might be risky to deal with directly, herein are two independent tycoons who feel that a level-playing field and genuine innovation are in the interests of national competitiveness. They are well plugged into the network and could be useful allies. Joining the business integrity forum would send a very strong signal that the IT consultancy is not interested in illicit advantages, but this possibility would need to be assessed against the risk of being seen as a foreign moral rabble rouser before the company has even proven its basic capabilities. The Investment Promotion Agency within the Ministry of Industry is a chaperone for foreign investors, but it is by no means a gatekeeper, and would only be one contact among others in this milieu. Thus, the map does not just capture the relevant network, but provides some hints of an engagement strategy.

Another exploratory question might concern the indirect or networked influence that a potentially hostile actor could bring to bear. In the West African case the rival regime faction, or "MF", was a key potential spoiler. Its network is shown in Figure 8.25.

Aside from its direct control over three ministries and two state companies, most of the faction's influence is via its southwestern ethnic links, deriving from shared tribal affiliations. The map does not show how strong the links are, and we noted in the previous MF summary that greater southern sub-nationalism, vis-à-vis Muslim northerners, is actually quite strong. Thus, the southwestern affiliation does not always translate to ardent mutual loyalty. Another thing to consider herein is that within several actor units linked to MF by tribal affiliation there is also a southeastern faction that would have ties to the presidential clique. Thus, MF might be able to spur some anti-company behaviour in these actors, but they would not act cohesively against the operation as long as the president remained favourable to the operation. Still, there is an indication that MF could cause disruption if it got its extended network on board. This discussion actually highlights the challenge

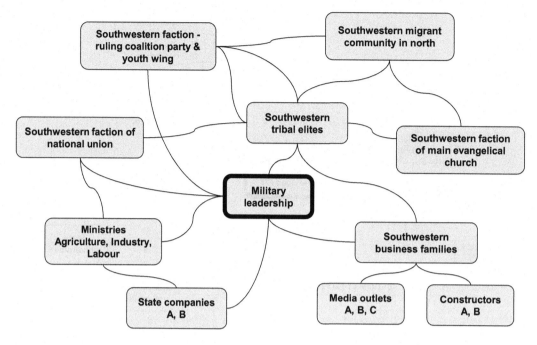

FIGURE 8.25 A hostile stakeholder's network.

of accounting for rivalries that cut across actor units. The church and union, for example, might be cohesive organisations from a functional perspective, but looking at affective bonds, they could appear to be split between ethnic factions, in effect creating two sub-units from one actor.

That last mention of the cross-cutting rivalries gives way to another exploratory question, which is how different axes of rivalry impinge on actor units and networks. Because armed conflicts are the epitome of rivalry, it can be assumed that rivalries are like conflicts in mainly being between clearly distinguishable sides and units. Consider the small conflict map in Figure 8.26.

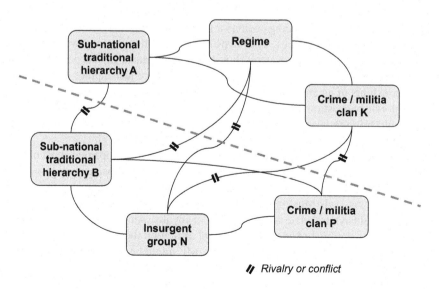

FIGURE 8.26 Basic conflict map.

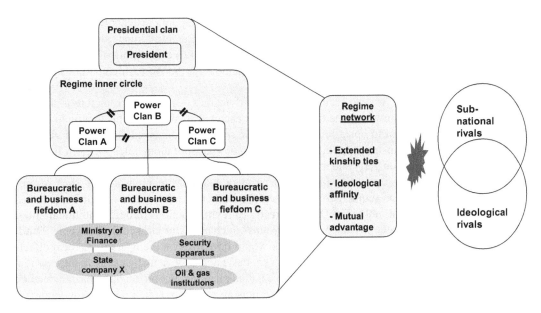

// *Rivalry or conflict*

FIGURE 8.27   Cross-cutting rivalries within larger ones.

Figure 8.26 would only be a small part of a more comprehensive conflict map. In broad outlines, it could be drawn from any number of countries. The main point is that the rivalry is between alliances of discrete actor units. This clear unit demarcation is not uncommon in violent conflict because its existential character imposes a position, and combatants exercise internal security to ensure the cohesion of their forces and defend against hostile penetration. Fractionalisation can happen, but when a conflict actor fractionalises, it usually splits into distinct units rather than lingering in an incoherent state (simply put, hostile armed factions cannot survive long together under the same tent). But short of violent conflict, rivalry patterns can be much more ambiguous, and as noted can cut across actor units. Figure 8.27 illustrates this phenomenon, loosely drawing on the MENA case country.

If this were Egypt, then the president sitting above clan rivalries and allocating influence to balance factional power is realistic, although the military retains considerable independent clout. In Algeria the presidential clique has been, and still is to a large degree, actually in the rival clan box, with the military uneasily playing the role of balancer. For purposes here and confining the discussion to the hypothetical country, there is a rivalry between the key families and cliques within the regime's circle. They have their own fiefdoms, but their turf war is ongoing. As they vie for more control over specific organisations, the others counter by supporting their own loyalists therein. Thus, several stakeholder units are actually split between clans. This would affect these units' cohesion, and for a foreign company it would complicate dealing with them. However, the factional rivalry exists in the context of wider national ones. In Algeria, for example, the regime has held together despite sometimes lethal internal enmity because of the shared threat of Islamist insurgency, pressure for democratic reform and pressure for Berber sub-national rights, all of which challenge the power structure that keeps all regime factions on top. The story is similar in many countries, with Russia being a particularly well-known example. Thus, there can be rivalry (between clan factions within organisations) within rivalry (between power clans), within rivalry (regime versus opponents). All levels can matter, but the factional ones within actor units can be the most elusive and thus offer more surprises.

The above focused on power clans, or cliques, but sub-national and ideological axes could be more relevant depending on the context, and often overlap with lines of elite factional competition.

A final exploratory exercise could be to aggregate detailed mapping insights for a more digestible summary schematic of the relevant stakeholder milieu. This top-level, impressionist perspective glosses over nuances, but provides a holistic picture that facilitates considerations around broader stakeholder responses and engagement strategies. An example for the West African highway case is shown in Figure 8.28.

Paring down the detail, we can focus on some key dynamics. Central to the picture is the government and regime, within which the two main rivals each has its own fiefdoms that include parts of the bureaucracy relevant to operational permits. The rivals are connected directly and via tribal elites to three influential institutions that are at least somewhat split along inter-southern lines, the main churches, the coalition party and the main unions. Again through tribal bonds, each side is also connected to elite business interests, which have a crony or patronage relationship with their respective regime champions. The southerner segments of the host community, or communities, is linked to the presidency via local authorities, and indirectly to regime factions through traditional elites. The local northerner segment has ties to bandit groups which are in turn linked to insurgents. Third-party observers, both domestic and international, would have eyes on the operation's local effects via national NGOs and independent media. This very basic depiction actually captures the essential stakeholder dynamics. It would not be useful for detailed planning, but on the other hand a detailed master map would not be very useful for creative musing about strategic options. Any summary schematic needs to be based on nuanced understanding, but at some point we need an uncluttered perspective or we remain mired in details.

As the above examples suggest, linkage mapping is not just one exercise yielding a single output. It is also an exploratory exercise to test linkages against emerging concerns and priorities and can be an initial foray into engagement planning and even political risk management strategy. More broadly, it provides much more nuance to our picture of the socio-political system, putting players and motives to what were once only abstract systemic dynamics.

On another note, we can see also see how mapping could significantly adjust our preliminary assessments of attitude and influence. Once we see an actor's wider links, we can better see who could influence their attitude, and also the alliances and rivalries that could affect their influence.

SENSE-MAKING

Before proceeding, one should note that if stakeholder analysis were a stand-alone intelligence exercise, all interpretation of results would occur in this step. In our context of a wider baseline intelligence exercise, in the planning stage stakeholder findings are taken alongside terrain outputs to formulate integrated planning foci. What follows here is broadly indicative of the finale of a stand-alone stakeholder process, but it would be taken further if there were not a separate planning exercise.

On a preliminary note, sense-making does not focus on prioritisation. In terrain analysis, it is possible to derive priorities, because challenges stem from exogenous factors which can be observed and assessed independently of company plans and interaction. A prioritisation of stakeholders does not easily translate to planning priorities, for several reasons. One is that unlike with terrain challenges, the sources of which a company cannot really affect, stakeholders can change position through company engagement. Thus, simply focusing on raw priorities misses opportunities to actually adjust the operation's stakeholder landscape. Another is that some lowly ranked stakeholders could be very important to the company's own values and concerns. For example, actors within a host community or in national civil society might not have strong assessment scores, but the company needs their buy-in in order to satisfy itself and its corporate stakeholders that its ethical standing and social acceptability are on firm ground. Finally, the company's strategy might call for entry with and through less influential actors, and hence their importance to the plan would be far higher than their position in a raw ranking. We will relate attitude and influence scores for a map of stakeholder positions, but the aim is to inform preliminary planning, not to depict priorities.

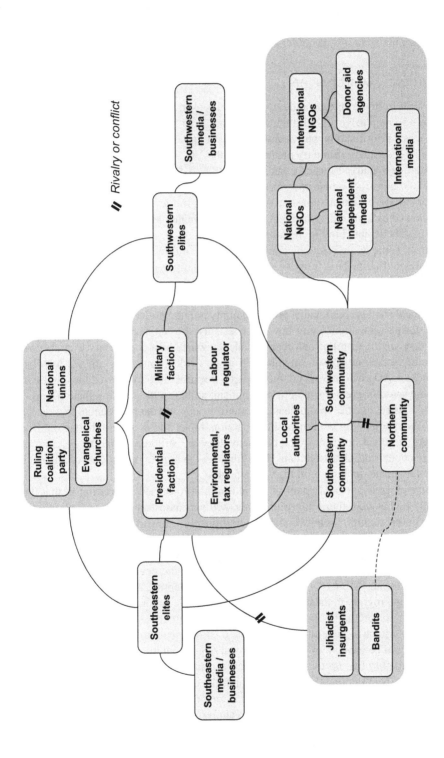

Rivalry or conflict

FIGURE 8.28 Holistic summary map.

One could devise a range of sense-making exercises but we confine this to three. We begin with the attitude-influence matrix and its interpretive challenges and uses. Following this, we apply findings to develop a clear sense of the main reasons for a given direction of attitude towards the operation. Finally, we summarise the main stakeholder-related issues and challenges, which often reflect terrain challenges but from a stakeholder-first perspective.

ATTITUDE-INFLUENCE MATRIX INSIGHTS

The matrix is built from the attitude and influence scales used in assessment. To reiterate, these were −5 (hostile) to +5 (supportive) for attitude and 1 (marginal) to 5 (major) for influence. The matrix does indicate a raw prioritisation, but, as noted, it is not particularly meaningful. More important is its application to generate preliminary planning insights.

We will examine a matrix for each case. It is possible to develop a matrix showing all individual actors, and also to construct a matrix for each domain. We could even show stakeholder links on a matrix. For parsimony, we can assume that we are building top-level summary versions. Each example will be followed by a brief discussion of some of the challenges in interpretation. The matrix for West African case is depicted in Figure 8.29.

In this matrix, some actor positions could seem rather quirky. The local police, present in and around both affected townships, might seem to be a relatively low-level player, and one might assume that being linked to the regime, they would be as favourable to the project as the national police or local authorities. Their lower favourability comes from their close relationships with the more extreme local southern nationalist groups. Simply put, the police might not be fair when maintaining order during relocations or in any other sensitive circumstances. Their influence is quite high because they are the frontline enforcement agency where host community friction could occur. Despite the military faction's power, members of its network are not fully aligned with its attitude towards the project. As previously noted, this is partly because intra-southern divisions are mitigated by at least some sense of greater southern nationalism, and even the military faction's allies would maintain some constructive ties to southeastern ethnic groups and the presidential faction. The army, controlled by and overlapping with the military faction, looks odd in a neutral position. But despite military leaders' political hostility to the company, they are still committed to ensuring territorial integrity and to countering jihadist threats. Thus, they let the army's operational command focus on its professional mandate, making it on the whole neutral.

The Ministry of Transport and donors involved in the project are interesting in that their influence is actually higher than the military faction's. MF was assessed as the second most powerful political actor in the country, so how could a mere transport ministry and foreign donors be more influential? MF would be higher than either if the focus were on the country itself, for example if we were assessing actors' roles in stability or long-term policy direction. But the object of the analysis is the company's project. From this perspective, as the constructor's direct customer and principal interlocutor, the Ministry of Transport is more influential. It will be assessing project performance, reporting progress to the president and handling any negotiations. From an operation-first perspective, donors too are highly influential: they are an indirect customer; their influence with the president could be critical to government support and commitment to fairness in community relocations; and they would be capable of inflicting considerable reputational and financial damage if the company badly failed to live up to expectations. A lesson in this, then, is that when interpreting a matrix, one needs to bear in mind that the operation is the object to which influence relates. It is easy to see influence in overall political terms, but that is only relevant if the country as a whole is under the microscope (and it actually will be in scenario analysis).

The matrix for the IT consultancy case is in Figure 8.30 on page 232. Note that "clan" therein refers to elite political-business cliques, whether or not kinship-based.

This too contains some interpretive idiosyncrasies. First, if the regime-linked clans are unfavourable to the operation, because of their interest in controlling it for their own purposes, then it would

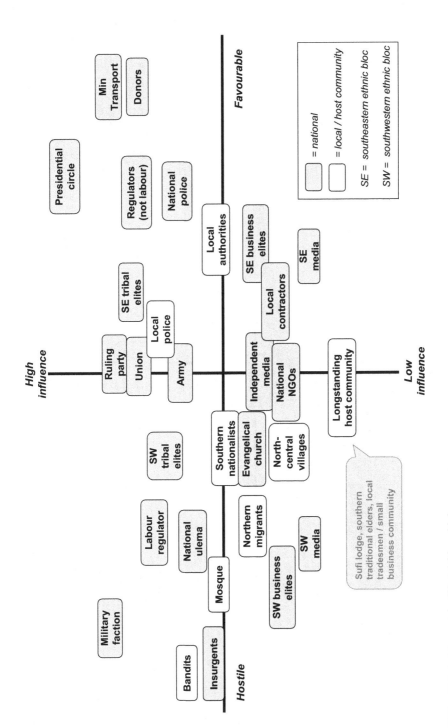

FIGURE 8.29 Stakeholder matrix, West African highway case.

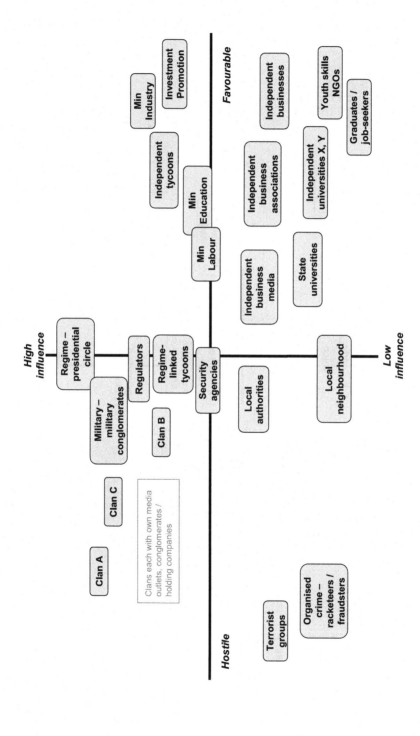

FIGURE 8.30 Stakeholder matrix, MENA IT consultancy case.

seem strange that their champion, the president, is neutral. It is often the case in developing and transitional countries that a regime is somewhat above the fray when it comes to vying for business advantages. It has myriad other things to think about, including how to stay in power partly through keeping a lid on socio-economic frustration. Even personalised regimes think about national development strategies, and in this case, perhaps prodded by the Ministry of Industry, the regime has a favourable view of growing legitimate knowledge sector FDI. Thus, its loyalty to the clans is countered by a degree of rational technocratic thinking. Another point is the slightly unfavourable attitude of regulators and local authorities. Some of this could be because of clan links. But a more mundane reason is also corruption. Even if both actors have no strong feelings about the operation, they will likely see some predatory opportunity in it, which, as we noted, equates to degrees of unfavourable attitude.

From a more macro-level perspective, the basic shape of the MENA country's matrix indicates a balance of power challenge. Most supportive stakeholders are in the less influential half, while most unfavourable ones are more influential. This might suggest that the IT consultancy is facing an uphill battle, lacking a critical mass of friendly influence to ward off or contain predatory interests. Before managers throw up their hands and scrap the venture, though, a more nuanced consideration is in order. The less influential, supportive actors have a low profile, especially to heavyweights concerned about mutual status competition. If the company were to slide into the friendly network and quietly work on building a local track record, it would take a while before it directly came up against powerful interests or was seen as a threat. By then it could be well ensconced. Its collaboration with actors around it could even boost mutual influence, for example by illustrating a successful FDI story that the regime could to refer to when making the case for the country's investment attractiveness. We noted how raw priorities are not necessarily strategic ones. Modestly influential, supportive actors could be the key to a sustainable country presence, and with mutual collaboration could become more influential over time.

The last point above suggests another application of the prioritisation matrix. It is not just useful as a schematic of actor positions, but it can also facilitate initial thinking about broader engagement and political risk strategies. Consider Figure 8.31, which posits some generic approaches to actors in different positions.

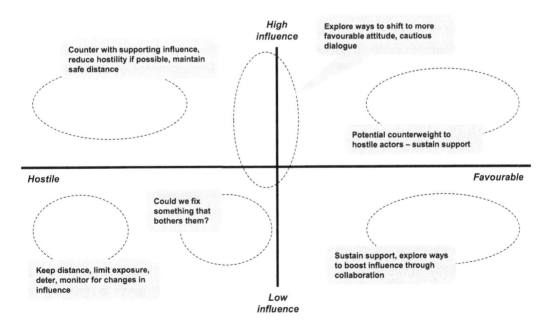

FIGURE 8.31 Stakeholder matrix for initial planning insights.

By way of example, in the highway case, there is a modestly influential grouping (host communities) that is wary about project-related disruptions and unfairness in relocations. The company already plans to ameliorate some of their concerns through compensation and assistance, but if we ask how to shift this set further right, more options could emerge, such as specific CSR initiatives aimed at addressing critical community-wide needs. In the IT company example, as noted above, developing success stories with actors in the low influence/favourable group could shift them into a higher influence bracket. If the regime, perhaps via the Ministry of Industry, learned of the company's successes, then it might deter the business clans from interfering in the operation. As long as we keep in mind the insights that brought us to this point, the matrix can be very helpful in generating ideas on how to shift the stakeholder picture to one more favourable to the operation's resilience and success.

Finally, we can subject the matrix to plausible contingencies to see what their effect might be on actor positions. As discussed in stakeholder investigation, changes to the operation could have a broad effect on attitudes. Recall from Chapter 3 that in one of the author's cases the client's plan was to start with relatively uncontroversial conventional gas extraction and then later shift to shale extraction. Testing the switch to shale operations, there was a marked overall reduction in favourability. We can also test potential power shifts in the country, such as coups, purges or electoral changes, to see how stakeholder influence positions could change. These experiments can help us to understand the wider implications of key contingencies, and the ones we need to pay particular attention to.

Interpretive exercises using the attitude-influence matrix are top-level and exploratory, but they are a definite shift from analysis to planning. By this point in the baseline intelligence exercise, armed with insights from both terrain and stakeholder analysis, thinking naturally starts to move from "what and who" to strategic implications and options.

Key Reasons for Directions of Attitude

Another useful summary that we can derive at this point is the principal reason for a given direction of stakeholder attitude. Prior to research, we developed the operation's socio-political profile as a way to extrapolate attitudes. With the research in hand, we now know the real reasons for positive and negative sentiment. Reasons can be extracted and summarised to provide planners with a clear indication of perceived attributes that the company can build on for trust and mutual understanding, or, where feasible, adjust or mitigate to reduce friction. Some relevant operational attributes, such as a company's nationality or the agreed cost of a project, are not adjustable, but if they are problematic, then we can at least account for them in the tone of our communications.

A top-level example of the outputs of this exercise for the West African case are depicted in Figure 8.32. The addition of actors holding certain perceptions adds some interpretive depth, but the more important insight is actually a socio-political profile directly based on actor investigation, not just on sketches that we used to extrapolate attitudes. In terms of utility, one can look at this way. Recall the example of getting a high-pressure job in a new and "office-politically challenged" company. If you try to fit into it and do not know how different actors perceive you, you have no way of managing perceptions and of preparing for potential responses. If you know, or at least have a reasonable idea, then you can tailor your profile for an optimal reception and prepare against hostile responses. If the summary in Figure 8.32 was about a real operation, even in its rough sketch form and as basic as it is, it would be very valuable.

A couple of explanatory points are in order. Note that several sets of actors have reasons for both favourable and unfavourable attitudes, in particular host community actors and NGOs which have reasons to be both wary hopeful. This split perception was noted in investigation, when nett attitude was estimated as favourable minus unfavourable perceptions. Even the president, who ultimately sought and approved the project, has one reason to be wary, which is the project's cost in

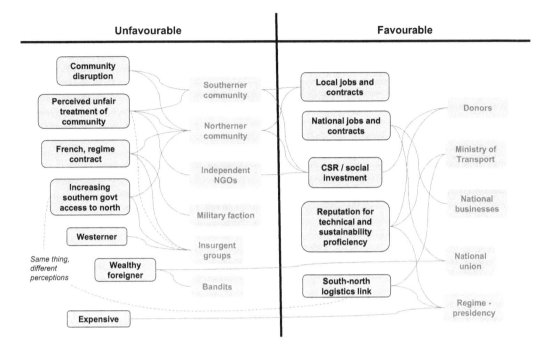

FIGURE 8.32   Attitude drivers, West African Highway case.

relation to budgetary concerns. Some perceptions seem to overlap but differ in nuance. For example, that the company is French and on a regime contract, and a Western organisation, are similar. But the Westerner aspect stands out in the ideologically coloured perception of jihadist insurgents, for whom any company from any "crusader imperialist" country is problematic.

Figure 8.33 on the next page is the output from the same exercise for the IT consultancy case.

In this case, an interesting twist is that the company's brand and business standing is the source of both positive and unfavourable attitudes. It would be of healthy interest to several sets of actors. For the crony elites, though, it makes the company a potentially lucrative target, to be captured in an "offer you can't refuse" (or if not captured, then disrupted to keep a rival from benefiting). As discussed earlier, predatory interest is a form of hostile attitude, and sometimes a company's positive attributes make it alluring for the wrong reasons. The dotted lines between two reasons for a favourable attitude and the presidency indicate that the operation is not especially important to the presidency, given other pressing concerns, but there is mild interest in the operation's socio-economic benefits, and this could be further sparked if the company made headway.

Summarising the Main Issues

Reflecting back on terrain analysis, terrain factors were examined to derive potential challenges to the operation. In principle, a given stakeholder could also be regarded as a factor, and its possible negative responses could be assessed and added to the list of terrain challenges for a more comprehensive set of problems that the operation could face. It is not that simple, though.

We will examine threat assessment in another chapter. It is an approach to prioritising hostile and predatory actors, as well as assessing the risk of different actions a threat actor could take. In that context, one can extract and assess specific potential challenges because there is seldom much, if any, interaction with threat actors. They are similar to terrain factors in being external to the operation and affecting it through potential intersections (which they contrive), not through twists and turns in a dynamic relationship.

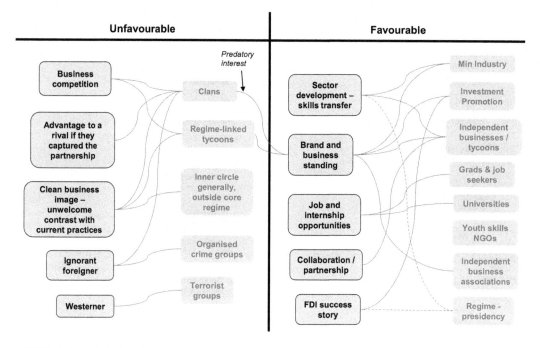

FIGURE 8.33　Attitude drivers, MENA IT consultancy case.

As noted earlier, most other potential stakeholder responses are tied to how the relationship between an actor and the operation evolves, and the company's decisions and behaviour are a major variable in this. Contingent "ifs", including about our own actions, abound, making an estimate of specific future actions quite speculative. Thus, a detailed list of possible stakeholder responses would be more distracting than informative. That said, within assessment, we did derive general, indicative responses for a sense of the direction and magnitude of potential effects, and now we can summarise these to lend nuance to subsequent planning. Instead of "responses", we will use the broader term, "issues", since responses would manifest in a wider situational context. As we will see, most issues are related to, or aspects of, terrain challenges. We noted how terrain factors are not just exogenous forces but also behavioural dynamics that can be channelled to the company through stakeholder interaction. The summary will provide a few new issues, but it will mainly put actors and motives to the challenges that came from a more abstract, bird's-eye view.

Table 8.1 is a top-level issue summary for the West African highway case; note that this omits a few issues that are nearly exact duplicates of terrain challenges, such as the military faction cancelling the project after a coup.

Doing the same exercise for the IT consultancy case, now that the company is seriously thinking about adjusting its strategy, crony partner manipulation is no longer an issue, but crony retribution against a foreign competitor would still come up. This could include the activation of networks in the bureaucracy and financial sector to try to impede the operation. An "if" in this instance would be the IT consultancy's profile and the degree of direct competition it posed. Opportunism and mild predation among regulatory agencies and the bureaucracy are also an issue, stemming from a perception of the company as both wealthy and gullible because of its lack of local experience. The security agencies might be very interested in what the company could bring to their surveillance capabilities and could press the company to assist in relevant technology projects.

An important point from the issue summary is that several "ifs" help to see how to prevent or mitigate the issue. At least for issues arising in interaction with the company, if we could ensure that "ifs" did not manifest, then overall political risk would be much reduced. In planning, for more complex issues we will use "ifs" to identify opportunities to forestall issue manifestation.

TABLE 8.1
Stakeholder Issue Summary

Issue	Main Actors	Main Ifs	Terrain Challenge Links
Host community backlash/clashes	Host communities, local authorities, police	Grievances, perceived unfairness, police violence, military faction agitation	Host community friction (system)
Strike – project workforce	Union, military faction union allies	Grievances, perceived opportunity, military faction agitation	Strike – project workforce
Workforce tensions/ violence	Union, local northern workers	Perceived ethnic discrimination, military faction agitation	Workforce tensions/violence
Military faction spoiling activity (see agitation in other issues)	Military faction, and its social, business, media, bureaucratic networks	Inherent in military faction's interests, but more acute if perceived discrimination against southwesterners	Rival faction obstruction
Friction with police over human rights compliance	National and local police	Company presses for compliance and monitoring	Host community friction system, potentially also security issues if police become less responsive to company needs
Public ethical criticism	NGOs, relevant media segments, donors	Perceived collusion with human rights abuses or unfair community treatment	Host community friction (system)
Association with integrity breaches/ nepotism	Local subcontractors	Perceived opportunity to use project for gain and to boost status	Nepotism/fraud among local contractors
Pressure for contract renegotiation	President and via him, Min. Transport	Cost perception changes because of economic problems	Political pressure on project (presidential)
Design and engineering decision interference	Highways Dept./Min. Transport	Likely, but matter of degree – could be motivated by anxiety, or seeking to pre-empt presidential whims	Could be an aspect of political pressure on project
Kidnapping	Local bandits in operating areas	Intention is inherent in bandits' role, but more acute if perception of unfairness towards northern communities; risk is higher if perceived security vulnerabilities	Bandit/insurgent kidnapping

There are more ways to extract top-line insights from stakeholder analysis. However, it does not readily lend itself to quick synopses. While terrain analysis yields a tiered list of challenges and key factors, stakeholder analysis provides less of a "to do" list and more of a navigational aid. Domain maps, stakeholder investigation and network mapping each provided invaluable insights on the socio-political milieu, and how the operation could deal with it for minimal mutual harm and a sustainable fit. The nuance on stakeholders and the company's relationship to them is a key finding in itself, and trying to distil this into discrete issues and a few priorities can defeat the purpose. We will find in planning that for each planning target there is a consideration of relevant actors and how to influence them to help achieve political risk management objectives. This draws on the overall awareness that stakeholder analysis provides, not just top-line findings.

We now have the results of the terrain and stakeholder stages. In the next chapter, we see how this intelligence can be applied to help an operation to stay safe, credible and sustainable.

9 Political Risk Management Planning

The objective of political risk management planning is to devise approaches to the challenges and issues that the country operation faces, and more generally to guide managers towards operational resilience. Strictly speaking, planning is not intelligence provision, but only by exploring a planning process can we clearly see how the garnered intelligence can make a difference. In Chapter 4 we noted that one of the main distinctions between intelligence and other kinds of information was its actionability. This chapter focuses on the link between intelligence and action. We address a few preliminary points before heading into the thought process.

First, although the operation's full duration is relevant, for practical purposes there are two time frames for planning. One is the period of the baseline exercise and the operational phases it covers, and again this is roughly 12 to 18 months depending on volatility in the environment. The other is long-range planning based on scenario analysis, and it might extend to three years and a few phases. We cover planning for the baseline period in this chapter and leave long-range planning for the next one on scenarios. In practice, one could do scenario analysis first and then do all planning afterwards. However, terrain and stakeholder analysis are both still fresh in our minds, and it makes sense to capitalise on this familiarity before introducing yet another analytical stage. Planning for the two timescales is also quite different, and in practice would be distinct. Near- to medium-term plans focus on broadly known challenges. Scenario planning guides preparation for country-wide change, the specific directions of which are often very uncertain.

Second, in Chapter 5 we noted that the baseline intelligence exercise is relatively high level, and its insights are like a navigational aid. Once people start working in a place, they will be able to explore the environment in detail, and the plans they develop will be nuanced compared to the upfront guidance developed here. We need to bear that in mind in this stage. Being too prescriptive now would be problematic, because it would pre-empt experiential learning and constrain subsequent adaptability. In addition, political risk intelligence is not an implementation function, and while intelligence team members will be familiar with the work of security, legal, CSR, labour relations and other relevant functions, they will not be nearly as knowledgeable in any given field as a dedicated functional manager. Each function that will be involved in implementation has its own best practices, and plans put forward in this stage usually undergo translation to functional processes. While it is realistic to give implementation a solid starting point, it is unrealistic to expect initial planning to be the final blueprints for action.

Another point concerns priorities. In terrain analysis, we undertook an explicit prioritisation exercise, and in stakeholder analysis an implied one when we assessed attitude and influence. A point made in terrain analysis was that prioritisation did not mean that lower priority issues were left on the shelf and only periodically dusted off to see if they were still safely unimportant. All challenges and actors that made it to end of each analysis matter, and their relative importance just indicates how much attention they get. As we proceed with planning, one will see a broad correlation between an issue's importance and the amount of cross-functional activity around it, but we will not set firm resource parameters a priori. We first let the issue decide what is needed to keep it from being problematic. Resource allocation can be adjusted later if mismatches are apparent or if we seem to exceed realistic resource limits.

A final preliminary note is that in practice political risk considerations are often integrated with operational and functional plans. That makes sense, since that is where the translation to detailed implementation occurs. However, there is merit to retaining a distinct, if high-level, political risk

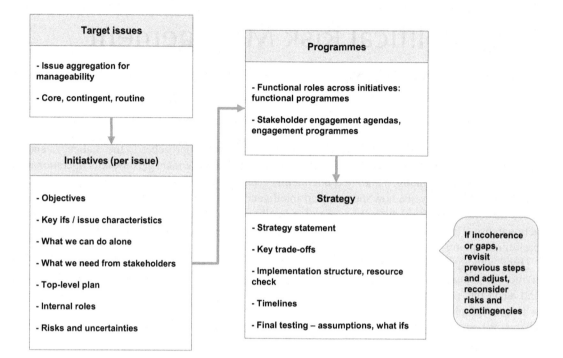

FIGURE 9.1   Planning process.

management plan. It helps people to see the end-to-end logic and how the pieces fit together, and the wider context of their own contributions. Additionally, it ensures that political risk is not subsumed by specific functions, and this is important since it is a cross-functional concern.

The chapter will follow the planning process, which is illustrated in Figure 9.1.

Before we introduce the process, a brief note on terminology is in order. This is what exactly we call the problems that we are planning for. For the most part we use "issue", as a somewhat broad term that incorporates both terrain challenges and stakeholder friction. When this becomes repetitive, "challenge" or "problem" or a similar term will pop up, but they all mean the potential situations, events, changes, responses and complications which political risk management addresses.

Within the process, first the issues derived from terrain and stakeholder analysis are combined based on linkages between them and the degree to which they can, or should, be managed as one wider problem. This might not condense the "to do" list very much, but the aim is to define manageable targets, not to achieve parsimony just for the sake of it. Issues are parsed into three categories: core, contingent and routine. This is not an academic typology; rather, each category suggests a general management approach that sets initial direction for the next step.

We then formulate initiatives to address each issue. Core, contingent and routine issues each has different formulation approaches, but the formulation step in Figure 9.1 broadly applies to all three. Noteworthy is key "ifs" and issue characteristics. Here, these are developed to reveal management opportunities, rather than for estimation as in the previous chapters. For core issues in particular, situational scenarios and backward thinking from a negative outcome help planners to steer away from the key "if" branches. Another point is the explicit inclusion of stakeholders as a planning consideration. What we need from them could be help or acceptance, but we might also need them to not enact a hostile response, or to fail if they do. The formulation of initiatives is where we directly tackle the challenges discerned in analysis, and thus it is the heart of the planning process. That being the case, this step will form a significant part of the chapter, and the examples that we discuss will reflect real experiences and lessons learned.

Unlike with initiatives, programme definition is not oriented to problem-solving. Rather, it is an organisational step that links what to do with who does what and ensures alignment between people and teams handling implementation. Initiatives are enacted by cross-functional teams or task forces. Each function relevant to political risk management will probably be involved in multiple initiatives, and the sum of its activities therein forms its functional programme. Likewise, various stakeholders will be relevant to multiple initiatives. The full set of a stakeholder's roles across different initiatives forms a stakeholder agenda, which in turn becomes the basis of an engagement programme.

From a strategic perspective, we then take stock of the overall plan. A clear strategy statement captures the way that initiatives work together for coherent political risk management. This is the conceptual glue between different initiatives and ensures that initiative task forces are aware of their place in the wider scheme. We also check resource allocation, explicitly note important trade-offs so that they can be carefully managed, and map a general implementation timeline. Finally, we knock the plan with a heavy stick and see how it holds up. If weaknesses become apparent, we can go back to previous stages and iron them out.

The above is somewhat abstract. As we proceed with each step, activities and outputs will become clearer, and again we will use the two cases for concrete illustration.

As we proceed, one can visualise how the insights from the previous two chapters would be put to use. In the final sections of each of the last two chapters, there were final assessments and sense-making. But planning does not just use those wrap-ups. It is based on a holistic awareness of the insights gained thus far, and the use of stakeholder intelligence in particular will draw on nuances from each step in that stage.

TARGET ISSUES

It might be feasible to approach each issue or challenge separately, but it could be inefficient, and it could lead to people working at cross-purposes when addressing closely related problems. Recall that in terrain analysis we defined at least one challenge system, and in stakeholder analysis we grouped some closely linked actors for the purposes of assessment. A similar grouping principle applies now, but specifically for coherence and efficiency in political risk management. Thus, one task here is defining integrated political risk management problems. As we do this, we can also consider whether target issues are in the core, contingent or routine category, for an initial sense of an appropriate management approach.

First, we will explain the three categories, and then see how the issues from the two cases can be shaped into coherent targets within them.

ISSUE CATEGORIES FROM A MANAGEMENT PERSPECTIVE

Categorisation schemes can just be ways of cataloguing facts for easy retrieval and of providing a quick characterisation of the objects they contain. But when they are based on characteristics relevant to how an issue would be managed, they can provide top-level guidance that helps to focus subsequent planning.

There are different possible schemes. One could, for example, divide issues according to the function that would manage them. For example, terrorism, crime and violent unrest would be security issues (handled by the security function), contract abrogation a legal issue (handled by the legal function) and community friction a CSR issue (handled by the CSR function). However, categorising by function can obscure an issue's ramifications for other functional remits. For example, if criminal threats were only dealt with by security, security might not take into account host community sensitivity to an obtrusive guard presence. Conversely, if community friction were only handled by CSR, there might be insufficient consideration of security vulnerabilities that could arise from being too open and interactive with people and groups whom we did not really know.

Another scheme might be the asset that an issue would affect. Assets, to reiterate, are people, reputation, continuity and control. There might be some indication of management approaches in this scheme, but as we noted in Chapter 3 and saw in terrain analysis, most issues affect multiple assets. We could try sorting by issue severity, but this really says little about how to approach an issue, and would only assist in broad considerations of resource allocation.

The categorisation scheme that we apply here is basic and not intended to be highly prescriptive, but it does provide some management guidance, including on the focus of a political risk management strategy. Again, the categories are core, contingent and routine. Each of these is explained in turn.

To begin with, a core issue could have serious and multifaceted consequences, and is inherent in the relationship between the company and the environment. In other words, the intersection with the relevant dynamics is built into the operational concept. Because core issues derive from a unique operation-country relationship, they are novel and require highly contextualised approaches. They are also complex, and it could be necessary to deal with different strands in an appropriate sequence.

The criticality of core issues necessarily puts them at the heart of a political risk management strategy. Thus, when developing initiatives for non-core issues, we will need to tailor them as far as possible to support core issue management, or at the least to not conflict with it. This can impose trade-offs when the optimal way to manage a lesser problem would hinder the treatment of core ones. For example, a management team might initially consider transferring the risk of labour friction by partnering with a local producer who manages its own workforce. But that could relinquish a critical lever, local job provision, in mitigating the core issue of host community hostility. Thus, core issues are the centre of gravity in political risk management, and their imperatives are the bones of a strategy.

There are two basic rules of thumb about core issues. One is that there will seldom be more than a small number of them, at the most five. This is not set in stone, but if one has too many, the "core" label has probably been used too liberally. Then there will be no strategic focus, and initiatives will end up competing with or undercutting each other when trade-offs arise. The other rule of thumb is that they are usually closely linked. Because they are at the nexus of the relationship between the operation and the environment, they can feed into each other, and how we manage one can affect the others. A strategy to address them therefore needs a healthy, if implicit, dose of systems thinking.

The next category is contingent issues, which are new events, actions and changes that could happen, contingent on certain combinations of precursors, triggers and actor decisions. Who the operation is and what it is doing can affect the plausibility of contingent issues, but they are not tightly bound up with the relationship between an operation and the environment. For this reason, and because their occurrence is not a given, contingent issues, while often important, are not usually central to a political risk management strategy.

When something could happen but is not inevitable, there are three parts to the management approach. One is to define observable indicators of the issue's causes and emergence so that we have some warning of it happening and can adjust preparedness accordingly. Another is to develop measures to reduce plausibility, not just of the issue's occurrence but of its more severe potential effects if it did occur (it could be impossible to prevent a political change or stop a harmful behaviour like terrorism, but we can control the company's exposure to dangerous dynamics). Finally, we devise contingency plans for occurrence, so that the company can act quickly to preserve assets and avoid further harm.

Contingent issues include the exogenous classics of coups, nationalisations, unrest, terrorism, strikes, sanctions and currency inconvertibility. But the category does not just contain issues that come from outside of the company's relationships. For example, a government cancelling a contract is contingent on some external variables, such as who is in power, but it also depends on the government's attitude to the company. Thus, stakeholder-related issues too can be contingent, since attitudes and relationships can change. As well, supportive stakeholders can often help to manage a contingent issue, even if it is an exogenous potential event.

The final category is routine issues. These derive from ongoing dynamics and behaviours in the environment, with which the operation will intersect from time to time. They also arise from ongoing relationships which will probably see periodic friction, and in which the same bones of contention are likely to come up now and then. Routine issues are somewhat predictable, since they follow a pattern, and this lends itself to the development of ongoing procedures and protocols to manage them. Standard corporate policies can be a basis for these, but the degree of required contextualisation will vary by issue. While patterns in issue manifestation could change, change is usually evolutionary at least within a given time frame, and approaches can be incrementally adjusted to remain current.

The above might make routine issues sound like a rather administrative or procedural matter, but they can be, or become, more complex management problems. For one thing, routine issues, whether arising from terrain factors or stakeholder attitudes, can give way to significant changes or spikes in intensity, depending on how their underlying drivers evolve. In stakeholder relationships, ongoing sources of minor friction can lead to rifts if left to fester. Thus, monitoring, adaptation and contingency planning are sometimes necessary corollaries of procedures and policies. As well, routine does not suggest that an issue cannot be proactively managed. There could be opportunities to reduce the frequency and intensity of negative intersections and interactions, and while stakeholders can be a source of routine issues, their support can also be essential to managing them. Routine issues, then, are not just dealt with through routine approaches.

It is worth noting that both routine and contingent issues are not necessarily less important than core ones. For example, a terrorist attack on the company could be a tragic show-stopper, and routine bureaucratic delays could lead to paralysis. Unlike core issues, though, contingent and routine ones can be managed at least partly as a separate support activity, or only as needed. Core issues, by contrast, are intrinsic to the operation and its socio-political identity, and cannot be managed without reference to operational decisions, activities and relationships. There tends to be a broad correlation between issue category and challenge severity, with core being severe, contingent moderately severe and routine less severe. However, this relationship is loose and exceptions are frequent. To reiterate a previous point, issue category is more about management approaches, while severity is more about resource allocation.

Issue Integration and Categorisation

With the above characterisation in hand, we can see how issues can be assembled for management coherence, and positioned in the three categories. The category fit will not always be precise, and for several issues there will be some crossover. We will examine the exercise in some detail for the West African highway project to illustrate some of the relevant thinking, and then more briefly see what it could yield for the IT consultancy case.

There are three core issues for the highway project, as follows:

- host community friction – the system of host community distrust, association with human rights abuses, police violence and discrimination, and unrest and antipathy during and as a result of relocations (this includes ethical criticism that could arise from perceived human rights abuses and unfair host community treatment);
- union responses/worker friction – all labour-related issues, including a strike, the union blocking local hiring, and workplace friction including violence; and
- military faction (MF) spoiling activity – potential bureaucratic hassles discerned in terrain analysis, but more importantly and linking to the other two core issues, MF's use of extended networks to incite union and southern nationalist unrest as a way of eroding the operation's credibility.

These are closely linked, as depicted in Figure 9.2.

Noteworthy is that in terrain analysis, the challenge of "rival faction obstruction" was mainly regarded as a potential source of bureaucratic and regulatory hassles, and not ranked as particularly severe. However, stakeholder analysis revealed how MF's connections could be used to incite spoiling activity among other important stakeholder groups. Thus, in any approach to labour and host

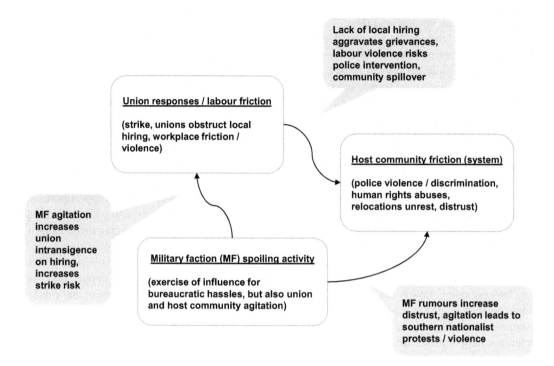

FIGURE 9.2   Core issues system, West African highway case.

community issues, MF would be a necessary consideration, and its potential behaviour joins them in the core set.

Not everything within the core issues is linked. MF bureaucratic obstruction might have little to do with either labour agitation or host community friction, and might be partly managed alongside routine bureaucratic issues. Similarly, a union strike could be motivated by standard labour grievances, and might be better positioned as a contingent issue. But these are both tied to the stakeholders involved in the core issues, and trying to extract them for separate treatment would fragment the stakeholder engagement aspect of core issue management.

Contingent issues for the highway project include the following:

- bandit/insurgent kidnapping;
- coup (both attempted and successful);
- electoral violence (local);
- anti-government unrest (democratic protest);
- insurgent attack on operation;
- port strike/sea piracy incident;
- contract renegotiation pressure (president); and
- donor-president friction.

One temptation here is to integrate the security-related issues under a security functional remit, but again a functional grouping would gloss over important nuances. For example, a kidnapping would most likely be carried out by local bandits, and managing the issue would include not just physical security, but building a relationship with local traditional elites who could dissuade would-be perpetrators from acting.

A coup and coup attempt are integrated, because the company would not know which issue it was dealing with until after the fact, so the same preparations are required. A port strike and sea piracy incident had very different rankings in terrain analysis, but they are both maritime logistical problems and the solution for either could be at least partly apply to the other.

Contract pressure and donor-president friction could be linked. If the president were annoyed with European donor criticism over his non-democratic tendencies, the donor-sponsored project could become a pawn and face political pressure. However, the more likely scenario for contract pressure is budget concerns, and hence the issues are kept separate. Either of these two issues could actually become routine. The government could start to haggle on a routine basis if it started to have qualms, and donor-president friction could become routine if donors decided to take a stand on non-democratic tendencies. At this point, though, at least the initial manifestation of both issues, to any degree, might not happen. If they did kick off and become routine, then there would be a switch from contingency planning and prevention to routine approaches.

Following are the routine issues:

- bureaucratic/customs delays;
- official corruption;
- contractor integrity breaches/friction;
- routine security issues (street crime, police hassles); and
- Ministry of Transport interference.

Bureaucratic and customs delays are integrated because while the agencies involved might be different, approaches would be very similar and any stakeholder support to address the problems would likely come from the same sources. Corruption is related to these two issues, and if we later see that an anti-corruption initiative overlaps with them, we could consider integrating the three initiatives into one. Both subcontractor issues are integrated, since they would be addressed in interaction with local partners. Despite street crime and police roadblock hassles having very different severity ratings, together they would affect staff moving in towns and the capital, and one could envision a package of personal security awareness measures and procedures that addressed both. Finally, Ministry of Transport (including the Highways Department) interference in project planning remains distinct, and would be handled through ongoing diplomacy.

The full set of challenges and issues from terrain and stakeholder analysis numbered 28 (or 31 if we count the parts of the host community friction system). We now have 16 target issues after integrating for management coherence. While the categorisation has not led to solid planning indications, we have at least a broad sense of how the issues in each set would be approached. For the highway project, we are now ready to proceed with the next step, the development of initiatives to manage each target issue.

Before moving on, though, we can see how the same exercise would have worked for the IT consultancy in a MENA country. With respect to core issues, there are two very significant distinctions from the highway case. One is that the core system is binary, and the other is that one core issue is not a negative challenge, but the positive challenge of achieving a sustainable presence. The core system is illustrated in Figure 9.3 on the following page.

This system directly follows from company ruminations following terrain analysis, which revealed the risks of partnering or otherwise engaging with major local players. A revised operational concept began to take shape during stakeholder analysis: the company would pursue a more gradual entry via the independent business network in order to build a sustainable track record before pursuing a higher market profile, which, if incurred too early, could attract concerted crony pressure. The two issues are closely interlinked. Crony spoiling activity would be aimed at impeding a successful entry, either to avert competition or to make a crony partnership the only effective option. Sustainably embedding would include a combination of avoiding and countering crony pressure, while at the same time moving towards the strategic aim of long-term, legitimate and lucrative operations.

It is a walk on wild side in political risk to posit the challenge of attaining a given business strategy as an issue to be managed. We could just posit the crony challenge as the single core issue, but

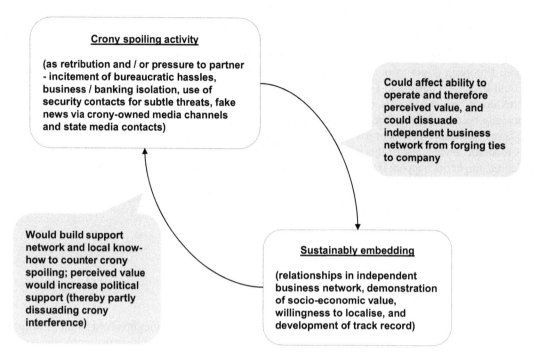

Crony spoiling activity

(as retribution and / or pressure to partner - incitement of bureaucratic hassles, business / banking isolation, use of security contacts for subtle threats, fake news via crony-owned media channels and state media contacts)

Could affect ability to operate and therefore perceived value, and could dissuade independent business network from forging ties to company

Would build support network and local know-how to counter crony spoiling; perceived value would increase political support (thereby partly dissuading crony interference)

Sustainably embedding

(relationships in independent business network, demonstration of socio-economic value, willingness to localise, and development of track record)

FIGURE 9.3   Core issues system, MENA IT consultancy case.

given that it could affect the solution to it and vice versa, explicitly recognising them as a system provides strategic clarity. In this case, even before developing initiatives there was reasonable confidence that the gradual, "stealth", approach was sensible, and when we have confidence in plans formed thus far, we can draw on that to accelerate the thought process. The above formulation was somewhat exceptional, but it illustrates that there is flexibility in the process, and that there can be opportunities for broader thinking along the way.

Contingent issues in the IT consultancy case would include staff detentions, terrorism, criminal extortion attempts, regulatory change and the introduction of currency controls. The two regulatory changes, one on FDI ownership rules and the other on local content, are kept distinct because of their different significance for the company. A high dose of local content actually fits well with the revised operational concept, while new FDI rules could open the company up to crony interference. Revolutionary unrest is another contingency, which would be a security and business continuity challenge.

Among routine issues, bureaucratic corruption and state nepotism pressure are integrated. This category also includes government pressure to assist in repressive surveillance projects, bureaucratic delays, and neighbourhood friction. Socio-economic protests might seem like a contingent issue, but they are quite regular and would require routine procedures on staff safety and movement.

As an aside, going back to stakeholder analysis, in the identification step one question posed was "who could help with terrain challenges?" For the IT consultancy, most of the types of actors which came up in that exercise were subsequently found to have actual constituents in the independent business ecosystem. Thus, the "sustainably embedding" approach to address crony pressure could actually help with a number of problems.

INITIATIVE FORMULATION

For each issue, initiative formulation directly addresses the question, "What should we do about it?" As noted earlier, the answers would be skeletal at this point, but they would still be instructive, providing a head start for on-the-ground planning, and guidance in remaining pre-entry decisions.

As we proceed, the main focus is on political risk problem-solving, as opposed to generic planning practicalities.

The issue categories in the last section provided a general characterisation of how each type would be managed. To reiterate, core issues receive highly tailored, programmatic approaches. Contingent issues are managed by prevention, warning, preparation and contingency plans. Routine issues are mainly dealt with through procedures and protocols, but sometimes also by reducing the frequency and severity of specific intersections, and preparing for a possible spike in intensity. All types involve both what the company can do on its own and how stakeholders can be engaged for beneficial effect. Rather than walking through the various considerations for each type, examples from the cases provide a more tangible illustration of the thinking involved in this step. For each type of issue, we will use one example from each of the two cases. The selected issues are quite distinct and together hint at the range of possibilities in initiative formulation.

INITIATIVES FOR CORE ISSUES

There is a significant contrast between the two examples that we apply here. The highway case's initiative to manage host community friction is illustrative of a systematic project-type approach. The IT consultancy's management of crony pressure comprises an emergent, learning approach closely aligned to the wider entry strategy.

Host Community Friction, West African Highway Case

On a preliminary note, for the sake of simplicity, we will assume that there is only one host community, perhaps Town A from the domain example in stakeholder analysis. In practice, if there were distinct communities, they would require tailored sub-initiatives, although ideas from each would feed into the others and they would be coordinated in a broader programme.

Recall that host community friction is a challenge system, involving a loss of trust, association with human rights abuses, police violence and discrimination, and unrest during relocations and lingering hostility afterwards. Relocations are a system lynchpin, in that they would be the main cause of resentment and ethnic unrest if badly managed. One can flesh out the wider problem with reference to the network map that we did for the issue in stakeholder analysis, which indicated the follow-on effects of ethical criticism and negative national-level reactions.

The company's objectives with respect to the issue are to avoid violence, resentment and insecurity, and to achieve smooth community relations, a peaceful and secure local environment (or at least to not contribute to tensions), and a reputation for fairness and credibility.

For initial hypotheses and direction, we can develop top-level pictures of the issue and possible solutions. In the issue picture, the company needs to know how a reasonable worst-case situation could develop, so that it can see where intervention in the pathway towards it is required and feasible. This is depicted in Figure 9.4 on the next page.

We can see that there are a number of problems at the front end, particularly around miscommunications and misinformation. MF has a role here as a source of agitation and rumour-mongering. Among affected northerners, there is frustration with a lack of local jobs, especially when they see southern union members in lucrative project employment. Impending relocations heighten northerner concerns and a sense of injustice. Among southern nationalists, the imminent rollout of northerner compensation crystallises a sense that their ethnic rivals are gaining unfair advantages. Relocations are thus the spark for protests and ethnic clashes. The police get involved to quell unrest, and heavily favouring southerners and lacking restraint, they perpetrate brutality against involved northerners. From here, backlashes ensue, and there would be a marked deterioration in the company's own security environment. It would be very difficult for the company to recover its standing at this point.

We can now examine the above for opportunities to intervene and avert the above outcome. Again, we are only aiming for initial ideas here, and Figure 9.5 on page 249 does not show a plan.

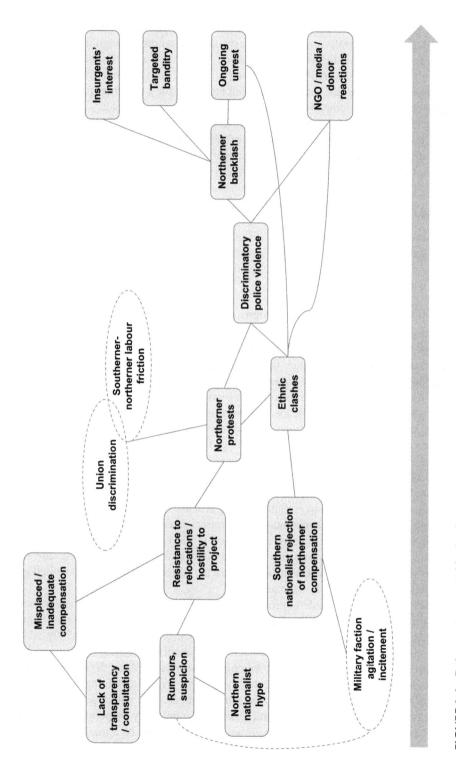

FIGURE 9.4   Pathways to a regrettable situation.

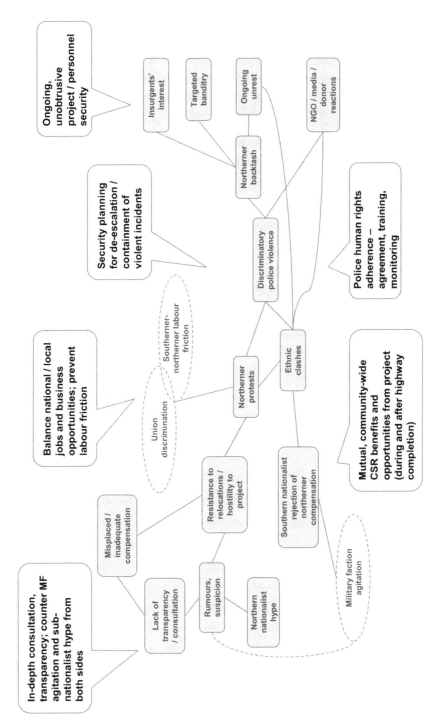

FIGURE 9.5 Opportunities to avert the situation.

Upfront and proactive local engagement prevents gauche mistakes in relocations planning, informs the company about other serious concerns, aligns mutual expectations and lays the groundwork for ongoing consultation and mediation throughout the project. Transparent and regular communication also counters hype and rumours. The company develops CSR initiatives that address the needs of all ethnic communities, thereby taking the edge off of southern nationalist ire, or at least reducing the effect of hyper-nationalist agitation among southern neighbourhoods. Development initiatives are planned for after highway completion, and positioned as helping people to make the most of the opportunities that a new transport link brings. This reduces wariness towards the project. Local northerners are included in project employment, giving them a positive stake. Proactively getting police commitment to human rights adherence, and establishing a human rights assurance programme, reduce the risk that police overreact to any unrest, and make police more capable of de-escalating incidents. Finally, on the premise that there would still be some extremist or predatory elements in the host community, the company needs its own local security coverage, but this is designed to be reasonably unobtrusive. Within this wider initiative, relocations form an intensive sub-initiative to ensure that it proceeds without serious incidents.

We know from both terrain and stakeholder analysis that there would be some hurdles to the above approaches, as well as some potential opportunities. These need to clarified before developing ideas further. This consideration is depicted in Figure 9.6. Note that this leaves aside the company's own security, since it is something the company has considerable control over, although greater police professionalism would certainly help with it.

The above indicates both problems and potential solutions to them. Inter-group mistrust in engagement and CSR could be reduced by including a significant representation from long-established community segments in consultation fora. As noted in the Town A sub-domain in stakeholder analysis, there is still a sense of shared community among those with long roots in the area, and they could be a moderating influence. A gender balance in such fora would also help to ease friction, since women tend to be less involved in sub-nationalist causes and more directly concerned about family economic security (a tendency that is well known to conflict resolution NGOs). An important point is that community engagement cannot just be window dressing. The company would have to be

Element	Hurdles	Opportunities
Proactive engagement - ongoing consultation / mediation forum, communication	- Mistrust between relevant groups	- Established communities / leaders more moderate, willing to interact
Community-wide CSR – needs that cut across ethnic divisions	- Sub-nationalist hype and intransigence	- Gender difference in sub-nationalist attitudes
Local job / opportunity creation – ensure northerners not excluded	- Union intransigence - Southerner reaction to specific opportunities for northerners	- Presidential sway with union leaders
Link highway completion to ongoing local development	- Depends on regime commitment, company would have no control	- Donor commitment to highway developmental benefits - Donor influence with regime
Police human rights programme – commitment, training, joint planning, monitoring	- Local authorities have limited control over police, and low interest in police fairness - Police links to southern nationalists - Low police professionalism - Local police autonomy – limited formal national oversight	- Donor commitment to human rights / human security - Presidential commitment to project completion - Donor influence with regime - Contract not yet finalised

FIGURE 9.6 Hurdles and opportunities.

willing to take legitimate concerns on board and actually make reasonable operational adjustments, or engagement would just look like a cynical PR exercise.

Unions would likely try to block local hiring, especially of northerners. However, the president and regime have direct links to southeastern elements in the union leadership, and if the president could be convinced of the necessity of local hiring, he could probably get union buy-in to at least hiring locals for work in proximity to their own communities. Northerner communities would be most directly affected by the project, and it might seem like they should be favoured in local employment schemes. But this would be seen as ethnic discrimination, and one could expect a severe southerner reaction. We cannot really address this now, but further implementation planning would need to explore the options for balanced local hiring which at the same time ensured that affected northerner communities felt that their hardship was offset. We have noted the role of functional expertise in implementation, and this is just the kind of issue that labour relations/human resources and CSR would have some ideas about, at least if they had much experience in ethnically divided societies.

Linking future socio-economic development initiatives with highway completion would be a good way to increase local acceptance of the project. Improved logistics would, in theory, mean more economic opportunity and the northward spread of development. But this theory would need to be transformed into actual programmes, which would only kick off after the company had left. Unless there were a credible case that such development initiatives would eventually ensue, just touting it would have no effect on local acceptance, and could even make northerners in particular wary of government spin. The company might not be around after completion, but some of the project's donor sponsors would be, and they also have some influence with the regime. The company could seek donor engagement on the initiative and propose that they work with the government to at least start laying the groundwork for development initiatives that would come later.

One of the most challenging issues is how to manage the role of the police, in general but especially with respect to relocations. The local police are the ones on the ground, but they are ethnically biased, not particularly professional, sometimes gratuitously violent, and for practical purposes run their own fiefdom, albeit alongside the local authorities. In a highly sensitive and volatile period in a divided community, they could be the bull in the china shop.

One consideration is if other police forces, perhaps from national units, might have more appropriate capacity for non-violent crowd control and incident management. Perhaps another unit could be brought in to assist in the phases most prone to unrest. Even then, however, all police would seem to lack sufficient commitment to human rights standards and ethnic fairness, and on their own would probably be resistant to a human rights assurance programme.

The only person in the country who could change this is the president, who has considerable influence over the police, since he has beefed up the Ministry of Interior as his own personal counterbalance to the military. Among the company's direct connections, donors and their respective diplomatic counterparts are the ones with access to the president, and they could seek commitment to police training and monitoring, arguing that the success of the project depends on it. In a plausible scenario, the president agrees but later lets the matter slide. The commercial and technical terms of the highway contract have been agreed on but there are some outstanding contract elements. The company and donors could write presidential commitment to human rights assurance into a final draft, thereby ensuring accountability on the issue. This is not just a nice-to-have. It would not be overstating the case to say that the government needs to give guarantees up front or the project's viability becomes questionable.

The above makes it clear that when a political risk intelligence exercise is undertaken can be quite critical. Had intelligence been sought after the contract was finalised, there would be little opportunity to even try to establish binding guarantees for human rights adherence. It also makes it clear that if an issue is sufficiently pressing, there is justification to apply pressure towards addressing it. In this case, if the company went ahead with no guarantees, it would be taking a serious chance with at least its own reputation, to the extent to which it might not be worth going ahead. It therefore has little to lose in using what leverage it can to gain a concession.

At this point, there is not much more that we can say about a police human rights programme. Again, functional (probably a combination of CSR and security) implementation expertise will need to discern and weigh the options, and develop detailed plans.

The above considerations on hurdles and opportunities can now be matched with the initial ideas on the elements of an approach, for a preliminary plan which takes sequencing into account. This is shown in Figure 9.7 on page 253. It is top level, although not far off from what would be feasible at this stage.

Note the NGO and aid agency partnerships in Figure 9.7. In a sensitive developing country context, partnerships with NGOs in particular, and sometimes aid agencies, can be very helpful for local engagement and CSR, given that the partners are professional and have area experience. When a company tries to directly handle local engagement on its own, it is often seen as trying to buy acquiescence for its primary commercial activities, and unless a company has deep experience in a place, these other organisations are usually better equipped to foresee and deal with local frictions. NGOs and international companies do not always see eye to eye, but criticism from a credible NGO partner is far better than learning about an issue through protests and violence. NGOs with their own operations in the area would also be relevant members of consultative fora.

There would be a few more steps to round out the skeletal initiative.

One would be a summary of the stakeholders involved and what the company was hoping to achieve with them. In the formulation thus far, these would include certain host community representatives, the government/president, the donor sponsors, the police, the union, relevant NGOs, and indirectly nationalist extremists and MF. This summary would contribute to the formulation of stakeholder agendas in the programme definition stage later on.

A second step would be summarising the main company functions and teams involved, again for contribution to programme definition, in which functional agendas are defined by their roles in different initiatives. CSR, security, labour relations and public relations are the main ones here, but senior management (responsible for overall project coordination and corporate diplomacy), legal (for contract adjustments) and potentially procurement (for local supply contracts) are also relevant. This is a complex initiative, and in fact most functions operating in the area would have at least a support role.

Another follow-up would be a risk assessment for the initiative. This could utilise a project risk assessment format, and would identify the principal contingencies that would need to be planned for. These could include, for example, presidential intransigence in making the necessary commitments, continued union intransigence or obfuscation on the question of local hiring, spoiling attacks by sub-national extremists hoping to derail the project or the compensation programme, police violence even after commitment to human rights training, and unrelated ethnic clashes that increase overall tensions during sensitive project phases.

Finally, the initiative would need to explicitly account for the links to the two other core issues, labour friction and MF spoiling activity. These were dealt with in the plan, but we would need to take a bird's-eye view of the links to check that what we do for the host community issue aligns with the treatment of the other two. The converse would be done when planning for those ones. Another related problem is electoral violence in the next local elections, which will take place just a couple of months after the relocations. That is a separate issue with its own planning, but it is germane here and there would need to be close coordination.

We can see that this initiative well characterises the holistic, programmatic approaches that core issues often call for. It is a project in itself, with several tasks and strands of activity that would need to be sequenced and coordinated. As for the utility of such a top-level outline, it is much too general to implement as it stands. However, even if there are significant adjustments later on, at least implementation planning would not be starting from a blank slate.

Crony Pressure, MENA IT Consultancy Case

We noted how the IT consultancy's entry strategy was interlinked with the management of crony pressure, to the extent that they formed a binary system. Crony activity could disrupt the strategy,

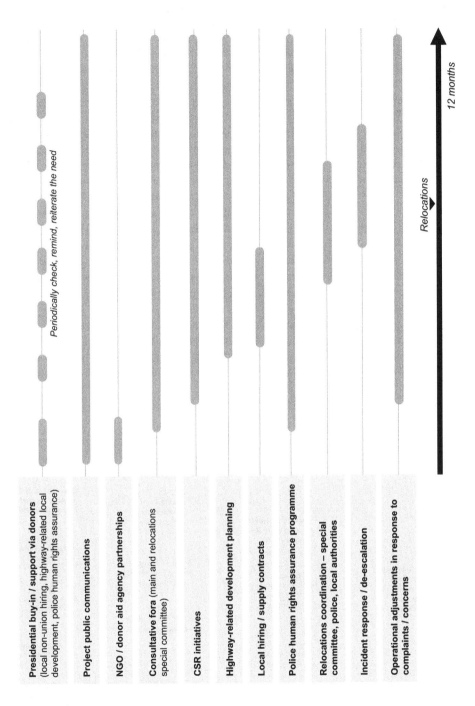

FIGURE 9.7 Preliminary host community friction initiative.

while the strategy is tailored to minimise crony pressure. There is a delicate balance in trying to use what is effectively a stealth approach to minimise spoiling activity by major players. Taken to its end logic, one would barely have a footprint or do much at all, in effect achieving what business-political players would want (if they felt that they could not force the consultancy into a one-sided partnership). Thus, while the approach needs to address crony spoiling activity, it also needs to have actual commercial merit, even if it takes somewhat longer to realise ambitions. This seems like a unique problem, but in fact many companies face this trade-off when setting out to establish a long-term country presence. There is no particular project which has been won and must be delivered on schedule, and hence how the company enters and operates is not pre-defined. They can take a risk and go quickly, or they can be slow and cautious, and to err on either side could be damaging.

An aspect of the above balancing act is the contradiction between the status of cronies and also military businesses as potential threats, and the fact that they comprise a considerable part of the market. While companies in the regime-business nexus are corrupt in some ways, they still undertake much normal and licit activity, and some parts of any such business operate like an ordinary, commercially ambitious firm. They could be lucrative customers for the consultancy, and any friction incurred in early stages could limit legitimate business opportunities later on.

Because the consultancy would need to find and carve out a safe niche and support network before pursuing hard growth targets, it would have an emergent strategy, or one that evolves with experience. This makes it somewhat amorphous compared to the scheduled, specific activities of the highway project's host community friction initiative. Nonetheless, for some tangible insights on how to manage the issue of crony pressure, we can try the same thought process of positing a pathway to a bad scenario and seeing where we could intervene to avert it. Figure 9.8 is a sketch of the route to a problematic outcome.

There are two triggers of a crony response. One is that the consultancy enters with a splash, touting its brand and technical prowess, and uses its business integrity track record as a selling point. If political-business clans felt that they could not control the consultancy, then it would look like a threat, not just in terms of lost business for their IT service arms but in terms of the contrast with

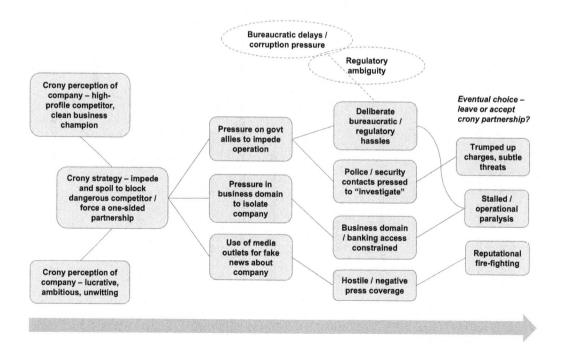

FIGURE 9.8 Pathways to paralysis and a hard choice.

their own rather unscrupulous image. The other trigger is that the company appears so eager to grab a piece of the action that it is open to pressure to engage in a partnership without knowing quite what it is getting into. If the consultancy then seems hesitant, pressure would block off opportunities until the only one left was "an offer you can't refuse". One could even posit a third trigger, which is that a clan senses that their rivals might get a partnership, and try to wreck the consultancy's prospects so that it becomes useless to anyone else.

All of these triggering perceptions would lead to the same reactions. The clans have considerable leverage in the government, banking and business, and their own media outlets, and these would be weaponised to squeeze the foreign interloper. If the consultancy did not cave in and take a local protector, pressure would intensify and even include threats. In the end, the consultancy would face a stark choice, join with a clan and imperil its reputation and freedom to manoeuvre, or leave.

Now we can see what interventions could be feasible, as depicted in Figure 9.9.

The consultancy reduces initial predatory interest with two related moves. First, it decides on a quiet, low-profile entry which is unlikely to appear threatening. Second, it communicates this intention, and even further downplays it, to the political-business clans, using its old contact with one particular company as one channel. Recall that early in the intelligence exercise, the consultancy's principal political risk "baggage" was its overenthusiastic early discussions with a well-connected local company. Expectations formed in those discussions are now reset, and the consultancy also uses public corporate statements to reposition the operation from a major launch to a market exploration.

Starting with a small presence, the company forges supportive ties in the independent business community, and with government agencies responsible for private sector development and FDI growth. With a niche carved out, the operation forms a partnership with an independent mid-sized IT service firm and starts to sell. As activity increases, other initiatives to build a fit ensue, including local hiring, educational CSR engagement and membership in independent business associations. A track record for successful projects and socio-economic impact accrues, and this meets with political approval that makes it harder for cronies to openly hinder the company.

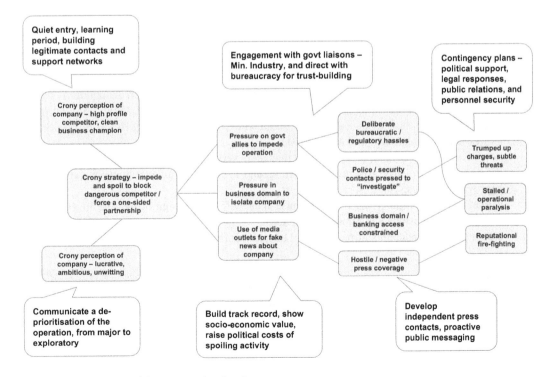

FIGURE 9.9 Opportunities to avert the situation.

At this point, the consultancy is on a safer footing and expands its activities. Its own public relations counter crony spin, and the firm retains contingency plans to address specific threats that could still arise. Eventually, after perhaps two or three years, the company is well embedded in the market, and grudgingly accepted as a fact by political-business clans. The clans realise that advantage could now lie not in subverting the consultancy, but in actually using its services to modernise and streamline their businesses to make them more competitive and to help prepare them for international opportunities.

An upfront project plan like the one for host community friction in the highway case would be quite speculative in the context of a learning phase. However, on the basis of intelligence, guiding imperatives for entry can be developed. These would include, for example, the following:

- retain a low profile until reasonably well embedded;
- engage in several parts of the independent business sub-domain (including tangent government and civil society) for learning and support from various angles;
- carefully manage expectations among stakeholders until the company is confident in its direction and is willing to commit to particular engagements;
- do not compromise integrity, since this would be a lever for opponents and any integrity breaches likely would be discerned through cronies' security agency ties;
- become valuable to the government in legitimate ways, as a case of the socio-economic benefits of FDI, as well as simply by becoming an FDI success story;
- do not antagonise organisations that could eventually be customers;
- but balanced with the above, be prepared to safeguard operational assets and the firm's legitimate interests, including through legal means – be a prickly target, and be prepared for hostile actions that could include at least implied physical threats.

Despite not forming a tangible project plan, the initiative would still need to be explicitly managed and tracked, including through routinely assessing interactions and problems that arise as ground-level intelligence for ongoing adaptation. Additionally, even a learning phase needs tangible guidelines and capabilities. Hence, early on, management would need to:

- set clear internal expectations of the operation, acknowledging that it has a learning phase which is a precursor to profitable operations;
- carefully craft and communicate messaging about company intentions in the country;
- establish a small beachhead office for an initial reconnaissance phase, with a mission of actually filling in the blanks in the above initial strategy, and supporting HQ in developing a more detailed interim plan down the road;
- hire a few trustworthy, experienced local managers very early on to help learn the environment, to assist in early government relations and to provide guidance with bureaucratic approval processes;
  - carefully vet initial local hires, because they will have a significant role in guiding important decisions and relationships; and
- assess potential independent partners and formulate criteria and options for engagement.

Because of the direct overlap of political risk management and the entry strategy, specific management functions relevant to the initiative would be quite diverse. Nearly all expat and local managers would have at least a tacit role. However, some would be more explicitly involved. Country management would lead the initiative in a corporate diplomacy and coordination role, and CSR, human resources, public relations, legal and security are relevant.

There would also be a range of relevant stakeholders. We already know several from that stage of the analysis, including the Investment Promotion Agency, relevant bureaucratic agencies, mid-sized companies, independent business tycoons, associations and educational organisations. But because of the exploratory character of the entry plan, it might be more appropriate to parse engagement into broader domains than by individual actors, and let domain-level interaction guide the selection of subsequent specific engagement targets.

A risk assessment for the initiative is still relevant even though it is a learning approach. One risk to consider is the effect of potential changes in FDI ownership rules. That warrants its own initiative, which could include lobbying and looking at alternative company legal structures for the country presence, but it would need to be closely coordinated with the core counter-crony initiative. Other risks might include specific forms of backlash if the stealth approach failed to sufficiently ameliorate crony concerns or predatory interest.

Despite there not being a step-by-step action plan, at least not yet, one can clearly see in the above considerations how intelligence guided a strong sense of how to proceed. Political-business challenges were defined in terrain analysis, whereupon the company realised that its high-profile partnership strategy had too many downsides. In stakeholder analysis, we learned more about the clans and how they might respond, but we also learned that there were alternative ecosystems where the company could find a fit, and that the government as a whole was broadly supportive of legitimate FDI success. Putting these indications together, a realistic option emerged.

INITIATIVES FOR CONTINGENT ISSUES

Herein we will examine the coup contingency from the highway case, as an illustration of the challenge of preparing for a significant potential change that might not actually happen. From the IT consultancy's operation, we will examine local staff detention, an interesting contrast to a coup because it is based on the potential intersection with a current harmful behaviour, rather than a possible future change in the environment.

Coup or Coup Attempt, West African Highway Case

We explored the possibility of a coup in terrain analysis, and in stakeholder analysis it came up in the investigation of the military faction. MF is concerned about its diminishing influence in the context of the president's increasing grip on power, and it would prefer a different, statist development trajectory and alignment with China rather than Europe. MF is hostile to the constructor's involvement in the highway project because it is a lost opportunity to work more closely with a Chinese state firm on one of the country's rare major infrastructure projects. Although MF still has strong inhibitions about launching a coup, its calculations could change. A coup or coup attempt would entail a period of volatility and some violence at least in the capital, and a successful coup would very likely see the company replaced by a Chinese firm. For planning purposes, we need to assume that a coup attempt would succeed, because we cannot know in advance which avenue the event could take, and we need to be ready for the worse of the two possibilities.

In planning for the coup contingency, an unrealistic objective would be to hang onto the project. Every indication now is that the company would lose the contract and probably have to leave soon after MF gained power. Thus, a reasonable objective would be to avoid harm to personnel because of coup-related violence, minimise losses, and recover as much as possible from the inevitable financial damage.

A potential coup well characterises a typical dilemma in preparation for political changes that could make an operation and country presence untenable. If we act too early, we can disrupt our own operation prematurely and, depending on how a situation plays out, perhaps unnecessarily. If we leave things too late, or sit tight and hope things go well, we can end up stuck in a quagmire, like the US constructor in Iran from the Introduction. The dilemma applies to resource allocation too. For example, if we keep a small fleet of planes on hand in case we need them for evacuation, it will soon affect the bottom line. If we do not have planes when we really need them, we would have an even bigger problem.

As an aside, the period of writing this book is spanning a number of significant global events and changes, and at the time of writing, early March 2022, the most recent one has been the Russian invasion of Ukraine. Foreign companies not only had to depart from Ukraine after months of uncertainty, but now many are trying to leave Russia because of Western sanctions. They are finding that Russia is making it very hard to withdraw assets. Thus, the above dilemma applies to a range of political change scenarios, and the Ukraine-Russian conflict is an excellent example.

An approach to addressing the above dilemma is to try to align preparedness for a contingency with the plausibility of it happening. Returning to the coup example, we can treat it like a scenario with degrees of emergence, each with indicators of relevant precursors and triggers. In political science, there are well-researched theories of why coups happen, but the causal chains therein tend to span several years. In our case, near- to medium-term indications are more useful. We can extract these from the analytical stages, particularly drawing on MF's motives and concerns from stakeholder analysis. Degrees of emergence of the coup scenario and associated indicators are depicted in Figure 9.10. Figure 9.10's contents still need some translation to observable, trackable phenomena, but it is the basis of a set of warning indicators which monitoring would use to spot relevant developments.

Note that the four degrees of emergence do not represent a specific sequence in one broader coup scenario. We can actually extract three scenarios from the menu of drivers and triggers. One is a progressive build-up of tension, until MF feels that it must act to preserve its core interests. From the current situation, this would probably take a year or so to reach breaking point, and it could stretch to coincide with any unrest around national elections. The second is linked to national elections. If these are clearly rigged, then in conjunction with related undemocratic changes they could lead to a popular backlash, distracting the presidential faction and giving MF a strong pretext for a coup. The third is that the president tries to take MF by surprise, and MF hastily plans and executes a coup. This scenario could unfold at any time, and from the president's initial moves to a coup could be as short as a month. In the elections and surprise presidential move scenarios, MF would nearly leapfrog planning and gamble that it could still succeed, and the whole sequence would be very condensed in time.

Returning to our own planning, to reiterate, for this type of issue an approach needs to decrease exposure and prepare for the worst while not leaping all the way to full exit until it seemed that the event in question was imminent. An analogy is taking a flight on a rickety plane. We know the plane is not in great shape, so we bring a parachute and sit near the door. If an engine starts sputtering, we put the chute on and stand with our hand on the door handle. We only jump when it seems quite clear that the situation will soon be dire. Until then, we can always go back and sit down if the flight resumes somewhat normally, sparing ourselves the risk and hassle of leaping into the countryside. This notion of graduated preparation is illustrated in Figure 9.11 on page 260.

In Figure 9.11, we could go up to the response to "imminent" and not incur too much operational disruption, and if a coup were averted, we could return to normal operations. In that case, however, unless there were a clear resolution of MF-presidential friction, we would not stop being prepared for the possibility, and at least the "latent" preparations would remain in place.

In terms of when the company has to be ready for a given stage, we can return to the three scenarios outlined above. In two scenarios, there is considerable warning time. However, for the surprise presidential move and MF reaction scenario, it could be as short as a month from the first indications to a coup attempt. This scenario and especially the shorter end of its timeline seem quite implausible, but that is the nature of surprises. Thus, although detailed preparations that cover the extraction of moveable assets could be left until indications of a shift to "planning", very soon after entering the country there should be a robust capability for crisis evacuation of staff based on a rapid leap to the "impending-imminent" stage.

Along with crisis evacuation, there would be two less urgent strands of preparation planning. One is how to reduce exposure as coup indicators edged towards occurrence. Personnel would be the main asset in this respect, but others, particularly data, intellectual property, cash and easily moveable assets, would be included in planning too. The other strand is how to seek financial compensation for the aftermath of a coup. Given that a successful coup would lead to contract abrogation

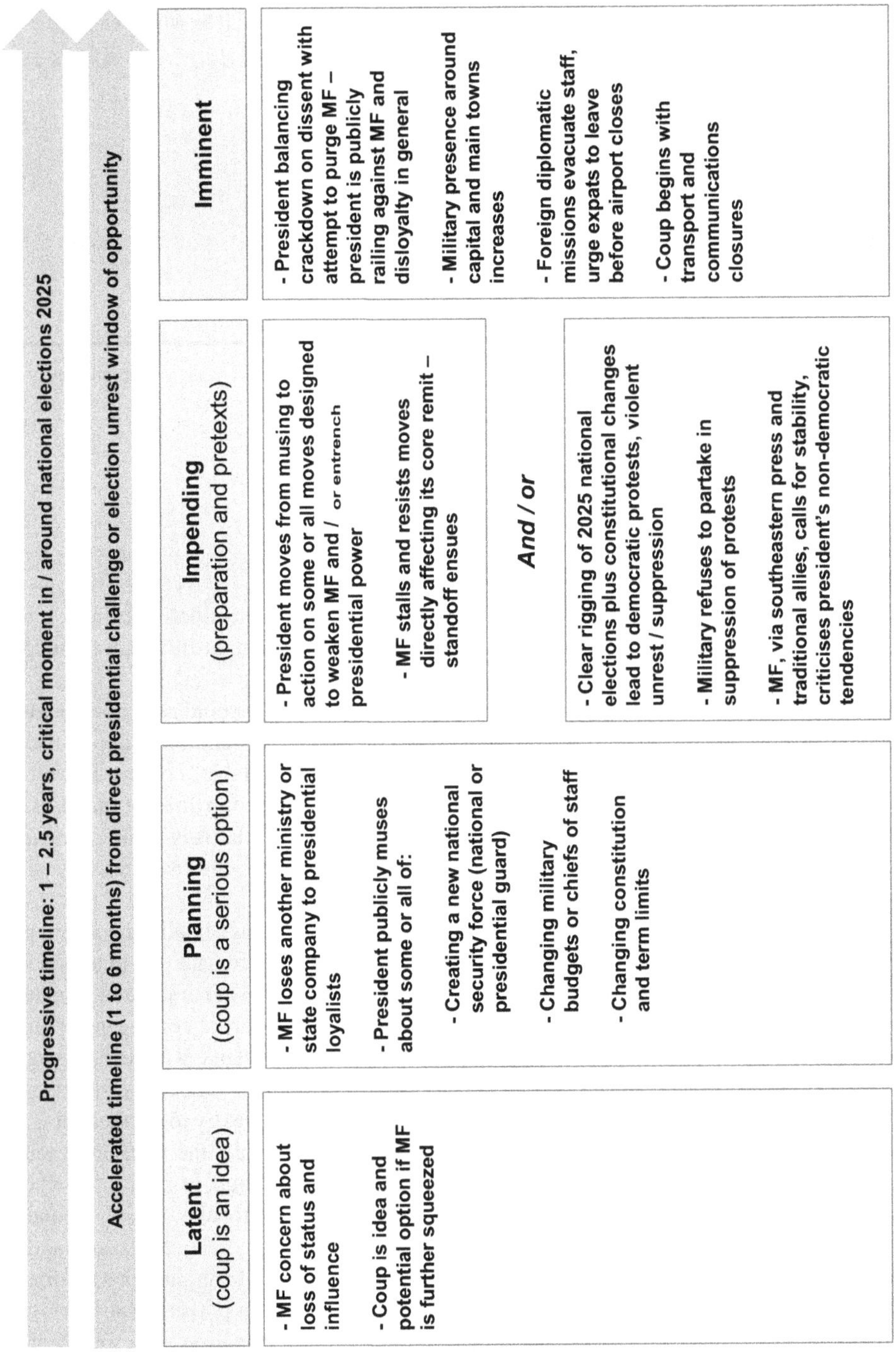

Progressive timeline: 1 – 2.5 years, critical moment in / around national elections 2025

Accelerated timeline (1 to 6 months) from direct presidential challenge or election unrest window of opportunity

Latent
(coup is an idea)

- MF concern about loss of status and influence

- Coup is idea and potential option if MF is further squeezed

Planning
(coup is a serious option)

- MF loses another ministry or state company to presidential loyalists

- President publicly muses about some or all of:

- Creating a new national security force (national or presidential guard)

- Changing military budgets or chiefs of staff

- Changing constitution and term limits

Impending
(preparation and pretexts)

- President moves from musing to action on some or all moves designed to weaken MF and / or entrench presidential power

- MF stalls and resists moves directly affecting its core remit – standoff ensues

And / or

- Clear rigging of 2025 national elections plus constitutional changes lead to democratic protests, violent unrest / suppression

- Military refuses to partake in suppression of protests

- MF, via southeastern press and traditional allies, calls for stability, criticises president's non-democratic tendencies

Imminent

- President balancing crackdown on dissent with attempt to purge MF – president is publicly railing against MF and disloyalty in general

- Military presence around capital and main towns increases

- Foreign diplomatic missions evacuate staff, urge expats to leave before airport closes

- Coup begins with transport and communications closures

FIGURE 9.10   Coup emergence indicators.

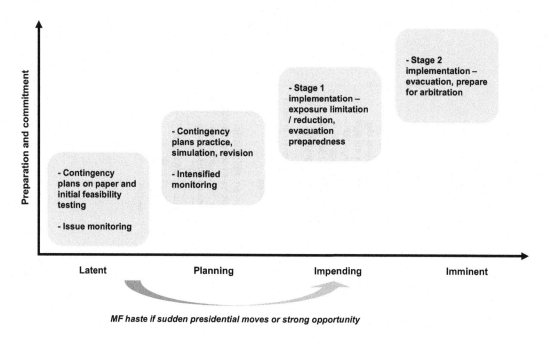

FIGURE 9.11   Graduated preparedness for a coup.

and possibly heavy equipment left behind, the company should have a prior notion of how it would respond to try to recover its losses, so that it could move into arbitration, or initiate a political risk insurance claim or legal case, as soon as possible after withdrawal.

We left aside the question of a failed coup aside because the company could not know in advance how a coup attempt would work out. There are options to hedge one's bets. For example, the company could temporarily relocate staff and portable assets to a nearby (stable) country to wait out a period of high tension, rather than flying them all the way home. If the coup attempt failed, it could then be faster to get back on track. However, the benefits would be relatively scant compared to being well clear of a violent and stressful situation, and that should be the main priority when a chaotic situation starts to appear imminent.

On a broader note, an important point in this example is that monitoring is actually an integral part of adaptive responses, enabling us to be as ready as possible without acting prematurely. In terrain analysis, we discussed how follow-up monitoring could reduce uncertainty around ambiguous challenges, by observing relevant dynamics as they become clearer with time. As a part of contingency planning, monitoring informs managers of when to move to the next level of preparedness, without being too late, and without taking irrevocable actions before there was a need to. There is a margin of error even in near-term monitoring and warnings can be wrong, but it is still the best way to try to get the timing right.

As for who would handle this initiative, security would probably take the lead on evacuation planning and on managing risk from any violence around an imminent coup. Logistics, by whatever label might be used, would also be involved in evacuation, and in the removal of assets. Finance and legal would prepare for the aftermath. If there were time for a tidy closure, labour relations and CSR might have time to close off local company engagements, although disclosing the possibility of an early exit could create unnecessary distractions, especially in terms of a potential union response. Country and project management would have an oversight and coordination role, and nearly all functions would have at least a tacit contribution.

Relevant stakeholders is a more ambiguous question, because an exit would be undertaken by the company itself, ideally on its own terms. But for monitoring insights, friendly contacts among NGOs, the police, the government and local businesses could be beneficial, and more trusted contacts could even help with a withdrawal. Importantly, the embassies of the company's own home government and those of involved donors might share intelligence updates, and would likely be able to lend a hand if a coup seemed imminent. They might even have their own expat evacuation initiatives that the company could consider as a fallback option.

A risk assessment of the initiative would probably focus on the potential for a sudden spike in MF-presidential friction and the possibility of being taken by surprise, impediments and missing pieces in evacuation logistics, and the potential for some stakeholders finding predatory opportunity in trying to impede a smooth company exit.

Local Staff Detention, MENA IT Consultancy Case

Staff detention refers to a local staff member being arrested or "disappeared" by government security forces. Local and expat staff can be detained in a number of scenarios, including in disputes with well-connected regime cronies, during acute unrest, in the course of sweeping purges and in periods of high tension between a foreign company's home and host governments. In the IT consultancy case, crony pressure is one potential cause of the issue, although the regime is trying to attract FDI and would look unfavourably on its crony allies directly threatening foreign firms. That context still needs to be considered, but the more important one is the potential spread of pro-democratic dissent, about which the regime is justifiably paranoid since it has not addressed many of the frustrations that drove the Arab Spring protests in 2011. If another round of dissent manifested, the regime would increase the use pre-emptive and arbitrary arrests to thwart opposition. Local staff are as vulnerable as any citizen to arbitrary detention, and sometimes more so because of their link to an employer from a country with political values antithetical to authoritarianism.

There are two broad points about this issue before we examine what a relevant initiative might look like. First, on a conceptual note, as a form of contingency staff detentions are a useful contrast to a coup. A coup and other disruptive political changes like a purge, revolution or civil war are the result of a build-up of pressure in the socio-political system. One can reduce exposure in line with indications of manifestation and respond to the event if it happens, but preventing it is not an option. Recall from terrain analysis that for political changes and events, intersection and manifestation are the same thing. For example, if a coup happened, it would be problematic, and the best we could do is control the extent of its effect on us.

Staff detentions are more like kidnappings and criminal and insurgent attacks, in that there is an existing behaviour, and its effects would be through its intersection with the operation. We have the opportunity to prevent the issue from manifesting in the first place by controlling the intersection, in other words by avoiding the harmful behaviour, reducing our target profile, protecting ourselves and deterring the actors involved. However, as with political changes, we still need crisis response plans in case the issue manifested. As well, monitoring is still relevant, because even if the harmful behaviour already exists, it can vary according to other socio-political dynamics, and if we track these, then we can adjust our preparations in line with the level of risk.

Second, and on a practical level, local staff detentions are often a blind spot for foreign companies. When a company goes to a country, HQ is well aware that it needs to look after its expat staff, because the company sent them to a new place where they do not have the usual personal support networks. In a sense, the whole country is an expat's workplace, not just a particular site or office building, and hence duty of care applies to an expat's entire experience while abroad. Local staff, on the other hand, are at home, and the problems they might have outside of work are not because the company sent them anywhere. The company has no particular obligation to them when they are on their own time. Compounding this sense of uninvolvement, the relationship between citizens and a government does not seem to be a company concern. If local staff get arrested or "disappeared", the matter is between the government and the citizenry.

For the above reasons, foreign companies seldom have policies or plans in place to address local staff detentions, and most HQs would probably prefer that managers on the ground not get involved in them. The crux, though, is that foreign managers often try to do something for detained local staff anyway, out of conscience and because of the effect on overall morale. Without guidance or support, their efforts can be unnecessarily risky and less likely to succeed. We can assume that the IT consultancy, being aware of the issue from analysis, has decided to avoid this unsatisfactory contradiction by at least sketching a top-level plan, which can be filled in and refined once the company has been on the ground for a while. What follows will not get into detail, but we can see what the broad outlines of an initiative might be.

The objective of an initiative is to prevent local staff from being arbitrarily detained or detained on trumped up charges, and if they were, then to get them released unharmed.

One relevant detention scenario, as noted, is regime cronies using their government contacts to pressure the company, a tactic which could extend to staff arrests. This is actually an aspect of the crony pressure issue, and within the initiative to address it was the company's legitimate self-defence against direct incursions. This general approach could have a sub-element tailored specifically for the staff detention contingency. Preventing a trumped-up arrest would come through deterrence in the form of a subtle message of willingness to use government relations and legal means to support any detained staff member, and to make some media noise about a case. A response to an actual case would combine those means with a message to the government that if the case were not resolved, it could become a stain on the country's reputation as an FDI destination. A strong response to one case would increase deterrence: the government would not want a repeat, and in turn it would raise the political costs for cronies. In this context, the importance of FDI to the state's development plans provides a lever. In other cases, there might not be an obvious lever, and a company might have to rely more on stakeholder relationships to support people detained in disputes.

The more complicated scenario, and separate from crony pressure, is detention linked to dissent and the resulting regime paranoia. Extra-legal arrests and disappearances occur now, although at a low level and for the most part the state targets people openly involved in opposition. The company would not need intensive preparations for local staff detentions in the current situation, and, as with the coup example, it would be constraining and wasteful to be on maximum alert unless and until the risk were higher. However, being underprepared in a high-risk situation would be dangerous. Again, then, we need a way to calibrate capabilities to relevant developments, ideally in advance of significant shifts. Renewed revolutionary unrest was discerned as an issue in itself in terrain analysis, and dissent will be monitored to inform appropriate company responses to an increase in bottom-up instability. That monitoring stream can also be used for the local staff detention initiative, to know when to elevate capabilities to prevent and respond to staff being detained or "disappeared". A resulting top-level planning framework is illustrated in Figure 9.12.

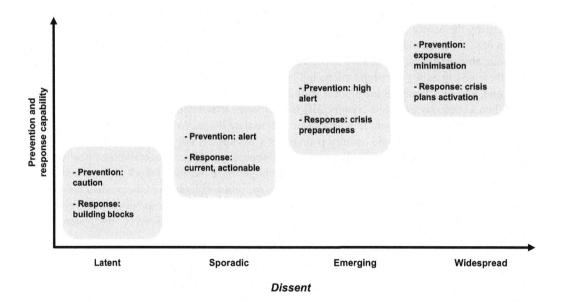

FIGURE 9.12   Staff detention planning aligned to level of dissent.

We can briefly examine what the different levels of dissent might look like. The current, latent, level sees periodic socio-economic protests but the regime does not regard them as a threat because thus far they have shown no political intent and tend to be short-lived. The sporadic level could see these become somewhat more intense and enduring and take on political overtones. In "emerging", a pro-democratic movement manifests and feeds into socio-economic protest while remaining somewhat distinct. Finally, in the widespread phase, socio-economic and political dissent merge, resulting in a mass movement that has organised direction. Along the way, regime paranoia would increase, and repression would intensify, up to widespread security sweeps, mass arrests and disappearances targeting anyone vaguely connected to the opposition. Thus, we have a sense of how the driver of arbitrary detentions could intensify and what to look for to increase our capabilities to handle it.

As noted in each box in Figure 9.12 there are two types of measures to address local staff detention, preventative and responsive, and each would be adjusted for the level of risk. At the current, latent, level, the company could minimise its own political symbolism to prevent an association between its staff and foreign democratic values. It would not be feasible to tell staff to avoid activism on their own time, but it could be made clear that company IT and other facilities are for work only: if security forces discerned that opposition messaging was being sent from inside the company, they would likely become suspicious of the consultancy's entire local workforce. A basic precaution is to physically avoid protests where arrests could occur. In the meantime, this period of low risk should be used to develop the building blocks of a capability to respond to a detention case. This forms both initial guidance and a blueprint for the development of more immediate response capabilities.

We will not explore each new level of planning in detail, but in periods of higher risk, prevention could include, for example, the following:

- providing basic risk awareness training and emergency contact numbers to staff;
- travelling to and from work in shared transport, like a company minibus, so that there are witnesses to any attempted arrest (arbitrary arrests are especially common at road blocks, witnesses can be a deterrent and witnesses would help to pinpoint someone's last-known whereabouts and potentially who undertook the arrest);
- similarly, using a buddy system when staff travel during the day;
- refraining from out-of-office travel on days when there are planned protests; and
- working from home during periods of prolonged or intense unrest.

Responses to arrests and disappearances would be facilitated by, and include the following:

- the use of itineraries and check-ins so that the last-known whereabouts of staff members were recorded, to facilitate searching for them in the event of disappearance;
- similarly, having tracking enabled on work phones, and monitoring staff locations during periods of unrest; and
- developing detailed crisis response capabilities, especially the extension of stakeholder networks to organisations and people who could help with an actual detention or disappearance case (by helping to locate detained staff, learning the charges against them, mediating with officials in the case of unsanctioned arrests and building an appropriate legal response).

In an acute, "widespread", situation, prevention and response would partly merge as the company minimised staff exposure, not just to the risk of detention but also to street violence (this would combine with the initiative to manage the separate issue of revolutionary unrest). Staff would "hibernate", in other words work from home with material support from the company. If the company's temporary evacuation became necessary, it could assist particularly exposed staff to exit the country.

Remaining local staff would still be paid and given sufficient cash to be able to survive a prolonged period of hibernation. They would also be connected to the company's local crisis response and monitoring network.

In the above, the most complicated element would be the development of detailed crisis response capabilities. Sometimes getting someone released can be as simple as going to the police station where someone is held and vouching for them. In other cases, someone's whereabouts might be unknown, and one meets a brick wall when making enquiries. Within a supportive stakeholder network, someone usually knows someone who could provide information about a case, or even call a contact in the authorities to suggest that there had been a mistake. This kind of extended network takes time to develop, but without local knowhow and contacts, an arrested employee could easily get lost in the system before the company could do anything for them.

Dilemmas are rife with this issue, including how far a foreign employer can go in trying to help someone without becoming a human rights activist in its own right. Bill Browder, the British-American head of Hermitage Capital in Russia, effectively went down this route in 2008 when seeking the release of tax advisor Sergei Magnitsky, although by then there was not much left of Hermitage in Russia. There are limits to what a company can do and to what it can get away with before it too is perceived as a threat by the state. Along with this is the question of at what point repression makes a country presence ethically or practically unviable. Having these discussions up front can make big decisions clearer if they become necessary. A risk assessment for this initiative would focus on these kinds of dilemmas, in addition to potentially problematic contacts made in trying to build a response capability (the more someone could help, the more likely it is that they are connected to the regime's inner circle), and the missteps that the company might make in addressing an actual case.

Several management functions would be involved in managing this issue. Security and human resources would be responsible for staff training, and the logistical side of prevention. Security would also handle police liaison. Legal would learn the relevant laws and develop sources of local legal support. Senior management, in a corporate diplomacy role, would be developing ties across the independent business ecosystem, and within this they would look for supportive contacts who might be able to assist in a detention case. All of these would coordinate on crisis planning and practice.

Stakeholders, on the other hand, would include the police or other relevant security forces, as well as contracted local lawyers and other advisors. Other specific potential sources of local support are hard to know in advance. As noted in previous chapters, in emerging markets there can be considerable overlap between business, government and social networks, and people with the right contacts might not have any obvious link to the legal or security system. Relevant ties would have to be discerned and developed over time. In addition to host country actors, home country diplomats could also be helpful. While they would not advocate for a host country citizen's release, diplomats often provide informal advice based on their own experience with a government.

Note that in practical terms, planning and specific measures to manage local staff detentions would be broadly similar for expat staff. There are two main differences. One is that with expats the company could coordinate with the detained person's embassy for additional support. The other is that if an expat's detention seemed to be linked to an international dispute and was a case of hostage diplomacy, it could well signal that the company should withdraw foreign staff at least until the dispute is resolved.

The staff detention example contains some useful broader points. First, it exemplifies how causal links between issues work in practice. The link to both crony pressure and revolutionary unrest leads to a need for close collaboration between initiatives, and to opportunities for shared monitoring. Second, it is clear that even though this is a contingent issue, routine measures are a part of the wider approach, since, unlike with major political changes, day-to-day precautions can help to prevent the issue from manifesting. Finally, the general logic of the approach to staff detentions, specifically the dual emphasis on prevention and response, applies to a range of contingent issues arising from a potential intersection with a particular behaviour. However, beyond a common top-level logic, it is hard to use one initiative as a detailed blueprint for others. For example, even within the staff detention issue, there was a distinction between managing detentions from crony disputes and from regime paranoia, specifically in the relevance of deterrence. There will be important nuances depending on the source of the problem and the assets affected.

INITIATIVES FOR ROUTINE ISSUES

Routine issues being less complicated, this discussion will be relatively brief. From the West African highway case, we will examine Ministry of Transport interference in project planning as an example addressing routine stakeholder friction. From the IT consultancy case, bureaucratic corruption is a useful contrast, since while it involves actors, it principally arises from routine intersection with an ongoing pattern of behaviour.

Ministry of Transport Interference, West African Highway Case

We did not go into this in detail in stakeholder analysis, but a common phenomenon in infrastructure projects in emerging markets is government interference in planning after a contract, based on agreed designs, has been signed. Recall the example of a Spanish consortium from Chapter 3. Three years after starting work on a high-speed railway in Saudi Arabia, the constructors were still wrangling with their customers over basic design questions, in spite of most of these having been agreed on up front. There are several reasons for this kind of interference. One is that the contracting authority is only the tip of a domestic stakeholder iceberg, and the authority did not manage its own consultations in advance of a contract. It then faces interest group pressure after commencement and transfers these onto the contractor. Another is that authorities sometimes have limited experience in the kind of work being undertaken and are anxious about how it will all come together. Finally, authorities might have to answer to a political executive or leader who is somewhat capricious, and there can be considerable anxiety about meeting the higher-ups' wishes and expectations. The last point was a significant cause of delays in the Iran highway project discussed in this book's Introduction.

We can assume that elements of all three apply in the West African highway project, but the last two reasons are especially relevant. The Ministry of Transport (MOT) and within it the Highways Department have not overseen a major highway project for a long time, and they ultimately answer to an overbearing president with a bent for micromanagement. Stakeholder analysis would have noted that the MOT will probably be a difficult customer, even if it is fully onboard with the concept and does not actually want to impede the project. Its anxiety could manifest in routinely revisiting old options and rationales, positing new ideas and insisting that they be explored, and raising potentially obscure risks and issues that the company would otherwise deal with in the normal course of operations. While including the customer in the journey is an ingredient of success, ultimately interference could add up to tangible delays, and even challenge the contractually agreed project schedule. Thus, there needs to be an approach to managing it, balanced with the need for the MOT's positive engagement and its support with other issues that the company could face.

At this point, the company does not know the MOT well, and hence ideas can only be preliminary. First, we need to minimise haggling over minor changes. This calls for a prior consideration of bargaining chips and negotiation redlines. If the MOT is insistent about a minor design change and the effect on the budget and schedule would be minimal, then in the interests of pace and goodwill, changes could be made. But this flexibility needs to be balanced with controlling expectations and ensuring that the MOT understands that any changes would be formally discussed and agreed, not decided on a whim through casual discussions.

Second, we need to be able put up some barriers to whimsical interference and change pressure, without offending the MOT. In most major infrastructure projects, there are joint project committees which constitute a formal forum to discuss any problems that either side has. Because of donor sponsorship in this case, donors would be a part of that forum. Donors are actually an indirect customer and a key project stakeholder. It would be perfectly reasonable for the company to tell the MOT that a given issue would need to be resolved in conjunction with donor representatives and that the MOT could put the issue on the agenda for the next meeting. This could minimise impulsive interference because the MOT would have to create some documentation and argue its case. Donors, who have a stake in the project's pace and efficiency, would likely question any specious requests. In sum, a degree of formal process would inhibit casual pressure without causing interpersonal offence, and donors would provide some political top-cover and act as a backstop.

Finally, we would need to ensure that there was reasonable mutual trust and respect with the MOT even if design differences arose, because the ministry could be a valuable supporter when trying to resolve cases of bureaucratic delays or corruption pressure, and in making the case to the president for sensitivity and consultation in dealing with affected communities. This calls for some informal interaction, consistent liaisons with specific MOT directors, and an appreciation of the MOT's political constraints and organisational culture. A level of informal diplomacy, then, needs to be a corollary of formal engagement processes.

We noted how routine issues can morph into a contingent change or event. In this case, there is a potential link between the routine issue of MOT interference and the contingent one of a change in the president's commitment to the project as it was agreed. The MOT's behaviour might be the first signs of presidential wavering. If interference becomes more frequent and intense, this could indicate that it is time for a serious discussion between the president, donors and company, and managing MOT interference would transit to managing the issue of presidential contract pressure. Thus, patterns in the MOT relationship need to be monitored for signals that a more serious problem could be manifesting.

The MOT and within it the Highways Department are the principal stakeholders in this initiative, but specific individuals and functions would also need to be discerned to enable consistent interpersonal engagement. Within the company, senior project managers would handle high-level MOT engagement, in both a formal and a diplomatic role. There would be a range of operational functions that would work with counterparts in the Highways Department, and senior management would need to ensure that messaging and protocols were broadly aligned across all MOT interactions.

A risk assessment of this initiative might consider the possibility of corruption and nepotism pressure from the MOT itself (this would form a link to the separate anti-corruption initiative), inadvertent cultural slights and misunderstandings, and the MOT being much more detail-oriented and nit-picky than initially assessed.

Bureaucratic Corruption, MENA IT Consultancy Case

As noted in terrain analysis, that a country has a bureaucratic corruption problem does not necessarily mean that bribery pressure occurs in every bureaucratic interaction. But if a company is in a country long enough, it will encounter pressure, and there needs to be procedures to deal with it or staff can feel compelled to muddle through, often incurring liabilities in the process. In the IT consultancy's case, liabilities are not the only concern. The company's strategy of initially building ties in the independent business community hinges in part on its image as a legitimate and respectable organisation. Additionally, any integrity breach could make the company more vulnerable to crony pressure. Cronies' ties in government could lead to exposure of company bribery, ties to security agencies could lead to investigations, and crony media outlets could make any pattern of bribery public.

Most international companies have standard anti-corruption policies as part of wider integrity standards which cover fraud, money laundering and other forms of white-collar crime. These are normally partly based on relevant home country law but broad enough to cover the main points of the OECD Anti-Bribery Convention (a basis for much OECD member state corruption regulation) and the US Foreign Corrupt Practices Act, or FCPA (for access to the US market and financial sector). Internal anti-corruption guidance for frontline staff usually contains not just a code of conduct but also practical advice on how to handle and report bribery pressure.

With adequate training, oversight and internal control, the above forms a reasonable baseline of effective anti-corruption practices. However, a corporate baseline usually needs to be adjusted for a specific country context. First, it probably would not account for local governance and cultural peculiarities, and it would need to accord with host country laws. Second, policies and procedures alone might tell us how to not inadvertently pay a bribe, but they do not necessarily tell us how to make progress in spite of facing bribery pressure for necessary services and permits. Based on preceding analysis, the IT consultancy can posit at least a preliminary approach for the host country. As an aside, note that in the company's home country law, facilitation payments (usually defined as payment to get an official to do what they should do anyway) are not allowed. They are allowed under the FCPA, but for the IT consultancy they are not an option.

First, the consultancy will adjust corporate practices to align with local cultural nuances. Many bureaucrats in the country position bribes as special service fees which help to ensure that applications are correctly filled in and given priority processing. The company can expect to be politely asked, "the regular or expedited service?" To the uninitiated, it sounds like a legitimate choice, somewhat like regular or priority mail, and over time one could rack up a hefty expenditure on "expedited service".

It is not just the culture of officialdom that matters, but also the host country management culture, since the consultancy plans on eventually having a sizeable proportion of local staff. There is a strong sense of hierarchy, and sense of duty to meet a supervisor's expectations. That can create pressure that causes people to take shortcuts. Sometimes staff even pay bribes out of their own pocket if it helps them to do their jobs. Additionally, written rules and regulations matter less than relationships, and unless compliance were somehow seen as a personal obligation to others in the company, a policy could well remain a mere abstraction. After all, local staff would be well accustomed to bureaucratic corruption and might not see it as more than a minor hassle.

Addressing such cultural variables, and also adapting to host country laws, informs the adjustment of policies and guidelines, and, importantly, it instructs plans for related training, communication and enforcement. The trickier side of the equation is how to still do business if paying bribes is not an option.

The consultancy is already going to use one general method, which is to take short-term profit pressure off the operation and give it time to learn. Immediate pressure and high expectations from HQ often signal to managers on the ground that corner-cutting is not just an option but expected. Second, when a manager is on a tight-time budget, taking time to learn a way around problems seems like a luxury. If bribery works, then it is a way to stay on track. Removing near-term profit pressure and explicitly tasking country managers with finding alternatives to bribery completely changes the incentives equation.

Another approach is seeking bureaucratic contacts higher up the hierarchy. Because of past politicised anti-corruption, or "transparency", campaigns, higher officials with any degree of political profile have become cautious about bribery. There is also a degree of legitimate professional interest in, and incentivisation for, genuine departmental performance. This is partly driven by the regime's desire to attract more FDI. Thus, the company can press for senior director intercession when it faces particularly obstinate and greedy junior officials.

The above can extend more broadly to proactively developing contacts among senior officials in relevant agencies. Trust and interpersonal relationships are taken seriously, and if the company can forge informal ties with the right people, it could have consistent channels for resolving corruption-related obstacles. This would not happen overnight, and it would be a part of the consultancy's wider approach of exploring potential support networks and slowly extending them. A good place to start would be business associations, whose members likely already have ties with relevant officials. Personal relationships should be carefully managed and kept above board, since a friendly approach to a senior official could be construed as interest in a longer-term "business" relationship.

Finally, some government agencies could help in dealing with the ones from which the company needs permits or services. For example, the Investment Promotion Agency is the main agency tasked with meeting the government's FDI growth objectives. It is pressing other agencies to reduce corruption and streamline processes to improve the country's FDI attractiveness. Again using patient trust-building, the consultancy can forge relationships within the agency, and eventually managers would be able seek its support with hassles from bribery pressure.

Note that in some contexts, particularly when dealing with corruption pressure from senior officials with a high public profile, it can make sense to pursue court cases when an operation is held up because of bribery pressure. A company might not win, but the hassle of going to court, plus the bad publicity for an agency, can create a deterrent over time. However, in this case, routine, uncoordinated corruption pressure by low- to mid-level bureaucratic officials does not form a very clear basis for legal action. More importantly, the consultancy explicitly decided on a low-profile entry, and to not needlessly antagonise the clans by becoming a vociferous champion of clean business. A legal strategy might have some deterrent effect in the long run, but court cases are more appropriate to countering potential aggressive crony behaviour than as a routine approach to bribery pressure.

The localisation of anti-corruption practices would be handled as a structured internal programme. On the other hand, building relationships to enable business activity without bribing would be one strand of the wider learning strategy, and hence the precise shape of the overall initiative is difficult to foresee. But there was sufficient insight from analysis to develop at least the broad-brush approach outlined above, and this would guide further investigation and experimentation towards an anti-corruption support network.

For the adjustment of corporate anti-corruption policies, functions related to corporate integrity assurance would have a leading role. These could include, depending on specific labels in the company, internal control and compliance. Legal would help to adjust policies to account for host country laws. Human resources have an important role in internal communication and training, and department managers, who have day-to-day interaction with local staff, would need to provide a degree of oversight and guidance.

Who among potential stakeholders might be able to help with bureaucratic corruption hassles will be learned over time, but we mentioned a few clearly relevant ones, including senior officials, the Investment Promotion Agency, and business associations. Local legal advisors would also have ideas on how to address the issue, although, as noted in Chapter 3, any local advisors who could learn details about the company should be carefully vetted.

Like MOT interference, bureaucratic corruption could go from being a routine issue to an indication of another type of problem. This is the core issue of crony pressure. The IT consultancy would need to track bureaucratic interactions and try to understand patterns which could suggest that corruption pressure has become orchestrated. This might be indicated by an increase in the frequency of bribery pressure and the obstinacy of officials, and by hesitation and cold shoulders among stakeholders who had previously been helpful. This could mean that the low-profile, or stealth approach, to market entry had failed, and that the clans were responding to a perceived threat. This would then put bureaucratic corruption into the core initiative of managing crony pressure, and approaches would need to be reconsidered in that context.

One last point on this initiative is that we had bureaucratic delays and bureaucratic corruption as separate issues. Sometimes dealing with delays is just a matter of planning ahead, whereas corruption requires more explicit treatment. In this case, though, it would seem that for practical purposes it would be useful to merge bureaucratic delays and corruption into one initiative. The anti-corruption initiative includes one of the main approaches to delays, namely time and patience, and the same stakeholders could help with both problems.

Before moving on, there are some wider points to extract from above six example initiatives. One is that sometimes an initiative cannot be particularly well defined up front because an operation will need to learn and adapt. The author has heard international managers say, "We don't explicitly worry about political risk and just get on with the job." When pressed on what this means, the reply is often some variant of, "We get to know the right people, and try to fit in. There are usually ways around problems if you're patient and get to know how things work." That sounds somewhat like an emergent strategy. However, the difference between an emergent strategy and muddling through is intelligence, and at least a general direction based on it.

Another point is the importance of monitoring in initiatives to manage contingent issues. Monitoring trends and changes in the environment is important for a number of reasons, not least simply learning about new potential problems that were not previously on the observable horizon. But for contingent issues, monitoring is how we know when to go from one level of preparation to the next. As noted in those examples, being on a hair trigger of preparedness is unfeasible, but being unprepared can be disastrous. Monitoring directly linked to planning is how we can get the balance more or less right.

Finally, an interesting and delicate point arises from the initiative to manage crony pressure, which would have a parallel in the constructor's core initiative to handle military faction spoiling activity. Sometimes political risk management means countering a political actor, and that can be strange new terrain for a company. Consider, for example, that the IT consultancy will essentially use deception to thwart crony interest. The company has every intention of eventually becoming a major player in the country, but cronies cannot know that until it is nearly a *fait accompli*. Political deterrence is another line of defence in the crony and MF initiatives, and it is usually associated with the hard game of national security, not business.

There are two concerns about a company actively trying to thwart a political actor's interests. One is that in so doing a company becomes a political player itself. This can be dangerous, because by comparison to business competition, the political variety can be very cutthroat. The other is ethical. If a company connives against legitimate socio-political actors with interests that run counter to the company's aims, it puts itself outside of the rules and standards that guarantee its own rights. This too is dangerous ground, and as noted in Chapter 3, while ethical corner-cutting can be good for next quarter's results, it can easily backfire and usually does at some point. There are clearly delicate balances to consider when explicitly planning against a political, or socio-political, actor. We address ethics in political risk management within the book's last chapter. For now, suffice to say that if a company is planning against a political actor, it needs to do so with its eyes wide open, and with a clear understanding of the risks, and its own limitations and moral red lines.

Initiative formulation is the heart of political risk management planning. It is where we directly apply the intelligence outputs to guide actions that make the operation more resilient. However, while we have the bones of a plan, we still need to design an organisation to enact it, and we turn to that question now.

PROGRAMME DEFINITION

Although we have a top-level plan for each issue, we need another layer of translation to action, how we organise for implementation. A given initiative will be cross-functional, as indicated in the above six examples. At this point, we can clarify who would be involved in each initiative, and if we aggregate each function's roles from across initiatives, we can derive functional political risk management programmes. This provides clear functional tasking. Stakeholders too often have roles in several initiatives, and their roles can also be aggregated to define an agenda and engagement programme for each stakeholder, led by a consistent company interlocutor. This ensures that stakeholder relationships are not fragmented or replicated between initiatives, and, from a stakeholder perspective, that the company's position is consistent and coherent. We will examine functional and engagement programmes in turn.

FUNCTIONAL PROGRAMMES

In every initiative example from the previous section, several different management functions were involved. The full set of participants in an initiative forms the cross-functional initiative team, or task force. Among involved functions, the one whose remit most directly covers the target issue is the appropriate task force leader, and others would have different supporting or oversight roles. A leader in one task force could well have a supporting role in another one. This cross-functional involvement, as opposed to simply assigning one issue to one function, ensures that all relevant expertise is brought to bear on a given problem, and that functional silos do form and impede political risk management coherence.

A basic example of the importance cross-functional task forces comes from a consulting case the author was involved with. The client's external affairs and security managers were on friendly terms but hardly discussed their own activities with each other. All security issues were firmly the security person's remit, while all local government relations belonged to external affairs. It turned out that the external relations manager had a very good understanding of how the local authorities would be able to help in a neighbourhood security incident such as a post-football match mob getting out of hand, or a flare-up of local economic protests. Since there was no basis for sharing this insight, it was not fed into security planning. Each function had its own little window on the world and their respective views did not join up.

Relevant functions are identified in initiative formulation; thus, to specify a cross-functional initiative task force, we only need to assign appropriate functional roles. But different functions need to clearly see what their roles are across initiatives, to be able to manage their own departmental resource allocation and coordinate their various contributions. A functional political risk management programme provides this clarity.

A matrix combining target issues and functions helps to map both the initiative task forces and functional programmes. The basic framework, which we can call the implementation matrix, is illustrated in Figure 9.13.

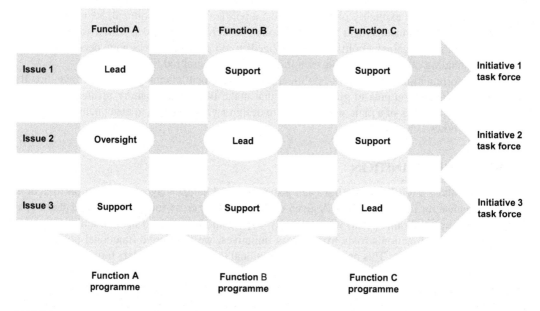

FIGURE 9.13 Implementation matrix.

To illustrate one axis of the matrix, a task force for the highway project's host community friction initiative might be as follows:

- CSR/community relations
  - Leader, since CSR is most directly involved with host community actors
- Security
  - Deputy leader, because of the importance of police liaison for human rights adherence, the need to quickly de-escalate violent incidents and the potential threats to company staff that could arise from local unrest
- Senior management
  - Oversight, because of the importance of the initiative to sustainable operations, and because it is complex and multi-stranded
  - Corporate diplomacy towards presidential agreement on the need to ensure fair community treatment and human rights, and on the need to link the project to post-completion local development
- Labour relations/human resources
  - Managing local hiring to increase local acceptance
  - Managing any resulting friction between union and local workers (labour issues overlap with host community friction)
- Procurement/supply chain
  - Managing local supply contracts to give local businesses and their workers a positive stake in the operation
- Legal
  - Building human rights adherence into the project contract
- Public relations
  - Clear public messaging about company intentions and activities, and countering sub-nationalist and military faction spin

In general, core initiative task forces have the most functions involved and require the most oversight, because they are multi-stranded. By contrast, an initiative to address a basic problem might only involve one or two functions. Again drawing on the highway case, the task force to address street crime and police roadblock hassles which could affect individual staff might only involve security, for obvious reasons, and human resources to facilitate personal security awareness training for staff.

Going down the vertical functional axis, we can develop a specific function's full contribution to political risk management, via their task force involvement. We can take human resources (HR) in the IT consultancy case as an example. HR's political risk management programme would constitute its roles in the following initiatives:

- Crony pressure: HR would hire trusted local managers who would help to navigate early relationship-building to offset crony pressure, and HR's lead on hiring local staff would contribute to raising the operation's socio-political value in the eyes of the government.
- Local staff detentions: HR would work with security to develop preventative measures and awareness training and would work with legal and senior management to address cases of staff detention.
- Bureaucratic corruption (and delays): Working with internal control, HR would facilitate tailored anti-corruption training for staff.
- Terrorism and other security issues: Alongside security, HR would organise staff training in how to avoid and respond to security incidents.
- Local content regulations: HR would lead in adapting to local content changes and manage the shift in the proportion of expat to local staff.

Along with generally guiding a function's political risk management role, a benefit of the functional programme perspective is that we can identify certain tasks that cross-cut a function's involvement in initiatives. For example, security might need to develop an evacuation plan for the possibility of a coup, serious unrest or the spillover of a nearby civil war. One evacuation plan, accounting for the nuances of each contingency, would suffice. Similarly, the corporate integrity function, by whatever label, could develop one tailored country policy that addressed the issues of bureaucratic corruption, supplier integrity lapses and nepotism in hiring, without having to start from scratch with each issue.

Note that even a function's routine tasks become a form of political risk management when there are a range of socio-political sensitivities and bureaucratic hurdles around them. For example, HR would also work on obtaining work permits for expat staff. This would mean understanding the relevant bureaucracy, developing a clear case for the need for a given visa and dealing with delays and corruption pressure. What is captured in task force participation is only a function's explicit political risk management contribution.

There are two questions that need to be addressed before moving onto stakeholder programmes. One is how explicit we actually make initiative task forces and functional programmes. The second is how we translate functional labels into political risk management roles.

On the question of explicitness, again it goes back to how challenging an environment is. For example, if a Western European company had an operation in a neighbouring Eastern European country, it would need the broad outlines of initiatives and programmes, but more as a guide to functional interaction and information-sharing than as a framework for specific activities. If the same company were going to Angola or Turkmenistan, it would need to treat initiatives and programmes as clearly defined parts of people's jobs, and oversight and coordination would need to be explicit.

On the second question, one might have noticed in the initiative formulation examples that functional labels somewhat varied, and indeed some, like "corporate diplomacy", seldom actually exist as titles in companies. Indeed, the same holds for "political risk management" itself, which is often done but almost never labelled as such. Differences in what functional titles mean and the responsibilities they encompass are a challenge when translating them into political risk management. Detailing every political risk management role and the functions that might fit them is unfeasible here, but we can point out of the more ambiguous correlations.

Corporate diplomacy, as noted, is one role with no clear corresponding function. It means handling high-level negotiations with political actors and strategic coordination with supportive stakeholders. In many companies, external and/or government affairs have a formal remit for political relationships. In practice, because of their limited decision authority, they tend to manage non-strategic relationships while providing intelligence on a range of political actors. Senior country or project managers, who can directly negotiate on behalf of the company, are usually the ones who handle corporate diplomacy as we define it here. They are often backed up by senior divisional managers from HQ or a regional hub. There is an argument that all expat staff in a country are "diplomats", and indeed their comportment and the relationships they forge with local counterparts are important, but that is not an explicit role.

Another tricky one is the distinction between HR and labour relations. In most companies, these are the same, and handled by HR, but in a political risk context there is a difference. HR would deal with a company's long-term, or permanent, staff, and support them with training and procedures aimed at keeping them safe and out of trouble. Labour relations, or in some cases industrial relations, is more about managing contracted or short-term labour and the relationship with the relevant union. HR usually has a softer, more nuanced touch, while labour relations includes a bargaining aspect and the ability to show some mettle if unions become opportunistic to the point of predatory. Both the HR and labour relations sub-functions would work with security, the former for staff security training and procedures, the latter to mitigate violence between groups in a workforce, or strike violence.

We have been calling the community relations role CSR. In some companies, CSR is the appropriate label for the relevant function, but in others it could be called sustainability, and sometimes external affairs has the community relations remit. Community relations often entails CSR activities, in terms of running programmes to offset hardship caused by the operation, but it also means building relationships with local civil society for the intangible but important purpose of mutual understanding and respect.

Communications is another role that corresponds to several possible relevant functions. Communications is aimed at countering fake news and rumours and at ensuring that people understand company intentions and what to expect from an operation. There is also a positive spin aspect, not in a cynical sense, rather to ensure that people know the company's values and its contribution to socio-economic development. Public relations, media relations and again the ubiquitous external affairs function can all have this role, depending on their precise remit in the company.

There is some ambiguity around local supplier contracting and logistics. Contracting is a political risk management role, because it handles sometimes sensitive relationships with local partners including state-connected companies, and it offers local business opportunities that help to improve acceptance of an operation (in both cases thereby also fulfilling part of local content requirements). Logistics, on the other hand, is about getting goods to and from the operation, and its political risk management aspect is ensuring reasonable resilience in supply chains, for example in the event of strikes, unrest or sea piracy. Both tend to be handled by the supply chain manager, but in some cases there is a distinction between the supply chain, procurement and logistics functions.

The above touches on another role, business continuity. There is a business continuity function in many companies, usually at the corporate level. Its job is to ensure that business can keep going through problems such as power outages, cyber-attacks and natural disasters. In a complex environment, business continuity would also need to focus on interruptions from terrorist attacks, unrest, conflict, strikes, sea piracy and bureaucratic delays. In the author's experience, there is seldom a business continuity person in a country operation's permanent staff. Rather, it tends to be handled by frontline operational managers, with support from logistics or its equivalent. Business continuity as an asset is exposed to so many factors that protecting it is nearly everyone's job in some form or another, and while corporate specialists can help, as a role it tends to be quite dispersed.

The role of integrity assurance helps an operation to avoid liabilities and to ensure legal and ethical comportment. In a complex environment, this includes preventing corruption and related white-collar crime, both within the company and in its dealings with other organisations, and avoiding affiliations with unscrupulous actors. Ethics and compliance, financial crime, fraud risk and other functional titles have a remit for integrity. Internal control is more general and sometimes covers those other functions. Given the proliferation of integrity-related regulations across OECD countries in recent years, the integrity assurance role has developed numerous sub-specialisations, and in turn relevant functional labels are diverse. Most of them relate to some aspect of political risk, but those which include a focus on anti-corruption and due diligence on local partners are particularly germane.

The last one that we will touch on here is the role of political risk transfer. Transferring political risk usually means buying political risk insurance. This has been touched on, but to reiterate, political risk insurance covers financial losses from certain types of political events, such as war (or political violence more generally), expropriation, cancellation and currency controls and devaluations. The latter two risks are also dealt with through financial hedging. While political risk insurance is a rather moot point after it has been acquired and an operation starts, the relationship with insurers can continue through an operation, and policies can be adjusted for different operational phases. It used to be that the risk management function in companies would handle insurance negotiation and acquisition, but since ERM's widespread uptake, risk management is now more of a corporate support function, and the finance function is more likely to handle political risk insurance.

There is a range of other political risk management roles and corresponding functions (two obvious ones, security and legal, were not mentioned because the roles and functions closely correspond).

If we use blank-slate initiative formulation to tell us what needs to be done, this indicates who is best positioned to be in a given task force, and their precise functional label does not really matter. Nonetheless, knowing what the company has on hand in terms of relevant expertise accelerates task force design, and the political risk aspect of functions helps to make that assessment.

A final point on roles and functions is that nearly anyone in a foreign operation can have a tacit political risk management role and get more directly involved if they are so inclined. The author is familiar with numerous instances when someone with a functional title that had nothing to do with political risk or a risk-related role played a significant part in managing issues that manifested. Particularly if someone has prior experience in developing and transitional country operations, they can have a very valuable contribution as long as there are channels and structures by which to partake and be heard.

STAKEHOLDER AGENDAS AND ENGAGEMENT PROGRAMMES

In many cases, an aspect of an initiative is to influence relevant stakeholders towards behaviour that helps to mitigate the target issue. Just as a given management function could be involved in a number of initiatives, a particular stakeholder could figure in multiple issues, as a potential cause of problems or source of support. Thus, several initiative task forces could end up engaging with the same stakeholder, each with different or overlapping objectives, and different messaging and protocols. Task forces might even start competing with each other for a stakeholder's attention. This is messy and counterproductive from an implementation perspective, and from a stakeholder's perspective it is at best confusing and at worst makes the company look disorganised and inept.

To avoid this not-uncommon scenario, we need to define coherent stakeholder agendas and engagement programmes based on them. When a stakeholder is somewhat peripheral or only figures in one issue, this would not be necessary, but it is important when an actor is relevant to a number of problems. We can again apply a basic matrix to derive an initial map of integrated stakeholder agendas, as depicted in Figure 9.14.

The action buttons in the illustration, such as "dialogue" or "deterrence", are quite basic, but from initiative formulation we would know what specific purpose each of these is aimed at. Horizontally, the matrix summarises stakeholder requirements for each issue's initiative. Vertically, it aggregates requirements across the issues, to define stakeholder agendas. An agenda in turn become the basis

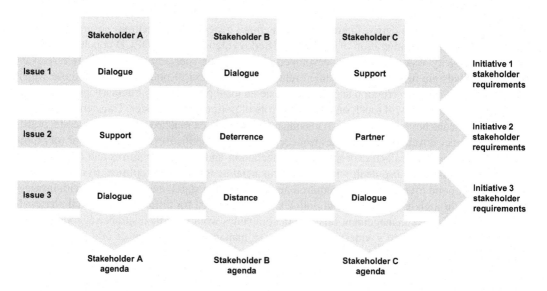

FIGURE 9.14 Stakeholder agenda matrix.

of an engagement programme, aimed at influencing a stakeholder towards meeting the full set of requirements.

We can try this on the president from the West African highway case. He is relevant to host community friction, where we hope to secure his promise to link long-term local development to highway completion and his commitment to ensuring fairness and human rights adherence during relocations. The president is central to the issue of contractual commitment, and we hope to sustain his commitment and to be able to negotiate any necessary changes in a fair and nonconflictual manner. He is also relevant to countering MF spoiling activity, since he has considerable clout with southern tribes in the host community, the union and the bureaucracy. A full agenda would combine these requirements. Thus, either in direct interaction or via donor country diplomatic interlocutors, the company's engagement with the president would be guided by a coherent set of objectives. For his part, the president would gain a comprehensive understanding of the company's concerns and interests, rather than dealing with seemingly disparate topics.

When defining holistic agendas, in some cases we can also more plainly see when there is a necessary balance between a need to address problematic behaviour and a need to get support. For example, the constructor wants to deter MF spoiling activity, but it also needs a dialogue with the regional army command for support with planning against a potential insurgent attack. If the company lacked circumspection in its deterrence approach, for example by telling the independent press what a bunch of thugs the generals were after evidence of shenanigans, managers would not be able to expect much help with security planning. With a holistic perspective, we might also see that dialogue on one issue could mitigate a hostile attitude that drives or worsens other ones. In the MF example, talking to the army about the insurgent threat could develop a degree of trust with local commanders, and this might filter up the chain of command, blunting MF's frustration with the company.

Engagement programmes are not just shaped by agendas. Because they focus on a particular actor, we can tailor a programme to its organisational culture, key personalities, our wider understanding of its interests and values, and appropriate protocols. Much of this would come from the supporting insight from stakeholder analysis, although at this point we might see where we need to go back and fill in some blanks.

Finally, while it might not be feasible to always have the same company person or functional team handling engagement with one stakeholder, there should at least be reasonable consistency in who deals with them, and a single point of engagement oversight. In this sense, a stakeholder is somewhat like the customer of a complex product or service. If a company has ten different sales people trying to sell their bits to the customer, no one will really get to know the customer or earn their trust. The customer, in turn, will not take kindly to disaggregated offers from different people they hardly know. To avoid this situation, no matter who in the company has something to sell, one account manager has overall responsibility for the relationship and ensures that it is strategically managed.

In our context, that person is the engagement leader. He or she could be from the function that will most directly deal with the stakeholder or have uniquely suitable experience. Note that engagement leadership applies not just to stakeholders with whom we will have a direct relationship but also to threat actors. We might not sit down and talk to them, but we still need consistency and accrued learning to optimise our approach to them over time. A final point is that the engagement leader is not a gatekeeper, rather an overseer, and importantly also an advisor. Gaining a nuanced understanding of the given actor, he or she is well positioned to guide task forces in shaping their stakeholder-related activities for best effect.

STRATEGY

We have target issues, initiatives designed to address them, and functional and stakeholder programmes. This has been a bottom-up thought process, and this final step weds the previous ones with an overarching concept and fixes any remaining gaps or weaknesses.

STRATEGY STATEMENT

The glue that binds initiatives and programmes is a strategy statement that concisely says how the operation is going to manage political risk. This does not list every initiative; rather, it is aimed at providing a beacon for the different teams and functions involved in political risk management. It helps them to see where their roles fit into the wider scheme and how the different threads some together. For senior management, it is also a high-level reference point that guides oversight and coordination. A possible, and abbreviated, rendition for the West African highway project is as follows:

> Political risk management will balance social responsibility and acceptance with reasonable assurance of the security of personnel. Its primary focus will be host community and labour friction, which will be approached with an eye to mutual understanding and fairness, but also to the company's right to protect itself from predation and opportunism. We will also develop legitimate relationships to counter the negative influence of the rival regime faction, which could affect social and labour relations in addition to bureaucratic expedition if left unchecked. Supportive relationships and tailored procedures will address bureaucratic delays and corruption pressure. Business continuity will account for customs delays, port strikes and sea piracy, and seek sufficient redundancy and alternative routes to ensure that these issues do not seriously affect the project schedule. We will work closely with the project's donors to put our case to the government for the fair treatment of affected communities, and to develop responses to any potential pressure for contract renegotiation. Should such pressure arise, we would balance our rights and legitimate interests with any genuine economic concerns for an appropriate resolution. Finally, we will monitor indications of a coup, an attack, and major unrest, and maintain reasonable preparedness for these contingencies.

Note that "balance" occurs twice, each time in the context of the company's legitimate concerns versus potentially harmful or disruptive socio-political interests. There is also an implied balance between self-preservation and acceptance, since security and countering hostile intentions goes hand in hand with preventing and reducing friction that could give rise to threats. Finally, the main contingencies, both from instability and from logistical disruptions, are included. Without the initiatives developed earlier, this could be fluff, like something a gung-ho manager might say to an investment screening committee concerned about a prospective operation's challenges. But by now we know that everything in here has been thought through on the basis of hard intelligence, and hence rather than being aspirational, this is a summary of actual, if preliminary, plans.

The statement for the IT consultancy in MENA would have a similar level of generality. Because of the revision to the company's concept (from getting a major partner for an accelerated presence to a more cautious entry via the independent business community), it would emphasise the need for building mutually supportive relationships, both to exploit the market opportunity and, just as importantly, to establish a legitimate presence that can withstand and counter potential spoiling activity. Supportive networks would also provide local insights to help the company to navigate bureaucratic hassles and corruption pressure and build a capability to support detained staff. A key element of the friendly network approach would be to maintain a relatively low profile until a local track record had been established, to avoid becoming the focus of crony concerns and exploitative interest while the company was still new and vulnerable. The statement would include security and other issues, but the core element would be sustainably embedding in the independent business ecosystem.

TRADE-OFFS

We noted when introducing the three general types of issues that trade-offs between initiatives could arise, and that when they did, core initiatives would usually take precedence. A trade-off means that we need to take a suboptimal approach to one objective in order to optimise the approach to another. Trade-offs are often unavoidable, but they can be problematic if not explicitly recognised and carefully managed.

For one thing, there is an implied assumption in trade-offs that one issue is more important than another. This assumption can become fixed and lead to complacency with respect to the secondary issue. For example, in the highway case, the company has prioritised managing the core issue of host community friction. Street crime, banditry and the threat from insurgents call for physical security measures. If these were the only issues the operation faced, the optimal solution would include obtrusive armed deterrence and hard perimeters. But in the interests of host community relations, we need to ensure that security is unobtrusive and does not burden local people. Now look about six months into the operation. Things are going well, and managers feel good about themselves for taking the high road and not hiding behind fences and guards. Low-profile security has become a group mantra. But the threat actors have not gone away and might well have noticed this complacency. Low-profile or not, security needs to adapt, and given the constraints imposed by the trade-off, security actually needs to be especially creative and dynamic. This will not happen if the trade-off becomes a fixed assumption or signifies that the threat environment is somehow unimportant.

Trade-offs also affect resource allocation, and this means that there needs to be realistic expectations about the initiatives on the receiving end of trade-offs. For example, if the corruption issue only gets one person because community relations are a more pressing priority, that person cannot be expected to have a contextualised policy and training regimen up and running in just a month. When we make trade-offs, we are accepting a slower pace and, indeed, lower performance on some issues than others. If this is not recognised, then unrealistic expectations create internal friction, which affects morale.

IMPLEMENTATION STRUCTURE AND RESOURCE CHECK

The implementation matrix depicted earlier can be expanded to depict the wider implementation organisation, which includes engagement leaders. When we have this picture, we can see the full set of human resources dedicated to political risk management. This is a reference point for future adaptation and adjustment in line with changes in the environment, which can bring up new issues and change the relative importance of the ones we already assessed. The structure can also reveal near-term resource imbalances, which are our principal concern now.

We noted that we would not get fixated too early on trying to align resources to issues' relative severity rankings and would let bottom-up design guide initial resource assignments. Now, however, we can have a look at the outcome and see how it aligns with the prioritisation undertaken in analysis. If, for example, we had a cross-functional team of three people dealing with a particular regulatory change, and that was given a relatively middling rating, we could ask where one of them could be reallocated for stronger overall political risk management. In general, though, it is rather premature to start worrying about precise person-time budgets. Detailed planning will be undertaken by implementors, and in practice task force resource-sharing can be quite fluid as long as there are open channels for collaboration. Nonetheless, it is still worth checking against priorities to make sure that important issues get the attention they warrant.

A more tangible problem is that some functions might be overburdened. For example, in the IT consultancy case, because of the importance of supportive relationships and the close link between the entry strategy and the initiative to counter crony pressure, there is a strong emphasis on corporate diplomacy led by senior managers. In fact, looking at the implementation structure, it might seem that senior managers will spend most of their time explicitly managing political risk. Since they will also be responsible for getting business and, eventually, managing projects, this is not ideal from a commercial standpoint. The company could consider sending an external affairs team to join the operation, thereby taking some burden off senior managers. If this were not feasible, then middle-level relationships could be managed by senior consultants, leaving senior managers to deal with correspondingly senior stakeholders.

In the West African case, as with many operations in volatile environments, security has a particularly heavy burden. It is responsible for issues ranging from street crime to the violent fallout of a potential coup, to police liaison and human rights training. It also needs to manage contracted security guarding. This is a specialist function and cannot just be shared with other ones. One or even two senior security people would be stretched. The company needs to ensure that security has the resources it needs to play its assigned role, regardless of original project budgeting. Given what analysis has indicated, trying to conform to original resource expectations could lead to dangerous vulnerabilities.

Resource scarcity can also be addressed by sequencing allocations. Some initiatives might not need to be fully up and running for several months, and the people involved in them can help with more immediate ones. The set-up phase of an initiative is often especially intense, and once an initiative is established, it might be able to pare down its team, freeing people up to help elsewhere. This kind of juggling can actually occur throughout an operation, and, as noted, that is why it is useful to have a schematic of the implementation structure as a reference point for resource tracking. We examine this in the next section on timelines.

Going beyond resource balancing, this discussion touches on the wider question of overall available resources. Overseas operations are sometimes planned without any consideration to how much time people will need to spend on preventing and managing "non-commercial/non-technical" issues. The basic assumption is that people will naturally spend most of their time on their "day jobs", and that they will adapt and muddle through if the unexpected comes up. Depending on how volatile a country is, this can lead to severe overall underperformance as people get drawn into de facto political risk management just out of necessity. In general, the more complex an environment is, the more time people will spend on non-routine activities. This calls for additional resource margin, and it is far better to know what could be required up front, based on intelligence, than scrambling to plug gaps later on, especially when new staff would be starting from scratch in learning the operational context.

Timelines

Each initiative would have its own timeline, including the sequencing of specific steps, and particularly sensitive or volatile periods during which the target issue would be especially prone to manifesting or flaring up. We can use these to develop a high-level view of all initiative timelines. Going back to the question of resource allocation, this can indicate opportunities to shift attention between initiatives depending on different requirements in a given period, and it can indicate when overall political risk management could be especially intensive, and hence demanding in human resource terms. The timeline in Figure 9.15 is purely conceptual and not drawn from a case, but it still illustrates some useful points.

In Figure 9.15, the thick grey bands are periods of focused activity, both in setting up initiatives and in managing foreseeable periods of high intensity. The horizontal initiative timelines range from narrow to thick, corresponding to how suddenly the issue could manifest, noted on the right-hand side of the diagram. We applied suddenness as an adjustment variable when prioritising terrain challenges, and it is also useful in planning. For gradual issues, we could spare resources between periods of activity and still have time to prepare if the issue began to emerge. For potentially sudden ones, if we reallocated resources, we might create dangerous vulnerabilities. Thus, we have a dashboard, or radar, of opportunities and constraints on resource flexibility.

To put this in more concrete terms, imagine that issue C above is the coup attempt from the highway case. In one coup scenario, there is little time to act on it, and it could happen at any point. Thus, one urgent initial task is to develop a rapid staff evacuation capability, so that we at least have the basics covered if the surprise scenario played out. After that, we know that the risk is higher near the time of national elections, and that would see another period of focused activity. But because of the need to be able to respond to a sudden crisis contingency, the initiative would not have slack periods. We would not need the whole task force poised for action at all times, but we should be careful about pulling them onto other initiatives too. Issue A, which we can imagine is host community friction from the same case, has a similar overall profile, but resource demands are driven

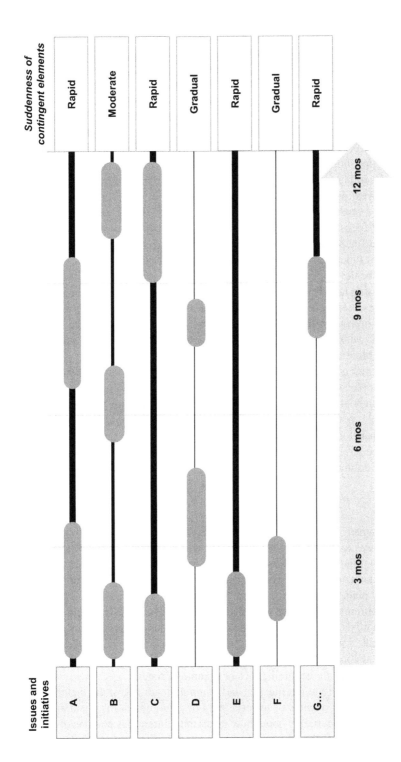

FIGURE 9.15 Overall timelines.

less by one potential event, and more by a need to manage several pressing problems so that they do not converge as one quagmire. Security-related issues, like a kidnapping or even just violent street crime, would also have high suddenness and therefore need a certain constant level of preparedness.

Issues D, F and G, by contrast, offer more opportunity for resource balancing. D might be about local sub-contractor integrity issues. We would have an early period of working intensively with partners on integrity assurance and setting up controls, but once this is done, routine monitoring and discussion would reveal any impending problems with reasonable warning. Perhaps down the road we would need to revise integrity standards in preparation for a new project phase, but after that we could go back to routine interaction. Issue F might be bureaucratic corruption, and upon establishing tailored procedures, the task force could scale back somewhat. We might not be able to foresee specific episodes of bribery pressure, but we would have our routine defences up and running. Issue G, which might be upcoming local elections that could lead to violence, will require an intensive focus, but not for several months. Until then, the initiative task force would be relatively free.

Timelines also reveal periods of especially high intensity in overall political risk management. For example, looking vertically down the diagram, we can see that around month eight to nine we have four periods of focused activity in addition to high preparedness on another issue. Knowing this, operational managers could actually plan ahead to get temporary support from HQ, which could second relevant functional specialists for a couple of months.

Timelines would be developed in detail prior to actual implementation on the ground. The main point worth emphasising here is the effect of issue suddenness on resource planning. Going back to plausibility as an assessment criteria, one can have a situation wherein an issue is highly implausible but could happen tomorrow, with serious implications. This is a balancing act. We would not task resources as though it were imminent, but the issue would warrant monitoring and sustaining at least a basic capability to blunt its more dire effects.

One final consideration in timelines is what needs to be done before the main body of commercial and technical people arrive in the country. In particularly challenging environments, it could be necessary to establish a small "pathfinder" office to set up capabilities that would be immediately required. For example, perhaps initial staff security procedures should be in place before people arrive, as well as a basic localised anti-corruption guide so that people do not make mistakes in their first few weeks on the ground. Then after the operation is underway, these initial capabilities can be developed into more comprehensive initiatives.

FINAL TESTING

As we discuss in Chapter 14, in an intelligence project, people can become very familiar with the factors and actors they are dealing with, to the point where their findings become a comfort zone. Various notorious intelligence failures have occurred not for lack of information and analysis, but because people could not get beyond fixed mindsets. Thus, there is still room for some testing before we finalise the initial plan.

Testing can take different forms, and we only suggest a few here. There could be a dose of devil's advocacy, whereby a mixed team of country specialists and operational planners are tasked to derive the top five to ten weak assumptions and flaws in the current plan. Devil's advocacy would not have to be long-winded and could just use a workshop format. Any significant findings could indicate a need to revisit certain points in the intelligence or planning process.

Another option is for the joint intelligence and planning team to test the factors and issues from analysis that had the highest degrees of uncertainty. For example, an insurgent attack was rated as implausible but there was uncertainty about how insurgents' intentions could evolve. This test could also focus on certain stakeholders, for whom we had to heavily rely on extrapolation as opposed to direct insight to estimate attitudes and reactions. We could run desktop simulations of the unexpected happening, assuming the preliminary plan had been implemented. If significant harm manifests in spite of our proposed measures, then we would know where to go back and plug some holes.

Finally, we can apply worst-case thinking, using a formulation such as "The company had to quickly leave after a year, it left assets behind and its people barely made it out in one piece – what happened?" The answers might point to some serious possibilities and vulnerabilities. Again, at the current time of writing, a recent political risk twist is the Russian invasion of Ukraine. If this exercise were undertaken a year ago from the time of writing, the invasion scenario might well have been an output, and ideally accounted for in planning.

Within the assessment period, the gaps or new insights from final testing might not be particularly dramatic. After all, we have been working within the observable horizon, reasonably able to see how the recent past and current dynamics will interact and play out. If we start prodding further out in time, though, uncertainty increases and the possibilities open up. Planning needs to account for potential change directions, because what we do now can help to prepare for the future. Discerning how the environment might evolve is the subject of the next chapter.

10 Scenario Analysis

To this point in the baseline intelligence exercise we have used scenario analysis, but tacitly and within broadly known horizons. In terrain analysis, some issues were formulated partly using postulations about twists and turns in a plotline, as when we derived the challenge of workplace tensions. In stakeholder analysis, stakeholder responses were partially formed through projecting how an actor might react to certain operational attributes based on a reading of their attitude and influence. In planning, scenarios were applied in working backwards from problematic situations to see how we could avert them. These were all applications of scenario thinking, but within a current system about which we had considerable information. In this chapter, we explicitly apply scenario analysis and set our sights beyond what we can currently see. Recall that this stage could have followed stakeholder analysis, but we went straight to planning to maintain continuity of focus. Following scenario analysis, planning will be augmented with options and contingencies aimed at preparation for longer-term developments and major discontinuities.

There is an important distinction between scenario analysis and prediction, and it is worth exploring this early on to set reasonable expectations. The distinction is almost philosophical. Prediction assumes that there is one future out there, while scenario analysis assumes that there could be at least a few. Prediction points a laser, trying to aim at that one future. Scenario analysis casts a net, aiming for the range of possibility. As noted in terrain analysis in the prioritisation section, some physicists propose that there is only one future, and that it is as fixed as the past. Even if this were the case, though, it is so obscured by the causal twists and turns between now and then that it is very hard, if not impossible, to see it in any detail, at least depending on how far out we are trying to look. Prediction has become a bit of fad, and even in political risk, replete with the effects of human eccentricity, some analysts and consultancies pride themselves on having predicted this or that specific event.

Prediction has its place in political risk, but only after we have a very clear understanding of certain potential events, and deriving those entails scenario analysis or a similar assessment. Among other things, a scenario analysis might yield an issue with a binary outcome, for example Country A might invade B, or not, within a given time frame. One can set up indicators, and when a critical mass of them light up, probability moves towards certainty. That seems to be the only context in which prediction makes sense. Failure to foresee something important could arise from a number of things in this context, whether wilful blindness to inconvenient possibilities, a lack of intelligence resources, a lack of imagination, or poor or badly executed process. But it would not arise from a lack of some ethereal power to predict, and seldom because analysts were not clever enough. Perhaps a brilliant analyst might have an intuitive leap and derive a seemingly obscure possibility out of the blue, and then correctly predict its occurrence, but such near-psychic abilities tend not to be replicable, nor often repeatable. Even when we think we predicted, we usually just put most chips on one bet among several, based on intelligence and hard thinking. Prediction is thus something of a chimera, and sometimes in fixating on the kinds of binary outcomes that lend themselves to prediction, we lose sight of wider system dynamics that could give rise to other possibilities.

The author came close to a prediction once, buried deep within a personnel risk policy project for an international NGO. The context section of the report contained very brief political synopses of 16 countries, one of which was Egypt. Included in the relevant paragraph was something like the following: "Unemployment, corruption, youth demographics and repression, combined with cynicism about Mubarak's aspiration to dynastic rule, make Egypt an archetype of a pre-revolutionary situation." That was written in 2008. Ironically, had the Arab Spring not happened, it still would

DOI: 10.1201/9781003149125-13

have been valid. It did happen so it looked like a prediction. But one can see the method herein. It was not brilliant nor sophisticated. Egypt just fit a well-known pattern. Any other time I came close to "getting it right" it was because one of several scenarios roughly looked like what actually happened, not because I managed to predict something.

For practical purposes, and from an ordinary human perspective, the future has not been written. It is a range of possibility, broader or narrower depending on inherent contextual volatility and how far out we look. We are aiming for a sense of possibility, not at estimating specific outcomes. In any case, prediction is only borne out after the fact. Before that, we still need to plan for the possibilities.

The basic objectives of scenario analysis are to:

- understand roughly how much more or less fragile or complex the country could become in the assessment period (approximately three years but it varies, as we discuss later);
- understand the outside possibilities, in particular how bad things could get;
- provide some warning of significant, systemic changes to enable early adaptation or avoidance;
- enable the operation to plot a path to adaptation to new environmental pressures (this path would be updated in subsequent analyses and incrementally adjusted based on monitored changes); and
- last but not least, to frame the host environment in a wider temporal setting, thereby increasing contextual awareness and intrinsic understanding.

There are different ways of meeting those objectives using scenario analysis. The basic scale is from "back of the envelope" doodling to mathematical correlations of change variables and a selection of relevant permutations. Assessed retrospectively, the back of the envelope method can be just as effective as the Excel-heavy mathematical ones, but just because it is done quickly and without much fuss, it does not mean that it involves a flash of brilliance or dumb luck. When someone has been intensively looking at an environment, there has been much thinking well before someone gets around to explicitly doing an analysis. In fact, much of the analysis has been done by that point. One problem with both extremes on the scale is that they are rather opaque to intelligence users. Both are a kind of black box that spits out an answer. Users tend not to like black boxes, because they like to see the logic behind results. The approach here is more on the side of the well-informed doodle. However, it unpacks what really goes on in that process so that we can critically watch our own thinking, and so that intelligence users can see how we worked or even partake in the process. This will be similar to other, more standardised, approaches, but in practice scenario analysis methodology is often eclectic and tailored, and this is too.

The approach is depicted in Figure 10.1, and each step will be briefly introduced.

The first step is scoping. Scenario analysis can be applied to different levels of questions, from broad (e.g., how a country could change) to narrow (such as whether and to what extent a government might be sanctioned). Broad scopes are fine but they still need boundaries so that we focus on relevant variables, and hence the question needs to be clearly framed. So does the time frame, because there is a big difference between trying to foresee the next few years and looking out a decade or more. The number of relevant variables dramatically changes. One can see this step as defining a clear brief, without which there would be considerable meandering, and fuzzy results later on.

Next, we need to decide what matters to the question, in the relevant time frame. We revisit the wider socio-political system from the context and focus stage, and, having much more information by now, fill in the blanks within its components. This forms the full menu of factors. We then map how the current system works to see what dynamics are behind change and change pressures. Finally, from ideas and hypotheses we apply a basic screening to decide on the factors that we will use as the lynchpins in scenario construction. We will not ignore other factors in the system. They will be part of the storylines too, whether directly or as context, but the lynchpins, or "swing variables", would be the most direct change drivers in the time horizon.

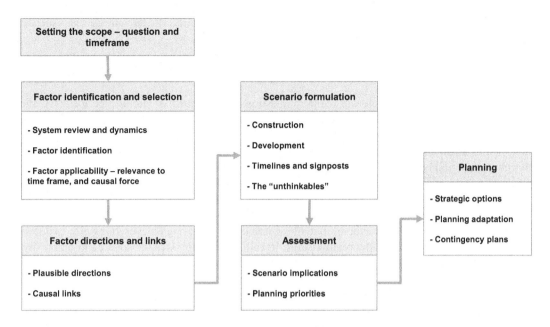

FIGURE 10.1 Scenario analysis process.

At this point, we see how each selected factor could move. For example, a factional rivalry could be resolved, or get more intense, or lead to a purge or coup, or a regulatory regime might or might not become more stringent. The directions are based on our understanding of the situation and are at least conceivable, but we keep an open mind. Then we map the relationship between factors and their different change directions to see what combinations are causally linked and compatible, so that when we construct scenarios, we develop internally consistent plots.

Formulating scenarios starts with rough construction, testing plausible combinations of factor movements to see what broader stories could emerge. The construction step can be an iterative, trial and error process, and it is seldom neat and tidy, but it yields the bare bones of our scenarios. Next, we decide how to integrate the different possibilities and which permutations to select, and develop these into coherent plotlines, which are our main scenarios. To enable later monitoring and warning, we then lay out each story in sequence and in time, and peg observable events or actions to different plot twists, giving us signposts of a scenario's emergence. We also go beyond the main scenarios and formal process, giving more rein to informed imagination to see how bad things could get. The results are the "unthinkables", and in many cases once we derive these, they no longer seem so farfetched. We do not integrate the unthinkables with our main scenarios, but we make sure that they sit visibly alongside them so that intelligence users keep a wary eye on them from time to time. They are like a shadow that could be nothing, or which could be a big spider hanging down from the ceiling. Now and then we feel compelled to go and check.

Scenarios are not assessed for plausibility or probability, since they are highly uncertain by definition, and if we prioritise by likelihood, we risk incurring surprises. But they can be assessed for general implications, and their effects can be compared with the results of other stages in the baseline exercise for a sense of how much better or worse they could make things for the operation.

Planning does not involve detailed programmes, since any given scenario might not play out, or not precisely as it was defined. Scenarios together suggest a range of possibility, and in fact that is precisely what we were looking for, not exact future states and pathways to them. Thus, rather than fine-tuned planning, scenario planning indicates the options that the company should develop and keep open at least until relevant uncertainties clarify, how political risk management efforts might need to shift over time, and some key contingencies that need to be planned for.

We will now examine the steps in the process, starting with scoping. Again, our two cases are the basis for illustration.

SCOPING

There could be a number of relevant scenario questions in political risk intelligence for a specific country operation. Bottom-up instability, regulatory developments, a conflict, relative preference for Western versus Chinese investment, and the shape and policy direction of a future ruling coalition, just as a few examples, could all be subjected to scenario analysis. The process presented in this chapter should be regarded as adaptable to a range of dynamics, and scenario exercises on specific questions could be undertaken as the need arises during an operation. However, as part of the baseline intelligence exercise, a big-picture focus is more useful. Terrain and stakeholder analysis already covered a number of specific dynamics. What we are still missing is a sense of how the whole ground might change or evolve. If and how it does has a bearing on everything else to different degrees, including stakeholder relationships. Recall that fragility was the source of complexity, and complexity was the main source of potential problems for an operation. When we say the big picture, we really mean potential new degrees of systemic fragility.

Given the breadth of the question, framing it can be a challenge. Fragility, to reach back to Chapter 2, was a country's propensity and proximity to state failure, which is a total breakdown of governance, law and order, and social cohesion leading to the outer limit of "politically risky". It is our interest, but it is a rather expansive and abstract concept. We can take a step back from it and borrow a page from old school foreign intelligence. Therein, the question might be framed around instability, using the term in its broader sense of unrest, violence, incohesive leadership and a general increase in the potential for major socio-political discontinuity. CIA assessments on Iran in the 1970s, for example, focused on instability, and the factors they considered included leftist agitation; religious, bazaari and tribal opposition; urban socio-economic frustration; the loyalty of the army; and the Shah's leadership and crisis management abilities (while the CIA downplayed the possibility, a revolution was among their scenarios). Instability in its general sense means the same thing as fragility, but it has a somewhat more common sense and concrete meaning, and for that reason it forms a better analytical target. We do not need an explicit benchmark of current instability to assess it, because from previous analyses we know where the situation stands and we are not doing country comparisons. Thus, our question is about how and to what extent the country could move from its current degree of instability (or stability, but we already know that both case countries are not exactly paragons of robust, well-functioning states).

The degree of instability will not always be a useful framing question. It is almost always relevant to the "complex emerging" bracket of countries, as discussed in Chapter 2. But if we move towards the less fragile and less complex, other questions might be more appropriate for a consideration of the overall degree of difficulty for an operation in a country. For example, in China instability is an issue, because there are some serious economic challenges and a contradiction between heavy-handed rule and the innovation needed for sustainable growth. But the regime is firmly in control and the country is still undergoing a shift to higher living standards. Thus, if one were only looking at the next three to five years, a better focus for an international company might be the business environment itself, for example how more or less state-dominated the economy will become, and the position of, and effect on, FDI. If we shoot far enough out, instability is a useful question, but for some places it could take a while to be relevant. In complex emerging markets, which are already at least somewhat shaky as socio-political entities, it is usually relevant even in the relatively near term.

With the above, we already entered into the second question in scoping, time horizons. Consider the two illustrations in Figure 10.2.

As the top diagram shows, the range of possibility increases over time, and this is true for any country. We cast our gaze out to between 1 year and 18 months in the rest of the baseline exercise. We can see that far, and while there could be major upsets in that time frame, we at least have a

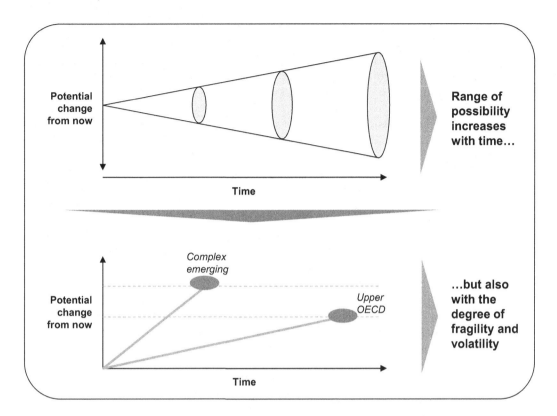

FIGURE 10.2   Calibrating time horizons.

strong sense of what they could be. If we go out a bit further, the possibilities open up somewhat, and if we were to list possible future states, there would be a couple of distinct conceivable ones. Going out further, it gets harder to say using just the facts and insights on hand. We need to decide how far out we can project and still have a reasonable idea of what could happen. If we aim too near, the exercise would not be very useful because it would just tweak terrain analysis. If we aim too far, it gets too speculative. But what exactly is too near and too far?

Now consider the lower diagram in Figure 10.2. Whether a certain time horizon is just a tweak or a stretch depends on volatility in the given environment or situation. If I projected three years ahead for an analysis of Canada, it could be a waste of effort. The country is so institutionalised, and institutions so solid, that most political change happens by and within known rules and is therefore incremental. Even if a major economic crisis occurred, absolute scarcity would probably not be an issue for most people, and hence the crisis would not drive violent resource competition or a breakdown in social relations. Canada has its own nationalist populist tendencies, and they are affecting social relations, but the country is so pluralistic that the effects are watered down by other axes of affinity. In political risk terms, it is a relatively boring country, and one would have to look quite far out, perhaps into speculative realms, to develop a significantly different state, or situation, from what exists now.

Now consider Lebanon, where even two years is a long time. In this case, it could be a waste of effort to project much longer than that, because the situation is so fragile that a number of significant changes could happen. It could be dragged into the Syria conflict even more than it has been, experience a renewed civil war, undergo a revolution, conceivably be invaded by Israel again depending on Hezbollah's perceived need for legitimising conflict and Israel's response, and it could remain teetering on the edge of all of these. Thus, the meaning of time depends on the pace of events, a factor of volatility, itself largely a product of fragility. When we calibrate time horizons, it is not absolute time that matters, but time in relation to volatility.

When introducing the baseline exercise, we already casually proposed three years as a time horizon for scenario analyses of complex environments. For both case countries, broadly represented by hybrids of Benin, Burkina Faso and Nigeria on the one hand, and Egypt and Algeria on the other, three years is probably appropriate, but it is worth being aware of the logic behind this choice. Two, four or five years could be appropriate in other cases. It is also possible to do longer-term projections, say of ten-plus years, just to explore a wide range of possibilities, but in complex environments this is more useful as a way to stretch the limits of one's own mindset than for planning purposes, since there would likely be a number of unforeseeable, significant twists and turns.

There are two other considerations in defining time horizons. One is the operation. We would not project beyond its duration, and it can be useful to align time horizons with a certain operational phase, if it is distinct in terms of exposure and socio-political profile. The other is significant planned or scheduled events or milestones in the host country. Elections, planned power transitions, ascension to regional blocs or alliances and leadership anniversaries of controversial presidents are examples. If our posited time horizon fell just short of such a planned event, we could stretch the horizon a bit to so that we do not miss a potentially relevant variable. However, if we had a reasonable time frame in mind based on inherent volatility, we would not stretch it by more than a few months, or the results would be too speculative. The effects of a given event could be assessed separately closer to the time of it happening, or, because scenario analysis is done on a rolling basis along with the whole baseline exercise, we could just cover it the next time around.

From the above considerations, we have our brief:

> How could overall stability in the country change in the next three years, what are the processes by which it could change, and what could the socio-political situation look like?

That is quite broad, but we already went into detail in the previous stages, working with relatively solid insights to see what specific changes and actions could occur within the observable horizon. Our interest now is actually how the bigger picture could evolve. This will add a sense of vision and give us a reasonable range of possibility in terms of the overall degree and forms of difficulty in the environment.

FACTOR IDENTIFICATION AND SELECTION

We have our scope, and now it is time to decide what factors are relevant to instability within the scenario time frame. As a preliminary note, we are back to using "factor", a nearly ubiquitous word in analytical methodology but which can mean different things. In terrain analysis, it meant a particular dynamic or behaviour that we might intersect with and which, in intersections, could cause challenges. Here it is similar, but what it affects is not us, at least not directly; rather, it is the wider socio-political system. We could also say "variable" and will use the terms interchangeably from time to time.

In this step, to briefly reiterate, first we lay out the full menu of factors, plugging our insights from the previous analytical stages into the socio-political complexity system model to flesh out its components. Then we see how the current system operates, using a top-level system map for an idea of what factors are causing the most change pressure on the system. These both give us ideas on factors relevant to instability in the given time frame. We screen these according to causal force, in other words their power to affect other parts of the system, and variability in the time frame, since we are not interested in things that will probably not change much within three years. This gives us our scenario factors.

We start with the full menu of factors within the socio-political system, not just the core one, but the wider system of complexity that includes external and long-term influences. Figure 10.3 is a reminder of the shape and components of the system.

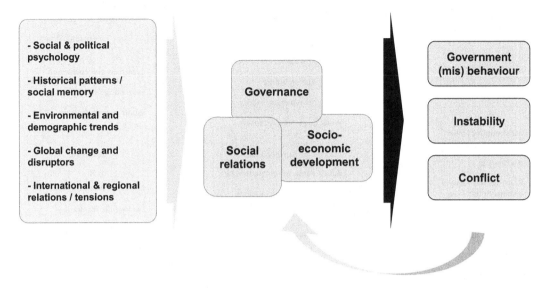

FIGURE 10.3   Socio-political complexity system.

In the context and focus stage, we derived a picture of the country's system to help identify relevant factors and to provide the forthcoming analysis with some background context. But we had not done much research at that point. Having completed terrain and stakeholder analysis, we can return to this picture and fill in actual dynamics in each element. An example is depicted in Figure 10.4 on the next page, using the county from the West African highway case.

For purposes now, we can call each bullet in this menu a factor. The specific factors herein probably speak for themselves after the last few chapters. In any case, this does not need to be a perfect explanation of how the system works. It just gives us a menu of possibilities. Some factors in Figure 10.4, such as ethnic tensions, seem to occur several times in different ways, but that is simply a reflection of systemic interaction. Factors often coalesce with other ones to produce particular dynamics.

We have the full factor menu, but to see what could be driving change in the relevant time frame it helps to see the sources of change pressure in the current system. A top-level system map provides the necessary perspective. In a system map, the factor links could have arrows to show the direction of causal pressure, but in practice there is often some bi-directionality and different degrees of causal force, and in our examples we leave arrows aside for the sake of visual parsimony. It can be useful to depict them, though, and in a real intelligence case there is ample whiteboard space or large sheets of paper to work with. We will start with the West African case country. Its system map is depicted on the following page in Figure 10.5.

It can take several iterations to get a system map more or less right, not so much in causal linkages but in visual fit and spacing. These are working models, though, not end user "deliverables", and one should not worry about visual appeal.

The map reveals some important causal relationships relevant to the next few years. For example, presidential authoritarian tendencies, and the rivalry with the military faction (MF) are directly linked. The president's aspirations to personal rule are partly driven by his near-term perception of the threat from MF, and conversely MF is vigilant because of its fear of a full presidential takeover. One should keep an eye out for "doom loops" or "spirals of doom" in system maps. These exist when factors keep enforcing negative behaviour in each other until eventually, if the causal chain is unbroken, they culminate in a significant discontinuity and a jump towards greater fragility. For example, we can see one in the relationship between socio-economic frustration, desertification and export vulnerabilities. Together these also contribute to ethnic tensions and insurgency, and

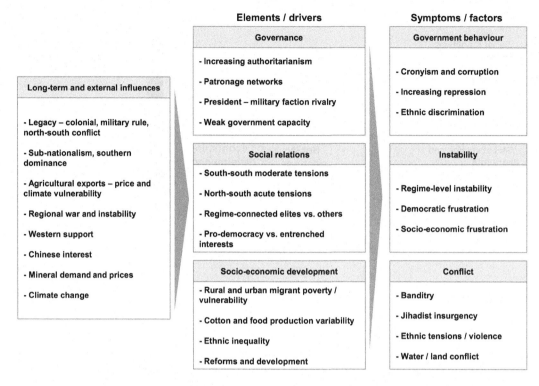

FIGURE 10.4   Full menu of factors, West African case country.

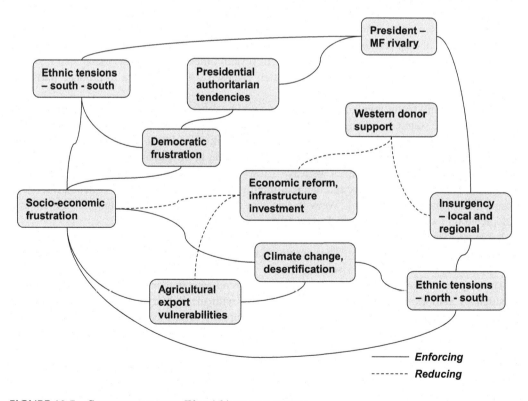

FIGURE 10.5   Current system map, West African case country.

to dissent. However, in this case there is an inhibitor on negative causal chains, economic reform, which is aimed at reducing agricultural export dependency, and at facilitating local and foreign business activity that creates at least some socio-economic improvement. We can see several factors herein which are causally important and quite volatile, but we will draw these out in the explicit screening process which follows. Before that, though, we will have a look at the other case.

We will not show the menu of factors, since the one for the West African case provided sufficient illustration of the idea. What is more interesting is the system map, or maps. As noted, the country in the IT consultancy case is a hybrid of Egypt and Algeria. This actually gives us two rather distinct possible angles on the case country, and the comparison is instructive. We will illustrate the system map that would be applicable if the country were more like Egypt, and then if it were more like Algeria. These are not based on research; rather, they are general characterisations to raise some useful interpretive points. The map for the Egypt-like variant is shown in Figure 10.6.

In the upper-left grouping, we see factors related to national governance. The country is a dictatorship, but not without a pragmatic aspect, driven by the executive's recognition that its legitimacy, and hence longevity, rests in part on actually delivering socio-economic development. Thus, there are reforms which help to ensure that hydrocarbons revenues are channelled to long-term development initiatives, and are grown alongside other sources of positive change, including FDI. However, looking again at the governance box, the president is not alone there, and both the military and the clans have some factional clout. Reforms, including a more transparent regulatory climate aimed at FDI attraction, might actually be threatening to these other regime interests, who thus far have benefited from preferential status in a rigged business game. We can imagine that this has already caused some factional machinations, and that the presidential clique faces some quiet but building discord. Other elements of the system also point to some pressure towards fragility, including a combination of socio-economic and democratic frustration, which is linked to the jihadist insurgency, thus far mainly confined to the Sinai but not for lack of ambition among insurgents. A defining aspect of

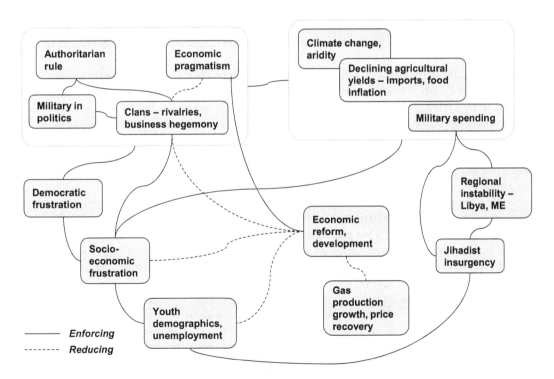

FIGURE 10.6   Current system map, Egyptian aspect of MENA case country.

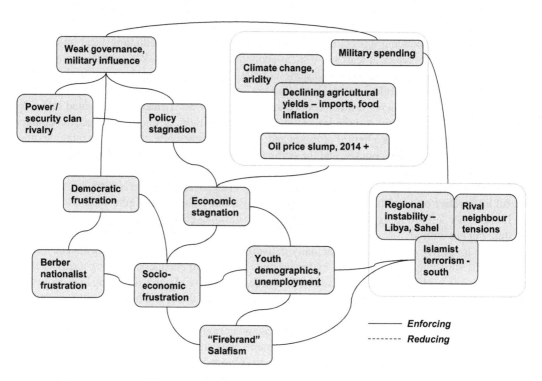

FIGURE 10.7   Current system map, Algerian aspect of MENA case country.

authoritarian rule is repression. The president has a balancing act between reform to ease frustration, and repression to contain dissent until reforms boost his legitimacy. There is considerable margin for error in this equation. Thus, we see several factors that are relevant to change in the three-year time horizon, including one, hydrocarbons-funded reforms, that actually slows movement towards greater fragility.

Now consider the map for Algeria-like variant in Figure 10.7. One thing to note is that if we only look at the current system, it is hard to explain why there has not been a major discontinuity, like a revolution or another civil war as in the 1990s. Going somewhat outside of the current system, some relevant factors would be lingering social memory of how bad direct confrontation was in the 1990s, and the Bouteflika period did at least start with some tangible positive changes to governance. But we can see a significant distinction from the Egyptian-type map, in that there are no "reducing" lines; in other words, there are no mitigators of pressure towards fragility.

At the time of writing, hydrocarbon revenues will improve as Europe tries to wean itself off of Russian gas, but unlike Egypt, Algeria has been highly dependent on oil and gas exports for decades, and price volatility since 2014 has played havoc with economic planning. The country would need several years of sustained price increases to make up for the slump years. Combined with high military spending (partly driven by a rather futile rivalry with Morocco), policy stagnation and the effects climate change, the economy is in bad shape. This has increased socio-economic frustration, which combines with frustration with fractious but military-dominated clique rule to create considerable bottom-up pressure. Socio-economic frustration also adds to the appeal of puritanical Islam. This helps jihadist groups in the south to gain recruits and risks a new insurgency in the urbanised north. One can see relevant factors similar to those in Egypt, but a critical dissimilarity is a lack of reducing or mitigating causal links. There are several doom loops in the Algeria-like system, and if this were the only basis for the case country, some scenarios deriving from it would hold some stark possibilities.

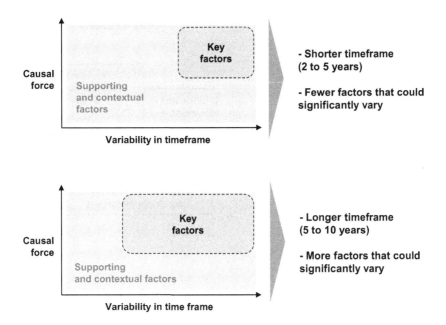

FIGURE 10.8 Factor selection matrix.

The system maps provide a useful schematic of factors, helping us to narrow down the search for those relevant to the timeframe. But we still need an explicit screening and selection step. In some scenario frameworks, the screening tool is the importance-uncertainty matrix, which indicates factors that are important to systemic change (or to change in whatever the target phenomenon is) and which could swing in different directions in the assessment period. For our purposes the concept is similar, but we can call the screening axes "causal force" and "variability in timeframe" instead. Casual force means a factor's ability to affect other ones in the system, and variability means how much it could change direction or intensity in the assessment period. The matrix is illustrated in Figure 10.8.

This step is where we explicitly, although broadly, consider how volatile or dynamic a factor is and the extent to which it could affect overall stability. There is no tidy formula for making these judgements. They will be based on intelligence from previous stages, team-based discussion and informed argumentation, and experiments with the system maps to test potential systemic outcomes based on changes in factor behaviour. However, we are only selecting factors to work with, not yet conducting an assessment. If in doubt, we can include factors on the margin, and their relevance will become clearer when we try to fit them into change stories.

Note the difference between factor selection for shorter- and longer-term assessments. For a shorter period, fewer factors will be lynchpins in scenario construction because fewer will significantly vary over a short time. For example, demographics, a long-standing regional rivalry, and country-level effects of changes in the global power structure might be excluded, whereas a certain acute rivalry, an ongoing conflict, or a reform programme could be selected. In the lower version in Figure 10.8, we have a longer-time horizon, and hence more factors are likely to change, going from context to being actual shapers of systemic outcomes.

Importantly, a factor selection process is not intended to suggest that unselected factors are irrelevant to the eventual scenarios. Note in Figure 10.8 that there are contextual and supporting factors. Without an explanation of how selected lynchpin factors became relevant or particularly volatile, the resulting scenarios would lack depth. Without a sense of how selected lynchpins impinged on less immediate factors, and hence on the wider system, a scenario would only be an assessment of the lynchpin factors, not of how the system might change. For example, a certain armed conflict might

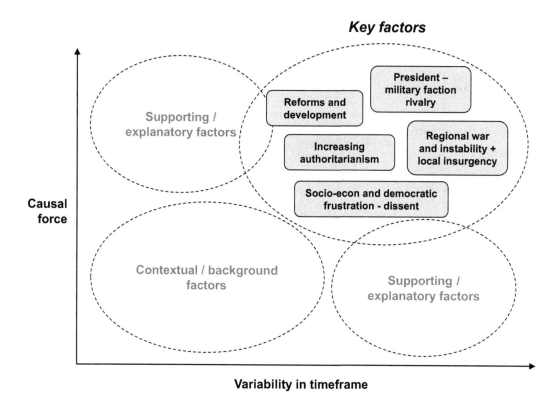

FIGURE 10.9   HERE: Factor selection, West African case country.

be a selected factor, but it stemmed from historical sub-national tensions. Depending on changes in the conflict's behaviour, it might accelerate long-term economic decline because of socio-economic disruption. That in turn would increase scarcity which could drive low-level, violent resource competition between groups not party to the main conflict. Thus, the lynchpins are connected to other dynamics which gave rise to them, and to factors which they would affect, thereby causing change to the wider system.

At this point, we can imagine that we have conducted the above exercise for both cases. The results for the West African country are presented in Figure 10.9.

It is no surprise that the president-MF rivalry is a selected factor, since it is a pressing issue that could move a number of ways within even a few months to a year. The president's increasing authoritarianism is also relevant, again because moves he could make to this effect could come soon and would affect dissent and MF's thinking about a coup. Reforms could be a longer-term variable, but we can assume that the current round of reforms, including national infrastructure development which gave rise to the decision to build a new highway, is quite recent and is intended to have near-term effects on jobs and growth. Regional, specifically Sahel, conflict and instability have been combined with the low-level local insurgency as one factor, since they are all closely related and together generate the risk of conflict spillover. For reasonable parsimony, dissent arising from socio-economic and democratic frustration has been aggregated, since there would be cross-effects and combined momentum in driving bottom-up instability and unrest. Thus, from a full menu of 30 factors, we have narrowed it down to 5 that could be change drivers in the three-year horizon.

Figure 10.10 shows the results for the IT consultancy case country, assuming a somewhat more Egyptian variant but with some Algerian characteristics (as we have done throughout our use of the case).

We mentioned how the president and his clique might face resistance to reforms from the military and clans. Power games were not relevant in the 12- to 18-month horizon of the baseline exercise,

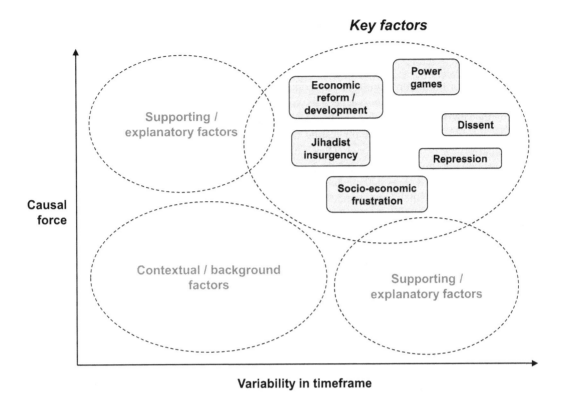

FIGURE 10.10   Factor selection, MENA case country.

since the president's control is quite firm for now. But since reforms could make factional tensions more acute, they become relevant in the three-year time frame. Reform itself is a variable, since it is aimed at having a near-term effect on socio-economic frustration. In this case, we kept socio-economic frustration distinct from overall dissent, because it already has recurrent manifestations. Dissent combines the socio-economic and political variants, given that socio-economic anger would provide the critical mass to a protest movement, while pro-democratic sentiment would channel it in a coherent direction. Dissent, as noted in the chapter on planning, is closely linked to repression. Repression is already a source of frustration and is likely to intensify if dissent gains momentum (this would form a binary spiral). Finally, the jihadist insurgency is relevant, because while it has been confined to a sub-region, its perpetrators aspire to extend activity to urban areas to increase pressure on the regime, and they would exploit any distraction or lapse to achieve this. The full menu for this case was not shown, but there were 32 factors in it, and this step has yielded 6 as lynchpins for scenario construction. Again, in both cases, unselected factors will still be a part of the stories, and if we had looked further out than three years, more factors would have been selected as change drivers.

We now have the factors with which to build our three-year scenarios, but we have not yet looked at how their behaviour could change, and how different directions of change could combine. We need to explicitly consider this before constructing scenarios, because as it stands we have our story components, but not a strong notion of potential plot twists.

FACTOR DIRECTIONS AND LINKS

At this point, we posit how factor behaviour could change in the time horizon, and see which changes are compatible with and linked to other ones. For example, the factor of economic development could accelerate, decline or remain static. Another factor might be a latent conflict that could flare up, get resolved or remain in a state of lingering tension. There would be a plausible link between the conflict being resolved and accelerated development, because the government could ease military spending and focus on socio-economic issues. Conversely, the conflict flaring up is not compatible with accelerated development. The economy would be damaged and the government too distracted for rational planning. A plot containing these two developments would be internally inconsistent and incredible. Thus, we need to work out what changes could be part of the same story, and how they could interact, before we begin scenario construction.

There are different approaches for testing factor relationships. Consistency matrices and cross-impact analysis are two common ones. They are readily covered in online sources and relevant literature, so we will not show them here, but the basic idea is that the relationship between each factor and its possible change directions is compared to each other one. Where factor behaviours are logically compatible, and where they have particularly strong causal links, the combination is highlighted for inclusion in a scenario. One can also generate every possible change permutation, and depending on the number of factors, a Monte Carlo simulation or similar computational method can be required. The art is then deciding which permutations to take forward as the bases of scenarios. Neither method actually tells us what the scenarios are, but they help in deciding what factor change combinations to use.

Another popular method is to form a matrix from two independent, in other words not causally related, factors. Each could go in two directions, for example better or worse, or more or less intense. Then each of the four matrix quadrants is the basis for a story, for example "the economy gets worse and the president becomes a full-blown dictator", or "the economy gets worse and the president commits to democratic reform". One pair of factors seldom suffices, and in this approach several pairings are usually done, and then the most plausible, or simply most instructive, boxes from across the matrices are assembled into different scenarios, based on the compatibility between them. This is a useful method, but one drawback is that it has only two directions of factor change, higher or lower, better or worse, or more or less. If there are several distinct directions for a given factor, it can require converting these into several binary possibilities, and one can end up with a somewhat unwieldy number of matrices.

The above methods are instructive, but one problem the author has faced when using more explicit, formulaic methods is that one loses sight of the forest for all the detail and mini assessments that need to be cleaned up and accounted for. When we already have a strong sense of a country's dynamics, sometimes it is useful just to gaze at a bigger picture and mentally test how the pieces could behave and how it could evolve. Scenario analysis is not modelled trend projection, after all, and at a certain point additional detail becomes mental clutter.

The approach here is conceptually similar to cross-impact analysis but tries not to lose the benefit of the contemplative gaze. Thus, rather than laying out factors and change directions in a table, we use a picture which allows us to visualise factor relationships and their potential wider effects. We can call this a factor relationship map for lack of a better term, and one is depicted for the West African case in Figure 10.11.

Each of the five selected lynchpin factors are shown, with possible change directions stemming from them. The change directions could be defined with more granularity, for example there could be a third possibility between conflict spillover and containment, or between low-level and widespread dissent. But we only need broad directions at this point, since when developing scenarios we will refine details for coherent plots.

At a top level, the map portrays broad factor linkages. For example, conflict spillover could impinge on the regime rivalry, because it would boost the military's relevance and standing, and if the president mishandled a response to the conflict, it could provide a pretext for a coup (as occurred in Mali, for example). The regime rivalry affects reforms and development, because it is distracting for the regime and it inhibits coherent economic policy implementation. Dissent is driven partly by increasing authoritarianism and partly by socio-economic frustration, and not only could it lead to

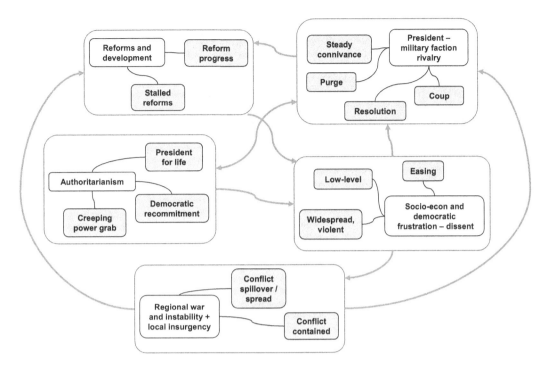

FIGURE 10.11 Factor relationship map, West African case country.

widespread protests, but among northerners an effect could be that membership in the insurgency has greater allure.

Below this broad level of factor interaction, specific factor changes and combinations thereof can be examined for linkage and compatibility. For example, stalled reforms and increasing authoritarianism are not compatible with easing dissent, since they would actually drive dissent. With the regime rivalry factor, if a coup happened, it would obviate the whole authoritarianism factor (which deals with presidential tendencies and does not refer to the character of any new military government). However, a presidential purge of MF as a change in the rivalry factor would be compatible with rising authoritarianism, and perhaps even with a recommitment to democracy. Thus, we can test each factor change against other ones to see which could, or indeed probably would, happen in combination, and which would need to be part of a different story.

An important thing to look for in the factor relationship map are potential wildcards. There is one in Figure 10.11, the insurgency and related regional instability. It has one arrow running into it, meaning that it is partly affected by what goes on in the immediate system, but if we used finer distinctions, then that arrow would be quite thin. The main decider of how the conflict factor might go actually does not lie in this system or even in the country. It lies in the Sahel, in the thoughts and assessments of jihadist commanders as they consider if and how to expand the insurgency beyond its current boundaries. We do not know their thinking in detail and perhaps they do not either at this point, but if they made it a priority, the war probably would spill over. This kind of factor, which does not depend on much else in the system, is known as a wildcard. When we construct and develop scenarios, wildcards could take any of their change directions in any given scenario. Thus, they complicate scenario development, just as they complicate real life for both governments and foreign companies. We do not have to play each wildcard direction in every plotline, but how and where they are played for instructive insight requires some judicious thinking.

Like consistency matrices and cross-impact analysis, the factor relationship map does not tell us what our scenarios are, but we know which changes are compatible and causally related, and when

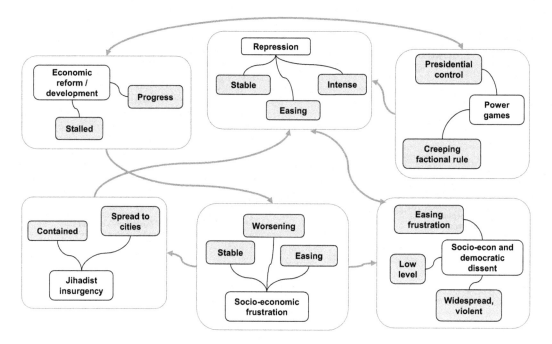

FIGURE 10.12   Factor relationship map, MENA case country.

we proceed to scenario construction, this will be critical to ensuring that we derive internally consistent plotlines. As noted earlier, we do not assess scenario plausibility, but taking account of compatibilities and causal links helps to ensure that the stories that we develop are not inconceivable.

The factor relationship map for the IT consultancy case country is presented in Figure 10.12. There are three noteworthy points about the MENA country map. One is in the factor of power games. The change direction of creeping factional rule was not a consideration in terrain analysis, but given potential elite resistance to reforms, it could become relevant within three years. We drew on prior intelligence to derive the power games factor and this particular change direction, but they are new and specific to our longer time horizon.

A second point in the map is the bidirectional arrow between dissent and repression. We already noted this combination. Where there is bidirectional causality, we can be aware that, like two orbiting neutron stars, there is a potential for some kind of culmination or jump which would be a significant subplot in the scenarios in which it features. Most revolutions, for example, involve the reinforcing interaction of dissent and repression, at least as one important stage.

Finally, we have a wildcard here too, and again this is conflict, specifically the jihadist insurgency and whether or not it extends to an urban terrorism campaign. If it did, it would probably increase repression as security forces sought to weed out urban cells, but there is only one arrow going into the factor, socio-economic frustration. Unemployed young men, as noted in Chapter 2, can become desperate for status and livelihoods, not to mention angry with the system that keeps them in purgatory. But otherwise, as with the West African case, what causes a potential move to urban terrorism is partly in the hands of people and organisations outside of the system. Although the insurgency is more or less home-grown, factions therein are affiliated with Al Qaeda and Islamic State, the leadership of which has some sway over the plans and capabilities of its branches. Even if state security is tight and prevents opportunistic attacks, if either umbrella organisation pushed for an urban campaign, then it could manifest. This factor change, as with conflict spillover in the other case, could happen alongside other factor change combinations because it is relatively independent.

We now turn to how factor links and change directions are applied in scenario formulation.

SCENARIO FORMULATION

This step leads from initial construction through to articulated scenarios. We begin with scenario construction, a somewhat experimental step in which we lay out scenario building blocks, namely factors and change directions, in skeletal combinations that cover a reasonable range of possibilities along the instability spectrum. This can be a messy step, and we are free to play with the number of scenarios and different combinations until we have some story outlines that we feel are reasonably robust and informative. Then we develop the outlines into coherent stories, taking wildcards into account, perhaps as variations on the main plotlines. In order to be able to foresee and plan for scenarios, they are then laid out in a timeline with an indication of how scenario emergence would look at different points in time, to provide signposts and warning indicators. Finally, we go beyond the main scenarios and ask what "unthinkable" plots could emerge, to give us a sense of the outside possibilities as a warning against surprise. We will walk through these in sequence, beginning with scenario construction.

SCENARIO CONSTRUCTION

There are different possible approaches to this step. The one used here is not sophisticated but it allows for testing and experimentation rather than just following a formulaic process.

First, we need an organising principle to guide thinking. If instability is the focus, then degrees of instability is an obvious principle to use. There will be a spectrum from stable to unstable, and our plotlines will fall along this. It also helps to have reference points or benchmarks. One that we can form quite quickly is a baseline, using a projection of current dynamics without much change. Then we can posit the outer edges of the spectrum, very stable and very unstable. From there, it is a bracketing exercise, seeing how the middle ground on either side could be reasonably parsed into stories that have instructive distinctions.

An example of this process applied to the West African case is illustrated in Figure 10.13 on the next page. This is not intended as a finished product, and even if it were, we would still need to deal with the wildcard of conflict spillover.

There are five skeletal scenarios in Figure 10.13, from A to E, and the baseline. The baseline is just a reference point, and we will not actually use it as a scenario. The "X" shows the application of a factor change in a scenario, and a question mark means that we are still testing whether or not that change would be useful in a given plotline. The instability spectrum goes from A, stable, to E, unstable.

Scenario A would lead to the most stable situation. It could be that the factional rivalry leads the president to democratic recommitment as a means to deter a coup, or democratic recommitment could follow a resolution of the rivalry and be driven more by anxiety about Western sanctions and criticism (note that this goes beyond the lynchpin factors, and we noted that these would not be the only ones taken into account). Either way, the regime moves back into the democratic fold and governance improves. This jives well with progress in reforms, which ease frustration. For this scenario, we have the wildcard of conflict spillover not playing out, because we are trying to explore the stable end of the range of possibility.

We then shift to the unstable end of the spectrum, E, to provide another reference point. This has the coup actually occur. The new regime is highly distracted by trying to secure its position. This along with at least limited Western and African regional sanctions bring reforms to a standstill, and indeed there is even socio-economic regression. Because of this, and because of the obvious leap away from any façade of democratic norms, socio-political frustration mounts and soon becomes widespread and violent. We thus have a situation of illegitimate and unpopular governance, socio-economic fragility and violent regime-societal contestation. Note that if we had a five-year scenario, we might project that Chinese investments and loans would rejuvenate development and that mining might start to bring in revenues. But those are probably not relevant to a three-year

Factor	Direction	A	B	Baseline	C	D	E
Regime factional rivalry	Steady connivance	X	X	X		X	
	Purge				X		
	Coup						X
	Resolution	?					
Presidential authoritarianism	Creeping			X			
	President for life				X	X	
	Democratic recommitment	X	X				
Reforms and development	Progress	X	X	X	?		
	Stalled				X	X	X
Frustration and dissent	Easing	X	X				
	Low level			X	?	?	
	Widespread / violent				X	X	X
Regional + local insurgency / conflict	Contained	X	X	X	?	?	?
	Spillover						

FIGURE 10.13   Scenario construction, West African case country.

horizon. The conflict wildcard shows up here as a question mark. A variant of this scenario would be if conflict spillover occurred after a coup, in which case political unrest would combine with armed conflict.

We can now start to fill in the middle ranges. There is only one between the baseline and most stable case, only varying from A in not having any prospect for resolution of the rivalry. Therefore, the rivalry continues even as democratic recommitment occurs. This is only a slightly less stable situation, since greater democracy would act as a deterrent against a coup, which would be all the more illegitimate if undertaken against an accountable government.

When constructing the matrix, there was originally only one scenario on the more unstable side between the baseline and E, but then it was found that this did not allow for a differentiation between a situation with a purge (by the president against the military faction) and one with continued rivalry. This was important because in a context of socio-economic and political frustration, a successful purge would at least obviate the chance of a coup and reduce the effects of discord within the regime. In C, greater regime cohesion after a purge could mean that there is continued reform progress, although given that we are exploring more unstable possibilities this was left as a question mark for now. In both C and D, which again are considering more negative contingencies, dissent was posited as reaching widespread and violent levels, but there could be variants in which it remains relatively contained.

The conflict spillover wildcard was left as a possibility for the three unstable scenarios, again not because it is directly linked to other outcomes in these, but because we are sketching more unstable stories and it would certainly complement those. It could have been played in the more stable scenarios too, but our aim is not to cover every possible permutation, rather to catch the range of possibility. Even in the more unstable cases, though, it is still only a question mark and represents potential variations of C, D and E.

Factor	Direction	A	Baseline	B	C	D	E
Power games	Presidential control	X	X	X	X	X	
	Creeping factional rule						X
Repression	Easing	X					
	Stable		X	X			
	Intense				X	X	X
Economic reform	Progress	X	X				
	Stalled			X	X	X	X
Socio-economic frustration	Easing	X					
	Stable		X				
	Worsening			X	X	X	X
Dissent	Easing frustration	X					
	Low level		X	X			
	Widespread / violent				X	X	X
Jihadist insurgency	Contained	X	X	X	X		
	Spread to cities					X	X

FIGURE 10.14 Scenario construction, MENA case country.

The process for the West African case country clearly shows that shaping scenarios is a dynamic and exploratory process. We could keep slicing finer combinations of factor changes until we have a numerous basic stories. However, as long as we have a few clear reference points for how things could go, it is enough to inform political risk management of how to at least partly "future proof" the operation. Additionally, having more than a few outlooks is impractical from a management perspective. We are not going to create plans based on every hypothetical twist and turn. We will return to how we derive specific scenarios from the above process after we have a look at the other case.

The same step for the IT consultancy case country is depicted in Figure 10.14.

We again started with the baseline as a reference point. In this case, we only have one more stable scenario, A. It sees reforms paying off in terms of easing frustration, and the regime feeling more confident as a result and, hence, easing repression. Jumping to the unstable end for another reference point we have E. Herein, elite resistance to reforms leads to factional power games that erode presidential control. This in turn leads to stalled reforms and worsens socio-economic frustration, which gives impetus to dissent. This triggers harsher repression, intensifying the spiral of repression and dissent. For the MENA country, conflict was a wildcard, but we decided to allocate it only to the two most unstable scenarios. Jihadist insurgency is more home-grown than in the West African case and more affected by socio-economic frustration, so there is some merit to this decision even if the variable is quite independent. Plus, we are exploring the unstable end of the spectrum, and urban terrorism fits well the more unstable possibilities.

When actually making the matrix, in the initial attempt there was only one story between the baseline case and E, but it was not enough for a reasonable range of variation. B sees stalled reforms and worsening frustration, but this has not yet translated into widespread dissent. In C they do, and this engenders more intense repression, kicking off the above-mentioned spiral. D is the same except for having played the wildcard of the insurgency spreading to cities. E is distinct from D in the fractionalisation of the regime, and this is where the Egypt-like case country starts to resemble Algeria prior to its civil war in the 1990s. One could add a scenario with creeping factional rule and no urban terrorism, but the combination of terrorism and incoherent leadership works because the latter would mean discordant and less effective responses to the challenge.

In conducting this exercise, the initial layout for each was the baseline in the middle and two scenarios on either side. How they turned out is a result of playing with combinations and finding that potentially instructive distinctions had to be examined. For other cases, the first layout we try might work, or we might end up with a couple of more outlines than we did here. The important point is that there is room to explore in this step, and that it does not have to yield tidy outcomes. We just needed the bare bones of our scenarios so that the next step, development, has a foundation to work from.

SCENARIO DEVELOPMENT

We have our basics, and now we can see what scenarios could form and then flesh them out. There is no rule on the number of scenarios that we should aim for. In more complex situations and with longer timelines, there tends to be more, and simple contexts and short horizons might only yield two. It is not entirely happenstance that we derive four for each of the cases, because in the author's experience four is a workable number. Five can be unwieldy, and three has a prominent middle ground that intelligence users often latch onto as the most plausible. There will be variations among the four to account for wildcards, and later in this step we also add the "unthinkables", but four main ones are a reasonable, if flexible, target.

Figure 10.15 summarises the four main scenarios for the West African case country. These only show a hint of story development but are sufficient for illustration.

The letter labels correspond to the skeletal construction plotlines that the scenarios draw on. Because of the fine distinction between the stable scenarios, A and B, they were integrated, and note that we used the earlier formulation of showing how a recommitment to democracy could happen with or without a resolution of the factional rivalry. C, stable authoritarian, sees the president coming out on top in the rivalry. We had question marks in the C column earlier, and in the final scenario

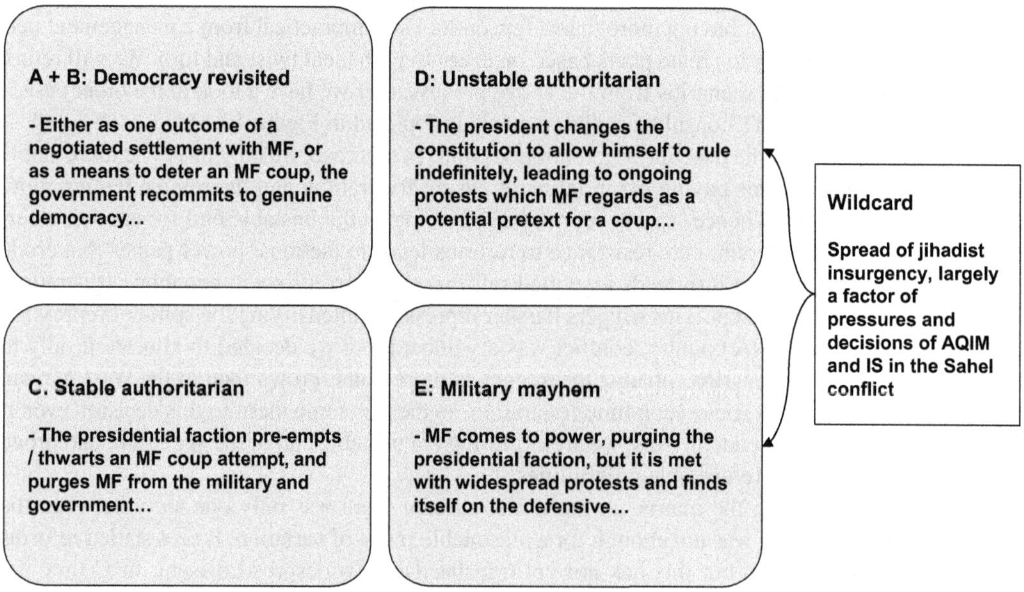

A + B: Democracy revisited

- Either as one outcome of a negotiated settlement with MF, or as a means to deter an MF coup, the government recommits to genuine democracy...

D: Unstable authoritarian

- The president changes the constitution to allow himself to rule indefinitely, leading to ongoing protests which MF regards as a potential pretext for a coup...

Wildcard

Spread of jihadist insurgency, largely a factor of pressures and decisions of AQIM and IS in the Sahel conflict

C. Stable authoritarian

- The presidential faction pre-empts / thwarts an MF coup attempt, and purges MF from the military and government...

E: Military mayhem

- MF comes to power, purging the presidential faction, but it is met with widespread protests and finds itself on the defensive...

FIGURE 10.15   Derived scenarios, West African case country.

we can imagine that we took a middle ground on these. For example, reforms are not stalled but they are not having much effect either. In C, we decide to leave out conflict spillover, because as it stands the scenario forms an instructive story of presidential control. D is a presidential power grab without the president having secured his position by first tackling MF, and this actually intensifies regime-level instability by giving MF a stronger pretext for a coup. Note how we do not have to resolve an uncertain situation in a scenario. An outcome can just be an even more hair-trigger situation. E is the military coup and subsequent unrest.

The wildcard of conflict spillover could apply to D and E. We would not need a completely different scenario for conflict spillover occurring. Instead, we would develop the progression up to the point where spillover impinged on other elements of the story, and then branch it out into two alternative endings. These might need to loop back to some other plot elements. For example, in D, spillover could weaken the president's hand in dealing with MF, and could even lead to scenario E, the coup, since it could reinforce MF's pretext. In E, conflict spillover would be a severe distraction for MF just as it was trying to develop its foothold in government. That would be destabilising, but we could also posit that MF might benefit somewhat from conflict, by blaming it on the ousted president's weakness and by using it to spur southern nationalist sentiment and allegiance to a hardline regime.

The four scenarios for the Middle East/North African country are in Figure 10.16.

Scenario A is the most stable one, with the technocratic aspect of the regime unhindered and yielding results, which lead to higher legitimacy. B contains a faltering of reforms and increasing frustration and dissent, but still sees the president in control. For this case, C and D have been combined, since the only distinction was urban insurgency. This distinction is then accounted for in a variation, again as an alternative ending rather than a separate story. Finally, E is taken directly from the construction step.

For both cases, the derived scenarios are not perfect and they could be finer. But if we look back to the scoping step and recall the "light cone" diagram and the notion of range of possibility, we have captured the range with credible stories. We are not assessing plausibility, but these are based on the intelligence that accrued over previous stages, and on judgements using that intelligence.

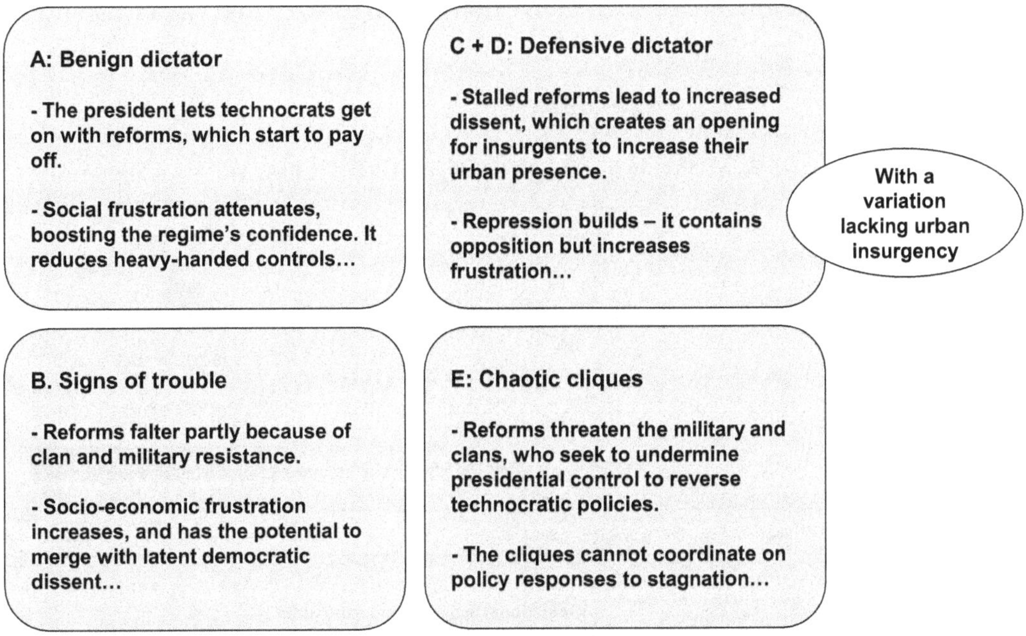

A: Benign dictator

- The president lets technocrats get on with reforms, which start to pay off.

- Social frustration attenuates, boosting the regime's confidence. It reduces heavy-handed controls...

C + D: Defensive dictator

- Stalled reforms lead to increased dissent, which creates an opening for insurgents to increase their urban presence.

- Repression builds – it contains opposition but increases frustration...

With a variation lacking urban insurgency

B. Signs of trouble

- Reforms falter partly because of clan and military resistance.

- Socio-economic frustration increases, and has the potential to merge with latent democratic dissent...

E: Chaotic cliques

- Reforms threaten the military and clans, who seek to undermine presidential control to reverse technocratic policies.

- The cliques cannot coordinate on policy responses to stagnation...

FIGURE 10.16 Derived scenarios, MENA case country.

Once we have developed the main scenarios, we can plot how they could unfold over time and what observable events and changes would mark their manifestation, to provide warning of their emergence.

TIMELINES AND SIGNPOSTS

In this step, we posit how a scenario would play out, in a time sequence marked by observable or at least knowable signpost events, which constitute warning indicators. Monitoring would keep an eye out for the general pattern of scenario emergence, and on specific indicators. If monitoring detected a shift towards emergence, this would trigger a tactical assessment to see what was really happening. Recall that we are using three-year projections. By the time indicators "blink", we would probably be further into the three-year period, and hence in a tactical assessment there would be greater clarity on relevant dynamics. The main point from this is that timelines and signposts are not the final word on how a scenario might play out. There is no way that we could know that from three years back in time. They only help to know when to look into the situation in detail, ahead of potential emergence so that the company can proactively plan for it.

With the above caveat in mind, we can see what a timeline would look like, using one scenario from the West African case, "unstable authoritarian", as depicted in Figure 10.17.

There are different possible depictions. This one is somewhat like a Gantt chart, with the sequence of events unfolding from top to bottom, each with an estimated time period. When we see a scenario laid out this way, it is clear that we would not be able to know an exact sequence or when things would happen. At the same time, it is not incredible. The sequence is causally logical, the timeline is based on an understanding of how similar patterns of change have unfolded, and we had considerable intelligence to work with. At a general level, it would serve its purpose of triggering a deeper look.

The signposts are the specific events that run down the left of the diagram. Some of these would be directly observable, and some would be widely reported in the press. Others, though, would not

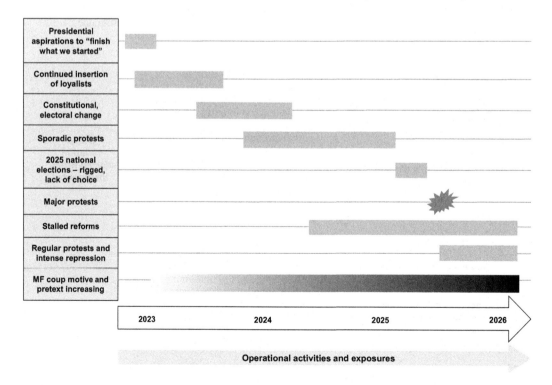

FIGURE 10.17 Timelines and signposts for unstable authoritarian scenario.

be readily apparent. The president's continued insertion of loyalists, an important indication of the president's intentions, would not be easy to track through open sources, and might only be revealed in conversations with people who had some insight on regime dynamics. Additionally, there is no way to see inside the heads of the military faction, although we could extrapolate their changing risk-reward calculation from what we learned in stakeholder analysis. Thus, not every signpost is going to be visible just by scanning open sources, and more in-depth methods might be required.

If the first few events in this scenario appeared to be playing out, the operation would intensify monitoring and conduct a tactical situation assessment for a nearer-term look at what could be happening. Assuming that it played out as posited, and that the company kept a close eye on the situation, it would be able to stay ahead of events. By the time the scenario got to sporadic protests, the company would be adjusting its operational exposures, especially of personnel. As we near the bottom of the sequence, a workable plan for at least temporary withdrawal would be on hand, as well as detailed crisis plans to address inadvertent encounters with violent activity. Thus, emergence, as indicated by monitoring, is linked to planning, which aims at reducing exposure in advance of harmful changes and dynamics. This approach is similar to one we used for contingent issues in the last chapter, although on a broader scale. Note the horizontal arrow at the bottom on the diagram. Broadly mapping the operation's activities and exposures alongside scenario emergence helps to visualise what would need to be covered in contingency plans and the actions they would guide.

We have the main scenarios, some variations on these, and timelines and signposts. In a calmer environment, we might be able to call scenario formulation complete. But especially in complex emerging markets, covering a reasonable range of possibility might be inadequate to prevent surprise. We now turn to the unthinkables, the outer, but still conceivable, limits of potential instability.

THE UNTHINKABLES

Even though plausibility is not assessed, the main scenarios were based on intelligence-led judgement, so they will be within the realm of plausibility. They are reasonable as opposed to seemingly absurd or specious. But the worst cases of political risk, and indeed national security crises, have involved things that were not reasonable, arising from weird twists of fate, sudden intensifications of what seemed to be mild trends, or apparently very irrational or uncharacteristically extreme behaviour. What was deemed unthinkable happens all the time in politics, yet instances continue to surprise. On this premise alone, it is worth prodding to see how strange things could get. Thus, now we extend beyond the realm of reasonable to see what possibilities could be out there. This is conceptually depicted in Figure 10.18 on the next page.

In both case countries' scenarios, there was one general pathway to a more stable situation, and three to less stable ones. They covered the range of reasonable possibility. Beyond this in either direction things get strange, at least according to the logic and insights we used thus far. There could be a somewhat miraculously improved situation compared to what we postulated for the more stable end of the spectrum. However, our remit in political risk is more about the darker possibilities, so we look in the other direction, beyond even our current worst-case scenario.

Deriving unthinkables is not a purely creative exercise. They might stretch the realm of plausibility, but they would still ultimately derive from the intelligence that we had on hand. Thus, we would not introduce entirely new factors or posit what intelligence tells us is simply not the case. However, where there was uncertainty and a high margin of error, we have some room to play. We can also look beyond the case country for similar situations elsewhere to see how they played out, since there are certain syndromes in the way that instability becomes acute. Elements of the Iranian Revolution, for example, have played out since in the Colour Revolutions and the Arab Spring, and the preconditions for military coups are quite similar across many instances. As discussed in Chapter 2, even wars and state failure seem to play out according to at least some common patterns. Finally, we do add in some creativity, not unbridled but free enough to surpass our preconceptions.

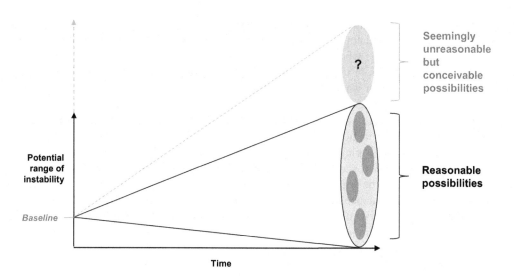

FIGURE 10.18 Looking beyond reasonable possibilities.

A failure of imagination is often the culprit when organisations incur surprise, and we do not want to make that mistake now. We might need to run through several iterations and tests, but again the aim is not prediction, rather it is providing an indicative picture of a certain degree of instability, in this case a high degree that goes beyond the old worst case. Assuming we conducted such thinking for the case countries, the results might be as summarised in Figure 10.19.

In the West African case, there are three possibilities. An insurgency and violent dissent could combine. This was a possibility considered in the main scenarios. A new one, though, is that either

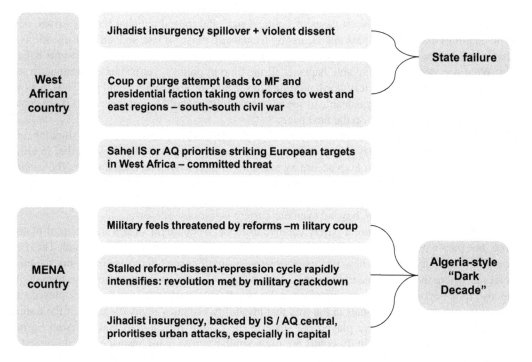

FIGURE 10.19 The unthinkables for the case countries.

an attempted coup or purge fails to yield a decisive victory, and both factions retreat to their tribal homelands and ratchet up tribal sub-nationalism to spur their own ethnic groups to take up arms against the other side. That might obviate dissent, which would be subsumed by sub-nationalist ardour, but it would be a clear opportunity for jihadist groups, and conflict spillover would accelerate. A south-south civil war overlaid with a north-south war would mean state failure. The country would be divided into warlord fiefdoms with much violence between them. What makes this seemingly inconceivable is that intra-southern friction is quite mild, but the situation would be unprecedented and we do not really know how southern sub-nationalism would behave in this context. A third, unconnected possibility derives from terrain analysis. This was the uncertainty around jihadist intentions towards foreign firms in the country. We now apply that uncertainty and posit that the insurgent groups in the Sahel decide to strike at Western companies in the region. Even without a major push to spread the conflict into the country, this could lead to sophisticated raids against foreign company staff and facilities. There is no indication of this now, but given the uncertainty it is not inconceivable.

In the IT case country, there might be a military coup, if the military feels threatened by economic reforms and pre-emptively acts to preserve its interests. Independently, there could still be a failure of economic reform, and growing frustration could coalesce with democratic dissent. The latter would become even more acute in the context of a coup, and a military regime would probably crack down hard. Because of the socio-economic impetus to dissent (which tends to add a very tangible sense of injustice), repression would just spur deeper anger. A spiral would ensue. If dissent were contained as street protests, there might be some accommodation in time. However, jihadists operating in sub-regions could see a chance to build an urban presence. We explored an urban campaign in the main scenarios, and it is an independent possibility. In the context of wider unrest, though, there is scope for a sustained jihadist urban presence drawing on frustrated youth for local recruits, and terrorism and guerrilla war could become a feature of urban life. Repression in this context would become pure state terrorism. The country would have reached the door of its own Algeria-style *décennie noire*, or Dark Decade, a period of intense and routine violence that caused many foreign companies to sharply reduce exposure. There are several uncertainties herein, a basic one being whether or not the military would ever break with the president, who was, and to a large extent still is, "the military's man". But this pathway and its outcome are not absurd by any means.

The main scenarios should inspire some broad forward planning. On the other hand, the main effect of the unthinkables is to induce awareness and ward off complacency. If we are alert and have a sense of how bad things could get, we can move a lot more quickly if we need to. If an unstable main scenario or variant thereof seemed to be emerging, a healthy question for tactical assessment is the potential for it to take the route to more extreme possibilities. However, even without indications of a main scenario manifesting, the unthinkables should remain on the radar, since they are not just about the degree of change, but also uncertainty about how quickly the situation could unravel.

SCENARIO ASSESSMENT

We have noted that scenarios will not be assessed for plausibility. This can vary. When the stakes are lower, say in a relatively stable context in which change might be more about the regulatory environment than state fragility, betting on a certain outcome and being wrong might only carry a moderate financial cost. In complex environments, there is a higher potential for surprise because of volatility and our own uncertainty, and the stakes are also higher. We could assess scenario plausibility, and it might well indicate that some of more dire outcomes are relatively implausible. The problem is that in many human endeavours and especially in business, positivity can make people latch onto good news and ignore or marginalise potential downsides. The historical fact is that when it comes to political risk, it is almost always outcomes deemed implausible that cause the most damage. In complex environments, the safest way to assess scenario plausibility is to monitor indicators and assess the situation as it evolves, not rate scenarios from three or more years back in time from the situation we are positing. Thus, while plausibility assessment is feasible, it clashes with an important political risk remit, avoiding disruptive and harmful surprise.

We can, however, examine scenarios to develop their potential meaning for the operation. We will not be able to develop very fine plans from scenario analysis, but if we understand scenarios' broad implications, we can at least posit future positions and preparations that the company might need to adopt, thereby enabling near-term decisions and plans to be made with an eye to the future.

Even though all of the scenarios are about degrees of instability, different pathways and situations could have different general effects. For example, we might have three scenarios for a country. One might posit that a demagogic leader comes to power and starts to chip away at democratic checks and balances, and "customises" the rule of law to favour his allies. In this scenario, his rule might be secure for the scenario period because he is still riding his initial wave of popularity, but corruption and legal ambiguity could increase. Another scenario might point not only to an ambitious economic reform programme but also to continued institutional weaknesses that would make programme implementation messy and confusing, especially for a foreign company trying to operate there. A third scenario might posit an uptick in violence, for example an increase in urban terrorism or a border war with a rival country, but include a subplot about progress in regulatory reform and an FDI attraction initiative. Thus, scenarios are not just about a general increase in fragility, and there is some, albeit general, grist for tailored planning.

A basic but still informative approach would be to broadly compare how the effect on the main operational assets, plus relationships, would vary between the baseline situation, as assessed in terrain and stakeholder analysis, and the scenarios. Figure 10.20 illustrates the idea.

The variants in Figure 10.20 are not drawn from the cases and are only illustrative. The top scenario is towards instability, and at its heart is the basic equation of a regime losing legitimacy, facing dissent, and cracking down, thereby risking an intensification spiral. We will not develop the story in detail, but as with most cases of increasing unrest with a potential for violence, the two most

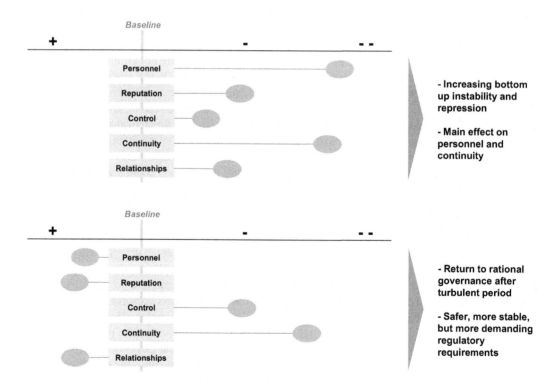

FIGURE 10.20 Scenario effects on baseline implications.

affected assets are people and continuity. The overall implications for these assets significantly vary from the baseline, which had a 12- to 18-month outlook. Assuming that these assets faced low to moderate exposure to violence and disruption in the baseline, this is a dramatic increase. If the scenario emerged, it would necessitate more intensive efforts to safeguard both assets and a workable exit and evacuation plan. Note that we also have relationships listed with the core assets. It could be possible to get a sense of how a company's overall standing with key stakeholders would be affected in a given scenario. For example, if a nationalist populist leader came to power and hyped rhetoric about exploitative foreign companies, an operation could expect cooler relations with bureaucrats who needed to show some adherence to the party line.

The bottom scenario is towards greater stability. While examining improvement scenarios is not our priority in political risk, it is a useful contrast for illustration. In this case, governance becomes more coherent and rational, but in taking development more seriously, the government has a hard look at FDI as a potential source of additional public revenue and skills transfers. Thus, while the prospects for personnel safety, a reputation for ethical performance, and legitimate relationships improve, control is more affected by higher obligations to work jointly with domestic players, and continuity by increasing bureaucratic hurdles arising from development-centric business regulations. Planning adaptation would therefore focus on these two assets.

Another, more nuanced exercise to understand scenarios' general implications is to see how both matrices from earlier assessments might shift in a given scenario. Recall that these were the plausibility-implications matrix from terrain analysis, and the attitude-influence one from stakeholder analysis. We can imagine that a given scenario manifested and then see how assessed positions on both matrices could change as a result. This is depicted in Figure 10.21 in conceptual terms, using the plausibility-implications matrix for illustration.

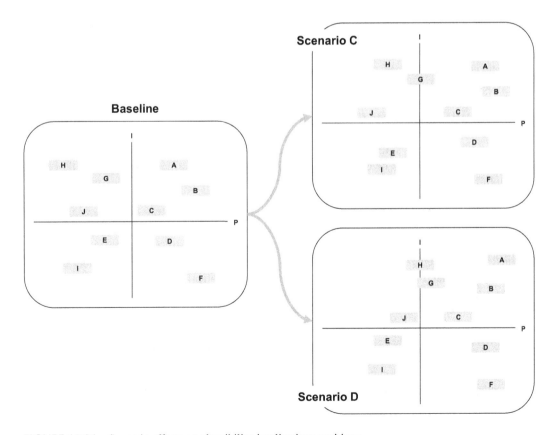

FIGURE 10.21   Scenario effects on plausibility-implications positions.

Assuming that scenarios C and D in the above were towards instability, we can see how some challenges would shift position, both in plausibility and in implications. For example, if we did this exercise for the West African highway case, and applied the scenario of "unstable authoritarian", a coup becomes much more plausible than in the current assessment. In the "defensive dictator" scenario for the MENA case, repression becomes much more intense. The plausibility of staff detentions increases, as do the implications in a given incident; for example, they might go from imprisonment to torture and disappearance. Some challenges might be obviated by a scenario, but the movement of those that would persist can indicate how political risk management might need to shift emphasis in the future. When we try the experiment with the stakeholder matrix, we might see a change in the relative status of supporters and opponents of the operation. This could indicate that the company might have to develop new relationships to maintain a workable level of socio-political acceptance or adapt to a significant change in the balance between stakeholder support and hostility.

The above exercises are more thought experiment than assessment, but they provide a stronger sense of what a scenario could mean for the operation, and by extension how planning would need to adapt. We now turn to planning, which lays the foundation for contingent adaptation.

PLANNING

As noted, planning for scenarios will not be precise, given the inherent uncertainty in future projections and the fact that we can only develop general pictures of alternative pathways and outcomes. However, in any planning horizon, for example the 12 to 18 months of the baseline exercise, an operation can take several steps to prepare for general future alternatives. These can be summarised as developing strategic options, preparing for shifts in the degree and direction of political risk, and devising specific contingency plans.

Strategic options aim at keeping the range of choice open for the operation, so that we do not make irrevocable decisions and moves that could turn out to be inappropriate or self-limiting depending on how the situation evolves. For example, if one scenario sees a significant improvement in stability while others indicate a more challenging environment, one would not wholly bet on either direction. To assume an improved environment could lead to entrenchment, making it harder to reduce exposure and even withdraw should the negative contingencies manifest. Conversely, betting on the unstable scenarios could lead to failing to take advantage of an improving situation. Skeletal plans for both general contingencies would be developed, and as the situation clarified with monitoring, the plan for the emerging situation would be developed in more detail. Thus, when the direction of change clarified, one would be equipped to act on it. Until that point, neither option would be discarded. In practice, there would be more than just two basic directions to consider, but the options spectrum aligns with the instability spectrum. Stability calls for expansion or deepening roots, while instability calls for exit, and between these there are more nuanced positions which would eventually coalesce into the appropriate response to an emerging situation.

The next level of planning is potential shifts in the emphasis of political risk management plans outlined in the last chapter. Terrain analysis in particular, but augmented by stakeholder analysis, would have indicated which assets were most exposed to political risk and the types of pressures the operation could face. Above we looked at how scenarios could affect those assessments. If a scenario indicated that a particular asset, say personnel or business continuity, would become more exposed to potential harm or disruption, the plans aimed at safeguarding these assets would be augmented with guidance on how they would need to adjust if the scenario began to emerge.

If we add in the explicit consideration of a scenario's potential effects on specific issues and actors, planning augmentation could be even more nuanced. For example, in the "stable authoritarian" scenario of the West African case, the situation might be more stable and somewhat safer, but an emboldened, even exuberant president might feel increasingly inclined to intervene in the project and to press for cost decreases. This would affect the plan to deal with Ministry of Transport (MOT) interference, which would need to be adapted to address more presidential pressure via the MOT. It would also shape contingent bargaining positions in the plan to address contract pressure. Finally, it would sharpen the challenge of president-donor friction over democratic standards, and the company would need to prepare for how this could affect the operation. Thus, we would have an indication of how to adapt plans under different conditions, and a jump on actual adaptation depending on which change direction emerged.

Finally, we develop contingency plans. Contingency plans based on scenario analysis are similar in structure to those developed for current contingent issues, like the coup and staff detention in the last chapter. The main difference is that they address the rapid deterioration of the wider environment rather than specific potential events. For example, an "unthinkable" scenario in the IT consultancy case saw a rapid descent into urban conflict and violent unrest. It would need much more stringent staff security measures rolled out very quickly, and could even require a quick exit. Given the seriousness of the hazards in the scenario, and its unpredictable timeline, these measures would need to be primed in advance. We might not need an actionable contingency plan for a while, but we would need a skeletal version to guide the rapid creation of a detailed one.

A final note on scenario planning concerns the outputs that would augment plans from the last chapter. One would be scenario descriptions, with indicators and timelines, which would be added to the list of monitoring targets. Another would be synopsis-level, skeletal plans, both strategic and tactical, that would need to be developed in more detail if and when different scenarios started to manifest. There would not be much additional planning documentation, since any given scenario might not emerge, and detailed planning at this point would be too speculative to be useful.

We noted how scenario analysis could, and often does, precede the planning stage. Although somewhat unconventional, having scenario analysis after planning seemed to be just as effective, because the plans laid in the last chapter provide scenario-based plans with a clear reference point. The baseline, focused on the 12- to 18-month horizon, is the foundation of operational resilience for that period, but also the object of modification to account for potential emergent change and the outside possibilities.

The above concludes the scenario analysis exercise, but a few closing remarks are in order. Scenario analysis is a rather speculative exercise compared to what we normally associate with intelligence, and its results can seem rather specious. It is worth briefly revisiting its character and value.

There are subject areas that lend themselves to detailed scenario analysis incorporating trend projections and modelling. Sector or country economics, environmental change, urban demographics and market growth are examples. These deal with relatively discrete sub-systems that ride quantifiable trends. Stability in complex emerging markets is affected by quantifiable trends, for example in demographics and economics, but it is highly subject to accidents of history, human eccentricity, risk-taking decisions and the interplay of myriad social and cultural dynamics. Thus, positing specific alternative futures in detail is seldom feasible. Neither is prediction, if that is defined as successfully describing key changes and events from years back in time.

It is instructive that just in writing this book the fluidity and pace of events often challenged the use of "current" examples. Chad was mentioned in the chapter on complexity. Just after writing that brief section (which was adjusted), the president was killed and his son, a somewhat unknown commodity, took over as head of a military council. Myanmar was going to be an example of the military in business and of crony politics, then its coup happened and it regressed into another round of violent unrest. Ethiopia was going to be an example of ethnic tension, but soon after sketching it, the civil war broke out. Trump's remarkable last stand, the covid pandemic and its myriad effects on political systems, and at the time of writing the war in Ukraine, have all come to pass since starting the book, and have challenged any tidy summary of how the world "currently" works. These are only a few examples of the pace of socio-political change and how quirky it can be.

The above accounts for a justifiable hesitancy to invest too much confidence in the outcome of scenario analysis. Again, without periodically keeping an eye on evolution as it happens, the scenarios that we derive years in advance are not very accurate guides to the future. However, imagine heading to a new, complex country without doing scenario analysis. We would have numerous insights on the situation as it stands, but no wider temporal context. Without shifting our gaze ahead, we would see things change with no sense of what it could mean, and mired in detail we would be unlikely to notice when the situation was becoming significantly different. Thus, while we cannot predict the future, we can extend our range of vision and at least characterise, with scenarios, the range of possibility. The tangible benefits aside, a key intangible one is that in our own minds the environment becomes a dynamic, evolving entity. Inherent in this character is change, and with a sense of the directions it could take, we are far more capable of reading the signs and adjusting to the future. Surprise remains a risk, but its prospect is much reduced if we have a sense of what could lie beyond the observable horizon, and do not lose sight of fact that the future will eventually be the situation we are in.

BASELINE INTELLIGENCE EXERCISE CONCLUSIONS

We have one more chapter in Part II, focusing on supplementary intelligence exercises, but this chapter was the final stage in the baseline intelligence exercise, the heart and bulk of the book. Therefore a summary and some concluding remarks are in order before moving on to related topics.

We started with the context and focus stage, which gave us broad intelligence targets and initial hypotheses on the challenges that the operation could face. This brought together the socio-political environment and the operation, to discern the overlaps wherein political risk could manifest. We derived ideas about both factors and actors, but the most tangible output was terrain factors, which provided the focus of the next stage. Importantly, the context and focus stage allowed us to develop intelligence targets directly relevant to the operation, rather than having to test and sift through broad, generic targets in a hit-and-miss fashion.

Terrain analysis examined the intersections between the operation and relevant factors. Intersections were the ways in which the operation encountered socio-political dynamics and behaviours, and from which potential challenges derived. Some challenges were based on interactions with current dynamics and could manifest by degree. Others arose from changes and significant events that a factor could give rise to, and which would affect the operation just through their occurrence. After accounting for links and overlaps, challenges were assessed for plausibility and implications. The resulting raw prioritisation was adjusted using interpretive exercises that added nuance and a dose of informed common sense. Finally, we summarised the principal planning indications.

Stakeholder analysis was the longest and most complex step, and this is befitting of an exercise that gets to grips with intangible human values and behaviours. After identifying stakeholders, they were mapped into domains within which socio-political interaction was particularly intense and direct. Domains were examined for relevant patterns of interaction and their effects on stakeholder behaviour. We then had a detailed look at stakeholders themselves. Their interests and values were examined against the operation's socio-political profile to see what attitudes they might form towards the operation. Then stakeholders' influence, both direct and indirect, gave us a sense of their capability to act on their attitudes. Possible stakeholder responses were informed by attitude and influence, but also from a reading of how stakeholders typically acted towards perceived opportunities and challenges. We mapped linkages between stakeholders, to understand what alliances and rivalries could form in reactions to the operation and, for one of the cases, to see where the operation could find a secure niche. Finally, stakeholders were mapped by attitude and influence to provide a coherent picture of the stakeholder landscape, and we applied accrued insights to derive the main drivers of positive and negative attitudes towards the operation.

The next stage, political risk management planning, showed that intelligence did not just lead to background insight for rumination, but was the basis for tangible guidance to make the operation safer and more resilient, and to safeguard its legitimacy. Specific issues derived in the last two stages were aggregated according to the appropriate general management approach. Within these were core issues which formed the basis of a political risk management strategy. We then formulated initiatives for each issue. These ranged from more programmatic responses, to contingency plans and tailored procedures. We examined the involvement of different management functions in initiatives and developed functional programmes to guide departmental participation in political risk management. The same exercise for stakeholders yielded coherent stakeholder agendas and engagement programmes, coordinated by stakeholder engagement leaders. A holistic view of plans yielded a political risk strategy statement, and clarified trade-offs, resource allocation and timelines. It was noted in this stage that on-the-ground learning and functional expertise would lead to ongoing adjustments in planning, but that planning in the intelligence exercise was both a head start and ensured that subsequent implementation remained coherent and coordinated.

Finally, we came to scenario analysis. This could have preceded planning, but since the most detailed plans aim at the baseline period of 12 to 18 months, we kept planning close to the intelligence stages that covered that period. Scenario analysis looked beyond the current system to see what forms and degrees of instability could manifest. It yielded not predictions or finely tuned estimates, but characterisations of different possible future states and the pathways towards them. Although we could not expect any given scenario to arise as postulated, we still derived timelines and signposts so that intelligence users would be able to notice and track significant changes in a given direction. This stage augmented planning with a consideration of strategic options, potential necessary adjustments to baseline plans, and outlines of contingencies plans to accelerate any necessary adaption to a sharp deterioration of the operating environment.

With the results of the baseline intelligence exercise in hand, operational managers would be well equipped to optimise the fit of the operation with its socio-political environment, avoid unnecessary or inadvertent friction, and prepare to minimise the effects of significant hazards and discontinuities. Without this intelligence and guidance, problems would be more likely to arise, and each would be a surprise for which the company was ill-prepared, leading to the darker possibility that the company's own reactive mistakes feed into the issues that it faces in an intensifying cycle of entanglement.

The baseline exercise part of the book sought to unpack and articulate the thinking that really goes on in trying to derive and shape actionable intelligence for an operation in complex terrain. One consideration in writing this book was that while the field has many insightful works, very few of them extend to what to actually do and how to do it. There was a need to get our hands dirty, and to get into a level of detail that might have been painful at times, but which was sufficient for practical illustration. The use of the two cases was an aspect of this, and hopefully helped to show how the concepts and methods herein could be applied to real-world problems and very different operational and country contexts.

There is more to add, however, for well-rounded and actionable guidance on political risk intelligence in complex environments. The next chapter will discuss other, more discrete, intelligence exercises that might be required before or during a foreign operation. Then Part III will examine the intelligence practices and capabilities which underpin any political risk intelligence exercise.

From this point, we will mainly be discussing established concepts, issues and methods that are well represented in the relevant literature. That being the case, there is no need to regurgitate current thinking and practice. Thus, what follows is light by comparison to the previous chapters, and mainly draws on the author's own experience with, and perspective on, these additional strands to provide a somewhat fresh and practical angle on them.

As a final note, we have come to the end of our use of the two cases. We will still draw on them for casual illustration, but for the most part they have served their purpose as analytical grist.

11 Supplementary Intelligence Exercises

The baseline intelligence exercise covered in the last few chapters is how a company develops sufficient insight for effective political risk management planning for a specific operation. As noted in Chapter 5, it can apply to different circumstances, not just to country entry, but in all cases it works from a blank slate to build a nuanced picture of the intersection of an operation and its socio-political environment. It covers a lot of ground, but is not the only intelligence exercise that might be required for a foreign operation. The decision to undertake the operation in the first place needs assessment, and once the operation is up and running, it needs to be able to adapt to changing circumstances. Thus, for a fuller picture of political risk intelligence, we will explore some supplementary intelligence exercises. We noted in Chapter 4 that intelligence, as a way of learning about the world around us, can be tailored to address myriad uncertainties and problems. This chapter does not try to cover all the ways that it can be used during a foreign operation, but we will look at some of the more common applications which together form reference points in the wider array of possibilities.

We will consider five different exercises. The first is monitoring, which we extensively referred to in the previous chapters as a way to ensure that we kept track of, and adjusted to, changes that occur after the baseline exercise is completed.

Next, we jump backwards in the business decision sequence to consider feasibility assessment, the intelligence that helps to make confident decisions about whether or not to pursue a prospective country operation.

We then have a look at tactical, or situation, assessments, which can shed light on both particular spikes in relevant country dynamics and problems that the operation is encountering.

Conflict analysis follows. While this was partly dealt with in stakeholder analysis, it can be a specific exercise aimed at conflict sensitivity, or how companies can operate without making socio-political tensions worse, and ideally how it can even help to mitigate them.

Finally, we indirectly covered threat assessment in the stakeholder stage, which considered adversarial stakeholders, but as an explicit exercise threat assessment focuses on intractably hostile and predatory actors whose plans and behaviour need to be understood for effective security and resilience.

As a holistic, strategic intelligence process, the baseline intelligence exercise is a rather rare beast in political risk. By contrast, these supplementary exercises are established practices, and hence what follows will be introductory on the premise that they are relatively easy to learn more about.

MONITORING

Monitoring was discussed in terrain analysis, where it was a useful fallback when we faced high uncertainty in assessing a challenge. If assessment was hard to pin down, an issue had to be monitored because indications would clarify over time. We did not directly discuss it in stakeholder analysis, but its importance was implied when we examined contingent changes in stakeholder positions. In planning, monitoring was how we knew whether and when to escalate preparations for contingent issues. Finally, in scenario analysis monitoring was essential to seeing if a given scenario was emerging, and to inform estimates of the wider direction of socio-political evolution. The fact that we would do monitoring was indeed a premise of the baseline exercise, which we acknowledged could become somewhat dated prior to the next one. Thus, monitoring is a way to ensure that

DOI: 10.1201/9781003149125-14

baseline insights remain alive and dynamic. In practical terms, this means that we remain abreast of both incremental and significant changes, and therefore capable of adapting to keep the operation safe and sustainable.

We noted in Chapter 4 that there was a systemic relationship between monitoring and more intensive intelligence exercises such as the baseline one. In Western foreign intelligence agencies, from where much intelligence practice derives, there is often a number of intelligence cycles, from long-term and strategic all the way through to short-term and routine. These do not occur as separate processes. Rather, there is a cascading of intelligence targets. The apex is national objectives from which strategic intelligence targets derive. Strategic assessment provides the big picture, but images therein then become intelligence targets in their own right, and so on until perhaps even a given pixel in the wider tableau becomes a target. The smaller the picture, the more dynamic the scene, and hence the more frequent the cycle. Look at a country from a bird's-eye view, for example, and we will see some patterns evolve over time. Stand on a street corner there and the scene will change from one moment to the next. Thus, we have rapid cycles, in other words monitoring, within the larger ones.

Once monitoring is underway, it can actually influence the direction of strategic intelligence. For example, if I am standing on the street corner doing my routine observation, and see a truck drive past carrying a nuclear bomb, when the country was not supposed to have any, this intelligence reverberates back up the chain. The development would quickly lead to an intensive tactical verification exercise, which in turn could lead to an early launch of the next strategic assessment with revised targets. Thus, monitoring can indicate when our big picture is out of date and needs to be redone.

Figure 11.1 captures the systemic and two-way relationship and will be the basis for some practical considerations.

In our context, the main intelligence cycle is the baseline exercise, which runs every 12 to 18 months, and which, depending on the context, takes several weeks to complete. Issues and uncertainties defined therein form monitoring targets. Depending on target volatility and criticality, monitoring cycles could be shorter or longer, but they are all much shorter than the baseline cycle.

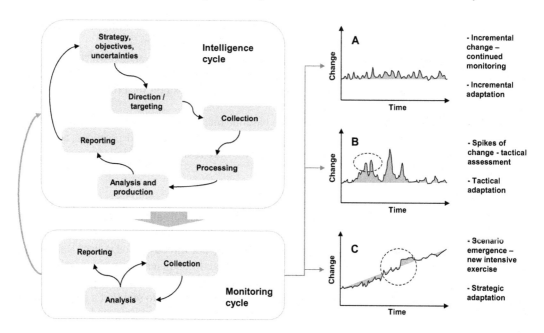

FIGURE 11.1   Monitoring within the intelligence cycle.

We can imagine that the monitoring target in Figure 11.1 is bottom-up instability which could lead to revolutionary pressure and a dissent-repression spiral. Chart A depicts a situation in which instability remains low-level, or nearly latent. We do not stop watching it, but the issue only requires incremental adaptation, for example avoiding certain areas when protests are likely to occur. Chart B shows some significant spikes in the manifestation of instability, for example large protest marches or major clashes in response to a particular scandal or unpopular economic policy. Monitoring notices the first round, and indications that there could be more. This leads to a tactical assessment looking at the drivers of unrest and what to expect in the near to medium-term. Based on this, the company takes proactive measures to reduce exposure until things calm down. In chart C, what at first seemed like minor spikes never really sink back to normal. Instead, they become a new baseline, and each time another spike occurs, unrest remains at a higher level of intensity. This indicates that an intensification spiral is forming and that a fundamentally new situation, or scenario, is emerging. The baseline assessment will need to be redone ahead of schedule to inform an appropriate strategy for this new context.

Notice in Figure 11.1 how the monitoring cycle differs from the main one. The baseline exercise covered in the previous chapters started from a blank slate. It had to scope what to look at (direction and targeting), collect information, sort and collate it (processing), analyse it, and then create reports and disseminate the results. Monitoring can rely on the groundwork that the baseline established to shorten the process. We know what to look at. Having specific targets, we do not need to gather reams of information that then needs to be sifted, and hence information directly feeds analysis. Assessed indications of change need verification and exploration, and directly become collection targets. A rapid analysis-collection sub-cycle forms. Standardised reports and briefings are issued through established channels. Truncated, standardised and highly focused, monitoring of any given issue is capable of keeping up with events.

Priority monitoring targets are factors, issues and stakeholders which present the greatest combination of uncertainty, volatility and potential effect on the operation. Most of these will be linked to political risk management initiatives or scenario plans, which can draw on shared monitoring programmes for insight on appropriate preparation and adaptation. In general, priorities receive more attention and more regular reporting. Less important targets can sometimes be tracked by proxy, in other words by looking at a few key factors that affect an array of specific issues. When this is not feasible, they will need their own focus, but monitoring can be periodic. We always need to bear in mind that less important issues could gain importance over time, and hence nothing that made it through the baseline assessment should be left to gather dust. Harking back to terrain analysis, issues that were assessed as having low plausibility but major implications should get much more attention than their raw severity rating would suggest. These are potential disruptive surprises, and an important aim of monitoring is to prevent being taken by surprise.

Reporting might need to balance a number of schedules and formats. Rapidly changing targets, like violence in a country experiencing conflict, might get 24/7 coverage, especially if we have staff working in locations where incidents recur. Policy or regulatory change, on the other hand, might only be reported on once a month or once a quarter. The full range of reporting, which is not uncommon for sizeable and more complex operations, can include the following:

- round-the-clock event monitoring in relation to staff geographic exposure, usually using a combination of spreadsheets and maps, or travel tracking systems that combine these;
- weekly or bi-weekly news-style reports for fast-paced targets, often with some general political news for contextual background;
- monthly to quarterly reports on more significant but slower-paced factors and issues, like government policy deliberations or the status of a long-running insurgency;
- ad hoc streams of reporting on specific issues of concern, for example a strike affecting logistics (or the company itself), or an impending election which could be divisive;

- stakeholder tracking using a system similar to customer relationship management but adapted for appropriate nuance (this is not very common but is useful);
- quarterly synopses of significant changes in the overall environment, and on the key differences between the situation "now" and as it stood upon completion of the baseline exercise; and
- importantly, incident reporting that captures staff experiences with political risk, for example security incidents and threats, instances of bribery pressure, and frictious stakeholder interactions.

Figure 11.2 shows a very top-level and general schematic of a monitoring programme, within which the above kinds of reporting would occur.

Figure 11.2 depicts only one target of each type just for simplicity, and the actual results of an entire monitoring programme would not fit together in one view. But it catches the notion of routinely tracking a number of different targets. There are political and security risk intelligence companies that use, and offer, integrated online monitoring platforms. These can be very useful, but one problem with over-relying on online systems is that they can replace human interaction and become seen as back office file-keeping. It is clear by now that monitoring is integral to political risk management and to warning in general. To ensure that it remains front of mind, the wider process should include considerable face-to-face interaction, such as mutual briefings, ad hoc workshops on the implications of specific changes and political risk management review meetings.

Thus far, we have mainly discussed monitoring in the context of change in the environment. However, there are two other aspects of it which are just as important, and often neglected in practice. These are the operation's political risk management performance and staff members' own

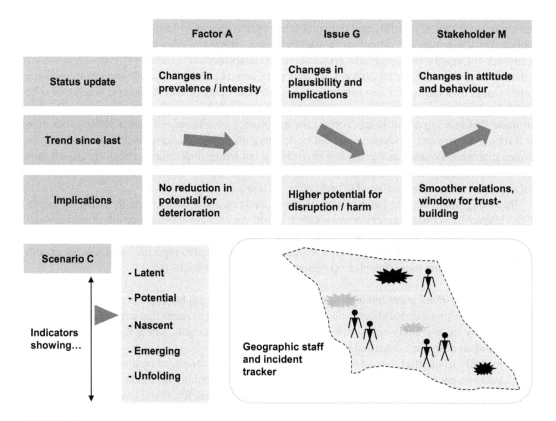

FIGURE 11.2   Monitoring programme.

experiences with political risk. Looking back to the planning stage, initiative task forces and stake-holder engagement leaders should scrutinise their own plans and activities to make sure that they are up to date and that causes of weak performance are discerned and corrected. Country or project management should periodically seek status reports and should pose some hard questions to chal-lenge any group thinking that might have set in. As for staff experiences, the author has found that quietly talking to people about incidents they have been through, the local relationships they have formed, and their perception of the operation and environment is indispensable. It not only sheds light on the actual status of the operation, but it can indicate problems that have gone unreported because of inhibitions or a lack of channels, and also concerns that are causing stress or depressing morale. This is not a whistle-blowing exercise; rather, it is just getting a sense of people's direct experience. People are the principal asset, and ultimately also the eyes and ears of the operation.

A final point is who does monitoring. Initiative task forces and engagement leaders could monitor targets within their own remits, and a monitoring coordinator could aggregate findings for access across the operation. Some operations even have a full-time intelligence coordinator or team, part of whose role is to liaise with external intelligence providers. Outsourcing monitoring to a political or security risk consultancy is an option, but while they might know about a country or region, they will not know enough about the operation and its relationships to meet the full requirement. Thus, if they are utilised, their roles should be scoped to support the company's own programme.

There is more that one could say about monitoring, but the above hopefully clarifies what it means and how it can work in a political risk context. It is integral to the baseline exercise, which is largely premised on routine follow up. The baseline exercise gets us off on the right foot, but from there, without monitoring we would effectively be living in the past.

FEASIBILITY ASSESSMENT

Feasibility assessment was discussed as one general role of intelligence in Chapter 4. In our context, this means understanding the potential effect of political risk on, or from, a prospective operation, so that we can make an informed choice on whether or not to pursue it. We noted in Chapter 5 how the baseline exercise itself could constitute this assessment, but that it would only be cost-effective when the stakes were particularly high. Otherwise, an intensive and nuanced intelligence exercise could be overkill. For example, perhaps sales or business development has discovered a potential opportunity in a new country, or the company is doing a scan of potential new regional service hubs. We do not want to be bogged down for weeks developing a nuanced political risk picture of a place we might not even bother with. Thus, here we consider some relatively simple approaches to checking feasibility from a political risk perspective.

As a preliminary point, we are focusing on early stages of an investment approval process, when the aim is partly to eliminate duds to save deeper investigation for prospects with better potential. Once a prospect shows promise and might really become a new operation, variants of the baseline exercise would become applicable in further assessment. As well, one can bear in mind that while we focus on political risk here, it would be only one strand of a wider assessment that would also look at market, financial and economic factors. Political risk, and overall risk, would ultimately be assessed against the potential reward and the company's own comfort with risk-taking.

We indirectly introduced one feasibility assessment method in the context and focus stage of the baseline exercise. This was comparative benchmarking. In that chapter, benchmarking the tar-get country against known ones helped to identify relevant factors. In this context, benchmarking can help to see if a country would be an acceptable location for a given type of commitment. As in Chapter 6, we can test the target country against known ones for a sense of how complex and risky the environment would be.

For a tangible reference point, the most complex country that the company has successfully worked in should be included. A nuanced option is to formulate the benchmarking criteria accord-ing to specific company concerns and red lines, and weight them if there is a sense of their relative importance. A challenge in formulating one's own criteria is standardising scores, and their meanings, when using different information sources and indices, but it yields a more customised perspective. Another, simpler option is to see how the target country compares to the benchmarks across different indices. For example, one could use the World Bank's *World Governance Indicators*, the Fund for Peace's *Fragile States Index*, Transparency International's *Corruption Perceptions Index*, Freedom House's *Freedom in the World* index and a commercially available "risk map" with an emphasis on security issues as a collective set of reference points covering different aspects of political risk. If the results of a benchmarking exercise were ambiguous or showed that the target country was not particularly challenging, then it would warrant further investigation. If the country were appreciably worse, then it might be time to call it a dud and look for better prospects, again depending on the potential risk-reward equation and the company's own attitude to risk.

Another exercise is testing the global portfolio of operations for overall political risk, and then using the output to see what the effect of a new operation would be on global exposure. If the new prospect could tip the balance into over-exposure, then the company could become vulnerable to strategic disruption. If, on the other hand, the company's current exposure was not particularly high, then it could have room to take on a challenging operation without risking disruption. Figure 11.3 captures the concept.

In this illustration, the company undertakes the mapping exercise and finds that it is actually more exposed to political risk than it expected, perhaps even well beyond its comfort zone. It decides to reduce the level of "acceptable" political risk for new prospects, so that only less risky ones make it to investment and implementation. Over time, the portfolio will rebalance, and eventually the company could become more adventurous again. New prospective Operation X is on the table. The company knows how important it would be, in terms of profit, competitive advantage, learning and the exposure of staff and other assets, but it does not yet know how politically risky the country is. Different brackets on the political risk axis are represented by benchmark countries. The new country is assessed against these, and Operation X takes its place on the map. If it ended up in the high political risk and high importance area, it would be unfeasible at least as it is currently conceived.

There are other uses of a political risk portfolio map. One is competitive benchmarking. We could use industry benchmarks for the political risk axis, with different brackets, from low to high risk, represented by countries where our major competitors are active. We might find that by comparison to competitors we are quite risk averse, and this could have implications for our long-term competitive advantage. It might also show if there is an opportunity to be more adventurous than the

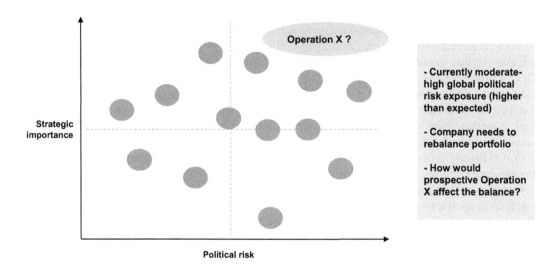

FIGURE 11.3   Global political risk exposure.

competition, using political risk management competencies to get a jump in higher-growth markets. The map can also be used for political risk management resource allocation. As part of one project, the author used variants of staff numbers (expat only, expat plus permanent local staff, all permanent and contracted staff) in different countries of operation instead of strategic importance, and then mapped the countries according to overall degrees of security-related political risk. Although there were additional considerations, the result was a top-level reference point for the allocation of security reviews and security management resources.

The strategic importance criteria for the exposure mapping exercise can be decided by the company, but they should include a notion of asset exposures and not just anticipated profits and other advantages. The political risk axis can be formed using standard indices or a commercial risk map, as in benchmarking, or the company could develop and model its own country political risk variables appropriate to its sector and types of operations. The security environment, governance as it relates to the rule of law and integrity issues, regulatory and legal stability, and political stability would be among the relevant components of a country political risk score, but there is considerable room for customisation.

As an aside, we have mentioned "risk map" twice in the above, and this warrants a brief clarification. Some security and political risk intelligence providers, business publications and political risk insurers update annual top-level assessments of political risk for each country in the world and then create maps with countries coloured by their political risk level, usually red (high) to green or blue (low). These can be very useful for political risk reference points, with two caveats. One is that they can use very different criteria. Some are more relevant to country risk (financial and economic), others more security-specific, and some are more about state fragility. Because of this, users need to know what went into a map's assessment, and any map should only be one of several inputs into a benchmarking or portfolio exercise. The other caveat is about quality. Risk maps from established advisories that have been tracking global and country trends for years draw on deep expertise and are backed up with explanatory reports. Risk maps from companies where political and related risk is not the core business might be done only using publicly available indices as inputs. These are more like snapshots and are not based on intrinsic understanding. They are not useless, but a decent one from a dedicated intelligence firm does not cost much and is usually a better option.

The final feasibility assessment method that we discuss here is top-level scenario analysis. The above exercises will use reference points that have a one-year projection, since most indices are updated annually. In deciding whether or not to pursue an operation, it would also be useful to know how the country might evolve during the projected operational timeline, or at least until it has paid for itself and earned some profit. We examined scenario analysis within the baseline exercise, and it was premised on the considerable intelligence that had accrued through the prior analytical stages. More top-level scenario analysis is feasible to get a sense of how the prospect country might evolve and how challenging the environment could become.

On approach is to project the current, or baseline, situation into the future, and then test it against plausible new shocks and pressures. Which ones are relevant would depend on the time frame. Longer-term forces might include climate change, global economic slowdowns and pandemics, while among shorter-term shocks could be a spike in regional tensions, a domestic economic crisis, or a major government scandal. A more resilient system would be able to withstand or contain plausible pressures, while a weaker one would edge towards fragility and a greater overall degree of political risk.

Another option is to develop and compare stories. Recall from terrain analysis how we tested plausibility assessments by comparing two arguments, one for and one against a challenge manifesting. A similar method can be used for a prospective operation. We develop two storylines, one of things going well, the other of entanglement and disruption. Then the plausibility of each is assessed. If the negative storyline is more robust, the prospect could be deemed unfeasible or at least potentially problematic. Company personnel might not know enough about a country to develop intelligence-based plotlines. Rather than dive into an intensive intelligence exercise, it can be efficient and sufficient to use a workshop format that includes both country experts and company managers familiar with the prospective operation. Managers can lay out what the operation would look like, and the subject experts can probe for its interactions with dynamics and actors in the environment. The team can then split into two to develop each story, and then rejoin to assess the stories' key assumptions and reasoning.

The above three feasibility assessment approaches are complementary and could be used in sequence. They are also not the only ones that would work. For example, another cost-effective approach is known as the Delphi method, named after the ancient Greek oracle. This invites different experts to answer specific questions about a country, or even about a type of operation in a country. The results are then collated, and both an overall indication of feasibility and specific indicated challenges are summarised. This, and other exercises, could again form part of a wider assessment process. However, because feasibility assessment is early in the investment approval process and deals with speculative prospects, if a definitive negative indication forms early on, it might not be worth trying more angles on the same question.

We touched on this earlier, but it is worth reiterating that a sense of feasibility is specific to a company's risk-reward attitude, in general and with respect to a particular operation. Another point is that political risk management itself can sometimes make what seemed unfeasible, feasible. Thus, one needs to be careful about discarding apparent duds. Avoidance is one political risk management option, but the analysis and planning that we examined in the previous chapters showed that much can be done to keep an operation safe and sustainable even in challenging terrain.

TACTICAL ANALYSIS

Going back to monitoring, it might show only minor change that requires incremental adaptation, but it could also show more significant change that needs to be investigated to fully understand the implications. This leads us to tactical analysis, tactical as opposed to the strategic perspective of the baseline exercise. Tactical analysis is a rather general label, and just means a highly targeted intelligence exercise which can be shaped to address an array of ad hoc uncertainties. We will examine three broad applications. One is the examination of recent changes in the environment. The second is estimating how a known, planned event might proceed. The third is identifying the reasons why an operation is facing problems when the environment itself seems to be more or less stable.

For an example of the first application, we can imagine that we are a foreign manager in Turkey in 2016, trying to understand the implications of the coup attempt in July that year. For most observers, despite acute tensions between the Gulenists and the ruling AK Party, this came out of the blue, and while it did not upend the political scene, it had significant implications beyond just the subsequent near-term crackdown. Any foreign on-the-ground operation there would have been very interested in what it really meant and how it might ultimately affect them.

The problem can be divided into what really happened, and the potential medium-term implications. Starting with what happened, observers at the time would have had two main hypotheses. One was that the coup attempt was, as the government said, conducted by Gulenists in the military. The other was that it was a false flag operation by the ruling AK Party to create a pretext to purge remaining Gulenists from any position of influence in Turkey and to increase its grip on power. Both hypotheses would have been examined, with an eye to the motives and capabilities, as well as relevant past behaviour, of the possible instigators. A complementary stream of analysis would have looked at the events of the coup attempt itself, including the chain and timing of actions and reactions. A genuine coup attempt would have seen the government initially taken by surprise but quickly responding. A false flag would have seen inconsistencies in government reactions, for example learning about the attempt but doing nothing for a while to build the drama.

To intelligence users' disappointment, what actually happened would have remained unclear. The government did have some apparent track record for creating pretexts, and a coup attempt would have been very useful for the AK Party in some ways. There were inconsistencies in the chain of events and communications that just seemed fishy. But the Gulenists were facing eradication from any position of influence, and they had a history of planning well ahead. A contingency plan to try to take over in the event of their impending demise would have been in character. Furthermore, a public TV announcement by a very temporarily victorious coup plotter did not sound at all like what the AK Party would have wanted to hear had they orchestrated things. Ultimately, there was some broad, and highly qualified, analytical consensus that the government had intelligence that the Gulenists would try a coup attempt, and decided to let it play out to expose the plotters and hammer home that the Gulenists were enemies of the state. In this view, the government was initially somewhat surprised by the pace of events and made a mistake in letting it play out further than it was supposed to. But in the end it was easily quashed and did lead to a major purge which might not have been feasible or publicly acceptable beforehand.

The implications would have been less challenging to estimate. The government had both a strong motive and pretext to purge Gulenists from their remaining vestiges of influence in the bureaucracy and in business. This would have led to organisational and leadership turbulence in the civil service and in major companies, and in turn this would have seen disruptions for foreign companies in terms of permits and authorisations, and state and private sector relationships. Additionally, President Erdogan had apparent aspirations to greater personal control, and it would have been foreseeable that he would use the coup attempt to reinforce the case for greater presidential powers and a reduction in checks and balances, thereby setting Turkey up for a more frictious relationship with Europe and other democratic powers. Had a foreign company done this kind of assessment, it would have been forewarned of disruptions, and of a more difficult act in balancing home and host country government expectations. What most assessments at the time missed was that the purges ended up going well beyond just influencers and leaders, and started to affect ordinary Turks, including foreign company local staff. This led to cases of staff detention, with consequent angst, organisational disruption and hard questions about the feasibility of remaining in the country.

There are a variety of ways to format a tactical analysis of political change, and the above was posited in relatively loose terms as a logical narrative exercise. However, the general framework of hypotheses on what happened, investigation of these to establish what really occurred and then the derivation of a medium-term outlook and its implications can apply to a range of types of events, from assassinations, to scandals, to spikes in a conflict or factional rivalry.

We now to turn to assessing how a planned event might proceed. A planned event might be an upcoming election or referendum, a summit, a constitutional change, the passage of a particular major law or policy, or the introduction of a new tax. The main distinction from assessing a potential discontinuity or manifestation of instability is that we are looking ahead at a known, planned occurrence with almost perfect plausibility. In this case, the question is how the event might proceed, and the implications of its likely mode of occurrence. For example, in 2007 Kenya was gripped by severe election violence. For a long time afterwards, this made election periods worrying for foreign companies there, and an obvious question to pose before an upcoming one was if there would be violence, and if so to what degree. Knowing the possibilities in advance, a company can adjust its exposure for a plausible worst case.

There are different approaches to event analysis. One can take an informed narrative approach or formulate and assess different mini-scenarios. There are also variants of the competing hypotheses method, which puts forward different possible outcomes and then sees how credible, relevant information aligns with each. Figure 11.4 on the next page is an illustration adapted from a real case, in which the team developed a basic interim thought experiment to help clarify emerging estimates.

The question was if, and to what potential extent, a planned regional summit in the country's capital would see unrest. This was of interest to the company, because violent protests were a recurrent security and continuity challenge, and sometimes high-profile events were the catalysts. In this case, three outlooks were posited, and the effects of known conditions were gauged for each outlook. This was not the basis of the final judgements, but it captures the idea of positing and comparing event outcomes to see what might actually play out.

What we know	Outlook for upcoming regional summit		
	Passes peacefully	Localised disruption / protest	Organised disruption
Main opposition does not want to be seen as spoiler	+	-	-
Govt and main opposition have negotiated an outcome	+	-	-
Fringe opposition questioning govt negotiation	-	+	+
Govt has extensive preventive security	+	-	-
High profile meetings have drawn crowds and triggered protest in the past	-	+	+
Indication	+	?	-

FIGURE 11.4 Alternative tactical outlooks.

The last application of tactical analysis covered here is how to understand why an operation is facing pressure when there is no obvious cause in environmental dynamics. We can loosely call this problem diagnosis. In previous chapters, we mentioned an Algerian case that the author worked on for an oil and gas company, and it was partly an example of this application. The company was facing a number of obstacles while many of their peers were doing fine. Part of the project was to find out why. AES in Georgia, as discussed in Chapter 1, would have benefited from a diagnosis after their operation started to hit turbulence. A thought process for problem diagnosis is depicted in Figure 11.5, using a hypothetical example of a company facing unexpected bureaucratic delays and unusual state company partner apathy.

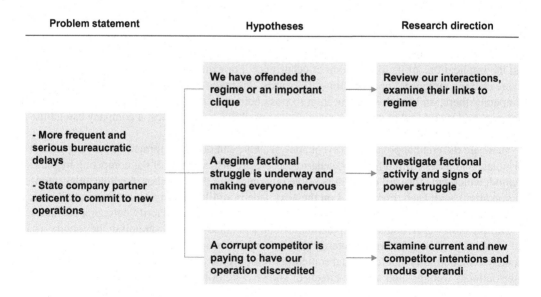

FIGURE 11.5 Problem diagnosis.

The process begins with a synopsis of the problem or situation. We will not know why we are having the problem, but we will know its manifestations. We then develop possible explanations for the problem as hypotheses. These indicate what needs to be examined. We could start with the most plausible hypotheses to potentially save time, bearing in mind that they could be wrong. The above is quite basic and more complicated problems would have more investigative branches, even splitting into sub-branches in a form of logic tree. What is not shown in the illustration, but which is the ultimate aim of such an exercise, is what the company could do to address the causes of the situation. Where causes are directly related to company relationships, there is an opportunity to proactively address them. When they stem from previously unnoticed environmental dynamics, the company could then apply the kind of assessment used in the Turkish coup example to see what it could mean and how to appropriately adapt.

The "five whys" is often posited as format for problem diagnosis. This is a thought tool that keeps drilling down through a series of whys until a root cause of the problem has been identified. This could be useful in some cases, but in the author's experience it works better for internal problems than political risk ones. In political risk, we simply do not know the answer to any given why until we formulate and test different hypotheses against the available evidence.

As noted at the start of this section, tactical analysis is a broad label for tailored, focused intelligence exercises that can apply to myriad political risk problems. The above three applications are just reference points. Of all the person-time in intelligence work, in political risk and probably in government too, monitoring accounts for the bulk of it, but tactical analysis is a close second. This stems from its character as an ad hoc method which, unlike comprehensive strategic assessments, can be quickly scoped and executed to address nearly any kind of socio-political uncertainty.

CONFLICT ANALYSIS

The illustration in Figure 11.6 on the next page is only a caricature, but it sets the scene for this section. Foreign Company (FCo) Inc. is dropping into a very fraught environment, and hopefully they have done their conflict analysis and developed plans on that basis.

Conflict analysis is aimed at understanding the drivers, axes, players and motives in a conflict. It clearly applies to armed conflict such as civil wars and insurgencies. But it is also germane to local contexts in which there are multiple axes of socio-political rivalry, some of which periodically manifest in violent clashes, but all of which hold that potential.

Conflict analysis as a practice stemmed from government intelligence on foreign conflicts and in support of peacekeeping missions. Starting in the 1990s, it evolved into a widely used tool of donor agencies and NGOs involved with conflict resolution and peace-building. It has made its way to business through UN, OECD and other transnational initiatives to try to mitigate and indeed reverse the negative effects that foreign business operations can have on conflict. We noted some in Chapter 3, but to reiterate, these can include the following: company security harming host communities; inadvertently empowering one side in a rivalry; indirectly funding conflict through payment of taxes, royalties and bribes to an abusive regime, and protection money to armed groups; raising the stakes in local conflict simply by being there as a perceived source of lucre or advantage to one side or another; contributing to scarcity-driven conflict by degrading local ecosystems on which livelihoods depend; and discriminatory labour management practices.

Thirty years ago, a company that did these things could well have escaped wider public notice, but international ethical scrutiny, including by governments, has become much more intense. There are serious reputational costs of ignoring one's effect on conflict, and on the ground if a company is seen as a conflict player, it can be treated like one. Thus, there are excellent reasons to understand the conflict environment, and to apply that learning through conflict sensitivity, which means programmatic approaches to not worsen conflict, or ideally to contribute to peace-building. Transnational organisations and NGOs offer a variety of guidance on conflict sensitivity, often in its wider context of business and human rights. Some examples include the OECD's *Guidelines for Multinational*

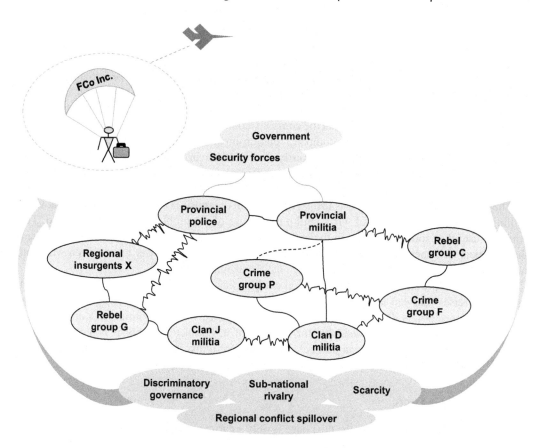

FIGURE 11.6 FCo Inc.'s new business environment.

Enterprises (on responsible business conduct and human rights), the UN's *Guiding Principles on Business and Human Rights,* International Alert's *Conflict-Sensitive Business Practice: Guidance for Extractive Industries* and the Voluntary Principles on Security and Human Rights' *Implementation Guidance Tools.* All of these and more contain detailed guidelines on relevant issues, analysis, and planning. As a hint, when a guidance paper says it applies to a certain sector or industry, there are usually lessons therein that are applicable to any on-the-ground operation.

When conflict is a factor in the host country, conflict analysis and sensitivity planning become a tacit element of a baseline intelligence exercise. For example, in previous chapters the socio-political system in the context and focus stage provided insights on the drivers and dynamics of conflict and rivalry. Terrain analysis further investigated the conflict factor. In stakeholder analysis, the Town A and conflict domain examples had attributes of conflict analysis, as did several of the exploratory linkage maps. Finally, in planning, the example of the initiative to address host community friction included aspects of conflict sensitivity. This indirect coverage can be sufficient when conflict is one factor among several. However, when conflict is a prevalent factor, or the key shaper of an operation's environment, a dedicated conflict analysis and sensitivity planning exercise is in order.

Given the abundance of guidance and literature on the subject, we do not need to provide a mini-manual here. Instead, we will focus more on the concept of the exercise. The ultimate objective of conflict analysis is to see how and where an operation will interact with and influence patterns of conflict. This starts with an understanding of conflict dynamics and players. Then the operation itself is mapped into the picture. Links into the socio-political system, at the national or local level depending on the context, are then examined for how they could raise the stakes for conflict actors, or empower or weaken different rivals. Activities, attributes and relationships with potentially acute effects on conflict actor perceptions, capability and status become targets for conflict sensitivity planning. This can lead to significant changes in the operation's location and physical processes, hiring and purchasing policies, anti-corruption policy, security arrangements, labour and government relations, CSR, and communications. It can also result in changes to the company's local relationships and lead to more intensive and focused stakeholder consultations. The operation's conflict sensitivity performance would then be monitored to inform continual adjustments and self-correction.

As an aside, a significant challenge in conflict sensitivity is when a government involved in abuses or waging suppressive military campaigns is the recipient of significant tax or royalty revenues from an operation. Conflict sensitivity might call for ensuring that the operation does not ultimately fund a regime's violent capability, but the only practical way to achieve that is to have major donor sponsors on board from the beginning, and with their help to get contractual guarantees. Even then, as Exxon and the World Bank found in Chad, the regime might renege if it would not suffer serious repercussions. In some cases, withdrawal from the country might be the only option to not make things worse.

Once in a conflict environment for a while, it can be very hard for a company to go back to the drawing board and redesign the operation for conflict sensitivity. It does not take long to get a local reputation for insensitivity or favouritism, and to actually do some real damage, if one is initially unattuned to rivalries. It can also be expensive and time-consuming to make significant changes to an operation after it is up and running. Thus, as with the baseline exercise, the ideal time to start conflict analysis and sensitivity planning is before an operation commences, or between major phases. Then, as with the baseline process, it would be redone between foreseeable time horizons, or when monitoring indicated a significant change in the environment.

There are two final points. First, on a practical level, we need to consider how conflict analysis and related planning works in conjunction with strategic political risk assessment as represented by the baseline exercise. When conflict is a major factor, the two exercises are very closely linked and should not become silos. One approach is to give conflict analysis its own distinct workstream in the baseline process, thereby ensuring that information is shared and insights are not fragmented. Another is to do a top-level conflict analysis as part of the baseline and then use these results to scope a more nuanced follow-on conflict analysis. The second might be preferable, since conflict sensitivity planning will have very detailed information requirements and immediately feed into an implementation programme. Either way, the close link between these exercises needs to be accounted for, or there is a risk of wasted time and effort through redundancies, and of a lack of overall coherence in both assessment and planning.

The final point is that conflict analysis and sensitivity have been construed as an ethical compliance exercise, aimed at showing audiences and observers that the company has done what it was expected to do. Conflict sensitivity is not mandated by law in any OECD country, and hence as opposed to anti-corruption programming there is no outside pressure to take it seriously. However, conflict and conflict-prone environments are potential quagmires, and intense rivalries affect nearly everything that people think and do. Direct experience usually enforces a switch from compliance-centric to substantive approaches. Genuine efforts early on can spare a company that awkward lag during which damage can be done, and incurred.

THREAT ASSESSMENT

Threat actors were included as stakeholders in that part of the baseline exercise, in a departure from conventional stakeholder analysis which generally sees stakeholders in somewhat euphemistic terms. Covering threats in stakeholder analysis is essential for a comprehensive stakeholder picture, but the framework therein was not threat-centric, and the security function in particular usually needs to conduct follow-up exercises to develop threat management plans. This would entail drilling down where threats were indicated in baseline intelligence, and developing a more nuanced threat assessment, the final supplementary exercise we cover here.

First some terminology is in order. We previously noted how "threat" is sometimes synonymous with "risk" or "risk factor". In casual usage, it can also mean a contingent warning or effort to deter or intimidate someone. In a political risk and security context, a threat is actually an actor. It becomes a threat when it has, or could develop, a capability and intention to harm an asset, which in our context could be an aspect or combination of people, reputation, control and continuity. Not every stakeholder who wants to hurt us in some way would be appropriately regarded as a threat. We need to draw a distinction between aggrieved and threatening. For example, if we infringed on someone's livelihood by building too close to their plot of land, they might start a court case or a local protest movement and might very well wish that we just disappeared. But they are responding because of how we hurt their basic interests, and had we not, then they might have had no particular attitude towards us. A threat, by contrast, wants to hurt us because of who we are and what we represent. An aggrieved actor can become a threat if their issue is left unaddressed, and once they are, they are assessed as such even if we could still explore avenues for remediation. As an aside, the last point highlights an important role of stakeholder analysis and engagement: simply put, it can reduce the number of threats that we face by forestalling aggrievement and mistrust.

A final distinction from other actors is that threats are or could become directly interested in us. They are stakeholders, after all, and one of the criteria for being a stakeholder is that an actor has some kind of relationship with us. There might be plenty of "bad actors" running around, but if they are involved in crime, terrorism, repression or insurgency that is not directed at us, then they are not threats. Rather, the activities that they are involved in are risk factors, and they are players in potentially harmful environmental dynamics. If they hurt us, it would be a side effect of their main activities. This is an important distinction, because there is a significant difference between how we manage environmental hazards, and people directly trying to harm us. For example, you cannot deter or deceive a hazard.

We can now examine some of the elements of the threat equation. Threats are usually assessed for capability and intent (which are threat-specific variants of influence and attitude as used in stakeholder analysis). Capability refers to their means to harm us, and intent is the strength of their motivation to do so. The degree to which an actor is a threat is a function of these variables. A severe threat would have high capability to harm, and strong intent. A minor threat would be low on both axes, or very low on one of them. Capability and intent also yield indications of threat activeness. A latent threat might not have noticed us yet or have bigger fish to fry for the time being. Their current intent is low, but we know that we broadly fit their target set, so this could change. They could also be latent because while we might be on their radar, they do not yet have the capability to attack. An active threat is one that is targeting us now, and is looking for an opportunity to attack. Specifically, they are trying to learn vulnerabilities, where our assets are unguarded and accessible. To capability, intent and vulnerability we can now add risk. A risk is a specific potential threat action which would cause a degree of harm. Risk probability in threat terms is therefore a function of the threat's capability and intent, and our vulnerability. If all of these are high, the probability of an attack is high. Impact, or implications, depends on the specific form of attack and its degree of success.

While we will not delve into security theory, the above makes it clear that threat management works on each of the elements of the threat equation to try to reduce the prospect and degree of harm. Let us imagine that there is a neighbourhood bully and I, being a nerdy weakling, fit the profile of his usual targets. I could alter his capability. That has rather dark connotations in this example but in other contexts it could be reasonable. I could also alter his intent. For example, I could spread a rumour that I just got my black belt in karate. With a preference for easy targets, he might be deterred. I could reduce my vulnerability to him, by avoiding him, going around in disguise, or walking around with a group of friends who would protect me if he tried something. If he did get me, I could activate a panic button that would call for help, thus limiting the damage and getting me to a clinic for rapid treatment. That would limit the impact of the manifested risk. If we changed the bully into a socio-political threat actor, the same generic options of capability-reduction, deterrence

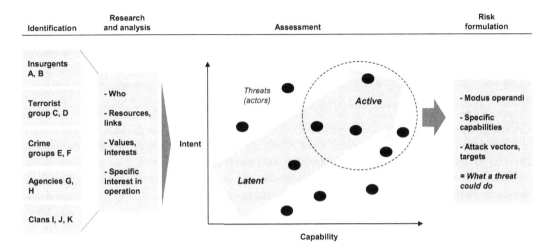

FIGURE 11.7 Threat assessment process.

(altering intent), avoidance/deception, protection and mitigation would apply. Interestingly, note how several of these actually applied to the IT consultancy's plan to counter crony pressure, including deterrence by raising the cost to the regime of crony incursions, thereby indirectly causing contingent negative consequences for the clans.

The above was rather conceptual, and a top-level schematic of threat assessment helps to clarify the exercise. This is shown in Figure 11.7.

This does not depict the whole process. Risk formulation for a given threat would inform planning to manage that threat, but all threat-driven risks would then be collated and assessed. That would reveal the array of different modes and forms of attack that the operation could face, and this would inform relevant cross-threat risk management preparations, for example for certain kinds of extortion attempts, armed attacks and criminal assaults. Planning would follow. One layer would be aimed at priority threats and would start with the generic options discussed earlier to formulate plans to forestall and avoid threat actions. Another would be risk management planning, a strong focus of which would be crisis management and mitigation for the event that a given type of threat action occurred.

Notice the similarity between this process and stakeholder analysis. Threat assessment would draw on stakeholder analysis and expand on the threat actor elements, doing a more detailed breakdown of identified actors if need be, and then conducting more threat-centric research on each entity. The two thought processes mainly differ in that threat assessment is now focused on stakeholders who were assessed as very hostile and/or predatory. In stakeholder analysis and planning, engagement included elements of threat management, but here that is the singular planning focus.

There are couple of other noteworthy points in the above schema. One is that a low capability does not always signify latency. Threat actors are not always rational and are sometimes desperate. They might not wait until they have the necessary capabilities before trying an attack, and if we think that they will wait until they are capable, we could be taken by surprise ("express" kidnappers are a good example). Notice also that agencies, referring to government agencies, are among the identified threats. When security agencies are corrupt or linked to criminal groups, perhaps through traditional ties or simply by being paid off, they can be threats in their own right, or support other ones. As with the IT consultancy's staff detention issue, they can even be threats just by doing their routine job if they lack restraint. On a wider note, as with the stages of the baseline exercise and scenario analysis in particular, threat assessment can be weak if it does not stretch assumptions and look beyond the plausible. Most failures in threat intelligence have more to do with underestimating threats than not identifying them in the first place. The Statoil Algeria case in Chapter 1 is a good example. The relevant groups were known. That they would conduct a complex operation from across a border seemed inconceivable given trends to that point. Threats often make use of deception and break patterns to achieve surprise, and this should be considered when estimating potential behaviours.

As with the baseline exercise, threat assessment should remain confidential for the user organisation, and actually be given an even higher confidentiality rating. There have been cases in which "insider threats" have reported threat assessments and security plans to kidnappers, hackers or terrorist groups. Additionally, sometimes an identified threat might be an organisation that the company needs to work with on some other level. A corrupt police force might be an example, and one can imagine their ire if they ever saw themselves on a threat matrix.

Threat assessment and threat management, or security, planning is a well-developed discipline. However, the language and methods can vary. Different sub-practices, for example physical and cyber security, can have their own approaches. The national security and defence context was where threat intelligence was born as a practice, and it still affords instructive reference points for the development of tailored frameworks.

CONCLUSIONS

We covered five supplementary intelligence exercises, but they should only be seen as reference points among the various possible ways that intelligence can be shaped in a political risk context. For example, to help inform specific negotiations or bargaining with political actors, intelligence-informed gaming can be used as the basis of simulations to help frame positions and develop a strategy. Due diligence investigations or in-depth profiles of specific people are another example. That can help to estimate potential responses of key influencers, and to make confident decisions on whether or not, or how, to engage. Specific communities where there are cross-cutting divisions that the company might trip over could be examined through the lens of human terrain analysis, a military application of social anthropology that has made its way to the private sector, and usefully complemented conflict analysis and community engagement planning. Intelligence is a practice and way of thinking rather than a specific tool or process, and as such its concepts and principles can be tailored to myriad situations of high uncertainty.

The above would seem to suggest that intelligence simply happens where it is needed, and benefits whoever has the requirement. Intelligence should be agile and serve specific needs, but there is a strong argument for maintaining organisation-wide visibility and coordination of political risk intelligence exercises, in general but especially for the same operation. The direct learning from one exercise can become useful contextual insight for another. Different exercises that address similar issues might develop different findings, and unless these were reconciled, one or all of them could remain weak and provide sub-optimal or simply wrong guidance. All intelligence on an issue or place contributes to a wider strategic picture. Finally, intelligence practices can be better or worse in certain pockets in the organisation. Without sharing and coordination, these gaps can persist when there was an opportunity for organisation-wide improvement. Going back to the section on monitoring, although many exercises will be routine and tactical, ultimately they all stem from strategic intelligence, which was directly targeted by strategic objectives and uncertainties. Thus, for organisational and planning cohesion, each subsequent exercise should contribute back up the chain, ultimately, if sometimes tacitly, informing strategic adaptation. That does not happen by itself.

Part III

The Practice of Intelligence

We have examined thought processes that go from uncertainties to information to actionable intelligence and initial planning. In the context of political risk to country operations, the baseline intelligence exercise provided a comprehensive picture of factors, actors and issues that needed to be accounted for to keep an operation safe, respected and on track. We then examined supplementary exercises as examples of how intelligence can be applied to a range of requirements before and during an operation. However, while the thought processes therein are a roadmap for intelligence production, we have not yet considered the basic practical thinking that underpins solid results. Thus, this part of the book goes behind the scenes to examine some of the operational aspects of political risk intelligence, in other words how to make it work.

There is an extensive body of thought and literature on the subject of intelligence operations, much of it coming from and oriented to government usage, but still highly applicable to international business. We cannot hope to scratch the surface if we attempt to cover the state of the art. Additionally, we need to stick to the knitting, which is political risk in complex environments. Therefore, we will cover only three main topics in this part of the book, and at a relatively high level, but they will be reference points in the broader theme of practical intelligence work.

Chapter 12 begins this part with an overview of the relevant aspects of intelligence management. This will revisit the intelligence cycle as a basis for an exploration of roles and workflows in intelligence creation. Next, we address how to structure and manage a relatively complex intelligence task such as the baseline exercise or stages within it. Intelligence reporting follows. While this is only one step in the intelligence cycle, it deserves attention as the point at which intelligence influences action.

Chapter 13 finally addresses a subject that we have referred to but saved for explicit treatment, intelligence sources and collection, or how to gather the information that becomes the grist for analysis. This will explore different types of information sources and some of the pitfalls and

DOI: 10.1201/9781003149125-15

sensitivities in collection. The main focus herein will be on human sources and fieldwork, since this is a lesser understood but potentially critical collection stream.

The last chapter in this part will concern quality control in intelligence. This will consider what quality in intelligence means, common sources of low quality, and how both intelligence practitioners and users can address quality issues. An aspect of this discussion will be some of the contradictions that arise between organisational imperatives and cultures, and the clear-sighted formulation and application of intelligence.

The three topics will mainly be examined through a political risk intelligence lens, drawing on the author's own experiences and perspectives as a practitioner. However, when dealing with these issues, touching on and drawing upon government foreign intelligence concepts and practices is nearly inevitable, since that domain remains the most active and abundant source of international intelligence practices.

Before we begin, a preliminary note is in order. This part of the book is about how to actually make intelligence happen, and as such it might seem like it is aimed at political risk practitioners. They are one audience, but users are too. Intelligence users might actually be the practitioners in the context of a specific operation, and we have made the argument elsewhere that managers should be involved in the intelligence process. Even when they are not direct participants, though, users are still part of the equation. They need to clearly task intelligence, ensure that it provides what they need, give helpful feedback to make it more effective and ask the right questions to be able to confidently act on it. If there is a distinct and separate intelligence team, ultimately, as in any type of organisation from government to business to NGO, users are the boss. Their needs are why intelligence is happening in the first place. And bosses have a responsibility to understand the processes that they rely on in shaping decisions. Thus, this can be seen as guidance for responsible and discerning customers as much as for those who make and deliver the product.

12 Intelligence Management

Imagine that I am trying to plan a high-stakes initiative in a place I do not know very well. Someone tells me that there is a library full of relevant information, and sitting therein are smart and knowledgeable people, some of whom are very capable of getting around in the target country and willing to go there on a whim. I visit the library and tell them what I am trying to do and where, and to kickstart things I even hand them outlines of the thought processes that I think are relevant. Then I leave. I come back some time later, and rather than getting a clear briefing and report to help with my initiative, I find some people working on pet problems in their own corners, others arguing about who should look at what, and others debating the whole point of the exercise. I reiterate my need, clearly I hope, and give them some more time. I come back. This time I get a long, detailed, rambling briefing about the country, and they leave me with a report that looks like something between an encyclopaedia volume and a printout of a massive database file. Luckily, the IT-savvy people on the team set me up with an online repository of findings and background. I log on, and I am amazed at the detail. There are interactive maps, graphs, statistics and indices. But I am no closer to getting any clarity on what I need to plan for to make my initiative as robust as possible.

Although aspects of the above scenario are not uncommon, it is a caricature. It demonstrates what can happen when we have all the resources we need, save one: management and coordination. This is the actual ability to effectively execute an intelligence task. Foreign intelligence in general, and political risk intelligence too if someone has actually heard of it, can seem rather exotic and mysterious from the outside. There is some fascination on the inside too, but behind the mystique is a great deal of ordinary, practical work that would look quite familiar to anyone whose job is to make something happen. Intelligence needs the linguist, the retired spy or international journalist, the academic with deep knowledge of an obscure and turbulent region, and the IT wizard who can conjure data from thin air, to name a few types. But expertise alone does not get coherent, reliable results. We need to manage and coordinate it to ensure that it walks in sync towards the optimal destination.

Herein, we first revisit the intelligence cycle for broad perspective on roles and workflows. The cycle has been scrutinised in recent years, and some shortcomings are apparent if it is applied too dogmatically. The shortcomings are actually instructive for our purposes, and hence we will consider them as even as we apply the cycle as a schematic of activities.

We then move onto the management of an intelligence task. In process terms, this is not unlike how research and planning exercises are scoped and managed across an array of disciplines; thus, we will skirt generic details on project management and emphasise what is particularly germane in a political risk intelligence context. A significant part of this discussion is on case teams and how they relate to external experts and consultants if they are included in an exercise.

Finally, we examine reporting and dissemination, the step in the intelligence cycle that directly links intelligence to planning. Again there are generic aspects to this activity, and we will confine the discussion to our own context. This will consider the mix between interactive and documented intelligence reporting, characteristics of effective reports and some considerations in report dissemination within the user organisation.

THE INTELLIGENCE CYCLE: ROLES AND WORKFLOWS

Having evolved into its current form by the 1940s, the intelligence cycle is ubiquitous in intelligence guidance and literature, and appears in many different domains, including of course government from where it originated. The depiction of intelligence production as a cycle emphasises the merits

DOI: 10.1201/9781003149125-16

of a learning-adaptation feedback loop. In the cycle's original home of national security, its closest correlation in practice is regular national threat assessments, which are often conducted on an annual, cyclical basis. Otherwise, strategic assessment only becomes a cycle when its target is both dynamic and of long duration. The baseline intelligence exercise in Part II is cyclical, although its interim tactical spinoffs can be ad hoc one-offs. Thus, the cyclical aspect of the process is a possibility, not a rule. Of more practical relevance here is that the steps and roles in the cycle are reflective of how new, intensive intelligence exercises are designed and executed, whether or not they become cycles. These steps, along with some identified problems within and between them, will be the basis for our overview of intelligence roles and workflows. We showed the cycle in the last chapter, and it is depicted again in Figure 12.1 for easy reference as we discuss its stages.

We begin with direction and targeting. Ad hoc assessments and monitoring while covering a strategic target can be launched by the intelligence organisation, but new intensive exercises are actuated by decision-makers in the user organisation, based on their strategic objectives, and concerns and uncertainties in achieving them. There are two roles in this step. One is tasking by users. They need to explain their concerns and questions so that the intelligence manager has a hook to probe and clarify, which is the second role. It is often difficult for intelligence to act on users' initial questions, which can be posed in general terms and without a clear understanding of the process that will get the answers. Scoping needs a consultative and questioning aspect to develop clear, actionable directives. Once there is a clear brief, or terms of reference, it in turn becomes the basis of intelligence case design. At this point, direction becomes internal to the intelligence team, as the manager allocates sub-targets and tasks according to the case framework.

The direction and targeting step is pivotal. Even if the rest of the cycle ran smoothly, without clarity it would probably be running to the wrong place. The author has seen fuzzy initial briefs taken at face value, and this has led to variants of the caricature that started this chapter, partly because intelligence overcompensated for a lack of clarity by covering all possible bases, creating a lot of noise for every nugget of actionable insight. Results can also simply be off-target, in other words partly irrelevant to users' genuine needs. The problem does not lie with one side or the other. The direction and targeting step is a two-way street. Users and intelligence managers need to have an open discussion about requirements, what would constitute being on target, and what is feasible and realistic in the context of intelligence capacity.

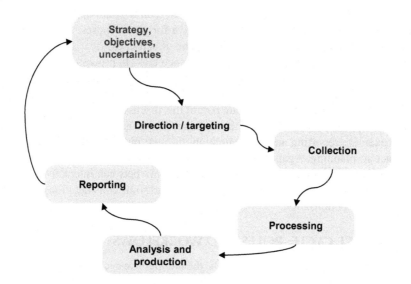

FIGURE 12.1   The intelligence cycle.

The next step is collection, or getting raw intelligence, and herein is some overlap with analysis as we examine one of the problems in the intelligence cycle. Much collection is tangibly distinct from analysis. For example, technicians managing satellite coverage or signals intercepts might not know much about the target, and do not have to know to do their jobs. Their information is processed for handover to analysis, which then makes sense of the data and uses it as an input to create actionable insight. However, if the collection-analysis distinction is dogmatically interpreted, it can lead to a missed opportunity for better intelligence. This is especially evident in the relationship between humint (human intelligence) collection and analysis.

Humint collectors, generally called intelligence officers or case officers, can spend years working in a certain region, or on a given adversary or issue. They develop deep first-hand insights on their targets, but from a narrow, tactical perspective. Analysts might have a fluid big-picture grasp of their targets, but if confined to a desk, remote from players and places, their insight remains rather sterile and abstract. Bringing the two roles closer together improves each. Case officers benefit from the big picture to adjust their lines of investigation to address critical gaps, and analysts gain from being closer to the ground to develop an innate sense of the reality behind the issues they report on. Accuracy and nuance increase on both sides. Another problem that closer proximity resolves is that some intelligence delivered from the field gets shelved or delayed in processing, which can be a complex bureaucracy in itself. A more direct collector-analyst relationship helps to ensure that when a case officer has a critical piece of intelligence, they can just take it directly to the analyst, and likewise, analysts can directly ask collectors to focus on holes in their picture of a situation.

In Western intelligence services, a formal interpretation of the collection-analysis distinction was less problematic during the Cold War, when the main target was a large adversarial bloc. For the most part, it was like watching the slow and steady construction of a massive machine. Collectors could nibble away at a known, slow-moving target, while analysts could adjust their picture of it without having to know the twists and turns at street level. Intelligence on the various fast-paced sideshows, such as regional wars, coups and revolutions, would have benefited from a stronger collector-analyst relationship, but these seldom constituted immediate national security risks. Fast-forward to the post–Cold War period. Big adversaries are still targets, but so too are insurgent and terrorist groups, global organised crime, cyber threats and middling powers trying to develop weapons of mass destruction. These might be global problems but they derive from rapid local dynamics, and getting intelligence wrong can lead not just to bad policy, but near-term vulnerabilities that asymmetric threats would readily exploit. Thus, many agencies have sought to bring collection and analysis closer together. More analysts are deployed overseas, and work alongside collectors in integrated target-centric task forces. This leads to a fluid relationship capable of keeping pace with events on the ground. The classical separation of the two roles still exists, but not as a matter of doctrine, rather just when it makes sense.

In a political risk context, the same problem of the separation of roles arises. In international companies, the corporate support or planning functions where the practice of political risk intelligence resides maintain some external stakeholder relationships and garner insight from these, which they analyse as part of their reporting on target issues. Thus, there is some melding of collection and analysis. However, intelligence-related functions are often remote from the operational action. In fact, the people in closest contact with target issues and places are frontline managers, who can develop profound insights and a deep feel for a place. Frontline staff benefit from specialist intelligence, but can see it as superficial and abstract when it does not correspond with their experience on the ground. There are seldom any formal channels by which their knowledge, or indeed feedback, flows back to the intelligence functions. The situation varies in risk and intelligence consultancies, but the story is often similar, with a rather rigid distinction between country and region desk analysts, and people in security and investigations who do considerable fieldwork but who tend to lack a contextual understanding of the places they travel to. In short, while the intelligence cycle's logic of "get information and then see what it means" seems basic, it becomes a drag on good practice if "get" and "see" have little to do with each other.

We now turn to analysis. In the intelligence cycle, analysis means taking the raw intelligence from collection, and turning it into meaningful insight. Analysts bring two things to the table. One is expertise on certain long-standing targets, which gives them a frame of reference to make sense of new insights. The other is analytical methodology, which allows them to extract tangible meaning from an apparent morass of information. In most cases, analysts also collect open source information, which they partly use to corroborate what dedicated collectors provide, and as noted, analyst-collector partnerships can form around specific targets.

A rigid notion of the intelligence cycle would see analytical thinking as only occurring in the analysis step. However, analysis applies not just to working with information. We need to analyse a problem before we even know what information to gather. Analytical thinking also underpins the design of appropriate case frameworks to address a given requirement. For example, the stages of the baseline exercise are not just how analysts use information. They guide how an entire team would work from start to finish to get the required results. When seen as problem-solving, and not just working with acquired information, analysis applies to all tasks within an intelligence exercise, including collection, which should be carefully planned to ensure that raw intelligence is relevant to the brief. Ironically, this clarification about the wider application of analytical thinking is largely irrelevant in most business and policy domains, since analysis is tacitly built into management decision-making. In intelligence, because analysis is a formal step, it can be interpreted in very narrow terms.

Moving on, production in analysis creates reports and briefing material, which are then disseminated to users in the reporting step. We have mentioned how intelligence formulation is not report-writing. Both collection and analysis generate considerable documentation, but most of this is for internal purposes, distilling what we know and using that to guide further investigation. Thus, even if we are sitting on reams of raw and interim reportage by the end of an exercise, intelligence still needs to be shaped to be digestible for users, with an eye to the clarity of key findings and the rationales behind them. In government agencies, analysts usually create user reports and deliver briefings, although collectors can be directly involved too.

A mechanistic adherence to the intelligence cycle can affect the reporting step too. When reporting is seen as distinct from analysis, it can put far too much emphasis on editorial standards and reader impact than on handing over qualified, credible intelligence. Not all intelligence has a tidy message, and insights need to be qualified for uncertainty. Users need to see rationales behind assessments so that they can understand why certain alternative conclusions were not selected, to be able to qualify their own confidence in the findings before acting on them. When reports are a publication exercise, they might read well, have a punchy plot and message, and look good, but at the expense of transmitting the often-messy reality that decision-makers will need to contend with. The temptation to over-produce reports comes partly from a concern that users will not pay attention to intelligence if it is boring, complicated or ambiguous (as an aside, the problem of users not reading intelligence also arises in a commercial context when clients are actually paying for a report). Better to round some edges if this means that users at least look at it. There is a fine balance. Reports and briefings need to be reasonably user-friendly, but not at the expense of getting an accurate picture.

Once when working alongside a team from a large risk consultancy, the author had the strange experience of seeing the case team's report go through "editing" before it could be delivered to the client. The company also produced subscription reports, and these appropriately went through a standardisation process, but that hardly seemed applicable to the results of a targeted intelligence exercise. By the time the results came back from the editing team, they were still recognisable, but had gone from careful qualification and appropriate nuance to something much like a news article. It took considerable negotiation and time to finally work out a variant amenable to both sides. That might seem odd, but it is not uncommon. Even intelligence agencies have experimented with newspaper formats and catchy synopses. However, they have also increasingly focused on educating users in how to read and interpret intelligence, so that results do not need to be dumbed down to make sure they get used.

At the end of the cycle, reporting feeds back into strategy and plans to achieve objectives, which are adjusted or augmented to account for critical issues. This is again where users take a primary role. They need to take intelligence seriously, and work to understand it in the context of organisational aims and exposures. However, intelligence has a role too, which actually began early on in the process. The whole intelligence exercise to this point should have been designed and managed with an eye to how results would fit into relevant organisational planning processes and functional remits, in other words how intelligence would be applied and implemented. User organisations also need to adapt to be able to apply intelligence, but this a longer-term endeavour. Within the context of a specific requirement, it is up to the intelligence manager to ensure that results are shaped to fit actual use. If not, there is a risk that results are translated into the language of practical implementation by junior managers before they end up with decision-makers, with a consequent risk of distortion, or again of dumbing down.

Assuming that user application was accounted for upfront in the cycle, at this point the intelligence team still has a role in helping users to interpret intelligence and make sense of its implications. There is a reasonable argument that if an intelligence team does not remain separated from decision-making, it will be biased by decision-maker preferences. However, just handing over a report or delivering a one-off briefing errs too far the other way. The intelligence team has been emersed in the target for weeks, and their knowledge of it goes well beyond what is just in a report or presentation. Users should have an opportunity to ask about nuances and implications, and the intelligence team should have a chance to ensure that users have a confident grasp of key findings and what they mean. Without an interactive and consultative element, the link between intelligence and action can remain tacit or even superficial. Recall our entire planning stage in the baseline exercise. That stage is not necessarily typical of intelligence projects, but when it occurs to any degree, via interaction between the intelligence team and users, it goes a long way towards ensuring that intelligence has an impact. Just throwing a report over the wall leaves a lot to chance.

Our walk through the intelligence cycle has yielded both key roles and lessons for intelligence management. There were four broad roles in the cycle. These are summarised below:

- Users are leaders, decision-makers, planners and doers who face uncertainties in the pursuit of organisational objectives. They task intelligence to help reduce uncertainty, and to reveal potential pitfalls that need to be planned for. They need to be open about their aims and concerns, and be ready to put in some effort to understand and apply intelligence.
- The intelligence manager probes users for clear targets and directives, and turns these into directions for the intelligence team, via a project framework that coordinates team efforts towards the required insights. After the team gets the results, the manager ensures that users have the confidence to act on them.
- Guided by the project scope, hypotheses and sub-targets, collectors search for the information that ultimately becomes intelligence (analysts and collectors can be one and the same in political risk cases, but even then there are often some specialist collection roles).
- Analysts make sense of collected information, and turn it into actionable insight. They also lead on developing users reports, and on delivering user briefings (again in political risk the analyst-collector distinction is often hazy, although some people on a case team could be primarily desk-based country or issue specialists).

We left out processing, but in our context of a small team and not an intelligence bureaucracy dealing with reams of information, processing is basic knowledge management handled in collection and analysis.

We can extract six main lessons from our review of the cycle:

- The direction and targeting step is a two-way street. Users need to be open and clear, and the intelligence manager needs to probe and refine. A brief, or terms of reference, should provide the intelligence team with clear direction, not just a topic.

- Direction within the intelligence team is based on a problem-solving framework that ensures that all activity ultimately leads back to the questions agreed with the users. Part of intelligence management is the development of the framework, and then coordinating activity within it. This is an application of analytical thinking that guides all roles in an intelligence exercise, and it overturns the notion that analysis only applies to working with garnered information in one formal step.
- The intelligence team needs to be aware of how intelligence will feed into the user organisation's planning and decision processes, so that results find a natural fit and are not discarded or reinterpreted because they are misaligned to how the organisation works.
- Separating collection and analysis can hurt intelligence performance. Collectors can dig without knowing exactly what picture they are helping to fill in, and analysts can ponder without knowing what the target looks like in real life. If these roles are brought closer together, each of them benefits from the other's perspective, and there is a more fluid, rapid focus on remaining unknowns.
- Production and report creation is not a publication exercise. The focus needs to be on relevance, clarity, qualification and rationalisation, not on contrived punchiness or an editorial house style. There is a fine line between digestible and user-friendly, and over-produced and dumbed down.
- Reporting and dissemination is not just a one-off handover. Users have a responsibility to apply intelligence, but the intelligence team has a responsibility to ensure that users understand it. Consultation and discussion should accompany standard reports and briefings, otherwise the beneficial effect on decisions and actions could be limited.

An examination of the intelligence cycle yields considerable insight on intelligence management, but it is still a top-level perspective. We now turn to a more narrow but tangible consideration in intelligence management, how to structure and manage an intelligence task. This will draw on what we learned from the cycle, but will focus specifically on what happens once the user's brief is clear and the intelligence manager needs to mobilise the team to fulfil it.

MANAGING AN INTELLIGENCE TASK

What follows applies to a relatively complex intelligence task that would involve breaking a general directive into manageable parts, and then bringing them back together for an integrated intelligence picture and key findings. Thus, we are not focusing on monitoring or highly tactical ad hoc investigations. Our illustrative target herein might be one stage of the baseline exercise, such as terrain or stakeholder analysis, or it might be a tactical assessment aimed at understanding significant changes and their implications. What follows will constitute some general pointers on managing a complex task, but given the diverse applications of intelligence, this will not apply to all requirements that could arise. It is also worth noting again that the aim here is not to explain project management practices in general, and we will stick to what is distinct about political risk intelligence.

We broadly divide this discussion into "what" and "who". The "what" is the project or case, as a framework and process to address the user brief. The "who" is the team that executes the case.

THE WHAT: AN INTELLIGENCE CASE

With a clear user brief in hand, the intelligence manager, or case manager at this point, will work with the team to understand what needs to be examined and how. Even a relatively discrete task will need its own variant of the context and focus stage, which we covered in Chapter 6, to provide shared contextual awareness and to break the main problem down into specific elements. This is in effect a mini-project to scope and target the main one, and as with the baseline's context and focus stage, it can be a somewhat messy combination of preliminary research and brainstorming.

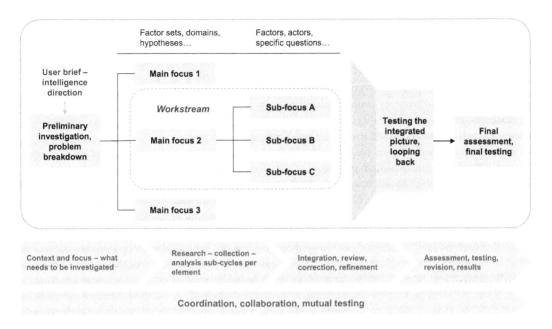

FIGURE 12.2   Intelligence case framework.

The above would result in a framework which forms a guide for intelligence team members, and a schematic with which the case manager can track and coordinate different workstreams once they are underway. Figure 12.2 is a top-level depiction of a generic case framework, along with general types of activities that occur through the execution process.

The user brief is the grist for the preliminary analysis that yields the main problem elements, which in turn can break down further, although that usually happens after research gets underway. A main element, or focus, with its constituent sub-foci, becomes a workstream which would be managed by one person. We discussed staging in terrain and stakeholder analysis. If there are not enough team members to simultaneously handle all workstreams, then the case manager needs to decide on an optimal sequence. Again, this usually goes from where we can gain broad contextual learning, to more specific and discrete targets. Jumping over a considerable amount of actual legwork in the workstreams, we get to the point where each workstream is more or less complete. There would have been collaboration along the way, but now there is an explicit integration of findings to test the intelligence picture for coherence and internal consistency. Discrepancies and gaps lead to looping back into collection and analysis, not for a re-do, but to resolve specific problems. When we are reasonably confident that we have ironed out the quirks, findings move into final assessment wherein key judgements and priorities are developed. These too undergo testing to check for weak assumptions and rationales. When we have accounted for these, analysis moves to production, specifically of user reports and briefing material.

The chevrons at the bottom of the main framework are generic activities that occur in most complex exercises. We can highlight two points therein. One is "research-collection-analysis sub-cycles". Going back to the earlier discussion about problems arising from a rigid separation of collection and analysis, in our context of a specific political risk intelligence task, we would be nearly paralysed if we tried to keep them distinct.

To illustrate the above assertion, imagine that I need to know something, but I am not sure exactly what. I research it. Now I have a target, so I investigate it. I build a picture of it, and analyse it to see if tells me anything useful. No, it does not, so I wonder if I shaped it properly, and do some more research. On that basis, I refocus my investigation. I analyse again, and I am starting to get some answers, but the picture is still somewhat fuzzy. I run another cycle with somewhat different parameters, and the picture clarifies. If instead of this fluid switch between activities, I sat at my desk waiting for the collectors to report, by the time they did, their raw intelligence would probably not be exactly what I need, and I would have wasted time. Similarly, if I gather reams of information between the rare period of reflection, I will end up spending much of my time later on sifting through noise, and my final analysis will be rushed and confused. There probably will be some specialist collection and analysis tasks in addition to the work of core team members, but within each workstream, the two roles are more or less fused in tight "research-collection-analysis" cycles. This even applies to fieldwork, since team members deployed to the target area will be using time outside of interviews and observations for research to corroborate what they learn, and to see what it might mean for the emerging analytical picture.

The other point to draw attention to is the bottom chevron, "coordination, collaboration, mutual testing". McKinsey & Company, one of the oldest strategy consultancies, developed the now popularised MECE (mutually exclusive, collectively exhaustive) principle in the 1960s, as a basic formula for defining project workstreams which together covered the whole client problem without tripping over each other. The idea of assigning clear and distinct sub-tasks to people makes sense, but even in business strategy research it is hard to imagine genuinely mutually exclusive workstreams. In political risk and related intelligence, it is even less conceivable. One reason is that most intelligence targets are a part of the socio-political system in which there is intense causal interaction. Thus, my workstream might be on conflict, but I am going to have to work closely with the people covering governance and ethnic relations to get a complete picture of my target. Another reason, as we discussed in stakeholder analysis, is that any given socio-political actor could have roles in several domains, and be linked to other actors along several axes of affiliation. I cannot fully know my targets without seeing how they come up in someone else's focus. The causal and networked connections between targets require ongoing and intensive collaboration.

We will discuss quality control in intelligence in a separate chapter, but as indicated in the above diagram, within a project would be several explicit review and testing exercises to identify and address weak assumptions, biases, groupthink and other sources of unreliability. Testing in intelligence goes to the root of thinking and interpretation, and hence it is far more intensive and dynamic than just checking editorial quality and factual accuracy.

THE WHO: THE INTELLIGENCE CASE TEAM

The above was about the "what", and now we move on to consider the "who", in other words the team which would undertake a specific intelligence task. Figure 12.3 is a very general illustration of a team structure for a political risk intelligence case, again perhaps a stage in the baseline exercise or an in-depth tactical assessment.

We introduced the role of intelligence manager when discussing the intelligence cycle. In a specific task, this role might become the case manager, or it could appoint one. Either way, the case manager is the leader of the exercise, and would also be the users' main interlocutor. Each workstream has its own manager, who is actually a doer too. They are managers in the sense that they are responsible not just for their own work but also for relationships with researchers and relevant external experts and facilitators. The support functions within the intelligence team's organisation (or sometimes seconded or subcontracted to it) include IT and data experts who can assist with things like dark web searches, social media analysis and geographic information system (GIS) data acquisition, in addition to secure knowledge management and communications. Research refers to junior analysts competent with open source research. The other two support functions are self-evident. We already discussed coordination and collaboration. They are not shown in the diagram but in addition to casual, ongoing collaboration there would be some regular coordination fora, as well as a shared project portal.

Nothing about the above is particularly remarkable. What is more interesting is who the intelligence team actually is, in the context of an international company seeking clarity on a political risk

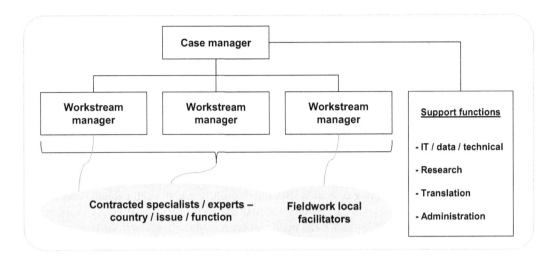

FIGURE 12.3   Intelligence case team.

question. An aspect of that question is how we, speaking now as members of the user organisation, utilise and relate to external experts and consultants. There is much that can be said about intelligence task management, but the "who" is both fundamental and open to a degree of misconception; thus, it is the focus of the remainder of this section. What follows mainly draws on the author's consulting experience, and inevitably there are models of intelligence team resourcing that are not represented here. Among the four variations that we review, two are examples of weak practice, and are instructive as lessons in what to avoid.

One variation is the creation of the case team from company roles with a formal remit for political risk and related types of issues. We discuss organisational capacity in a later chapter. For purposes here, we can be aware that some companies have their own internal case management resources. Recall from Chapter 1 that political risk units were not uncommon in the 1980s, but fell out of favour the following decade. Not all companies ditched this capacity, and as complexity reared its head again, others rebuilt it. The situation of a political risk capacity varies. It can be in strategy, external/government affairs, security or sustainability, and there are cross-functional structures that draw on relevant capabilities in each. When a country operation needs an assessment, it is effectively the customer of the in-house corporate intelligence function. In better examples, this function will work with country management to scope the brief and collaborate with the country team to ensure that local insights and on-the-ground experiences feed into analysis.

When there is a capable in-house team, usually with access to country monitoring subscriptions and its own ongoing reporting, external consultants and experts can be used very selectively. One common use is the provision of an independent perspective. Intelligence people in companies can be well aware that as part of the user organisation they risk being swayed by corporate ambitions and culture. Discrepancies between in-house and external assessments of the same target can be very revealing, and help to adjust the team's intelligence picture. The second main use is to plug specific holes in the picture, and in such instances the relevant external specialists are usually narrow and deep country and issue experts with unique local sources. In neither instance does the external provider replace or partner with the case team. Extra team resources or intelligence skills are not required, just a fresh point of view or very specific additional knowledge.

In general, how well the in-house model works depends on how integrated the intelligence function is with operational units in the company. Intelligence should remain reasonably independent of user preferences. However, confining the intelligence function to an office can lead to abstract results that do not provide a solid basis for planning. That was one reason why in-house political risk units did not seem particularly valuable after their initial decade in fashion. When the function is well integrated, despite the risk of bias from proximity to users, there is considerable merit to having an intelligence team that intimately knows the user organisation, including its approach to operations and political risk management. Additionally, an in-house team means that intelligence capacity does not need to be sourced each time it is needed. Sourcing a consultancy takes times, not just to verify that there will be value for money, but to assure its trustworthiness given its potential access to sensitive company information. There will be a need for external experts from time to time, but not for every requirement.

A second variant is the formation of an ad hoc intelligence case team from among the people and functions who are going to be managing a country operation, supported by consultants, but not dependent on them. This is seldom a formal model, and when it occurs, it is usually the result of managers' personal experiences in complex environments and, based on this, a gut sense that there will be challenges in the upcoming operation. Because it pulls in people with a direct stake in how the operation goes, an ad hoc team can be very focused and energetic, even if nearly everyone on the team still has their routine "day job". The main risk is probably self-evident: the team's stake in the operation also means that it might have some bias towards making it sound doable, and in not raising doubts or worries. This is partly countered by an awareness that discerning potential issues will help the operation to succeed, but it can be a fine balance.

An example of this approach, which includes the use of consultants, comes from one of the author's old cases. The operation was launching soon, and some months prior the country manager had organised a part-time task force to identify and plan for the challenges that could arise. The task force consisted of the country manager and senior representatives of several functions including security, legal, CSR, supply chain management, HR and engineering. The government affairs manager for the operation acted as the coordinator and helped to chaperone the initiative.

As the launch date grew closer, the team was concerned that while it had accruing knowledge and myriad reports, it lacked a coherent intelligence picture. A consultancy was selected to provide its own assessment of potential challenges and stakeholder attitudes that would need to be planned for. However, this was not just for an independent cross-check. At that point, just handing over a brief and then taking the results two months later would not have worked. There were near-term decisions that needed guidance, and the in-house team's own research was ongoing and there was no point in duplication. Thus, while the consultancy had a clear brief, collaboration and flexibility were built into the case framework.

The consultants' case team resembled the above illustration. We had a case manager, several workstreams, support functions, and, importantly, our own expert sources and fieldwork facilitators. We address fieldwork in more detail in the chapter on collection and sources, but for now, facilitators are usually citizens of the target country, and they support fieldwork undertaken by case team members. Unlike in the above diagram, though, because of the collaborative and interactive aspect of the project, we were directly linked into the client's own team, both through individual liaisons and through participation in the team's meetings.

The flexibility built into this model allowed for exploring hypotheses and honing direction without worrying about a rigid scope set in a consulting proposal. Close collaboration between operational people and intelligence specialists meant that results were very much about the operation, and oriented to tangible problem-solving. Overall, it was a very effective case team model, and aside from the results, both sides learned a lot from the interaction. The only downside in this instance was that the company did not have a wider concept of political risk, and no channel or forum to capture the model for future country operations led by other people. Ironically, the absence of standard practices and functional ownership was a factor in the flexibility that made the case uniquely effective. No one tried to cram it into a box. But without any basis for institutional learning, even that lesson was probably never captured. This raises a point about the balance between flexibility and functional ownership, and we will explore that in the book's concluding chapter.

We now move onto instructive examples of how not to handle a case and its human resourcing, including the use of consultants. The first of these we can call offloading, when a company manager needs political risk intelligence, but instead of having it feed into a company initiative, they just hand the whole process to a consultancy. An example comes from another case the author was involved with, in which a functional manager in the operation was tasked by the country manager to develop a comprehensive picture of the challenges and stakeholder issues that the company could face. He in turn had limited resources to do the job, so he found a consultancy to do it for him.

The reason for the brief might have been clear to the country manager, but there was no clear rationale for it when it landed with the consultancy. The country was not particularly stable but it was not bad either, and the company's operation did not seem to be experiencing an unusual degree of friction. Despite our efforts to learn more, the functional manager remained the vigilant gate keeper and the brief remained rather vague. As usual when the "why" is unclear, the resulting report was huge and had no particularly pointed finding. The main benefit for the company actually came through interviews conducted with staff at the country office. These disclosed some serious concerns about friction and cultural misunderstandings. Those issues actually warranted further investigation and would have made a useful focus for the case, but in this instance, they were just discerned in passing as we continued to march towards our hazy target.

There is some irony in the offloading approach. It is particularly alluring when an operation does not have its own intelligence activity or relevant resources on hand, but because of the lack of intelligence behind direction and targeting, the brief is vague and so too are the results. Additionally, in the absence of an ongoing intelligence initiative, once the results are handed over, priorities and indicators are not monitored, and the whole report is stale in about six months. The above example clearly shows the risks and missed opportunities in offloading a task, and how consultants are no substitute for an in-house intelligence capacity. Indeed, effectively using external intelligence expertise requires having some of that same expertise ourselves, or we will not know how to utilise it for best effect.

The second mode of weak practice is a variant of the above and is so dull that it hardly merits a paragraph, but while we are the subject, it is at least a stark lesson in what not to bother with. In this variation, there is no internal case team, de facto or otherwise. A manager responsible for some aspect of project due diligence needs to show that they have done their homework. They send a brief to a consultancy, who writes a report and sends it back. The next time someone asks how the due diligence is going, the report comes out of the drawer and gets waved around for a second or two. This is the proverbial box-ticking exercise. Two parties, the stressed-out middle manager and the consultancy, win, the latter with an easy ride to a fee. The operation in a complex environment loses, at least if this is as far as political risk intelligence goes. As an aside, this attitude to intelligence often goes hand in hand with the notion that political risk insurance is political risk management: as long as the potential financial pitfalls are covered, then the operation is just like any business initiative anywhere. This perspective is increasingly rare, but it is not uncommon. In short, the box-ticking approach really has no case team, because there is no case, just a paying client, and an analyst writing a generic country profile. Value for money aside, there are far better uses of time and attention when planning an operation in a complex setting.

We have touched on several topics that will be dealt with in more detail later, including collection and sources, quality control and organisational considerations. These are all part of managing an intelligence task. What we examined here was case structuring for a clear workflow and as a reference point for oversight, and case teams, particularly the interplay between in-house teams and external advisors. These would have made it clear that intelligence work only produces actionable insight if it is targeted on what matters, approached in an organised way that leads to required answers and staffed by a dedicated and collaborative team. Even more importantly, intelligence is not just a report from an intelligence provider. If a company lacks its own means to decide what to target and to follow up on intelligence results, then external specialists cannot make much difference no matter how profound their knowledge of the target environment.

We now proceed to the last theme in this chapter, intelligence reporting. We have already touched on this, but as the point where intelligence informs decisions and actions, it bears further consideration.

INTELLIGENCE REPORTING

Again for illustration we assume that there is a discrete but relatively complex intelligence task. Going back to the earlier case framework, reporting usually begins after research and analysis is complete, and the results have been tested and refined. We say usually, because in some cases the user has near-term decisions to make, and a case can be staged to provide specific interim insights. Interim and final reporting follow similar principles, and for purposes here we just focus on final reporting.

We have discussed reporting, and two insights thus far are, first, that there is a delicate balance in written reports between user-friendliness and providing a robust and accurate picture and, second, that a degree of interaction and consultation needs to accompany documented reports. We build on these here with a more in-depth look into what makes for effective reports. First, we examine the relationship between the intelligence process and reports. Next, we consider written reports. The interactive, consultative aspect of reporting is then addressed. We finish with a note on dissemination, specifically on the balance between accessibility and confidentiality.

INTELLIGENCE PROCESS VERSUS REPORTS

We have noted that an effective intelligence process is not a report-writing exercise, nor is it guided by a report format. Now that we approach reporting, and because there is some confusion over the distinction, it is worth revisiting why. This difference is conceptually illustrated in Figure 12.4.

The process of deriving intelligence on the target is represented on the left of the picture. It is dynamic, iterative and interactive. A report, on the right, is a static summary of the key learning from the intelligence process. In the process, what we learn later can influence, or even obviate, what we learned early on. Thus, there is no point in tying the process to the step by step completion of a report. That would entail constant revision, which is a waste of time especially given that report-writing entails considerable attention to editorial quality. If we insist on writing as we proceed, we also risk getting attached to completed sections, and unwilling to alter them as new information comes in and shows them to be inaccurate.

The intelligence process is a like a caricature of a police or journalistic investigation, with open files, cluttered network maps pinned to the wall and team members hunched over each other's desk in constant give and take, until the target has been sketched and understood with reasonable accuracy. Considerable documentation, including summaries, experiments, doodled diagrams and notes, will accrue during the process, but little of this would be suitable as report material, and indeed some early synopses will likely turn out to be downright wrong further down the road. If one had to guess, a two-month case undertaken by four or five core people would result in about 600 to 1,000 pages of summaries and tests, not counting raw intelligence that is only read. The final, full intelligence report for users might be 80 or so. That in itself tells us about the distinction between the intelligence process and report-writing.

It is necessary to make the above case because there is still a tendency in political risk, and in other social and business research fields, to treat the report as the project template and to regard filling it in as project execution. This can be fine if an analyst with a deep understanding of a subject is asked to write a background paper. Then there is not much required new learning and no specific problem to solve. The analyst only needs to structure their thinking with a table of contents. In any complex task, though, 90 percent of the work is not about report-writing, which only captures key learning after we have confidence in our knowledge about the target.

While the process / report distinction is worth some emphasis, there is a relationship between the two beyond their obvious link in the transmission of learning. First, when shaping the intelligence brief, users would want some idea of what they are going to get. An indicative report outline broadly tells them what to expect. The parts therein might just have generic labels, but at least they show the types of things that will be covered. Second, the intelligence process can be very fluid, and it is easy

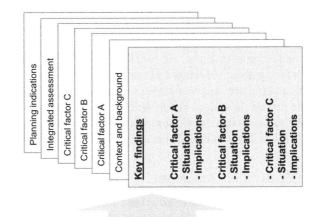

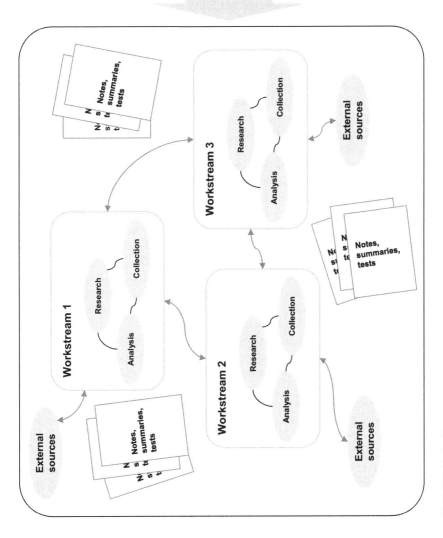

FIGURE 12.4 Process versus report.

for people to get sidetracked by interesting nuggets and rare opportunities for unique intelligence access. Having the report outline in mind, and knowing that soon they will have to produce the report, keeps people focused on the user requirement and the agreed brief. The final report structure might change from the original outline, depending on how hypotheses evolve during research, but it still represents the brief and a tangible output.

A case framework and a report structure will usually roughly correspond at least at a top level, since one is aimed at learning about the target and the other at explaining this learning to someone else. However, both for an effective intelligence process and clear, digestible reports, the two must not be confused. If the process is seen as report-writing, intelligence accuracy will suffer. If the report is structured like the case framework, and walks through the process of getting results in detail, readers will suffer, and this will impede the application of intelligence.

DOCUMENTED REPORT FORMATS AND ATTRIBUTES

This is not the place to expound on generic essay and report-writing skills. There will be some inevitable overlap with general good habits, but we will mainly confine this to what is unique about political risk intelligence. There is considerable flexibility in report formats. What we cover herein will not always be relevant to a given case, but it will provide some guidelines.

As a general reference point, we can assume that our target readership is the senior management team of a country operation, along with relevant corporate, divisional and regional executives. This will not always be the case, and who the readers will be is something that should be established in the direction and targeting step of the intelligence cycle, when the user brief is defined.

Documented reporting on a relatively complex case usually consists of four specific outputs. One is an executive summary, which summarises key findings and their implications. This might only be two or three pages. Its purpose is to ensure that no matter how busy or distracted a user is, he or she will get at least the bare essentials.

Next is the synopsis. For a 60- to 100-page main report, a synopsis might be 15 to 25 pages. It replicates the main report's top-line structure, but each section is trimmed down to the basics. This will have more supporting information than the executive summary, in terms of context, rationales for the main judgements and planning indications, but again the emphasis is on transmitting what the users must be aware of. Synopses do not replace a main report, but they are useful as a top-level guide to one, and they are also handy references for workshops and planning sessions, when thumbing through the main report could be cumbersome in the midst of fluid discussion.

The main report has the full findings and supporting evidence and argumentation. Even this, however, considers digestibility, and as noted in the previous section, much of the nuts and bolts thinking that occurred in the intelligence process is not included. We only present what we need to in order for readers to have confidence in the findings and judgements.

Finally, there is an appendix. This is for tangent and supporting information, statistics and data, notes on methodology, models we used and, in some cases, a list of sources or at least types of sources. This is also where we can show the case framework without distracting readers from the main findings.

The main report is the principal output and the basis for both of the summary versions, and hence it will be our focus as we consider report attributes. We first characterise some general stylistic attributes, then the principal distinctions from analysis, and finish with the use of qualification, rationalisation and dissenting opinion.

General tone and style in intelligence writing tends to be unembellished even if thoughtful narratives can create interesting subplots. Writing does not have to be deliberately dry, and in fact it should be as compelling as confidence permits. In general, when it comes to flow and logic within a given subject, or sub-target, a report will briefly explain what the subject is and why it matters, the key finding or judgement about it, the main evidence and rationales for the judgement, and what it could mean for the users. The last point can vary. Not every case will have a brief that includes drawing out implications and planning priorities. But to be a solution as opposed to just information, a report should link back to the users' aims and concerns. This might be general, or it might go as far as explicitly recommending a top-level user action. The whole report should likewise flow to a point of high significance and relevance for the user. What is most important should be clear, as should key uncertainties that bear further scrutiny. The end of the report should be a springboard to decisions and planning.

The first, and main, distinction between analysis and what is in the report is the relative emphasis on models. Recall from the stages of the baseline exercise how many diagrams, mind maps, matrices and linkage maps we used to eventually derive findings. Only a few of those would be useful for users, and even then they would need to be cleaned up and simplified. Some tools, like a master stakeholder linkage map, would be very useful for some specialist functions, but irrelevant for others. If the main report is aimed at senior decision-makers, we need to be aware that they would have neither the time nor the inclination to ponder and play with the intelligence toolkit. Any graphic or model we show should directly support key findings. The appendix is a good place for anything else.

A second distinction from analysis is that we slim down contextual background and write it specifically to frame the forthcoming findings. In analysis, because we started from a blank slate, we would have developed extensive contextual insight to inform ourselves about relevant variables and dynamics. Readers benefit from some context, but to guide their interpretation of findings, not as a way to discern what to focus on.

A final distinction that we can draw is that in the report, all assessment (the formulation of judgements) of a given subject, be it a factor, challenge, actor or hypothesis, occurs in the section on the subject. In analysis, we often save assessment until after we have a picture of all subjects, because a comparative perspective helps to see their relative importance, and because systemic linkages mean that we often need to see the big picture to know the full character of each piece. Separating discussion of a subject into different parts of a report risks users losing the thread. If we have a final assessment section, instead of conducting assessment therein, we just use it to show and discuss comparative results and the holistic picture.

One hallmark of intelligence reports is the use of qualification. Recall from the terrain analysis stage in particular how we were sometimes faced with estimative uncertainty. That was not necessarily because something was unknowable; rather, we ourselves were uncertain about it. Therein we discussed the need to clearly state our uncertainty, usually alongside the recommendation that the subject be monitored and revisited later in time. That was a form of qualification.

Qualification is routinely used in all intelligence reports, but it varies according to the level and type of report. In our context of a final report, it is usually used to clarify to what degree and why we are uncertain about an important finding. That can be explicit, as noted above, but qualification also takes the form of estimative, or probabilistic, language. For example, rather than saying, "The government is planning to introduce new regulations", it could be, "There are strong indications/ There is strong evidence that…", or "The government will very likely…". If we were less confident, we might preface the assertion with "It is possible that /There are indications that…". Estimative language can be rather subtle and not every reader will give an adverb or brief expression much thought, but it is a reasonable balance between routinely showing distracting mini-assessments of confidence, and not qualifying at all. A basic formula for qualification would be: (implications of getting a judgement wrong) × (uncertainty) = how explicit a qualification should be. In some government reports, there is a brief upfront guide to estimative language, and this might be useful in political risk too just to ensure that readers do not miss the more subdued qualifications.

Qualification is necessarily much more explicit in raw intelligence reporting, which is not really our concern here but it bears mention. In this context, it often has to do with the credibility of a source. For example, a human source tells a foreign intelligence officer that the military is planning a coup and it will happen within three months. That gets sent to HQ, along with the intelligence officer's assessment of the source's track record, access and potential motives for telling the truth, fabricating or deceiving. The desk officer seeks corroboration but cannot find any. Assuming the source is credible, this presents a problem. Is this information a rare nugget that we should apply in our estimate, or it is so niche and contrarian that we can safely discard it? If the issue in question is sufficiently important, the information would be used in analyst reports to users, and would have an effect on the overall assessment of a coup's plausibility. Before that information came in, perhaps a coup was not even on the radar, or it was rated as highly speculative. Now it goes up a notch, but alongside an explicit qualification that the assessment was based on one credible source and there was no corroboration. The possibility would be further investigated, but until more intelligence came in, it would be up to users to decide what to do about it. In a final political risk case report, we would probably not need such explicit and detailed qualification, but it can be necessary, and when it is, we should not gloss over it just to maintain our report's narrative flow.

Explicit rationalisation is another hallmark of intelligence reports. We need to provide clear rationales for why we decided on one of several possible alternative interpretations on a subject. For example, in analysis it might become clear to us that a government is trying to improve the investment climate for foreign companies. However, the government has had a dismal track record, and some politicians continue to evince a suspicious and nationalistic attitude towards foreign investors. We are quite confident in our interpretation, but readers could well have seen other ones. They might not have confidence in our finding if we do not explain why it is more sensible than the alternatives. In analysis, we would have examined competing hypotheses and tested rationales and evidence for different perspectives, so we did not ignore the alternatives and in fact gave them all a fair hearing. Now we need to show just enough of this thought process to rationalise our conclusion.

Note that rationalisation, as a general method, is not always aimed at arguing for the view we feel is correct. Sometimes readers should be aware of alternative interpretations and see the arguments for each, especially when our confidence in the one we bet on is only moderate. Then readers will, ideally, at least keep their eye on other possibilities. Just by way of illustration, recently I have been reading a lot about the war in Ukraine, and some think tanks aggregate and present the opinions of different experts on the same question, such as under what circumstances Russia would use a nuclear weapon and how it might do so. Each contributor on a given question is highly credible and has good arguments, but the answers they give are very different. If I were a national security planner, I would not be able to close off any of them even if I mainly oriented planning towards the ones that seem most sensible now.

The final point about written reports is how to deal with dissenting opinion within the intelligence organisation or team. In a government context, a strategic assessment can involve several agencies with different angles on the same issue, and in some cases their interpretations do not line up. The inter-agency team would try to achieve analytical consensus, but if there are some holdouts, then dissenting opinions are noted in the sections where interpretations diverge, alongside the majority or mainstream interpretation. Dissent in a report is not ideal for users, because it complicates planning, but sometimes it is unavoidable. In a political risk context, a joint client-consultant team is quite small and does not consist of competing bureaucracies. Thus, dissent can be discussed and ironed out more easily. But even in this context, sometimes it has to be explicitly accounted for. Dissent can look messy, and sometimes intelligence people worry that it makes them look inept or like they were not cooperating well. But as the earlier example of different expert opinions on the Ukraine war illustrates, sometimes even well-informed and robust judgements diverge.

There is much more that could be said about reports. For interested readers, examples of old government intelligence reports in national security archives give a flavour of the tone and style of intelligence writing, and these are not dissimilar to political risk reports. For our purposes, the above suffices as an introduction, and we turn our attention to the interactive aspect of reporting.

INTERACTIVE REPORTING

Interactive reporting consists of briefings and preliminary planning sessions. Briefings transmit key findings and rationales, and provide a forum for questions as well as discussion about implications.

Briefings are more about ensuring that users understand the case results, as opposed to what to do about them. Planning sessions, by contrast, start with briefings but then move into an interactive thought process aimed at sketching an initial strategy and at least the types of initiatives that would be required to address priority issues. Any intelligence case should be able to yield coherent briefings. Planning sessions, on other hand, would arise from an initial brief that specifically asked for planning indications, and consequently from casework premised on a robust understanding of operational aims, plans and exposures. Sometimes briefings turn into ad hoc planning sessions just because that is where the discussion goes. In that case, rather than trying to chaperone the session, the intelligence team can take a back seat and just help to keep the users' discussion grounded in the facts.

Briefings can be presentations, in the sense of talking through findings to an audience. That is usually a part of the process, but perhaps a more important one is quiet one-on-one or small team briefings with senior users. The informal character of individual or small meetings allows users to ask more probing questions, and there is more time for the discussion of complex findings. In some cases, there could also be sensitive findings which should have a restricted audience. This is not a matter of facilitating cover ups. There have been instances when case teams have blithely presented somewhat depressing or shocking results to a roomful of people, who then erupted in anxious discussion and later shared the information with colleagues far and wide, kicking off a chain of embellishment in the organisation. Senior managers would much prefer to convey sensitive findings through appropriate channels, and after they have had time to think about how to address any pressing issues. In such cases a wider presentation can still occur, but the tone and degree of detail would be worked out with senior users in advance.

Given how diverse intelligence requirements and subsequent reporting can be, rather than outline more variations of interactive handovers, we will conclude this section with a few key suggestions on how to make them effective.

A basic point is to ensure that the right people are in the room. Everyone in a session should be aware of the case and have a professional interest in it. Superfluous invitees often derail discussions with basic questions about the entire exercise, and going back to the above point about discretion, it is preferable if those present have a need to know.

In the case of planning sessions, the case team and their user counterparts should work out the thought process in advance. Unstructured planning sessions tend to be messy and yield opinion more than reasoned consideration. We do not want to stifle creativity, but people need to be working in the same direction. Recall that cases are guided by frameworks whose purpose is to maintain cohesion while still encouraging alternative thinking. Discussion frameworks have a similar purpose.

The case team can present dissenting opinions, but they should not be positioned as, "It could be this way, or it could be that way." There should be a consensus position on the given issue, with dissent noted but not expounded on as an alternative reality. The case team needs to get its story straight well in advance and iron out any friction, because while reasoned dissenting opinion is fine, a case team arguing with itself in front of users is no cause for confidence. The author has been in briefings in which a delicately crafted approach to dissent was thrown out the window by a subject expert with a very strong attachment to their perspective, derailing a considered rendition of a complex finding.

General good practice for presentations and workshops applies in an intelligence context, but there is one noteworthy distinction from most business presentations. In business, interactive sessions are often aimed at generating enthusiasm for the initiative being discussed, and speakers are expected to sound passionate and inspiring. In intelligence, clarity and accuracy predominate, and while an experienced case manager might have presentation and facilitation skills, many subject experts and analysts do not even like being in front of an audience. They might not be what typical business users expect, but if we want the goods from the horse's mouth, we need them in the room, and users should put aside their notions about motivational speaking and be ready to listen.

We noted in an earlier example that it can be useful for a case team to be available for some time after the results have been handed over. This is a final aspect of interactive reporting. Questions are bound to arise after the formal completion of a case. The case manager should make it clear that the team is available for follow-up discussions, and case files should be in easy reach for a while.

Intelligence Dissemination

Dissemination is the process and structures by which intelligence reports end up in the right hands. Delivering a report to the users who agreed on the intelligence brief is only the first step. Once the report is in the user organisation, it needs to get to other people who would benefit from it. Whichever distribution channels are used, there is an important consideration which we mentioned above in the context of briefings. This is how restricted the report should be.

Many political risk reports are not much more sensitive than think tank reports. For example, reports that only derive from terrain or scenario analysis do not say anything too pointed about particular groups or people, even if the findings might not paint a very flattering picture of a government. They also do not give much away about the company and its concerns. However, other kinds of assessments are inherently more sensitive. A stakeholder analysis report would almost certainly contain information that made some socio-political actors grind their teeth. Threat assessments would be very valuable to threat actors trying to know where we will target our defences. A problem diagnosis could tell certain socio-political actors that we are having serious problems, and that we think they are responsible. If more sensitive intelligence reports ever made it into the public domain, or were somehow gleaned by an adversarial intelligence actor, we could have some serious headaches.

We have no a priori assumption that companies are full of careless people who would post a report on their Facebook page just to gain a few likes. But the more accessible a piece of intelligence is, the more likely it is that someone either inadvertently leaks it, or, less likely but worse, the intelligence finds its way to someone who is actually being induced or coerced to pass on sensitive information about the company.

Intelligence agencies have a number of ways of dealing with this challenge, and corporate practices for the handling of sensitive information have adopted some of these. For example, classification ratings for reports correspond to security clearances, so that only someone with a given clearance can gain access to a report. There can restricted channels, so that reports can only flow among those with a need to know. Reports can be redacted, so that many users have access to some findings, but only a few have access to the full ones.

The precise formula will vary. The main point is that we should carefully consider the implications of a piece of intelligence falling into the wrong hands and control dissemination accordingly. Much political risk intelligence is about threats and our vulnerabilities, and contains frank and unflattering assessments of specific powerful actors. The less they know what we know, the better.

That concludes this chapter. For practitioners, it was perhaps a few new angles on a familiar subject. On the other hand, for international managers who could be intelligence users, the chapter aimed at providing enough reference points to be an effective and participatory customer. In summary, intelligence might be a product, but it is also the way that the product is made. Like any productive process, it needs clear direction and careful management to get high-value results.

The next chapter continues our introduction to the hands-on aspect of intelligence, with a look at information sources and how we can use them to obtain the raw insights that feed into analysis.

13 Intelligence Sources

From Part II on the baseline process and supplementary exercises, we have a strong sense of how acquired knowledge is used to generate actionable insight, and in the last chapter we explored how an intelligence case is managed. Thus, we now have a strong contextual framework for an explicit look at the raw ingredient of intelligence, information, which collection extracts from sources. The aim of this chapter is to introduce the main types of sources and some key considerations in using them. This will include the principal caveats and pitfalls in raw intelligence acquisition, both in general and with respect to types of sources. Fieldwork and human sources will receive a disproportionate emphasis, since in a political risk context these are both uniquely valuable and less well known than open sources.

The chapter begins with the relationship between types and sources and stages of learning, and some general principles in assessing sources to enable accurate interpretation. Next, we examine general open sources suitable for honing a contextual understanding of an intelligence target. We then consider more focused open sources which would come into play once we have defined sub-targets. Fieldwork and human sources follow. This includes types of on-the-ground sources in a complex case, observation and targeted interviews, and the risks that we need to consider when undertaking fieldwork.

Throughout this chapter, the working assumption is that there is a case team, whether in-house or an in-house-consultancy hybrid, and hence herein we will not revisit discussions on how to set up a collection apparatus. Collection is a significant part of any case team's work, and it is planned and conducted within the case framework. Within this, we noted that aside from fieldwork, collection was seldom a discrete project phase but was an element of work cycles that combined basic research, targeted collection and analysis for ongoing and accelerated learning.

SOME GROUNDWORK: SOURCES AND LEARNING, SOURCE ATTRIBUTES

In general, assuming that we are working on a new situation or country, our learning will move from broad and contextual, to specific and nuanced. At each phase, the kinds of sources we use will broadly align with our level of knowledge and be aimed at helping us to get to next level. This is depicted in general terms in Figure 13.1 on the next page. The types of sources therein are only indicative.

The tree stemming from the initial haze of deciding what to focus on can be interpreted as starting with the main case workstreams and their sub-targets, going towards more specific questions as learning accrues. As noted in the last chapter, it can take some upfront research just to get an outline of the intelligence picture that we are aiming to fill in. With a bit more work, we can identify broad elements of the picture. As we progress, we see how these further break down into sub-elements and so on until we have very granular pieces. In illuminating those, each broader element starts to clarify, until our original outline has become a detailed, coherent tableau from which we can extract key findings.

Different types of sources are more applicable to different learning stages. If the case involved a country that we were not very familiar with, there would be no point in starting with local news articles on current events in the country, or discussions with specific people there. We would have no preliminary understanding from which to derive relevant questions, and no context to interpret what we learn. Conversely, if it is the sixth week of an eight-week case and our picture is quite detailed, there would be little value in reading a general country study. Our evolving understanding and requirements would have rendered top-level sources obsolete for practical purposes.

DOI: 10.1201/9781003149125-17

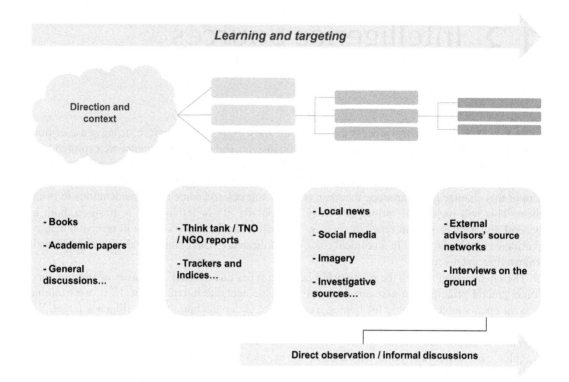

FIGURE 13.1   Sources in the learning process.

The general pattern in a case is from contextual "about the country" sources, to more granular open sources, to fieldwork for observation and human source discussions. Each level guides our selection of sources in the subsequent one. There are some exceptions to this. If the company already has an office in the country, casework could actually start in the field. It would still proceed from general to nuanced, but just being in the country would help to accelerate learning. Discussions with knowledgeable contacts can also occur at any time, with our questions going from general to specific as learning evolves.

We should note that the learning and source sequence depicted above also broadly corresponds to the intelligence team's proximity to socio-political actors involved in the situation or issues that we are trying to understand. We can start from a desk far away for context and an initial breakdown of the picture's outline into manageable pieces. As we progress, we might still be remote, but we will be using local news sources and perhaps plugging into social media feeds from the host society. At some point, we cannot learn much more from a desk and need to see the place, to directly observe and experience dynamics therein. We finally approach actors directly involved in the target situation to try to understand their perspectives and motives. Cost and risk are aspects of this directional flow. It costs more to have people on location than it does at their office desks and hence we should have a good idea of what we need to learn before we undertake fieldwork. In complex environments, it can be somewhat risky to be on the ground asking questions, and the risk is more manageable if we have a clear picture of dynamics that could affect us before heading off.

Workstream managers on a case usually set and adjust their own collection agendas, but the above considerations on the flow of learning and accruing nuance would guide at least a top-level collection plan for a case team. Because learning breakthroughs and leaps can happen, this would need to be flexible. But fieldwork in particular needs to be planned ahead; thus, a certain amount of open-source learning would need to precede it, partly so that we knew the gaps and key questions that fieldwork should target and partly to identify relevant local sources.

Different types of sources carry different opportunities and risks, but before we launch into a more detailed examination, we can review some general source attributes. At a general level, for an accurate interpretation of the information conveyed or proffered by a source, we need to know three characteristics of it.

One is the source's purpose. Whether someone writes a publicly available report or article, or agrees to talk to us, they have a motive in doing so. Purposes range from a professional commitment to high-quality news or academic principles, all the way to trying to influence people to support a particular perspective in a socio-political rivalry. If we understand the purpose behind proffering information, we can account for its potential effect on the accuracy of presented facts and the validity of the accompanying interpretation.

The next one is the source's perspective. This is somewhat different from purpose. Purpose is intentional. A source's perspective can be intrinsic and unselfconscious. Especially in discussions of political issues, nearly everyone has an ideological or national bias, however much they try to be, or think they are, objective. An academic think tank in the US or EU, for example, might look like it is offering solid, objective analysis. But the very choice of issues they cover betrays where they are from, as do the research angles they take in their reports. With effort, people can control the effect of perspective on the accuracy of their knowledge and the validity of their interpretations, but it is nearly impossible for someone to negate. If we know a source's perspective, again we can better account for it when interpreting the source for our own learning. The question of perspective and unconscious bias comes up again in the next chapter when we actually turn it onto ourselves, as a factor in intelligence quality.

A final attribute is access, meaning how close the source is to the situation in question or how direct their channels are to actors therein. Access gives a source first-hand insights, and as a result their information is more accurate and nuanced by comparison to a remote source which relies on a chain of intermediaries for information. For example, if our interest were the organisational health and dynamics of a state company, a senior manager therein would have high access. A local business reporter with company contacts would have reasonably high access. An analyst sitting in New York or London who only read about the company in the news would have low access. Similarly, if I am trying to learn the ins and outs of Moroccan politics, local papers staffed by journalists with their own political contacts would have higher access than an international news outlet that drew its information from wire services.

We can lay out the three source attributes in schematic terms to get a sense of how they relate to generate source quality:

- (transparency and legitimacy of purpose) × (control for, or neutrality of, perspective) = credibility; and
- credibility × access = source quality.

Thus, a high-quality, or ideal source, has a transparent purpose, a neutral perspective on the target issue, and high access. In political risk, the ideal hardly exists, but knowing these attributes, we can control for them in our interpretation of a source's information. Limited access can be a showstopper if we are at a point in a case where we need nuanced insights. However, the other two attributes are actually information in themselves if properly accounted for. The information that we seek in political risk is not just facts, but perspectives, values, motives and interpretations. I would not directly learn these by talking to a highly skilled and credible analyst. I would learn them by reading a political party newspaper, or by talking to someone directly involved in a rivalry, and whose threat perception clearly comes through in their interpretation of an issue. As we proceed, we will see how the above attributes manifest and affect different types of sources. For now, as conceptual groundwork, we can bear in mind that source quality is not always related to source value. Knowing a source's angle, we can filter it out when seeking facts, and actually learn from it when seeking less tangible insights.

We now proceed with a look at types of sources, roughly following the sequence from contextual to nuanced as illustrated earlier. This review will be relatively brief for open sources, so that we can focus more on fieldwork and human sources, which are far more complex.

CONTEXTUAL AND BACKGROUND OPEN SOURCES

At least in political risk consulting, it is somewhat rare that a case team does not already know something about the picture they are tasked to investigate. After all, a consultancy's experience with a place or an issue is often a selection criterion. However, even then a case team's understanding might not be current, or it might not relate to a specific user requirement. Speaking from my own experience, being more on the case management side, I am not a country or region expert, and while I can learn from colleagues on a given case, I still need to develop my own background knowledge of the target. With respect to in-house intelligence units, they can be quite small and have limited routine coverage of a place or subject, and ad hoc case teams formed from operational management might well be facing a new situation. Thus, for any type of case team, there can be a need to develop a holistic contextual picture of the target before we can begin to break it down into specific elements. A variety of sources would be useful in this early phase, but we will narrow it down to four reference points. These include the following: books; academic papers; reports by think tanks, NGOs and transnational organisations (TNOs); and finally general discussions with knowledgeable contacts.

Books are not in vogue these days, when it is easier to just enter a search term in Google and read snippets that satisfy our immediate curiosity. For most of us, a book is a slog by comparison and requires more patience and persistence than we are accustomed to. However, for getting a grip on a bigger picture, books remain invaluable, especially those written by one author with a single wider argument or plot which helps to facilitate our cognitive structuring of the learned information. When it comes to countries, speaking from experience, books on recent political history reach far enough back in time for historical context, but also explain current dynamics, key players and potential trajectories. While few authors explicitly apply systems thinking in such works, the interplay between key actors and dynamics in a book's plot or argument often provides a systemic perspective. After reading a carefully selected book, one would have a holistic, if basic, grasp of the subject, and an initial conceptual framework for the interpretation of subsequent learning. We should challenge the framework as we learn more, but we need to start somewhere.

Books that are useful for political risk intelligence can be written by academics, journalists, ex-government foreign service personnel and professionals whose work involved long experience in a certain region or country. Going back to source attributes, we need to understand an author's purpose, perspective and access before committing to a book. Again, we are not looking for an ideal source, but given that the book is for background learning, it would be premature to read a highly polemic work or one from a very specific ideological perspective. That might come in handy later, but for now the less baggage the better as long as the author had reasonable access. There is a balance, though. Almost any book on a country or government will have a perspective, and there actually tends to be a correlation between the intensity of perspective and access. The closer an author is or has been to the subject, the stronger their feelings about it. The more remote, the more detached. Thus, we should not avoid contentious or pointed works, as long as we account for where the author is coming from.

The next contextual source is academic papers. Unlike books by a single author, academic papers can be distinctly unfun to read. Academic works are often required to include a literature review to position their contribution, and to explain their research methodology in detail. The actual substantive content and findings can be difficult to extract from methodology. Nonetheless, an academic paper on the subject of interest is potentially very valuable. Many academic papers are based on original research and fieldwork, which means that they are not regurgitations of past works, and that authors have had direct access to the subject. Papers are also peer reviewed, and this helps to weed out bias and inaccuracy. Academic standards are similar in some ways to intelligence standards.

Weak or dubious findings can arise in both fields, but at least there are clear guidelines. Finally, even a PhD thesis would have been written by someone with a long-held knowledge of the subject, and on that basis can offer profound insights.

In our context, relevant information can derive from two broad types of papers. One is country specific and would examine factors in the country's overall socio-political evolution. The other has a principal focus on a certain dynamic, such as instability or cronyism, and then draws evidence from country cases, among which would be the country of interest to us. The latter type has less total information on the target country, but often more detail on a factor within it. As a bonus, papers on specific socio-political phenomena also contain insights into patterns of socio-political change that recur across countries. Theoretical learning is not usually part of casework, but it does not hurt to pick up some relevant political science along the way.

Just because a study is academic, we still need to assess its quality for our own interpretation. Adherence to standards of scholarship can vary between academic institutions. Less rigorous works can sometimes make it through the peer review process. Academics tend to save their more personal insights for non-academic books, but perspectives certainly affect papers too. Not all papers are based on original research and fieldwork, and authors did not always have much access to the subject. Finally, while papers from academics based in the country of interest have the potential to be very useful, if the government constrains academic freedom, then we need to beware that there could be some self-censorship to avoid incurring official hassles.

We now come to reports. Reports are publications on specific topics which fall under the remit of the authoring organisation, which as noted can be think tanks, NGOs and TNOs, the last of which include international and regional development banks. Think tanks, or privately funded research institutes, include everything from one person at a computer to a large organisation that resembles a small university. The size is not an indication of the quality of their work. More important in interpreting their reports is their purpose and perspective. As noted earlier, even the better think tanks have baggage in terms of ideological outlook. More broadly, we can be aware that any think tank exists for a purpose, which in turn partly derives from the purpose behind its funding, in other words what its funders are trying to achieve. Think tank reports can be very well researched, have high currency, and be right on target in terms of the country or issue of interest to us, but we will still need to adjust our interpretation to account for the organisation's leanings.

By comparison to think tanks, NGOs which publish research reports have a clear stated purpose, which is actually their value proposition to key audiences, including home and host region societies, governments, and the UN and other international organisations. Reports are aimed at inspiring social momentum and official action to address NGOs' priority issues, which derive from clearly articulated values. Thus, at least for legitimate international NGOs, determining purpose and perspective is relatively straightforward. NGOs tend to have high access, with either a permanent presence in particular countries or long-term partnerships or missions. NGO reports seldom directly meet our need for contextual background on a country, but they can still offer insights on particular dynamics. For example, reports on human rights and corruption provide a sense of the quality of governance, and reports on development challenges include socio-economic trends relevant to stability. One form of report that is very germane background reading is conflict analyses published by peacebuilding and conflict resolution NGOs. A side benefit of NGO reports is that we can sometimes learn about NGO perceptions of international companies working in the target country, and the kinds of company behaviour likely to trigger criticism and local reactions.

There are a few caveats about NGO publications. Legitimate, genuine NGOs are on a mission and have strongly held organisational values. A thick value lens can lead to a blurring between research and analysis, and advocacy. In another vein, if we use reports from NGOs based in the region or country of interest, we need to be aware that governments can tightly control NGO formation, funding and activities. More "successful" NGOs, in terms of size and resources, might be regime-linked, or even fronts for regime social manipulation. We discussed cronyism mainly in the overlap between business and politics, but it applies to NGOs too. Finally, even legitimate NGOs in authoritarian countries or "flawed democracies" need to be careful not to cross the regime. Where civil society clampdowns are in effect, the actual information in NGO reports tends to be quite superficial, and there is little pointed analysis.

Finally, TNOs, including development banks, publish socio-economic data and indices, routine country development reports, and reports on specific development challenges in a country. For top-level information on governance and socio-economic trends, these sources can be very useful. The authoring organisations tend to be very technocratic, in other words led in part by functional and academic specialists, and analysts are often highly qualified economists or other experts. Global and regional TNOs have a direct presence in their member countries or countries which they assist, and therefore a reasonable degree of access to local dynamics and players. Access is not always reflected in their reports, which seldom focus on highly localised issues, but it provides TNOs with an opportunity for a degree of first-hand verification of the data they gather.

It might seem like a TNO is a safe bet for accurate, if perhaps un-nuanced, information. However, TNOs are comprised of people from member governments, which have at least some stake in influencing TNO policy and reporting to favour national interest. TNOs also derive their funding from member states, and some, like the US or China, see influence over major TNOs as a source of competitive strategic advantage. As for perspective, neo-liberal economic values tend to underpin economic assessments. This is even the case for regional development banks, which in spite of a regional perspective are still very plugged into the global financial system. For these reasons, we cannot assume that just because a TNO is large, technocratic and nationally pluralistic that its reported information is always accurate. An illustration of issues that can arise in TNO reporting was the World Bank's investigation into its own *Ease of Doing Business* index in 2020, which indicated, although did not definitively conclude, that governments had sought to influence their countries' scores. On a slightly different note, the author has often been surprised by the sharp difference between country governance and doing business scores. Governance scores can make a country look very challenging, yet its doing business scores can paint a relatively rosy picture. For the most part, data from TNOs is sufficiently sound for a top-level contextual picture. However, as an input into specific assessments it should be corroborated and adjusted based on credible alternative sources.

We conclude contextual sources with knowledgeable casual contacts. We have noted that field-work and interviews with human sources usually occur in the latter half of a learning process, when we have specific intelligence gaps that only up-close and personal discussions can resolve. However, there is nothing to stop us from arranging a phone call or meeting with knowledgeable people simply to help get a clearer contextual picture. We might know an executive who managed a project in the target country, or we could arrange call with a diplomat based there. Even political risk analysts and county experts can be happy to casually share knowledge (if their bosses insist on charging, a one-hour call could still be worth it). We cannot expect much from a general chat, but listening to someone with considerable experience on the ground can be instructive and simply make the country seem more three-dimensional than what we get from reports. How much we reveal about our interest depends on our relationship with the source. We can also assume that in a casual discussion a source will not strive to be particularly objective.

MID-STAGE OPEN SOURCES

We can assume that we now have a reasonable contextual picture of the target, and have broken it down into smaller pieces for investigation. Bear in mind, however, that the learning process is a continuum rather than having certain cut-off points where one stage ends and the next begins. We would usually continue to build contextual insight even as we start more detailed research, and we would also use a blend of general and highly targeted information. Thus, the types of sources we examined in the last section remain relevant now, and it is mainly our use of them that becomes more specific. One key difference from contextual learning is that now we will go beyond a search for accurate information and start to examine some sources which are instructive specifically because they could be skewed by values and interests. Bearing in mind that contextual sources could remain useful, here we will examine a few additional types, again only as reference points in a wide array of possibilities. These include trackers and indices, social media and websites, and local news media. More briefly, we will also consider imagery, company records and the dark web.

There are a variety of online trackers and publicly available indices that capture trends in specific socio-political dynamics. These sometimes come with little context or analysis, but as part of our own analysis they can be useful for indications of the prevalence and frequency of potentially problematic behaviours. One typical example is the Armed Conflict Location & Event Data Project (ACLED), which tracks armed conflict and violent unrest. The Global Initiative Against Transnational and Organized Crime publishes the *Global Organized Crime Index*, and the *Global Terrorism Index*, produced by Institute for Economics and Peace, provides data on global terrorist activity. These just scratch the surface, though. One can find trackers for specific regions, such as the Oxus Society for International Affairs' *Central Asia Protest Tracker*, and for labour strikes in particular countries, for example the China Labour Bulletin's *Strike Map*. Trackers and indices provided by established NGOs, think tanks and universities tend to be reasonably accurate, but how they define the target activities can affect what they include. If we were seeking precise data for our own modelling, we would need to corroborate sources and aggregate the most relevant data. However, the better sources are suitable for a general assessment of a given problematic activity. They save us considerable legwork, since they rely on the same sources, such as media reports, social media and government travel advisories, that we would need to go through to get similar results.

Next, social media use is often constrained in more authoritarian countries, but even then it can offer insights into public perspectives on political issues and rivalries, government disinformation campaigns and the concerns that underlie it, and sometimes the status of bottom-up dissent. Especially since the Arab Spring, because of government information controls in most complex emerging markets, there is seldom a sufficient volume of social media commentary around sensitive political issues to apply data and network analysis. But we can plug into social media feeds and discussion boards, and with a quiet profile observe communications on the subject of interest. Analysts have also used Twitter and similar platforms to learn about specific events and incidents long before they made the news, if indeed they did at all.

Social media, along with the websites of specific political organisations, government agencies or religious groups are seldom useful for accurate information. Their utility mainly comes from their direction of inaccuracy, or skewing, which can reveal important patterns in social and state-society relations. For example, hyperbolic or rabid language for or against a sub-nation or ideology, apparent consensus on an issue that objectively would seem quite divisive, and a nearly total absence of commentary on what we know is a key event or change could all be instructive depending on our intelligence target. Interpreting social media and website information relies on solid contextual awareness and an understanding of relevant dynamics in a country, but after that it not only fills in some important blanks but provides unique insights into the fears and ambitions that drive problematic behaviour.

Moving on to news, international news outlets are an obvious source, and we would no doubt read much of their reporting in the course of a case. But as our need for nuance increases, local, in-country news is more instructive for two reasons. One is that local news outlets can provide relatively granular insight on socio-political dynamics, based on journalists' direct presence in the environment, and sources within the socio-political milieu. In other words, they have high access. Another reason, though, is that national mainstream news can be ordinary people's main source of information, and, as with social media and websites, how news is skewed can reveal how and why powerful interests, not least a government, are trying to influence public opinion.

We discussed local news outlets in stakeholder analysis when looking at the civil society domain. The media sub-domain within that mapped the media landscape, so that we had an idea of who controlled different outlets and how they might exercise control. It is difficult to know how to interpret a given article or report without first having this broader understanding of how the media works in a country. In one case I worked on, media ownership and links between the government and owners seemed deliberately opaque. Thus, upon starting fieldwork, some of our earlier discussions were actually with editors and journalists from some of the major papers. They were reasonably forthright. Once we had a better picture of the sector, it was possible not only to extract factual reporting from the news to learn about actual twists and turns in national politics, but to get a sense of the evolving concerns and aspirations of owners, who were often influential business leaders. State press is also instructive, less for potential facts that we might glean, and more for a regime's influencing priorities.

In terms of journalistic standards, in all but the most authoritarian countries there are various shades of grey. Individual journalists often aspire to high standards, and it is quite feasible to obtain factual information from news even in countries where the government and business-political cronies control much of the media. Again, however, knowing the media landscape and interests therein helps to weed out spin and misdirection. Sometimes committed journalists need to write between the lines in order to avoid hassles, and we will need to be able to read between the lines in order to learn what they are trying to convey.

The above types of sources were only indicative. One can find an array of relevant reporting online, sometimes from unexpected sources. For example, donor agencies that partly sponsor developing country infrastructure projects sometimes publish project appraisals and even risk assessments which can be useful, and even travel blogs or "vlogs" can be instructive.

We now turn to some less common sources. One is imagery, a relatively new source for private sector intelligence. Up until the 2000s, governments had a near monopoly on satellite imagery, but along with Google Earth came the growth in private satellite providers and space transport companies. At the time of writing, satellite imagery is being used for analysis and planning by news organisations, urban planners, climate scientists, academics and companies. Closer to the political risk context, it is also used for social-environmental impact assessments. Directly within our context, imagery on a given community, like the Town A example in stakeholder analysis, can be highly instructive, giving analysts a tangible sense of the socio-political terrain, and an ability to see what flashpoints and high-risk areas actually look like. Evacuation planning benefits from the analysis of routes, potential bottlenecks and other attributes of the ground that could affect staff movement to extraction sites. Finally, imagery can inform conflict analysis. Troop and refugee movements, and physical evidence of battle, can provide indications of armed activity that might not make it into the mainstream news for some time.

In the late 1970s, US and other Western intelligence services saw such rapid improvements in satellite and signals collection that it seemed that traditional spying was becoming a thing of the past. Not only was spying risky, but by comparison to technology, the human factor was complicated and hard to control. This perception actually led to cutbacks in clandestine capabilities, which left a very noticeable intelligence gap, and led to a stark realisation that "techint" was no substitute for knowing values, attitudes and intentions, not to mention capabilities hidden from view. While imagery and other technological sources do not suffer from bias or fabricate, a bias towards technology is a potential pitfall in itself. As others have learned, however handy or wondrous it seems, it can augment but not replace other types of sources.

The next source, company records, is usually more applicable to corporate investigations, but it can still be instructive in our context. If we know that certain local companies will be relevant to the user's initiative, records can shed light on ownership structures, legal status and liabilities, and tax status. There are a variety of company information services that one can subscribe to or purchase data from, but in developing countries records might not be online or otherwise readily available to such services. One might need to use a local investigator, or an international law or accountancy firm with a presence in the country, to garner company information, or save that research for fieldwork when records can be directly sought. Note that in many developing and transitional countries records can be patchy, and there is often low official interest in ensuring their accuracy; thus, they cannot always be taken at face value despite being in an official registry.

The other source is not really a source, rather a tool. This is the dark web (as an aside, this is often confused with the deep web, which contains unindexed web pages). The dark web contains pages and sites which are deliberately unavailable to a public search. It does not just contain criminal services and transaction hubs, but that is a significant part of it. A dark web search might turn up information on illicit activities of organisations that users might need to deal with, and just as importantly, it can show if the user organisation has been compromised. For example, the user organisation or its staff could turn up in offers of stolen data or false identities, or as a prospective target for cyber-attacks. Knowing this, users could initiate an internal investigation to trace the source of data leaks and remedy vulnerabilities. Using the dark web for research is potentially risky since other actors therein might notice us. The Tor browser, which provides access, anonymises searches, but even so, a VPN, a separate computer and IP address, a robust alias and other precautions are warranted.

Both company records and dark web searches are usually more relevant to due diligence investigations on specific companies and people, and general corporate security, than they are to political risk cases. However, there is a fine line between investigation and stakeholder analysis, and some cases bridge the two exercises. Additionally, operations in highly charged environments or contexts can easily attract the wrong attention or incur hostility. When an operation is contentious or subject to acute predatory interest, it is sensible to more regularly check the integrity of operational and company data.

FIELDWORK AND HUMAN SOURCES

We now turn to fieldwork and human sources, which particularly apply to cases when the user will be in or facing a complex environment or situation, as opposed to just considering where to go or how feasible a presence might be. Note that for brevity we often use "fieldwork" to include human source discussions. Discussions can occur anywhere, but access to human sources is a significant reason for fieldwork, and hence the two are closely linked. To reiterate, because fieldwork and human sources are potentially very valuable and quite complex, this section constitutes the bulk of the chapter.

This section begins with the rationale for fieldwork. There is a need to state the case, because it is an underutilised approach in political risk intelligence, yet it can be the key to robust results. We then examine the chain of human sources, and human source assessment. Next, we consider observation visits, both as a specific exercise and as an element of casework in a country, before moving onto source interviewing. We wrap up this section, and the chapter, with some thoughts on managing the risks that political risk intelligence collectors can face in sensitive environments.

THE RATIONALE

To begin this discussion, Figure 13.2 on the next page is a basic conceptual depiction of the rationale for the use of fieldwork and human sources.

To this point, we have considered open sources that can be accessed remotely. For some intelligence requirements, like initial feasibility analysis or scenario analysis, we can usually get all we need from a desk and a computer in our home town. For more in-depth requirements, though, open sources run out of steam at a certain point. A case brief might call for the detailed illumination of certain targets, or an attuned sense of what is going on in a place and in the minds of relevant actors therein. If fieldwork is not a part of the exercise, we can end up going around in circles, trying this or that research avenue with increasing desperation. In the end, we face a stark choice: heavily extrapolate from what we know to make general suppositions about what we do not, and then extensively qualify findings, or tell users that certain parts of the brief cannot be confidently addressed and just report what we know. Both are less than ideal. Fieldwork is what can take us that last mile, from a second-hand open-source picture in which we can only interpret vague shapes, to a clear and nuanced one from which we can extract actionable findings.

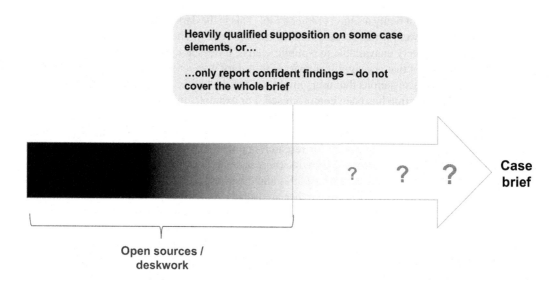

FIGURE 13.2   The rationale for fieldwork.

The rationale for fieldwork and the use of human sources is not always clear in political risk. This is mainly because of an increasing, and mutually reinforcing, tendency among both user organisations, namely international companies, and political risk consultancies to regard open sources as a magic bullet. For users, open-source results are relatively quick and cheap. For consultancies, open sources allow for price competition, with the low price per project is offset by the volume of quick pieces and open-source report subscription sales. This tendency is linked to the exponential growth in online information and the technology to extract, model and present it. Dense and data-heavy reports, visually appealing interactive dashboards and user-friendly databases all give the appearance that open sources can do the job. As noted, in some cases they can. But if we assume that open sources alone work for every requirement, intelligence will be weak when we need it the most, specifically when we will be in particularly sensitive, complex and potentially dangerous circumstances.

Open-source information is what other people and organisations report and publish for their own purposes. They will probably never know about our complex intelligence requirement, let alone the attributes of our organisation. No matter how apparently relevant a piece of open-source information is, it is tangent to, as opposed to directly pointed at, our problem. Thus, using open sources is always an exercise in extrapolation. We might know A, B and C, but they were not derived and conveyed for our purpose, so we need to triangulate their meaning to us. Fieldwork, by contrast, puts me as the questioner at, or much closer to, the heart of the thing I need to know about. I derive the information that I need, so it directly intersects with my requirement.

At risk of belabouring the relevance of fieldwork, there is a good argument that one should not even bother trying to address certain intelligence needs if open sources are the only option. By way of illustration, I and a colleague with military intelligence experience in recent conflicts met a prospective client who expressed a need for stakeholder analysis in a complex country. The manager explained that the results were needed quite quickly and there was no budget for fieldwork, and helpfully suggested that deskwork and open sources would suffice. My colleague, who had made a career out of trying to understand communities and rivalries in tense environments, told him that a desk-based exercise would do more harm than good. Trying to engage with stakeholders in the country on the basis of only open-source intelligence would lead to serious mistakes. It was better to go with no preconceptions than weak intelligence, because at least then the company would be cautious and learn on the ground. In short, some things are not worth doing if you cannot do them well. In a political risk context, doing it well means resources, such as the right team and enough time, but it can also mean fieldwork.

We can conclude the rationale not with more argumentation, rather with a few concrete illustrations of things that never would have been confidently learned just from a desk:

- An important organisation that looked fine from the outside was riven by sub-national factional rivalries, to the point to which different directors would hardly speak to each other and indeed seemed to harbour the worst of mutual intentions. Core functions undertaken by junior staff were reasonably sound, but senior in-fighting meant that the organisation's contribution within the wider institutional framework was limited. It did not speak with one voice and its inter-organisational diplomacy was incoherent because of competing senior agendas.
- The town in the south where the company was looking at a potential infrastructure project was wholly controlled by an armed faction that formed the de facto government in the area, and this effectively made the location part a separate political entity with its own laws, police and even "state" TV channels. Working on a "government" project there would have actually meant dealing with two distinct governments. There would have been no way to verify and understand the depth of the faction's control without seeing it first-hand and talking to people in the area.
- The regime was paranoid to the point to which it had created eight security services (six with an independent power of arrest and their own jails) that routinely spied on each other and the public. Despite this, armed clan factions still ran their own fiefdoms and uneasily shared a monopoly on the use of force with the central government. The initiative in question would require an ongoing, delicate balancing act, and adaptation to the paranoid political culture.
- A major state company partner was paralysed by senior-level purges, a politicised anti-corruption campaign, and competing factional pressure for control over company contract allocations and indeed even company profits. Unless or until the president managed to reassert control, the state company would be incapable of making important strategic decisions and would be hesitant to commit to new major projects with foreign partners.
- When dealing with host communities in the area of operation, managers needed to understand and consult with heads of traditionally powerful families who were simultaneously community leaders, landowners, businessmen, arbitrators and, in some ways, mafia dons. It was possible to get central government help to deal with them, but direct negotiation on local issues and seeking mutual understanding was far preferable for a smooth long-term relationship.
- Despite the country's reputation as highly unstable and riven by sub-national tensions, for the most part normal life continued unaffected by sporadic violence, and this extended to business, where business leaders were more interested in mutual opportunity than ethnic advantage. The country's portrayal in open sources was based on serious but relatively infrequent ethnic clashes, and was not reflective of day-to-day interaction.
- A few local staff with access to company information subtly threatened to disclose internal reports of labour and safety issues unless they were given better promotion prospects. The relevant manager had struggled to deal with this on their own, since there had been no formal channels to seek specialist guidance. This risk factor in information integrity would have remained obscure and its treatment ad hoc unless quiet, on-site management discussions had been a part of the intelligence exercise.

Just to be clear, a couple of the above examples came from engagements with non-commercial organisations.

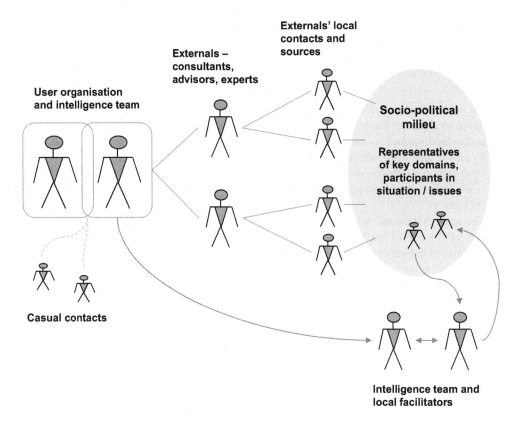

FIGURE 13.3   The chain of human sources.

HUMAN SOURCES

Figure 13.3 is a depiction of the types of human sources that a political risk intelligence case might engage with. Sources are shown in a chain from the user organisation through to the socio-political milieu in and involved with the target environment or situation. This is broadly typical for a more complex case, although any given requirement can yield its own variation.

We already discussed casual contacts in the context of background sources, and hence we leave them aside, although they could be revisited later in a case. The main chain, or network, of sources goes from us, namely the joint user-intelligence team, to the target. One could regard the distance between these points as a line of decreasing trust or confidence. The core case team is directly working with and for the user organisation, and they know each other well. One step removed are contracted externals, specialists we bring on board for their unique expertise and access. We might have long-standing relationships with some of them, but they are not "us". We will learn about the externals' contacts and sources in the target milieu, but we will probably not meet them, and hence not know them. Their contacts in turn could have their own sources, and we would rarely have a chance to even know who they are. Thus, with each step removed from the core team, there is more access to the target, but less knowledge of and control over human sources. Core case team members' fieldwork provides a direct channel to the target milieu and hence mitigates some uncertainty in the source chain, but the trade-off between access and confidence still needs to be recognised and managed.

We will walk through the chain, from externals and their sources, to fieldwork, which includes facilitators and direct interview subjects in the target milieu. As we proceed, we will consider some of the means of managing the issue of confidence and some other challenges that arise with human sources. The section will conclude by briefly addressing human source assessment.

Externals contracted to the case or engaged for specific sub-elements might be specialist consultancies or other kinds of advisories, or freelance experts. Assuming that we have our own core intelligence team, externals would be selected based on their particular subject expertise and access. They would be able to directly answer some of our questions themselves, but we would also rely on them to activate and manage their own sources to get the insights we need. This means that, like the case team, externals need to be reasonably proficient at assessing and reporting information, which becomes raw intelligence for the case workstreams.

There are several considerations in managing externals. One is trust. The more we trust an external, the more we can tell them about ourselves, and the more relevant and targeted their intelligence will be. If we only hire them for their expertise and access, without trusting them and sharing information, then their results might be useful but not directly for and about us. Trust comes from a prior relationship, vetting and/or referral from a trusted contact. It also comes from personal interaction prior to mutual commitment. For example, selecting a local consultancy at arm's length on the basis of a tender seldom affords the chance to test a prospective relationship. Trust then builds over time through a case, particularly if externals are not just given a task and told to run with it but are included in at least some case discussions and reviews. Finally, our confidence in externals is linked to quality checks and verification. Core team members doing fieldwork can spend some time jointly working with externals both for their own learning and to check on the externals' activities and methods. Asking externals to provide interim reports and briefings allows us to test their emerging findings against other sources, and to ensure that their work is on target.

Assuming we trust an external, we need to make sure that they have the information they need to get relevant results. In one of the author's old cases, we contracted an expert on NGOs and the media in the target country. He came back with his results, which seemed strangely off base. It turned out that no one had informed him of a critical operational attribute which would have had a significant effect on local attitudes if not carefully managed. He managed to do a last-minute reinterpretation of his findings based on his understanding of the target milieu before the client workshop, but it was not ideal and it was a wasted opportunity for something better. We already discussed how users and intelligence managers need to have a frank discussion about user concerns and interests. The same applies to externals, as long as we can trust them with information about us.

In a similar vein, we need to decide how much externals can tell their sources about the user organisation when they seek information. If we trust an external to apply good judgement, we can leave this up to them. However, if the case is particularly sensitive, we might need a blanket stipulation that the external should not say who they are working for, and just describe the user organisation in broad terms. As we will see, case team members doing fieldwork will face the same decision, but with respect to particular interview subjects.

A final consideration was reflected in our discussion about authors, and how proximity to the subject often went hand in hand with a passionate perspective on it. Freelance experts in particular can have deep attachments to their subjects and very strong views. They are also seldom "intelligence people", and hence they do not proactively try to weed out normative judgements. Their findings are often uniquely valuable because of their access, but we might need to account for an intense perspective in our interpretation. In another case that I was involved with, one external expert with deep knowledge of the country and issues had a long and close association with a dissident group, and was himself highly critical of the regime. If we took his reports at face value, we would have concluded that the government was led by a venal cabal with zero interest in development or in attracting legitimate FDI. That was plainly countered by other more corroborated findings, which did not yield such a stark portrayal. Thus, his judgements only had some effect on the emerging picture, but the details he provided on regime dynamics and factional cliques were highly instructive. Because we have a working relationship with externals, there are opportunities to talk and test, but in the end, we might need to extract the facts and take the judgement with a grain of salt.

We should note that externals are not always brought in as an extension of the case team. In one instance, we realised that we were missing appropriate nuance on the rather convoluted and shifting institutional framework that governed FDI in the client's sector. We hired an industry analyst with expertise on the country to deliver a one-day workshop to the case team, and a good part of that was discussion around our outstanding questions. We could trust his expertise because we knew his public writing on the subject, and we did not need to trust his character because in that context he could be effective without knowing anything about the user aside from its sector.

Just for a flavour of who and what externals can be, below are a few types that have been involved in past casework:

- a sociologist and journalist with expertise on civil society and society-state relations in the target country, tasked to develop the civil society domain;
- a master's student and son of a state company director in the target country, tasked to report on the status of recent business reforms (in this case, there were low confidentiality requirements);
- an anthropologist with extensive academic fieldwork in the target country and area of operations, tasked to examine local traditional authorities and clan/tribal dynamics;
- an ex-special forces freelance security consultant with first-hand knowledge of the security situation and the security services in the target country;
- a retired diplomat (and perhaps intelligence officer) who had once been posted to the target country and who maintained contacts there, tasked to report on regime dynamics;
- a retired senior director with the target country's national oil company, tasked to report on decision processes in the formation of foreign partnerships (again there were low confidentiality requirements in this instance); and
- a local business consultancy with extensive business and government contacts, tasked to provide a picture of the business domain and profiles of key influencers.

We turn to the next layer, externals' sources. Consultants and freelancers usually rely on their social contacts and extended networks in a country for insights. Indeed, much of what an external learns is usually over a coffee or phone call with an old colleague or friend with insights on specific sub-targets. These discussions are relatively informal. In some cases, an external's sources will also be in the information business, and there would be tacit agreement that they would receive the same courtesy of a discussion if someday they needed help with their own work.

Sometimes an external will pay their sources for time and expenses, and local consultancies obviously factor in the costs of their own staff utilisation and retained specialists. This would be accounted for as a cost in the external's fee. That should be the extent of monetary payments to sources. Especially where official corruption is pervasive, it might be relatively easy to pay an official or business person for confidential information. Sometimes international investigations on specific people or organisations bribe for confidential insights. In our context, payment should not be an inducement to breach ethics or laws to provide information. One reason is that it would be corruption, and, if traced back to the user organisation, it would hurt credibility. Another is that it could look like attempted espionage and that carries serious risks and liabilities. Finally, confidential, or secret, information obtained from a single source is rarely reliable. Financial opportunity easily leads to fabrication, and a single piece of exclusive information is usually so hard to corroborate that it has little effect on an overall assessment. Intelligence agencies have the resources to manage the risks of paying for secrets and to verify them. Political risk case teams seldom do. In short, paying for confidential information carries high risk for scant reward.

The above does not suggest that externals' sources should only provide information already in the public domain. The value of source information is that it derives from interaction between people active in the target milieu and those who keep their ears to the ground on certain issues and topics. This results in highly nuanced and instructive insights, without any need for seeking secrets. Some source information could make governments or other actors uncomfortable even if it were acquired without subterfuge, and hence sources and the externals managing them might need to exercise discretion, but this is the extent of any relationship to espionage practices.

This brings us to human sources involved in fieldwork undertaken by members of the core case team. However, before talking about people, we should address why core team fieldwork is valuable even when we have externals with access on board.

First, the case team will be doing the final assessment and reporting, and a direct, unfiltered sense of attitudes and dynamics in the target environment puts both tasks on firmer ground. The author has seen complex cases in which those doing the final interpretation had never even been to the target country or even region. Their second-hand sense of it showed in stilted, somewhat generalised results. Those responsible for the final results should be able to convey a living, three-dimensional target to users, not an abstraction built from data points. Fieldwork also allows the case team to better verify and corroborate information coming from externals and their sources, and through some overlap with externals to build trust in the relationship. Third, core case team members should handle the more sensitive stakeholder discussions, so that they retain control over tone and discretion and can fluidly adjust questions to address key gaps in the total intelligence picture. Finally, if the user organisational already has a presence in the environment, fieldwork allows for sensitive in-company discussions to discern relevant concerns and experiences and to assess political risk management practices.

Turning to people involved in fieldwork, one or two core case team members would undertake it, usually after open-source research and interim reporting from externals have identified at least initial fieldwork information targets. Fieldwork would be assigned to case team members on the basis of their prior knowledge of the country, language skills if relevant, fieldwork experience and the relevance of fieldwork to their assigned parts of the case. Again, if the user organisation already had offices in the target environment, then case team members could deploy earlier than the actual fieldwork stage, and indeed a whole case could be handled from the local office. Just being in the country accelerates learning, even in the initial contextual stages.

The fieldwork facilitator is another key person. As a citizen embedded in the target country, they are a source in themselves, but also a door-opener and, in some ways, a chaperone. Their main roles are helping the case team to find and access relevant interview subjects, and sometimes to partake in interviews to help handle cultural sensitivities or the subject's wariness about speaking to a foreigner. Translation can be a role too. "Fixer" is another, perhaps more common, label for facilitator, but it often suggests helping to get bureaucratic permits, which are not relevant to our context.

Fieldwork does not always need a facilitator, or not for the whole fieldwork exercise. For example, in one of the author's cases, we managed to organise some source interviews before leaving for the target country, and once there, we obtained more. However, these were mainly with easily identifiable and accessible sources, including foreign diplomats and NGO workers, and local law firms, press editors and business managers. These were useful but we wanted a flavour of regime dynamics too, and so activated a facilitator whom we had dealt with in the past. He set up discussions with members of the ruling party and political scientists focusing on domestic politics. He attended the discussions with the ruling party representatives because of their hesitancy about meeting foreign consultants without a mutually trusted interlocutor. The blend of our own wide-angle sources and his more politically informed ones was instructive. If the exercise had had less-specific requirements, we could have made do on our own. Conversely, sometimes we might benefit from more than one facilitator. For example, a facilitator might be well plugged into civil society and could help with access to traditional authorities and NGOs, and another might be well connected in the business domain.

Depending on how much, and specifically how, we need to rely on a facilitator, trust and a good working relationship are critical. It is ideal if we know them well beforehand. Political risk consultancies that have a fieldwork capability often proactively seek and retain potential facilitators, so that vetted and trusted support is on hand should the need arise. Likewise, in-company intelligence teams might have access to either current or past local company staff who have proven to be professional and trustworthy. If we need to recruit a facilitator from scratch, we can rely on trusted contacts for recommendations, but even then there should be a trial engagement to test the relationship before committing. In one instance, for example, the author had a workshop with an international organisation in a country, and decided to see how a local contact there would work in a facilitation role. I asked him to set up a few meetings. The contact proved to be well plugged-in and energetic, but he lacked the appropriate subtlety for political risk work. There had been no mention of a more enduring arrangement, so we parted ways and stayed in touch on a friendly basis.

There can be trade-offs between a facilitator's access and their trustworthiness and appropriateness for the role. For example, an ex-state company executive or military officer would have access to some interesting parts of the target milieu, but if they would intimidate subjects, or not accept that they are only playing a support role, then a conscientious and mature graduate student could be preferable even if they lacked the same access. We need to accept that we need to adapt too. In another case, my facilitator was assigned by the client organisation, and at first I found him to be too boisterous and laid-back. I decided to hang in there for a while, and it became clear that I had misinterpreted his persona, which was more of an easy-going gregariousness that helped to put people at ease. After some mutual annoyance, we eventually made a good team.

Given that facilitators would have at least some understanding of our interests and learn more about our lines of enquiry as fieldwork proceeded, there are risks. We will not consider every possibility and angle. Rather, if we are confident that we have planned for the two worst-case scenarios, then we are probably reasonably well covered. One is that they learn enough about us to do damage if they told the wrong people, and then apply this lever if we ever try to end the relationship. Another is that they are actually working for and reporting to someone else. How concerned we should be depends on how well we know them, the sensitivity of the case, and how much we need to rely on them. If the first is low and the next two are high, then due diligence and considerable testing prior to any commitment would be warranted.

We now turn to the final cog in the human source chain, interview subjects. There is no specific type. Depending on the case, we will seek discussions with people in different domains, from different perspectives, and from different socio-political strata. There are source discussions for contextual awareness, for detailed facts and for perspectives and attitudes, and the same source could be appropriate for more than one of these angles. In general, it is instructive to have discussions both with knowledgeable people on the outside of an issue or situation, and with direct participants therein. The outside view helps with an understanding of relevant dynamics and socio-political structures, and the inside one helps to obtain a direct sense of the interests and values that drive relevant behaviours.

Sources in the target milieu can be motivated to share insights for several reasons. A common one among other professionals is learning. They will tell us something, but they expect us to share some insights too, and some might be seeking contacts for their own future research on other topics. Curiosity is a motive as well, especially in a developing country where foreigners seldom show up asking for a chat. Another motive is to convey their perspective, or to persuade us of the validity of their beliefs or position. Finally, people can have an earnest interest in mutual understanding, or ensuring that we know the ins and outs of a situation, and that they grasp the position that we represent. In the last instance, there would be an expectation that we share information about ourselves and the user organisation. Sometimes it is risky to share what they want to know, and if we are not prepared to do so, we need to accept that we might not get much more than generalities.

Along with sources in the milieu, as noted earlier, if the user company has an ongoing operation in the country, fieldwork can, and often should, include interviews with both expat and local staff. The aim is to learn first-hand experiences of working in the country, problems and concerns that formal channels might not have accounted for, and perceived gaps in how political risk is dealt with. We had some prior examples of issues that were revealed in internal discussions. To recount, these were friction between local staff and expat managers, threats to disclose company information as part of a pay and promotion bid, and a lack of information-sharing between functions involved in political risk management. In other cases, the author learned from internal discussions junior staff's concerns about executive managers' blasé attitude to personnel risk, concerns about the integrity and intentions of local partners, and the anxious dilemmas that managers had faced in dealing with local staff detentions and disappearances. Internal interviews are not an invitation for whistle-blowing, but we need to be ready for the instance of learning about perceived misdeeds and negligence, and prepared to pass on sensitive information to the appropriate level of management. For the most part, internal discussions simply help us to obtain a tangible, living picture of the object of the intelligence exercise, the operation and its people, and to learn what they know about the place, but if urgent issues are revealed, all the better for operational integrity and resilience.

All human sources, including externals and their contacts, facilitators, interview subjects and company personnel, have their foibles and weaknesses. Most people that we end up dealing with will be sincere and provide something useful, but we cannot assume that. Thus, we conclude the discussion of human sources with a brief consideration of source assessment. We already discussed the basic components of source quality. Applied to human sources, the framework in Figure 13.4 is a basic guide. The specific contents of each box are illustrative, and there could be other variations.

The matrix only has four boxes, but in practice each axis would be a continuum and motives can be mixed. The only box that contains relatively useless sources is the darker one on the bottom left. Low access and low credibility mean that someone cannot tell us much. They might try, but their credibility is so questionable that we can safely doubt their veracity. We can learn something from sources in each of the other boxes. Ideal sources, in the upper right, are rare but valuable. Low access but sincere sources can be useful for contextual insights. Players in rivalries or other high-stakes situations are prone to providing one-sided and distorted insights, but as long as we know where they are coming from, their perspectives are instructive. Note that this can even apply to in-company sources, since office-political feuds can give rise to one-sided information. Aside from externals and facilitators, we will not be able to vet sources before we talk to them, but we will have some prior sense of where they fit in the above framework. This can be further understood during interaction, and afterwards when we compare the information obtained in a discussion with information from other sources. We will seldom be getting the fully accurate, unvarnished truth from human sources,

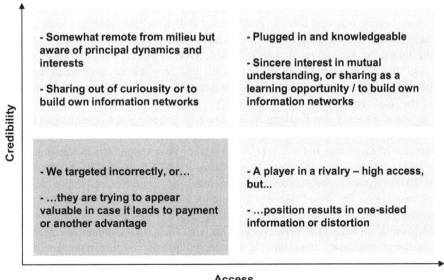

FIGURE 13.4 Human source assessment.

but as long as we targeted the right people, and account for their blind spots and biases, their contributions are usually very instructive.

We now proceed to observation visits, which make use of human sources, but in casual and ad hoc ways that build our direct sense of the target environment.

OBSERVATION

An observation visit can be a reconnaissance of a location to help inform a user about the feasibility of working there, and it can be conducted well before the launch of an operation for a stronger sense of what to expect upon entering a country. Observation can also occur during a case conducted in the target location, or as an aspect of a wider fieldwork exercise. In the latter two instances, the observation aspect is usually what a case team member does on their own to build a better feel for a place, even while working on more structured tasks most of the week. There is no particular formula for observation. It is mainly for intangible learning and is somewhat opportunistic. Rather than discuss it in abstract terms, two examples help to illustrate the exercise and its potential value. One was an actual observation visit and the other was observation done alongside structured casework.

The first example was one of my earliest political risk cases. An international construction company was considering a port project in Nouakchott, Mauritania. No one in the company knew anything about the country, which in those days was quite obscure to most people in Europe and North America. My task was to provide a background report on the overall business environment, and a sense of what it was really like on the ground there. After some research, I spent ten days in the country's capital city on a tourist visa.

My first instructive experience was upon arrival, when I encountered a rather strange permutation of official corruption. An airport police officer insisted on escorting me to my hotel, told the taxi driver to charge a high fee and then pocketed most of it for himself, and then insisted that he would pick me up in the morning to visit his village. I arranged not to see him, thanks to helpful hotel staff, and then proceeded to explore. The port area was one target, but so too were shantytowns around the city centre, the embassy and government neighbourhood, and the commercial district. My relationship with the hotel staff, and in particular the manager, was helped by my being only one of two guests. The manager was a Lebanese émigré, and his extended family had been well plugged into the local social scene for decades. I ended up spending a considerable amount of time with him and his cousins, and in the process learned their perspectives on national and local politics, ethnic relations and the business landscape. The hotel staff were from different local ethnic groups and were happy to share their insights. In the end, while a rather bizarre trip in some ways, it added considerable nuance to the final report, particularly in terms of a genuine flavour of what it would be like to live and work in the city. As an addendum, the first person I encountered at the airport upon departure was the friendly officer, who this time insisted on personally chaperoning me through exit procedures (no "fee" required).

In the second example, I was working in-country on a donor agency case in conjunction with a small NGO. The assessment involved interviews in different locations, but that was nearly the extent of my awareness of the place, and local socio-political divisions were actually an important aspect of the research. After mainly being glued to a desk for a while, I decided to see things for myself. There were always the same few taxi drivers taking breaks at the hotel, and I got to know them. Our discussions were useful, but then I began to arrange for long evening and weekend tours of the city and its environs. These excursions included visiting common flashpoints in the area and the key geographic lines of division. The drivers would provide their own commentary, which was one-sided but passionate and instructive, since their social groups were important players in local issues. Complemented by several long walks in socially divided areas, my formal work was increasingly supported by a tangible feel for the socio-political geography. Without the observation aspect, the experience would have been as if I had been based in a foreign city and only teleported in for the odd discussion. With this additional aspect, I had a much better sense of the subject that I was supposed to be assessing. Just being somewhere does not mean much if we spend most of our time at a desk.

There are different possible occasions for observation, but in all of them, directly seeing and experiencing the target environment makes a significant difference. Observation is often underutilised by both users and intelligence teams, who can feel that as long as they have someone in the field reporting in, they can stay in their offices and just make sense of what arrives in the inbox. As noted earlier, though, doing a final interpretation and report with no idea of what the target environment even looks like leads to somewhat abstract results. Additionally, our externals' sources might be working the same ground, but they are likely so familiar with it that significant local quirks seem entirely normal to them. If we are ultimately reporting to a foreign organisation, itself a prospective newcomer and outsider, it helps to bring an outsider's perspective to the table.

INTERVIEWS

We covered much that was relevant to interviews in the section on human sources. Thus, rather than explain variations and approaches in detail, here we will briefly present some important considerations in interview planning and conduct:

- Have an agenda but be flexible. We will have a sense of how a source can help, and we can build an agenda on that basis. However, sources can take discussions in directions of particular interest to them, and if we prioritise an agenda over a conversation's flow, we can hinder spontaneity and even inhibit them from being open.
- Break the ice and follow up. Someone might need to get to know us over casual conversation before openly talking with us. We can keep an initial discussion general, and then ask for another chat later on to follow up on specifics. Multiple discussions with someone can be beneficial anyway, and we should try to keep the possibility open.
- Beforehand, decide whether or not the facilitator should be involved. A facilitator's presence can help to put a source at ease, but too many people could be intimidating, or the facilitator might not have the appropriate style for a given conversation.
- Also beforehand, decide how much we can share about our purpose and the user organisation. As with all sources, the more we tell them about our interests, the more pointed the results, but sometimes it could be risky to identify the intelligence user.
- Translators, if required, should not have a stake in our interpretation of the discussion, or they might put their own slant on the source's words. We also need to assess the potential risk of a translator hearing the exchange, and accordingly be cautious about who fills the role.
- Consider sensitivities. A source might be worried about being known to have spoken with us. They might have strong values and could easily be offended. They could have particular expectations in terms of cultural protocols. Finally, they might not want to share much information about themselves. We should adapt to sensitivities, including, if need be, by providing reasonable assurances that the source's identity would not be linked to any particular finding, or even mentioned in any reports. We should also ask before taking notes.
- Do not appear to judge a source. A source could have an unsavoury role or past, or they might come across as unethical. It might be hard to control our inner reaction to a source, but we should not let our judgement show, and should focus on getting relevant insights.
- Be careful about paranoid governments and surveillance. Sometimes a source finds a discussion with a foreigner to be a refreshing chance to vent political frustrations. We can control for the discretion that the location of an interview affords, but even then, in the source's and our own interests, we should steer a discussion back to safer ground if it could lead to unwanted government interest.

As journalists, HR managers, academics and investigators know, interviewing is an art in itself, and there is much more that could be listed by way of general good practice. One point that is worth stressing is that it helps to spend some time in a place before starting interviews. General, casual social interaction in the local culture helps to mentally prepare oneself for in-depth engagement with specific people. The point about the risk of incurring government concern will be revisited in the next section on managing risks in fieldwork.

In my own casework, I have come across reluctance and misdirection, but also passion and a sincere willingness to share. In some instances, we might have to sit through a dull, scripted monologue or lecture, and there is hardly an occasion to lift the pencil. In others, we realise that we struck a potential mother lode, and there is every reason to ask for another chat later on. In short, it is hard to know what to expect, and we need to be ready to adapt. A final practical point is that we should plan for everything to take longer than we might be accustomed to. In developing and transitional country cities, traffic can be terrible, and it can take a while to break the ice before a conversation flows. We should not try to squeeze too much into a day.

Managing Fieldwork Risks

There are number of professions that face risks in fieldwork. Humanitarian aid workers in conflict environments, academics researching armed groups and state violence, and human and animal rights groups conducting covert investigations all face considerable hazard. There is a range of guides and manuals on managing risks in sensitive or dangerous terrain. As a political risk intelligence team working for a company, hopefully not much in such material applies to us, but it is useful to be aware of it. Just a few examples of relevant guidance freely available online at the time of writing are:

- *Workbook on Security – Practical Steps for Human Rights Defenders at Risk* (Front Line Defenders, 2011);
- *Security Guidelines – for Research in Complex, Remote and Hazardous Places* (Hilhorst, Hodgson, Jansen, & Mena, 2016);
- *Security Considerations for Conducting Fieldwork in Highly Dangerous Places or on Highly Dangerous Subjects* (Felbab-Brown, 2014); and
- *Operational Security in Violent Environments – A Field Manual for Aid Agencies* (Humanitarian Practice Network, 2010).

Much of what is in these and other guides might seem extreme for an intelligence team that is essentially the extension of a foreign company seeking legitimate opportunities in a country. A case team is not going to a country to change anything, seek confidential information or develop a case against a government or other powerful actors. However, we are foreigners going to a complex environment, asking questions about politics and socio-political actors, thus, there is a need to be aware of the risks and to take reasonable precautions. It would be ironic, after all, if a political risk intelligence team did not turn their assessment and planning capabilities on themselves when they were the ones exposed to a challenging environment.

Personnel risk management in complex environments has grown into an extensive body of thought and practice, some of which overlaps with corporate security. It is impossible to make a dent in the subject in one subsection of a chapter, and it would be very distracting from our main focus on political risk intelligence if we tried. However, we can at least summarise the main issues that most directly pertain to political risk fieldwork, and some general risk management pointers. To be clear, wider duty of care processes and capabilities would be relevant. A case team member would face the same risks as any other foreigner in the place. A general risk assessment would indicate what needed to be accounted for, and a case team member should have the same kinds of support and insurance that would be appropriate for any foreign staff member.

Specifically concerning political risk intelligence fieldwork, the main challenge is that we are perceived as conducting espionage or as engaged in subversive activities. Our activities will not be typical of a foreign businessperson. Many of our meetings will be with non-business people. If we are surveilled, which can happen, it would be clear that we are interested in politics and different socio-political perspectives. If the security services accessed our full notes, and again this can happen especially since hotels are often required to support official snooping, things could seem even more suspicious. Ultimately, if we looked like we were in the country for the wrong reasons, we could be detained, interrogated and deported, or perhaps worse. The people we talked to could also be in for a rough ride.

While I have heard of private investigators and security consultants being detained, I have not heard of this happening to political risk professionals. However, political risk consultants have had their rooms searched, been under obtrusive surveillance and been stopped and asked some rather pointed questions about what they were doing in the country. Thus, depending on the place, the issue is entirely plausible, and I have had a couple of creepy experiences myself.

There are several ways of managing it. A basic one that is not going to fool a curious security service but which suffices for others is just to avoid using "political" and "intelligence" in any documentation we bring to the country, including business cards if we are consultants. We can tell people that we are international business advisors or use whatever other broad label would describe our activities. If the regime and, by extension, security services are paranoid, then they would likely know who we are quite soon, if they had not already learned after we had applied for a visa, but there is no point in wearing a political risk intelligence nametag.

Avoiding the label is as far as we want to go in looking like we are trying to conceal anything. A good rule of thumb for notes from discussions is to write down what we would not mind anyone seeing, and just remember the rest with the help of brief written cues. Trying to hide or code notes or using VPNs or different tricks with email to send notes back to HQ might work on casual snoopers, but for professionals it would probably just arouse suspicion. Bear in mind that as non-espionage people, any trick we learn is probably at least five years out of date. We might look like bad spies, but we could still look like spies. Aside from documentation, looking dodgy in our movements is another potential red flag. It is fine to have a meeting in a discrete location, but using clever manoeuvres to get there is not going to help. Even intelligence services in poor developing countries are very adept at what they do, and we should not underestimate their ability to keep tabs on someone who arouses their curiosity.

Academics and human rights investigators often meet people who are on a government watch list, or who might even be arrested for meeting a foreigner. I have met dissidents before, but they were grudgingly left more or less alone by the regime to avoid making them martyrs for their cause. In a political risk case, there is no need to meet people hiding from the regime. It might be very interesting, but it is not going to provide enough to be worth the risk of raising suspicions.

As noted earlier, we should be careful not to invite or even allow sources to expound at length on the regime's shortcomings. It can be instructive to hear dissenting perspectives first-hand, but we can get the picture pretty quickly and there is no point in risking our mutual security. We can politely refocus discussions onto less-sensitive topics. We also need to exercise discretion ourselves. In many emerging market countries, it is fine to talk about politics with casual contacts or in public places, but where a regime is paranoid, it can lead to problems. There is a chance that someone in the vicinity is an informant.

Going back to an earlier point, we should be aware that hotel rooms and hotel communications could be compromised. A number of people in one country told me that in hotels where foreigners stayed, there was an informant network and routine surveillance. In fact, hotels are favourite haunts for foreign intelligence services too, who regard them as hubs of international interaction and ideal targets for bugging and observation. In hotels, we need to behave as though we are periodically surveilled just to be on the safe side, and we should be careful what we leave in the room.

If the user company has an office in a country, it can provide a reasonably secure base, and if we work from there, it also assuages security service concerns about what we are doing and for whom. We could also try to arrange office space from an external or a facilitator if they run their own local business and if we trust them. Any friendly government contacts that they, or the user company, have could also be used to communicate the benign purpose of our work, and called upon if we experienced official hassles. In short, if there is a potential support base, we should certainly make the most of it.

We might also need to accept that certain types of sources would be too risky in a given context. For example, in a highly security conscious official environment, meeting with unofficial union leaders, or independent social justice NGOs, could inspire excessive official curiosity. We could tailor our plan to instead focus on sources that the regime has fewer concerns about, such as business executives, academics or members of the mainstream press. For those not familiar with tense environments, this might seem like a cop-out, but where a regime is unusually paranoid, it might be the only way to safely operate. We can still get useful, ground-level insights from more mainstream local sources.

A final approach is to include influential officials and diplomatic staff among our interview sources even if we do not really need their perspectives. Discussions with local officials increase our transparency to them, and if they report anything to security services, it would likely sound safely uninteresting. Diplomatic officials, including but not just from our home country, become aware of us and what we are doing, and could be able to assist if we had problems. Another benefit of both types of meetings is that if we are surveilled, security agencies might feel that we are too well connected to bother casually hassling. Keeping business cards from such meetings on hand is a good idea too, not just to be able to call someone if we got into trouble, but because if we were searched, the cards would be evidence of influential contacts and could be a subtle deterrent against further trouble. If a security agency has a serious concern about us, then these methods would be moot, but they can work to deter informal or unsanctioned hassle or intimidation.

As an aside, it is not unfeasible to actually meet security officials too, perhaps through diplomatic contacts. However, this needs to be carefully considered. The author has met security officials in the course of non-commercial casework, and some were helpful and open, but those were unique contexts. The main risk in such meetings for a commercial political risk case is that we inadvertently spark interest when there was none before or raise more questions in the minds of officials than they otherwise had.

A couple of points round out the above suggestions. One is that while we need to behave transparently, we still need to be discrete, especially when it comes to civil society interview sources. Being cautious about notes, locations and names is just common sense and professional in this context and would not look like we were exercising tradecraft.

The second point is that even if we were periodically surveilled, governments and security services usually have little interest in what foreign companies do to inform themselves, and this extends to what a case team is doing. It can vary tremendously by country and context, but even where a regime is very security conscious, they tend to have bigger things to worry about. However, we would be remiss if we did not assess the risk before setting out and conduct ourselves accordingly. Our own safety is one thing, but the whole point of the exercise is to help the user organisation to have a smooth experience in the country. It would not be a very good start if one of their earliest problems was how to get the political risk team out of jail, or how to convince a government that the company did not really send a team of covert operatives.

This concludes the discussion of intelligence sources. All types of sources are useful, but we obviously emphasised fieldwork and human sources. One can probably understand why at this point. They hold very high potential value, but they require much more sensitivity, planning and caution than any of the others. Again, on-the-ground methods tend to be downplayed in political risk, and this is ironic given how critical sound political risk intelligence can be for an operation. These approaches are not appropriate for every requirement, but when a company is, or will be, in a challenging environment, it needs actionable intelligence, not just more "about the country" knowledge. This is when fieldwork and human sources can make the difference.

REFERENCES

Felbab-Brown, V. (2014). *Security Considerations for Conducting Fieldwork in Highly Dangerous Places or on Highly Dangerous Subjects*. Washington D.C.: The Brookings Institution. Retrieved July 17, 2022, from https://www.brookings.edu/research/security-considerations-for-conducting-fieldwork-in-highly-dangerous-places-or-on-highly-dangerous-subjects/#:~:text=The%20full%20list%20of%20elements,supplies)%3B%20keeping%20a%20low

Front Line Defenders. (2011). *Workbook on Security: Practical Steps for Human Rights Defenders at Risk*. Retrieved July 17, 2022, from https://www.frontlinedefenders.org/en/workbook-security

Hilhorst, D., Hodgson, L., Jansen, B., & Mena, R. (2016). *Security Guidelines for Research in Complex, Remote and Hazardous Places*. The Hague: International Institute of Social Studies. Retrieved July 17, 2022, from https://ihsa.info/security-guidelines-for-field-research-in-complex-remote-and-hazardous-places/

Humanitarian Practice Network. (2010). *Operational Security Management in Violent Environments*. London: Overseas Development Institute. Retrieved July 17, 2022, from https://odihpn.org/publication/operational-security-management-in-violent-environments-revised-edition/

14 Intelligence Quality Pitfalls and Remedies

This chapter will complete the review of intelligence practices that underpin political risk exercises. As a brief recap, we started with intelligence management, particularly as it pertains to a political risk case. That took us through roles and workflows in the intelligence cycle, case design, case teams and reporting. Next, we examined political risk intelligence sources and their use and interpretation, with emphasis on fieldwork and human sources for nuanced insight on complex targets. Here, we will consider quality assurance in intelligence, again drawing on general principles but applying them to the context of political risk. However, for a tangible sense of why quality matters and to set the scene for this chapter, we begin with a brief prelude discussing some actual cases in which intelligence suffered from low quality and ultimately failed to have a beneficial effect.

Writings on quality in intelligence often take the backward approach of deconstructing cases of intelligence failure to discern what could have been done better. This approach is instructive, and we will apply it here. First, we will examine some elucidating national security cases and then briefly revisit the company cases discussed early in the book.

The menu of national security cases is extensive, and we will only examine four, beginning with the 1973 Arab-Israeli War. Despite solid intelligence on the build-up of Arab forces, Israel was slow to prepare for an attack, and only fully mobilised as it was happening. The main reason was overconfidence: Israeli planners thought that their Arab neighbours would simply not try a serious attack for fear of losing much of their armed forces and even more land. Along with this, Israel failed to grasp the more subtle point that at least for Egypt a clear Arab victory was not necessarily the aim. Rather, just reminding Israel of its vulnerability and hence of the value of negotiations was an end in itself (despite Egypt's battlefield losses during the war, this was actually partly achieved). Finally, overconfidence combined with the considerable inconvenience of, and political inhibition against, mobilising troops on the eve of Yom Kippur when the country was in a celebratory mood. Thus, a lack of information was not the problem. Rather, fixed mindsets and political inhibitions led to misreading information and to downplaying the immediacy of the threat.

The Vietnam War is another case. By the mid-point of the US intervention, there was an increasing realisation in the US government that the war was unwinnable, at least without invading North Vietnam, which no one was prepared to do. Yet with the USSR and China, not to mention the American public, looking on, there was no political will to risk losing face by leaving. Muddying the waters were competing assessments from the Defence Department and the CIA. Defence was somewhat optimistic about American prospects, a view partly aimed at convincing politicians to augment the US military presence and its freedom of action. Defence was concerned that if the war were "lost", its reputation would suffer. The CIA, by contrast, factored in the respective political wills and patience of the two sides in the war, as well as South Vietnam's ill-preparedness to stand on its own two feet. Its assessments were far more pessimistic. Thus, both hawks and doves in the US government had intelligence to support their own perspectives. Again, information was abundant, but competing political imperatives hindered a coherent interpretation and impeded clear-sighted decisions.

The Iranian Revolution, as seen by its principal Western ally, again the US, is another instructive case. From 1977, US intelligence was regularly reporting on building opposition to the Shah, and by 1978 instability in Iran had become a major intelligence target. As that year went on, a revolution was among the scenarios under consideration, but most assessments indicated that the opposition

DOI: 10.1201/9781003149125-18

was fragmented or would fragment, and the Shah would use his considerable security forces before his regime faced an imminent threat. Hindsight is always a safe vantage point for criticism, but the direction of events should have been reasonably foreseeable at the time.

Information actually was one problem in this case. The CIA did have its own assets in Iran, but it heavily relied on its partnership with SAVAK, the Shah's secret police, for information. SAVAK, in turn, faced a common problem in dictatorships. It was too close to the regime to have a clear perspective, and its bosses were wary of telling the Shad bad news, so it watered down its reports. There were also issues in the CIA's analyses. Breaking the mindset that Iran was a stable regional power, partly because of US backing, was a challenge. It might be shaken, but it was, to use an expression from the 2008 financial crisis, "too big to fail". As well, to that point US intelligence had had little experience with Islamist political movements, and for a while could not wrap its head around the Shiite clergy being the key political adversary. These shortcomings led to another one: CIA analyses were incrementalistic, in that they were premised on the lynchpin of the Shah's power and only probed slightly beyond it. Had the seemingly radical hypothesis of a revolution been seriously tested, it would have looked quite plausible.

There are plenty of historical cases to choose from, but at the time of writing there is a very recent one which, after some time, will no doubt go down in history as particularly notorious. This is the Russian invasion of Ukraine in 2022. The initial Russian plan was a multipronged attack aimed at a rapid and total invasion. Indeed, the Russian regime was expecting a near fait accompli, with Ukraine brought so quickly into the Russian orbit that Western powers would only shrug and see no further point in mutually inconvenient sanctions. Even Western intelligence agencies were surprised when Ukraine ruined the plan, and despite Russian progress in the east of the country, the campaign has become a costly quagmire. While Western agencies certainly made mistakes in their assessments, Russian failures were starker and more consequential.

This was a case of the total politicisation of intelligence. Uncorroborated evidence is trickling out that some clear-sighted assessments indicated that the invasion was overly ambitious and would likely fail as planned. But even if such reports had made it up the food chain, they were apparently not taken seriously or were simply discarded. The regime was set on a victory and had already put it in the bank. The Russian regime is characterised by highly centralised, personalised power ruling through myriad cliques connected to the security apparatus, competing for status and favour with the president. In this system, senior intelligence and defence officials had nothing to gain by telling Putin that his plan was a bad one. Additionally, the regime's tight control on news and information actually worked on itself. The country became an echo chamber devoid of public alternative perspectives. It is well known that Western politicians often watch the news to gauge public opinion and to hear perspectives not reported in intelligence. If Putin or others turned on the TV, they would have heard exactly what they already told everyone to report. There has been an apparent factional scramble to shift blame for the resulting fiasco, but while there was still time to prevent it, no one dared raise their voice or go against the regime's "truth". The regime has adapted to the actual situation, but current prospects are still a shadow of initial ambitions, and the price has been far higher than expected.

We have already examined several cases of failure in a political risk context, and to bring our scene-setting back to political risk, we can briefly revisit these to summarise the main pitfalls encountered. The US highway project in Iran was our first case. The company therein was partly hindered by being American, and hence having access to some of the same blinkered analyses that hurt US policy makers. More pointedly, however, the company was optimistic given its previous experience in the country, and had a sense of safety in the herd of other foreign companies in Iran. Its people were individually well informed, but it had no intelligence structures or processes that could have aggregated and made sense of insights from around the operation. Finally, it did not have a clear notion of political risk, and hence no conceptual basis to inform itself of potential socio-political challenges.

AES in Georgia was among the three cases recounted in Chapter 1 on political risk. We suggested therein that the company might have had to be somewhat paranoid to foresee the issues it faced and that it did a reasonable job of identifying and handling the more evident issues such as corruption and initial resistance to metred electricity. But it failed to ask a very basic question germane to operations that involve control over high-value resources in a country: Who might the project affect, and how could they respond? Even though political risk was considered, this points to a fundamental shortcoming in the intelligence process, which needs to test potential frictions in the relationship between the company and the socio-political milieu. The company was both ambitious and optimistic, as many businesses are, and hence when problems did manifest, it tried to muddle through without stepping back and asking what the fundamental issues were. Thus, manifestations of connected root issues continued to look like discrete problems, until it was even too late for a graceful exit. Information would have been a problem in this case, because stakeholder interests were so varied and entangled, but the need for an intensive diagnosis should have been apparent.

Sainsbury's experience in Egypt was not, objectively, particularly bad, but the company was unaccustomed to the kinds of problems that complex environments can pose, and from the corporate perspective the company's run-in with local interests probably looked alarming. Coming from a relatively safe and stable home region and with limited emerging market experience, the company did not know the kinds of questions that needed asking, and again an obvious one in a complex environment is whose interests could be hurt and how they might react. The cultural friction it experienced also points to a lack of acculturation that could have been developed through a prior period of quiet learning. Commercial ambition often makes the accrual of less tangible knowhow seem like a waste of time. In sensitive environments, the intangibles are just as important.

Finally, we revisit Statoil in Algeria. Along with its partners it had an intelligence capability and was well aware of the current risk environment. However, while monitoring brought in pieces of intelligence, they were seldom integrated for a holistic perspective which could form the basis of "what if" types of analysis. The recent turmoil in Libya and Mali should have inspired an in-depth tactical assessment, but updates continued to predominate. The prospect of an attack was not clearly distinguished from other terrorism risks, and the upper-left quadrant of the risk matrix (where potential surprises lie, as we discussed in challenge prioritisation) was not explored in detail. Additionally, a lynchpin of security planning was that the Algerian military would detect and respond to an incursion, but this assumption was not thoroughly tested. The army was in fact a project stakeholder, but was regarded as a fixed element of situation. In short, there was intelligence, but as with the CIA's assessments of Iran, it was incrementalistic: a bolt-from-the-blue attack was a stretch beyond the limits of thinking, even though recent events across the border strongly suggested that the regional security environment had fundamentally changed.

From a common-sense perspective, we often associate tripping up with a lack of information. For example, if a traveller had known that the visa line on arrival would be mayhem, they would have obtained a visa at the consulate and saved three hours of hassle. However, across the cases, a lack of information was only a significant problem when the organisation did not understand what it needed to learn or that learning was even important. Along with that lack of conceptual understanding, the main issues were embedded mindsets and beliefs, the intrusion of political considerations and organisational culture into clear thinking, ambition and optimism, and a sense that things would only ever change bit by bit. There is a fine line between intelligence failures and bad luck. Sometimes change is so dramatic, or a situation so seemingly absurd, that even a robust intelligence capability would have missed it. However, most cases of intelligence failure would have been preventable if the organisation had sought and used the information it had access to with careful attention to mitigating its own blinkers, and with a healthy dose of scepticism about how easy anything would be.

As a transition to how we approach this chapter, note that in the cases, the seat of responsibility for intelligence failure varied. There has been a tendency in intelligence literature to examine the intelligence organisation as the source of failure. Intelligence often is the culprit, but the cases make clear that user organisations also bear responsibility. They can be obtuse, divided or overconfident. They might not listen to what intelligence tells them, and they might not even let intelligence do its job. The intersection of the intelligence and user organisations, where directives are shaped and reports rendered, is also where things can go wrong. Thus, we have three angles to a consideration of sources of weakness and their converse, remedies: the intelligence organisation, the intelligence-user relationship and the user organisation.

Note that by including users and how intelligence is, or is not, applied, it is clear that our principal quality criterion is actionability. In other words, intelligence can be, and is, acted on to benefit the user organisation. Good intelligence is often described as relevant, accurate (which can only be assessed after the fact) and timely. These are elements of actionability, but intelligence that has all three traits can still gather dust. We will not explicitly use specific criteria in the forthcoming discussion, but one can bear in mind that actionability and the positive impact of intelligence form the overarching reference point.

The rest of the chapter is structured as follows. First, we examine the intelligence practitioner side. This is usefully divided into different levels of practice, from individual practitioners to the wider intelligence profession. Next, we consider the intersection of the intelligence and user sides, focusing on the general relationship as well as interaction during a given exercise. Finally, we move to the user organisation, where we consider constraints on intelligence application arising from both attitudes and organisational structure.

Within each section there will be a consideration of how problems can be prevented or managed. However, these can only be indicative of the possibilities, because organisational contexts are very different and require tailored approaches.

INTELLIGENCE PRACTITIONERS

Literature on intelligence failures often emphasises cognitive and epistemological shortcomings in analysis, and in analysts, as the source of weak intelligence products. That is important, but it is just one factor in intelligence quality. We need to examine several levels of practice for a complete picture. These are the individual practitioner, with emphasis on analysts and analytical thinking; the team or group; the intelligence organisation; and the intelligence profession.

Note that herein we leave aside critical reviews and structured devil's advocacy. These should be inherent to any intelligence exercise. Such exercises are valuable, but whether or not they are used, and to what effect, are affected by the broader quality issues that we discuss herein.

At the individual level, the relevant factor is how people think and the influences on their thinking. If we do not think clearly, then we might look for information that is irrelevant to the problem, or interpret information towards a concept or a story that is quite distinct from an actual situation. An irony about thinking is that we do much of it unconsciously. The end result might be an articulate and well reasoned briefing or report, but at any given instant towards the result, if someone suddenly interrupted us and asked what we were doing, we would not be able to give a very clear account. As an aside, one challenge in writing the analytical chapters of this book was in trying to unpack what really goes on in those analyses. On a real case, no one has a checklist 100 pages long, and much relevant thinking happens unconsciously. Unconscious thought is faster and more fluid than confining ourselves to a step-by-step method, but because we (speaking from the self-conscious level) cannot see it, we cannot easily control it, and a variety of non-analytic impulses and shortcuts can occur.

The seminal piece on pitfalls in analytic thinking is *Psychology of Intelligence Analysis* (Heuer Jr., 1999), by Richards J. Heuer, Jr., compiled in 1999 from writings mainly produced in the 1970s, by which time cognitive psychology was a well-established field. Heuer was a senior CIA officer with both operational and analytic experience, and his main concern was that the CIA's analytical processes did not sufficiently control for the intrusion of subconscious habits and beliefs. The understanding of cognitive bias, as well as of the elusive but valuable nexus between knowledge and wisdom, has expanded since Heuer's work, but the book remains very instructive, and readers are urged to consult it if they want to explore thinking problems in more detail. A PDF version is freely available online from the CIA's Center for the Study of Intelligence (it also contains other relevant material).

One thinking problem is entrenched mindsets, or pictures of a place or situation that have gone unchallenged for a long time and have grown roots that are hard to shake even with evidence of change, or that we were wrong to begin with. Biases can also intrude. One type is values. For example, if I do not like a regime because of its human rights record, I might be inclined to overestimate its challenges. We are also biased towards simplification. It is well known that our brains construct a basic interpretation of reality, and to help keep things simple it can even prevent us from registering what our sensory organs perceive. In intelligence, this bias shows up as our imposing known patterns onto new situations, and latching onto our first hypothesis instead of exploring alternatives. More information in the absence of clear lines of questioning does not help. It can overload cognitive abilities and reinforce our bent to simplify. We also do not like uncertainty and ambiguity, and prefer strong causal stories, and protagonists with clear motives. This can lead to our imposing a plot or narrative that mischaracterises a complex, dynamic situation. There are many more thinking pitfalls, but together they add up to the same problem. We fail to stretch beyond our comfort zones, and even as we get new information, we unconsciously seek to confirm what we already thought we knew. The real situation is out there, and we remain relatively oblivious to it.

Heuer had several recommendations to help analysts get beyond these and other thinking traps. The principal one was the analysis of competing hypotheses, which he developed into a structured methodology that remains widely used. The precise method aside, the idea is to push ourselves to develop distinct alternative ways of looking at a situation, and to gather and test evidence to see which ones make sense. That is actually similar to the scientific method, although in intelligence there is seldom enough hard data to fully confirm a theory. More generally, if analysts are well aware of the pitfalls, then they can be more self-conscious and explicit in their thinking, not only laying it out schematically from time to time to see what it is going on, but becoming their own devil's advocates to critically test emerging conclusions. However, it is hard for an individual to get beyond themselves, thus collaboration and inter-subjective testing is critical. This brings us to the next level of the intelligence practitioner side, teams and groups.

Even in long-established intelligence services, prior to post–Cold War reforms to adapt to more dynamic and messier problems, there had been a tendency for analyses to be conducted by individual specialists, or parsed out between them with their separate results glued together in an editorial review process. This has given way to more collaborative working, using integrated teams, to account for the cognitive problems discussed above. Private sector political risk intelligence has followed this practice, albeit more slowly. The principal benefit of integrated teams is that they enables mutual testing and challenging. Team members can tacitly be each other's devil's advocates even outside of a formal review process. However, more integrated teams also lead to a group identity, and this can lead to groupthink and leader-follower dynamics which erode teamwork's advantages.

Groupthink is when members of a team or other small group seek consensus to try to maintain smooth intragroup relations. This is fine if the issue is the distribution of some shared good, but in the context of analysing ambiguous and complex problems, it can lead to individual team members reining in their own ideas and perspectives to better align with an emerging mainstream view. Team leaders often set the tone for this, by pressing for a rapid resolution of outstanding questions in order to meet a deadline, or for team agreement to avoid the uncomfortable situation of dissenting opinion. Teams are also prone to the social dynamic of admiring strong and risk-taking personalities, and being intimidated by them. An informal hierarchy can develop even when a team leader tries to allow for individual creativity. This can cause individuals with distinctly different points of view to curtail their input to avoid confrontation. Thus, the irony of teams is that they can easily lead to the very problem that they were supposed to prevent, a lack of exploration of alternative hypotheses and latching onto quick fixes. Without explicit awareness of, and control for, groupthink and hierarchies, teams can be little better than just relying on one specialist to handle an analysis. This brings us to the next practitioner level, the intelligence organisation, from which the training, practices and culture to address groupthink would ideally derive.

Whether an intelligence agency, an in-company political risk unit or a consultancy, intelligence organisations have their own political imperatives, cultures, cliques and bureaucracies, and these do not always support the core mission of providing actionable insight. Government agencies tend not to like political hot potatoes, and intelligence leaders can subtly hint that assessments on divisive issues should appear very balanced and not too pointed, even if a robust intelligence process might have definite conclusions. In any type of intelligence organisation, the organisational culture can take on shades of groupthink. Excessive professional politeness and deference to authority can hinder creativity and even force out mavericks, leading to a lack of diversity and dissent. Organisations are always concerned about looking valuable. This can lead to catering to user hopes and expectations instead of prioritising actionable insight. In consultancies, there is a concern for the bottom line. Deadlines are enforced not just to meet user needs, but to free up a team for the next fee-earning task. This can lead to lead to rushed results, or to an overreliance on boilerplate templates that favour pace over actual problem-solving.

An intelligence organisation that minimises these kinds of issues has probably failed several times because of them, and after some soul-searching has had to pull up its collective socks. Failure is actually the best medicine. An intelligence organisation can get away with mediocrity for a long time as long as it does not lead to any serious damage. Complacency and even contentment with organisational processes and culture can set in even when, objectively, the organisation is hardly an example of best practice. The principal benchmark for organisational performance is how well users' genuine, legitimate needs for actionable intelligence are met. Thus, ultimately, an organisation finds its reference points in the relationship with users, which we examine in the next section.

We address one more level of practice, the profession. Certain practices, trends and fads within the intelligence profession can hinder development towards strong performance. If everyone is doing certain things, then there is comfort in the herd, even if these things are not particularly useful. For example, in Western agencies, as we discussed, the sharp division between collection and analysis was engrained largely because it was just the way things were done, by nearly everyone in the business. So too was the assignment of specific reports to individual specialists who actually did use a report-centric approach to analysis, something we already argued was problematic. When collection and data analysis technology took off, a strong reliance on technology became a fad, to the detriment of more nuanced human intelligence capabilities. In consultancies and in-house units, technology fed by open-source intelligence remains fashionable, promising quick fixes at a cheap price. Another fad has been ERM. Seeing clients' hyped interest in ERM, some political risk consultancies began to position themselves in that space, losing their edge in what they had actually been good at.

Intelligence has not become a well-defined profession, but professional standards are developing, and some experienced practitioners strongly argue that intelligence should become a discipline. This would be founded on solid, tried and tested principles and approaches that underpin genuinely actionable intelligence. Professional standards would evolve not with fads, but with learning by deconstructing cases of success and failure. There has been movement towards professional standards and learning. Just within, and accessible to, the private sector, this includes the growing number of credible master's programmes either focusing on intelligence or with an important intelligence aspect. While it is arguable how much standardisation intelligence could bear without actually adding blinkers to practitioners' thinking, there are widely available reference points of good practice and an opportunity for self-education therein.

Before moving on, we can note how each level on the practitioner side of intelligence quality depends on other ones for its contribution to robust practices. The individual can strive to overcome their own limitations through self-conscious awareness, but they benefit from working within a team in which members test and challenge each other. Teams can be prone to groupthink and pack-like hierarchies, and the intelligence organisation provides the leadership, cultural context and training to overcome those shortcomings. In turn, the organisation can develop weak practices through political imperatives and complacency, and hence it must remain aware of professional standards. Professional standards themselves arise from advocacy by individual practitioners, some of whom become practitioner-thinkers or academics feeding their experience-based knowhow back into the profession. The most important element herein is probably leadership at the level of the organisation. Leaders need to keep the mission of actionable intelligence provision front of mind, benchmark their own performance and apply user feedback to improve, and ensure that teams are well led and hospitable to a range of perspectives and personalities.

INTELLIGENCE-USER RELATIONSHIP

There could be a relatively robust intelligence capability, but unless this translates into informed user actions, then actionability, our overarching measure of intelligence quality, is not achieved. Usage is partly up to users, and we address their issues later. Here, we focus on the relationship between the intelligence and user organisations. This is where direction is set, mutual perspectives form and results are developed for application by users. Each side is fully half of the actionability equation, and hence what goes on in this intersection is critical. We already addressed some issues and fixes in Chapter 12. Those points are relevant to this discussion, but here we take a broader perspective on the relationship.

The intelligence-user relationship is well represented in intelligence literature, but almost exclusively in a government context, which is instructive for us but not always transferrable. Again, we will draw on government experiences, but ensure relevance to the political risk context. As with the last section, we will only examine a few issues by way of introduction to a more complex space than we can fully cover. These are the effects of hierarchy on intelligence independence, low mutual understanding, haste in direction setting and a lack of user involvement in the intelligence process.

An axiom of good intelligence is that it should be sufficiently independent from users such that it does not feel pressured to stray from quality. If intelligence had to consider user political imperatives, ambitions and inhibitions, it would spin its results for political acceptability, and users would be acting on an inaccurate picture. In practice, independence is an ideal. There is a hierarchical relationship between the two sides. Users are the boss or the customer, and no instance comes to mind where the independence of intelligence is enshrined in a constitution or corporate charter. Independence is a matter of degree, and problems arise at the lower end of the spectrum.

In a government context, if users exert their power to get results skewed to support political imperatives, then intelligence has only a few choices. One is to push back and restate the case for independence, another is to resign and a third is to acquiesce to user pressure (a fourth is to blackmail leaders or try a coup, but while those happen, we leave them aside for purposes here). In well-governed democracies, there have been some stark cases of intelligence collusion with political interests, but for the most part the response to pressure is a combination of pushback, minor accommodation and the rare resignation. An example of a better response to political arm-twisting comes from the US in the run-up to the invasion of Iraq, when senior political figures sought the CIA's agreement that Saddam Hussein had formed an alliance of convenience with Al Qaeda. The CIA declined to play ball, and the administration formed its own ad hoc intelligence unit to reassess and try to spin relevant intelligence. In flawed democracies and authoritarian states, acquiescence is the main response, because not only is intelligence under and even within the regime, but it is usually led by people appointed because of their personal loyalty to the leader. This does not necessarily mean that the regime gets inaccurate information, but it will get skewed information that tends to confirm its political narrative, and which heavily focuses on the regime's domestic critics as opposed to threats to the nation-state as a whole.

The above is conceptually instructive for political risk, but we need to contextualise. There are two types of political risk intelligence organisation, in-company units and consultancies. In-company units are staffed by company employees, who would have gone through the same acculturation process as anyone else and who would be expected to support the company's values and brand. They are also embedded in the corporate hierarchy. The corporate purpose is profit generation, on which everyone's status and jobs depend. Any given decision or initiative which intelligence could be tasked to inform is ultimately driven by a profit ambition, and originated with specific people or units who have a high stake in their own success. Bad news in this context can be problematic. If intelligence said that a proposed initiative would encounter serious challenges, or pointed out significant issues in an initiative underway, initiative owners might see executive management or a board committee pull the plug. If, say over the course of a year, intelligence caused this to happen several times, it would start to look like a spoiler, not just to initiative owners, but also to senior leaders. Most corporate cultures emphasise ambition and positivity, and intelligence would not be a very good "company man". Intelligence managers and their bosses up the hierarchy know this, and if they do not have the fortitude to stand by quality, and if corporate leaders do not back them, then they would be inclined to proactively censor insights to reduce organisational friction.

In the case of consultancies, they too can sense users' stakes. Consultants are not in the hierarchy, and hence would not experience ongoing friction with colleagues or bosses because of apparent naysaying. But they do experience customers' frustrations. Consultants are being paid to provide actionable insight, but as a business it is inescapable that they are also being paid for customer satisfaction. A concern for the latter can lead to taking the edge off of unwelcome results, in other words reducing accuracy, usually not of reported facts, but of interpretation.

Just focusing on the private sector context, both intelligence and users have a role in resolving the effect of hierarchy on independence. The intelligence organisation can make a clear case for the value of independence, and not be afraid to restate the case if need be. The value proposition is simply that clear-sighted intelligence keeps the organisation safer and enables it to navigate potential pitfalls, thus making it more capable of fulfilling its mission. As part of this, intelligence managers can stress that intelligence is not about making decisions, only ensuring that decisions are based on the best possible information. Users, for their part, need to understand that intelligence is not telling them to be risk averse, but it is telling them to be informed risk-takers. It is up to users to decide how cautious or freewheeling they should be, but any chance they take is more likely to succeed, with less harm to assets, if they have a clear picture of the potential issues. Making the case for independence would require not just a memo or a chat, but an ongoing dialogue, and it is up to both sides to enable this. All of this depends on will, and here we are assuming that intelligence is not just supposed to provide a veneer of due diligence or show that certain compliance boxes have been ticked.

A second challenge in the intelligence-user relationship is a lack of mutual understanding. On the intelligence side, this can arise from several tendencies. One is a purist intelligence perspective. Purists can emphasise intelligence practice over user needs and concerns. Purists avoid associating with users beyond direction setting and reporting, because getting too close can taint objectivity. Purists can even be disdainful of users, seeing them as too close to the action to have any objectivity, and as ambitious to the point of wishful thinking. This intellectual arrogance not only inhibits understanding users, but it can show and make users hesitant to deal with intelligence even when they need help. Another issue is that intelligence can be very removed from the action. It does not have to make high-stakes decisions, handle difficult negotiations or manage complex challenges on the ground. As a result, intelligence sometimes fails to grasp how it can really help. Adding to this is that intelligence people might not understand what users actually do. Whether a military officer, engineer or financial planner, users' jobs and the technology and processes involved can be obscure for people specialised in political intelligence and regional or area studies. The nett result is that intelligence has a hard time shaping results as tangible guidance, and in the worse cases is perceived by users as unhelpful and disinterested.

Users can also contribute to the gap. They rely on intelligence, but they might never bother trying to understand how it actually works. Not knowing how it works, their tasking can be too blunt and abrupt to give intelligence a useful hook, their expectations can be unrealistic in the context of intelligence resources and they can take objection to bad news. Users can also see intelligence as a report vending machine which can be activated by an email, with minimal discussion or context. Just as intelligence purists can be disdainful of users, users can be disparaging towards intelligence people, whom they regard as flaky intellectuals or dangerous anachronisms with no real-world utility.

Intelligence can pick up on this attitude, making it more than happy to keep users at arm's length, leading to an even weaker understanding of users' genuine needs.

Some governments have partly addressed the misunderstanding problem by seconding intelligence officers to policy-making departments, where they can get a direct sense of user needs and how intelligence is applied. This goes hand in hand with explicit educational initiatives to help users to grasp how intelligence works and how it can realistically help. In the case of in-company intelligence units, because they are embedded within the user organisation, there is plenty of opportunity for sharing and cross-learning, but it takes time and commitment. For example, some companies actually send intelligence case team members to the operations that they are assisting, enabling them to work directly with users, and to get a first-hand sense of the operation and its needs. This might take people away from their routine monitoring work, but it is very effective both in a given case and for building mutual understanding for the long term. This could be augmented with corporate workshops aimed at generating insights on how to build the link between intelligence and real-world operational challenges. With respect to consulting, we discussed an example in Chapter 12 in which the case team included users and consultants. That is a mode of working that bridges the user-intelligence gap, and it builds mutual knowledge that applies well beyond just one case. The onus is on both sides to reduce misunderstandings and increase trust. While a purist intelligence perspective might hold that getting closer to users could harm independence, not knowing them hurts actionability. Likewise, not knowing how intelligence works prevents users from making the most of it.

The next problem is haste in developing the intelligence direction, or the brief. This applies to a range of intelligence-user arrangements but particularly to the use of consultants, which is a useful context to illustrate the problem. We already discussed the problem of haste and fuzzy briefs in Chapter 12. To put it in perspective, imagine this regrettably common scenario. A company manager needs an assessment of relevant dynamics in a country. They email a request for proposal (RFP) to a few consultancies. A consulting company sees it, writes a proposal with a fee and sends it back. The consulting company wins the task.

Whatever more the consultancy finds out about the client's problem, it cannot change its approach or scope, because that was the basis of the fee, which has been contractually agreed. However, the approach and scope were decided on scant information and are bound to be at least somewhat inappropriate for the genuine need. As it learns more, the consultancy could adjust its approach, but this risks exceeding the deadline and reducing the case's profitability. Or it can plough through and deliver something that fails to hit the mark but which adheres to the proposal. Why did this happen? The manager did not have much time and thought that a detailed RFP would be faster than talking to five different consultancies. In fact, the RFP even stipulated that "for fairness", there can be no prior contact with the user company. The consultancy is hungry for the fees, and is willing to take a chance that it can meet reasonable quality, or somehow appear to, even with a superficial understanding of the requirement and the real reasons behind it.

Speaking from experience, the above situation or even degrees of it is a formula for bland, abstract, generic, off-base results that are overly detailed to compensate for a lack of direction. The detail just makes the results even harder to use. Actionability is negligible. So too is trust, which has not been built at all through personal interaction prior to commitment, and which later turns to mistrust because of ineffective results.

One obvious remedy is consultative, interactive and interpersonal pre-commitment discussion. A company could use an expression of interest process to narrow down the prospective suppliers, but at some point before either side commits, there needs to be an open discourse. Even if a given supplier does not accept or win the task, both sides would have learned something. For the supplier that does the job, its approach will be based on a much deeper understanding of the need, how the intelligence will be used and who their users are.

Another, complementary, fix is to divide an initial requirement into two separate cases. In political risk sales interaction, there can be an assumption that one can propose for a complex task even without knowing what is involved. In other words, upfront and before any research, everyone seems to agree that an engagement with a certain fee, duration, scope and approach is going to be exactly the right size and have precisely the right focus to address the requirement. If we really knew that, then we probably already had the answers. There is enormous uncertainty in more complex political risk cases. When an intelligence case happens without concern for adherence to a proposal, it can test and explore to derive the optimal directions for subsequent learning stages. If we are bound to a proposal, this cannot happen. We just march through the list of "deliverables", not exploring potentially relevant avenues or changing course if the scope proved to be misinformed.

In more complex cases, it would make a lot more sense to do one case, for a specific fee, focusing on identifying and prioritising relevant factors or research directions, and then a second one scoped and priced specifically to explore priorities. The result would be far less noise, much higher relevance and more nuance where it mattered. Staging is not popular. Users see it as taking too long and potentially costing more (it could actually be cheaper), and consultancies see it as risking the second part of their fees, since a user might ask someone else to handle the second stage. However, if intelligence actionability were the priority, staging would be much preferable to blind adherence to an approach set before we even knew what mattered.

We come to the final challenge in the intelligence-user relationship, a lack of user participation in an intelligence case. We have already discussed this and can be brief here. With direct experience managing operations in foreign countries, users can bring a lot to the table. Left to their own devices, intelligence teams often focus on major change factors like instability and factional rivalries, but based on experience users might suggest that some far less newsworthy problems, like customs delays or being mobbed by desperate job seekers, can be very significant. Users also have a sense of what does not matter. For example, we might derive a number of prospective official stakeholders. Country management, with a deep understanding of the structure of the operation, might be able to confirm that in the institutional framework regulating the project certain agencies in the list are actually irrelevant or would be dealt with by local partners. Engagement with users also ensures that if there were interim indications of pressing issues, they could be fluidly discussed without relying on formal reporting channels. More generally, a working relationship allows the intelligence team to maintain a concrete sense of what they are contributing to. A purist perspective on intelligence would hold that to avoid bias; it is better to have minimal user interaction after a brief has been agreed. That might help to preserve objectivity, but it foregoes potentially significant gains in actionability.

USER ORGANISATION

Most user organisations, whether a government, NGO or company, cannot be ideal intelligence customers and users, simply because they need to achieve something, and to remain relevant they need a certain momentum. This often means acting without full information, even when there are potential downsides. Culturally, user organisations need to be action oriented, or they get lost in indecision. To paraphrase, Sun Tzu wrote that in war blundering speed is better than informed hesitation. This is not always good advice, but pace and risk-taking can be essential to an organisation's survival. If it is seen by core stakeholders as stale or inactive, then they can withdraw their support and transfer it to other organisations that seem more committed to the given mission. Thus, realistically we cannot ask too much of users. That said, there are a number of problems in intelligence usage that are usually addressable without sacrificing momentum. Again, we cannot cover the full gamut here; thus, by way of introduction we focus on three, specifically concerning businesses: an insular business mindset, hyper-positivity and organisational stovepiping or silos. We briefly addressed the first two of these problems in Chapter 3's discussion on company attitudes as a political risk factor, but they are germane to intelligence usage and will be expanded on here in the usage context. Note that weak corporate governance could be another, but it is a general challenge, and the issues that we examine can arise even when governance is reasonably sound, at least by conventional standards.

An insular business mindset is often responsible for companies and managers not even knowing that political risk could be a challenge, and thus not seeking intelligence. Most managers come from two general backgrounds, commercial and technical (or engineering), and in neither is there much education about, nor consideration of, socio-political issues. This is changing as sustainability makes inroads into the corporate psyche, but by and large most managers see the world in business terms. Regulation is a fact of life, like the weather, and the human world is confined to the "Three Cs" of company, customer and competitor. There is also a common assumption that business is a universal language, and that everyone else also thinks in win-win commercial terms. Thus, if launching an operation in a new country, a company need only convince everyone of the mutual commercial benefits in order to have a smooth reception. Within this mindset, the type and character of the government is largely irrelevant. It might be despotic or hyper-nationalist, but that is politics, not business. When it comes to business negotiations, everyone will put on their rationality hat and look for a deal. While this might overstate the case, degrees of this mindset exist in nearly every company, and especially in those which have not had to face challenging socio-political environments or situations. It can be a tremendous impediment to intelligence usage, again by obscuring the need for it in the first place, or by making even garnered, disseminated intelligence seem irrelevant to the "real world".

Closely related to the above mindset problem is a culture of hyper-positivity. Because pace and momentum are important to an organisation's appeal to core stakeholders, and therefore to survival, companies can emphasise raw progress above all else. In this perspective, higher growth, higher margins and bigger market share are the keys to survival. Additionally, the company fears that if it does not exceed itself each year, the market and other stakeholders will think that it has lost its magic. Fear leads to its flip side, hyper-positivity. People need to feel that they are on a high-speed journey to excellence to sustain the energy and enthusiasm on which pace depends. When it comes to foreign initiatives, if there are already a number of competitors in the country, then its viability is confirmed, and the company can try to outpace the herd. If there are few other international firms there, even better, because then the company can gain first-mover advantages. Questions only show dithering and doubt, and slow things down.

Again, we pose this attitude in somewhat exaggerated terms for illustration, but as with a business-centric mindset, degrees of it exist in most companies. It can lead to flimsy strategies that mistake "stretch" targets for plans, and enthusiasm for planning. In our context, it can inhibit seeking intelligence, because asking about impediments to success can look defeatist. If there is intelligence on an initiative, managers can be disinclined to study or act on it, because this reduces pace and distracts people from their core profit-making activities. Sometimes, as I have directly seen, managers entirely shrug off any discussion of political risk as completely irrelevant in the face of drive and ambition, which are like magic charms or mantras. Ironically, ERM is often an established function in hyper-positive organisations, but it runs in the background disconnected from specific decisions, and like intelligence it has a hard time having much impact.

A business-centric mindset is often entirely unconscious, and a hyper-positive culture might start out as someone's idea to get better results, but usually becomes unconscious. We noted that for complacent and mediocre intelligence organisations, failure was often the best remedy. Likewise, very few companies that have experienced serious manifested political risk, or have spent much time in complex countries, will remain unconscious of the benefits of intelligence. But difficult experiences are a regrettable way to learn.

A potential fix is to combine bottom-up and top-down approaches to increasing the awareness of socio-political challenges and the benefits of intelligence and planning. From the top, an initiative could start with the relevant board committee and senior management. They could task the most relevant functions to develop training and educational initiatives, including but not just for managers who could be leading overseas operations. Along with this could be the internal communication of the intelligence value proposition, as outlined earlier. From the bottom, there are usually pockets of awareness and intelligence practice, either in risk-related functions or among experienced country managers. With senior executive support, these pockets could link as a knowledge hub, which runs informal educational initiatives in their immediate organisational vicinity. These ideas are starting to overlap with considerations about how to build a political risk intelligence capability, and we address that in the book's conclusions. Suffice to say, it does not take much to build awareness. It would certainly not mean a change programme or even new costs. However, the key to it is senior management commitment, and enabling people to partake without being penalised for sometimes stepping away from the daily grind. Once there is awareness, there would be more work to do, but it is the first step. Until then, intelligence itself would remain an unknown unknown, as would the ways it could help the business.

The next problem is organisational stovepiping, not in general but with respect to political risk intelligence and management. This issue arises from if and how political risk is conceptualised in the company. We start with the "if", then move onto the "how". First, even though managers might seek ad hoc intelligence now and then, if political risk is not a defined, shared concept in the company, the intelligence will remain with the manager who commissioned it. They would have no basis to share it or to involve others in how to deal with political risk. For them, it arose as a specific concern about the aspect of the operation they are responsible for, and the brief was tailored to their functional requirements. Several functions might actually seek intelligence, but their insights are not joined up for a holistic picture that informs operation-wide political risk management. This is not uncommon. The author has even seen instances of different functions using the same consultancy for very similar requirements, without even knowing this until the consultancy finally asked what was going on. Chapter 9 on planning made it clear that political risk management requires a cross-functional effort, and this stovepiping severely reduces the potential overall benefits of intelligence.

The second aspect of the stovepiping problem arises from how political risk is conceptualised. In this case, there is a concept of political risk, but it is so narrowly defined that intelligence is, again, not targeted at the multifaceted issues that could affect an operation. In some cases, political risk is seated in a specific function, such as external affairs or security. If an operational manager seeks intelligence, the brief goes to that function. What comes back will be framed and interpreted from the functional perspective, for example external affairs will focus on relationship and reputational issues, and security on threats and violent unrest. Even if a manager had access to a dedicated "political risk" unit in the company, or hired a consultancy bearing the label, they still might not get back a holistic perspective. "Political risk" as a specialty is often seen as applied political science and international relations, and political risk analysts often focus on macroscopic political dynamics, at the expense of more nitty-gritty behaviours and relationships that are often more responsible for wear and tear on an operation. Thus, "political risk" can be a stovepipe in itself. In short, even when there is a concept of political risk, if it is narrowly defined, it leads to an incomplete intelligence picture, and in turn to piecemeal or incomplete political risk management approaches.

The solution to both stovepiped reporting and silo-centric intelligence production is a shared, cross-functional concept of political risk, and a cross-functional political risk management process. Developing both would be an extension of the suggestions concerning awareness raising. If some functions are already using intelligence or have intelligence capabilities, they could collaborate towards a stronger shared concept of political risk, and then focus on how it can best be elucidated and planned for. These discussions would need some specific baseline contexts. Ours is operations in challenging environments, and that would certainly be one basis of discussion. Another could be global corporate planning and supply chain management. Risk and intelligence-related functions, such as security or external affairs, would necessarily retain their own specialisations, but become capable of contributing to wider cross-functional initiatives. Again, developments could come from both the top and the bottom ends of the organisation, but more coordination would be required than in the case of just educating people about what intelligence is. This too enters into a discussion of organisational considerations, which we reserve for the book's concluding thoughts.

To summarise, political risk intelligence usage is most strongly inhibited by simply being unaware of the concept and why it matters. Overcoming organisational obtuseness means tackling entrenched mindsets and cultures. The main question at this level is that if intelligence is simply unknown, who learns enough about it to know that it needs more explicit attention, and how? There needs to be that initial grain of doubt, telling us that we lack a capability that we need, and it is far preferable if that doubt does not arise from negative experiences. By comparison, if intelligence is already undertaken then low awareness is less problematic, although addressing rigidities and silos is necessarily a more explicit, coordinated endeavour. There is also the question of how far the organisation needs to go. Not every company needs a permanent political risk intelligence capability, and would need to find the most cost-effective model that also aligned with the better aspects of corporate culture. We examine some options in the book's concluding chapter.

With the quality of intelligence defined as actionability, we saw that it can suffer in three places: within and among intelligence practitioners, at the intersection of intelligence and users, and in the user organisation. Of the three, the user organisation is the lynchpin. If users know what good intelligence is and how to apply it, then their feedback to the intelligence organisation can help to improve the actionability of its results. An intelligence organisation is bereft of a mission and slides into being a think tank if users do not use it, and help it to improve its impact. We said that users are the boss, and a good boss does not quietly grumble about someone's low performance; they look for ways to improve it. Thus, to the suggestions in this chapter for improving quality we can add another, user feedback, rendered not just through surveys and forms, but through discussion about the merits of a given exercise and how to do better next time.

REFERENCES

Heuer Jr., R. J. (1999). *Psychology of Intelligence Analysis.* Washington, DC: Center for the Study of Intelligence, Central Intelligence Agency. Retrieved July 17, 2022, from https://www.cia.gov/resources/csi/books-and-monographs/

Concluding Thoughts

We have covered the substantive elements of the central subject, political risk intelligence for operations in complex environments. Thus, this final chapter can look beyond the subject itself, and consider some broader but still very relevant questions. Readers will no doubt have their own thoughts on these, and this chapter is aimed contributing to wider discussions rather than providing specific insights. Much would be interesting here, but we confine it to three main topics.

One is a direct continuation of the discussion in Chapter 14 on the organisational aspects of political risk intelligence and management. Therein we looked at organisational rigidity as a factor in weak intelligence usage. Here we consider the question of an appropriate political risk structure, not in a single operation, which we covered in Chapter 9, but in the company as a whole.

Next, we consider the changing global landscape. The last decade or so has seen an acceleration of several trends that are having increasingly direct effects at a national level, particularly in less developed countries that are more susceptible to external pressures. We examine a few key trends herein, with an eye to their implications for country-level political risk.

Finally, we address business ethics. Ethics are a significant factor in how a company approaches political risk management, and in previous chapters we have made a case for their serious consideration, if not centrality. Here we take a broader look at the meaning of being a good company, but also at the forces which seem to be working against that concept, along with suggestions on how to interpret and adapt to these forces.

Before commencing these final thoughts, we might need a quick reminder of how we got to this point in the book. That journey could well be a bit of a blur by now, and for retention a brief synopsis would help.

We began with the core concepts of political risk intelligence, including political risk, complex environments, operations and intelligence. These provided the foundation for the exploration of the baseline, or strategic, intelligence exercise, aimed at guiding an operation through a 1-year to 18-period, at which point it would have lost its currency and would need to be redone.

The baseline exercise was preceded by an explanation of the shortcomings of generic or a priori approaches, which led to either too much noise or too narrow a picture, and which were seldom directly about the object of the exercise, the foreign operation. The baseline exercise was informed by these shortcomings, and in particular strived to be very much about the unique operation.

From there we entered into the baseline exercise with the context and focus stage, which ensured that we had meaningful intelligence targets and a contextual picture of the operation and its environment.

Terrain analysis followed. It focused on the factors identified in the prior step and sought to understand how these could affect the operation. Specific potential challenges were then assessed and prioritised to give planning a clear focus.

We then examined stakeholder analysis. This was the most in-depth and intensive stage, which gave us a strong sense of who mattered to the operation, the interests and attitudes that we would have to engage with, and both individual and networked potential stakeholder responses.

Next, for the purposes of continuity, we delayed scenario analysis and went straight to planning. Herein, we recognised that the baseline's results could only inform top-level plans and that on-the-ground learning and functional expertise would need to refine more specific elements of political risk management. Nonetheless, planning provided a robust starting point. Plans addressed integrated priority issues and included both what the company could do on its own and how relevant stakeholders could be engaged with for operational resilience.

DOI: 10.1201/9781003149125-19

We then went back to complete the full analysis, this time to see what scenarios could unfold and how they could affect the operating environment. We developed scenarios for country stability, but in addition we stretched ourselves to consider the effects of wildcards and how seemingly inconceivable states could emerge. Plans derived in scenario analysis then augmented our previous planning results.

That completed the baseline exercise, but we knew that it was not the only intelligence requirement that a company might have when considering, or in, a complex country. Thus, we examined supplementary exercises. Monitoring was one, and it was a way to keep the baseline results alive and current during the baseline cycle. We also examined pre- and post-entry exercises, from top-level feasibility assessment to in-depth problem diagnoses.

With the above complete, we had moved beyond intelligence frameworks, and it was time to understand the core intelligence practices that underpin any exercise. We began with an examination of intelligence management. This started with the intelligence cycle for ideas on relevant roles and activities, then moved onto case management and staffing, and finally reporting to intelligence users.

Next, we looked at sources and collection, from which came the raw information ingredients of intelligence. Different kinds of sources applied to different stages of learning, until ultimately for a complex, high-stakes case we needed to do fieldwork and actually talk to people on the ground. We spent most time here on fieldwork and human sources, since they are critical in complex cases, but also uniquely sensitive.

Finally, after defining quality as actionability, we examined quality pitfalls and assurance in intelligence. We found that issues and remedies lay in three places: among intelligence practitioners, in the intelligence-user relationship, and within user organisations. Of the three, user organisations were the lynchpin, because without them intelligence had no raison d'être.

By this point, hopefully the book has provided the conceptual background, guidelines and practical insights required for at least some confidence in leading or guiding a political risk intelligence exercise. However, while the size and detail of preceding chapters might suggest otherwise, there is much more to learn, and other places to learn from. The book was principally based on the author's own experiences, accumulated learning, and thoughts, and as we said in the chapter on sources, every source has its purpose and perspective. I would expect that some of my own personal perspectives are quite clear. This is only one angle on broad subject, and readers who will be managing operations in complex environments, or leading intelligence cases, are urged to explore more widely.

With that, we proceed to final thoughts. Note that while this will discuss actual trends and phenomena, final thoughts mean exactly that. There is a definite perspective to much that comes, not least that I am writing from a Western democratic point of view. What follows has not been subjected to an intelligence process. Additionally, as it has been for whole book, the intended audience is better characterised as a private company from a democratic country than a state company from an authoritarian one. Finally, since this discusses some recent developments, be aware that this chapter was written in mid-2022, and that recent could be historical depending on when this is read.

ORGANISATIONAL CONSIDERATIONS

In Chapter 9 on planning, we considered organisational structures for political risk management in an operation. These included cross-functional initiative task forces, and functional and engagement programmes. In Chapter 12, we looked at case teams that formed to handle specific intelligence exercises. Then in Chapter 14, the organisation came up again in the context of stovepipes and silos. These discussions were instructive, but only indirectly addressed the question of how a company could develop and position a political risk intelligence capability at the corporate level. This is unfinished business for us, because any intelligence and planning exercise for an operation would ultimately rest to an important degree on wider corporate capabilities. We cannot address this question in detail, but it is possible to suggest some options and reference points. These might be instructive even for companies who already feel that they have relevant structures in place, since organisations evolve and nothing is fixed in stone.

A look at the situation as it stands is a useful backdrop. Where there is an explicit capability for political risk intelligence and planning guidance, it tends to be situated in, or across, a few different functions. One is external or government affairs, wherein political risk is a sub-focus of the wider concern for communications, relationship-building and government stakeholder engagement. Another is in the security function, where it tends to manifest as threat intelligence or political-security risk intelligence. Following the In Amenas attack in 2013, several oil and gas companies decided to give political risk more prominence and a wider corporate perspective by situating it in the strategy department, or the strategy unit of frontline business units. In these models, there are other functions, such as legal and community relations, handling aspects of political risk, and wider cross-functional coordination can be a challenge, but at least political risk is known about and someone is holding the fort. In most international companies, it remains a tacit and ad hoc aspect of various functional remits at different levels of the organisation, and there is no defined concept of political risk, by whatever label, anywhere in the company. Thus, there are very different starting points for developing and honing a corporate political risk capability, although most companies would be starting near the beginning if they decided to undertake the journey.

Aside from the need for cross-functional collaboration and shared awareness, there is no prescriptive formula or one-size-fits-all model for a political risk capacity. Different company contexts and exposures, types of operations and corporate cultures are all factors in what would be appropriate and workable. Thus, here we will examine a few options and their pros and cons to provide some reference points in scoping a relevant organisational model. The basic spectrum of models ranges from tacit and ad hoc through to explicit and permanent. Along this we will select three stops for consideration. These are the light touch, the hub and the unit. These could be seen as stages in evolution, since they do build on each other, but each of them could be appropriate in itself. These are not standard organisational templates, and the sketches that follow are only indicative.

A light-touch capability would mean that corporate leaders, concerned functions and frontline operational units share a common understanding of what political risk means in the company's context, as a baseline for internal discussions, ad hoc coordination on intelligence exercises and joint planning. In addition, practice guidelines would provide managers with the basic knowledge to guide or oversee an intelligence and planning exercise. Finally, a curated knowledge portal or library would contain an archive of political risk reports, a folder of current news and analysis, practice guidelines, synopses of lessons learned from past exercises and country experiences, and links to other relevant resources. To actuate this model, there would need to be some explicit ownership over the capability, or it would probably not even get off the ground, but the assigned function or manager would not be working on it fulltime. They would ensure that relevant units were aware of the initiative, and would organise a political risk network of interested people across the organisation to raise awareness in their own units. Importantly, there would be clear contexts and triggers for the activation of a political risk exercise, so that people knew when it was relevant and how it could help.

While corporate HQ would develop and host the practice guidelines, and different corporate functions could assist in a given intelligence exercise, a country operation team would be responsible for its own intelligence and planning. Knowing about political risk intelligence, if the team needed to draw on external consultants, it would be well placed to brief and guide externals and to work with them towards actionable results.

There are several benefits to the light-touch model, either as outlined above or in some other form. One is that it helps to ensure that political risk does not become a niche specialist capability remote from the action. If it is integrated with other responsibilities, it would be closer to the units that needed guidance. This approach also reduces the chance that political risk gets stovepiped into a single function. Finally, when political risk knowhow is positioned as helping frontline units to do their jobs, and not forced upon people as a routine process, it is not perceived as a ball and chain or compliance box-ticking.

The obvious downside to this model is that it might be so light that political risk is easily brushed aside and forgotten in the normal course of people's day jobs. This is especially likely if people are not granted the time and space to develop the capability. Then it would be a distraction from their core functional roles on which performance reviews are based. There is a fine balance between sub-tlety and simply being unnoticed and deprioritised. If this option were to stand any chance of making a difference, that balance would need to be managed. Ultimately, the initiative would need board committee or senior management commitment and oversight to make sure it had an enduring effect.

The mid-point on the spectrum is an advisory hub. This builds on the light-touch model by creating one or a few fulltime political risk advisory positions to curate the knowledge portal and coordinate networks and to independently build their own expertise in political risk management and planning. Additionally, the advisors would provide continuity and oversight in any relationships with external monitoring services, and with consultancies if there were consistent suppliers. When a requirement for an exercise arose, the advisors would draw on relevant functional expertise from around the company to mutually decide on their respective involvement, help to scope and develop the brief, and advise on execution. For complex exercises, an advisor might even be seconded to the relevant team to directly lend a guiding hand.

One benefit of this approach is that it remains quite light and well integrated with the rest of the organisation. The hub would be too small to handle tasks on its own, and would be firmly positioned as an enabler rather than the sole owner of political risk capabilities. Conversely, having a few full-time people means that there is always an eye on the ball, and hence less risk that the capability is ignored or forgotten. Finally, it provides a seat of institutional learning and knowledge capture, so that the company's overall capabilities continue to improve.

A challenge with this model is where to situate the advisory hub. It might make sense to append it to an established function with a related remit. However, if the hub just added to a department's costs, it would be under pressure to support the host function with its day-to-day activities and would in effect be subsumed by it. I have seen this happen in a different context, when a consultancy was trying to set up a new capability and sat it with an existing one. The new, little team was quickly saddled with routine work and the venture never got off the ground. Thus, making the hub its own cost centre might be a prerequisite for its positive impact.

Finally, we examine the other end of the spectrum, a fulltime political risk unit or team capable of balancing routine monitoring with the management of at least more complex intelligence exercises. One approach is to have a small core team augmented with staff rotating in from relevant units, including security, external affairs, CSR, legal, integrity and international operations. This would retain a cross-functional aspect and also bring learning back into other functions. Another is to keep the core team relatively small, but to extend it with staff in other departments who have a permanent part-time remit as team members. Finally, it could be established as an independent, permanent unit, rather like the company's own in-house political risk consultancy. In the last option, the team would need to ensure that it maintained cross-functional networks and close relationships to operating units in order to avoid friction, and to remain relevant and accessible. Even an independent unit should not directly handle all political risk cases. While it might lead on more complex ones, it would also have an advisory remit, helping country teams and operating units to manage their own exercises.

The fulltime, permanent in-house consultancy is the model that several oil and gas firms set up in the wake of the In Amenas attack, and notably also the kind that failed to gain traction back in the 1990s, when many such teams became seen as an irrelevant appendage. The key to impact would be cross-functionality, avoiding sole ownership of political risk and collaborative engagement with intelligence users as opposed to handling tasks for them, in the offloading mode discussed in Chapter 12. The last point means working on the ground where possible, from country offices directly alongside operational managers. There is still a risk that such a unit begins to look like a specialist silo. It would have its work cut out in terms of internal diplomacy and stakeholder engage-ment. However, if it were well received the benefits would be significant. It would ensure consistent skills development, institutional learning and the capacity to have an effect in multiple places around the company, unlike the smaller hub model.

In all three models or variants thereof, the capability would need a mandate, and senior-level commitment and oversight. Without these, as with so many other seemingly good ideas that turned out to be a flash in the pan, it is hard to see how the capability would endure. This is especially so since it is not a standard business specialisation and would have only an indirect effect on profit.

We should briefly consider relevant individual skills and backgrounds, since these are the bedrock of any capability. On one case for an international NGO, I learned about its initiative to set up a political risk capability, and this is instructive. The initiative was started by one experienced operational manager, who was concerned that the organisation was working across an array of unstable countries without any relevant guidance for country management and staff. He established a hub and network of interested people throughout the organisation, and over the course of a year or so they developed and refined political (and security) risk intelligence and management guidelines. The network also ran a knowledge portal and held virtual and face-to-face educational seminars. The NGO began to conduct intelligence and planning exercises, usually led by country teams but with the network's support. No one in the network started off as a political risk intelligence expert, yet their work had a very positive effect. That there was an established forum for sharing concerns was also valuable, not least because people realised that they were not alone in having worries about socio-political issues.

After writing a book on political risk intelligence, it would be disingenuous to suggest that anyone can do it well as long as they have an interest. At least a few people with a solid understanding of relevant socio-political dynamics, intelligence principles and case management need to be on board. But as we noted in the last chapter, user participation in cases generally raises quality by bringing direct experience to the table. With self-education and accruing case learning, people with overseas operational experience could become proficient intelligence practitioners. The NGO example above actually started with no intelligence expertise, but by the time I looked at the situation, it was a credible capability. People had read extensively, shared ideas with each other and with experienced external experts, and over time actually became the necessary core of understanding. Thus, while expertise is necessary, and while interaction with experts accelerates learning, expertise does not necessarily have to be imported, and indeed organic growth is often the most enduring.

THE CHANGING LANDSCAPE

Every era seems to the people living in it to be especially dynamic and problematic. Perhaps every subsequent era is, because since human communities formed, we have made things more complex with each generation, with more people in more diverse groupings, and technological advances that accelerate change. Still, we tend to overestimate just how bad our times really are, and there is a currency tendency in political risk commentary to hype the dire and chaotic state of the world. The Cold War era preceding the current one saw much more war and conflict-related death, probably just as much terrorism, although of a less-shocking variety, abundant severely repressive dictatorships, economic meltdowns, tumultuous great power rivalry and moments in which nuclear war seemed more than conceivable.

To put things in perspective, then, we are no worse off than we were. What is different is that, as a result of technology and globalisation, the pace of change is accelerating, and this means that lynchpin assumptions keep getting stressed. Another difference is that we are closer to experiencing a fundamental shift that will, if not controlled in the little time we have left, actually make the world much more problematic. This is climate change. There is much that we could discuss here, but we will confine it to three current dynamics that have implications for political risk: democratic backsliding, great power and system rivalry, and climate change including its close concomitant, pandemics.

Even in the 1980s, but especially in the decade following the Cold War, democratisation seemed to be ascendent. We discussed why in Chapter 1, but to briefly refresh, reasons included the economic dysfunction of statist, centralised systems; governance conditions in Western donor support; and the fact that democracy helped to mitigate social frustration arising from poor economic performance. Since 2005, there has been a democratic backsliding, more in quality rather than the number of countries that still use elections. The Colour Revolutions scared less legitimate governments and caused them to crack down on civil liberties. The Arab Spring had the same effect but even more strongly. China's rise and global prominence provided a model of successful authoritarianism and regime longevity, as did Russia's to a lesser degree, and both readily engage with and support undemocratic regimes with no concern for their governance standards. While most countries are still democracies, many are deeply flawed, and for people living in them they can seem much like dictatorships.

An important stream within democratic backsliding was discussed in Chapter 2. This was nationalist populism and demagoguery which stokes a nativist in-group identity and then claims to be the real nation's champion. When combined with adroit information manipulation, this has led not only to fracture lines in liberal democracies but also to highly persistent regimes that rely on the continued ardent support of the tribe to undermine checks and balances and democratic institutions.

One underlying enabler of this tendency is that disadvantaged segments see mainstream politics as inextricably linked to globalisation, which itself is problematic because it erodes tradition and economic security. That global interaction has at least some cultural homogenisation effect is quite clear, but there is also some validity to the economic complaint. The economic ideology of liberal democracy, liberalism or neoliberalism, regards trade as good for profit, which is good in itself, no matter how many people might get marginalised in the raw pursuit of it. Frustration with a lack of social mobility, even as overall wealth grows, has created fertile ground for demagogues and aspirants to personal rule, types of political players that often overlap.

The other enabler is information technology, specifically the explosion of new information channels and the means of manipulating them. These help fully fledged dictatorships, which can more easily control political narratives and refine surveillance capabilities. But with respect to illiberal leaders, these channels cut out the annoying intermediary of professional journalism. While no media outlet is without bias, journalistic standards used to filter out at least some hyperbole and lies from facts. Now, demagogues have direct channels to the tribe, which creates its own echo chambers too. Informed criticism is drowned out or just called fake. There might be freedom of the press, but the press itself, once regarded as one of the pillars of democracy, is increasingly irrelevant.

Dictatorship carries various risks for international companies, and we covered some, including eccentric policy, repression and regime intervention in business. Illiberal democracy and populism, even if still within an electoral framework, is often more eccentric, and in the long run poses greater challenges to national and international stability. Populists are elected as disruptors, and their support from the tribe depends to some extent on acting like rebels with respect to national institutions and international norms. They do not just get away with outrageous policies and behaviour, but they depend on it. Second, a nationalist regime needs outsiders and enemies to keep supporters mobilised and to distract people from the eventual decay that self-aggrandising disruption inevitably gives rise to. Stoking divisions and reducing overall national cohesion is therefore instrumental. If that gets stale, then foreign enemies are required. This leads to regional and international adventurism, and a higher risk of conflict. There is some irony in how the populist right in Western countries collude against common mainstream liberal and globalist enemies, because if they ever did succeed in displacing them, they would need to turn on each other to sustain nationalist ardour at home.

From a political risk perspective, democratic backsliding has combined the usual challenges of dealing with dictatorships with increasing social polarisation and intentionally disruptive government behaviour. Along with these, bottom-up instability in states led by nationalist regimes is not just of the government-versus-people variety, but it is about the leader's tribe versus outside groups. In other words, it has a much higher potential for social violence. And when change does occur, however rational or well-intended new leaders are, they will be severely hindered by corroded institutions and a lack of national cohesion. Given that nationalist populism and effective, strategic governance are nearly mutually exclusive, most such regimes will eventually face serious bottom-up pressure if they persist in that mode. Electoral change can forestall messy outcomes or a devolution into outright repression, but only if there is any meaningful electoral system left intact.

The next issue is global rivalry, between great powers and by extension the political systems which they operate and espouse. On one side is the West, a shadow of its Cold War self after decades of complacency following the collapse of the USSR, and weakened by various flirtations with nationalist populism. Once the West's principal adversaries, China and Russia, decided that confrontation was essential to the survival of their own autocratic systems, it took a while for the West to wake up to the threat. Speaking of business-centric mindsets, Western governments far preferred business as usual and dealing with their own problems to any grand strategic game. The Chinese regime's wolf warrior style and Russia's increasingly aggressive assaults on international norms eventually made them hard to ignore. The West is hardly cohesive, but within national and joint policy-making circles are committed defenders of liberal democracy, and a good number of national security hawks were finally wheeled out of the closet. For the first time since Mao, China has been designated as a national security challenge, and the Ukraine War cemented Russia's status as a threat.

The regimes of China and Russia, friends if not quite allies, share a dual perception of the West. On the one hand, it remains a threat to their respective autocratic regimes. Liberal democracy is antithetical to autocracy, and the West has made spreading its system sound like a crusade in the past. With social changes and greater information access in their own countries, China and Russia both fear that aspirations to liberal democracy could drive dissent, and they need look no further back than the Arab Spring to see how even entrenched dictatorships can be taken by surprise. The other side of the perception is that the West is weaker than ever before, and is too incoherent and complacent to stand up to committed pressure on its geostrategic reach and global soft power. Within this broad shared perception, though, there are differences between the two countries.

For Putin, the most pressing issue is the threat from democracy. Putin's regime, desperately short of domestic socio-economic achievements since initially bringing order from Yeltsin's chaos, does not feel that it can undertake meaningful reforms without risking the control necessary to stay on top. However, without reforms the regime understands that discontent will grow, and could well manifest in democratic aspirations and serious bottom-up pressure. In the absence of positive change on the domestic front, the regime has opted for a hyper-nationalist agenda, including the reclamation of European parts of the old USSR. Putin has manufactured a variety of specious national security concerns to justify this position, and these were laid out in plain view as rationales for the invasion of Ukraine. If NATO ever had a plan sitting on the shelf to subjugate Russia, it has been the best-kept secret since planetary rule by super-intelligent alien lizards. The revanchist and anti-Western orientation is mainly aimed at stoking and corralling nationalist sentiment to stave off dissent. Trying to weaken the West has three benefits. One is that a weaker West is less capable of responding to the regime's moves to rebuild the lost empire, itself a pillar of the nationalist narrative. Another is that it makes Western democracy look dysfunctional and reduces its appeal. Finally, it creates an external enemy to keep people behind their national champion, namely Putin, and provides someone else to blame for the country's problems. Contention with the West, then, is indeed self-defence, but for the regime, not the country.

China has more complex motives. The CCP, which since 2012 has tightly centred on Xi and his immediate coterie, knows that its survival is dependent on a social contract. It will deliver a transition to enduring, advanced economy status with commensurate prosperity, in exchange for acquiescence to indefinite and unchallenged CCP rule.

With ageing demographics, aridity and shrinking arable land, structural economic weaknesses and middling productivity (not to mention more recently the cumulative effects of repeated disruptions from tight covid restrictions), the regime perceives that the time window to achieve the transition is closing. The patient, frictionless approach of Xi's predecessors could take too long to stave off a middle-income trap. The Chinese regime, too, benefits from having an external enemy to sustain support, and this has driven some of its wolf warrior behaviour. It is also worried about the intrusion of democratic ideas, which would be especially problematic if the social contract comes under pressure. But more concretely, in its perspective, it needs the West to not resist, or be capable of resisting, China's development of and control over a global and regional network of resources and markets, unconstrained by the "rules-based international order". Only then can it achieve the growth essential to the CCP's continued legitimacy and dominance.

The CCP has always had aspirations to superpower status, and national security and grandeur are factors in its global ambition. But it seemed to be getting there without having to be confrontational. Indeed, if China had carried on with business as usual, Western countries might well have been too enamoured with their own gains from the win-win relationship to see China's rise as a serious problem. Xi's personality aside, the above feeling that time is short, plus the West's perceived vulnerability, created the sense that this is a make-or-break moment. Confrontation, then, is not just an excuse for and distraction from bad rule as in Russia's case. Rather, it is seen as essential to the creation of a global, unfettered China Inc. (to borrow from the title of Ted C. Fishman's 2012 book) capable of achieving enduring prosperity. The win-win status quo is no longer enough. China needs to win a lot more, or the CCP will be in trouble.

Both Russia and China have in fact already partly succeeded in undermining the rules-based order. Both regimes have gained the transactional loyalty of many emerging market governments, who can take the proffered security and economic support, loans and infrastructure projects without the attached strings of criticism about human rights and irrational economic planning. A loosening of the rules is not problematic for companies from Russia and China, or other countries where governments only enforce ethical business regulations when it suits them. However, it is problematic for companies based in the West. Western governments expect reasonable adherence to anti-corruption and environmental standards, and Western investors, markets and employees are also interested stakeholders. When the game has fewer rules, it begins to favour players who are not constrained by rules. The economics of a US or a European company's foreign operation factors in local content compliance, environmental standards, community relations, responsible security and anti-corruption. A Chinese state company need only factor in whatever it takes to get the acquiescence of the host country regime.

With the Ukraine War, we have seen some very direct effects of confrontation. Foreign companies in Ukraine had to leave or curtail operations, and Western sanctions made it hard to keep a presence in, or dealings with, Russia. Business is not given any preferential space. When governments decide that a given relationship is a national security problem, companies are expected to take a side and do their part. Additionally, Western-based companies have had to watch out for market and public opinion. While not quite jingoistic, the Western public is generally very frustrated with the invasion of Ukraine, and critical of companies that still try to make a buck by dealing with Russia. Finally, the war has come at a very bad time for global energy demand, and everyone, including businesses, are feeling the effects. The Ukraine War will likely be drawn out and not come to a definitive resolution for a long time. Western focus and ire will recede, but Russia will pose similar challenges again, and it is hard to see a full return to business as usual until the Russian regime prioritises the country's socio-economic development over rebuilding the old USSR. That seems unlikely under Putin and most of the people who could replace him in short order.

The situation with China is more complicated and puts many companies between a rock and a hard place. China remains too big for most international companies to risk leaving to competitors, yet working there is increasingly difficult. As part of its anti-Western nationalist narrative, the regime routinely warns people about the threat of subversion and espionage from foreign organisations and stokes xenophobic reactions when a Western company comments on human rights or tries to avoid using forced labour. Local staff of foreign firms can come under suspicion, and expats face becoming pawns in hostage diplomacy if their home countries have an acute dispute with China.

The current crackdown on the independence of private Chinese companies, including the mandated formation of internal party committees, is already affecting foreign firms' JV partners, and could extend to foreign subsidiaries.

From the Western side is an increasingly complex array of rules on technology and skills transfer, the use of Chinese suppliers for sensitive technologies, and collusion with Chinese firms that benefit from forced labour. Along with this are market and social expectations that companies avoid even indirect complicity with human rights abuses in Chinese supply chains. There is talk in official circles of decoupling. A company with a strong presence in both sides of the divide has good reason to be concerned about the disruption that this might lead to. Finally, if China engaged in armed conflict to solidify its claims to the South China Sea or against Taiwan, the resulting sanctions would be a regulatory minefield and supply chain disruptions would be acute.

On another level, the conceivable risk of global or regional war aside, like the Cold War, the current confrontation is likely to manifest in proxy conflicts. Russian mercenaries are already active in a number of hotspots, propping up dictators in the expectation that they will grant Russia cheap access to commodities and allow a more permanent military presence. Thus far, China has not undertaken military action abroad, but it does support violent regimes and has obtained, and seeks, overseas military bases. Among Western states, as the US in particular slides back into a Cold War mindset, it too will see alliances in terms of strategic advantage and could have few qualms about trading arms for loyalty. Thus, the global rivalry, both for political leverage and for resources, could eventually affect the frequency and intensity of conflicts in emerging market regions.

A final point about the global rivalry is that while Russia and China share a common enemy, the relationship is somewhat transactional and could conceivably fracture. Indeed, in the long term this is more than conceivable. China's pressing concerns include water, arable land and commodities, and Russia's sparsely populated far east looks very alluring. Russia is also anxious about Chinese influence in Central Asia, and the two friends continue to back opposite sides in the India–Pakistan rivalry. Should the West ever not quite suffice as a bogyman to rally nationalist support, China could easily look quite scary to Russia, and vice versa. There are few deep social links between the two countries to mitigate any official manipulation of threat perception. Thus, buried within the wider global rivalry between two systems and philosophies of governance are the seeds of a more basic binational one, and few observers have even pondered what the effects for international business would be if it manifested.

Finally, we turn to climate change and pandemics. There is still some scientific debate about the exact causes and pace of global warming, but there is widespread consensus that human activity is a significant factor, and that at least the initial effects of climate change are upon us. The frequency of extreme weather events and the pace of desertification in arid regions are causing disruption and scarcity to varying degrees in all regions. Rising sea levels will also have an increasing effect. The challenge has been on the world's radar for decades, but like the proverbial frog in a pot, governments have delayed addressing the issue until quite recently.

There have been three reasons for the delay. One is that moving towards a low-emissions economy would be disruptive, and even though many ordinary people support action on global warming, they still tend to blame the government of the day for short-term economic pain. A democratically elected government has low incentives to be the one to pull the trigger on climate action, especially since any political gains would likely not be realised during their tenure. A second reason is climate change denial, which is typically led by the same populist right that sees any coordinated international action as a reduction in national sovereignty. Denial has also come from regimes, politicians and business interests with a stake in fossil fuel, industrial agriculture and lumber production. Finally, although the global rivalry discussed above has only recently become sharply defined, governments have long been wary of working together to address global challenges. Some see others as free riders, some perceive strategic disadvantage in being among the first to take a problem seriously, and others say that the problem should be addressed by those who first started it. Now, with a global rivalry in full swing, it is probably going to be even harder to achieve a coordinated response, not least because control over rare earth minerals used in green technology is becoming another axis of strategic competition.

We have already noted some of the socio-political effects of climate change. They include local-ised conflict as social groups and subnations vie for control over shrinking water and land resources. This affects not just rural communities, but also urban agglomerations, where sub-national tensions can already be acute because of migration from different areas of a country. The risk of international conflict is also increasing. Damming or channelling river systems that plenish whole sub-regions is a major source of interstate friction. This even affects relations between areas of a country; for example, southern Chinese are well aware that their native water resources are being channelled to the arid north, and there has been serious consternation about the local effects on the environ-ment and livelihoods. Another impact is socio-economic protest. Left to their own devices, political-economic systems nearly everywhere tend to increase inequality, and this accelerates when there are significant stressors – the poor cannot cope and get poorer, while the wealthy can fence themselves off from the effects. Alongside increasing inequality, climate change drives absolute scarcity, for obvious reasons. While a given government might not be responsible for climate-related hardship, any existing perception of underperformance or illegitimacy is amplified by it, and protests are a result. On top of this, uncomfortably hot weather tends to drive violence in protests. If unchecked, all of these effects will intensify.

It is not yet known precisely how the war in Ukraine will affect responses to climate change, but there is no clear reason to be hopeful. For years prior to the war, oil and gas companies were curtail-ing investment in new exploration, and refining and transit facilities saw underinvestment. This was partly because of hyped political promises to go green. The post-covid rebound has strained energy supplies, while at the same time the West is now acutely aware that reliance on Russian hydrocar-bons is a serious vulnerability. Reductions in imports from Russia might hurt its economy but it has also driven up prices. There is no way that green energy can soon compensate for current energy shortages or price rises. Thus, an immediate response has been to try to boost conventional energy production and to diversify sources of imports. There is of course talk of accelerating the growth of green energy, and how the war might be the kick that the world needed to finally commit to it. But those discussions have taken a back seat to the urgent problem of near-term supply. How this lapse back into conventional power sources eventually balances out with a push to renewables remains to be seen. Recall, however, that particularly for solar power the necessary resources are a pawn in global strategic contention. Specifically, China controls most of the required minerals, and also produces most of the hardware, in part using Uighur slave labour which Western governments are loath to be associated with. As well, recall from the stakeholder analysis chapter how acute rivalries tend to predominate in an actor's thinking. Simply put, the transition to green energy is looking somewhat like a nice-to-have in the current geostrategic context.

Closely associated with global warming is the challenge of pandemics. Covid has put this issue firmly in the spotlight, and the world's experience with it is instructive. But it is unfortunately not going to be a unique case. Just anecdotally, we can hope anyway, at the time of writing there have been hundreds of cases of monkeypox occurring well beyond its reservoir in West Africa, from which it had previously rarely spread. Its transmission rate is quite low, but it is still very surprising, and, more importantly, it could have been something much worse. Pandemics are likely to be a recurrent challenge for two principal reasons.

The main reason for an increase in pandemic risk is the combination of climate change and human population growth. Together they lead to the encroachment of human settlements and cities onto natural habitats, partly for living space but also for arable land and water. Shrinking natural habitats cram different species closer together, increasing the chance of inter-species viral transmis-sion and mutation. The stress that individual animals experience from shrinking habitats weakens their immune systems, just as occurs in humans, and this also increases susceptibility to latent viruses which then spread. Species with high immune responses, including rats and bats, tend to weather outbreaks even as they become carriers, and they also adapt well to human environments.

Thus, human encroachment creates a cauldron in which disease breaks out, spreads and mutates. Now if we add in greater human proximity to wildlife, and in many countries the consumption of wildlife, we get high human exposure, and extant animal diseases have a chance to become zoonotic, or able to survive the jump from animals to people. This was the origin of covid and previous SARS strains, just to give one example.

The second, and related cause, is global movement, which continually increases. Viruses spread with air travel. Someone can be in a new continent in hours, and from the point of arrival can be anywhere in a country or move onto another one in only a few more hours. Tracing diseases and controlling outbreaks is enormously challenging, and in fact exotic diseases routinely travel far and wide. We are lucky that not many of them turn out to be especially contagious, but as covid showed, it only takes one to run the risk of a major spread, and with climate change increasing localised outbreaks and mutations, more dangerous diseases will travel.

Most readers have had direct individual experience with some of the effects of covid. We might have been locked down, had trouble shopping or seen our employers go out of business or cut staff, not to mention lost family and friends or been ill ourselves. In countries that had reasonably fair and effective responses, individual experiences were what mattered most. In many countries, though, the effects extended to the socio-political realm, and we can expect that future outbreaks will see broadly similar patterns. Many of these would matter to international business in general and we cannot cover the gamut here. However, we can note several effects that contribute to political risk for foreign operations.

One is an increase in socio-economic and political protest, and bottom-up instability more generally, adding spikes to the upward trend created by climate change. Government responses to covid were often maladroit, but even when they were reasonably sound, in divided or polarised societies they were bound to stir contention on one side or another, with some segments welcoming restrictions and others claiming that they were infringement on individual rights. The disease surveillance systems that many governments put in place looked suspiciously like repressive surveillance. Where state responses seemed inept because of corruption or cronyism, public ire was further stoked. The socio-economic effects often followed existing socio-economic divisions. Upper classes or regime-connected groups sustained livelihoods and lifestyles and had access to decent healthcare, while the bottom half had little to no state support. Thus, existing fault lines in the socio-political fabric were severely stressed, and cracks manifested as spontaneous protests and organised dissent. It was interesting to watch over the covid period how societies were on the one hand locked down and cautious, but on the other brewing with street movements that obviated any benefits from social distancing.

Few governments have come out of the height of the pandemic with their legitimacy intact, and they and citizens are in for another rough ride as the full economic effects finally catch up. Alongside the spike in energy prices, and in food prices because of Ukraine's inability to export grain, a global recession is plausible, and unrest might hardly abate before it picks up again. If this pattern does repeat with future outbreaks, even without the squeeze on gas and grain, then foreign operations, especially, but not just, in developing and transitional countries, can expect pandemics to make their operating environments considerably more restive and unstable.

Lockdowns, quarantines, illness and staff layoffs have had a dire effect on the transport sector and revealed a lack of resilience in just-in-time supply chains. This affected international business generally, foreign operations included. On a more immediate level, though, lockdowns and travel restrictions meant that expat staff in foreign operations often had a very hard time making it home or even leaving the country. Given that evacuation is a political risk management contingency for dire circumstances, this was clearly a serious security and safety issue, particularly in light of increasing violent unrest. Likewise, travel restrictions made it hard for expert crisis management personnel to get to foreign operations in need of assistance, for example in the event of a kidnapping or a spike in local armed violence. Country staff were often left largely to their own devices with only remote guidance, similar to how people try to land planes after the pilot has a heart attack. For companies working in more challenging environments, it was an unnerving period. For many types of operations, the need for a direct presence and expat staff will not go away, but based on the covid experience, both evacuation and security options, and localisation options to reduce the need for expat staff, have been under serious discussion. By the time another pandemic strikes, hopefully there will be tangible plans and ideas derived in a period of relative calm. A mistake now would be to shelve such considerations just because covid has become less problematic. It was only a harbinger.

In my last book on political risk, an introductory text published in 2010, I had a similar section on global changes. They included global multipolarity, asymmetric warfare and the potential use of chemical and biological agents by non-state actors, and failed states along with their contagion effects and relationship to international terrorism. Aside from multipolarity, which has morphed into rivalry, the other challenges remain, but it is interesting to take stock of how much has changed since. As noted at the start of this section, the world is not necessarily a more difficult place, but the pace of change is a challenge in itself. Paradoxically, globalisation continues even as nationalism and rivalries put up barriers to consensus and mutual understanding, and hence we will continue to be exposed to the effects of specific hostilities wherever we may be. Recall from Chapter 2 how we noted that more fragile countries, with Chad as an example, tended to be affected by global and regional influences as much as by their own system dynamics. All countries are increasingly buffeted by external influences, and we could turn that on its head to suggest that all countries are somewhat more fragile, even if their inner workings have been quite healthy in the recent past.

QUESTIONS OF ETHICS

A discussion of ethics in our context is necessary because intelligence, and planning based on it, can be quite powerful, and if abused or misused, it can cause harm and bring disrepute. History is replete with spying and scheming to undermine legitimate governments or launch coups to put abusive regimes into power. On the corporate side, it has been applied to impede social activism, counter scientific findings about harm caused by lucrative products, thwart legitimate competition, intimidate rivals and buy off corrupt politicos. An intelligence and planning capability does not contain its own ethical boundaries. We need to bring those ourselves, or we risk at least inadvertently misusing the capability, or being lured to its darker applications to achieve quick fixes and cunning but shallow victories. We have discussed ethics at various points, and here we bring the key elements of the issue together for a holistic, if brief, consideration.

We already addressed some ethical considerations in intelligence practice. This is a relatively straightforward issue. The ethical standards in academic, journalistic, scientific and market research are not dissimilar to intelligence for legitimate commercial endeavours. We should avoid inducing or coercing people to disclose secrets, ensure that human sources know the purpose of our enquiries and how information they provide will be used, and take reasonable precautions to respect source privacy. Likewise, we should protect the privacy of the user organisation, at least within the limits of their lawful activity. We should avoid breaking the law. We should tell users when they could risk breaking the law or causing harm through planned activities. Finally, we should qualify findings so that users do not end up confidently acting on uncertain indications. One could add to this, but again it is not particularly complicated as long as we see political risk intelligence as an extension of legitimate business activity and not as a covert espionage capability.

When it comes to political risk management, the question of ethics is more complex. It would be easy enough to say that plans and initiatives based on intelligence should account for sustainability, the 'do no harm' principle in conflict-prone environments, effects on rights and livelihoods, and integrity. However, that assumes that these "shoulds" are important to us in the first place. That is not just a question of political risk management; rather, it is about how an organisation perceives its role in the world and its intrinsic priorities.

The notion of corporate citizenship, that companies had an opportunity and reason to be good, developed and spread over the last three decades, and most international firms based in Western countries or other established democracies have taken being good on board. At the heart of the concept is that most people, including investors, customers and employees, dislike bullies and cunning manipulators, but respect fairness and honesty. As media and NGO reporting on corporate social performance grew, so too did corporate interest in trying to ensure that companies were not at odds with basic social values. Trying to meet expectations is seldom straightforward. There can be difficult trade-offs with the profit imperative. It is easy to find chinks, or even large holes, in any company's ethical armour. But by and large, the era of cowboy capitalism, when roaming the world on the hunt for raw opportunity was a splendid endeavour, has come to a close. Even if a boss thinks that short-term profit should come before anything, acting on that notion has painful repercussions. A common critique of corporate ethics and sustainability is that they are just veneers void of deeper commitment. Maybe so to varying degrees, but to maintain the veneer, one actually needs to do things differently, and even acknowledging that a veneer is required is at least partial acceptance that ethical expectations matter.

As beneficial and accepted as corporate goodness seems, when looking at the global political landscape, we can see several serious challenges to the goodness imperative, either making it harder to be good and profitable at the same time or actually challenging what good means. These could give rise to cynicism, and to the temptation to see political risk capabilities as a means to scheme and connive, rather than to inform a responsible fit with host societies while legitimately safeguarding people and assets. We will examine these pressures, and how and why corporate citizenship can be maintained in spite of them without sacrificing commercial performance.

In emerging markets, the coexistence of goodness and profitability is challenged by two factors. One is the spread of authoritarian governance, mainly of the flawed democracy type but also dictatorship. Authoritarian regimes reduce checks and balances, and hence there is more opportunity and incentives for official corruption and abuse of power. Since they cannot rely on institutional legitimacy, they are more repressive. They also rely more on hardcore nationalism to bolster support, and this means discriminating against minorities and outside groups. In short, authoritarian regimes are not good, to varying degrees. This is a problem for a good company seeking emerging market opportunities. Their very presence in a country could help a bad government look more credible, and taxes, royalties and technology transfers can actually bolster a regime's ability to do harm or to continue in power without creating a concrete basis for legitimacy.

If we were to suggest that a company only work in well-governed countries, it would be confined to a few niches and probably wither, not to mention there would not be any rationale for this book. Both of the imaginary, but realistic, cases in the baseline exercise chapters included significant elements of trying to remain good in weakly governed host countries. As the cases indicated, one can sustain company ethics, but to do so needs nuanced insight and fine-tuned planning. Additionally, it depends on what the company is bringing to the table. In both cases, it was doing something of value to the host government, one by building a high-quality highway, the other by potentially becoming an FDI success story and bringing rare expertise to the local market. The operation's value is its bargaining chip. In the construction case we saw that this was played to get presidential acceptance of the need for fair and non-abusive community relocations and union acceptance of local employment. In the IT company case, it could have been played to avoid pressure to partake in projects to boost state surveillance capabilities. In each case, the operation was to the advantage of the regime, but the principal benefit was for the host society and private sector.

The point about an operation's value is nuanced. In both hypothetical cases, the operation's value to the regime came through its socio-economic developmental value. Even though both case countries suffered from a degree of bad governance, neither was a tyranny or kleptocracy. There was a strand of rationality which recognised that what was good for society was good for the regime, because development staves off frustration and makes a government more legitimate. There are utterly venal governments who care almost nothing about genuine development, but in most cases the picture is more ambiguous. An operation with strong socio-economic merit, and of high quality and a clean bill of integrity health, can be a significant boon to an overall bad government that still tries to boost its credentials where it can. And frankly, a lot of bad governments do not necessarily like being that way but are stuck in that mode for lack of clear avenues to become better without risking their own collapse and sometimes the collapse of the state. In other words, bad governance and a genuine interest in development are not mutually exclusive.

It might not be entirely possible to do business in badly governed countries without an operation somehow supporting the regime, but it can be a question of relative benefit. An operation might directly benefit the regime, but if by being there it also provides jobs, opportunities, learning, social investment and contact with outside ideas, then the balance of benefit is a consideration in an operation's ethical merit. Additionally, within this balance, there are ways to build in at least some guarantees that an operation will not fund or support abusive capabilities. For example, the Extractive Industries Transparency Initiative and similar sets of principles can be the basis of contractual agreements that ensure that state earnings from an operation are prioritised for development. Donors can be brought on board to provide rights and sustainability oversight. The company itself could have the bargaining power to impose contractual conditions that ensure non-collusion with abusive labour practices, abusive security or sub-national discrimination, and it can invite independent monitors to ensure that all sides stick to the terms.

While a company can sustain ethical standards in badly governed countries, it still needs to know its moral redlines, as we discussed before. These can tell a company when it is not possible to undertake an operation without breaking core principles, and if in a country and under pressure to breach ethics, defined redlines can provide the moral backbone to either bargain hard or leave. While astute political risk intelligence and management can make it possible to ethically navigate badly governed countries, sometimes just to work in a country one needs to make too many compromises. Persisting in the face of moral hazard risks liability, reputational damage, extortion, entanglement and our own self-identity. We can avoid those possibilities by having clearly defined principles and limits, and the courage to stick to them. Recall the case of Talisman Energy in Sudan during the civil war. If the company had had clear redlines, it would have left Sudan well before it became embroiled in a human rights scandal that was a significant factor in the company's decline.

As for pressure for bribes or other inducements, it is a two-way street. I have actually heard the question before, "Who do we have to pay to do business there?", and have listened to discussions of cunning plans to somehow avoid scrutiny while cutting corners to get access. We mentioned a business-centric mindset and hyper-positivity in the last chapter. In their more extreme manifestations, they can both lead to corner-cutting and fudging redlines. An irony of these perspectives is that they tend to emphasise cunning collusion over a fundamental variable in business competitiveness, namely quality. In our context, quality is a wider package. It means technical quality and proficiency, but it also means that we do not come with baggage or act in ways that could bring liability onto partners or customers. Going back to the fact that even in badly governed states there is usually some interest in genuine development, and in simply getting what you pay for with minimal complication, this rarer notion of quality can have much higher appeal than a tawdry package premised on complex side deals and closet liabilities. In short, just by sticking to the business knitting, we can get clean business even when corruption is pervasive. If we cannot, fine, but at least we came armed with a solid proposition and gave it a chance.

To summarise, there are more authoritarian countries in the world, and many are weakly or badly governed. A good company can still find legitimate opportunity and safeguard its principles, although it takes learning, and there will be some delicate balances to maintain. A clear sense of our moral limits is how we know when there is no way to be good and work in a place. On that note, one might suppose that a bad company would have a wider geographic reach than a good one, because it has fewer inhibitions. Ironically, the reverse is true. Bad companies are usually known as such and have a hard time finding a footing where clean business is respected and appreciated. Conversely, a good one has free range in those markets, and a solid proposition for anyone, anywhere who wants a decent partner, product or project without strings attached.

Authoritarian governance is one challenge in balancing profit and corporate citizenship in emerging markets. The second is that there is increasing competition in emerging markets from companies who are incentivised to get business and maximise revenues any way they can. Specifically, these are state or state-affiliated companies from transitional countries, including but not just China and Russia. We discussed this challenge earlier. These players are backed by the flag and by official inducements to host governments to grant their companies access and contracts. These firms' guiding principle is supporting their governments' global agendas by bringing home revenues and resources, and by leading the way in establishing strategic outposts.

It can look like it is hard for a good company to compete. Western diplomats do lobby on their companies' behalf, and Western countries have a number of trade agreements and bilateral investment treaties. However, Western governments do not directly back their international companies, or give them any official recognition or power to wave the flag. They seldom offer side deals, cheap infrastructure or loans to ensure that "their" companies win work. And rather than telling companies to do whatever they must to get business, they actually tell them that if they contravene anti-corruption regulations or other legal standards, they will be in serious trouble. Thus, by comparison to their state company counterparts, Western firms are more or less on their own, and cannot cut many corners even if they wanted to.

This imbalance in state backing and permissiveness has had consequences for Western companies' commercial performance and market shares. This could lead to a temptation to play their competitors' game, and to apply political risk capabilities to develop plans not just to stay safe and resilient, but to actually skew the playing field to even the odds. In the short term, playing the game might make some difference, though with serious risks which we have already discussed. In the medium to long term, it is a reasonable bet that the playing field will even out by itself, and that a clean and conscientious proposition will start to look compelling compared to the entangling offers of state firms.

We mentioned cowboy capitalism, a mode of business conduct that emphasised opportunity-seeking over sustainable operations. In the 1960s and 1970s, corporate meeting rooms in Europe and the US hosted discussions that would seem outrageous now. Bribery, playing off sides in a political rivalry and even organising coups or trying to get the CIA to do one were all on the table. Environmental and labour standards were a shadow of their present forms. Verve mattered, and so did loyalty to the company, probably a lifelong employer and a close-knit tribe. That sounds exciting, but there are reasons why that mode of international business went by the wayside. The world became more complex and interconnected, host societies became better organised and more aware of the pitfalls of quick and dirty foreign business operations, and companies could no longer simply hide behind the raw logic of capitalism. Bad reputations and bad business performance made it hard to win the right friends and attract the right people. Low credibility made would-be stakeholders suspicious. Sequential mini-crises incurred through blind opportunity-seeking impeded effective strategic thinking. By the late 1980s, the cowboy model was waning, and in the interests of sustainable and resilient overseas growth, it was time to play by some rules.

It is easy to forget how relatively inexperienced transitional market companies, even their state behemoths, are in foreign emerging markets. The lessons learned by their Western counterparts were based on decades of experience. The state players are only just starting to learn that business without principles is problematic. Chinese companies have already experienced considerable friction in Africa by dodging local content rules, ignoring environmental impacts and using heavy-handed security. Russian companies are tainted by association with the escapades of Wagner Group and other state-linked private military companies that combine mercenary activities with negotiation for mineral rights. Companies from China, Russia and other states with weak integrity regulation are automatically expected to offer something above and beyond just a solid project at a fair price, and this clouds expectations and drags out negotiations. While such firms do not have to worry about social expectations at home, and even less about their home governments' expectations, they are finding that despite official backing and often because of it, their operations increasingly face political entanglement and social hostility. These issues have actually prompted an interest in social responsibility, at least among some Chinese firms, and hence they are just starting to apply political risk management approaches that Western firms have been using for decades.

While the rise and reach of state and state-affiliated companies will continue to have an effect on the market shares of independent, rules-bound firms, there is no reason to panic or to abandon hard-earned lessons. The state players will go through their own cowboy period, with the additional baggage of having a flag glued to their chests, and will learn the hard way that ethics matter. Meanwhile, the best antidote for Western firms is the concept of quality mentioned above. Even in poorly governed countries, politicians and senior officials often seek legitimate FDI and need something done well, with no political strings or liabilities attached. And not everyone wants the Chinese state in their backyard either. Dept-trap diplomacy is not exactly the conspiracy that it is made out to be, but the experience of countries indebted to China has raised valid worries. Many developing countries are desperate for foreign support, but still wary of the political overtones in state company approaches. In short, the water is muddy enough without playing by state company rules, and the appeal of a competent, transparent and fair proposition is going be all the stronger as host governments and societies gain experience with the alternative. There is still a need for adroit navigation and multifaceted stakeholder engagement, but cutting corners in being good, when it could well become a key competitive advantage, would be a self-inflicted wound.

We mentioned that not only was there a challenge in balancing profit and ethics in emerging markets, but that the very notion of good was itself being challenged. We now turn to this final ethical conundrum. Even within long-established democracies and Western systems, the notion of good as we have outlined it is under pressure. We already discussed the sources of pressure, right-wing nationalism and the global rivalry, and here we see what they mean for corporate citizenship.

Right-wing nationalism has been a strand of Western political thought for decades, but it went from being niche to significant following the 2008 financial crisis. By 2015, it was gaining momentum as an alternative to liberalism, which was tainted by its association with globalisation and its effects on jobs, and with neo-liberal economic policies that were ultimately responsible for the deregulation that made the financial crisis possible. The critique of liberalism is not without merit, and there is certainly a lesson herein on how, and why, to address its systemic defects. But when the critique was hijacked by populist right-wing politicians, its finer points were lost in raw demagoguery and political opportunism.

As we noted earlier, the nationalist populist phenomenon sees the definition of an authentic tribe which a leader then claims to be protecting, thereby gaining ardent support in pursuit of power. Few such leaders have gained power in Western states, but they are firmly in the political arena and have a high pulpit to espouse their views. Their promises of putting the real people first, combined with a slick propaganda operation, have gained followings on par with mainstream parties. Even where the nationalist right has little chance of gaining power, it still makes elected parties nervous, and they cater to nationalist sentiment in an effort to prevent voter defection.

The result is that within the very societies where the meaning of "good company" was defined, there is a sizeable segment with a completely different notion of it. For the nationalist right, a good company would be one that created jobs at home, did whatever it had to do overseas with brutal efficiency, and made sure the profits came back to the nation. Being concerned about the rights and wellbeing of foreigners is a sign of disloyalty, as is hiring overseas and partaking in transnational initiatives that challenge sovereignty. Environmentalism hurts jobs and near-term domestic growth, plus climate change is overhyped, so companies who espouse their sustainability credentials are suspect. If these are becoming mainstream social values, then it would seem that companies' notion of good is misaligned, and that they need to inject a strong dose of nationalism into their concept.

While the nationalist right is noisy, and politically has made a splash, it is important to distinguish the appeal of its full proposition from its appeal as a critique of the effects of globalisation and neo-liberal economics. The far left used to have some credentials in the latter respect, but its ideology remained an abstraction to most mainstream voters, and it failed to account for concerns about cultural erosion. The right talks about "us", and anyone in that group feels included and finds common ground in the face of global forces and a political-economic system that seems rigged against the average citizen. Beyond that, though, the average nationalist voter is not racist or xenophobic.

Thus, that right-wing nationalist parties have gained traction does not mean that most of their supporters have taken the full package on board.

Not only is the average nationalist voter not an ardent right-winger, but recent generations of citizens are very aware and critical of bad corporate behaviour, as the converse of the current notion of good. By and large, then, while the question of offshoring and overseas jobs is a cross-ideological complaint about companies, most people agree on what makes a company good. Fair, honest and socially and environmentally responsible are still by far the preferred corporate characteristics.

We already discussed another consideration. While the nationalist critique of liberalism holds some water, the kinds of politicians that opportunistically leverage nationalism tend to be very bad leaders, and those still on the sidelines are not showing much potential either. Hyped promises of upholding the people's interests, domestic jobs, anti-immigration, social spending and sustaining tradition are seldom backed by any realistic policy or strategy. In the face of complex domestic and global dynamics, achieving such aims falls by the wayside, and to compensate for poor performance leaders blame hard times on outside groups and globalists. Polarisation increases as governance standards and capacity decline. It would be interesting to ever see a genuine success story from right-wing nationalist government, but thus far the track record is varying degrees of chaos. For this reason alone, it is doubtful that this tendency ever will displace mainstream liberal politics. The nationalist critique holds some lessons and Western governments should listen. The nationalist phenomenon needed fertile ground to get as far as it did. But because it is almost invariably hijacked by ardent ideologues and demagogues mired in their own narrow perspectives, it will seldom show itself to be better than centrist leadership. The wave came quickly, and as people experience nationalist rule or even its indirect effects on policy, it could well prove to be a disruptive sideshow.

In short, while right-wing nationalism has made a splash, to glom onto the nationalist perspective as a reference point for society's concept of good would be a detour and a distraction. It would undo years of adaptation to widely held, cross-ideological values. For an international company, suddenly trying to be a nationalist champion would also be a serious, and unnecessary, cramp in one's international credentials and capabilities.

The global rivalry as a challenge to the notion of good is a more nuanced question. As noted earlier, when a relationship becomes a national security matter, the idea that private business is somehow sacrosanct and fenced off from politics quickly goes up in smoke. That is happening now for sectors with even minor national security significance, and that is a surprising number when one thinks about what sustains national strategic capability including societal resilience. Thus, there is a new and very large elephant in the room when it comes to what "good company" means. To Western governments, and indeed to many Western citizens, it means not doing anything that could make rivals stronger, and in any trade-off between national interests, to prioritise the Western side.

This is hardly the position that an international, and especially a genuinely multinational, company wants to be in. On a purely business level, a company could well have very close and friendly relationships with perfectly decent people and organisations in China and Russia. An international company also hesitates to bear its country's or bloc's flag. A political identity, as we discussed concerning socio-political profiles, is usually unhelpful in gaining trust and support overseas. But there is not much wriggle room. As we noted, when an existential rivalry manifests, and the current one is taking on that shade, it makes for singlemindedness. If a Western company failed to account for official, and to a lesser extent public, expectations, it risks repercussions.

The problem for the notion of good is that strategic government imperatives and business ethics often misalign. If a company got on board with every strategic rivalry or conflict that its government had, it would hardly have an ethical leg to stand on. The Iraq War and the sanctions that preceded it were a moral quagmire. Sanctions on Cuba are an anachronism and impede the country's development, and if its authoritarianism is an excuse, then one wonders how Saudi Arabia escapes similar treatment. Helping to kill Qaddafi without any notion of what would come after was irresponsible and contributed to the chaos in Libya and the region now. The list goes on. If it is "my country right or wrong", we will often be wrong. Thus, it is astute to ask if the current pressure to take sides is a threat to good corporate citizenship. There is a reasonable argument that by and large it is not, at least not currently and as long as companies avoid taking a direct role as enablers of Western strategic advantage.

Perhaps politicians everywhere are at least somewhat self-obsessed and cynical, and no government or political system escapes valid ethical criticism. But while everything is a shade of grey, some patches on the spectrum are pale grey and some are nearly black. The global rivalry is between a system in which people do not have to live in fear of their governments and have at least some means to hold them to account, and systems in which people must abide by the whims of a narrow, unaccountable elite or face harm. From a Western perspective, China after Mao was morally ambiguous. Deng ensured that after him there were defences against personal rule and an in-party dictatorship. While China had one-party rule and was certainly not democratic, its system did not lack consensus-building, criticism and accountability. Currently, a person could risk arrest in China just by posting or discussing Deng's own criticism of personality cults. China is not just different now, it represents a model of oppression that few Western citizens could live with. Both the Chinese and Russian regimes seem to have scant notion of universal human values. Xi and Putin both equate "good" with what keeps them on top and in full control, and secondarily with what makes their countries capable of rewriting global norms and building, or rebuilding, empires.

Russia's destructive invasion of Ukraine and before that its devastation of Syrian cities in support of Assad, not to mention use of nerve toxins and radioactive poisons in foreign cities and on dissidents, are just a few examples of the regime's misalignment with common norms. China's assault on Uighur and other minorities' culture and identity, its ecologically ruinous fishing armada raiding other countries' shorelines, its hostage diplomacy and the routine disappearing of merely outspoken citizens are again just a few visible indications of its regime's attitudes towards rights and fairness. They would argue that they need to break a few eggs to secure their countries against Western connivance. From another point of view, the West was more than happy to overlook their unsavoury aspects if it meant business as usual, and was practically sleepwalking when it finally realised that they were playing a zero-sum game and knew few limits.

While Western governments have engaged in needless adventurism in the past, the current rivalry is based on well-founded concerns about the effects for reasonably free societies, human rights and global stability if Russian and Chinese aspirations go unchecked. Thus, from a corporate citizenship perspective, there is no significant misalignment between playing one's prescribed part and being a good company.

We noted two possible exceptions to this alignment. One is if Western states move from a containment and pushback posture to an increasingly hawkish one and become aggressive and cavalier in their pursuit of security. As occurred in the Cold War, this could lead to a very instrumentalist foreign and security policy that rewarded tyrants and warmongers as long as they took the Western side. This has actually happened in the "War on Terror" too, with the US and European governments providing military and intelligence support to a number of dictatorial regimes in exchange for security cooperation (ironically, Qaddafi was one such "partner" before his demise partly at the hands of NATO jets). Thus far, Western action in the rivalry has been cautious, but if it intensifies, then an all-or-nothing attitude could lead to ignoring or discarding humanitarian principles to gain strategic advantage. At that point, Western companies could be regarded as de facto agents of an uncaring foreign and security policy agenda. While removing oneself from the fray might not be an option, companies could join civil society actors to call out the hypocrisy of resisting autocracy by imitating it, and to appeal for a more balanced and conscientious approach that favoured diplomacy, business engagement and development assistance over manipulation and coercion by proxy.

The other exception would be if a company went too far in directly supporting Western government protagonists. Jingoistic communications aimed at appearing to be "on the side of right", offering the use of the company as a front for espionage, and in general going well beyond what a company simply needs to do would unnecessarily infringe on corporate citizenship. Companies are civil society actors. They have no social mandate to act against national security threats. Abiding by government rules and being cautious about one's potential strategic impacts is one thing. Proactively becoming a geopolitical player challenges the notion of good, and would likely lead to confusion and suspicion among societies where the company operated.

The rivalry was only clearly defined quite recently, at least in the West. It might not go very far. Russia and China both have pressing domestic problems and simply might not have the means to pursue their broader ambitions. The world might well default to business as usual again after a realisation that the costs of contention are too high all around, especially with the pressing climate challenge. Thus, some of the above considerations might not be relevant for some time, or not at all. However, it is plausible that the standoff escalates into a new, acute cold war. There is no misalignment now between a good company and one that fulfils expectations in supporting Western imperatives, but this could change as pressure mounts. Companies should beware of the potential effects and consider how they could push back to maintain their own independence and business ethics. This could be a delicate balancing act, especially if Western civil societies develop a sharp "us versus them" attitude towards global rivals.

A discussion of ethics is an appropriate place to bring the book to a close. On one level, political risk intelligence and management is about looking after our assets and interests, but on another, it is about how to achieve and sustain the alignment between ethical principles and measurable performance. Thus, what those principles are and our commitment to them are very significant factors in why and how political risk capabilities are applied. Principles and commitment cannot just be instrumental, in other words adopted and adhered to because they make life easier. They are not themselves part of some cunning strategy for enhanced performance. Without them, we have no grounding. We mentioned company tribalism is Chapter 3, and how people start to identify so closely with their group, and its immediate ambitions and struggles, that together they lose perspective. They throw themselves into projects and initiatives with abandon. Being part of a team fighting for the good of the tribe is exciting, like being in a war minus the risk of being maimed. Doing well for the tribe earns status, which is highly gratifying. There is no wider questioning of why it all matters, or if we should be doing something else in an entirely different way. I have personally seen and been involved in cases where the task at hand became everything, only to later realise that it was irrelevant in the grand scheme of things, and indeed that there had probably been far better uses of everyone's time and cortisol.

A final thought, then, is that we need to be able to step back from what we are doing and question why. Wisdom is an aspect of human intelligence, and if we include that in our concept of political risk intelligence, we will ultimately be reducing the gap between what is meaningful to us, and the decisions we make and what we actually do. Grounded in what really matters, we will not be distracted, lured or pushed into frivolous undertakings or schemes, and will retain a clear perspective on a given situation as the basis for sound judgement. As previous chapters revealed, there are myriad techniques and approaches in political risk intelligence, and with agile thinking and appropriate method one can get a detailed picture of a target. It is a powerful tool, but that is all it is unless we know, and are guided by, the greater why behind its application.

Index

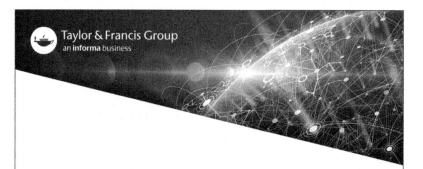

Printed in the United States
by Baker & Taylor Publisher Services